Encyclopedia of the Mexican-American War

Encyclopedia of the
Mexican-American War

Mark Crawford

David S. Heidler and Jeanne T. Heidler
Consulting editors

ABC-CLIO

Santa-Barbara, California
Denver, Colorado
Oxford, England

Copyright ©1999 by Mark Crawford

All rights reserved. No part of this publication may be reproduced, stored in a retrieval system, or transmitted, in any form or by any means, electronic, mechanical, photocopying, recording, or otherwise, except for the inclusion of brief quotations in a review, without prior permission in writing from the publishers.

Library of Congress Cataloging-in-Publication Data
    Crawford, Mark
    Encyclopedia of the Mexican-American War / Mark Crawford.
      p.   cm.
    Includes bibliographical references and index.
    Summary: An encyclopedia fo the Mexican-American War, including excerpts from eyewitness accounts that highlight the day-to-day reality of marching and fighting.
    ISBN 1-57607-059-X
    1. Mexican War, 1846–1848 Encyclopedias. [1. Mexican War, 1846–1848 Encyclopedias.] I. Title
    E404.C93   1999
    973.6'2'03--dc21

03 02 01 00 99 10 9 8 7 6 5 4 3 2 1

ABC-CLIO, Inc.
130 Cremona Drive, P.O. Box 1911
Santa Barbara, California 93116-1911

This book is printed on acid-free paper.
Manufactured in the United States of America.

To the memory of my mother, Janet Patricia Crawford, who kindled my interest in history and writing at age five by reading me "Old Glory at the Crossroads" from the Chicago Tribune *comics, hundreds of other historical tales, and by somehow complimenting every story I ever wrote. That fire has never died.*

Contents

Preface, xiii

Acknowledgments, xv

Introduction, xvii

Maps, xxi

Encyclopedia of the Mexican-American War

Abolitionists, 1
Aburto, Juan, 1
Adams, John Quincy (1767–1848), 2
African Americans, 3
Agua Fria, Skirmish of (June 4, 1848), 3
Agua Nueva, 4
Aguascalientes, Plan of, 5
Alamán y Escalada, Lucas (1792–1853), 5
Alcorta, Lino José (ca. 1794–1854), 6
Alexander, Edmund Brooke (1800–1888), 6
"All of Mexico" Movement, 7
Almonte, Juan Nepomuceno (1803–1869), 7
Alvarado, 8
Álvarez, Juan (1790–1867), 9
Alvarez, Manuel (1794–1856), 10
Ampudia, Pedro de (1805–1868), 10
Anaya, Pedro María (1795–1854), 11
Anderson, Robert (1805–1871), 12
Andrade, Manuel (1800–ca. 1860), 12
Anglo-American Press in Mexico, 13
Apache Canyon, 13
Arab, 14
Archuleta, Diego, 14
Arista, Mariano (1802–1855), 15

Arizona, 16
Armijo, Manuel (1801–1854), 16
Armistead, Lewis Addison (1817–1863), 17
Army, Mexico, 17
Army, United States, 21
Arroyo Colorado, 28
Arroyo Hondo, Skirmish at (January 1847), 28
Atlixco, Skirmish at (October 19, 1847), 29
Atocha, Alexander J., 29
Aztec Club, 30

Backus, Electus (1804–1862), 31
Baker, Edward Dickinson (1811–1861), 31
Balbontín, Manuel (1824–1894), 32
Balderas, Lucas (1797–1847), 32
Bancroft, George (1800–1891), 33
Barbour, Philip Norbourne (1813–1846), 33
Bartlett, John Russell (1805–1886), 34
Bartlett-Condé Agreement, 34
Baz, Juan José (1820–1887), 35
Beach, Moses Y. (1800–1868), 35
Beale, Edward Fitzgerald (1822–1893), 36
Bear Flag Revolt (June–July 1846), 37

Beaubien, Carlos (1800–1864), 37
Beauregard, Pierre Gustave Toutant (1818–1893), 38
Bee, Barnard Elliott (1824–1861), 38
Belknap, William Goldsmith (d. 1851), 39
Bent, Charles (1799–1847), 39
Benton, Thomas Hart (1782–1858), 40
Bent's Old Fort, 41
Biddle, James (1783–1848), 42
Billings, Eliza Allen, 42
Bishop's Palace, Monterrey, 42
Bissell, William Henry (1811–1860), 43
Black, John, 44
Blake, Jacob E. (1812–1846), 44
Blanco, Santiago (1815–1883), 45
Bliss, William Wallace Smith (1815–1853), 45
Bocachicacampo, Skirmish at (February 13, 1848), 46
Bonham, Milledge Luke (1813–1890), 46
Borginnis, Sarah (1812–1866), 46
Borland, Solon (1808–1864), 47
Bowles, William Augustus (1799–1873), 47
Boyd, Linn (1800–1859), 48
Bragg, Braxton (1817–1876), 48
Bravo Rueda, Nicolás (1787–1854), 49

vii

Brevet Rank, 50
Brooks, Horace B. (ca. 1815–1894), 50
Brooks, William Thomas Harbaugh (1821–1879), 51
Brown, Jacob (ca. 1788–1846), 51
Buchanan, James (1791–1868), 52
Buchanan, Robert Christie (1811–1878), 53
Buena Vista, Battle of (February 23, 1847), 53
Burnett, Ward B. (1810–1884), 56
Bustamante, Anastasio (1780–1853), 56
Butler, Pierce M. (1798–1847), 57
Butler, William Orlando (1791–1880), 57

Cadwalader, George (1806–1879), 59
Cahuenga, Treaty of (1847), 59
Calhoun, John Caldwell (1782–1850), 60
California, 60
California Battalion, 61
Californios, 62
Camargo, 62
Campuzano, Antonio (1810–1866), 63
Canales Rosillo, Antonio (ca. 1800–1869), 63
Canalizo, Valentín (1794–1850), 64
Carbajal, José María Jesús (ca. 1805–1874), 65
Carmen, 65
Carrasco, José María (1813–1851), 65
Carricitos Ranch, Skirmish at (April 25, 1846), 66
Carson, Christopher ("Kit") (1809–1868), 66
Casey, Silas (1807–1882), 67
Castro, José María (ca. 1810–1860), 67
Casualties, Mexico, 68
Casualties, United States, 68
Catana, Massacre at (February 10, 1847), 69
Catholic Church, Mexico, 69
Cerro Gordo, Battle of (April 17–18, 1847), 71
Chapita, 74

Chapultepec, Battle of (September 13, 1847), 74
Chase, Anna McClarmonde (1809–1874), 76
Chaves, Manuel Antonio (1818–1889), 76
Chihuahua, 77
Childs, Thomas (1796–1852), 78
China, 78
Churubusco, Battle of (August 20, 1847), 79
Citadel, Monterrey, 80
Clark, Meriwether Lewis (1809–1881), 81
Clay, Cassius Marcellus (1810–1903), 81
Clay, Henry (1777–1852), 82
Clay, Henry, Jr. (1811–1847), 82
Clifford, Nathan (1803–1881), 82
Coahuila y Texas, 83
Cochori, Skirmish at (January 30, 1848), 84
Collado Beach, 84
Collins, John L., 84
Colorado, 85
Conner, David (1792–1856), 85
Contreras, Battle of (August 20, 1847), 85
Cooke, Philip St. George (1809–1895), 86
Cooper, James Fenimore (1789–1851), 87
Corpus Christi, 87
Corwin, Thomas (1794–1865), 88
Cos, Martín Perfecto de (1800–1854), 88
Couch, Darius (1822–1897), 89
Court of Inquiry, Scott (1847), 89
Couto, José Bernardo (1803–1862), 90
Cross, Trueman (ca. 1795–1846), 90
Cuevas, Luis Gonzago (1800–1867), 91
Cushing, Caleb (1800–1879), 91

Dallas, George Mifflin (1792–1864), 93
Dalton, Patrick (ca. 1824–1847), 93
Davis, Jefferson (1808–1889), 94

Davis, John (1787–1854), 94
Dayton, Wreck of (September 13, 1845), 95
De la Rosa, Luis (1804–1856), 95
Delaware Indians, 96
Dent, Frederick Tracy (1821–1892), 96
Desertion, 96
Diarrhea, 98
Díaz de la Vega, Rómulo (ca. 1804–1877), 98
Dimick, Justin (1800–1871), 99
Dominguez, Manuel, 99
Dominguez's Spy Company (Mexican Spy Company), 100
Donelson, Andrew Jackson (1799–1871), 100
Doniphan, Alexander William (1808–1887), 101
Doniphan's March (1846–1847), 102
Dos Amades, 104
Dragoons, 104
Drum, Simon H. (1807–1847), 104
Du Pont, Samuel Francis (1803–1865), 104
Duran, Augustín, 105

Echeagaray, Miguel María (1816–1891), 107
El Brazito, Battle of (December 25, 1846), 107
El Embudo Pass, Skirmish at (January 29, 1847), 108
El Molino del Rey, Battle of (September 8, 1847), 108
El Rincón del Diablo, 110
El Tomacito (Tomás Baca), 110
Emerson, Ralph Waldo (1803–1882), 110
Emory, William Hemsley (1811–1887), 111
Ewell, Richard Stoddert (1817–1872), 111

Falcón, Rámon (d. 1847), 113
Flores, José María (1818–1866), 113
Flying Artillery, 114
Ford, John Salmon (1815–1897), 114
Forrest, French (1796–1866), 115
Fort Brown, 115
Fort Jesup, 116
Fort Marcy, 116

Fort Polk, 116
Fort Tenería, 117
Foster, John Gray (1823–1874), 117
Frémont, John C. (1813–1890), 117
French, Samuel Gibbs (1818–1910), 119

Gadsden Treaty (1853), 121
Gaines, John Pollard (1795–1857), 121
Galaxara, Skirmish at (November 24, 1847), 122
Gaona, Antonio (1793–1848), 122
García Condé, Pedro (1806–1851), 122
Garrison, William Lloyd (1805–1879), 123
Gillespie, Archibald H. (ca. 1812–1873), 123
Gillespie, Robert Addison (1815–1846), 124
Gómez Farías, Valentín (1781–1851), 124
Graham, Richard H. (ca. 1817–1846), 125
Grant, Ulysses S. (1822–1885), 125
Gray, Andrew Belcher (1820–1862), 126
Gray, Mabry B. (1817–1848), 127
Green, Duff (1791–1875), 127
Guadalupe Hidalgo, Treaty of (1848), 128
Guaymas, Battle of (October 20, 1847), 128
Guerrilla Warfare, 129

Hall, Willard Preble (1820–1882), 133
Halleck, Henry Wager (1815–1872), 133
Halls of the Montezumas, Mexico City, 134
Hamer, Thomas Lyon (1800–1846), 134
Hannegan, Edward Allen (1807–1859), 134
Hardee, William Joseph (1815–1873), 135
Hardin, John J. (1810–1847), 135
Harney, William Selby (1800–1889), 135
Hawk's Peak, 136

Hays, John Coffee (1817–1883), 137
Hébert, Paul Octave (1818–1880), 137
Henderson, James Pinckney (1808–1858), 138
Henrie, Daniel Drake, 138
Heredia, José Antonio de (ca. 1800–ca 1870), 138
Herrera, José Joaquín de (1792–1854), 139
Hill, Daniel Harvey (1821–1889), 139
Hitchcock, Ethan Allen (1798–1870), 140
Holzinger, Sebastián, 140
Hooker, Joseph (1814–1879), 140
Houston, Samuel (1793–1863), 141
Huamantla, Battle of (October 9, 1847), 141
Huger, Benjamin (1805–1877), 142
Hughes, John Joseph (1797–1864), 142
Hunt, Henry Jackson (1819–1889), 143
Hunter, Charles G. (1813–1873), 143

Ide, William Brown (1796–1852), 145
Immortal 14, 145
Indians, 145
Ingraham, Duncan N. (1802–1891), 146

Jackson, Andrew (1767–1845), 147
Jackson, Samuel, 147
Jackson, Thomas Jonathan ("Stonewall") (1824–1863), 148
Jalapa, 148
Jarauta, Celestino Domeco de (1814–1848), 149
Jarero, José María (1801–1867), 150
Jesup, Thomas Sidney (1788–1860), 150
Johnston, Albert Sidney (1803–1862), 150
Johnston, Joseph Eggleston (1807–1891), 151
Jones, Anson (1798–1858), 151
Jornada del Muerta, 152
Juvera, Julián (1784–1860), 152

Kearny, Philip (1814–1862), 153
Kearny, Stephen Watts (1794–1848), 153
Kearny's March (1846), 154
Kendall, George Wilkins (1809–1867), 155
Kinney, Henry Lawrence (1814–1862), 156
Kirker, James (1793–1853), 157
Klamath Indians, 157

La Cañada, Battle of (January 24, 1847), 159
La Encarnación, 159
La Hoya, Skirmish at (June 20, 1847), 160
La Mesa, Battle of (January 9, 1847), 160
La Paz, 161
Lamy, Jean Baptiste (1814–1888), 161
Landero Bauza, José Juan (1802–1869), 162
Lane, Joseph (1801–1881), 162
Larkin, Thomas Oliver (1802–1858), 162
Lee, Robert Edward (1807–1870), 163
León, Antonio (1794–1847), 164
Lincoln, Abraham (1809–1865), 164
Lombardini, Manuel María (1802–1853), 165
Longstreet, James (1821–1904), 165
Loreto, 166
Loring, William Wing (1818–1886), 166
Los Angeles, 166
Lowell, James Russell (1819–1891), 167

Mackenzie, Alexander Slidell (1803–1848), 169
Magoffin, James Wiley (1799–1868), 169
Magruder, John Bankhead (1810–1871), 170
Manifest Destiny, 170
Mansfield, Joseph King Fenno (1803–1862), 171
Marcy, William Learned (1786–1857), 172
Marshall, Thomas (1793–1853), 172

Martinez, Antonio José (1793–1867), 173
Mason, Richard Barnes (1797–1850), 173
Matamoros, 174
Mazatlán, 174
McClellan, George Brinton (1826–1885), 175
McCulloch, Ben (1811–1862), 175
McElroy, John (1782–1877), 176
Meade, George Gordon (1815–1872), 176
Medical Practices, Mexico, 177
Medical Practices, United States, 178
Mejía, Francisco (1822–1901), 180
Mervine, William (1791–1868), 180
Mexico, 181
Mexico City, 182
Mexico City, Battle of (September 13–14, 1847), 183
Mier Expedition (1842), 184
Miñón, José Vicente (1802–1878), 185
Moderados, 185
Monclova, 186
Monroe Doctrine (1823), 186
Monterey, 186
Monterrey, Armistice of (1846), 187
Monterrey, Battle of (September 21–23, 1846), 187
Mora, Skirmish at (January 25, 1847), 191
Mora y Villamil, Ignacio (1791–1870), 191
Mormon Battalion, 191
Mule Hill, 192
Mulejé, Skirmish at (October 1, 1846), 192
Munroe, John (ca. 1795–1861), 193

National Road, 195
Navy, Mexico, 195
Navy, United States, 196
Nevada, 200
New Mexico, 200
Niños Héroes, 201
Nueces River, 201

O'Brien, John Paul Jones (ca. 1818–1850), 203

Ojo Oso, 203
Olompali, Skirmish at (June 23, 1846), 204
Ortega, José María (1793–1871), 205
Ortiz, Tomás, 205

Palo Alto, Battle of (May 8, 1846), 207
Pánuco, 208
Paredes y Arrillaga, Mariano (1797–1849), 209
Parras, 210
Parrodi, Anastasio (1805–1867), 210
Parrott, William S. (1798–1863), 210
Patterson, Robert (1792–1881), 211
Pedregal, 211
Pemberton, John Clifford (1814–1881), 212
Peña y Barragán, Matías de la (ca. 1798–1850), 212
Peña y Peña, Manuel de la (1789–1850), 212
Pérez, Francisco (ca. 1810–1864), 213
Perote Castle, 213
Perry, Matthew Calbraith (1794–1858), 214
Petrita, USS, 214
Pico, Andrés (1810–1876), 215
Pico, Pío de Jesús (1801–1894), 215
Pierce, Franklin (1804–1869), 216
Pike, Albert (1809–1891), 216
Pillow, Gideon Johnson (1806–1878), 217
Point Isabel, 217
Polk, James Knox (1795–1849), 218
Polkos Revolt (1847), 219
Porter, Caroline, 220
Posada y Garduño, Manuel, 220
Price, Sterling (1809–1867), 221
Puebla, 221
Puebla, Siege of (September–October 1847), 222
Pueblo de Taos, Skirmish at (February 4, 1847), 222
Puros, 223

Quartermaster Departments, 225

Quijano, Benito (1800–1865), 226
Quitman, John Anthony (1799–1858), 226

Ramos, 229
Rancho Dominguez, Skirmish at (October 8, 1846), 229
Rangel, Joaquín (1803–1874), 230
Rea, Joaquín (ca. 1791–1850), 230
Reily (Reilly, Riley, O'Reilly), John, 231
Rejón, Manuel Crecencio (1799–1849), 231
Reno, Jesse L. (1823–1862), 232
Repatriation, 232
Resaca de la Palma, Battle of (May 9, 1846), 232
Rey, Antony (d. 1847), 234
Reynolds, John Fulton (1820–1863), 234
Reynosa, 234
Richey, John A. (1825–1847), 235
Ridgely, Randolph (1814–1846), 235
Riley, Bennet (1787–1853), 236
Rincón, Manuel E. (1784–1849), 236
Ringgold, Samuel (1800–1846), 236
Río Calaboso, Skirmish at (July 12, 1847), 237
Río Colorado, 237
Río Grande, 238
Río Sacramento, Battle of (February 28, 1847), 238
Roberts, William (d. 1847)/, 239
Robidoux, Antoine (1794–1860), 239
Rockets, 240
Rogers, R. Clay, 240

Saint Joseph's Island, 241
Salas, José Mariano (1797–1867), 241
Saltillo, 241
San Antonio, Skirmish at (March 25, 1848), 243
San Francisco, 243
San Gabriel River (Bartolo Ford), Battle of (January 8, 1847), 243
San José del Cabo, 244

San José del Pozo, Skirmish at (May 13, 1847), 245
San Juan, Skirmish at (July 30, 1847), 245
San Juan de Ulúa, 245
San Luis Potosí, 246
San Pascual, Battle of (December 6, 1846), 246
San Patricio Battalion, 246
Sands, Joshua Ratoon (1795–1883), 247
Santa Anna, Antonio López de (1794–1876), 248
Santa Clara, Battle of (January 2, 1847), 249
Santa Cruz de Rosales, Battle of (March 16, 1848), 250
Santa Fe, 251
Scott, Winfield (1786–1866), 251
Semmes, Raphael (1809–1877), 253
Sequalteplan, Skirmish at (February 25, 1848), 254
Sevier, Ambrose Hundley (1801–1848), 254
Sherman, Thomas West (1813–1879), 254
Shields, James (1806–1879), 255
Shubrick, William Branford (1790–1874), 255
Slavery, 256
Slidell, John (1793–1871), 256
Sloat, John Drake (1781–1867), 257
Smallpox, 258
Smith, Persifor Frazer (1798–1858), 258
Soldado River, Skirmish at (April 9, 1848), 258
Somers, USS, 259
Stevens, Isaac Ingalls (1818–1862), 259
Stockton, Robert Field (1795–1866), 259
Storms, Jane McManus (1807–1878), 260
Surfboats, 261

Sutter, John Augustus (1803–1880), 261
Tabasco, Battles of (October 25, 1846; July 16, 1847), 263
Tacubaya, 265
Tacubaya, Armistice of (1847), 265
Tampico, 266
Taos Rebellion (January–February 1847), 266
Tattnall, Josiah (1795–1871), 267
Taylor, Zachary (1784–1850), 268
Téllez, Rafael, 270
Terrés, Andrés (1777–1850), 270
Texas, 271
Texas Rangers, 271
Thoreau, Henry David (1817–1862), 273
Thornton, Seth B. (d. 1847), 274
Tilghman, Lloyd (1816–1863), 274
Todos Santos, Skirmish at (March 28, 1848), 275
Tornel y Mendivil, José María (1789–1853), 275
Torrejón, Anastasio (ca. 1802–ca. 1861), 275
Tower, Zealous Bates (1819–1900), 276
Transcontinental Treaty (1819), 276
Trías Álvarez, Ángel (1809–1867), 277
Trist, Nicholas Philip (1800–1874), 277
Truxtun, USS, 278
Tuxpan, 279
Twiggs, David Emanuel (1790–1862), 279
Tyler, John (1790–1862), 280

Urrea, José (1797–1849), 281
Utah, 281

Valencia, Gabriel (1799–1848), 283
Vallejo, Mariano Guadalupe (1808–1890), 284
Van Dorn, Earl (1820–1863), 284
Vázquez, Ciriaco (1794–1847), 285
Veracruz, 285
Veracruz, Battle of (March 9–29, 1847), 285
Walker, Robert John (1801–1869), 289
Walker, Samuel H. (1817–1847), 289
Walnut Springs, 290
War Address, James K. Polk, 290
War Message, Mariano Paredes y Arrillaga, 292
Washington, John Macrea (1797–1853), 293
Weapons, Mexico, 294
Weapons, United States, 294
Webster, Daniel (1782–1852), 295
Whitman, Walt (1819–1892), 295
Wickliffe, Charles Anderson (1788–1869), 296
Wilmot, David (1814–1868), 296
Women, Mexico, 297
Women, United States, 299
Wool, John Ellis (1784–1869), 299
Wool's Chihuahua Expedition (1846), 301
Worth, William Jenkins (1794–1849), 301
Wright, George (1803–1865), 302

Yell, Archibald (1797–1847), 303
Yellow Fever, 303
Yucatán, 304

Zozaya, María Josefa (d. 1846), 305

Chronology, 307

Selected References, 313

Index, 339

Preface

The Mexican-American War was fought from 1846 to 1848 between the Republic of Mexico and the United States. It is one of the least-understood conflicts in U.S. history and generally forgotten when compared with larger wars. Yet it had one of the highest U.S. mortality rates of any U.S. war, gave the United States California and the Southwest, and devastated the struggling new Republic of Mexico, including taking over half its territory. The Treaty of Guadalupe Hidalgo continues to affect Mexican Americans and is still used in litigation with the federal government today.

The purpose of the *Encyclopedia of the Mexican-American War* is to increase the reader's awareness of the Mexican-American War by exploring people and events—some big, some small, but all of them important. Histories of wars tend to focus on commanders and troop movements, and the personal drama of the common soldier is forgotten. I have included entries, and excerpts from eyewitness narratives, that highlight the day-to-day reality of marching and fighting. Few of us today can imagine the magnitude of the hardships, sacrifices, and accomplishments. In addition to the major battles, marches, and commanders, I have included some smaller events that are rarely mentioned, such as Mexicans and U.S. soldiers fighting side by side against raiding Apache warriors, the funeral of an unnamed Mexican officer after the Battle of Cerro Gordo, Santa Anna's death march to Buena Vista, and the young Mexican woman who was shot to death helping wounded men of both armies during the Battle of Monterrey. These entries capture more fully the reality for the U.S. and Mexican soldier.

Compared with the number of U.S. writings, diaries, letters, and journals that record the conflict, first-person Mexican accounts are few in number. Most Mexican soldiers were poor, illiterate, and pressed hurriedly into service. They often told the events of the day to their wives and loved ones, who frequently followed the army. This lack of Mexican material creates an imbalance in the descriptions for certain events; the more accounts that are available from both sides, of course, the more accurately military events can be reconstructed. Many of the accounts of Mexican activities were generated from U.S. reports or from those of high-ranking Mexican generals, and these accounts were often exaggerated to support the writer's own decisions on the battlefield. Fortunately, some historians, especially Justin H. Smith, William A. DePalo, and K. Jack Bauer, have made special efforts to examine Mexican archival material, and their detailed footnotes are a tremendous source of information.

This book contains more biographical profiles of U.S. officers than of Mexican officers, simply because the former are easier to find. The feats of bravery on the U.S. side are well documented; the feats of bravery on the Mexican side are harder to locate. Their mention is fleeting in reports and books, and the heroes are often nameless: the brave color bearers at Palo Alto, the San Blas Battalion at Chapultepec, a badly wounded sergeant staying with his sons in battle to help them reload.

Each of the many secondary works on the war are subject to the author's interpretation of primary accounts and occasionally conflict. Some entries in this book are documented by only one or two accounts; others have been documented by hundreds. Postwar reminiscences, although valuable, are often inaccurate, especially if 20 or 30 years have elapsed before memories are written down. The entries I present in this book draw on a variety of primary and secondary sources, and I have strived to make them as accurate as possible. I have corrected misspellings in quoted material to make it more readable.

Acknowledgments

Many thanks to ABC-CLIO for undertaking this project. My editor, Alicia Merritt, has been supportive, patient, and a pleasure to work with. The vast majority of readily available research material on the Mexican-American War is written in English from the U.S. perspective. In an effort to make this work as balanced as possible, Eric and Maria Wolf and Alfonzo Zepeda-Capistrán have kindly translated Mexican documents written in Spanish, in return for very little. Their generosity with their time and their belief in the importance of this project are much appreciated. Historians Jeanne and David Heidler reviewed the manuscript. I wish to thank the entire staff at the Pinney branch of the Madison Public Library. In addition to supplying me with numerous rare volumes through their efficient interlibrary loan service, they were always helpful with even my toughest questions and entrusted me with restricted reference materials overnight. My research was made that much easier by the excellent collections (and reference assistance) at the Wisconsin Historical Society.

Introduction

At first glance, it would seem that Mexico and the United States should have been good neighbors in the nineteenth century—they were both relatively young countries that had rebelled against a mother nation to establish republics. As they grew, they both had to deal with states with populations that believed that their needs were not being met by the federal government.

However, one of the biggest differences was that the U.S. population was mostly European in origin. They had come to "America" as political or economic refugees and banded together to drive out the British, French, Spanish, and Native American cultures. Feeling morally and religiously superior, they were swept along by the concept of Manifest Destiny. In the United States, the economy, especially industry and transportation, was growing quickly.

Mexico, on the other hand, under Spanish rule, had established a caste system and provincial isolationism. Its immigrant population was largely Spanish and in Mexico primarily as an occupational force. Mexico's northern frontier was huge, politically adrift, and difficult to govern. The communication, transportation, social, and economic ties among the provinces were limited. Mexico's new fragile republic, founded in 1821, was wracked by political revolutions for its first 25 years as different factions tried to wrest control of the government. This instability damaged economic and industrial development, and the treasury department was often in a state of near-bankruptcy.

These divergent economic, social, and political paths led to friction and misunderstanding between the two countries, especially along the U.S.-Mexico border. As the rebellious population of U.S. settlers in the Mexican state of Tejas (Texas) grew, General Antonio López de Santa Anna and a formidable army marched northward to suppress them. Blood was spilled at the Alamo, Goliad, and San Jacinto in 1836. Mexico was forced to surrender Texas, and the anger and embarrassment of this surrender smoldered for a decade. The United States continued to pressure Mexico to sell New Mexico and California. When the Republic of Texas decided to join the United States in 1845, Mexico broke its diplomatic ties in Washington, D.C. Mexico believed that Texas was still Mexican territory and feared that the insatiable United States would take more land.

In the spring of 1846, two armies gathered along the Río Grande near Matamoros. Zachary Taylor's Army of Occupation arrived on the north side of the river to protect the new U.S. state of Texas and began to build a fort. General Mariano Arista's Army of the North watched the U.S. troops warily from Matamoros on the south side of the Río Grande. Mexican cavalry patrols splashed across the river and skirmished with U.S. dragoons. By the time President James K. Polk received official word of the first U.S. casualties, several skirmishes and two major battles had been fought in the thick chaparral along the Río Grande. Claiming that Mexico had "invaded our territory and shed American blood upon the American soil," President Polk stirred Congress into declaring war on May 13, 1846.

The Battles of Palo Alto and Resaca de la Palma in May 1846 were startling victories for Taylor's outnumbered force and shocking losses for the proud Mexican army. In the choking heat, dust, and smoke, the U.S. army had demonstrated its cohesiveness as a unit, its fighting spirit, and the deadly effectiveness of its artillery. The Mexican retreat to Matamoros and southward to Monterrey was the start of a slow, inexorable advance by Taylor and his army into northern Mexico.

After occupying Matamoros and Camargo and breaking in new volunteer soldiers, Taylor marched southward to Monterrey, where he defeated the Mexicans again in a brutal, four-day fight in September in the city's streets and among demolished homes.

As Taylor pondered his next move, the U.S. navy continued its blockading activity along both Pacific and Gulf of Mexico coasts, chasing down Mexican vessels and seizing port cities. President Polk had begun operations to seize New Mexico and California by sending Brigadier General Stephen W. Kearny and the Army of the West to occupy both provinces. Although Kearny's occupation of New Mexico and the combined army-navy subjugation of California were triumphs that inspired the U.S. public, they had little impact on the outcome of the war. Who won and who lost and the resultant spoils would be determined on the battlefields in northern and eastern Mexico, where the casualty count was steadily climbing.

Desperate for leadership, in August 1846 the Mexican government welcomed back General Santa Anna, who had been living in exile in Cuba. Using his dictatorial power, motivational skills, and negotiating prowess, Santa Anna quickly rebuilt the Army of the North into a 20,000-man army in the winter of 1846–1847. Full of hope and confidence, Santa Anna marched northward to find Taylor. On February 23, 1847, the two armies collided in the rugged hills near hacienda Buena Vista. Taylor held on during the desperate Mexican assaults, and Santa Anna reluctantly retreated during the night. In a pattern that would haunt the Mexican army for the rest of the war, high-ranking commanders failed to support each other in battle. And once again, the U.S. artillery ripped fearful holes in the Mexican ranks. By the time Santa Anna had returned to his base at San Luis Potosí, he had lost more than half his army.

The restless Polk was never satisfied with Taylor's pace of warfare and chaffed at Taylor's reluctance to advance deeper into Mexico. Polk assigned Major General Winfield Scott the task of organizing a 10,000-man army to attack Veracruz and march inland to take the capital, Mexico City. In March 1847, Scott's forces waded ashore at Veracruz, accomplishing the first major amphibious landing in U.S. history. The city was shelled into submission at the cost of hundreds of civilian lives. Anxious to avoid the dreaded season of "black vomit," or yellow fever, along the coast, Scott quickly moved his men along the National Road that led inland to Mexico City.

Refusing to give up, Santa Anna assembled a makeshift army of soldiers, guardsmen, militia, teenaged conscripts, and old men. Barely trained and poorly clothed and equipped, Santa Anna's new army faced Scott's army at the Battles of Cerro Gordo, Contreras, Churubusco, El Molino del Rey, and Chapultepec. Although the Mexicans fought well, each engagement was a U.S. victory. As the U.S. soldiers streamed into the defeated fortress at Chapultepec, a weary Mexican officer watching from a distance shook his head and muttered, "God is a Yankee" (Alcaraz 1850). The decimated Mexican army could not keep the victorious U.S. force from the gates of Mexico City, which fell on September 14, 1847. On February 2, 1848, the Treaty of Guadalupe Hidalgo was signed. In return for $15 million, Mexico surrendered New Mexico and California—more than half its territory—to the United States. In July 1848, the last U.S. soldiers boarded ships for their long return home. The war was over.

Causes of the Mexican-American War

The causes of the conflict are still argued today. The animosity that ultimately erupted in warfare between the two neighbors was rooted in decades of territorial and political friction. The grievances gathered a momentum that, once started, continued to lurch toward more misunderstandings, reactionary responses, and finally the costly Mexican-American War. The following are the principal reasons that have been mentioned by historians as contributing to the Mexican-American War; they are all, to some degree, interrelated.

(1) Mexico, independent from Spain since 1821, was weak, wracked by political upheavals, and vulnerable to takeover (23 administrations had governed Mexico from 1836 to 1848—almost two governments per year). Many of Mexico's states, especially the northern ones, were rebellious and objected to absolute Mexican rule. The United States feared that France, England, or Russia might invade Mexico and threaten U.S. borders.

Many U.S. leaders reasoned that, if Mexico were to be invaded, it might as well be by the United States, which could guarantee democratic rule and likely economic improvement.

(2) The United States was swept along by the imperialistic concept of Manifest Destiny and wanted to occupy North America from coast to coast. This drive reached an almost religious fervor with the idea that the United States with a democratic government would relieve Mexicans of its dictatorship. God's will was often invoked as justification for expansion. U.S. expansionist inclinations had already been well demonstrated by the acquisition of Florida, Louisiana Territory, and the Republic of Texas and by conflict with Great Britain over Oregon. After many offers of purchase, the United States had clearly made it known that it wanted to own New Mexico and California. Many U.S. citizens developed the belief that they were morally, intellectually, and politically superior to the Mexicans, which they viewed as a separate "race." This enthnocentric view was demonstrated by interactions along the border, the treatment of Mexican ministers in Washington, D.C., and treatment of Mexicans by U.S. dignitaries in Mexico.

(3) Mexico had allowed thousands of U.S. immigrants to settle in its northern state of Texas, yet many of these settlers refused to comply with the Mexican laws that they had promised to obey. Mexico had hoped that the U.S. settlers could be integrated into Mexican society, but there were too many ideological and cultural differences for this to occur. Mexican dictator Santa Anna had abolished the constitution and stripped the state of Texas of its independent government, actions that led to further disillusionment in Texas, especially by the Anglo-American population, and to resentment in other northern Mexican states, which further weakened Mexico's control over its northern frontier.

(4) By the 1830s, more than four times as many Anglo-Americans as Mexicans resided in Texas. Some Mexican leaders worried that the United States would take over more than Texas, especially New Mexico and California, as the United States continued to push westward. In a harsh campaign, Santa Anna crushed rebellious U.S. forces in Texas in 1836 at the Alamo and Goliad. An uprising by Sam Houston's army, already begun at the time of the Alamo and Goliad, defeated Santa Anna. Santa Anna was forced to sign the Treaties of Velasco, which acknowledged the Republic of Texas, whose southern border with Mexico would be the Río Grande. The loss of Texas created intense resentment toward the United States.

(5) The Mexican government refused to recognize the Treaties of Velasco and still considered Texas to be part of Mexico. (It claimed that the treaties were invalid because they had been signed by Santa Anna when he was a prisoner of war.) Texas and the United States recognized the southern border of Texas as the Río Grande; Mexico regarded the border as either the Nueces River or the Sabine River, a huge difference in land area. Santa Anna stepped up raids, which inflicted damages on some Anglo-Americans.

(6) The Mexican government defaulted on its agreement to pay the United States approximately $2 million for damages claimed by U.S. citizens during various periods of unrest within Mexico and along the border. Knowing that the Mexican treasury was nearly bankrupt, President Polk argued for U.S. ownership of California and New Mexico in lieu of payment.

(7) The José Joaquín Herrera administration, which favored a peaceful settlement with the United States, fell in a military coup. Herrera was replaced by General Mariano Paredes y Arrillaga, who wanted to fight the United States.

(8) Slave owners in the South and the majority of southern leaders in the U.S. Congress wanted Texas and any other Mexican territory that might be acquired to be open for slavery. They lobbied hard for the annexation of Texas. In 1845, Texas accepted an annexation offer from the United States, which again recognized the Río Grande as the southern border of Texas. Mexicans believed that the United States had accepted territory that was still rightfully theirs. Mexico reacted angrily by withdrawing its minister from Washington, D.C., and prepared for war.

(9) Regarding race and slavery, Mexico had different ideas from those of the United States. African slavery had never been an important institution under Spanish or Mexican rule. The Mexican government initially encouraged Texas settlers to bring in slaves as a way to increase the population. However, in an effort to slow settlement of Anglo-Americans in Texas, Mexico abolished slavery in 1829. Yet slavery continued to thrive in Texas because the no-slavery law was too difficult for the government to enforce. In Mexico, persons of Indian or mixed descent were habitually discriminated against, but Mexico had made some efforts to assimilate several of its native cultures. Some Mexicans feared that they would be treated the same way that the U.S. government treated its African American and Native American populations.

(10) President Polk wanted to use the unpaid U.S. claims against Mexico to leverage the purchase of California and New Mexico. When U.S. consul John Black told Polk that the Mexican government would receive a minister to discuss this issue, Polk sent John Slidell to Mexico City. Upon his arrival, Slidell was shocked to learn that Mexico had planned to discuss only Texas. In an embarrassing incident, Slidell was refused by the government and eventually returned to the United States empty-handed. This further irritated relations between the two countries and put Polk in a more warlike mood.

(11) After Texas was annexed by the United States in December 1845, Taylor moved to the north bank of the Río Grande (which the United States claimed was its territory) and built a fort along the river. Mexicans believed that the U.S. army was trespassing on what was still their land and considered the trespass as an overt act of war. Before any warfare had commenced, on April 15, 1846, Taylor ordered a naval blockade of the Río Grande—another warlike act. About a week later, a U.S. patrol was ambushed by Mexican cavalry north of the river and resulted in 16 U.S. casualties. Taylor then fought General Mariano Arista's Army of the North in the Battles of Palo Alto and Resaca de la Palma on May 8 and May 9, respectively. Polk's declaration of war passed resoundingly on May 13, 1846. The Mexican-American War had officially begun.

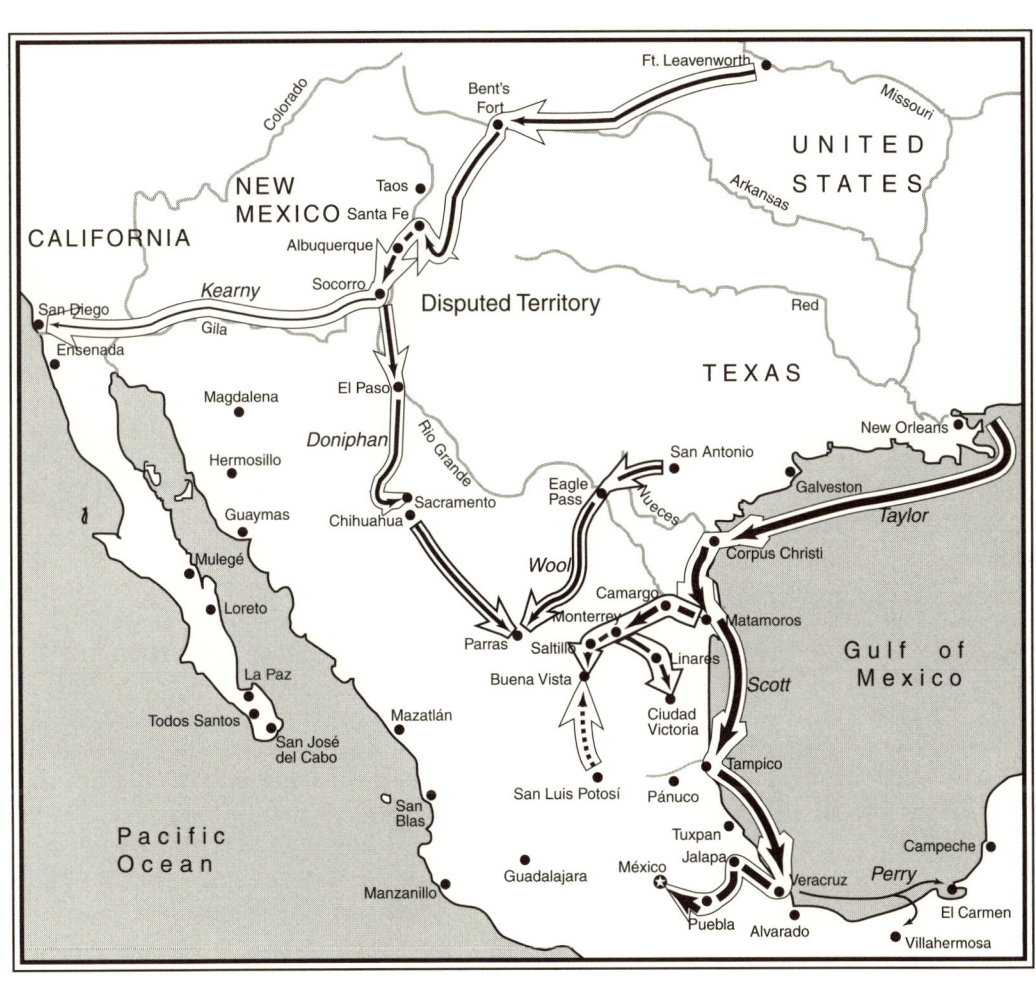

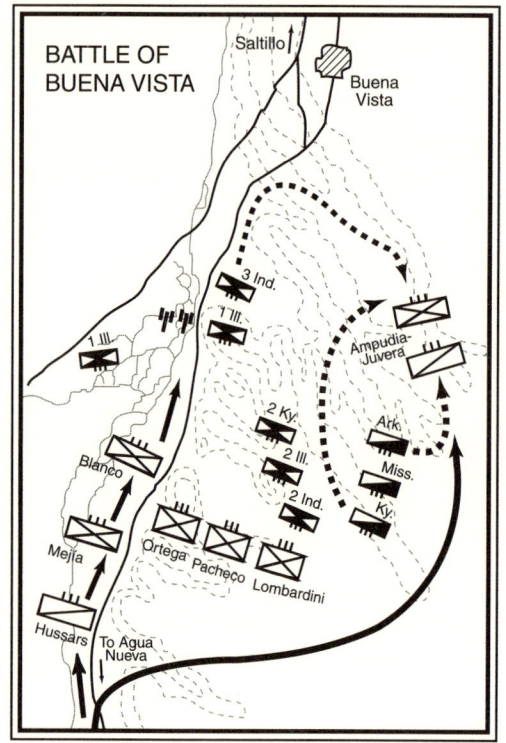
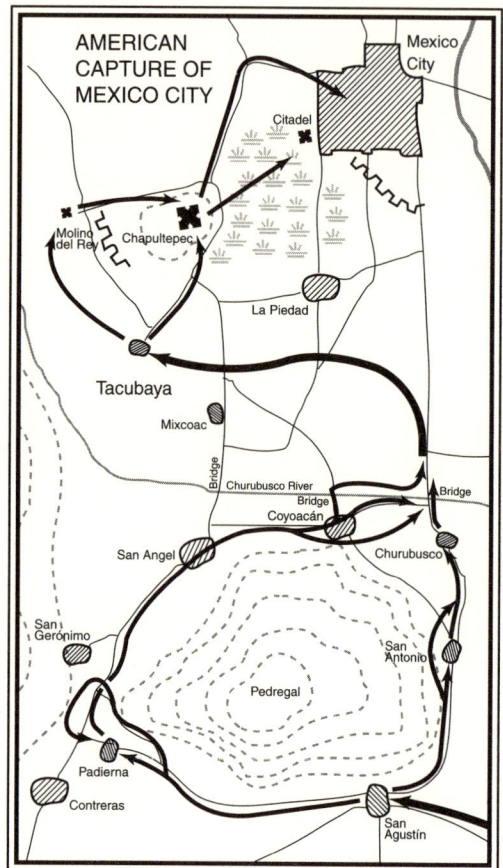
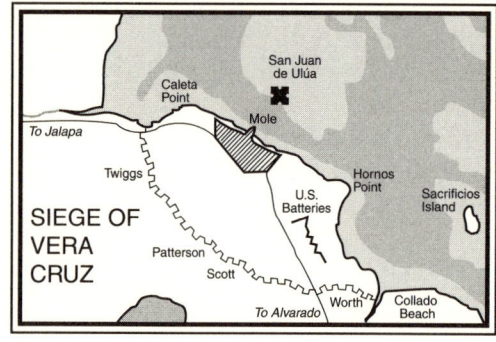

A

Abolitionists

Abolitionists were one of the most outspoken groups in the United States, and they vehemently denounced the war. They feared that the war was being fought to gain new territory for slavery and tried to sway public opinion against it.

William Lloyd Garrison used his abolitionist journal, *The Liberator*, to crusade against the U.S. war effort. For example, Garrison wrote:

> If ever war was waged for basest ends,
> By means perfidious, profligate and low,
> It is the present war with Mexico,
> Which in deep guilt all other wars transcends.

Abolitionist writers often accused U.S. soldiers of being murderers who preyed upon a weak and defenseless country. John Greenleaf Whittier and James Russell Lowell were two of the foremost antiwar poets in the United States. Two weeks after the war began, Whittier called it "miserably wicked" and maintained that "every conquered Mexican village becomes a market-place for human flesh." In 1847, as editor of the abolitionist *National Era*, Whittier continued to publish numerous antiwar pieces. Lowell wrote that the war was a "national crime committed in behoof of Slavery, our common sin." He assailed the war in his biting, sarcastic style in the highly popular *The Biglow Papers*.

Although they were widely published, abolitionist writers and lecturers were not successful in changing the public's patriotic support of the war. Leading abolitionists themselves did not unanimously agree that the war was evil. For example, Kentucky abolitionist Cassius M. Clay left his antislavery newspaper to join the army and fight in Mexico. Although he had opposed the war, he explained that it was his duty to serve his country. Other editors decided to not publish antiwar material if it threatened the safety and morale of U.S. soldiers in Mexico.

The actions of extremists helped alienate the public against abolitionism during the war. Extremists prayed for Mexican victories, wrote to Mexican leaders pledging support, and hoped foreign countries would enter the conflict against the United States. Ohio senator Thomas Corwin delivered such a harsh antiwar speech in February 1847 that he damaged the credibility of his fellow antiwar supporters.

See also Corwin, Thomas; Garrison, William Lloyd; Lowell, James Russell.

For further reading: Johannsen, *To the Halls of the Montezumas*, 1985; Merk, *Slavery and the Annexation of Texas*, 1972; Schroeder, *Mr. Polk's War*, 1973; Sewell, *Ballots for Freedom*, 1976.

Aburto, Juan

One of several prominent Mexican guerrilla leaders, Juan Aburto harassed Major General Winfield Scott's army as it moved from Veracruz to Mexico City in 1847. He frequently combined forces with guerrilla Padre Celestino Domeco de Jarauta and struck smaller columns that marched along the National Road between Veracruz and Jalapa. The losses they inflicted caused Scott to detach large numbers of his army to keep the highway open and protect shipments of supplies.

Aburto's guerrillas, numbered up to 1,500, are most remembered for attacking a 1,000-man U.S. force under Major Folliot T. Lally near Paso de Ovejas on August 10, 1847. Brisk fighting occurred until the U.S. troops finally reached Jalapa on August 20. U.S. casualties were 24 killed and 68 wounded.

Shortly after this fight, Aburto contracted a fever and died. He had been one of the most active and locally supported partisan leaders along the National Road. The loss of his leadership, combined with increased antiguerrilla operations by Scott, reduced guerrilla attacks on the U.S. army.

See also Guerrilla Warfare; Jarauta, Celestino Domeco de.

For further reading: Alcaraz, *The Other Side*, 1850; Brackett, *General Lane's Brigade in Central Mexico*, 1854; Oswandel, *Notes of the Mexican War*, 1885.

Adams, John Quincy
(1767–1848)

One of the most prominent political figures in U.S. history, John Quincy Adams served as a U.S. senator, representative, secretary of state, and president. He ardently opposed the Mexican-American War, which he maintained was unconstitutional, immoral, and designed to propagate slavery. He led the antiwar minority in Congress during the war.

Adams, the son of U.S. President John Adams, was born in Braintree (Quincy), Massachusetts. After an excellent formal education, Adams became a lawyer and was later an interpreter for the U.S. minister in Russia. Finding he enjoyed governmental affairs, Adams launched a political career in which he was active until the last day of his life. His early accomplishments included serving as a U.S. senator (1803–1808) and secretary of state (1817–1825).

In 1819, Secretary of State Adams negotiated the Adams-Onís Treaty with Spain, which gave Florida and West Florida to the United States in return for the United States' relinquishing all present or future U.S. claims to Texas or any other Spanish territory. The boundary between Louisiana and New Spain (later Mexico) was drawn at the Sabine River. (When James K. Polk was elected president, he emphasized the *re*annexation of Texas, implying that it had been part of the Louisiana Purchase that Adams had traded away.)

John Quincy Adams, ca. 1847
(Library of Congress)

Adams became the sixth U.S. president (1825–1829) when he defeated Andrew Jackson in a bitter campaign. His presidency was marked by constant battles in Congress with pro-Jackson politicians. With the help of Henry Clay, Adams tried to purchase Texas from the new Republic of Mexico, but with no success. He ran for reelection in 1828 and was overwhelmingly defeated by Andrew Jackson.

Adams occupied a seat in the House of Representatives from 1831 to 1848. During the Mexican-American War, he was known as an abolitionist, "Radical Whig," and member of the "Conscience Whigs" (so-called because their consciences were repelled by the war). Adams and other antislavery leaders believed that the war was designed to propagate slavery. On May 11, 1846, Congress listened to Polk's War Address for almost two hours and voted 173 to 14 to accept it. The 14 dissenting votes—later to be known in New England as the Immortal 14—were led by Adams.

In the Thirtieth Session of Congress (January 1848), Adams spearheaded a resolution that maintained that the war was unconstitutional. The resolution called for the immediate withdrawal of U.S. troops, peace without indemnity, a boundary somewhere between the Nueces River and the Río Grande, and financial compensation to Mexico. It passed by a vote of 85 to 81, but was not acted upon because Mexico signed the Treaty of Guadalupe Hidalgo one month later.

On February 22, 1848, Adams suffered a stroke in the House as he spoke against the Mexican-American War. He died the following day. "Where could death have found him," asked Senator Thomas Hart Benton of Missouri, "but at the post of duty?"

See also Abolitionists; Immortal 14.

For further reading: Adams, *The Diary of John Quincy Adams*, 1928; Bemis, *John Quincy Adams and the Union*, 1970; Clarke, *John Quincy Adams*, 1932; Richards, *The Life and Times of Congressman John Quincy Adams*, 1986.

Adams-Onís Treaty

See Transcontinental Treaty.

African Americans

Because of their low social status or enslavement in the United States, African Americans did not usually play the soldier's role during the Mexican-American War. Most southern blacks were owned as slaves. As "men of color," free blacks were prohibited from serving in the U.S. army, although a few served in the U.S. Navy. Many opponents to the war viewed the war as an effort to extend the enslavement of African Americans into new western territories. Prominent free blacks such as Frederick Douglass and Henry Garnet spoke out vigorously against the war.

Despite the army regulations, a few lighter-skinned African Americans did serve in the army. Slaves also tried to join the service to escape their masters. One slave was drummed out of the army at Veracruz after it was discovered that he was black.

The most prominent role for African Americans in the U.S. army was as servants. Hundreds of blacks, both free and slave, were personal attendants to officers. Junior officers were allowed one servant; major generals could have four. Blacks suffered constant physical and emotional abuse by the U.S. army and were occasionally murdered. Blacks were attracted to Mexicans because they treated them more kindly than did their Anglo-American masters. Knowing slavery was illegal in Mexico, some black servants deserted to join the Mexicans as free men. At one point, many U.S. officers considered switching to white servants because they were losing so many blacks to the Mexican ranks.

Blacks were part of every U.S. force during the war. During his expedition, John C. Frémont depended on a black servant for his roping skills. Although most of the servants were men, a few black women were also present, including a mulatto woman named Blanche who served an officer from the 2nd Indiana Volunteers.

Most African American servants tended to the personal needs of their officers, such as cooking and cleaning, or drove wagons. They also brought food and supplies to the front during combat and helped collect and nurse the wounded both during and after combat. Servants were frequently in the line of fire, for example, holding the reins of their masters' horses. The slave of a southern army captain threw himself in front of a Mexican lance at the Battle of Huamantla, thus saving the life of his owner.

Jacob Dodson, a black man who served with Frémont, later applied for and won Mexican War service pay from Congress. No African American accounts of the war have yet been discovered.

For further reading: May, "Invisible Men," 1987.

Agua Fria, Skirmish of
(June 4, 1848)

Fought on June 4, 1848, the skirmish at Agua Fria near Marin, Mexico, was the last fight of the Mexican-American War. A command of 23 men from the U.S. 2nd Dragoons was ambushed and pinned down by a large band of mounted Mexican guerrillas.

While both nations waited for the ratification of the Treaty of Guadalupe Hidalgo, the remnants of U.S. General John E. Wool's army (formerly General Zachary Taylor's) were still camped at Walnut Springs, near Monterrey. Their primary duties involved chasing smugglers and guerrillas. A twenty-three-man force from the 2nd Dragoons was ordered to Seralbo on June 2. Returning two days later, they were attacked by mounted guerrillas after passing through Marin. The ambush quickly turned into a violent collision of mounted men. Thick dust and impenetrable chaparral made it difficult to form a battle line. U.S. carbine fire eventually drove the guerrillas back a short distance.

More than half the U.S. command had been killed or wounded. U.S. survivors built a protective wall of dead horses, branches, and cacti, and discarded Mexican lances were used to form a makeshift abatis. A wounded German trooper rode through a gauntlet of small-arms fire to bring reinforcements. The heat became unbearable. A volunteer who went to get water from the nearby river was lassoed and dragged to his death in the chaparral. The guerrilla chief rode forward, was fired upon, and fell wounded beside his horse. The chief tied his lasso under his arms, and his well-trained horse dragged him from the field. The guerrillas attacked briefly one more time before a mounted column from the 2nd Dragoons appeared in the afternoon. The guerrillas then dispersed quickly in the chaparral. U.S. casualties were 7 killed and 12 wounded; 29 Mexican dead were counted by the U.S. troopers.

The following day, the dragoons brought in 22 guerrilla prisoners. After an examination, the prisoners were released by the order of General Wool. (The same day, Wool received official notification that the war was over.) Samuel Chamberlain, one of the survivors of the original expedition, indicated that dragoons and Texas Rangers went "a hunting that day" and killed every one of the released guerrillas.

For further reading: Chamberlain, *My Confession*, 1956.

Agua Nueva

Located in the Mexican state of Coahuila, the small community of Agua Nueva, about 17 miles south of Saltillo, was an important staging area for Mexican and U.S. troops in the northern theater of the war. Agua Nueva was occupied by both sides during the Buena Vista campaign in 1847.

The citizens of Agua Nueva likely saw their first U.S. soldiers when General John E. Wool's force occupied the town on December 21, 1846. Wool's men had been en route to Chihuahua, before they turned south in response to a call for reinforcements from Brigadier General William J. Worth at Saltillo. Wool's remarkable forced march of 120 miles surprised General Antonio López de Santa Anna, who then canceled his planned attack on the U.S. forces at Saltillo. The inhabitants of Agua Nueva were shocked on Christmas Day in 1846, when a group of Arkansas volunteer soldiers attacked and raped several women. U.S. soldiers traveled frequently through the village on scouting missions until mid-February 1847, when General Zachary Taylor ordered his men to advance from Saltillo to Agua Nueva. The U.S. army of nearly 5,000 men soon established a sprawling campsite outside the village.

While waiting for the northward advance of Santa Anna's army from San Luis Potosí, one of Taylor's Arkansas soldiers was found murdered near the U.S. camp on February 9, 1847—apparently in retaliation for the incident on Christmas Day. A group of about 100 Arkansas cavalrymen rode out "hunting" from Agua Nueva the following day and murdered a group of Mexican refugees in a cave near the settlement of Catana. Taylor was outraged. The resulting military commission failed to identify the actual killers, and the soldiers involved were sent to the Río Grande. "Such deeds," wrote Taylor, "cast indelible disgrace upon our arms and reputation of our country."

Captain Ben McCulloch of the Texas Rangers scouted the enemy position to the south at La Encarnacíon, where Santa Anna was camped, and rode back to Agua Nueva on February 21 with the news. Taylor's men moved back to a better defensive position called La Angostura (the narrows), three miles south of the hacienda Buena Vista. Colonel Archibald Yell's command, left behind to bring up the remaining supplies, made contact with the lead elements of the Mexican army and quickly withdrew, burning buildings and remaining supplies. When Santa Anna reached the village, he found the abandoned campsites and burning wagons and assumed that Taylor had made a hasty retreat.

After the Battle of Buena Vista on February 23, 1847, the defeated Mexican army retreated to Agua Nueva. On February 25, Santa Anna held a council of war in the village, and his officers recommended withdrawal. An envoy of U.S. soldiers arrived to arrange for the exchange of prisoners and the care of the wounded. The Mexican army left the following day for a dreaded 35-mile night march to La Encarnacíon. The U.S. army occupied Agua Nueva from February 27 to March 9, 1847. Reconnaissance patrols from this staging area located a group of more than 200 wounded Mexican soldiers in a chapel in La Encarnacíon. The wounded had been abandoned during Santa Anna's retreat.

See also Buena Vista, Battle of; Catana, Massacre at; La Encarnacíon.

For further reading: Alcaraz, *The Other Side*, 1850; Chamberlain, *My Confession*, 1956.

Aguascalientes, Plan of

General and ex-president Mariano Paredes y Arrillaga, displeased with the Mexican government, led a short-lived rebellion in 1848 that called for a new government under his Plan of Aguascalientes. The rebellion never gained any serious momentum and was suppressed by military forces in 1848 and early 1849.

Shortly after the signing of the Treaty of Guadalupe Hidalgo on February 2, 1848, and the ascendancy of new president José Joaquín de Herrera, General Paredes y Arrillaga began to raise an army and incite civil unrest. In June, he denounced the treaty and the Herrera government (which he had toppled in a coup in December 1845) and urged rebellion against the *moderado* government. Paredes y Arrillaga's Plan of Aguascalientes called for individual states to resume their own sovereign leadership until a better government (presumably under his leadership) could be established. The war-weary public failed to embrace the rebellion, and military troops crushed Paredes y Arrillaga's small band of insurgents in 1848 and 1849 and executed the popular guerrilla Celestino Domeco de Jarauta, Paredes y Arrillaga's ally.

See also Jarauta, Celestino Domeco de; Paredes y Arrillaga, Mariano.

For further reading: DePalo, *The Mexican National Army, 1822–1852*, 1997.

Alamán y Escalada, Lucas
(1792–1853)

Lucas Alamán y Escalada was one of the most prominent Mexican statesmen during the Mexican-American War. He favored finding a European ally to help run the Mexican government and fight the United States. He also plotted with General Mariano Paredes y Arrillaga to overthrow the administration of President José Joaquín de Herrera in 1845.

Born to wealthy parents in Guanajuato, Alamán y Escalada was well schooled and excelled in the natural sciences. He traveled and studied in Europe and served as a delegate of New Spain to the Spanish congress. He returned to Mexico in 1823 after the overthrow of Agustín de Iturbide and held various governmental posts.

Alamán y Escalada's diplomatic skills were quickly recognized, and he was appointed minister of foreign relations in 1823–1825 and 1830–1832. Concerned about the large number of rebellious U.S. settlers in Texas, he spearheaded a law in 1830 aimed at stopping the flow of U.S. settlers. He also tried to attract settlers from other countries.

Alamán y Escalada published numerous essays and political articles. His argument in 1840 that Mexico should recognize Texas as an independent republic to avoid conflict with the United States led to his being called a traitor by citizens and government officials alike.

Realizing the need for a strong government, and that Mexico was ill-prepared to fight a war with the United States, Alamán sought European intervention in Mexican affairs. He plotted with Spanish minister Salvador Bermúdez de Castro and General Paredes y Arrillaga to establish a new government. When Paredes y Arrillaga overthrew José Joaquín de Herrera and assumed a warlike stance, Alamán was dismayed but supportive.

Despite Alamán y Escalada's appeals to European nations, none entered the conflict with the United States. When the Paredes y Arrillaga administration fell, Alamán fled and was absent from Mexican politics during the war. After the war, he wrote an abundance of material on Mexican sovereignty, politics, and his famous *Historia de Méjico*. He still feared U.S. expansionism and called for European intervention to solve Mexican problems. He later served as President Antonio López de Santa Anna's minister of foreign relations and died in office in 1853.

See also Paredes y Arrillaga, Mariano.

For further reading: Green, *The Mexican Republic*, 1987; Hale, *Mexican Liberalism in the Age of Mora, 1821–1853*, 1968; Soto, *La conspiración monárquica en México, 1845–1846*, 1988; Valadés, *Alamán, estadista e historiador*, 1938; Webb, *The Handbook of Texas*, 1952.

Alcorta, Lino José
(ca. 1794–1854)

As did many of the Mexican leaders during the Mexican-American War, Lino José Alcorta first gained fame as a patriot fighter during the War for Independence. He worked closely with influential leader Antonio López de Santa Anna and became Santa Anna's minister of war and chief of general staff. Alcorta argued strongly for a well-organized guerrilla war to drive U.S. forces from Mexico.

Alcorta was born in Veracruz around 1794. He enlisted in the army in 1813 and was seriously wounded battling insurgents. In 1821, he joined the forces of Agustín de Iturbide and became known as a courageous fighter. His capable leadership won him a promotion to the rank of brigadier general. In 1840, while commanding loyalist troops in Mexico City, he was wounded again in suppressing Brigadier General José Urrea's attempt to overthrow President Anastasio Bustamante. Alcorta was military commander in San Luis Potosí in 1844. During the Mexican-American War, Alcorta was chief of general staff and later became minister of war in 1847. He became one of Santa Anna's most trusted advisors. Realizing the hopeless situation of the Mexican army, Alcorta favored quick, multiple attacks on the U.S. army by small, well-armed, mounted forces of up to 2,000 men that could then disappear into the rugged hills and chaparral.

Alcorta conveyed messages from Santa Anna to U.S. generals regarding an armistice toward the end of the war. When Santa Anna called a junta after the defeats outside Mexico City, Alcorta urged the surrender of the city to avoid needless destruction and civilian deaths.

After the war, Alcorta remained active in politics and was vice-president of the Mexican Society of Geography and Statistics in 1851. He also wrote about military operations. As Santa Anna's minister of war, he died in office in 1854.

For further reading: Carreño, *Jefes del ejército mexicano en 1847*, 1914; *Diccionario Porrúa*, 1995.

Alexander, Edmund Brooke
(1800–1888)

A member of the U.S. Third Infantry, Captain Edmund Brooke Alexander served with distinction during the Mexican-American War. He is most remembered for leading a bayonet charge against the heavily defended ramparts of the convent during the Battle of Churubusco.

Alexander, who was born in Virginia, graduated thirty-third of 35 in his class from the U.S. Military Academy at West Point in 1823. He served in various duties on the western frontier until the outbreak of the Mexican-American War.

Alexander performed capably during General Winfield Scott's march from Veracruz to Mexico City. During the Battle of Churubusco on August 20, 1847, Alexander led 3rd Infantry soldiers in a charge over the ramparts and bastion of the convent in brutal hand-to-hand fighting. This final charge quickly demoralized the Mexican troops and almost immediately resulted in their surrender. Alexander received two brevets during the war for "gallant and meritorious service."

Alexander was part of the Utah Expedition in 1858. During the Civil War, he was stationed in Nebraska, the Dakotas, and Missouri. He retired from active service in 1868 as a brevet brigadier general.

See also Churubusco, Battle of.

For further reading: Cullum, *Biographical Register of*

the Officers and Graduates of the United States Military Academy from 1802 to 1867, 1879; Smith, To Mexico with Scott, 1917.

"All of Mexico" Movement

When the Mexican-American War began in 1846, a few of the more radical politicians and members of the press in the United States advocated seizing the entire Republic of Mexico. As Mexico continued to resist and the war became bloodier and more expensive, the "All of Mexico" movement gained serious momentum. The Treaty of Guadalupe Hidalgo, which secured New Mexico and California for the United States, effectively ended the movement.

The public, distraught at the rising death toll in the fall of 1847, began to feel that demanding more territory, and possibly the entire country, would be the only way to force Mexico to surrender. This idea was propagated by congressmen such as Robert Dale Owen of Indiana, Ambrose H. Sevier of Arkansas, John W. Tibbatts of Kentucky, and Alexander D. Sims of South Carolina. President James K. Polk discussed this idea with his cabinet in September of 1847, and high-ranking officers, such as Brigadier General John A. Quitman, urged taking the entire country. Most proponents were drawn by the economic benefits of owning all of Mexico, including its mineral resources and the isthmus of Tehuantepec.

Public support for the seizure of the entire country was at its peak in February 1848, after peace talks had dragged on for six months. Polk had already decided to demand more territory (including Baja California) when U.S. envoy Nicholas P. Trist, against direct orders from the president, concluded the Treaty of Guadalupe Hidalgo in February 1848. The war-weary public embraced the announcement of the treaty. Polk could not viably reject it, but was disappointed that more territory was not gained. The timely signing of the treaty quite possibly saved Mexico's sovereignty.

See also Trist, Nicholas Philip.

For further reading: Bourne, "The Proposed Absorption of Mexico, 1847–1848," 1901; Fuller, *The Movement for the Acquisition of All Mexico, 1846–1848*, 1936; Lambert, "The Movement for the Acquisition of All Mexico," 1972; Pletcher, *The Diplomacy of Annexation*, 1973.

Almonte, Juan Nepomuceno
(1803–1869)

An important Mexican military and political figure, Juan N. Almonte opposed foreign intervention in Mexican affairs, especially by the United States. As Mexico's minister in Washington, D.C., he broke diplomatic relations with the United States in 1845 when he returned to Mexico after President James K. Polk offered annexation to Texas. Almonte accompanied the exiled Antonio López de Santa Anna from Cuba to Veracruz in 1846 and served as an advisor.

Born to an influential family in Michoacán, Almonte was sent to the United States in 1815 for his education. He became involved in political affairs at an early age when he joined the movement for Mexico's independence from Spain. His diplomatic skills were soon recognized, and in 1825 he helped negotiate one of Mexico's first treaties with England. At this stage of his life, he vehemently opposed foreign intervention in Mexican affairs. His reports from the Texas frontier in 1834 helped

Juan N. Almonte
(Library of Congress)

the government track the simmering unrest along the border. As an officer in the Mexican army and aide-de-camp to General Santa Anna, Almonte was captured at the Battle of San Jacinto in 1836.

The following year, Almonte became increasingly prominent in Mexican affairs. He was appointed a brigadier general and secretary of war from 1839 to 1841. The following year, he was sent to Washington, D.C., as Mexico's foreign minister. After Polk was elected U.S. president and the U.S. Congress passed the joint resolution that offered annexation to Texas in 1845, Almonte broke diplomatic relations by leaving the city and called the resolution "the greatest injustice recorded in the annals of modern history…despoiling a friendly nation…of a considerable part of its territory."

A candidate in Mexico's national election in 1845, Almonte lost to José Joaquín de Herrera, the acting president. Opposed to the negotiations with the United States that Herrera was pursuing, Almonte was part of the military group that deposed Herrera and installed General Mariano Paredes y Arrillaga as president of the country in December 1845.

Almonte approved of the aggressive stance of the new government. Appointed secretary of war in January 1846, he held the position for less than a year before resigning. He was also temporarily secretary of the treasury in 1846. His influence helped bring Santa Anna back to Mexico from exile; he accompanied Santa Anna's entourage from Cuba to Mexico City. Some sources indicate he fought bravely during the Battle of Churubusco.

Almonte became Mexico's minister to Great Britain in 1856. He spent several years in Europe and was instrumental in convincing the French to intervene in Mexico. Intent on establishing a monarchy, Almonte landed with French troops in 1862 at Veracruz. His continued efforts brought Maximilian, who trusted Almonte as his deputy, to the throne in 1864. Almonte was also vice-president of the Mexican Association of Geography and Statistics and a member of various scientific organizations in Europe and North America. He returned to France as an envoy and died in Paris on March 21, 1869.

See also Herrera, José Joaquín de.

For further reading: Cotner, *The Military and Political Career of José Joaquín de Herrera, 1792–1854*, 1949; Harris, "The Public Life of Juan Nepomuceno Almonte," 1935; Ramirez, *Mexico during the War with the United States*, 1950.

Alvarado

Alvarado, in the state of Veracruz, was one of the more important Mexican ports along the Gulf of Mexico. The United States wanted to seize the port and capture or destroy Mexican vessels, some of which belonged to the Mexican Navy, that were moored in the Alvarado River.

Alvarado, two miles inland from the Gulf of Mexico, is located along the Alvarado River. In 1846, the city of 1,500 inhabitants and river were refuge for the small Mexican Navy—brigs and several smaller vessels. (Three were sunk deliberately by the Mexican commander to block the river channel, and the others were burned when U.S. forces occupied the city in April 1847.) The mouth of the river was defended by a fort on the beach and a number of shallows and sandbars. The town, located on a peninsula, was protected by five artillery pieces and a force of about 200 militia.

Commodore David E. Conner of the U.S. Home Squadron wanted to seize the smaller vessels at Alvarado for his own fleet. The entrance to the harbor was as shallow as eight feet, a channel through which only his schooner-gunboats could navigate. The Mexican ships consisted of brigs *Zempoalteca*, *Mexicano*, and *Veracruzano Libre*, gunboats *Guerrero*, *Queretana*, and *Victoria*, and schooners *Aguila*, *Libertad*, and *Morelos*.

Part of Conner's Home Squadron attacked the harbor entrance on August 7, 1846. Gunboats loaded with sailors tried to land under the cover of artillery fire from the *Mississippi* and *Princeton*, two swift steamers, but the river current was too strong, the weather had turned rough, and brisk fire came from Mexicans on the beach and in gunboats. Conner withdrew, but his attack compelled the Mexicans to improve its coastal defenses by adding more soldiers and a 16-gun fort.

Embarrassed by the failure, Conner tried again on October 16 with an attacking force consisting of the *Mississippi*, the steamers *Vixen* and *McClane*, three gunboats, and the schooners *Nonata* and *Forward*. Conner's plans of advancing the gunboats under the protective fire of the *Mississippi* immediately fell apart when *McClane* became grounded on a sandbar. The strong currents and winds hindered the progress of the gunboats, and shelling from the Mexican battery (commanded by Captain Pedro A. Díaz of the Mexican Navy) struck the *Vixen*. With Commodore Tomás Marín commanding the Mexican defenses, the Mexican vessels *Veracruzano Libre*, *Zempoalteca*, and *Aguila* came down the river to meet the U.S. force, and Conner decided to withdraw. The U.S. government had hoped for a victory to advertise naval successes in the U.S. papers and was chagrined by this second "defeat." A number of Conner's officers were also embarrassed by the poorly executed assault. As a result of the two failed missions to capture Alvarado, the approach to the harbor had been strengthened by six new forts and a total of 49 guns.

Immediately after the seizure of Veracruz in March 1847, Major General Winfield Scott ordered Brigadier General John A. Quitman and three volunteer regiments from Georgia, South Carolina, and Alabama on a 50-mile march to occupy Alvarado. Scott viewed the city as a possible source of supplies, horses, mules, and cattle. Commodore Matthew Perry of the Home Squadron wanted the fishing village as a harbor for his small ships and a source of drinking water. Although the seaward approach was well defended, the city was vulnerable to an overland attack. Quitman moved out on March 30. That evening, the steamer *Scourge* fired on Mexican works at the mouth of the river and discovered the following morning that the city had been evacuated, cannon spiked, and the Mexican vessels burned. Lieutenant Charles G. Hunter immediately occupied the city with a skeleton crew of six men under the command of Passed Midshipman William G. Temple.

The joint army-navy operation arrived at the village on April 1, 1847. To their amazement the troops found that it had been occupied the previous day by Lieutenant Hunter and sailors from the *Scourge*. Hunter's orders had been only to blockade Alvarado; in fact, Hunter and his men had gone upriver and also captured the town of Tlacotalpán. Some of Perry's ships went upriver on April 2 and returned on April 4. Quitman arranged for the purchase of beef, horses, and other supplies from the citizens of Alvarado and Tlacotalpán. Both Perry and Scott were incensed that Hunter had exceeded his orders and taken the city, which apparently had resulted in the Mexicans driving off horses and cattle. (It is likely that Perry and Scott were annoyed also because they had not been the first to occupy Alvarado.) Hunter was court-martialed and found guilty of disobeying his orders. This fairly pointless expedition resulted in the deaths of a number of U.S. soldiers from sickness that swept their ranks during the grueling march.

See also Hunter, Charles G.; Navy, Mexico.

For further reading: Bauer, *Surfboats and Horse Marines*, 1969; Knox, *A History of the United States Navy*, 1936.

Álvarez, Juan
(1790–1867)

As a cavalry general during the Mexican-American War and popular political and military figure in southern Mexico, Juan Álvarez had no problem raising troops. His military leadership, however, was hesitant and ineffective. His failure to attack the U.S. left flank during the Battle of El Molino del Rey helped turn the hard-fought battle into one of Mexico's most disheartening losses.

Álvarez was born to wealthy parents in Santa María de la Concepción Atoyac (today the city of Alvarez). He joined the revolutionary forces in 1810 as a private and was quickly promoted to colonel. In 1821, he became the military commander of the Acapulco region. His popularity continued to rise, and he was given a division to command as a general in 1841.

Álvarez had developed a strong alliance with Antonio López de Santa Anna in the decades prior to the Mexican-American War. Álvarez commanded the 2,700-man Army of the South in the Acapulco area in 1847. Although he was a popular figure, he was an ineffective leader during the war. As General Winfield Scott advanced from Veracruz ership skills were recognized by his promotion to captain in 1819. He fought for independence from Spain in 1821 when he supported the revolutionary movement of Agustín de Iturbide. As the new republic became established, Anaya grew more prominent in military and political affairs. By 1833, he was a brigadier general. José Joaquín de Herrera selected him as his war minister in 1845, which Anaya held until Herrera was deposed by General Mariano Paredes y Arrillaga at the end of the year.

Anaya helped organize the movement that ultimately resulted in the removal of acting president Valentín Gómez Farías in early 1847 for seizing church funds. Santa Anna then appointed Anaya as provisional president from April 2 to May 30, 1847. Anaya left that post to command the defense of Mexico City. He fought valiantly at the Battle of Churubusco on August 20, 1847. He was captured and released and, as an advisor to Santa Anna, helped negotiate and signed the armistice after the battle. He resumed his post as provisional president from November 1847 to January 8, 1848.

Anaya remained a popular and respected leader after the war. He later served as minister of war and postmaster general and died in office in 1854.

See also Churubusco, Battle of.

For further reading: Carreño, *Jefes del ejército mexicano en 1847*, 1914.

Anderson, Robert
(1805–1871)

Known as one of the U.S. army's foremost artillery specialists, Robert Anderson wrote the advanced artillery training manuals that helped transform U.S. artillerists into some of the best in the world. Anderson also helped direct the siege mortars during the Battle of Veracruz.

The son of a Revolutionary War officer, Robert Anderson was raised in Kentucky. He entered the U.S. Military Academy at West Point at the age of 16. He graduated fifteenth of a class of 37 in 1825 and was assigned to the 3rd Artillery Regiment. Anderson saw service in the Black Hawk and Florida Wars, during which he was brevetted for gallantry.

His artillery talents led him to teach artillery tactics at West Point, where he also translated French artillery training publications. Artillerists learned these new tactics in 1845, just prior to the Mexican-American War. Major Samuel Ringgold further developed Anderson's ideas into the Flying Artillery that was so effective during the war.

In March 1847, Anderson helped command the siege mortars during the Battle of Veracruz. He fought bravely in the subsequent battles along the National Road and was brevetted major for "gallant and meritorious conduct" during the Battle of El Molino del Rey, in which he was wounded in the arm, on September 8, 1847.

Anderson is most remembered for surrendering Fort Sumter, South Carolina, in 1861 to the Confederate forces whose attack on the fort began the Civil War. He was later appointed brigadier general and commanded the Department of Kentucky. He was brevetted major general in 1865. Anderson died in Nice, France, on October 26, 1871.

For further reading: Anderson, *An Artillery Officer in the Mexican War, 1846–1847*, 1911; Cullum, *Biographical Register of the Officers and Graduates of the United States Military Academy from 1802 to 1867*, 1879; Dillon, *American Artillery in the Mexican War 1846–1847*, 1975.

Andrade, Manuel
(1800–ca. 1860)

General Manuel Andrade was one of the highest-ranking Mexican cavalry officers during the Mexican-American War. His poor performance on the battlefield at El Molino del Rey led to his court-martial by General Antonio López de Santa Anna.

Andrade, who was born in Puebla, joined the Spanish army at the age of 14. After Mexico gained its independence from Spain in 1821, he became a cavalry officer and participated in various military actions.

During the war with the United States, Andrade was an ineffectual leader, partly because he was under the command of General Juan Álvarez, who was not aggressive or decisive on the battlefield. Andrade did not cooperate during the attack on the U.S. rear during the Battle of Buena Vista. He also quarreled with Álvarez during the fighting outside Mexico City, disobeyed orders, and made only a single, halfhearted charge during the Battle of El Molino del Rey. Incensed, Santa Anna ordered his court-martial. Andrade was acquitted because the commission ruled that his commanding officer, General Álvarez, was as much to blame for the failure to attack the exposed flank of the U.S. army.

After the war, Andrade remained in the military and, somewhat ironically, was assigned the task of upgrading the quality of officer training in the Mexican army.

For further reading: Alcaraz, *The Other Side*, 1850; Balbontín, *La invasión americana, 1846 a 1848*, 1888.

Anglo-American Press in Mexico

Operated by experienced printers and newspaper people, a number of small newspapers were quickly established where large groups of U.S. soldiers camped for extended periods of time. The English (and often bilingual) newspapers boosted the morale of the soldiers, explained military orders to both Anglo-Americans and Mexicans, and attempted to influence Anglo-American and Mexican thinking through political editorials.

The first Anglo-American newspaper was the Corpus Christi *Gazette*, established in January 1846 by Samuel Bangs, an experienced printer. In a few months Bangs moved with General Taylor's Army of Occupation to the Río Grande across from Matamoros. Other printers arrived, many of them volunteer soldiers. The *Republic of the Rio Grande*, published in Spanish and English in Matamoros, editorialized for the secession of Mexico's northern states. Its name was later changed to the *American Flag* and was operated by volunteer soldiers from Louisiana. Two or three other newspapers competed for readership in the city before the army moved to Camargo.

Soon after California was seized by the United States, the *Californian* appeared in Monterey, California, and lobbied for English as the first language of the province. Another English-language newspaper was published in Yerba Buena.

During its prolonged stay in Monterrey, Taylor's army was in desperate need of a newspaper. The *American Pioneer* appeared in February 1847, followed later by the *Monterrey Gazette*. Louisiana journalists established the *Sentinel* for a few months in Tampico, a U.S. staging area prior to the invasion of Veracruz. Another paper appeared for a brief time in Saltillo. Within a week of the occupation of Veracruz, the *Eagle* was distributed to U.S. soldiers. Even small forces were quick to print newspapers—Colonel Alexander Doniphan and his Missouri volunteers published the *Anglo-Saxon* during its brief occupation of Chihuahua (March 1847).

The *American-Star* became the prominent Anglo-American newspaper in the City of Mexico after it fell to General Winfield Scott's victorious forces in the fall of 1847. Because it was considered an important means of disseminating information to the Mexican population, it was printed in both English and Spanish. Other newspapers sprang up in Puebla, Mexico City, and Veracruz—wherever large groups of soldiers were stationed. The newspapers folded or relocated when the U.S. troops left Mexico. A few of the more successful ones operated for a number of years in Texas, California, and New Mexico.

For further reading: Bodson, "A Description of the United States Occupation of Mexico as Reported by American Newspapers Published in Vera Cruz, Puebla, and Mexico City," 1970; Spell, "The Anglo-Saxon Press in Mexico, 1846–1848," 1932.

Angostura (La), Battle of

See Buena Vista, Battle of.

Apache Canyon

Apache Canyon (also known as Cañoncito) is a narrow opening through a line of rugged hills about 15 miles north of Santa Fe, in what was the Mexican province of New Mexico during the Mexican-American War. Governor Manuel Armijo had planned to defend the canyon against the approaching Army of the West, but abandoned it before Brigadier General Stephen W. Kearny and his men arrived.

President James K. Polk had selected General Kearny and his Army of the West to occupy New Mexico. Kearny entered the province in early August 1846 with no resistance. As he approached Santa Fe, his scouts reported that Governor Armijo wanted to fight the U.S. army. Armijo began to assemble a force and drew men from nearby Chihuahua and Durango. His 3,000-man army consisted of soldiers, militiamen, guerrillas, and Indians with a variety of arms, including bows and arrows. Although they outnumbered Kearny's army, they had not been trained and were not a cohesive unit. The force was placed under the command of Colonel Manuel Pino, who set the army to work building defenses at Apache Canyon. The three leaders—Armijo, Pino, and Diego Archuleta—began to quarrel about what to do next. On August 17, a junta voted to disband the force and retreat. The cannon were spiked and the men scattered into the hills. As Kearny cautiously advanced toward the canyon, a citizen on a mule rode up and announced that "Armijo and his troops have gone to hell and the canyon is all clear." Welcomed by the acting governor of Santa Fe, Kearny's men occupied the capital city of adobe huts and shops.

See also Archuleta, Diego; Armijo, Manuel; Army, United States.

For further reading: Bancroft, *History of Arizona and New Mexico 1530–1888*, 1889; Clarke, *Stephen Watts Kearny, Soldier of the West*, 1961; Hughes, *Doniphan's Expedition, Containing an Account of the Conquest of New Mexico*, 1973.

Arab

President James K. Polk ordered Commodore David E. Conner of the U.S. Home Squadron to allow exiled Antonio López de Santa Anna to sail through Conner's blockade to Veracruz. Santa Anna and his entourage boarded the hired British vessel *Arab* in Havana, Cuba, on August 8, 1846. En route to Veracruz, it was boarded by officers from *St. Mary's*, a sloop of war from Conner's fleet. Important political or military figures with Santa Anna were Juan N. Almonte, the former Mexican minister to the United States, and Manuel C. Rejón, an influential politician. *Arab* docked in Veracruz on August 16, and that evening, cannonades and rockets celebrated the return of Santa Anna to Mexican soil.

See also Atocha, Alexander J.

For further reading: Henry, *The Story of the Mexican War*, 1950; Semmes, *Service Afloat and Ashore during the Mexican War*, 1851.

Archuleta, Diego

As one of the more militant leaders in New Mexico, Diego Archuleta wanted to resist the invasion of New Mexico by U.S. forces in 1846. He helped raise an army to fight General Stephen W. Kearny's Army of the West, but it was disbanded before it saw any action. Archuleta was a main conspirator in the uprisings against the U.S. territorial government that struck Santa Fe and Taos in 1847.

As Kearny and his men approached Santa Fe in August 1846, Diego Archuleta, Governor Manuel Armijo, and Colonel Manuel Pino had assembled a makeshift, 3,000-man army to fight Kearny at Apache Canyon. A council of war decided to abandon the position, and the force fell apart. Many of the men fled to Chihuahua (including Armijo), but Archuleta remained in the Santa Fe area.

It is likely that after Kearny's advance emissary, James Magoffin, arrived in Santa Fe, he spoke secretly with Archuleta about abandoning Armijo and becoming the commander of the western half of New Mexico, which at the time U.S. President James K. Polk had not considered seizing. (Kearny had claimed only the disputed land from the Río Grande eastward to Texas.) Archuleta accepted, only to find out later that Kearny had taken all of New Mexico and would march on to California. Archuleta was incensed.

After Kearny and 300 men departed for California in September 1846, Archuleta, Tomás Ortiz, and Augustín Duran continued to incite unrest in Santa Fe. Padre Antonio José Martinez, an influential priest and fellow insurgent, probably was also involved. Their growing plans included assassinating Acting Governor Charles Bent and Colonel Sterling Price, the commander of the occupational force. Hearing about the conspiracy, Price chased down seven of the rebels, but never captured Archuleta, Duran, or Ortiz. The murder of Bent and others by a huge mob in the Taos area sparked the Taos Rebellion in January 1847. After the war, Archuleta became a prominent politician in the U.S. territory of New Mexico.

See also Apache Canyon; Taos Rebellion.

For further reading: Bancroft, *History of Arizona and New Mexico 1530–1888,* 1889; Lavender, *Bent's Fort,* 1954.

Arista, Mariano
(1802–1855)

General Mariano Arista commanded Mexico's Army of the North during its first two battles with the U.S. army under General Zachary Taylor. Both battles were disheartening losses during which Arista displayed uninspired leadership. He was removed from command by General Antonio López de Santa Anna and court-martialed.

Arista, who was born in San Luis Potosí, attended a military academy at the age of 15. He joined the Spanish army in 1819, suppressed rebellions, and was promoted to lieutenant in 1821. After supporting the Agustín de Iturbide revolution, he steadily rose through the officer corp to the rank of brigadier general. A political rebellion in 1833 resulted in his exile to the United States, where he lived for three years. Returning to Mexico in 1836, he became the commanding general at Tamaulipas in 1839 and put down various rebellions. By the time of the Mexican-American War, Arista was one of the most respected military leaders in Mexico.

Like many of Mexico's military leaders, Arista was involved in political rebellions. After General Mariano Paredes y Arrillaga seized power in December 1845, a group of prominent Mexicans considered declaring northern Mexico an independent country with Arista as its president. A coconspirator, General Antonio Canales Rosillo, had actually contacted General Taylor about U.S. financing and weapons.

In April 1846, President Paredes y Arrillaga chose Arista to be the commander in chief of the Army of the North at Matamoros. Arista's demeanor in dealing with Taylor was polite and professional. He wrote to Taylor that the "Mexicans have been calumniated as barbarous, in the most caustic and unjust manner…I do not believe that the troops under my command will do anything to confirm such an aspersion; they will exhibit the feelings of humanity and generosity which are genial to them." Arista proposed an armistice, which Taylor refused.

The Mexican army did little during the loss to Taylor at the Battle of Palo Alto, which led Arista's men to question Arista's loyalty to Mexico. Arista posted his men in a strong defensive position at Resaca de Guerrero (Resaca de la Palma) the following day, but was inexplicably absent during the main U.S. attack; instead of being at the front, he was writing reports in his tent as the battle raged. It quickly turned into a rout, and the disillusioned Mexican soldiers fled across the Río Grande to Matamoros. Santa Anna relieved Arista of command on July 3 and later requested a court-martial. The tribunal absolved Arista of all accusations.

In June 1848, Arista became Mexico's secretary of war. He was constitutional president from 1851 to January 1853, but had many difficulties with the military. Tired and in ill health, he resigned and sailed for Portugal. Arista died in Lisbon on August 7, 1855.

Mariano Arista
(Library of Congress)

See also Palo Alto, Battle of; Resaca de la Palma, Battle of.

For further reading: Alcaraz, *The Other Side*, 1850; DePalo, *The Mexican National Army, 1822–1852*, 1997; *Diccionario Porrúa*, 1995; Haecker, *A Thunder of Cannon*, 1994; Webb, *The Handbook of Texas*, 1952.

Arizona

Arizona was mostly part of Mexico's northern province of Sonora y Sinaloa. Approximately the northern half of Sonora was given to the United States according to the Treaty of Guadalupe Hidalgo.

The first expeditions from New Spain (later Mexico) entered the area of present-day Arizona in the 1530s. Franciscan priests and Spanish explorer Francisco Vasquez de Coronado visited Hopi and Zuni native villages. Missionaries from the Roman Catholic Church developed missions in the late 1600s and early 1700s, and the discovery of silver in 1736 near the Indian village of Arizonac led to increased settlement, which led to increased fighting between the Spanish forces and the Indians. By the mid-1700s, the Spanish built walled forts, including Tucson.

When Mexico won independence from Spain in 1821, it took ownership of Sonora y Sinaloa. Spanish and U.S. fur traders, and later U.S. settlers, began to explore Arizona in the 1820s, but these activities were largely abandoned during the 1830s and 1840s because of incessant warfare with the Apache Nation.

During the Mexican-American War, General Stephen Watts Kearny and 300 men, and later the Mormon Battalion, crossed what is now Arizona en route to California in 1846. The United States took possession of present-day Arizona north of the Gila River according to the Treaty of Guadalupe Hidalgo in 1848. In 1853, the Gadsden Purchase (Treaty of La Mesilla) added the territory south of the Gila River. This area forms part of the present boundary between the United States and Mexico. Arizona became the forty-eighth U.S. state in 1912.

See also Gadsden Treaty; Kearny, Stephen Watts; Mormon Battalion.

For further reading: Bancroft, *History of Arizona and New Mexico 1530–1888*, 1889; Cooke, *The Conquest of New Mexico and California*, 1878; Mattison, "Early Spanish and Mexican Settlements in Arizona," 1946; Sheridan, *Arizona: A History*, 1995; Trimble, *Arizona: A Panoramic History of a Frontier State*, 1977; Wyllys, *Arizona: The History of a Frontier State*, 1950.

Armijo, Manuel
(1801–1854)

As governor of the remote Mexican province of New Mexico, Manuel Armijo had a reputation for being a powerful and scandalous administrator. He initially wanted to fight the U.S. soldiers who entered New Mexico in 1846. After raising a 3,000-man force, he fled south and left Santa Fe and New Mexico to be occupied by Brigadier General Stephen W. Kearny.

Manuel Armijo was born into poverty near Albuquerque. By the time he was 20, he had taught himself how to read and write and had become established as a trader in Santa Fe. As governor during 1837–1844 and 1845–1846 and as commander general, he oversaw civic and military affairs in the province.

Armijo was disliked by most of the populace for awarding large grants of land to his friends and allies. He claimed undue valor for capturing a small group of Texans in 1841 and, as prisoners of war, treated them cruelly. Also, he had plans for controlling New Mexico as a republic separate from Mexico.

On August 8, 1846, as General Kearny and the Army of the West approached, Armijo called for New Mexicans to rise up and fight: "Fellow Patriots: The moment has come at last when the country requires from her sons, the unlimited decision and reserveless sacrifices, which circumstances, extreme under any point of view, claim for its salvation…. Behold, fellow citizens, the [U.S.] invasion is the sign of alarm that must prepare us for the combat…. Let us be ready for war since we are provoked to it." Armijo met Kearny's advance guard, led by Captain Philip St. George Cooke and James W. Magoffin, on August 12, 1846. Cooke recalled there was "no mistaking the governor, a large fine looking man…he wore a blue frock coat, with a rolling collar and a general's shoulder straps, blue striped trousers with gold lace, and a red sash."

With the help of Diego Archuleta, Armijo had assembled a 3,000-man force to challenge Kearny's passage through New Mexico at Apache Canyon. However, Armijo fled before the U.S. troops arrived, and his men scattered into the hills. This allowed Kearny to occupy Santa Fe on August 16 without any fighting.

Armijo was later charged with treason by the Mexican government, tried, and acquitted. After the war, he returned to New Mexico and settled on a ranch near Socorro. He continued his involvement in politics, but on a more local level. Armijo died in 1854 and left $1,000 to establish a public school.

See also Apache Canyon; Archuleta, Diego; Army, United States.

For further reading: Diccionario Porrúa, 1995; Keleher, *Turmoil in New Mexico, 1846–1848,* 1952; Lavender, *Bent's Fort,* 1954; Meier and Rivera, *Dictionary of Mexican American History,* 1981; Tyler, "Governor Armijo's Moment of Truth," 1972.

Armistead, Lewis Addison
(1817–1863)

A lieutenant in the U.S. 6th Infantry, Lewis Addison Armistead distinguished himself during the Battles of Contreras, Churubusco, and El Molino del Rey in 1847. He received two brevets during the war and was wounded at Churubusco.

Armistead was born in New Bern, North Carolina. Seeking a career in the military, he was admitted to the U.S. Military Academy in 1834 and was later appointed second lieutenant in the U.S. 6th Infantry.

During the Mexican-American War, Armistead fought bravely with Major General Winfield Scott's army as it marched from Veracruz to Mexico City, and he received two brevets for "gallant and meritorious conduct." He was one of the first of the U.S. soldiers to leap into the ditch that surrounded Chapultepec to begin scaling its western slope on September 13, 1847. Armistead faced tremendous musket fire and was immediately felled with a serious wound.

After the war, he served on the western frontier. Armistead joined the Confederate Army in 1861 and was appointed brigadier general commanding a brigade in General George E. Pickett's division of the Army of Northern Virginia. He led his brigade during Pickett's Charge at the Battle of Gettysburg on July 3, 1863, with his hat on the point of his sword, and was mortally wounded a few steps within the Union line.

For further reading: Cullum, *Biographical Register of the Officers and Graduates of the United States Military Academy from 1802 to 1867,* 1879; Henry, *The Story of the Mexican War,* 1950.

Armistice

See Monterrey, Armistice of; Tacubaya, Armistice of.

Army, Mexico

The Mexican army was woefully unprepared to fight a protracted war with the United States. A great proportion of the army was hastily assembled, poorly trained, and armed with inferior weapons. When the Mexican-American War began, the Mexican army totalled about 20,000 men. Its Army of the North lost the Battles of Palo Alto, Resaca de la Guerrero (Resaca de la Palma), and Monterrey to the U.S. army under General Zachary Taylor in 1846. The Mexican army's shattered remnants and nearly 10,000 conscripts were molded into a "second" Army of the North by General Antonio López de Santa Anna. This 20,000-man unit was narrowly defeated by Taylor at the Battle of La Angostura (Buena Vista) in 1847. Elements from this army, combined with more conscripts, national guardsmen, and militia, as the Army of the East, were rushed to the front to defend Mexico City against the advance of General Winfield Scott. The Army of the East was defeated also. Nevertheless, the Mexican soldiers fought with a determination that won the respect of the U.S. army.

After the War of Independence from Spain in 1821, the Mexican army was a combination of royalists and insurgents, trained in the Spanish military tradition. The officer corp became polarized between federalism and centralism; this split created political dissension within the ranks. The army was broken down into provincial forces that were commanded by a host of different generals, who usually responded to affairs only within their own districts. The army was further fragmented by the lack of consistent military training, especially among the junior officers. Because of the distance and self-interests of the provincial commands, the training and discipline required for a large army could not be accomplished. Funds were misused; for example, officers and elite troops were beautifully clothed in expensive, colorful uniforms, and not enough money was spent on weapons and ammunition. Unity within the army was further disrupted by conspiracies and the frequent revolts led by high-ranking officers. Military actions from 1821 to 1846 consisted mostly of putting down local insurgencies.

When the war started, the 20,000-man Mexican army had an overabundance of officers, many of whom were political or social appointees with no military experience. The Mexican generals, who had served in the Spanish army, adopted Spanish tactics, uniforms, and other army traditions. Twelve infantry regiments, eight cavalry regiments, three brigades of artillery, and various groups of foot artillery, sappers (engineers), and dragoons made up the army. The cavalry troopers were well outfitted with carbine, pistol, saber, lasso, and sometimes a long lance. The infantry was filled with mostly poor, illiterate conscripts drafted for at least a six-year term. All able-bodied single men and childless married men were expected to serve. The typical soldier was about five feet two inches in height. The quick assembly of the army resulted in communication problems (numerous Indian dialects), split political loyalties, conflicting leadership, and poor training. The drilling was kept simple, and target practice was reserved for the elite regiments. Most of the men had never fired their weapon until they faced U.S. soldiers in combat.

In the Spanish tradition, the soldiers wore a great variety of colorful, Napoleonic-style uniforms. Infantrymen wore a woolen tailcoat with cloth facings in a combination of bright colors that was distinctive of each regiment. Militia companies had blue tailcoats, red collars, and white pants. Different colors on the collars, lapels, cuffs, and piping denoted rank and regiment. Plain white canvas pants were worn in the summer; dark blue wool pants in the winter. Most of the men wore sandals or were barefoot. The line cavalry were dressed in sky blue coats with scarlet collars and trim. Artillerists wore blue pants and tailcoats with red collars embroidered with an exploding bomb. Even bands had their own uniform colors. Other equipment included a canvas knapsack, blanket, cross and waist belts, and canteen.

Camp followers, or *soldaderas*, were an integral part of the army. Largely women and children who followed their husbands, fathers, brothers, or sweethearts, they carried food, clothing, and firewood, helped maintain morale, and nursed the sick and wounded. A U.S. soldier recalled that the "camp followers were a sight to behold, men, women and children of every grade, colour and condition on foot, on donkeys, mules, half-starved little ponys, carrying immense bundles of household goods, with chattering parrots, hens, chickens and monkeys...."

With little money and no formal quartermaster system, the army took supplies from communities, foraged off the land, and relied on the thousands of camp followers. The troops were usually hungry, irritable, and sometimes rebellious. Their meager rations and poor treatment by officers led to high desertion rates. As the war progressed and the army's losses were replenished, conscripts, national guardsmen, local militia, prisoners, and rural peasants were forced into the ranks. They were typically illiterate and poorly clothed and fed. Desertion continued to escalate as the war progressed.

Advance of the Army of the North (1847)

After the heavy losses of the Battles of Palo Alto, Resaca de la Guerrero (Resaca de la Palma), and Monterrey in 1846, the survivors of the Army of the North gathered in San Luis Potosí. Anxious to strengthen the army, the federal government established a national levy/quota system that called for all males between the ages of 16 and 50.

Santa Anna, newly installed as the general in chief, arrived in San Luis Potosí from Mexico City in mid-October 1846 to take control of the army. About 7,000 men were assembled, many of them forcibly conscripted. Men continued to arrive from a variety of districts across the country. In November, 2,000 men and a corp of national guardsmen reported from Guadalajara. General Gabriel Valencia, a popular leader and commander, brought nearly 5,000 auxiliary troops from Guanajuato.

Santa Anna and his officers began to organize and train this makeshift army in January 1847. Funds were scarce. Santa Anna's favorite regiments were issued the better equipment. In an effort to save gunpowder and bullets, only the elite units were allowed target practice. In fact, the majority of the soldiers fired their weapons for the first time as they charged Taylor's U.S. troops at La Angostura nearly two months later. The troops were poorly sheltered and fed during their month's training and had barely learned the basics of maneuvering.

After intercepting U.S. correspondence that revealed Taylor was understrength, Santa Anna was eager to move northward and destroy him. By the end of January, Santa Anna's army had about 20,000 men and officers and 39 artillery pieces. (The Army of the North gained another 1,000 men under General Anastasio Parrodi at Matehuala later during the march.) The magnificent cavalry, under General Anastasio Torrejón, led the advance. Their target was about 250 miles to the north at Saltillo, where the U.S. army was gathered. Trailing behind the army's wagons were the numerous camp followers, mostly women and children, who carried firewood and the personal belongings of the soldiers.

The hardships of the march immediately began to thin the army's ranks as they traveled through Peñasco, Bocas, Hedionda, Venado, Charcas, Laguna Seco, Solis, and the Presa. Many soldiers became desperately sick and died from the cold. Spirits were briefly lifted when they saw U.S. prisoners who had been captured by the cavalry. One of the U.S. captives remembered that

> We met the great army…. First came his splendid park of artillery of fifty guns; then a body of five thousand infantry; then a huge body of cavalry; then infantry and cavalry, together in large bodies; then Santa Anna in person, seated in a chariot of war drawn by eight mules and surrounded by his staff elegantly and gorgeously equipped; then he fluttered on his rear a bevy of wanton women; and lastly, covering his rear, his baggage train in the midst of which were five mules loaded with chicken cocks from the "best coups" of Mexico. (Scott 1848)

A strong norther raged across the plains on February 3, bringing rain, sleet, and biting cold. With no shelter, the men slept together to stay warm. The weather then became hot and sunny. With few water holes, the soldiers suffered terribly from thirst in the desert climate. After a day's rest at Matehuala, they were joined by Parrodi's command. More cold and wet weather continued to plague the army. The sick fell in great numbers at the side of the road. Deaths and desertions continued to mount. After marching through the Cedral, Las Animas, and Vanegas, the troops received mail on February 14 and stopped in the desert to read their letters.

The first to arrive at La Encarnación was General Francisco Pacheco's division on February 17, followed by General Manuel María Lombardini on the 18th, General José María Ortega on the 19th, and the cavalry brigade over the next two days. An inspection revealed that approximately 4,000 men had been lost to death or desertion. The loss among the *soldaderas* that followed them will never be known.

After eating and filling their canteens and gourds with water, the Mexicans continued northward on February 21, 1847. They raced through the burning village of Agua Nueva that had been set aflame by Taylor's retreating men. On February 23, the exhausted Mexican army was repelled by Taylor's stubborn defense at the Battle of La Angostura (Buena Vista).

Retreat of the Army of the North (1847)

As the Mexican army retreated to the south, General Torrejón's cavalry stayed behind and built campfires to deceive Taylor into thinking the army was holding its position. Hundreds of the wounded were left behind, shivering and desperately thirsty in the cold night. The first troops arrived at Agua Nueva near midnight and, desperate for water, drank from a pond that was tainted by scum and blood and died. Women and children wept over the dead bodies of loved ones. On the morning of February 24, the army was reassembled by Santa Anna. Three U.S. officers arrived to inform him that the Mexican wounded had been collected and sent to Saltillo. They suggested a treaty, but Santa Anna refused.

After an evening junta with his senior officers, Santa Anna decided to retreat to San Luis Potosí. The less seriously wounded (those with the greatest chances of recovery) were hauled in ox-drawn carts; others were carried on makeshift stretchers made from rifles. Desertion was rampant as the starving army marched slowly toward La Encarnación. After arriving at the Salado on February 27, the hungry soldiers ate tainted provisions that led to more illness and death. Alcaraz wrote that "the army seemed made up of dead men: the miserable condition to which the sick were reduced caused the skin of many to stick to their bones, and its shrinking exposed their teeth." On February 29, the army reached the Cedral, where the popular José María Oronoz, a 23-year-old adjutant for Santa Anna, died from his wounds. His funeral was well attended. The army trudged on to Matehuala and rested there for two days. It was during this time that Santa Anna had General José Vicente Miñón arrested for failing to charge the enemy during the Battle of Buena Vista. The exhausted and starved men entered the somber city of San Luis Potosí on March 9.

During the army's return, Valentín Gómez Farías had been deposed as acting president during the Polkos Rebellion. When Santa Anna left for Mexico City to deal with this new complication, he left General Ignacio Mora y Villamil in charge of the army. In all, the Army of the North had marched over 500 miles in 40 days, fought a desperate battle, and lost over 10,500 men to battlefield deaths, disease, and desertion.

The best portion of the army was taken by Santa Anna to form the core of the new Army of the East. The remainder of the Army of the North was commanded by General Gabriel Valencia at the Battle of Contreras, and the remnants later joined the Army of the East in the subsequent battles near Mexico City.

Army of the East

After General Winfield Scott's army had landed at Veracruz in March of 1847, Santa Anna, with his typical energy and resolve, scraped together a force to defend Mexico City. Many of the soldiers came from the Army of the North infantry brigade of General Ciriaco Vázquez, General Pedro de Ampudia's 3rd, 4th, 5th, and 11th Infantry Regiments, and General Julián Juvera's remaining cavalry regiments. These troops totalled about 6,000 men. More conscripts, militia, and national guardsmen were gathered, especially from Mexico City and Puebla. The army was quickly moved to Cerro Gordo on the National Road, where Santa Anna planned his first defense against Scott's army. The Army of the East had grown to nearly 12,000 men, but was not strong enough to win the series of battles that led Scott to the gates of Mexico City.

Armies of the South and Center

The smaller Army of the South had little impact on the outcome of the war. Perhaps because of his mistrust of cavalry general Juan Álvarez, Santa Anna assigned his 3,000-man Army of the South a peripheral role during Scott's advance from Veracruz. Álvarez's mission was to harass the rear of Scott's army, which he did with little success. Again assigned a support position during the Battle of El Molino del Rey, Álvarez refused to commit his troops in a flank attack at a crucial juncture of the battle. The Army of the South was absorbed into the remaining army that fell back toward Mexico City. The Army of the Center, a 3,500-man force under popular leader General Nicolás Bravo, was pulled in from its defensive position near San Antonio to join the remnants of the other armies at the battles of Churubusco, Chapultepec, and the gates of Mexico City.

See also Agua Nueva; Buena Vista, Battle of; Casualties, Mexico; Women, Mexico.

For further reading: Alcaraz, *The Other Side*, 1850; Alvear Acevedo, *La guerra del 47*, 1957; Balbontín, *Estado militar de la República Mexicana en 1846*, 1891; Berruto Ramón, *En defensa de un soldado Méxicano*, 1957; Chamberlain, *My Confession*, 1956; DePalo, *The Mexican National Army, 1822–1852*, 1997; Hefter, *El soldado mexicano*, 1958; Jones, *Santa*

Anna, 1968; Marchena Fernández, *Oficiales y soldados en el ejército de América*, 1983; Roa Bárcena, *Recuerdos de la invasión norte-americana*, 1947; Salas, *Soldaderas in the Mexican Military*, 1990; Scott, *Encarnación Prisoners, Comprising an Account of the March of the Kentucky Cavalry from Louisville to the Rio Grande*, 1848.

Army, United States

The U.S. army had a total of about 8,000 men and officers at the outbreak of the Mexican-American War. Directed by President James K. Polk, the commander in chief, the army operated on three different fronts: northern Mexico (General Zachary Taylor), Veracruz–Mexico City (Major General Winfield Scott), and New Mexico–California (General Stephen W. Kearny and Captain John C. Frémont). Although outnumbered, the U.S. army won all its battles in Mexico as a result of superior training, leadership, and weaponry.

Before the Mexican-American War, the infantry, dragoon, and artillery regiments had seen combat against Native Americans in the Black Hawk and Florida Wars. The routine of the U.S. soldier had been well established in other military operations on the western and northern frontiers. The army was well disciplined, thoroughly trained, and well armed. Unlike their counterparts in the Mexican army, a number of the higher-ranking U.S. officers had undergone an intensive, four-year officer training at a military academy (U.S. Military Academy).

English, Irish, German, and Norwegian immigrants composed a significant portion of the army. Some of them had European military backgrounds and had served in European wars. A few groups of Native Americans were also in the ranks, including the Tonkawas, Choctaw, and Cherokee. When the war began, about 47 percent of Taylor's Army of Occupation were immigrants, and nearly a quarter of all his men were Irish. (The Mexicans tried to take advantage of this ethnic diversity by circulating propaganda leaflets that stressed to the Irish Catholics that the United States was waging war against the Roman Catholic Church.)

The typical, "regular" U.S. soldier wore a sky blue jacket and trousers made from lightweight, coarse wool. The forage cap was dark blue. The men also wore white shoulder and waist belts and carried cotton haversacks. Artillerists were identified by their darker blue uniforms, red facings, and closer-fitting coats. Mounted dragoons wore dark blue woolen jackets, blue-gray woolen pants, and a dark blue wool forage cap with a stiff visor.

Although the quartermaster department was much maligned by U.S. soldiers and press throughout the war, the soldiers were generally adequately supplied. In contrast to the Mexican army, the U.S. army was well funded and contracted with the industrious private sector for supplies, which were delivered to the front via U.S. naval vessels or hired private ships.

The initial battles of the war at Palo Alto (May 8, 1846) and Resaca de la Palma (May 9, 1846) were fought by Taylor and his Army of Occupation—about 3,600 "regular army" soldiers. Taylor's victories electrified the United States and made everyone anticipate a short war. New Yorker Herman Melville wrote that "people here are all in a state of delirium.... Nothing is talked of but the 'Halls of the Montezumas.'"

In 1846, President Polk stated "It has never been our policy to maintain large standing armies in time of peace. They are contrary to the genius of our free institutions, would impose heavy burdens on the people and be dangerous to public liberty. Our reliance for protection and defense on the land must be mainly on our citizen soldiers, who will be ever ready, as they ever have been ready in times past, to rush with alacrity, at the call of their country, to her defense." In mid-May Secretary of War William L. Marcy announced that the U.S. government needed 50,000 volunteer soldiers. Despite Taylor's victories, the Mexicans continued to stubbornly resist, and in February 1847 Congress added ten new regiments to the regular army.

There was no shortage of volunteer soldiers. For example, in Tennessee 30,000 men reported for only 3,000 volunteer positions. Eager to fight, men turned away by their home states often joined the volunteer regiments of bordering states. Volunteers represented all social classes, from doctors and lawyers to farmers. One volunteer soldier wrote that he was surrounded by "lead-miners from Galena; wharf rats and dock loafers from Chicago;

farmers on unpurchased lands from the interior; small pattern politicians…[and] village statesmen, pregnant with undeveloped greatness…." (Smith and Judah 1968)

Early war legislation allowed the volunteers to dress as they wished, resulting in a colorful and bizarre mixture of styles, shades, and hues. Many of them dressed in deerskins and straw hats, and had wild hair and beards. The Mexicans thought the volunteers looked like "clowns at a carnival" and were shocked that such irregular-looking men could defeat them in battle.

Volunteer regiments were well known for their undisciplined behavior. Regular soldiers detested the volunteers and believed that they ruined the reputation of the U.S. army. Volunteers were reluctant to follow standard military procedures, such as posting pickets at night. Captain Philip N. Barbour wrote before the Battle of Palo Alto that the army must win "before the arrival of the volunteers or the army will be disgraced." During its occupation in 1846 and 1847, volunteers were greatly responsible for turning Matamoros into a "theatre of drunkeness [sic]." Brawls and killings were commonplace. In August 1846, a Georgia regiment had a brawl in which three Georgians were killed. Daniel Harvey Hill wrote that the "vile Volunteers had committed the usual excesses & the lovely town was in good part deserted."

Although the war was supposed to be against the Mexican government and its army and the Mexican citizens were to be treated with kindness and respect, the volunteers' behavior was often otherwise. Nicknamed the "Ransackers," the Arkansas volunteer cavalry assaulted women in the town of Agua Nueva in 1846 and slaughtered 30 men, women, and children in a cave near Catana in February 1847. Although indispensable as scouts and fighters, the Texas Rangers were brutally undisciplined. Driven by a deep hatred of Mexicans developed from years of border fighting, they frequently launched acts of murder and destruction called "Texas vengeance." Their wanton killing of Mexican civilians in northern Mexico led to an increase in guerrilla activity that claimed many U.S. lives. Taylor wrote that "On the day of battle I am glad to have Texas soldiers with me, for they are brave and gallant; but I never want to see them before or afterward." The death of Texas Ranger Captain Samuel H. Walker during the Battle of Huamantla in October 1847 triggered a wave of burning, murder, and rape by Pennsylvania and Indiana volunteers in one of the ugliest incidents of the war.

After being camped in Saltillo for months and receiving orders to leave, Captain E. Kirby Smith wrote that "the inhabitants had rapidly gained confidence in the regulars and were much alarmed when they found we were about leaving them to the mercy of the volunteers, of whom they have the utmost dread, and by whom they are generally treated with the utmost barbarity."

A large group of "amateur" soldiers—men who wanted to fight but who could not get into regiments—also followed the army. "Adventurers" were those who had decided to fight on their own against Mexico, without any attachment to the army. The army recognized both groups, who were allowed to draw supplies and rations from the quartermaster. A contingent of civilian teamsters, reporters, printers, and entertainers also worked for the army and sometimes fought as soldiers. Also an undisciplined lot, these men also committed atrocities that were quickly blamed on the volunteer regiments.

Army of Observation

In 1844, President John Tyler, fearing Mexican hostilities over Texas, ordered General Zachary Taylor to assemble an "Army of Observation" at Fort Jesup, Louisiana, just across the Sabine River from the Republic of Texas. Taylor gathered nearly 2,000 men, about one-quarter of the total U.S. army. Most of them were members of the 3rd and 4th Infantry Regiments and the 2nd Dragoons. Expecting the annexation of Texas to result in serious conflict with Mexico, President Polk ordered Taylor in July 1845 to take his army to the Nueces River boundary as a show of strength. Secretary of War William L. Marcy stressed to Taylor that the Texans would be "entitled…to defence and protection from foreign invasion and Indian incursions" and that Taylor's force was to be "kept in readiness to perform this duty." Taylor selected the site of

Corpus Christi and by the end of October 1845 had transferred four infantry regiments, four artillery regiments, and one regiment of dragoons for a total of about 3,600 men. The mobilization of the troops effectively changed the name of the army from the Army of Observation to the Army of Occupation.

Army of Occupation, Taylor-Wool

Taylor's 3,600-man army was officially designated the Army of Occupation when it was mobilized in 1845 from Fort Jesup, Louisiana, to Corpus Christi, Texas, where it spent a miserable winter. Soon after the annexation of Texas in December 1845, Taylor was ordered to advance to the Río Grande to protect the new state. The army broke camp at Corpus Christi on March 8, 1846. As most of the army moved overland, U.S. naval vessels brought the sick, extra supplies, and an artillery company to Point Isabel, near the mouth of the Río Grande.

After a long winter, the troops were eager to move south. The weather was good and the roads were dry. Following the "Road of the Arroyo Colorado"—a well-worn trail between Corpus Christi and Matamoros frequently used by traders and smugglers—the soldiers passed prairie expanses filled with colorful wildflowers. Soon the terrain changed, and they struggled across salt flats and deep sand that felt like "hot ashes." Mexicans had burned the vegetation in their front, and the soldiers quickly became coated in black ash. The heat was unbearable, and the thirsty soldiers frequently broke ranks at the sight of water, which usually proved brackish. During one point in the march, the soldiers went 36 hours without water. General Taylor himself was badly sunburned with cracked, peeling skin.

The army entered a vast expanse of mesquite as they approached the Arroyo Colorado, where they easily drove away a small force of Mexicans on the opposite bank on March 20 and crossed the salty lagoon uncontested. On March 27, they reached the Río Grande after having marched more than 200 miles. The main camp was assembled in a plowed field on the north bank of the river, directly opposite the Mexican city of Matamoros and Mexico's Army of the North. Engineers began to direct the construction of the earthen Fort Texas (later named Fort Brown). The U.S. and Mexican forces quickly clashed in the next few weeks. The Battles of Palo Alto

A bird's-eye view of the campsite of the Army of Occupation under the command of General Zachary Taylor in 1845, Corpus Christi, Texas (Library of Congress)

(May 8) and Resaca de la Palma (May 9) resulted in the earliest victories for the Army of Occupation.

The Army of Occupation later occupied Matamoros and continued to be strengthened by new volunteer regiments that arrived in Matamoros and Camargo. Now reinforced with volunteer regiments, Taylor's Army of Occupation won the hard-fought Battles of Monterrey (September 21–23, 1846) and Buena Vista (February 23, 1847). When Taylor showed his reluctance to advance deeper into Mexico, President Polk decided to open a second front at the port city of Veracruz. The best troops in Taylor's army were reassigned to General Winfield Scott for his assault on Veracruz. The remaining portion of the army became a truly occupational force in northern Mexico under Taylor, and later Brigadier General John E. Wool. The "second" Army of Occupation under Scott advanced inland from Veracruz and fought a series of battles that led to the capture of Mexico City. The army continued to be reinforced by new volunteer regiments that arrived at Veracruz.

Army of Occupation, Scott

With orders from President Polk to open a second front at the port city of Veracruz, General Scott arrived at the Río Grande on January 1, 1847, to assemble his army. Authorized to take

A typical camp kitchen in the U.S. Army of Occupation, as depicted in John Frost's *Pictorial History of Mexico and the Mexican War*, 1849 (Library of Congress)

Wash day in the camp of the U.S. Army of Occupation, from a wood engraving that first appeared in *The Journal of Wm. H. Richardson*, 1849 (Library of Congress)

4,000 regulars from Taylor's army, he was also to receive ten volunteer regiments. With a force of more than 10,000 men, Scott landed his troops at Veracruz on March 9, 1847. After a furious artillery barrage, the city surrendered on March 27. The Army of Occupation quickly moved inland along the National Road and defeated the Mexican army at Cerro Gordo on April 18, 1847. Volunteers were exchanged and trained at Puebla from May to August. Once he was satisfied with his new forces, Scott marched them into battle at Contreras, Churubusco, El Molino del Rey, Chapultepec, and the gates of Mexico City. The army served as an occupational force in Mexico City until it was sent home in June and July 1848.

Army of the West

When the United States declared war on Mexico, President Polk decided to send a U.S. force into New Mexico to occupy Mexico's northern territory, especially the town of Santa Fe. New Mexico was an important trading partner to the United States, relatively friendly, and disenchanted with Mexican rule.

Under the command of Brigadier General Stephen Watts Kearny, the force consisted largely of the 1st Dragoons and volunteer cavalrymen from Missouri, a total of about 1,600 men. Leaving Fort Leavenworth, Kansas, on June 5, 1846, the Army of the West traveled via Bent's Old Fort on the Arkansas River (in present-day Colorado) into New Mexico. It entered Santa Fe without any bloodshed in mid-August 1846.

After establishing a military government, Kearny took 300 dragoons and marched westward for California. By September, the remaining Army of the West had been reinforced by 1,220 Missouri volunteers under Colonel Sterling Price and the 500-man Mormon Battalion. Kearny saw action in California at the Battle of San Pascual, where he was severely lanced. The Mormon Battalion also marched to California, blazing a new wagon trail.

Colonel Alexander Doniphan and 900 Missourians left New Mexico in December 1846 to occupy the city of Chihuahua. After an arduous march across the desert and fighting two battles, Doniphan's forces occupied the city on March 1. Afterward, they marched to Saltillo to

VOLUNTEERS!

Men of the Granite State!

Men of Old Rockingham!!

the strawberry-bed of patriotism, renowned for bravery and devotion to Country, rally at this call. Santa Anna, reeking with the generous confidence and magnanimity of your countrymen, is in arms, eager to plunge his traitor-dagger in their bosoms. To arms, then, and rush to the standard of the fearless and gallant CUSHING----put to the blush the dastardly meanness and rank toryism of Massachusetts. Let the half civilized Mexicans hear the crack of the unerring New Hampshire rifleman, and illustrate on the plains of San Luis Potosi, the fierce, determined, and undaunted bravery that has always characterized her sons.

Col. THEODORE F. ROWE, at No. 31 Daniel-street, is authorized and will enlist men this week for the Massachusetts Regiment of Volunteers. The compensation is $10 per month---$30 in advance. Congress will grant a handsome bounty in money and ONE HUNDRED AND SIXTY ACRES OF LAND.

Portsmouth, Feb. 2. 1847.

A recruitment poster that appeared in New England ca. 1847 promises land as well as payment to any men who enlist. (Library of Congress)

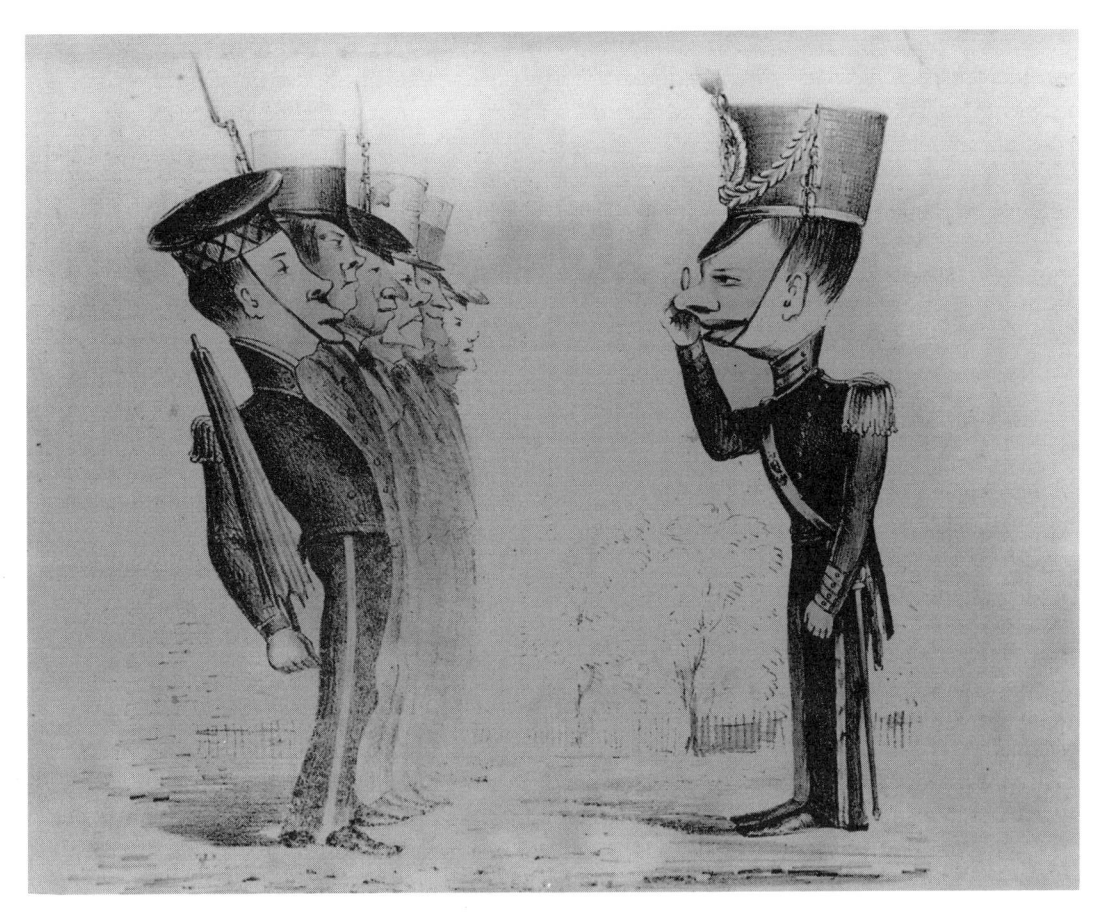

A scornful portrayal of the men who responded to the U.S. call for volunteers for the Mexican War, ca. 1846. Notice the only volunteer in uniform carries an umbrella instead of a musket. (Library of Congress)

join General Taylor's army. The remaining portion of the Army of the West under Colonel Price in Santa Fe chased guerrillas, suppressed the Taos Rebellion, and occupied the cities of Chihuahua and Rosales in March 1848 after the Treaty of Guadalupe Hidalgo had been signed.

Army of the Center

The Army of the Center was the name given to a U.S. force under the command of Brigadier General John E. Wool. To expand U.S. control in northern Mexico beyond General Kearny's occupation of New Mexico in August 1846, President Polk wanted an army to seize the city of Chihuahua, an important trading center in northern Mexico.

Organized in San Antonio, Texas, from July to September 1846, the largely volunteer, 1,400-man Army of the Center went through a rigorous training period. It finally moved out of San Antonio on September 23, 1846. The army occupied the town of Monclova for 27 days because of Taylor's armistice at Monterrey. After reaching Parras on December 5, Wool received orders to change course and march to the Saltillo area to reinforce Taylor against a possible assault from General Antonio López de Santa Anna. On December 21, the Army of the Center arrived at Agua Nueva, a few miles south of Saltillo, after a grueling march. The Mexican attack never materialized, and the Army of the Center became part of Taylor's Army of Occupation.

For further reading: Baylies, *A Narrative of Major General Wool's Campaign in Mexico,* 1851; Chamberlain, *My Confession,* 1956; Cuncliffe, *Soldiers & Civilians,* 1968; Ganoe, *The History of the United States Army,* 1964; Hitchcock, *Fifty Years in Camp and Field,* 1909; Johannsen, *To the Halls of the Montezumas,* 1985; McCaffrey, *Army of Manifest Destiny,*

1992; Risch, *Quartermaster Support of the Army*, 1962; Skelton, *An American Profession of Arms*, 1992; Smith and Judah, *Chronicles of the Gringos*, 1968; Winders, *Mr. Polk's Army*, 1997.

Arroyo Colorado

The stream crossing at Arroyo Colorado, Texas, was the first contact between General Zachary Taylor's Army of Occupation and elements of Mexico's Army of the North. After seeing the hostile Mexican force on the other side of the stream on March 19, Taylor deployed his men for battle and crossed the stream; the Mexicans retreated toward Matamoros.

On March 8, 1846, Taylor's 3,600-man Army of Occupation broke camp at Corpus Christi, Texas, and marched south toward Matamoros, Mexico, on the Río Grande. As they approached Arroyo Colorado, a steep-sided, brackish stream about 30 miles north of Matamoros, Taylor halted the army to scout the crossing. On March 19, Taylor sent forward a squadron from the 2nd Dragoons, who were immediately challenged by Mexican cavalry whose position was hidden by woods and thick brush on the other side of the stream. Although no shots were exchanged, the Mexicans made it clear that any crossing would be regarded as an act of aggression.

The following day, Taylor decided to cross the arroyo. His engineers cut down the bank for easy fording. Mexican bugles and drums could be heard on the other side of the 80-yard-wide stream. Lieutenant Ulysses S. Grant recalled that if the "[Mexican] troops were in proportion to the noise, they were sufficient to devour General Taylor and his army." After careful deployment of the 1st and 2nd brigades of the 2nd Dragoons and his artillery, Taylor marched his army across the river in perfect order with General William J. Worth in the lead and the bands playing "Yankee Doodle." Eager for action, the U.S. forces were disappointed to learn that the Mexican force had retreated to Matamoros.

For further reading: Barbour, *Journals of the Late Brevet Major Philip Norbourne Barbour, Captain in the 3rd Regiment, United States Infantry, and His Wife Martha Isabella Hopkins Barbour, Written during the War with Mexico, 1846*, 1936; French, *Two Wars, an Autobiography*, 1901; Grant, *Personal Memoirs of U. S. Grant*, 1885.

Arroyo Hondo, Skirmish at

(January 1847)

Approximately six U.S. citizens were killed in the small New Mexico community of Arroyo Hondo in January 1847 during the Taos Rebellion, a revolt against the U.S. government in Santa Fe that had been installed by General Stephen W. Kearny in August of the previous year.

Brigadier General Kearny had brought his Army of the West to New Mexico in August 1846. Kearny was successful in winning acceptance from many of the New Mexicans. His subordinate, Colonel Alexander Doniphan, also maintained the good relationship and even signed a peace treaty with the aggressive Navajo Nation. By January 1847, both Kearny and Doniphan had left with independent commands, and the occupational force was headed by Colonel Sterling Price, a poor leader and disciplinarian. The increase in drunkenness and rough behavior by his soldiers aggravated the citizens of Santa Fe. Rebel leaders including Diego Archuleta and Tomás Ortiz began to develop a plot to overthrow the U.S. government there.

Violence erupted in Taos when visiting military governor Charles Bent and others were murdered on January 19, 1847. The killing frenzy spilled over to nearby Arroyo Hondo, a tiny settlement built around Simeon Turley's distillery and mill. (Turley, a U.S. citizen, had lived there since 1830 and employed local New Mexicans and Indians to manufacture his famous "Taos Lightning.") Receiving warning before an angry mob of 500 rebels arrived, Turley closed the gates to the stockade that surrounded his distillery complex.

Turley and his eight to ten defenders were besieged for two days. The rebels slaughtered the cows and horses in the corrals, and some of the main buildings were set fire and burned to the ground. The rain of bullets and arrows over the walls had killed some of Turley's men. Running low on ammunition, the rest tried to escape at dark; all but three were hunted down and killed.

Price eventually subjugated the New Mexican and Pueblo rebels by killing 150 of them in a fight at the Taos Pueblo and hanging their leaders in the Taos town square.

See also Archuleta, Diego; Price, Sterling; Taos Rebellion.

For further reading: Lavender, *Bent's Fort*, 1954; McNierney, *Taos 1847*, 1980; Twitchell, *The History of the Military Occupation of the Territory of New Mexico from 1846 to 1851 by the Government of the United States*, 1909.

Atlixco, Skirmish at
(October 19, 1847)

The bloody skirmish at the small community of Atlixco, state of Puebla, was one of the last serious engagements between Mexican guerrillas and U.S. forces. A band of guerrillas under Brigadier General Joaquín Rea was overtaken by troops under Brigadier General Joseph Lane on October 19, 1847. Rea's force took heavy losses in the fight and, between casualties and subsequent desertion, was too reduced in number to remain an effective fighting unit.

After the passage of General Winfield Scott's army toward Mexico City, the small U.S. force that garrisoned Puebla was besieged by forces under General Antonio López de Santa Anna and Brigadier General Rea. The siege lasted nearly a month, during which 52 U.S. troops were killed or wounded. The arrival of Brigadier General Lane and a large force on October 13, 1847, finally liberated the garrison, and Rea's cavalry/guerrillas dissipated southward into the hills.

Rea and his 2,500 followers had withdrawn to Atlixco, about 25 miles southwest of Puebla. When Puebla had fallen to the U.S. force, the state government had moved its headquarters to this quaint, well-kept town. The hillside community was surrounded by gardens, orchards, and cultivated fields.

Lane and 1,500 dragoons and infantry left Puebla on October 19 in pursuit of Rea. They encountered Rea's advance late in the afternoon, which began a running fight of heavy skirmishing. Eventually a short, pitched battle was fought on a hillside outside Atlixco near sunset. According to Lane, "the whole body of the enemy was discovered on a hillside, covered with chaparral, forming hedges, behind which they had posted themselves.... So thick was the chaparral that the dragoons were ordered to dismount and fight them on foot. A most bloody conflict ensued...." Rea and his men retreated into Atlixco at dark. Under a bright, full moon, Lane ordered an artillery barrage that lasted about an hour. Distraught, the citizens quickly surrendered the town and informed Lane that the rebels had fled further south toward Izucar de Matamoros. Lane claimed that 219 rebels were killed and 300 wounded; he lost only two men. Civilian losses were not recorded. About a month later, Lane struck Rea again at Izucar de Matamoros and inflicted about 80 casualties, which further reduced Rea's fighting force.

See also Lane, Joseph; Puebla; Rea, Joaquín.

For further reading: Brackett, *General Lane's Brigade in Central Mexico*, 1854; Frost, *The Mexican War and Its Warriors*, 1848; Oswandel, *Notes of the Mexican War*, 1885.

Atocha, Alexander J.

Alexander J. Atocha met with President James K. Polk in 1846 to convince him that, if allowed to return to Mexico, exiled leader Antonio López de Santa Anna would pursue peace negotiations. Accordingly, Polk allowed Santa Anna to pass through the U.S. naval blockade in August 1846. As Santa Anna quickly escalated the war effort, it became obvious that he had no intentions of negotiating with the United States.

Atocha, who was born in Spain, was a naturalized U.S. citizen with banking interests in Mexico. As one of Santa Anna's close associates, he too was exiled from the country with Santa Anna in January 1845. Atocha met with President Polk in June regarding personal claims he held against the Mexican government. On February 13, 1846, he confided to Polk in Washington that, although Santa Anna was in exile in Havana, Cuba, he had a strong support network in Mexico and believed that he could easily return to power. Polk recorded in his diary that Atocha said, "Santa Anna was in favor of a treaty with the United States, and that in adjusting a boundary line between the two countries the [Rio Grande] should be the western Texas line, and the Colorado of the West down through the Bay of San Francisco to the sea should be the line on the north, and that Mexico should cede all east and north of these natural boundaries to the United States for a pecuniary consideration and mentioned thirty millions of dollars as the sum." Atocha stressed that the money would stabilize Mexico and help pay its numerous debts. He went on to tell Polk that Santa Anna felt a strong military presence was imperative to force the Mexican Congress into a peace settlement.

Three days later, on February 16, Polk and Atocha met again for more than an hour and discussed various ideas. Atocha, speaking for Santa Anna, applauded General Zachary Taylor's march to the Río Grande and the naval blockade of Mexican ports. Atocha stressed that the United States should also demand payment for its claims. He reasoned that, because the Mexican government was essentially bankrupt, it would be forced to agree to the boundaries to avert war. Atocha claimed that Santa Anna's last words to him were "When you see the President, tell him to take measures, and such a treaty can be made and I will sustain it."

Although Polk had his reservations ("Colonel Atocha is a person to whom I would not give my confidence…"), he was intrigued by the possibility of a quick end to the war. Polk sent U.S. naval commander Alexander Slidell Mackenzie to Cuba in July to negotiate personally with Santa Anna. Corroborative reports from Mackenzie compelled Polk to allow Santa Anna safe passage through the naval blockade to land at Veracruz in August 1846. Once in power, Santa Anna showed no interest in negotiating a treaty with the United States, as Polk had been led to believe, and began to rebuild the Army of the North for an offensive strike against General Taylor.

In mid-January 1847, Atocha again approached the U.S. government, proclaiming a desire for peace. He told Secretary of State James Buchanan that Mexico would accept the Río Grande as the U.S. border with certain conditions and that California could be purchased. Polk submitted a counterproposal that called for giving California and New Mexico to the United States and keeping the Río Grande border with no concessions. Atocha carried this back to Mexico City, where it was flatly refused by the Mexican government on February 22. Ever persistent, Atocha tried again to interest the president in a surrender plan in February 1848, but was dismissed by Polk as a "great scoundrel."

For further reading: Pletcher, *The Diplomacy of Annexation,* 1973; Polk, *The Diary of James K. Polk,* 1910.

Aztec Club

After General Winfield Scott's army entered Mexico City in September 1847 and became an occupational force, a number of its officers formed the Military Society of the Mexican War, more commonly known as the Aztec Club. Its first meeting was October 13, 1847. Patterned after the Society of Cincinnati that was founded during the Revolutionary War, its initial enrollment was about 160 officers. Membership descended from father to son or to the nearest male blood relative. After some constitutional changes, the purpose of the club was defined in 1892 as "cherishing the memories and keeping alive the traditions that cluster about the names of those officers who took part in the Mexican War…and also to aiding other patriotic Societies in efforts to inculcate and stimulate patriotism.…" Today, approximately 400 members compose the Aztec Club, which focuses on preserving the history of the Mexican-American War.

For further reading: The Aztec Club of 1847, *Military Society of the Mexican War,* 1964; *Constitution of the Aztec Club,* 1893.

B

Backus, Electus
(1804–1862)

A captain in the U.S. 1st Infantry, Electus Backus led a command of 75 men that held a strong advance position during the Battle of Monterrey in 1846. They poured a hot fire into the Mexican soldiers operating the guns at Fort Tenería, an act that inspired a U.S. charge that overran the fort. Its seizure was one of the key turning points in the battle.

Born in New York in 1804, Backus graduated from the U.S. Military Academy in 1824 as a second lieutenant in the 1st U.S. Infantry. He served in New York, the Second Seminole War, and later on the Minnesota frontier. He was promoted to captain in 1837.

Part of General Zachary Taylor's Army of Occupation, Backus performed well during the Battles of Palo Alto and Resaca de la Palma in May 1846. On September 21, 1846, during the Battle of Monterrey, Backus had led an advance of the 1st Infantry and did not hear the order to retire. Having seized a building in the rear of El Tenería, a Mexican fort with batteries that guarded the eastern approach to the city, his men took position behind a two-foot-high parapet of sandbags and fired constantly at the Mexican artillerymen. The 1st Infantry's firing was so rapid that they ran low on ammunition, and the rifles began to foul. The sandbags caught fire and smoldered, creating choking smoke and heat. Inspired, the U.S. troops charged again and seized the Mexican guns. The fall of El Tenería demoralized the Mexican forces and allowed the United States to gain a key position that helped turn the battle into a U.S. victory.

Following the war, Backus was assigned to various frontier positions in New Mexico and skirmished with hostile Indians. As a colonel of the 6th U.S. Infantry, he was a mustering officer in the Union Army during the Civil War. He died in Detroit, Michigan, at the age of 58.

See also Monterrey, Battle of.

For further reading: Backus, "Brief Sketch of the Battle of Monterey," 1866; Cullum, *Biographical Register of the Officers and Graduates of the United States Military Academy from 1802 to 1867*, 1879.

Baker, Edward Dickinson
(1811–1861)

A colonel of Illinois volunteers, Edward Dickinson Baker was one of the better volunteer officers during the Mexican-American War. He led General James Shield's brigade during the Battle of Cerro Gordo after Shields was wounded, and he continued to command it until the end of the war.

Baker, who was born in London, England, moved with his family to Philadelphia in 1815. He later moved to Illinois, opened a law practice in Springfield in 1835, and became associated with Abraham Lincoln.

Baker was a senator in Washington, D.C., when the Mexican-American War erupted. He quickly raised a regiment of Illinois volunteer soldiers and joined General Zachary Taylor's army on the Río Grande. Shortly afterward, Baker was wounded while trying to break up a camp brawl. Later, in General Winfield Scott's army, he served with distinction at the Battle of Cerro Gordo in 1847, when he assumed the command of General James Shield's brigade after Shields was seriously wounded. Baker led the brigade in a charge that overran the Mexican rear. He also commanded the brigade in the subsequent battles that led to the capture of Mexico City.

In 1848, Baker resumed his political career in Illinois and then later moved to Oregon and won a seat as senator against the heavily favored Joseph Lane, another Mexican-American War veteran. During the Civil War, Baker joined the Union Army. He was killed in action during the 1861 Battle of Ball's Bluff, Virginia, where his leadership was criticized.

See also Cerro Gordo, Battle of.

For further reading: Bauer, *The Mexican War, 1846–1848,* 1974; Dodd, "The West and the War with Mexico," 1912.

Balbontín, Manuel
(1824–1894)

Manuel Balbontín was one of the few Mexican veterans who recorded the Mexican perspective in his *La invasión americana, 1846 a 1848,* a standard reference work on the Mexican-American War.

Balbontín, who was born in Mexico City, enlisted in the Mexican army in 1846 at the age of 22 to fight the "norteamericana." He saw his first action at the Battle of La Angostura (Buena Vista) in February 1847 and later fought with those who resisted General Winfield Scott's advance on Mexico City from Veracruz.

After surviving the war, he joined liberal political factions and participated in rebellions at Michoacán and Julisco. A soldier again, he fought against the conservatives in Puebla in 1856, and his liberal contingent later occupied Veracruz. Balbontín was the military commander in Tampico from 1861 to 1862. He also resisted the French invasion of Mexico.

In his later years, as a noted military historian and author, he wrote *La invasión americana, 1846 a 1848* in 1888. Balbontín died in Mexico City in 1894.

For further reading: Diccionario Porrúa, 1995.

Balderas, Lucas
(1797–1847)

One of the officers of the Mina Battalion, Lucas Balderas had fought bravely throughout the Mexican-American War before he was killed by a bullet at the Battle of El Molino del Rey on September 8, 1847.

Balderas was born to a family of modest means in San Miguel el Grande. He worked in a tailor's shop at a very young age in Mexico City. By 1827, Balderas was captain of the local militia, and later an inspector. He helped suppress a number of local uprisings and rebellions, and by 1841 he was a colonel of infantry and was later transferred to the artillery.

In the thickest of the severe fighting at El Molino del Rey on September 8, 1847, Balderas was wounded in the foot but refused to leave the field. He was leading a charge to retake some of his artillery, which had been seized by U.S. soldiers, when he was killed and fell into the arms of his son. Alcaraz wrote that "war deprived us of one of the best citizens; one of the military's bravest; one of the men most honorable."

For further reading: Alcaraz, *The Other Side,* 1850; Bauer, *The Mexican War, 1846–1848,* 1974; Carreño,

Lucas Balderas
(Library of Congress)

Jefes del ejército mexicano en 1847, 1914; *Diccionario Porrúa*, 1995.

Bancroft, George
(1800–1891)

Regarded as one of the most brilliant minds of his time, George Bancroft played an important role in the election of President James K. Polk in 1845. Bancroft served as Polk's secretary of war and secretary of the navy and helped establish the U.S. Naval Academy.

Born in Massachusetts, Bancroft's intellectual gifts became evident at an early age. He was well educated at private academies and entered Harvard University at the age of 13. His education continued overseas. A noted traditionalist, he was one of the last citizens in Worcester to wear a tricornered hat.

Bancroft was drawn to politics in the 1830s and joined the Democratic Party in Massachusetts. As a delegate in the 1844 Democratic National Convention, his influence was instrumental in securing the nomination for Polk.

Polk trusted Bancroft and appointed him secretary of the navy in March 1845. Aware of the potential for warfare over Mexico and Oregon Territory, and the resultant need to upgrade the U.S. navy, Bancroft spent much of his time establishing the U.S. Naval Academy in Annapolis, Maryland. Assuming that Congress would reject any proposed budget for the project, much of the funding was covert and often was obtained through vaguely worded requisitions. Bancroft used an old army fort at Annapolis and hired new faculty and gunnery instructors. The school opened on October 10, 1845. Midshipmen from docked vessels were immediately sent there for training.

Bancroft served as secretary of the navy for 18 months. As a temporary secretary of war in 1845, he signed the order that sent General Zachary Taylor and the Army of Occupation from Corpus Christi across disputed Mexican territory to the Río Grande. He also advised Commodore John D. Sloat and his Pacific fleet to begin operations along the California coast.

He became increasingly unpopular in Massachusetts because of his support of the Mexican-American War. Polk satisfied Bancroft's wish for an overseas post and in September 1846 appointed him U.S. minister to Great Britain. Bancroft was well regarded in England and France, where he conducted historical research. He returned to live in New York, where he finished his multivolume *History of the United States*. During the Civil War, he supported Lincoln and opposed slavery. He died at the age of 90 on January 17, 1891.

For further reading: Handlin, *George Bancroft*, 1984; Howe, *The Life and Letters of George Bancroft*, 1908; Nye, *George Bancroft*, 1944.

Barbour, Philip Norbourne
(1813–1846)

A promising young officer from the U.S. Military Academy, Philip Norbourne Barbour received a brevet to major for his "meritorious conduct" during the Battle of Resaca de la Palma in 1846. He was killed a few months later at the Battle of Monterrey.

Barbour was born in Kentucky. He attended the U.S. Military Academy from 1829 to 1834. He was commissioned as a second lieutenant of the 3rd U.S. Infantry and served on the western frontier. Barbour was brevetted to captain for gallantry during the Florida Wars.

Barbour and the 3rd Infantry were part of General Zachary Taylor's Army of Occupation that marched from Corpus Christie to the Río Grande in 1846. An eager soldier, Barbour led from exposed positions during the Battles of Palo Alto and Resaca de la Palma in May. His charge at Resaca de la Palma helped break the Mexican line and resulted in Barbour's brevet to major.

The night before the battle for Monterrey, Barbour wrote in his journal: "During a time of war, my life is the rightful property of my country, and cannot be taken from me, or preserved, except by the fiat of the great God who gave it. And to His will, whatever it be, I am perfectly resigned." The following day, on September 21, 1846, he was killed by a bullet through his heart as he rallied his men in heavy fighting.

For further reading: Barbour, *Journals of the Late Brevet Major Philip Norbourne Barbour, Captain in the 3rd Regiment, United States Infantry, and His Wife Martha Isabella Hopkins Barbour, Written during the War with Mexico, 1846*, 1936; Cullum, *Biographical*

Register of the Officers and Graduates of the United States Military Academy from 1802 to 1867, 1879.

For further reading: Bartlett, *Personal Narrative*, 1854; Garber, *The Gadsden Treaty*, 1959; Johnson and Malone, *Dictionary of American Biography*, 1928–1936.

Bartlett, John Russell
(1805–1886)

In 1850, President Zachary Taylor appointed John Russell Bartlett as the U.S. commissioner for surveying the new boundary between Mexico and the United States. Bartlett and his Mexican counterpart, General Pedro García Condé, signed the Bartlett-Condé Agreement, which fixed the starting point for the survey.

Bartlett was born in Providence, Rhode Island, and raised in New York and Canada. His love of writing was evident at an early age. He excelled in history and literature as a university student and opened a bookstore in New York City in 1836. He also had a lifelong interest in ethnology and linguistics.

In 1850, he was chosen by President Taylor to be the U.S. commissioner responsible for surveying the boundary, as defined by the 1848 Treaty of Guadalupe Hidalgo, between the United States and Mexico. Eager to work in Spanish-speaking Mexico, Bartlett took his well-equipped group of surveyors and engineers to Texas, and, on December 3, 1850, he met Mexican commissioner General Condé in El Paso. Contradictions immediately arose regarding the location of the starting point because their map locations did not agree with descriptions in the text of the treaty. To expedite the survey, they agreed to a starting point according to a document that they prepared and signed, called the Bartlett-Condé Agreement. The four-year surveying project required extensive fieldwork in Texas, New Mexico, Chihuahua, Sonora, California, and Arizona. Bartlett's findings were published in 1854 in the two-volume *Personal Narrative of Explorations and Incidents Connected with the United States and Mexican Boundary Commission*.

Bartlett returned to Rhode Island in 1855 and became its secretary of state from 1855 to 1872. He worked tirelessly to organize all of Rhode Island's historical papers that had been generated over the past two centuries. Bartlett died at the age of 79.

See also Bartlett-Condé Agreement; García Condé, Pedro.

Bartlett-Condé Agreement

A document signed by U.S. boundary commissioner John Russell Bartlett and Mexican boundary commissioner General Pedro García Condé, the Bartlett-Condé Agreement pinpointed the starting point for the survey of the new border of Mexico and the United States.

The written instructions for determining the Mexico-U.S. boundary were included in Article V of the Treaty of Guadalupe Hidalgo: the border was to follow the Río Grande to the southwestern boundary of New Mexico, then follow the Gila and Colorado Rivers, and finally continue as a straight line to the Pacific Ocean, just south of San Diego. The borders of New Mexico were arbitrarily defined according to an 1847 J. Disturnell map that was known to be inaccurate. In fact, the two maps that were used during the treaty ratification process were not the same—the United States used the seventh edition, and Mexico used the twelfth.

Article V also called for a commissioner and surveyor from each country to conduct the survey. General Condé represented Mexico, and Bartlett was chosen by President Zachary Taylor. The two commissioners met in El Paso, Texas, on December 3, 1850.

Initial surveys quickly indicated that the Río Grande on the Disturnell map was mislocated by two degrees and that El Paso was too far to the north. The contradictions among the instructions in the treaty, the maps, and the actual location of the key starting points made a huge difference in the amount of land that could be gained or lost by either country. After making mutual concessions, the two commissioners agreed to fix the initial point on the Río Grande at the latitude stated on the map, without reference to El Paso, and to extend the line westward from the initial point three degrees. All this was detailed in the formal document that they signed and was immediately contested in the United States and discussed by the Committee on Foreign Relations. Bartlett's interpretation of Article V was supported by Nicholas P. Trist, who had negotiated the treaty. After exhaustive congressional debate, the agreement was accepted and the survey completed.

Much of the land that would have been within the U.S. border if the original starting points had been used, including the fertile Mesilla Valley, was later acquired by the United States in 1853 through the Gadsden Treaty.

See also Gadsden Treaty; García Condé, Pedro.

For further reading: Bartlett, *Personal Narrative*, 1854; Garber, *The Gadsden Treaty*, 1959; Goetzmann, "The United States–Mexico Boundary Survey, 1848–1853," 1985; Webb, *The Handbook of Texas*, 1952.

Bartolo Ford

See San Gabriel River (Bartolo Ford), Battle of.

Baz, Juan José
(1820–1887)

A close ally of liberal Valentín Gómez Farías, Juan José Baz was a wealthy and influential citizen in Mexico City during the Mexican-American War. His unflagging support of Gómez Farías's plan to seize Catholic Church property in 1847 helped lead to the *Polkos* Revolt.

Baz was born to an affluent family in Guadalajara. He was drawn to politics at an early age and became a spokesperson for radical liberalism in Mexico City. Opposed to foreign intervention in Mexican affairs, Baz supported the war against the United States and was one of the first to propose drawing from the vast wealth of the Catholic Church to finance the war effort.

Sharing the same political views as acting president Gómez Farías, Baz was appointed governor of the Federal District in Mexico City in 1847. As a supporter of Gómez Farías, he signed the legislation that authorized the seizure of 20 million pesos from the Roman Catholic Church. This action resulted in the *Polkos* Revolt, which ultimately removed Gómez Farías from power. Baz retained his position after the return of General Antonio López de Santa Anna to the city. As the commander of the capital's national guard, Baz was involved in the city's defense against General Winfield Scott's advancing army in August 1847. Baz helped mediate Mexican-American affairs during Scott's occupation of the city.

After the war, Baz remained an outspoken supporter of liberalism and clashed with Santa Anna when he returned to power in 1853. Baz remained in contact with influential political leaders such as Benito Juárez and fought as a military officer against the French in the 1860s. His continual efforts at liberal reform resulted in the building of new schools and orphanages before he died in 1887.

See also Gómez Farías, Valentín; *Polkos* Revolt.

For further reading: Carreño, *Jefes del ejército mexicano en 1847*, 1914; Robinson, *Mexico and Her Military Chieftains, from the Revolution of Hidalgo to the Present Time*, 1848; Santoni, *Mexicans at Arms*, 1996.

Beach, Moses Y.
(1800–1868)

Newspaperman Moses Y. Beach was selected by President James K. Polk to travel to Mexico at the onset of the Mexican-American War to persuade leading governmental and Catholic Church officials to lobby for peace. His efforts were unsuccessful, and he was nearly imprisoned before he escaped the country.

Moses Y. Beach was born in Connecticut. As a young child, he invented mechanical toys. Continuing his interest in mechanics, he moved to New York City in 1834 to oversee the printing press at the *Sun*. He later purchased the newspaper and turned it into a successful business. As editor, he frequently championed the Democratic Party. An avid expansionist, he often editorialized in 1845 about seizing California.

In the summer of 1846, Beach received a proposal from a group of prominent Mexicans that involved surrendering part of northern Mexico to the United States. He discussed this with Secretary of State James Buchanan and President Polk in person in Washington in November and volunteered to go to Mexico. Polk accepted, and Beach was instructed to discuss the peaceful settlement of the war with Mexican and church officials.

First sailing to Cuba, he entered Veracruz

with a false British passport in January 1847, accompanied by his 26-year-old daughter and Jane Maria Eliza (McManus) Storms, a journalist and political activist. They interacted with other agents and U.S. consul John Black in Mexico City. Despite his efforts at disguise, Beach's mission was well known to Antonio López de Santa Anna through Santa Anna's loyal contacts in Cuba.

Beach spoke with high-level businessmen, priests, and government officials, including acting president Valentín Gómez Farías, about how the United States could help industrialize Mexico. He had convinced several bishops that Santa Anna's war efforts were dangerous to the church and that the U.S. government would protect its assets. Shortly afterward, the *Polkos* Revolt against Gómez Farías erupted. Believing that Beach was at least partly to blame, Santa Anna posted a $1,000 reward for Beach and announced that anyone with a copy of the *Sun* would be punished as a traitor. Beach, his daughter, and Storms narrowly escaped the country. Upon his return to the United States, Beach met with President Polk in Washington, D.C., on May 11, 1847.

During the Mexican-American War, Beach helped found the New York Associated Press, a cooperative of some of the biggest newspapers in the country. In 1848, he retired to Wallingford, Connecticut, where he died at the age of 68.

See also Storms, Jane McManus.

For further reading: Caruso, *The Mexican Spy Company*, 1991; Johnson and Malone, *Dictionary of American Biography*, 1928–1936; Nelson, "Mission to Mexico—Moses Y. Beach, Secret Agent," 1975; O'Brien, *The Story of the* Sun, 1928.

Beale, Edward Fitzgerald
(1822–1893)

As part of Brigadier General Stephen W. Kearny's force that was besieged by Californian rebels after the Battle of San Pascual in 1846, naval officer Edward Fitzgerald Beale was one of three volunteers who walked 35 miles to bring back reinforcements.

The son of a War of 1812 soldier, Beale was born in the District of Columbia. Through an appeal from his widowed mother, Beale was

Edward F. Beale
(Library of Congress)

appointed by President Andrew Jackson to the U.S. Naval School. In October 1845, Beale sailed on the frigate *Congress* under Commodore Robert F. Stockton to California.

Brigadier General Kearny and 300 dragoons had left Santa Fe, New Mexico, in September 1846 to join Stockton's force in San Diego. Lieutenant Beale was part of a group of sailors led by Lieutenant Archibald Gillespie that had left San Diego and joined Kearny just before the disastrous Battle of San Pascual on December 6. After the battle, the Californio rebels trapped Kearny's men on a rocky hill. Beale, Delaware Indian scout Chemuctah, and frontiersman Kit Carson crept through the Californian lines at night and walked to San Diego for help. Barefoot, Beale traveled over 35 miles of rocky ground to report Kearny's plight to Commodore Stockton. It took Beale nearly two years to fully recover his health after the ordeal. He traveled in February 1847 with important dispatches to Washington and participated in the court-martial of John C. Frémont. A highly respected officer, Beale resigned from the navy in 1850.

In 1852, President Millard Fillmore appointed Beale as superintendent of Indian affairs in California and Nevada. He was later brigadier general of militia in California and conducted railroad surveys for the federal government. In 1876, President Ulysses S. Grant appointed him minister to Austria-Hungary. Beale remained close friends with Grant, Frémont, and Carson and died peacefully in his Washington home.

See also San Pascual, Battle of.

For further reading: Bauer, *Surfboats and Horse Marines*, 1969; Bonsal, *Edward Fitzgerald Beale, a Pioneer in the Path of Empire, 1822–1903*, 1912; Johnson and Malone, *Dictionary of American Biography*, 1928–1936.

Bear Flag Revolt
(June–July 1846)

Inspired by the hostile actions between Mexico and the United States, a small group of mostly U.S. settlers in California fought one skirmish and occupied the towns of Sonoma and San Francisco in June–July 1846. Named for the grizzly bear on their flag, they declared California to be free of Mexican rule.

At the beginning of the Mexican-American War, California was in a state of turmoil. Too far from Mexico City to be effectively governed, Californians were rebellious and spoke of self-rule. Although ardent, the state's government was poorly developed, inexperienced, and not totally unified in policy. In December of 1845, John C. Frémont and a group of about 60 well-armed, warlike riflemen arrived in California. Frémont's belligerence resulted in Mexican commandant José Castro ordering him to leave California in March 1846. Frémont refused and began to incite the settlers in the Sacramento Valley, who were already displeased with Mexican rule, to rebel.

On June 14, a group of about 30 armed men, led by William B. Ide and Ezekiel Merritt, seized prominent Sonoran citizen General Mariano Vallejo. Colonel Frémont oversaw the two-month imprisonment of Vallejo at Sutter's Fort. The party declared California's independence at Sonoma and raised a homemade flag decorated with a star and a grizzly. On June 24, the Bear Flaggers, as they were to be known, skirmished with a small force under Castro south of Sonoma at the Battle of Olompali. Emboldened by their victory, they occupied San Francisco on July 1. A few days later, Frémont assumed official command of the Bear Flaggers and merged them with his unit. By July 11, Commodore John D. Sloat had captured Monterey, raised the U.S. flag, and claimed California officially for the United States. The Bear Flag Revolt had lasted less than one month.

See also Frémont, John C.; Olompali, Skirmish at.

For further reading: Bancroft, *History of California*, 1886; Cleland, *From Wilderness to Empire*, 1970; Goodwin, *John Charles Frémont*, 1930; Harlow, *California Conquered*, 1982; Nevins, *Frémont, Pathmaker of the West*, 1955.

Beaubien, Carlos
(1800–1864)

A successful trader in New Mexico, Carlos Beaubien supported the U.S. invasion of New Mexico in 1846. Also a judge, he issued death sentences to those tried for murder during the Taos Rebellion in 1847.

Beaubien, who was born in Canada, became an active member in the St. Louis fur trade in the 1820s. Moving gradually westward, he and other trappers were drawn to New Mexico in the mid-1820s. He developed a prosperous fur business in Taos and learned Spanish. Well liked and regarded as a fair man, he married a New Mexican woman and became a citizen of New Mexico. Beaubien began to invest in land and received a large land grant from the government in about 1841.

Beaubien was a strong supporter of General Stephen W. Kearny and the Army of Occupation when they arrived in August 1846. Kearny quickly recognized his ally by appointing him judge in his military government. In January 1847, Beaubien's son was brutally murdered during the Taos Rebellion, when rebels killed U.S. citizens and pro-U.S. New Mexicans in Taos and nearby communities. As judge, Beaubien issued the death sentences for the captured rebel leaders accused of murder. They were later hung. After the war, Beaubien remained a prominent and popular figure in New Mexican politics and culture.

See also Taos Rebellion.

For further reading: McNierney, *Taos 1847*, 1980; Meier and Rivera, *Dictionary of Mexican American History*, 1981; Twitchell, *The History of the Military Occupation of the Territory of New Mexico from 1846 to 1851 by the Government of the United States*, 1909; Weber, *The Taos Trappers*, 1971.

Beauregard, Pierre Gustave Toutant
(1818–1893)

Second Lieutenant Pierre Gustave Toutant Beauregard was an engineer with the U.S. Army of Occupation. He performed important reconnaissance missions as General Winfield Scott moved inland from Veracruz, especially before the Battles of Cerro Gordo and Contreras in 1847.

Born of French ancestry in New Orleans, Beauregard was later educated in New Orleans and New York. He graduated near the top of his class from West Point in 1838 and was assigned to the corps of engineers.

During the Mexican-American War, Beauregard was part of General Winfield Scott's forces as a second lieutenant of engineers. Beauregard and Robert E. Lee scouted the defenses around Veracruz in March 1847 before Beauregard was stricken with fever and bedridden for most of March and April. Riding ahead of Scott's army as it moved forward from Veracruz, Beauregard was instrumental in scouting out a route for flanking the Mexican army at the Battle of Cerro Gordo. Again teamed with Lee, they found a twisting path through the almost-impenetrable *pedregal* (lava field) before the Battle of Contreras in August 1847. With 500 men, they opened a road through the lava fields for artillery and the wagons. His services at Contreras won Beauregard a brevet. Most accounts indicate that he was influential in convincing Scott to attack Mexico City via Chapultepec, which proved to be successful. Beauregard won another brevet after receiving two slight wounds during the taking of Mexico City in September. During Scott's occupation of the city, Beauregard continued to perform as a scout.

Never having fully regained his health in Mexico, Beauregard resigned in 1858. He returned to New Orleans and was employed as an engineer, overseeing the construction of the canal system that drained the wetlands around the city. In 1860, he was chosen as the superintendent of West Point. He resigned five days later to join the Confederate army as a brigadier general. His bombardment against Fort Sumter in South Carolina was the first action of the Civil War. One of the South's most consistent commanders, he performed capably in a number of campaigns throughout that war.

After the Civil War, Beauregard was employed as the president of a railroad company, commissioner of public works in New Orleans, and adjutant general of Louisiana. He wrote frequently about the Civil War and died from heart disease at his home in New Orleans.

See also Cerro Gordo, Battle of; Contreras, Battle of.

For further reading: Cullum, *Biographical Register of the Officers and Graduates of the United States Military Academy from 1802 to 1867*, 1879; Johnson and Malone, *Dictionary of American Biography*, 1928–1936; Semmes, *Service Afloat and Ashore during the Mexican War*, 1851; Williams, *P. G. T. Beauregard*, 1954.

Pierre G. T. Beauregard
(Library of Congress)

Bee, Barnard Elliott
(1824–1861)

Lieutenant Barnard Elliott Bee served in the 3rd U.S. Infantry during the Mexican-American War. A trusted and capable leader, he was severely wounded during the Battle of Cerro Gordo in April 1847.

Born in Charleston, South Carolina, Bee and his family moved to the Texas frontier in

1835. After attending the U.S. Military Academy from 1841 to 1845, he was commissioned as lieutenant in the 3rd U.S. Infantry and joined General Zachary Taylor's Army of Occupation at Corpus Christi. Bee fought at the Battles of Palo Alto and Resaca de la Palma in May 1846.

He later joined Major General Winfield Scott's Army of Occupation that landed at Veracruz in March 1847. Wounded at Cerro Gordo in April, Bee received brevets for "gallant and meritorious conduct" at the Battles of Cerro Gordo and Chapultepec, where he was part of the storming party.

A popular officer, Bee continued his military service on the western frontier. By 1855, he was captain of the 10th U.S. Infantry. He resigned in 1861 to join the Confederate service as a brigadier general. His brigade suffered heavy losses during the First Battle of Bull Run in 1861. It was Bee who pointed to Jackson and shouted out that there he stood "like a stone wall." Shortly afterward, Bee was wounded and died the following day.

See also Cerro Gordo, Battle of; Chapultepec, Battle of.

For further reading: Cullum, *Biographical Register of the Officers and Graduates of the United States Military Academy from 1802 to 1867*, 1879; Johnson and Malone, *Dictionary of American Biography*, 1928–1936.

Belknap, William Goldsmith

(d. 1851)

One of the more seasoned officers in the U.S. army, Lieutenant Colonel William Goldsmith Belknap commanded the left wing of General Zachary Taylor's Army of Occupation during the Battles of Palo Alto and Resaca de la Palma in 1846. He also participated in the Mexico City campaign under Major General Winfield Scott in 1847.

Born and raised in New York State, William G. Belknap joined the U.S. Army in 1813 during the War of 1812. He later fought the Seminole Indians during the Florida Wars and served on the western frontier.

Belknap ably commanded Taylor's left wing (8th U.S. Infantry and artillery units) during the Battle of Palo Alto in May 1846. He also commanded Taylor's left wing the following day during the Battle of Resaca de la Palma. In the midst of the fighting, he led the 5th U.S. Infantry in a charge that overran a Mexican artillery position and was wounded during hand-to-hand fighting. Belknap received a brevet to colonel for his leadership in these engagements. Following the path of the retreating Mexican army after the Battle of Buena Vista, Belknap and a small patrol rode into La Encarnación on March 1, 1847. Here they found 222 wounded Mexican soldiers in deplorable conditions in a small chapel and cared for them as best they could.

Colonel Belknap served with Major General Winfield Scott's Army of Occupation as it marched from Veracruz to Mexico City in 1847, and he helped establish the military government in the city. As one of Scott's senior officers, Belknap participated in the military court of inquiry on March 13, 1848, that investigated the conduct of General Gideon Pillow.

See also Buena Vista, Battle of; Palo Alto, Battle of; Resaca de la Palma, Battle of.

For further reading: Chamberlain, *My Confession*, 1956; Cullum, *Biographical Register of the Officers and Graduates of the United States Military Academy from 1802 to 1867*, 1879; Frost, *The Mexican War and Its Warriors*, 1848.

Bent, Charles

(1799–1847)

Charles Bent was one of the most prominent citizens and businessmen in New Mexico at the outbreak of the Mexican-American War. His popularity led Brigadier General Stephen W. Kearny to appoint him military governor in August 1846. Bent's brutal murder five months later by a mob of rebels was the beginning of the Taos Rebellion.

Born in Charleston, West Virginia, Charles Bent was six years old when his family moved to St. Louis, Missouri. As a young man, he moved west in 1826 as an employee of the Missouri Fur Company. After spending years in the fur trade, he and his brother William built Bent's Old Fort during 1833–1834 along the Arkansas River. Although most of the Bent family lived at the fort, Charles Bent promoted the family trade from his home in Taos, where he lived with his Mexican wife and children. Bent was well known and respected throughout New Mexico and Chihuahua and received large land grants from New Mexican Governor Manuel Armijo.

Bent's Old Fort was a stopping point for Brigadier General Stephen W. Kearny's Army of the West on its way to occupy New Mexico in the summer of 1846. Bent and Kearny had long conversations about the political and military situation in New Mexico. Once Kearny was established in Santa Fe, he appointed Bent as the new military governor on September 22, 1846. Many of the governmental officials that Bent selected were friends and family, including native New Mexicans.

Bent took his new job seriously. Immediately after his appointment, he wrote to Secretary of State James Buchanan and Senator Thomas Hart Benton about the need for a government library, raw materials, translators, mail service, a school system, and a mining code.

Discontent with the new government, New Mexican insurgents Tomás Ortiz and Diego Archuleta began to organize a rebellion that involved killing Governor Bent. Apparently unconcerned, Bent wrote to Buchanan on December 26, 1846, that "the men considered as leaders in [this conspiracy] can not be said to be men of much standing."

Against advice to stay in Santa Fe for his own protection, Bent returned home to Taos to visit friends and family on January 14, 1847. Five days later, a drunken mob of Pueblo Indians and New Mexicans led by Pablo Montoyo and Tomás Romero attacked Bent at his home. Wounded by arrows and scalped alive, he was finally killed and decapitated. His wife, children, and guests were spared. The frenzied killing spread to outlying regions—in addition to Bent, 17 other Anglo-Americans and New Mexicans were murdered before the insurrection was stopped by U.S. troops commanded by Colonel Sterling Price. Sixteen of the leaders, including Tomás Romero, were sentenced to death and hanged in the Taos plaza in April 1847.

See also Bent's Old Fort; Taos Rebellion.

For further reading: Grinnel, *Bent's Old Fort*, 1923; Keleher, *Turmoil in New Mexico 1846–1848*, 1952; Lavender, *Bent's Fort*, 1954; McNierney, *Taos 1847,* 1980; Twitchell, *The History of the Military Occupation of the Territory of New Mexico from 1846 to 1851 by the Government of the United States*, 1909.

Benton, Thomas Hart
(1782–1858)

An influential member of the U.S. Senate, Thomas Hart Benton was involved in the planning of Colonel John C. Frémont's California expedition. He was also a close political and military advisor to President James K. Polk during most of the Mexican-American War.

Born in Hillsboro, North Carolina, Thomas Hart Benton was raised near Nashville, Tennessee. He became the head of the household at the age of 8 when his father died and worked hard during his teenage years to support the family. When he was 27 years old he entered state politics and later fought in the War of 1812. After that war, he moved to St. Louis, Missouri, and opened a legal practice.

Known as a hot-headed Democrat, Benton killed a young district attorney in a duel in 1817. Four years later, he became a member of the U.S. Senate. His lifelong interest in expansion and land management favored methodical exploration followed by settlement, rather than simple speculation. Benton opposed slavery in the 1820s, but not for the usual moral reasons: he viewed it as interfering with the acquisition and settlement of new territory. As Senate floor leader, he fought the National Bank in the 1830s and supported free homesteads to settlers who had worked and improved their land for five years. Benton was quick to favor any new ideas, such as the telegraph and railroad, that would open up western lands.

Against his wishes, his daughter married explorer and U.S. hero John C. Frémont. Benton then became involved in planning the details of Frémont's expeditions. To stress the importance of Oregon and California, they both visited President James K. Polk before Frémont's third expedition in 1845. Benton remained an important political and military advisor to Polk during the Mexican-American War.

Benton believed that the annexation of Texas was an unnecessary affront to Mexico. He wanted to negotiate a Texas boundary that would satisfy Mexico and disapproved of Polk's eagerness for war. Despite his disapproval, when war became imminent, Benton sought a generalship. He and Secretary of War William Marcy proposed a bill that called for six new generals (one of whom would have been Benton), but it was defeated in the House of Representatives.

In November 1846, Benton visited Polk at the White House to discuss the possibility of an invasion centered on Veracruz and again offered his services as overall commander. Polk preferred Benton, but fearing political backlash if he granted such a high-level position to someone of little military experience, Polk instead offered Benton a position under Major General Winfield Scott, which Benton declined. Benton defended his son-in-law John C. Frémont during his 1847 court-martial in Washington, D.C., and resigned from his chairmanship of the Senate Military Affairs Committee in outrage over the verdict. His relentless attacks on the reputation of Brigadier General Stephen W. Kearny during and after the trial damaged Kearny's reputation. Benton's lingering resentment of Polk over military command and the court-martial of his son-in-law made him one of the few senators who voted against the Treaty of Guadalupe Hidalgo.

Thomas Hart Benton
(Library of Congress)

Benton continued to oppose secession and slavery in the 1850s. His biting criticism of the Missouri Compromise, and secessionists in general, almost resulted in his murder by an outraged senator. As the Civil War approached, his popularity in Missouri faded because of his unwavering opposition to slavery. Benton spent the last years of his life writing his memoirs and died from cancer in 1858.

See also Frémont, John C.; Kearny, Stephen Watts.

For further reading: Benton, *Thirty Years' View*, 1856; Chambers, *Old Bullion Benton, Senator from the New West*, 1956; Meigs, *The Life of Thomas Hart Benton*, 1904; Polk, *The Diary of James K. Polk*, 1910; Roosevelt, *Thomas Hart Benton*, 1886; Smith, *The Magnificent Missourian*, 1958.

Bent's Old Fort

This massive adobe structure in Colorado, built by brothers Charles and William Bent during 1833–1834, was an important link in the trade between Santa Fe, New Mexico, and St. Louis, Missouri. Explorer John C. Frémont visited the Bents there during some of his western travels, and Brigadier General Stephen Watts Kearny's Army of the West used it as a resupply base on its way to Santa Fe in July 1846.

Located in present-day southeastern Colorado on the north side of the Arkansas River near Las Animas, Bent's Old Fort was called an adobe "castle" by those who visited there. The fort was an important trading center and gathering place for Indians, trappers, merchants, and migrating settlers.

Approximately 150 New Mexican laborers from Taos built the fort. The rectangular structure faced east, its walls between 137 and 178 feet long, 14 feet high, and nearly 4 feet thick. The southeast and northwest corners were protected by 18-foot-tall round towers that were equipped with muskets and artillery pieces. A two-story square of rooms and offices, capped by a watchtower, was located in the inner court.

After leaving Fort Leavenworth, Kansas, Kearny's Army of the West reassembled, rested, and reoutfitted in a grassy meadow about 9 miles from the fort along the river in late July 1846 after a 650-mile march. The Bent brothers were besieged by officers with special point, Davis became so enraged that he challenged Bissell to a duel, but President Zachary Taylor dissuaded them.

In 1852, Bissell suffered a stroke that left his legs paralyzed, and he walked on crutches for the rest of his life. Four years later, he won the governorship of Illinois over the popular Abraham Lincoln. He died from pneumonia in the last year of office.

See also Buena Vista, Battle of.

For further reading: Carleton, *The Battle of Buena Vista,* 1848; Engelmann, "The Second Illinois in the Mexican War," 1934; Lavender, *Climax at Buena Vista,* 1966.

Black, John

As U.S. consul in Mexico City, John Black was a important link in communications between the Mexican and U.S. governments during 1845–1846. His efforts to bring U.S. minister John Slidell to Mexico to resolve the issues of Texas, California, and New Mexico fell apart when Slidell was summarily rejected by Mexican authorities after he arrived in Mexico City.

Little is known about Black, other than his Mexican-American War activities. As U.S. consul in Mexico City in 1845, he was deeply involved in facilitating peace discussions and meeting with other U.S. representatives, some of whom were Polk "secret agents" such as Moses Y. Beach. In September 1845, Black was given the task by Secretary of State James Buchanan of finding out if the Mexican government would receive an envoy "entrusted with full power to adjust all the questions in dispute between the two governments." Black met with Mexico's Minister of Foreign Affairs Manuel de la Peña y Peña on October 11, 1845, to discuss this possibility. After long discussions, Black reported to Washington that Mexico had agreed to receive a commissioner; Polk then sent John Slidell as U.S. minister to Mexico to negotiate U.S. claims against Mexico, the Texas border, and the purchase of California and New Mexico.

Upon Slidell's arrival in Mexico City on December 6, it became painfully clear that there had been a miscommunication between Black and Peña y Peña; Mexico was prepared to discuss only the matter of Texas, which it considered to be the foremost issue. Remarkably, it appears that Black and Peña y Peña never discussed what "all the questions in dispute" actually were. Mexico refused to discuss U.S. claims against Mexico or the purchase of New Mexico and California. In fact, the Mexican government refused to even meet with Slidell, who waited for months before returning home to Washington in May 1846. This snub irritated the U.S. government and heightened its warlike feeling toward Mexico.

Black remained in Mexico during the war and met with other U.S. agents from time to time. When Veracruz fell, he was expelled from the country. After the war ended, he returned to Mexico City, again as U.S. consul.

See also Peña y Peña, Manuel de la; Slidell, John.

For further reading: Caruso, *The Mexican Spy Company,* 1991; McAfee and Robinson, *Origins of the Mexican War,* 1982; Pletcher, *The Diplomacy of Annexation,* 1973; Sears, *John Slidell,* 1925.

Blake, Jacob E.
(1812–1846)

Lieutenant Jacob E. Blake was a topographic engineer in General Zachary Taylor's Army of Occupation along the Río Grande. He rode forward in an exposed position to reconnoiter the Mexican Army before the Battle of Palo Alto.

Blake was born in Pennsylvania. He attended the U.S. Military Academy from 1829 to 1833 and was commissioned as a second lieutenant in the 6th U.S. Infantry. He joined the Topographic Engineers in 1838, fought in the Second Seminole War, and helped survey the Texas-Mexico border in 1842.

As his army approached the already-deployed Army of the North under General Mariano Arista before the Battle of Palo Alto on May 8, 1846, General Taylor sent two men forward to examine the Mexican position. Engineers Blake and Lloyd Tilghman rode to within 100 yards of the Mexican line and dismounted. They peered through field glasses at the gleaming weapons and colorful uniforms and looked for artillery pieces hidden in the tall grass. Although within range of the Mexican muskets, no shots were fired. A U.S. officer remembered that General Arista, in holding his men's fire, had acted with the "courtesy becoming a knight of the Middle Ages."

After surviving the ensuing battle, Blake was killed by a gunshot from his own revolver on May 9. General William J. Worth remembered of Blake that, after stopping for water and "casting aside his weapons, one of his pistols accidentally discharged, and gave him a mortal wound." He was 34 years of age.

See also Palo Alto, Battle of.

For further reading: Bauer, *The Mexican War, 1846–1848*, 1974; Cullum, *Biographical Register of the Officers and Graduates of the United States Military Academy from 1802 to 1867*, 1879; Frost, *The Mexican War and Its Warriors*, 1848.

Blanco, Santiago

(1815–1883)

General Santiago Blanco was one of the Mexican Army's steadiest and most loyal commanders during the Mexican-American War. His leadership at the Battle of Buena Vista in 1847 was recognized by his promotion to the rank of general.

Blanco was born in Campeche in 1815 and later moved to Mexico City. He joined the army in 1827 after graduating from the Colegio Militar (Military College) at Chapultepec. His excellence in mathematics led to assignments in the artillery and engineers. Lieutenant Blanco helped suppress regional rebellions, led surveying expeditions, and built fortifications. In the early 1840s, he traveled to the United States to study railroad systems. In 1843, he had attained the rank of colonel.

Blanco was an active participant throughout the Mexican-American War. Unlike some high-ranking Mexican officers whose personal or political agendas often affected their military cooperation, Blanco worked well with other commanders. On February 22, 1847, his troops skirmished with U.S. defenders in the rugged hills near hacienda Buena Vista. During the Battle of La Angostura (Buena Vista) the following day, Blanco's men anchored General Antonio López de Santa Anna's left flank on the road at La Angostura (the narrows). His advance was checked by the deadly fire from U.S. artillery batteries posted in the road. His brave leadership, however, earned him a promotion to general of the Battalion of Engineers.

As part of the Mexican resistance at the Battle of Padierna (Contreras) on August 20, 1847, General Blanco expertly directed artillery fire at the U.S. troops that were coming through the *pedregal* (lava fields) toward the vulnerable position of General Gabriel Valencia's Army of the North. Constantly exposed, Blanco was seriously wounded during the battle.

After the war, he retained his role as commander of the Battalion of Engineers, was minister of war in 1853, and was later commandant of the Colegio Militar in 1854. An outspoken conservative and critic of liberal policies, he was jailed as a political prisoner for two years in Tacubaya and eventually released. Blanco died in Mexico City in 1883.

See also Buena Vista, Battle of; Contreras, Battle of.

For further reading: Carreño, *Jefes del ejército mexicano en 1847*, 1914; *Diccionario Porrúa*, 1995.

Bliss, William Wallace Smith

(1815–1853)

As adjutant to General Zachary Taylor during the Mexican-American War, Major William Wallace Smith Bliss handled all of Taylor's paperwork. His close relationship with Taylor allowed Bliss to offer important diplomatic and strategic advice during Taylor's campaign in northern Mexico.

The son of a West Point officer, Bliss was born in New York. He attended the U.S. Military Academy at the age of 14 and was appointed a lieutenant in the 4th U.S. Infantry in 1833. Bliss taught mathematics at the academy from 1834 to 1837 and saw action in the Second Seminole War. He gained the nickname "Perfect" because of his attention to the smallest details in any work he performed.

Well aware of Captain Bliss's military and diplomatic skills and Taylor's lack of attention to details, especially in correspondence, Major General Winfield Scott assigned Bliss to be Taylor's adjutant when the Mexican-American War began. One officer wrote that he could not imagine "one man's being more indebted to another than Taylor was to his assistant." Almost always by Taylor's side, Bliss wrote all his correspondence and official reports and occasionally tactfully reworded Taylor's gruff responses to Mexican authorities.

Bliss was brevetted to major after his performance at the Battles of Palo Alto and Resaca de la Palma in 1846 and to lieutenant colonel after the Battle of Buena Vista in 1847. Following the battle, he rode into the Mexican camp at Agua Nueva to propose an exchange of prisoners and care for the wounded.

After the war, Bliss continued his role from 1849 to 1850 as personal secretary to Taylor, now his father-in-law and U.S. president. Bliss was later appointed adjutant general of the army's Western Division from 1850 to 1853 and died of yellow fever in Mississippi at the age of 38.

For further reading: Bauer, *Zachary Taylor*, 1985; Cullum, *Biographical Register of the Officers and Graduates of the United States Military Academy from 1802 to 1867*, 1879; Dyer, *Zachary Taylor*, 1946; Frost, *The Mexican War and Its Warriors*, 1848; Hamilton, *Zachary Taylor, Soldier in the White House*, 1951.

Blockades

See Navy, United States.

Bocachicacampo, Skirmish at

(February 13, 1848)

A skirmish between Mexican soldiers and a small U.S. naval force in 1848 at Bocachicacampo in Baja California was one of the last actions of the Mexican-American War along the Pacific coast.

Bocachicacampo, a rocky peninsula along the Baja California coast, was the headquarters for a small, refugee Mexican force under the command of Antonio Campuzano. Facilities included a barracks and storage buildings. On February 12, 1848, approximately 60 men from the U.S. naval force at Guaymas sailed for Bocachicacampo. The group landed at midnight on February 13, encircled the sleeping Mexican camp, and attacked. The Mexican soldiers were captured or fled, and most of their equipment, arms, ammunition, and artillery was seized. The buildings were burned a week later.

For further reading: Bauer, *Surfboats and Horse Marines*, 1969.

Bonham, Milledge Luke

(1813–1890)

Appointed by President James K. Polk, Lieutenant Colonel Milledge Luke Bonham of the 12th U.S. Infantry was an aggressive and able commander whose leadership during the Battle of Contreras was highly acclaimed.

Born and raised in South Carolina, Bonham graduated from South Carolina College in 1834. He left his law practice to command South Carolina troops in the Second Seminole War and later the state militia. From 1840 to 1844, he was a member of the South Carolina legislature.

Assigned to the 12th U.S. Infantry as a lieutenant colonel by order of President Polk, Bonham served under Brigadier General Franklin Pierce during Scott's advance toward Mexico City in 1847. Before the Battle of Contreras, Bonham and a battalion of the 12th advanced to within 200 yards of the Mexican position. Bonham was later wounded at the Battle of Churubusco. Pierce praised his leadership at Contreras and throughout the rest of the campaign. Bonham later served as governor of one of the Mexican provinces.

Bonham resumed his political and law career upon his return to South Carolina. A brigadier general in the Confederate army during the Civil War, he fought at the First Battle of Bull Run, resigned, and was elected to the Confederate Congress. After that war, he became governor of South Carolina and, later, state railroad commissioner. He died in 1890 from a burst blood vessel.

For further reading: Bauer, *The Mexican War, 1846–1848*, 1974; Johnson and Malone, *Dictionary of American Biography*, 1928–1936.

Borginnis, Sarah

(1812–1866)

Unlike other laundresses who were in the U.S. Army, Sarah Borginnis accompanied her regiment on the march and at the front. She exposed herself to constant shelling during the siege of Fort Texas (later Fort Brown) in 1846, as she tended the wounded and assisted the soldiers.

Borginnis was born in Clay County, Missouri. She enlisted as an army laundress in 1840 and later married a soldier in the 7th U.S.

Infantry. Her six-foot-tall stature won her the nickname "Great Western," presumably after the large British steamer of the same name.

The 7th U.S. Infantry was part of General Zachary Taylor's Army of Occupation at Corpus Christi, Texas, during the winter of 1845–1846. When the other army laundresses left by ship from Corpus Christi to the Río Grande that spring, Borginnis insisted on marching with the regiment. She drove her donkey cart full of utensils and supplies with skills that the "best teamster in the train might have envied." Impatient at the delay in crossing Arroyo Colorado, where the army saw its first Mexican troops, she is said to have threatened to cross on her own and fight them herself.

She became the laundress, cook, and nurse for the 7th Infantry during the siege of Fort Texas in May 1846. Unlike the other laundresses who hid in the bomb shelters during the incessant shelling, she constantly exposed herself to fire as she served coffee, food, and soup, bandaged wounds, and loaded rifles.

Borginnis accompanied the Army of Occupation through the Battles of Palo Alto, Resaca de la Palma, and Monterrey and marched on to Saltillo. During the Battle of Buena Vista, she cared for the wounded and packed cartridges for muskets.

The events of her later life are less clear. She managed hotels (some claim brothels) in the Saltillo and Monterrey areas, married several other men, and later traveled with a regiment of dragoons to California. Finally settling in Fort Yuma, she ran a saloon there until she died from a tarantula bite in 1866. Remembered for her kindnesses to soldiers, she was buried with full military honors.

See also Fort Brown.

For further reading: Chamberlain, My Confession, 1956; Elliot, "The Great Western," 1989; Ferguson, The Port of Brownsville, a Maritime History of the Rio Grande Valley, 1976; Johannsen, To the Halls of the Montezumas, 1985; Sandwich, The Great Western, 1990.

Borland, Solon
(1808–1864)

A volunteer soldier from Arkansas, Major Solon Borland is most remembered for his embarrassing capture by General Antonio López de Santa Anna's cavalry at an abandoned hacienda a few days before the Battle of Buena Vista in 1847.

Borland was born in Virginia. He studied medicine in North Carolina and later moved to Little Rock, Arkansas. He volunteered to serve in the Mexican War and was part of the Arkansas cavalry.

As ordered by General John E. Wool on January 18, 1847, Major Borland, Major John P. Gaines, and a scouting party of about 90 men moved out from Victoria, looking for the lead elements of General Santa Anna's Army of the North. On the night of January 22, they camped in the ranch building of the abandoned hacienda La Encarnación. Typical of the volunteer contempt for military regulations, Borland posted no pickets. The scouting party awoke in the morning to find themselves surrounded by about 3,000 Mexican cavalrymen under General José Vicente Miñón, who was said to have apologized for rousing them so early. The presence of U.S. prisoners buoyed the spirits of the tired Mexican army as it passed them on their march northward.

Despite his carelessness, Borland's reputation remained intact and he was elected to the U.S. Senate in 1848. In 1853, he became minister to Nicaragua and other Central American states. In 1854, he declined the governorship of New Mexico to resume his medical practice in Little Rock. Borland joined the Confederacy during the Civil War and was promoted to brigadier general, but resigned for health reasons and died in Texas in 1864.

See also La Encarnación.

For further reading: Chamberlain, My Confession, 1956; Johnson and Malone, Dictionary of American Biography, 1928–1936; Scott, Encarnación Prisoners, Comprising an Account of the March of the Kentucky Cavalry from Louisville to the Rio Grande, 1848.

Bowles, William Augustus
(1799–1873)

Colonel William Augustus Bowles was a volunteer officer from Indiana with no formal military training. His confusion and poor leadership led to the premature retreat of the U.S. left flank during the Battle of Buena Vista in

1847. The retreat nearly resulted in a Mexican victory.

Born in Maryland, Bowles moved to Washington County, Indiana, in 1812. He had several jobs, including doctor, hotel owner, and newspaper editor. In 1832, Bowles helped found the town of French Lick, which became his permanent home.

When the Mexican-American War began, Bowles became the colonel of the volunteer 2nd Indiana Infantry. As ordered by General John E. Wool, he positioned his men on the left flank of General Zachary Taylor's Army of Occupation at the beginning of the Battle of Buena Vista on February 23, 1847. The 2nd Indiana faced a fierce attack from General Manuel Lombardini's and General Francisco Pacheco's divisions. Bowles misunderstood his orders and commanded his men to retreat, which quickly led to the collapse of the entire left flank. Even after the Mississippi Rifles arrived as reinforcements, the Indiana men continued to fall back. Bowles stayed with the Mississippians, picked up a rifle, and fought as an infantryman. His poor performance during the battle led to charges of incompetence; Generals Taylor and Wool were quick to blame Bowles for the collapse of the left flank, and Bowles was quick to accuse his men of being cowards.

His postwar life was also checkered by poor decisions and business dealings. He was caught bringing slaves into Indiana in the 1850s. In 1864, he was sentenced to death for treason by the U.S. government for attempting to destroy federal property. The death sentence was later reduced to imprisonment in the Ohio Penitentiary. Bowles died in 1873, still trying to rebuild his reputation.

See also Buena Vista, Battle of.

For further reading: Chamberlain, *My Confession*, 1956; Indiana State Library, *Indiana Biography Series*, Volume 65; Perry, *Indiana in the Mexican War*, 1908; Shepherd, *A Biographical Directory of the Indiana General Assembly*, 1980; Thompson, *Indiana Authors and Their Books*, 1981.

Boyd, Linn
(1800–1859)

Linn Boyd was an influential Democrat in the U.S. Congress during the Mexican-American War. He strongly supported the war, chaired the committee on military affairs, and helped organize the new postwar U.S. territories.

Born in Nashville, Tennessee, Boyd grew up in Kentucky. His father, a Revolutionary War veteran, could not afford early schooling for his son, and Boyd labored in the fields when he was a boy. His resolve, intellect, and oral skills enabled him to secure an education as a lawyer. Boyd developed his political career as a Democrat, first in the state legislature and later in the U.S. Congress from 1839 to 1855. He was also good friends with Andrew Jackson.

An ardent expansionist, Boyd helped guide the discussions that led to the joint resolution to offer annexation to Texas in 1845. During the Mexican-American War, he was chairman of the committee on military affairs and had frequent discussions with President James K. Polk. Eager to overpower Mexico, Boyd proposed an amendment to Polk's War Bill that called for 50,000 troops and an appropriation of $10 million to bring the "existing" war to a "speedy and successful term."

After the war, Boyd was chairman of the committee that organized the lands ceded by Mexico into new territories. One of the most powerful and influential men in U.S. politics in the 1850s, Boyd became speaker of the house in his last term (1851–1855). He died suddenly in 1859 before he could take office as the newly elected lieutenant governor of Kentucky.

For further reading: Johnson and Malone, *Dictionary of American Biography*, 1928–1936; Nevin, *The Mexican War*, 1978.

Bragg, Braxton
(1817–1876)

Known as one of the ablest and most aggressive artillery commanders in the Mexican-American War, Braxton Bragg's batteries played decisive roles in the Battles of Monterrey and Buena Vista.

Bragg was born in North Carolina. He graduated from the U.S. Military Academy in 1837 as a second lieutenant in the 3rd Artillery and performed capably during the Second Seminole War.

In 1845, Bragg was assigned to General

Zachary Taylor's Army of Occupation at Corpus Christi, Texas. After performing bravely at Fort Texas (later Fort Brown) and Monterrey, Bragg was promoted to captain in the 3rd Artillery. His expert placement of his extremely mobile guns during the Battle of Buena Vista on February 23, 1847, helped fill gaps in the U.S. lines and break the attacks of waves of Mexican infantrymen. This leadership under heavy enemy fire resulted in his brevet to lieutenant colonel.

Despite his accomplishments, he was regarded as arrogant by his men and fellow officers and was generally disliked. In fact, some of his men twice tried to kill him, in August and October of 1847. Throughout the war he suffered from headaches and chronic dysentery, holdovers from illnesses contracted during the Florida Wars.

Bragg returned to Louisiana after the war and was employed as an engineer and commissioner of public works. Given the rank of brigadier general in the Confederate Army in 1861, he was highly praised for his leadership during the Battle of Shiloh in Tennessee. But as the war progressed, he developed a reputation of inconsistency, caution, and not being able to handle larger commands. Although he was a great organizer, Bragg's quarrelsome temperament and communication breakdowns with other generals led to several costly defeats, such as the Battle of Chattanooga in November 1863.

Bragg conducted engineering projects in Texas and Alabama after the Civil War. He died from heart disease in Texas in 1876.

See also Buena Vista, Battle of; Monterrey, Battle of.

For further reading: Johnson and Malone, *Dictionary of American Biography,* 1928–1936; Seitz, *Braxton Bragg,* 1924; Welsh, *Medical Histories of Confederate Generals,* 1995.

Bravo Rueda, Nicolás

(1787–1854)

One of the most influential military and political figures in Mexico from 1821 through the Mexican-American War, Nicolás Bravo Rueda commanded the Army of the East that resisted the advance of General Winfield Scott toward Mexico City in 1847.

Nicolás Bravo Rueda was born in 1787 in

Nicolás Bravo
(Library of Congress)

Chilpancingo, in what is now Guerrero. He fought against the Spanish until independence was won in 1821. Revered for his principles and humanity, he released 300 prisoners that he was ordered to execute during a rebellion against the Spanish in 1814, despite the fact that they had murdered his father.

For his valorous leadership during the War of Independence in 1821, Bravo Rueda was given the title of national hero the following year. A staunch conservative, he helped overthrow the Iturbide regime in 1823 and became the vice-president under Guadalupe Victoria. Bravo Rueda and other conspirators were defeated in an attempt to overthrow Victoria in 1827 and were imprisoned.

Disturbed by the keen interest of the United States in Texas, New Mexico, and California, Bravo Rueda warned that the United States was "at present occupied about the dismemberment" of Mexico. Bravo was vice-president from 1824 to 1828, led troops during General Antonio López de Santa Anna's invasion of Texas in 1836, and commanded all the troops in the Federal District in 1843 under President Pedro María Anaya. After Mariano Paredes y Arrillaga seized power in December 1845, Bravo Rueda became vice-president of Mexico for a second time. Following the toppling of the Paredes y Arrillaga administration, Bravo Rueda was acting president in July and August 1846.

Despite their antagonistic relationship, General Santa Anna gave Bravo Rueda command of the hastily constructed Army of the East in 1847 to stop General Scott's advance on Mexico City. The Army of the East was barely trained and desperately undersupplied. While headquartered in Puebla, Bravo Rueda tried to organize a guerrilla force to harass Scott. The guerrillas were too ill behaved to be effective and were more interested in plundering churches and the homes of civilians. In September, Bravo Rueda commanded the small Mexican force—barely 1,000 men, including the San Patricio Battalion and the college's young cadets—that held the military college at Chapultepec. Ramon Alcaraz recalled that Bravo Rueda, "thickset and erect, with deep eyes and a powerful chin—though he was cold and unenterprising, had flawless courage, and he stood with folded arms or marched calmly from post to post" during the furious U.S. attack in September 1847. Bravo Rueda surrendered his diamond-studded sword, which was gracefully returned to him by his U.S. captors. In typical fashion, Santa Anna was quick to court-martial him for the defeat, but Bravo Rueda was fully exonerated.

After the war, Bravo Rueda held a variety other military and political positions, including that of governor of the state of Puebla in 1848. Bravo died mysteriously in April 1854, the day after Santa Anna, his old nemesis, had visited his home city of Chilpancingo.

For further reading: Bravo, "Don Nicolás Bravo y la defensa de Chapultepec," 1947; *Diccionario Porrúa*, 1995; Parrish, "The Life of Nicolas Bravo, Mexican Patriot (1786–1854)," 1951; Ramirez, *Mexico during the War with the United States*, 1950.

Brazito, Battle of

See El Brazito, Battle of.

Brevet Rank

A form of temporary promotion adopted from the British army system, a brevet rank was higher than an officer's regular grade. It was introduced into the U.S. Army in 1812 as a reward for "gallant conduct" or "meritorious service."

Junior officers coveted brevets because it increased their reputation and sometimes allowed them to outrank their regular-grade superiors. In fact, this often created friction in the officer corps and shouting matches on the battlefield. Because of a smoldering conflict between two of General Zachary Taylor's commanders, Colonel David E. Twiggs and Brevet Brigadier General William J. Worth, President James K. Polk intervened to rule that brevet rank was inferior to regular rank.

Knowing how slow the regular process of promotion could be, generals used brevets as a way of recognizing promising officers and giving them more responsibility. Brevets could also be deadly: officers competed for brevets, which often led to daring and sometimes reckless exposure on the battlefield. Brevet rank did not bring higher pay or benefits, and, after the war, brevet officers returned to their regular rank.

For further reading: Boatner, *The Civil War Dictionary*, 1959; Skelton, *An American Profession of Arms*, 1992; Winders, *Mr. Polk's Army*, 1997.

Brooks, Horace B.
(ca. 1815–1894)

A talented officer with the 2nd U.S. Artillery, Horace B. Brooks was highly regarded by his superiors for the artillery work he performed during the battles General Winfield Scott fought on his way to Mexico City in 1847.

Brooks, who was born in Massachusetts, graduated ninth of 56 cadets from the U.S. Military Academy in 1835. He was commissioned a second lieutenant in the 2nd U.S. Artillery. Various assignments included the Second Florida War (one brevet), teaching math at the academy, and patrolling the New York border with Canada.

As captain of the 2nd Artillery, Brooks saw action in Scott's 1847 campaign from Veracruz to the capture of Mexico City. Brooks was brevetted to major for his conduct during the Battles of Contreras and Churubusco and to lieutenant colonel after the Battle of El Molino del Rey. The guns of the 2nd Artillery played an important part in defeating Mexican fortifications along the causeway toward the San Cosmé garita outside Mexico City on September 13, 1847.

Various duties after the war included fighting Indians in Utah and commanding garrisons along the East Coast. His role for the Union during the Civil War was mostly administrative. Brooks retired from active service in 1872.

For further reading: Cullum, *Biographical Register of the Officers and Graduates of the United States Military Academy from 1802 to 1867*, 1879; Dillon, *American Artillery in the Mexican War 1846–1847*, 1975.

Brooks, William Thomas Harbaugh
(1821–1879)

An officer in the 3rd U.S. Infantry, William Thomas Harbaugh Brooks performed daring reconnaissance work near Mexican positions before the Battles of Cerro Gordo and Contreras in 1847. His findings allowed General Winfield Scott to outflank the Mexican army.

Born in Ohio, Brooks left for the U.S. Military Academy in 1837. Although he was known as a thorough and dedicated student, he graduated near the bottom of his class in 1841. Assigned to the 3rd U.S. Infantry, he was stationed at isolated posts on the western frontier.

The 3rd U.S. Infantry was part of General Zachary Taylor's Army of Occupation that wintered at Corpus Christi, Texas, in 1845. Brooks fought at the Battles of Palo Alto, Resaca de la Palma, and Monterrey, where he was brevetted to captain for "gallant and meritorious service."

Reassigned in 1847, Brooks and his men landed as part of General Winfield Scott's Army of Occupation at Veracruz in March. Marching inland along the National Road, Brooks fought from Cerro Gordo to Mexico City. His work as a scout at Cerro Gordo helped find a mule path that allowed the U.S. forces to turn the left flank of General Antonio López de Santa Anna's Army of the East. At the Battle of Contreras, Brooks and Robert E. Lee undertook a hazardous night reconnaissance of the ground in front of the Mexican position the night before the battle. They selected a primary assault path that proved to be effective the following morning. For his expert reconnaissance work, Brooks was rewarded with a brevet to major.

Considered to be one of the most resourceful, energetic, and quick-witted officers in the army, Brooks served as the adjutant to General David E. Twiggs from 1848 to 1851. Fighting Indians in harsh frontier conditions began to weaken his health in the 1850s.

A Union general in the Civil War, Brooks led his troops with distinction in most of the major eastern campaigns and was wounded at Savage Station and Antietam. His failing health finally forced him to retire in 1864. Brooks had developed a painful, recurrent urinary tract problem during the Mexican-American War that ultimately contributed to his death.

See also Cerro Gordo, Battle of; Contreras, Battle of.

For further reading: Cullum, *Biographical Register of the Officers and Graduates of the United States Military Academy from 1802 to 1867*, 1879; Johnson and Malone, *Dictionary of American Biography*, 1928–1936; Semmes, *Service Afloat and Ashore during the Mexican War*, 1851; Welsh, *Medical Histories of Union Generals*, 1997.

Brown, Jacob
(ca. 1788–1846)

Major Jacob Brown of the 7th U.S. Infantry became one of the first U.S. casualties of the war when he was mortally wounded by an artillery shell on May 6, 1846.

Brown was born in Massachusetts. At the outbreak of the Mexican-American War, he, at 58, was one of the more senior officers in the U.S. Army. A natural officer, Brown had enlisted during the War of 1812 as a private and rose quickly to the rank of lieutenant. As commander of the 7th U.S. Infantry, Brown and his men were left to defend Fort Texas on the north bank of the Río Grande after General Zachary Taylor took the rest of the Army of Occupation to his staging area at Point Isabel. Fort Texas lay directly across the river from the Mexican town of Matamoros and its fortifications.

General Mariano Arista, commander of Mexico's Army of the North, decided to lay siege to Fort Texas to force the return of General Taylor. Arista sent Colonel Francisco Mejía and a small force to Matamoros to begin shelling the fort on May 2, 1846. After four days of incessant artillery fire, only one U.S. soldier had been killed. On May 6, during an inspection of his artillery positions, Major Brown had most of his right leg torn off by an exploding shell. Tended faithfully by nurse and laundress Sarah Borginnis, Brown lingered in agony for nearly four days before he died. On May 17, Taylor renamed the garrison Fort Brown in his honor. The city of Brownsville, Texas, later grew around the fort.

See also Borginnis, Sarah; Fort Brown.

For further reading: Frost, *The Mexican War and Its Warriors,* 1848; Smith, *The War with Mexico,* 1919.

Buchanan, James
(1791–1868)

As U.S. secretary of state, James Buchanan, later president, was an important advisor to President James K. Polk during the Mexican-American War. Perhaps Buchanan's most important accomplishment was negotiating a peaceful settlement regarding Britain's claim to Oregon Territory. Mexico had hoped that a protracted struggle over Oregon would keep the United States from invading Mexican territory.

James Buchanan, ca. 1847
(Library of Congress)

Resolving the Oregon issue allowed the United States to focus its war efforts on Mexico.

Born near Mercersburg, Pennsylvania, James Buchanan received much of his education from Dickinson College. Graduating in 1809, he chose a law career. He quickly became known as an excellent speaker and one of the best lawyers in the state. Buchanan's personal life was completely shattered when Ann Coleman, his young bride-to-be, died suddenly. (He never married.)

Having always enjoyed debate, Buchanan was drawn to politics and became a member of the state government in 1814. A popular state leader, he was elected to the House of Representatives from 1821 to 1831 and the Senate from 1834 to 1835. Always a believer in compromise, Buchanan opposed the spread of slavery, but believed it should be tolerated where it already existed.

Although he had hoped to be the Democratic candidate for president, Buchanan fully supported the nomination of James K. Polk, who then appointed Buchanan secretary of state. Buchanan's communication and diplomatic skills helped present Polk's decisions to the U.S. public. Buchanan's tireless and creative efforts at negotiating a settlement with Great Britain over Oregon helped Polk's cause regarding Mexico: by not going to war over Oregon, Congress was more willing to approve money and manpower for a war against Mexico.

Always a courteous diplomat, Buchanan frequently addressed Mexico in a considerate manner regarding the annexation of Texas. He instructed U.S. minister John Slidell to focus on acquiring New Mexico and California in return for unpaid debts, and not to discuss the issue of the Texas boundary, when he visited Mexico City in 1845. Some historians speculate that this may have been a delaying tactic to derail the José Joaquín de Herrera administration, which was seeking a peaceful settlement with the United States. (Herrera was overthrown the last day of the year by Mariano Paredes y Arrillaga, a more likely candidate with whom to incite war.) In fact, Slidell was summarily rejected by Herrera, and negotiations stalled.

Buchanan closely advised Polk on a number of issues, such as Polk's restatement of the

Monroe Doctrine to discourage British interest in occupying California. He alienated Polk when he maintained that early versions of the Treaty of Guadalupe Hidalgo did not offer enough compensation to Mexico. Buchanan was keenly interested in Central America and Cuba and offered Spain $120 million for Cuba in 1848.

After a brief retirement, Buchanan became a foreign minister for President Franklin Pierce and continued in his efforts to purchase Cuba. Buchanan defeated candidate John C. Frémont to become the fifteenth president of the United States from 1856 to 1861. Buchanan supported the Dred Scott decision and in Kansas the pro-slavery Lecompton Constitution, which increased sectional friction. Buchanan retired to his estate in Pennsylvania, where he died at the age of 77.

For further reading: Johnson and Malone, *Dictionary of American Biography*, 1928–1936; Klein, *President James Buchanan*, 1962; Pletcher, *The Diplomacy of Annexation*, 1973.

Buchanan, Robert Christie

(1811–1878)

Captain Robert Christie Buchanan of the 4th U.S. Infantry discovered a path through the chaparral that flanked the Mexican left during the Battle of Resaca de la Palma. He led a portion of the 4th U.S. Infantry down the trail and seized a Mexican battery, a move that began the panicked Mexican retreat that ended the battle.

Buchanan, who was born in Maryland, graduated from the U.S. Military Academy in 1830. He participated in the Black Hawk War and the Second Florida War and later served on the western frontier.

In 1845, Buchanan and the 4th U.S. Infantry were part of General Zachary Taylor's Army of Occupation at Corpus Christi, Texas. In the spring of 1846, the Army of Occupation marched to the Río Grande and defeated General Mariano Arista's Army of the North at the Battle of Palo Alto on May 8, 1846. The following day, Taylor's forces engaged the Mexican army at the Battle of Resaca de la Palma. Captain Buchanan discovered a path through the chaparral that circled the Mexican left flank. Taking some companies from the 4th with him, Buchanan raced down the path and seized a Mexican battery in severe hand-to-hand fighting. The Mexicans counterattacked, but could not drive the U.S. troops from the gun emplacement. This action inspired the rest of the U.S. attack along the *resaca* (swampy ravines) and panicked the Mexican defenders, who soon began a retreat to the Río Grande and Matamoros. After the battle, Buchanan received a brevet to lieutenant colonel for turning the Mexican left flank.

Buchanan was stationed at various garrisons on the western frontier after the war. In 1862, he was appointed brigadier general of Union volunteers during the Civil War. After performing well in the Antietam and Fredericksburg campaigns, he developed severe rheumatism. His failing health forced him to retire in 1870, and he died in Washington, D.C., from apoplexy.

See also Resaca de la Palma, Battle of.

For further reading: Cullum, *Biographical Register of the Officers and Graduates of the United States Military Academy from 1802 to 1867*, 1879; Welsh, *Medical Histories of Union Generals*, 1997.

Buena Vista, Battle of

(February 23, 1847)

Known to the Mexicans as La Angostura (the narrows), the Battle of Buena Vista (good view) was fought on February 23, 1847, between General Antonio López de Santa Anna's Army of the North and General Zachary Taylor's Army of Occupation. It resulted in a heartbreaking loss for the Mexican army, which had been on the verge of victory all day. The U.S. troops were relieved to win; a Mexican victory could have changed the outcome of the war.

After the hard-fought victory at Monterrey in September 1846, General Taylor rested his Army of Occupation near that city. The armistice signed between Taylor and General Pedro de Ampudia forbade any deep U.S. penetration to the south for eight weeks. General Santa Anna began to reconstruct the Army of the North with new conscripts at San Luis Potosí. Meanwhile, General John E. Wool's detached force occupied the city of Monclova on its way to Chihuahua.

View of the battleground at Buena Vista taken from a sketch made at the time, February 23, 1847 (Library of Congress)

On November 5, by order of an exasperated President James K. Polk, Taylor notified Santa Anna that the armistice was terminated. Wool abandoned his march to Chihuahua and joined Taylor near Saltillo. On the move after nearly two months, Taylor's army occupied Victoria on January 4, 1847.

Impatient as always, President Polk had decided to open a second front under the command of General Winfield Scott at the port city of Veracruz. Arriving in January, Scott took most of Taylor's regular regiments to be the core of his invasion force. Taylor's role was to be reduced to guarding Monterrey and northern Mexico. Reluctant to obey, Taylor advanced his remaining force to Agua Nueva, about 17 miles south of Saltillo.

Santa Anna's far-ranging cavalry kept him informed about Taylor's activities and even captured a messenger from Scott who detailed Scott's plans to remove men from Taylor's army and attack Veracruz. Delighted with this information, Santa Anna hurried at the end of January to start his poorly fed and ill-supplied Army of the North toward Saltillo to overwhelm the understrength Taylor. The Army of the North was followed by thousands of women and other family members who carried firewood and clothing for the soldiers. (Although each soldier could bring only one shirt and scant cooking equipment, Santa Anna rode in a coach pulled by eight mules.) After losing nearly 5,000 men on the march, by February 21 Santa Anna's forces had gathered at La Encarnación, about 35 miles south of the U.S. encampment at Agua Nueva.

A bold reconnaissance by Captain Ben McCulloch of the Texas Rangers revealed the location and strength of the Mexican force. Dressed as a Mexican, McCulloch penetrated the Mexican camp at night, climbed a small hill, counted campfires, and reported back to Taylor on February 21. After consulting with General Wool, Taylor pulled back from Agua Nueva on the 21st to a better defensive position that Wool had chosen about 3 miles south of hacienda Buena Vista. (This proved to be the only U.S. retreat during the war.)

Santa Anna pushed on relentlessly the night of the 21st, arriving at Taylor's hastily evacuated campsite at Agua Nueva on the morning of February 22. Thinking that the U.S.

troops were fleeing, Santa Anna refused to let his exhausted men stop for water and continued the march.

Wool had chosen a good place to defend: La Angostura, a narrow, 40-foot-wide opening in the rugged hills through which the road to Agua Nueva passed. Because Taylor decided to return to Saltillo that evening, Wool placed the 4,759 troops in position on the 22nd. His right was anchored in the road with Captain J. M. Washington's battery from the 4th Artillery. The artillery was protected on both sides by Colonel John J. Hardin's 1st Illinois Infantry. Wool positioned the rest of his troops to form a line that extended from Washington's battery southeastward along a plateau that was bordered by ravines and gullies. His extreme left was anchored by the 2nd Indiana Infantry, the 1st Kentucky and 1st Arkansas cavalry regiments, and three artillery pieces under Captain John Paul Jones O'Brien. Six companies and three pieces of artillery were held in reserve at Buena Vista to protect the rear and supply wagons. Only 700 of Taylor's 4,759 troops had seen combat: the Mississippi Rifles, 2nd Dragoons, and artillery.

About 11 A.M. on the morning on February 22, Santa Anna demanded surrender: "You…cannot in any human probability avoid suffering a rout and being cut to pieces with your troops; but as you deserve consideration and particular esteem, I wish to save you from a catastrophe…." Taylor flatly rejected the offer. Santa Anna deployed his men slowly: two divisions of infantry under Major Generals Manuel María Lombardini and Francisco Pacheco held the center; the left flank, facing Washington's guns, was manned by Colonel Santiago Blanco's Battalion of Engineers; and the right flank was anchored by Major General Pedro de Ampudia's infantry and Brigadier General Julián Juvera's cavalry brigade. Major General José María Ortega's division was held in reserve. Using the rough terrain as a screen, Ampudia's men crept close enough to skirmish with the U.S. left. The night was cold, windy, and rainy, and fires were forbidden.

At dawn on the 23rd, the U.S. troops discovered that the Mexicans had positioned a battery on a higher slope that could enfilade their line. Mexican bands played, priests blessed soldiers, and the smoke of incense filled the air. Santa Anna rode along the lines on horseback, and the assault soon began. Colonel Blanco's division was turned back by Washington's deadly battery in the road. The divisions of Lombardini and Pacheco moved toward the U.S. left. Lombardini was wounded, and command devolved to General Francisco Pérez. The raw recruits of Pacheco's division fled to the rear in terror.

Despite the collapse of Pacheco's division, the Mexican pressure was too great and the U.S. left flank began to waver. Colonel William A. Bowles of the 2nd Indiana became confused and ordered his men to retreat, which made the entire left flank, including O'Brien's artillery, fall back toward the center. Mexican forces began to curl around the bent U.S. line. Mexican lancers rode through the scattered volunteers, "using their lances freely on every side." Colonel Archibald Yell of the 1st Arkansas Cavalry was killed. General Juvera led a cavalry charge that swept around the U.S. left toward the supply trains in the rear at hacienda Buena Vista. The reserves, firing from the protective buildings of the hacienda, repelled the attack. Free U.S. batteries roamed the field, filling gaps in the line and blasting the Mexican advance with double canister. The reserve Mississippi Rifles and 3rd Indiana Infantry formed a V to accept the charging cavalry, which was caught in a murderous crossfire. The cavalry retreated, and Mississippians came forward to ruthlessly kill the wounded with bowie knives.

A final, furious charge by a makeshift division under General Pérez was directed at the U.S. left flank. The charge was met by a handful of infantry soldiers and some artillery. The fighting became desperate and hand to hand. Lieutenant Braxton Bragg and Captain Thomas W. Sherman frantically moved their artillery to strike Pérez's unit from the rear. Having stopped the cavalry charge, the Mississippi Rifles and 3rd Indiana Infantry came running to help. "Without our artillery," noted General Wool, "we could not have maintained our position a single hour." Pérez finally retreated.

The battle ended at nightfall. Luckily for the U.S. army, the Mexican attack had been a series of separate, poorly coordinated advances. The U.S. soldiers expected another attack at dawn and lay on their arms. Fires were forbidden. The following morning, February 24, the U.S. troops were surprised to see that the Mexicans, who had kept their campfires burning at night as a diversion, had fallen back to Agua Nueva. Taylor and Wool were so relieved that they hugged each other. Patrols combed the hills and ravines for the wounded from both sides. On February 25, Major William Bliss, Taylor's adjutant, rode forward into the Mexican camp to arrange for an exchange of prisoners and wounded.

Santa Anna remained at Agua Nueva until February 26 and then began an agonizing, 35-mile night march to La Encarnación. When the Army of the North entered San Luis Potosí, nearly 10,500 men had died, been captured, or had deserted. Santa Anna reported a loss of 591 killed, 1,048 wounded, and 1,894 missing in the battle. Taylor lost about 280 killed, 450 wounded, and 23 missing (about 6 percent of his fighting force). Taylor had fought his last battle against Mexico. His men withdrew to Monterrey and remained there as an occupational force for the rest of the war.

The Battle of Buena Vista was a tremendous turning point in the Mexican-American War. Santa Anna with a numerically superior force had failed to defeat Taylor. Santa Anna's uncoordinated attacks allowed Taylor to rearrange his outnumbered forces, especially his Flying Artillery, to meet each threat as it arose. The last battle in northern Mexico, Buena Vista was a demoralizing and costly loss for Mexico and wrecked the Army of the North.

See also Agua Nueva; Army, Mexico; La Encarnación; Monterrey, Armistice of.

For further reading: Alcaraz, *The Other Side*, 1850; Balbontín, "The Battle of Angostura (Buena Vista)," 1894; Brooks, *A Complete History of the Mexican War, 1846–1848*, 1849; Carleton, *The Battle of Buena Vista*, 1848; Lavender, *Climax at Buena Vista*, 1966.

Burnett, Ward B.

(1810–1884)

Colonel Ward B. Burnett led the 2nd New York Volunteer Regiment during the Mexican-American War. He was severely wounded leading his regiment during the Battle of Chapultepec in 1847.

Burnett, who was born in Pennsylvania, attended the U.S. Military Academy from 1828 to 1832. He was commissioned a second lieutenant in the 2nd U.S. Artillery. Various duties included service in the Black Hawk War, teaching infantry tactics at the academy, and being assigned to the Corps of Engineers. He resigned in 1836 to pursue a career as a civil engineer.

Burnett volunteered for service during the Mexican-American War and became colonel of the 2nd New York Volunteer Infantry. He performed capably during the Battles of Vera Cruz, Cerro Gordo, Contreras, and Churubusco in 1847. In September during the Battle of Chapultepec, Burnett was seriously wounded as he led his men through heavy fire and across a minefield to scale the walls of the fortress.

After the war, Burnett supervised military installations in Pennsylvania before resigning to resume his engineering career in New York City. He was later the U.S. surveyor general of Kansas and Nebraska Territory. Burnett died in Washington, D.C., at the age of 74.

See also Chapultepec, Battle of.

For further reading: Cullum, *Biographical Register of the Officers and Graduates of the United States Military Academy from 1802 to 1867*, 1879; Smith, *The War with Mexico*, 1919.

Bustamante, Anastasio

(1780–1853)

Former two-time president, Anastasio Bustamante was an influential member of the Mexican Congress during the Mexican-American War and later joined the Mexican army.

Bustamante was born to affluent Spanish parents in Jiquilpan, Michoacán. He was well educated, and his education included medical studies in Mexico City. A lieutenant in the Spanish army in 1810, he helped suppress numerous rebel uprisings. In 1821, he defected to Lieutenant Colonel Agustín de Iturbide's rebel forces, and his resultant friendship with the new emperor led to a series of prominent military appointments.

Veering into politics, Bustamante was elected vice-president to Vicente Guerrero in 1829. Their political ideals quickly clashed, and

Bustamante managed to overthrow Guerrero late in the year and ruled as president until 1833. Discontent over his conservative government brewed, and the liberals gained the presidency when Antonio López de Santa Anna drove Bustamante into exile.

Mexico was again leaderless and adrift after Santa Anna was deposed in 1836. Bustamante returned and was elected president. Overwhelmed by the economic, political, and social problems in the country, Bustamante was perceived as being indecisive and ineffectual. He was overthrown again in 1841 and left shortly thereafter for Europe.

Bustamante returned in 1844 and became a member of the Mexican Congress. He rejoined the military, but contributed little to the Mexican-American War. Considered by most to be too old for field command, his assignments were largely peripheral in nature. His planned mission to invade California in 1847 fell through because other troops refused to cooperate in the plan. The frustrated military commander did, however, suppress General Mariano Paredes y Arrillaga's rebellion against the government in 1848. Bustamante died on his private estate in 1853.

For further reading: Alamán, *Historia de Méjico desde los primeros movimientos que prepararon su independencia en el año de 1808 hasta la época presente,* 1850; Bancroft, *The History of Mexico,* 1966; Costeloe, *The Central Republic in Mexico, 1835–1846,* 1993; *Diccionario Porrúa,* 1995; Green, *The Mexican Republic,* 1987.

Butler, Pierce M.

(1798–1847)

A volunteer officer with previous military experience, Colonel Pierce M. Butler commanded the volunteer South Carolina Regiment during General Winfield Scott's march from Veracruz to Mexico City in 1847. Butler was killed in action during the Battle of Churubusco.

A son of a Revolutionary War soldier, Butler was born and raised in South Carolina. He joined the U.S. Army in 1818 as a lieutenant. Butler resigned in 1829 with the rank of captain to become involved in politics and banking. After reenlisting to fight the Seminole Nation in Florida, he was elected governor of South Carolina in 1836. His administration reflected his interests in social programs, such as developing a public education system. Butler was also known as a fair and sympathetic agent to the Cherokee Nation in South Carolina.

During the Mexican-American War, Butler was colonel of the Palmetto Regiment, a volunteer infantry unit from South Carolina that landed at Veracruz in 1847 to join General Winfield Scott's Army of Occupation. The Palmettos were attached to General James Shields's brigade. Bedridden before the Battle of Churubusco on August 20, Butler was adamant about leading his regiment. Quickly wounded, he continued to lead his men until he was killed by a bullet through his head. General James Shields remembered the assault as being "one of the most terrific fires to which soldiers were ever subjected." Shields lost nearly a third of his brigade in the bloody assault.

See also Churubusco, Battle of.

For further reading: Frost, *The Mexican War and Its Warriors,* 1848; Johnson and Malone, *Dictionary of American Biography,* 1928–1936.

Butler, William Orlando

(1791–1880)

A volunteer general from Kentucky, William Orlando Butler was one of General Zachary Taylor's better volunteer commanders during the Mexican-American War. Butler commanded the Army of Occupation in Mexico City after Major General Winfield Scott was relieved of command.

Butler, who was born in Kentucky, received a good education and chose a career in law. He served in the War of 1812 and won the respect of Andrew Jackson at the Battle of New Orleans by leading a daring night charge. Recognizing Butler's military ability, Jackson was disappointed that he resigned from the army after the war. A natural politician as well, Butler served two terms in the U.S. House of Representatives as a Democrat.

Eager to serve in the Mexican-American War, Butler was appointed major general of volunteers by President James K. Polk and was given command of the all-volunteer 3rd Division in General Taylor's Army of Occupation. Butler suffered a bullet wound in the leg while

William O. Butler
(Library of Congress)

"leading the Ohio regiment to storm two of the most formidable batteries in the town" during the Battle of Monterrey on September 21, 1846. His wound failed to heal properly, and Butler was sent home in early 1847 to recuperate. After General Scott had captured Mexico City in September 1847, General Butler, finally recovered, arrived with more volunteer troops. On January 8, 1847, Polk chose Butler to succeed Scott, who was being investigated by a court of inquiry. Butler took command on April 22, 1848, and oversaw the occupation force until it left Mexico City in June 1848.

Butler returned to Kentucky to try farming. In 1848, he was nominated as vice-president for presidential candidate Lewis Cass. Butler declined the governorship of Nebraska from President Franklin Pierce in 1855. Opposed to secession, he was a strong supporter of the Union during the Civil War. He retired in Carrollton, Kentucky, and wrote poetry in his later years.

See also Monterrey, Battle of; Scott, Winfield.

For further reading: Frost, *The Mexican War and Its Warriors,* 1848; Johnson and Malone, *Dictionary of American Biography,* 1928–1936; Smith, *The War with Mexico,* 1919.

C

Cadwalader, George
(1806–1879)

A volunteer general, George Cadwalader joined General Winfield Scott's Army of Occupation on the road to Mexico City in August 1847. He fought well in the subsequent battles that led to Mexico City and was brevetted to major general.

The son of a Revolutionary War general, George Cadwalader was born in Philadelphia. He received a good education and became a lawyer. A general in the Pennsylvania State Militia, he was well known for ordering his troops to fire into a crowd during an anti-Catholic riot in Philadelphia in 1844.

Cadwalader was appointed brigadier general of volunteers on March 3, 1847. After arriving in Veracruz, Cadwalader's regiment moved out along the National Road in June and finally joined General Winfield Scott's Army of Occupation at Puebla on August 8 after several guerrilla skirmishes. Cadwalader's men were assigned to General Gideon J. Pillow's division.

Cadwalader led capably at the Battles of Contreras, Churubusco, Chapultepec, and San Cosmé *garita* (gate) at Mexico City. His quick response in protecting the exposed U.S. left flank during the Battle of El Molino del Rey helped prevent a cavalry attack that could have driven the U.S. troops back. Cadwalader supported General William J. Worth during the fighting at San Cosmé *garita* at Mexico City. He was brevetted to major general of volunteers for his Mexican War performance.

During the Civil War, Cadwalader was commissioned a Union major general of volunteers. He held combat commands during the first two years of the war and retired in 1865. He died in 1879 at the age of 73.

See also Contreras, Battle of; El Molino del Rey, Battle of.

For further reading: Bauer, *The Mexican War, 1846–1848*, 1974; Frost, *The Mexican War and Its Warriors*, 1848; Semmes, *Service Afloat and Ashore during the Mexican War*, 1851; Winders, *Mr. Polk's Army*, 1997.

Cahuenga, Treaty of
(1847)

The Treaty of Cahuenga, signed between Lieutenant Colonel John C. Frémont and Captain Andrés Pico, officially ended the Californio resistance in northern California during the Mexican-American War.

After fighting two small-scale battles in early January 1847, a combined U.S. army-navy force led by Commodore Robert F. Stockton and Brigadier General Stephen W. Kearny reoccupied the city of Los Angeles on January 10, 1847. Colonel John C. Frémont and his California Battalion were still advancing toward Los Angeles from the north on January 11 when they encountered the remnants of the Californio army near Rancho Los Verdugos. The commander, Captain José María Flores, having violated his parole and fearful of being hanged, rode for Sonora that night and turned command over to Captain Andrés Pico.

Pico sent Francisco de la Guerra and Francisco Rico to negotiate with Frémont. The details of the treaty were worked out on January 12, 1847. The next morning, at Rancho Cahuenga, the treaty was signed by Major P. B. Reading, Major William H. Russell, Captain Louis McLane, and Agustín Olvera for the Californios. Terms included the right for Californios to return home on parole or leave the country after the war. Those who surrendered would be protected, no oath of allegiance was required, and all Californians would enjoy equal rights. This document effectively ended the war in Upper California.

Frémont actually had no authority to create or sign the treaty, especially when his commanding officers were nearby. This conduct was another indication of his inclination for insubordination. In fact, the first word that Stockton or Kearny received from Frémont was when an officer appeared with the surrender papers in Los Angeles on January 13. Frémont and his 400 men rode victoriously into Los Angeles the following day. The civic leaders in Los Angeles arranged a ball for the U.S. officers to celebrate.

See also Flores, José María; Frémont, John C.; Los Angeles; Pico, Andrés.

For further reading: Bancroft, *History of California*, 1886; Cleland, *From Wilderness to Empire*, 1970; Harlow, *California Conquered*, 1982.

Calhoun, John Caldwell
(1782–1850)

Senator John C. Calhoun was one of the most outspoken U.S. politicians who opposed the Mexican-American War. A supporter of slavery, he maintained that the defeat of Mexico would increase the power of the federal government and destroy the plantation system in the South.

Born in South Carolina, Calhoun worked on a farm as a youth. He graduated from Yale in 1804 and became a successful attorney. A natural politician, he was part of the South Carolina legislature and later was elected to Congress in 1810. Calhoun worked tirelessly during the War of 1812 to raise troops, funds, and equipment and to regulate commerce. By 1816, he was described by J. C. Jewett as the "most elegant speaker that sits in the House.... His gestures are easy and graceful, his manner forcible, and language elegant; but above all, he confines himself closely to the subject, which he always understands...." As secretary of war to President James Monroe, he expanded the military and established the offices of the surgeon general, commissary general, and quartermaster general.

Calhoun served two terms as vice-president to President Andrew Jackson and supported the annexation of Texas. A South Carolina plantation owner, he stimulated debate by admitting that slave-holding states had a special interest in Texas. As a U.S. senator, Calhoun advocated peaceful settlements with Great Britain over Oregon and the same with Mexico. Calhoun, as secretary of state, helped craft the joint resolution to acquire Texas in 1845 for President John Tyler.

An outspoken critic of the looming Mexican-American War, Calhoun favored continued negotiations with Mexico. He worried that a U.S. victory would increase the power of the federal government and lead to new tariffs, which would damage the southern economy. Calhoun fought David Wilmot's proposal to prohibit slavery in any new territory that would be acquired as a result of the Mexican War; he argued that slaveholders should not be barred from entering any new U.S. territory with their slaves.

In 1849, Calhoun lobbied southern senators to address the slavery issue and predicted that the Union would dissolve if southern rights were not protected. His dire visions were rejected as being too extreme. Just before he died a year later, his last words from his deathbed in Washington, D.C., were "The South, the poor South."

See also Wilmot, David.

For further reading: Bartlett, *John C. Calhoun*, 1993; Capers, *John C. Calhoun, Opportunist*, 1960; Coit, *John C. Calhoun*, 1950; Cralle, *The Works of John C. Calhoun*, 1854–1861; Current, *John C. Calhoun*, 1963; Lander, *Reluctant Imperialists*, 1980; Niven, *John C. Calhoun and the Price of Union*, 1988; Wiltse, *John C. Calhoun*, 1951.

California

First claimed by Spain and then Mexico, present-day California was part of the larger Alta California province that included much of the

Great Basin. Alta California was ceded to the United States according to the Treaty of Guadalupe Hidalgo in 1848.

European exploration of Alta California began in the mid-1500s, when both Spain and Great Britain were interested in controlling this region of North America. The first explorer from New Spain (later Mexico) was Juan Rodríguez Cabrillo, a Portuguese explorer employed by Spain. In 1602, Sebastian Vizcaino conducted the first serious exploration, named landmarks, and recommended that Spain colonize California and Mexico.

Missions and *presidios* (military forts) were built from Baja (Lower) California northward to San Francisco from about 1697 to 1780. A few Russian fur-trading posts appeared along the northern coast. Franciscan friars from the Roman Catholic Church were active in establishing missions and trying to convert the native people to Christianity. The friars also taught the native people farming, weaving, and other skills. Only approximately 10 percent of the native population was successfully converted. In the 1830s, the Mexican government began to break the hold of the missions by selling the missions' best grazing lands to citizens to stimulate new settlement. This secularization of the missions led to great resentment of the Mexican government by the Californians. Large, wealthy, patriarchal families began to form an upper class that dominated political affairs, and they frequently aligned themselves with U.S. merchants and ranchers who were settling the newly available lands. Livestock became the key industry.

Following Mexico's independence from Spain in 1821, Alta California became a province of Mexico. It had its own legislature and military force. Beginning in 1825, Mexico sent to California a series of governors who were unpopular with the California citizens who wished to maintain their own government. The cruel leadership of Manuel Victoria, who became governor in 1831, led to fighting between Mexican troops and insurgent Pió Pico and his followers. Victoria finally left, and Mexican control over California was tenuous.

The first organized group of U.S. settlers arrived in 1841. Others began to follow. Mexico refused an offer by the U.S. government to purchase California. California citizens were equally distrustful of U.S. interest in their province.

Just before the Mexican-American War, a party of rough frontiersmen led by explorer John C. Frémont entered California in 1845. They were hostile and warlike and disobeyed Mexican directives. By the time war was declared, Frémont's activities had been supported by U.S. naval forces. Small-scale fighting against bands of Californians ultimately resulted in California's surrender to the United States (Treaty of Cahuenga).

California joined the United States according to the Treaty of Guadalupe Hidalgo in 1848 and became the thirty-first state in 1850. Despite treaty language that guaranteed their property rights, Californians were frequently stripped of their lands. Many were driven out of the newly discovered goldfields or simply killed. This led to bloody guerrilla raids and other retaliatory violence in the southern California frontier. By the end of the 1880s, most Californians had been forced out or were living in Spanish-speaking ghettos.

See also Bear Flag Revolt; Cahuenga, Treaty of; California Battalion; Frémont, John C.

For further reading: Bancroft, *History of California,* 1886; Cleland, *From Wilderness to Empire,* 1970; Crosby, *Antigua California,* 1994; Kelsey, *Juan Rodríguez Cabrillo,* 1986; Richman, *California under Spain and Mexico,* 1911.

California Battalion

Led by Colonel John C. Frémont, the California Battalion was officially recognized by the U.S. government in July 1846. It was mostly used as an occupational force in Los Angeles, San Diego, and other coastal cities during 1846–1847.

Frémont first entered California in late 1845 with a band of about 60 men. Headquartered near Sutter's Fort, his men were heavily armed and warlike and defied directives from the Mexican government. They antagonized local citizens and took property.

In June 1846, emboldened by the presence of Frémont, a group of Californians and U.S. settlers seized Sonoma, skirmished with Californian troops, and declared California free from Mexico. The exact role of Frémont in planning this Bear Flag Revolt is unclear; he did, however, cooperate with the rebels, who later joined his command.

Frémont's growing force was officially authorized by Commodore Robert F. Stockton on July 24, 1846, as the California Battalion of Mounted Riflemen; Frémont's second in command was U.S. Marine Corps Captain Archibald H. Gillespie. The 300-man battalion was the military force that Stockton used in occupying Los Angeles in August and enforcing the new U.S. government he had proclaimed. Broken into smaller units of 25 to 50 men, part of the battalion was used to occupy the cities of Los Angeles, San Diego, Santa Barbara, Monterey, and San Francisco.

Captain Gillespie's 48-man portion of the battalion in Los Angeles surrendered to California insurgents in September 1846. San Diego and Santa Barbara also fell. While this was occurring, Frémont and the rest of the California Battalion remained in the Sacramento Valley. Brigadier General Stephen Watts Kearny and his exhausted command (they had marched westward from Santa Fe, New Mexico, and fought two battles) arrived in San Diego in December. Early in January, a combined U.S. navy-army force led by Commodore Stockton retook Los Angeles after fighting the Battle of San Gabriel River. On January 14, 1847, Frémont and the rest of the battalion rode casually into the U.S. camp, where Frémont proudly presented the Treaty of Cahuenga, which he had signed with rebel leader General Andrés Pico two days before and which ended the fighting in California.

Against orders from President James K. Polk and over the protestations of Kearny, Stockton appointed Frémont the military governor of California on January 16, 1847. About two weeks later Stockton was replaced with Commodore Branford Shubrick, who, with new presidential orders, promptly replaced Frémont with Colonel Richard B. Mason. Soon afterward, Stockton, Kearny, and Frémont left for court-martial proceedings against Frémont in Washington, D.C. By this time, most of Frémont's California Battalion had dispersed into the California hills; the few remaining members were "regularized" into the U.S. army stationed in Los Angeles.

See also Bear Flag Revolt; Cahuenga, Treaty of; Los Angeles.

For further reading: Cleland, *From Wilderness to Empire*, 1970; Cutts, *The Conquest of California and New Mexico by the Forces of the United States in the Years 1846 and 1847*, 1847; Grivas, *Military Governments in California, 1846–1850*, 1963; Harlow, *California Conquered*, 1982; Revere, *A Tour of Duty in California*, 1849.

Californios

Californios are generally defined as those Mexicans, and their descendants, who were residents in Alta California during the Mexican-American War. The term also had social implications during this period because a number of Californios were wealthy and owned prosperous ranches, thus forming an elite upper class.

For further reading: Pitt, *The Decline of the Californios*, 1966; Richman, *California under Spain and Mexico*, 1911.

Camargo

An important staging area for General Zachary Taylor's invasion of northern Mexico, the town of Camargo, Tamaulipas, was filled with U.S. soldiers, wagons, supplies, and tents during the Mexican-American War. The climate and camp conditions led to epidemics of sickness that swept the camps, killing about 1,500 soldiers.

After the U.S. Army of Occupation had won the Battles of Palo Alto and Resaca de la Palma in May 1846, it occupied the town of Matamoros. Intent on taking the city of Monterrey, Taylor moved his army up the Río Grande to the town of Camargo, which became his new staging area. Most of the army arrived by steamer in July and August 1846.

Camargo is located on the San Juan River, about three miles upstream from its confluence with the Río Grande. In 1846, it had a population of approximately 3,000. Described by one visitor as being in a "sunbaked, rocky bowl," temperatures in the city typically climbed higher than 100 degrees. The U.S. camps along the San Juan River were plagued by dust, insects, ants, scorpions, snakes, and tarantulas. The soldiers drank water from the San Juan River, which was muddy and polluted by human waste.

Poor sanitation and contaminated drinking water quickly led to epidemics of dysentery, yellow fever, and diarrhea. The hospital tents were filled with sick soldiers, and corpses were removed daily at sunrise and sunset. After running out of wood for coffins, the dead were buried in blankets. At one point, almost one-third of Taylor's entire command was bedridden. It was not uncommon for nearly half of newly arrived volunteer regiments to become seriously ill. (The regular troops were healthier because they occupied the choicest campsites on higher ground.)

Boredom and sickness exacerbated the army's ill will toward the Mexican citizens, and numerous acts of violence and lawlessness erupted. Taylor remained in Camargo to receive new volunteer regiments. Desperate to leave because of the failing health of his army and the impatience of President James K. Polk, he began to move his undersupplied force—the last of the army left—southward to Monterrey on September 6, 1846. About 2,000 men were left behind to maintain the camp, care for the wounded, and transport supplies and dispatches. Of the nearly 12,000 men who were stationed in Camargo, 1,500 perished from disease. Many of them are buried in unmarked graves along the San Juan River.

For further reading: Blackwood, *To Mexico with Scott*, 1917; Chamberlain, *My Confession*, 1956; Henry, *Campaign Sketches of the War with Mexico*, 1847.

Campuzano, Antonio

(1810–1866)

Colonel Antonio Campuzano defended coastal Sonora and the port city of Guaymas against attacks from the U.S. Pacific Squadron during 1847–1848. His forces were never strong enough to really challenge the U.S. naval actions in the area.

Campuzano, who was born in Mexico City, joined the military at a young age. After serving at Veracruz and in Texas, he resigned in 1839. In 1841, he became one of General Antonio López de Santa Anna's officers and commanded troops in Sonora.

In 1847, Colonel Campuzano was determined to resist the attack of U.S. forces at Guaymas. He refused to surrender his army of 600 to 800 men and approximately six artillery pieces to the U.S. warship *Cyane* and Commander Samuel F. Du Pont on October 6, 1847. Eleven days later, Captain Elie A. F. La Vallette, the commander of the *Congress*, also demanded his surrender. Campuzano rationed the remaining food and water supplies in Guaymas, mostly for his own soldiers. Staying in the area, he launched a surprise attack that pinned down a landing party from the *Dale* on November 17. Hindered by a lack of men, supplies, and morale, Campuzano's force had disintegrated by April 1848.

In his postwar years, Campuzano was prefect at Guaymas in 1853 and suppressed various insurrections. A dedicated follower of Santa Anna, Campuzano served in Santa Anna's last administration as an inspector and as military commander of Guaymas. Campuzano was driven out of Guaymas by conservative forces in April 1858. After grudgingly accepting the French Intervention, he died in Mexico City in 1866.

See also Guaymas, Battle of.

For further reading: Bauer, *Surfboats and Horse Marines*, 1969; *Diccionario Porrúa*, 1995.

Canales Rosillo, Antonio

(ca. 1800–1869)

Known as the "Chaparral Fox" to Texans along the Mexican border, General Antonio Canales Rosillo led guerrilla forces that attacked U.S. patrols and supply lines and occasionally Mexican citizens in northern Mexico during the Mexican-American War.

Canales was born in Monterrey, Nuevo León, and spent most of his life in the Camargo area. A prominent local figure, he was employed as a lawyer, surveyor, and commandant of the garrison in Tamaulipas. He fought Apaches in the early 1830s and opposed General Antonio López de Santa Anna's centralist government. From 1838 to 1840, Canales tried to establish a Republic of the Río Grande between the Nueces River and Río Grande.

His plans did not succeed, and by 1840 he had realigned with the centralist government. Rewarded with a generalship in the army, he helped capture the Texas Mier Expedition in 1842. Canales developed a reputation for cruelty and cunning during years of border warfare with the Texas Rangers and was hated by Texans and some Mexicans, whom he also plundered.

In 1846, Canales commanded an auxiliary regiment from Tamaulipas. During the Battle of Palo Alto in May 1846, he led about 500 cavalrymen in an unsuccessful attempt to flank General Zachary Taylor's army. Canales bravely led his lancers the following day at the Battle of Resaca de Guerrero (Resaca de la Palma). He was later detached in June to conduct raiding and guerrilla work with a loosely organized band of 600 guerrillas and rancheros.

As General Taylor and his Army of Occupation left Monterrey for Saltillo, Canales' guerrilla raids became more focused. Operating with General José Urrea's cavalry in February 1847, Canales was effective in harassing Taylor's ever-lengthening supply lines. Canales' forces killed more than 150 U.S. soldiers that month. The U.S. troops retaliated, burning homes and villages suspected of harboring guerrillas. By April 1847, Canales' fighting force had been greatly reduced by battle deaths, desertion, and the reluctance of civilians to give them supplies and shelter.

After the war, Canales became governor of Tamaulipas in 1851, a local representative, and senator in the Mexican Congress. Continuing his military role, Canales suppressed border disturbances and broke up illegal trading. He died at the age of 67 in Miquihuana.

See also Mier Expedition.

For further reading: Chamberlain, *My Confession,* 1956; *Diccionario Porrúa,* 1995; Zorilla and Salas, *Diccionario biográfico de Tamaulipas,* 1984.

Canalizo, Valentín

(1794–1850)

A follower of General Antonio López de Santa Anna, Valentín Canalizo served as Santa Anna's minister of war, a cavalry general, and commander of the Army of the East during the Mexican-American War. Canalizo's leadership during Scott's Veracruz–Mexico City campaign in 1847 was high criticized.

Canalizo, who was born in Monterrey, Nuevo León, joined the Spanish army at the age of 17. He participated in suppressing various rebellions until 1821, when he joined the ranks of Agustín de Iturbide's army. Canalizo held various political and military positions in the new republic, including the governorship of the Department of Mexico. His loyalty to General and President Santa Anna resulted in Canalizo's appointment as interim vice-president from October 1843 to May 1844 and from September to December 1844. The administration was toppled by General Mariano Paredes y Arrillaga in December, and Canalizo was exiled.

Returning to Mexico City in 1846, Canalizo, again aligned with Santa Anna, became his minister of war until February 1847, when Santa Anna appointed him general of the Army of the East to fight the advance of General Winfield Scott toward Mexico City. All available troops and militia and new conscripts young and old were sent to Jalapa to be assembled into the new army. Canalizo was instructed by Santa Anna to hold the National Bridge (over Río Antigua) on the National Road between Veracruz and Cerro Gordo so that Santa Anna would have enough time to organize his defense at Cerro Gordo.

Canalizo's 2,000-man force constructed only some light fortifications at the bridge and then fled at the sight of the approaching U.S. forces. Canalizo's actions were further questioned when, protecting the rear during the Battle of Cerro Gordo in April, his cavalry failed to attack the flanking movement by General James Shields's brigade, which captured the highway. This created the panicked retreat that ended the battle. In July and August 1947, Canalizo was a coconspirator with General Mariano Paredes y Arrillaga in a plot to overthrow Santa Anna. In September, Canalizo had a minor role in the fighting at the gates of Mexico City.

See also Cerro Gordo, Battle of.

For further reading: Bauer, *The Mexican War, 1846–1848,* 1974; Carreño, *Jefes del ejército mexicano en 1847,* 1914; Costeloe, *The Central Republic in Mexico, 1835–1846,* 1993.

Carbajal, José María Jesús
(ca. 1805–1874)

A militant Mexican leader who lived along the Texas-Mexico border, José María Jesús Carbajal led numerous political uprisings and commanded troops during the Mexican-American War.

Carbajal was born near San Antonio and in 1823 moved to Kentucky. There he worked for two years as a tanner and leather maker. After a brief stay in Virginia, he returned to Texas as a surveyor and worked with Stephen F. Austin. Carbajal later moved into politics and served in the Coahuila y Texas legislature. Exiled in 1835 for rebellious behavior, he moved to New Orleans. He was later imprisoned in Matamoros for aiding Texans, but eventually escaped and returned to Texas. A constant advocate for an independent republic in northern Mexico, he aligned himself with whatever Mexican or U.S. faction was attempting to establish a new government. In 1939, he led Texan volunteers in a raid near Mier and was wounded severely in the arm.

In 1846, Carbajal worked with General Antonio Canales from Camargo in trying to gain U.S. support for Canales's proposed Republic of the Río Grande, which ultimately failed. Strongly opposed to U.S. intervention in Mexico, Carbajal commanded Mexican troops during the Mexican-American War.

Between 1850 and 1853, Carbajal led U.S. merchants and filibusters in border raids called the Merchants War (sometimes called the Carbajal Disturbances), was arrested, and later released. In 1862, he joined the liberal army to fight against the French. After residing in Texas, he was later governor of the state of Tamaulipas.

For further reading: Bancroft, *The History of Mexico*, 1966; Bancroft, *History of the North Mexican States and Texas*, 1884–1889; Webb, *The Handbook of Texas*, 1952.

Carmen

Located in the province of Campeche, the town of Carmen was an important center for the movement of contraband goods between Yucatán and the rest of Mexico during the Mexican-American War.

Sheltered by barrier islands at the entrance to Laguna de Términos, small coastal vessels carrying contraband cargo were able to evade the U.S. naval blockade at the beginning of the war and dock at Carmen. Commodore David Conner of the Home Squadron was eager to eliminate the flow of goods by occupying Carmen. On December 16, 1846, Conner ordered Commodore Matthew C. Perry to go there with the *Mississippi*, *Vixen*, *Bonita*, and *Petrel* and destroy or seize all military supplies. Four days later, Perry's squadron was anchored in Laguna de Términos and received Carmen's unconditional surrender on December 18. Perry's men seized stores of gunpowder and destroyed other munitions and military supplies.

Perry appointed Commander Joshua R. Sands as the military governor of Carmen. Sands was a fair governor and treated the Mexicans and their property respectfully. The blockade of the Yucatán coast was maintained until the deposed, pro-U.S. government in the province regained control.

For further reading: Bauer, *Surfboats and Horse Marines*, 1969; Emmons, *The Navy of the United States*, 1853; Knox, *A History of the United States Navy*, 1936; Nugent, *Rural Revolt in Mexico and U.S. Intervention*, 1988.

Carrasco, José María
(1813–1851)

Colonel José María Carrasco commanded the 2nd Mexican Infantry Regiment during the Battles of Palo Alto, Resaca de Guerrero, and Monterrey in 1846. He was not regarded as a strong leader and saw little action after Monterrey.

Little is known about the early life of Carrasco. A lieutenant in the Mexican army, he helped suppress various revolutions. In 1833, he joined General Mariano Arista in his failed attempt to overthrow the government. In May 1846, Colonel Carrasco led the 2nd Infantry Regiment at the Battles of Palo Alto and Resaca de Guerrero (Resaca de la Palma), during which his troops broke and ran. During the Battle of Monterrey in September, he commanded 200 men from the 2nd Infantry and the Querétaro Battalion at La Tenería, a fort on the eastern edge of the city, a critical position, which he eventually evacuated.

In 1851, Carrasco was given command of the 4th Battalion of Infantry in Sonora and occupied the town of Junos. He died that year in the port city of Guaymas.

For further reading: Bauer, *The Mexican War, 1846–1848,* 1974; Carreño, *Jefes del ejército mexicano en 1847,* 1914.

Carricitos Ranch, Skirmish at
(April 25, 1846)

About 80 U.S. dragoons from General Zachary Taylor's newly arrived army were attacked at Carricitos Ranch, Texas, on April 25, 1846, by General Anastasio Torrejón's cavalry. It was this first military engagement that led President James K. Polk to proclaim that U.S. blood had been spilled on U.S. soil.

General Taylor moved his Army of Occupation from its winter camp at Corpus Christi, Texas, to the north bank of the Río Grande opposite Matamoros in the first few months of 1846. Hearing that a Mexican force had crossed the river, Taylor dispatched Captain Seth B. Thornton and 80 dragoons to check the river crossings on April 24. Against the advice of Chapita, his Mexican guide, Thornton pushed on the following day. While the dragoons were exploring the buildings of the abandoned Rancho de Carricitos, General Anastasio Torrejón's Mexican cavalry closed the gates and opened fire on the trapped U.S. troopers from the cover of the surrounding thick chaparral. Eleven U.S. soldiers were killed and six were wounded. The survivors were sent across the Río Grande to Matamoros as prisoners of war. Torrejón sent one wounded U.S. soldier back to Taylor's camp in an oxcart with a note stating that he could not adequately treat the soldier's wounds.

This first major armed conflict between the Mexican and U.S. forces along the Río Grande gave Polk the opportunity to claim that "Mexico...has invaded our territory and shed American blood upon the American soil." Two days later, the U.S. Congress declared war on the Republic of Mexico.

See also Chapita.

For further reading: Frost, *The Mexican War and Its Warriors,* 1848; Heitman, *Historical Register and Dictionary of the United States Army,* 1903.

Carson, Christopher ("Kit")
(1809–1868)

A famous frontiersman, Christopher "Kit" Carson guided the western expeditions of explorer John C. Frémont. As the guide for General Stephen Watts Kearny's command that marched from Santa Fe to San Diego in 1846–1847, Carson fought in the Battle of San Pascual and, after slipping through the Californian line, sent back reinforcements.

Born in Kentucky, Carson later moved to Missouri. An illiterate youth, Carson ran away to the western mountains from an apprenticeship as a saddler. Over the next few years, he became an accomplished trapper and frontier guide in the Mojave Desert and California, Utah, Idaho, and New Mexico. After his Arapaho wife died, he took his five-year-old daughter to St. Louis, Missouri, placed her with relatives, and financed her education.

On his way back from Missouri in 1842, Carson met Frémont on a steamboat. Frémont hired Carson as the guide for his first expedition, and Frémont's official report of his adventures brought them both immediate fame. Carson also participated in Frémont's subsequent explorations of the West, including his expedition into California in 1845. He helped Frémont's 60-man force battle Klamath Indians in northern California in 1846. Appointed a second lieutenant in Frémont's California Battalion, Carson was later promoted to lieutenant and transported messages to Washington, D.C.

After his return to the West, Carson met General Stephen Watts Kearny's 300-man column near Socorro, New Mexico, on October 6, 1846. En route to San Diego, Kearny compelled Carson to guide them. They were surprised by Californian forces led by Major Andrés Pico at the Battle of San Pascual on December 6. Urged by Carson to attack, Kearny and his command fell into a trap that killed or wounded a third of his force, including three officers. Kearny himself received a painful lance wound in the groin. The crippled command found a small hill to defend, and Pico was content to surround them and begin a siege.

Desperate for help, Carson, Lieutenant Edward F. Beale, and Delaware Indian scout Chemuctah, often crawling on their bellies, slipped through the Californian defenses on the night of December 9. After they had successfully penetrated the line, the three split up and walked with bare feet over 35 miles of rocky ground to reach Commodore Robert F. Stockton's reinforcements in San Diego. Carson's injured feet kept him bedridden for nearly a week afterward.

As part of the joint U.S. army-navy force that left San Diego to reoccupy Los Angeles, Carson participated in the Battles of San Gabriel River and La Mesa in January 1847. He escorted more dispatches to Washington and on June 9 was appointed by President James K. Polk as a lieutenant in the California Battalion. The Senate, however, denied his appointment on January 28, 1848, because of his close relationship to the court-martialed Frémont.

At the conclusion of the Mexican-American War, Carson returned to Taos, New Mexico, where he married a local woman. Continuing his frontier lifestyle, he became a popular and influential figure in New Mexican governmental affairs and a well-respected Indian agent. Still illiterate, Carson dictated his autobiography in 1857–1858.

During the Civil War, Carson organized the 1st New Mexican Volunteer Infantry in 1861 and was commissioned lieutenant colonel. He spent most of his time fighting Indians and suppressed the Navajo by burning their crops and killing their horses and livestock. Carson was brevetted to brigadier general in 1865 for "gallantry in the Battle of Valverde and for distinguished services in New Mexico." His health failing, he resigned in 1866 and died two years later at Fort Lyon, Colorado.

See also Frémont, John C.; Klamath Indians; San Pascual, Battle of.

For further reading: Bonsal, *Edward Fitzgerald Beale, a Pioneer in the Path of Empire, 1822–1903,* 1912; Brewerton, *Overland with Kit Carson,* 1993; Carter, *"Dear Old Kit,"* 1990; Estergreen, *The Real Kit Carson,* 1955; Frémont, *Memoirs of My Life,* 1886; Guild and Carter, *Kit Carson,* 1984; Peters, *The Life and Adventures of Kit Carson,* 1858.

Casey, Silas

(1807–1882)

A talented U.S. infantry officer, Captain Silas Casey was brevetted twice during the Mexican-American War and severely wounded leading a dangerous charge during the Battle of Chapultepec in 1847.

Casey was born in Rhode Island. He was admitted to the U.S. Military Academy at the age of 15 and was commissioned second lieutenant of the 2nd Infantry upon his graduation in 1826. Casey saw duty in the Great Lakes area and along the western frontier. From 1837 to 1842, he fought the Seminole Nation in the swamps of Florida. Promoted to captain in 1839, Casey was highly regarded for his analytical and mathematical talents.

As part of General Winfield Scott's Army of Occupation during the Mexican-American War, Casey fought in the Battles of Contreras, Churubusco, El Molino del Rey, and Chapultepec. He was brevetted to major for "gallantry in action" at Contreras and Churubusco. Another brevet to lieutenant colonel followed his performance at Chapultepec, where he was severely wounded leading a storming party of 265 selected men under concentrated rifle fire from the fortress.

Assignments along the Pacific coast followed the war. Casey also wrote a manual of infantry tactics that became standard for both Union and Confederate armies during the Civil War. As a brigadier general of volunteers for the Union, Casey was brevetted for distinguished service during the Battle of Fair Oaks, Virginia. He also recruited African American troops. Retired from service in 1868, Casey died in Brooklyn, New York.

See also Chapultepec, Battle of.

For further reading: Cullum, *Biographical Register of the Officers and Graduates of the United States Military Academy from 1802 to 1867,* 1879; Johnson and Malone, *Dictionary of American Biography,* 1928–1936; Smith, *The War with Mexico,* 1919.

Castro, José María

(ca. 1810–1860)

José María Castro was an important political and military figure in California during the Mexican-American War. As military commander for the province, he helped fight the Bear Flag Revolt, John C. Frémont's California Battalion, and the joint U.S. navy-army force led by Commodore Robert F. Stockton.

Little is known about Castro's earlier years. A patriotic Californio, Castro was eager for his province to be totally independent from Mexican (and U.S.) rule. As the military commandant, he took care of matters in the northern half of the province. Although a patriot, he was aligned closely with wealthy settler John A. Sutter and had a reputation regarding the unscrupulous use of provincial funds.

Having arrived at Sutter's Fort in December 1845, Captain John C. Frémont and his 60-man force traveled to Monterey to meet General Castro. Suspicious, Castro gave them permission to stay in the Sacramento Valley. Frémont refused to stay there, and Castro ordered him to leave California. Again Frémont refused. After the Bear Flag Revolt, Castro's 50-man force skirmished with the Bear Flaggers in June 1846 at the Battle of Olompali. Castro was further irritated by the sudden activity of the U.S. Navy's Pacific Squadron, which seized Monterey in July.

Castro rode south to Los Angeles and joined forces with his occasional nemesis Pío Pico, the governor of the province and chief political and military authority in southern California. Together they tried to convince Great Britain to challenge the U.S. invasion. They also appealed to Commodore Stockton for California to be a free republic instead of a U.S. territory. Neither plan worked, and both leaders left Los Angeles on August 10, three days before the city was seized by Stockton.

Castro's pleas to the Mexican government for troops and weapons went unfulfilled. He later joined forces with Captain José María Flores, whose 300 followers captured the small U.S. garrisons at San Diego and Santa Barbara in the fall of 1846. The rebels enjoyed their success only until January 1847, when a joint U.S. navy-army force under Stockton and General Stephen Watts Kearny retook the cities, thus ending Californio resistance.

After the war, Castro lived quietly in Monterey and held a variety of government positions. He died in Baja California in 1860.

See also Bear Flag Revolt; Olompali, Skirmish at.

For further reading: Bancroft, *History of California*, 1886; Cleland, *From Wilderness to Empire*, 1970; Cutts, *The Conquest of California and New Mexico by the Forces of the United States in the Years 1846 and 1847*, 1847; Harlow, *California Conquered*, 1982; Richman, *California under Spain and Mexico*, 1911.

Casualties, Mexico

Mexican casualties during the Mexican-American War can be only approximated. It is likely that at least 82,000 men served as regular or guerrilla troops; of these, approximately 14,700 were reported as killed or wounded.

Exact casualty figures for the Mexican army are not known. Citations for killed, wounded, captured, and missing vary tremendously from source to source. Some estimates come only from U.S. battlefield reports.

Probably at least 70,000 men served in the northern Mexico and Veracruz–Mexico City campaigns. Of these, 12,600 were killed or wounded, and nearly 8,000 were captured. Desertion figures probably approach 8,000 to 10,000.

Mexican forces, including guerrillas and "irregular" troops, in smaller battles and skirmishes probably totalled approximately 12,000 men. Tabulations from various accounts and reports indicate that approximately 2,100 of these men were killed and wounded, and an undetermined number were missing or captured.

Civilian losses are even harder to approximate. A total of approximately 1,000 civilians were killed or wounded during the Battles of Monterrey, Veracruz, Mexico City, and Huamantla. Civilian losses in atrocities by U.S. soldiers and guerrillas number in the hundreds.

Casualties, United States

By the end of the Mexican-American War, 104,556 regular and volunteer U.S. soldiers had served during the conflict. Of these men, 13,768—or approximately 13 percent—died. Thousands more were so grievously injured from their wounds, or the diseases they contracted, that they died prematurely.

Three percent (944) of the 31,024 regular soldiers were killed in action or died from wounds, and 19 percent (5,821) died from diseases and accidents. In comparison, less than 1 percent (607) of the 73,532 volunteers died in battle or from wounds, and 9 percent (6,408) died from disease or accidents. In all, approximately 1 in 8 deaths was battle-related.

The greatest number of deaths for a single

regiment was the 15th U.S. Infantry: 37 died in battle, and 373 from disease and accidents, for a total of 410. The 15th Infantry was closely followed by the 1st South Carolina Volunteers: 405 men perished on the battlefield or in hospitals. The highest number of battle deaths was recorded by the 8th U.S. Infantry (102), followed by the 5th U.S. Infantry (90).

For further reading: Upton, *The Military Policy of the United States,* 1968; Winders, *Mr. Polk's Army,* 1997.

Catana, Massacre at (February 10, 1847)

Volunteer Arkansas troops committed one of the worst atrocities of the war when they murdered and mutilated about 25 Mexican citizens in a cave near Catana, Coahuila, in February 1847.

Following its victory at the Battle of Monterrey in September 1846, General Zachary Taylor's army was camped at Agua Nueva, a small community about 17 miles south of Saltillo. By mid-February 1847, more than 4,500 troops were sprawled on the wide plain around the town. Taylor was waiting for General Antonio López de Santa Anna and the Army of the North to advance northward from San Luis Potosí.

The volunteer soldiers, especially the Arkansas volunteer cavalry, nicknamed the "Ransackers," treated the townspeople roughly, and several women were raped on Christmas Day, 1846. According to Samuel Chamberlain, a U.S. dragoon, "the place was full of volunteers, who were committing all manner of outrages on the few women left in the ranchero. They were fighting over their poor victims like dogs...." In apparent retaliation, an Arkansas private was murdered outside the U.S. camp on February 9.

The following day, more than 100 men from Colonel Archibald Yell's Arkansas cavalry brigade went hunting for the killers and murdered a group of Mexican refugees in a cave near the settlement of Catana. Chamberlain recalled that "the cave was full of volunteers, yelling like fiends, while on the rocky floor lay over 20 Mexicans, dead and dying...." Several bodies had been scalped. The volunteers were stopped by a detachment of regulars sent out by General John E. Wool. Most accounts indicate that between 20 and 30 Mexicans were killed.

Despite an investigation ordered by Wool, Colonel Yell failed to produce the murderers. General Taylor ordered the two guilty companies, B and G, to the mouth of the Río Grande, a surprisingly light punishment. "Such deeds," said Taylor, "cast indelible disgrace upon our arms and reputation of our country." Taylor, however, failed to invoke harsher treatments such as flogging, branding, or execution.

See also Agua Nueva.

For further reading: Chamberlain, *My Confession,* 1956; Eisenhower, *So Far from God,* 1989.

Catholic Church, Mexico

The Roman Catholic Church was one of the most powerful institutions in Mexico during the Mexican-American War. To help finance the war, many of its assets were seized, which ultimately resulted in the *Polkos* Revolt in 1847. In an effort to get Catholic soldiers to desert from the U.S. army, Mexican generals circulated pamphlets that claimed that the war was directed against the Catholic Church in Mexico.

At the time of the Mexican-American War, the Roman Catholic Church had been the only permitted religion in Mexico for nearly 300 years. It was the most powerful institution in Mexico, and life in every Mexican town centered around its church and included daily masses, holy days, funerals, marriages, baptisms, town meetings, and church suppers. Fiestas were held on religious holidays, which began with a mass and ended with fireworks and a rollicking fandango. The church and its clergy enjoyed special political and economic privileges (such as being exempt from civil trials), which led to corruption at various levels. The church was the largest landowner in Mexico, and many Mexican families depended on farming church lands for employment.

The Mexican government asked the Catholic Church to help finance the war, which it refused to do, and then voted to take 20 million pesos from the once-protected church treasury. This resulted in the March 1847 *Polkos* Revolt, which paralyzed the central government. General Antonio López de

The anti-Catholic view of the Mexican clergy prevalent in the United States at the time of the Mexican-American War is illustrated in this sarcastic 1846 lithograph. The title is "The Mexican Rulers Migrating from Matamoros with Their Treasures." (Library of Congress)

Santa Anna, weary from his defeat at La Angostura (Buena Vista), returned to the capital and negotiated a 2-million-peso settlement with the church and rebellious factions.

Priests traveled with the Mexican army and were part of most military ceremonies. Each infantry regiment was assigned two chaplains; cavalry regiments had only one. Because General Zachary Taylor had only two Catholic chaplains for his entire army, the Mexicans took advantage of this opportunity to woo unhappy Catholics from the U.S. ranks. A number of Irish Catholics deserted Taylor when he was camped along the Río Grande in 1846. Some Catholic priests were active in convincing U.S. soldiers to desert. In Monterrey, the Mexican priests succeeded in getting more than 50 U.S. soldiers to join the Mexican army. Regarding a priest who was captured in November soliciting soldiers, a U.S. captain wrote that "he should be hung, spite of his sanctity." (Miller 1989)

Mexican generals frequently resorted to propaganda pamphlets to increase dissension among U.S. Catholic soldiers. General Santa Anna's leaflet targeted Irish Catholics: "Irishmen! Listen to the words of your brothers, hear the accents of a Catholic people.… Is religion no longer the strongest of human bonds?… Can you fight by the side of those who put fire to your temples in Boston and Philadelphia?"

Mexican soldiers expected to be blessed by their priests before battle. U.S. soldier Sam Chamberlain witnessed with fascination, before the Battle of La Angostura (Buena Vista) on February 23, 1847, as the "procession of ecclesiastical dignitaries with all the gorgeous paraphernalia of the Catholic Church advanced along the lines.…"

Mexican priests tried to get U.S. troops to desert during General Winfield Scott's Veracruz–Mexico City campaign in 1847, especially at Veracruz and Jalapa, where the sheer number of priests amazed the U.S. forces. Father Rafael Ignacio Cortez and Father Eugene McNamara, an Irish priest and missionary in Mexico, were two of the most persistent clergy.

Although the Catholic Church actually supported the war effort, it was reluctant to finance it. This refusal to donate its wealth dismayed the Mexican government, which became increasingly hostile toward the church. While President and General Santa Anna was in the field, vice-president Valentín Gómez Farías tried to wrest 20 million pesos from the church. The resultant domestic revolt, called the *Polkos* Revolt, crippled the government for over a month and kept it from reinforcing the city of Veracruz during Scott's amphibious assault in March 1847. Santa Anna later negotiated a settlement with the church for a donation of 2 million pesos.

Archbishops and priests fervently prayed for Mexican victory. As Scott's army moved ever closer toward Mexico City, the archbishop of Mexico spoke to an assembled mass in August 1847 that, if the U.S. forces won, it would "see altars re-erected against altars, and sects and dissident communions formed, which secretly and openly will make cruel and incessant war on our sacred, uniquely true religion...."

The 1830s in the United States was a decade of intense anti-Catholicism. Protestant U.S. citizens fought with Irish immigrants, most of whom were Catholic and coming to the United States in great numbers. In fact, a growing nativism promoted attacks on all residents and immigrants of foreign birth. Anti-Catholic riots occurred in eastern cities such as Philadelphia, and churches and homes were burned. Foreign-born soldiers in the U.S. army were often insulted and held back from promotion. Some radical elements (Protestant and Baptist) in the United States maintained that the war was necessary to control the spread of Catholicism.

Thus, many U.S. citizens in Mexico began to feel hostile toward the Catholic Church. They saw the incredible power of the church in all the towns they passed through, and corrupt local priests, and began to believe that the church kept the Mexicans oppressed and impoverished. Some U.S. citizens also disapproved of the holiday atmosphere of the Mexican Sabbath, which was generally packed with social events such as cockfights, bullfights, gambling, dancing, and fandangos.

Catholic U.S. soldiers acted respectfully toward the church and clergy and regularly attended mass. Others, especially Texan units, occasionally desecrated and burned church property and harassed religious processions and ceremonies. Josiah Gregg, after witnessing armed soldiers during a church service in Monclova in November 1846, wrote that "We wish to conciliate these people, and especially to put down all suspicion of domineering over their religion.... I think it to have been decidedly—very decidedly, improper, not only for [General Shields] and all other officers to go to church with arms...but still more so for his guard of 12 or 15 dragoons to march, in regular file, & armed, into the church...."

President James K. Polk, eager to convey to the Mexican populace that the United States was not at war with the Catholic Church, attached two Catholic priests to General Zachary Taylor's army as civilian acting chaplains. Fathers John McElroy and Antony Rey, both Jesuits, were to serve U.S. Catholics in the army, help the sick and wounded, and reaffirm to Mexican citizens that the United States would not destroy their religion. After arriving in June 1846, Rey was murdered by guerrillas in January 1847; McElroy became seriously ill, and returned to the U.S. in May 1847.

For further reading: Callcott, *Church and State in Mexico,* 1926; Johannsen, *To the Halls of the Montezumas,* 1985; Miller, *Mexico,* 1985; Miller, *Shamrock and Sword,* 1989; Ramirez, *Mexico during the War with the United States,* 1950; Santoni, *Mexicans at Arms,* 1996; Winders, *Mr. Polk's Army,* 1997.

Cerro Gordo, Battle of
(April 17–18, 1847)

General Winfield Scott's first battle along the National Road on the way to Mexico City, the Battle of Cerro Gordo was an impressive U.S. victory against a larger Mexican force that defended a superior position on higher ground. It confirmed the fighting ability of Scott's half-volunteer army and dashed Mexican hopes for a desperately needed victory.

After taking Veracruz in March 1847 and assembling his army in that city, General Scott prepared to move toward Mexico City along the National Road. Communities along the route included Santa Fe, Paso de Ovejas, Cerro Gordo, Jalapa, La Hoya, and Perote. Anxious to leave before the yellow fever season struck,

Scott moved out before he had received all the wagons, mules, and other supplies he needed. His quick departure surprised Mexican leaders, who had hoped that the tropical climate and yellow fever would decimate his ranks and force him to wait for more troops.

As General Antonio López de Santa Anna scraped together the makeshift Army of the East, he gave the task of defeating Scott to General Valentín Canalizo. Under him were Generals Rómulo Díaz de La Vega, Gregorio Gómez, and Antonio Gaona. Other troops included 2,000 national guardsmen from Puebla and thousands of new conscripts between the ages of 15 and 50.

Santa Anna left Mexico City on April 2 to personally command the army at Cerro Gordo, the place he had chosen to fight Scott. Located in rugged highlands, the National Road descended into a steep ravine before it entered the village of Cerro Gordo. Two steep hills, El Telégrafo and La Atalaya, dominated the approach to the village. Fortifications and redoubts were constructed along the heights. Santa Anna was confident that these hills were too rugged for the U.S. troops to attack from the rear. The Army of the East totalled approximately 12,000 men, many of whom had never fired a rifle. Santa Anna's quick organization of the army and its placement at Cerro Gordo was a remarkable achievement; it even amazed Scott when he learned about it. Mexican camp conditions were harsh—drinking water was contaminated, and a cholera epidemic swept the army. Many of the soldiers were frightened, morale was low, and Santa Anna ordered deserters to be shot on sight.

Brigadier General David E. Twiggs was the first to move out from Veracruz with artillery and 2,600 men. The march was wickedly hot. Numerous soldiers fell sick by the roadside; some of them died. On April 11, Twiggs's advance skirmished with a small force of Mexican lancers. When Twiggs's scouts returned with reports of the well-defended heights at Cerro Gordo, Twiggs wanted to attack immediately. General Robert Patterson, however, insisted that he wait for General Scott and the rest of the Army of Occupation.

Skillful reconnaissance by Lieutenant P. G. T. Beauregard and Lieutenant Zebulon B. Towers discovered an unprotected mule path that led around the Mexican left. Scott then sent out for more reconnaissance from Captain Robert E. Lee, who found a way to attack La Atalaya and seize the highway behind the village of Cerro Gordo. By the time the reconnaissance had been completed and Lee's path cleared with axes, General William J. Worth and 1,600 more men arrived, bringing Scott's force to a total of 8,500.

At 8:00 in the morning on April 17, Twiggs advanced slowly toward La Atalaya along the road cut through the chaparral of oak, mesquite, and cactus. When it was discovered that La Atalaya was occupied by only a small force of men and three artillery pieces, Twiggs launched an attack that seized the heights and sent the Mexican gunners running to El Telégrafo. Led by Colonel William S. Harney, the U.S. troops pursued the Mexicans halfway up the slope of El Telégrafo before they were repulsed by heavy musket fire. Determined to utilize La Atalaya, Twiggs managed to haul three artillery pieces up its rocky sides, which took most of the day. That night, Santa Anna reinforced his positions at El Telégrafo.

The following day, April 18, Colonel Bennet Riley's force (2nd U.S. Infantry and artillerists from the 4th U.S. Artillery deployed as infantrymen) moved westward around the lower slope of El Telégrafo, intent on joining Brigadier General James Shields's brigade in a flanking movement on the Mexican rear. Artillery fire from El Telégrafo began to open holes in their ranks. Twiggs then ordered Riley and Harney to charge El Telégrafo. Many of Harney's men were killed by artillery fire as they descended the rocky slope of La Atalaya. Bitter hand-to-hand fighting erupted at the wooden palisade defenses that Santa Anna had built at the base of El Telégrafo. As the U.S. troops began to ascend the steep incline, they were protected by rocks and trees.

Led by Harney, the U.S. soldiers broke into the open, cleared ground near the summit and collided in hand-to-hand combat with the Mexican defenders. A bullet in the head killed General Ciriaco Vázquez as he tried to rally his troops. As Riley's force approached the summit, Captain James B. Magruder turned the Mexican guns on the fleeing defenders. The collapse of El Telégrafo began a general retreat, and the jubilant U.S. forces surged down the other side of the hill toward the Mexican camp at Cerro Gordo. By this time, General Shields and his volunteers appeared behind the Mexican camp after flanking El Telégrafo and faced artillery and 2,000 cavalry under General Valentín Canalizo. A burst of artillery fire seriously wounded Shields, but Canalizo and his men fled into the ravines that led to the Río del Plan.

Scott had planned for General Gideon Pillow's men to attack the Mexican right flank at the same time that the left flank was being attacked. Pillow was several hours late in launching his attack, which was poorly organized. Charging into a blast of grape and cannister from Mexican artillery commanded by General José María Jarero, Pillow lost about 80 men killed or wounded in less than five minutes, including most of his field officers. By this time, the Mexican army was in full retreat from the early morning attacks on its left flank.

"Our reverse at Cerro Gordo was a rout as complete as it was shameful," wrote Ramon Alcaraz. "Everything was lost. Absolutely nothing was saved; not even hope.... A small portion of our troops fought and died heroically; the rest surrendered their arms almost without putting up any defense, or else they ran away...."

U.S. pursuit of the Mexican army continued toward Jalapa. As the Mexicans streamed through La Hoya, its garrison under General Gregorio Gómez joined in the retreat. Thousands of Mexican soldiers were captured and paroled. U.S. losses in two days of fighting were surprisingly light: 63 men were killed and 368 wounded. Santa Anna's losses were more severe: approximately 1,100 were killed or wounded, and 3,036 were captured. The following day, the U.S. army marched through Jalapa with bands playing "Yankee Doodle Dandy," in pursuit of the Mexican army.

J. J. Oswandel, a member of the 1st Pennsylvania Volunteers, visited the battlefield on April 19. "The Mexican wounded were strewn all over the field; some with their arms and legs off, some shot almost in two and still gasping," he recalled. "We gave them water out of our canteens, and eased them of their misery all we could.... We saw the paroled Mexicans hunting up their dead and wounded comrades; to some of the dead they gave a decent burial, and the wounded they took proper care of; others of the dead they gathered in heaps and burned. The wounded were taken up and put in the ambulance wagon and taken to the hospital.... We also saw the body of the gallant Mexican General Vásquez. He was shot through the head. I regret to state, that some of our *moral* soldiers, who, after the battle of yesterday were sent out to bring in our dead and wounded soldiers, not only rifled his pockets, but took off his boots and all his mountings. In fact nearly all the dead Mexicans had their pockets turned inside out, to see whether they had anything in them. This thieving operation on the dead seems to be the custom among all victorious parties...."

The burial of a Mexican officer after the battle was recorded by U.S. officer Raphael Semmes: "A captain in the 4th Light-Infantry, who had been mortally wounded at the battle of Cerro Gordo, was buried hence with the honors of war. The corpse was borne by six Mexican soldiers, under the direction of a Mexican officer—all without arms—and was deposited on its bier in the center of the [cathedral].... The solemn ritual of the Catholic Church was read in a slow and distinct manner, by a venerable old priest...while clouds of incense rose from a burning and burnished censer in the hands of an attendant. General Scott, General Twiggs, Colonel Childs, Colonel Hitchcock, and others of the distinguished officers of the American army, entered soon after the commencement of the service, and ranging themselves around the corpse, listened attentively and reverently to the solemn words.... Around the fancifully decorated coffin [stood] Americans and Mexicans intermingled—who had so recently met in deadly conflict on the battle-field—uncovered, and paying the last tribute of respect to a fallen brother.... The coffin was removed from the church, and escorted to the grave by a company of our infantry, with the band of our regiment playing that most solemn and impressive of all tunes—the Dead March. A cavalcade of American officers brought up the rear...."

For further reading: Alcaraz, *The Other Side*, 1850; Brooks, *A Complete History of the Mexican War, 1846–1848*, 1849; Grant, *Personal Memoirs of U. S. Grant*, 1885; Oswandel, *Notes of the Mexican War,*

1885; Ramirez, *Mexico during the War with the United States*, 1950; Semmes, *Service Afloat and Ashore during the Mexican War*, 1851.

Chapita

An employee of Texas rancher Henry Lawrence Kinney, Chapita served as a scout for General Zachary Taylor's army as it moved from Corpus Christi, Texas, to the Río Grande in 1846. He also led Captain Seth B. Thornton's squad of dragoons, who were attacked at Carricitos Ranch on April 25, 1846.

Little is known about Chapita, a Mexican who was employed by Texas rancher H. L. Kinney in the 1840s. Kinney had helped Chapita escape from a prison in Matamoros, and Chapita became his spy and go-between in illegal trading along the border. Chapita worked alone, and frequently traveled the trails between Corpus Christi and the Río Grande at night. Devoted to Kinney, Chapita was described by W. S. Henry as a "man in the prime of life, middling height, broad shoulders, muscles like whipcords, a dark, piercing eye, prominent forehead, and bushy eyebrows; having the determined expression of countenance common to one who follows so dangerous an occupation."

When Kinney joined Taylor's army, Chapita became Taylor's guide and spy. Once along the Río Grande, Chapita entered Matamoros at will and brought back estimates of troop strengths. Chapita led Captain Seth B. Thornton and approximately 60 dragoons on a reconnaissance on April 24, 1846. After going about 20 miles, and learning that there was a strong force of Mexican cavalry ahead, Chapita insisted it was too dangerous to go further. Thornton ignored him and was embarrassed the following day when his command was captured at Carricitos Ranch by General Anastasio Torrejón's cavalry. Chapita returned to Taylor's camp on April 26 with the news that Thornton had been captured.

Chapita remained with Kinney during Taylor's subsequent movements along the Río Grande and beyond during 1846–1847. Chapita served as a scout, translator, and assistant to Kinney, who was responsible for procuring supplies, often from Mexican sources, for the U.S. army.

See also Carricitos Ranch, Skirmish at; Kinney, Henry Lawrence.

For further reading: Dufour, *The Mexican War, a Compact History, 1846–1848*, 1968; Smith, *To Mexico with Scott*, 1917.

Chapultepec, Battle of
(September 13, 1847)

Chapultepec, a hill less than two miles from Mexico City, was heavily fortified and guarded the city's western approaches. Defended by approximately 1,000 men under General Nicolás Bravo Rueda, the Mexican defenses were overrun by General Winfield Scott's army on the morning of September 13, 1847. By nightfall, the victorious U.S. troops had seized two of the entrances to Mexico City.

Following the Battle of El Molino del Rey, the Mexican army fell back to its next stronghold outside the City of Mexico: Chapultepec, a hill rising 200 feet above the marshy plain and crowned with an abandoned, castlelike summer palace and the Colegio Militar (Military College). The hill was a commanding defensive position. Improvements were begun in May 1847, and bells were melted down into new cannon. In violation of the Armistice of Tacubaya, the Mexicans worked busily on fortifying the castle under General Antonio López de Santa Anna's watchful eye in early September. The masonry walls were reinforced with thousands of sandbags and stout beams, and parapets were constructed on the roofs of the buildings. Explosive mines were placed on the lower slopes of the hill. Santa Anna had approximately 14,000 men who were positioned behind walls and entrenchments around the hill. Most of those troops were protecting the western approach. General Bravo Rueda and approximately 1,000 men defended the buildings of the Colegio Militar on the heights.

The defenders at Chapultepec had anxiously watched the Battle of El Molino del Rey on September 8 from the battlements. During the fight, Lieutenant Colonel Miguel María Echeagaray of the 3rd Light Infantry, on his own

The storming of Chapultepec by Quitman and his troops, from a lithograph that first appeared in George Kendall's *War between the United States and Mexico,* 1851 (Library of Congress)

resolve, launched a hard-hitting counterattack from Chapultepec that retook a Mexican artillery position. His troops inflicted heavy casualties, but could not hold the position and were forced to fall back.

On September 11, howitzers under Captain Simon Drum were placed about 1,000 yards from Chapultepec. An artillery duel began the following morning. Not sure where Scott would strike, Santa Anna removed some men and cannon from Chapultepec and placed them to the east. Although the U.S. fire was quite accurate, it did not induce a surrender, and Scott realized a frontal assault would be required to take the position. The Mexicans left the dead and wounded where they had fallen and worked through the night to repair the damage. The young cadets at the military academy were ordered to leave, but approximately 50 remained to fight with the troops. Bravo Rueda placed about half his men on the lower slopes of the hill behind earthworks.

Scott selected the divisions of Generals John Quitman and Gideon Pillow for the morning assault. Each commander picked a "forlorn hope"—a group of approximately 300 men who would be the first to race across the deadly ground as storming parties. These were led by Captain Silas Casey and Captain Samuel Mackenzie. Pillow's men would cross the rubble of El Molino del Rey's fortifications, elaborate walled gardens, and a cypress swamp in a direct assault from the west. Quitman would advance from the south along a causeway and attack the southeast corner of the defenses. U.S. officers were gloomy, and even Scott was worried.

The following morning (September 13) the U.S. guns began an artillery barrage at dawn that continued for more than two hours. Colonel William Trousdale with the 11th and 14th Infantry, and some artillery under the command of Lieutenant T. J. Jackson, were positioned to guard Pillow's left flank and discourage any reinforcement from Mexico City. Lieutenant Colonel Joseph E. Johnston led a charge that drove the Mexicans from the defenses at the perimeter of the hill and then opened an intense fire on the southern parapets of the college. U.S. batteries continued their deadly fire. Pillow's men (9th and 15th Infantry) took heavy losses as they crossed the swamp in front of Chapultepec. The high garden walls also frustrated their advance until, enlarged with bayonets, a breach funneled more soldiers toward the hill. After reaching the walls they were forced to wait in an exposed position until the storming parties arrived with scaling ladders. U.S. batteries held their fire. (The mines on the slopes below the castle failed to detonate because the canvas powder trains had been discovered and cut by U.S. soldiers.)

When the ladders finally arrived, the U.S. troops quickly scaled the parapets and flowed into the college. Having witnessed Mexican soldiers slitting the throats of U.S. soldiers wounded during the Battle of El Molino del Rey, the U.S. troops killed surrendering Mexicans in retaliation and bayoneted the wounded. Six young cadets chose to die rather than surrender; one of them leaped or fell from the wall clutching the Mexican flag. By 9:30 in the morning a U.S. flag was flying over the east wall of Chapultepec. The flag was a grim sight to 30 U.S. deserters captured at Churubusco and who were immediately hung when the flag appeared over the castle.

An officer with Santa Anna, watching the defeat from a distance, shook his head and muttered "God is a Yankee" (Alcaraz 1850). About 1,800 of Santa Anna's force were killed, wounded, or missing; Scott lost about 450. Once Chapultepec was secure, the U.S. forces swarmed down the causeways that led to the gates of the City of Mexico, which would be seized by the end of the day.

See also Bravo Rueda, Nicolás; Casey, Silas; Niños Héroes; San Patricio Battalion.

For further reading: Alcaraz, *The Other Side*, 1850; Bravo, "Don Nicolás Bravo y la defensa de Chapultepec," 1947; Echánove Trujillo, *Juan Crisóstomo Cano*, 1947; Gordon, "Battles of Molino del Rey and Chapultepec," 1913; Grant, *Personal Memoirs of U. S. Grant*, 1885; Molina, "El asalto al castillo de Chapultepec el día 13 de Septiembre de 1847," 1902; Sánchez Lamego, *El Colegio Militar y la defensa de Chapultepec en Septiembre de 1847*, 1947.

Chase, Anna McClarmonde

(1809–1874)

The wife of U.S. consul Franklin Chase, Anna McClarmonde Chase was a U.S. spy in Tampico, Mexico, during the Mexican-American War. She informed the U.S. Navy of the withdrawal of troops from Tampico, which allowed the port to be seized without loss of life.

McClarmonde, who was born in Ireland, was living in Tampico when she met, and later married, Franklin Chase, the U.S. consul. With the outbreak of the Mexican-American War, Franklin Chase and other U.S. citizens were ordered to leave the country. Her British citizenship allowed Anna Chase to remain behind to manage the couple's business.

In the summer of 1846, she forwarded information about military activities and plans in the area via British sailors to Commodore David E. Conner of the U.S. Home Squadron in the Gulf of Mexico. She observed improvements to harbor defenses and Mexican troop movements. She also circulated false rumors that up to 30,000 U.S. troops were going to be landing at Tampico, which may have prompted General Antonio López de Santa Anna to withdraw the Tampico garrison. Mexican authorities began to suspect her and tried to seize her property. As soon as Tampico was evacuated, she informed the U.S. Navy, which then moved in to occupy the town. When U.S. sailors came ashore, she raised the U.S. flag over her home.

See also Tampico.

For further reading: Bauer, *Surfboats and Horse Marines*, 1969; Franklin and Anna Chase Collection, Dallas Historical Society, Dallas, TX; Nevin, *The Mexican War*, 1978; Smith, *The War with Mexico*, 1919.

Chaves, Manuel Antonio

(1818–1889)

A prominent rancher and trader in Santa Fe, Manuel Antonio Chaves was involved in the Taos Revolt in New Mexico in January 1847. He later supported the U.S. occupation of New Mexico.

Chaves was born near Albuquerque, New Mexico. He became involved in the active trading along the Santa Fe Trail. He lived briefly in St. Louis before returning in 1841 to Santa Fe, where he married and became a prominent rancher and influential citizen.

After General Stephen Watts Kearny's

Army of the West seized New Mexico in 1846, Chaves became involved with other rebels in plotting the Taos Rebellion. Suspicious U.S. authorities arrested him, but he was acquitted of treason in January 1847. When the revolt was launched one week later, he switched sides and helped suppress it.

Chaves became well known in the 1850s as an Indian fighter. Nicknamed the "Little Lion," he scouted for the Union army during the Civil War. Chaves moved his family to a large ranch in southwestern New Mexico, where he commanded the local militia. Suffering from old wounds, he died there in 1889.

See also Taos Rebellion.

For further reading: Meier and Rivera, *Dictionary of Mexican American History,* 1981; Simmons, *The Little Lion of the Southwest,* 1923.

Chihuahua

The city of Chihuahua, the capital of the province of Chihuahua, was an active trading center in the 1840s. Its prosperity depended on U.S. trading via the Santa Fe Trail. It was occupied by Colonel Alexander Doniphan and his Missourians in 1847.

The city of Chihuahua contained shady trees and gardens, an attractive plaza and public walk, and an impressive, white marble cathedral. "From afar," wrote a visitor, "wayfarers could descry the great stone arches of the aqueduct and the soaring towers of the cathedral, whose statue-embellished facade convinced many a Missouri backwoodsman that it must be one of the world's great structures. Smelting furnaces spewed smoke, the streets had some semblance of plan, and the better houses were actually built of stone rather than of adobe." (Lavender 1954)

At the outbreak of the Mexican-American War, President James K. Polk wanted to occupy all of the northern Mexican states. Brigadier General John E. Wool was detached from General Zachary Taylor's army in 1846 to organize a force that would march 500 miles west from San Antonio to occupy Chihuahua. His 2,500-man force moved out on September 25, 1846. While occupying Monclova, Wool was informed that General Antonio López de Santa Anna was advancing with his army to attack Taylor at Saltillo. With Taylor's permission, Wool changed course and headed toward Saltillo.

A second U.S. force was also en route to Chihuahua: about 1,100 men (mostly Missouri volunteers) under the command of Colonel Alexander Doniphan. Doniphan had been left to hold Santa Fe when General Stephen Watts Kearny marched for California in September 1846. On December 16, Doniphan left Valverde, New Mexico, to join Wool at Chihuahua. After learning that Wool had changed course, and having no other orders, Doniphan pushed on toward Chihuahua.

Chihuahua sought federal assistance for supplies, weapons, and soldiers. Ángel Trías Álvarez, a wealthy hacienda owner and governor of the province, had assembled a force of infantry and cavalry with almost no resources. Damaged weapons were repaired, a cannon foundry built, and uniforms made. As Doniphan approached the city in February 1847, General Pedro García Condé arrived from Mexico City to help organize the defense of the city. The total Mexican force numbered approximately 3,000 soldiers, 1,000 loosely organized rancheros, and ten cannon.

About 15 miles north of Chihuahua, the Chihuahuan force was routed with heavy losses by Doniphan at the Battle of Río Sacramento on February 28, 1847. Trías Álvarez fled to Parras. Mexican historian Ramon Alcaraz wrote that "in the city, where, blinded by the expectation of victory, they were preparing with enthusiasm for a triumphal festival, the sound of cannon had been heard in the evening, with the liveliest anxiety; and, when news was received of the disaster, the utmost terror was spread among the people, and many families...rushed into the streets."

Doniphan's men occupied the city on March 1. Many of the townspeople had fled, and the homes and buildings were used at will by ill-mannered soldiers as bunkhouses and stables. Susan Magoffin wrote that the Mexican citizens were shocked that "their lovely homes would be turned into quarters for common soldiers, their fine houses turned into stables, and their public drinking fountain used as a bathing trough."

Doniphan had also escorted a group of traders with wagons full of merchandise. The traders immediately set up business in the city.

After a stay of nearly two months, Doniphan departed on April 28 to join Taylor at Saltillo. Some of the U.S. traders remained behind. Wanting to improve the economic prosperity from U.S. business, several prominent Chihuahuans lobbied unsuccessfully to join the United States in 1848.

See also Doniphan's March; Río Sacramento, Battle of.

For further reading: Alcaraz, *The Other Side*, 1850; Hughes, *Doniphan's Expedition, Containing an Account of the Conquest of New Mexico*, 1973; Lavender, *Bent's Fort*, 1954; Magoffin, *Down the Santa Fe Trail and into Mexico*, 1926.

Childs, Thomas
(1796–1852)

Thomas Childs served with both General Zachary Taylor and General Winfield Scott during the Mexican-American War. A highly respected officer, Childs is most remembered for storming Independence Hill during the Battle of Monterrey and withstanding a monthlong siege while he was the military governor of Puebla.

The son of a Revolutionary soldier, Childs was born in Pittsfield, Massachusetts. After graduating from the U.S. Military Academy in 1814, Childs was commissioned a third lieutenant of artillery. He had an excellent service record during the War of 1812 and the Florida Wars.

Part of General Taylor's Army of Occupation along the Río Grande in 1846, Childs was brevetted to lieutenant colonel for "gallant conduct and repeated successes" during the Battles of Palo Alto and Resaca de la Palma. On September 22, 1846, Childs led an assault force up the rugged slopes of Independence Hill, an 800-foot-tall rise that guards the western approach to the city of Monterrey. His men climbed the almost vertical rock face in a rainstorm at 3:00 in the morning and at dawn overran a position that Mexican General Pedro de Ampudia had thought was impregnable. The fall of Federation Hill allowed General William J. Worth's men to attack the western end of the city. Childs led his troops in hand-to-hand street fighting the following day.

During General Scott's 1847 campaign, Childs was chief of staff to General Worth at Veracruz. Childs was installed as military governor in Jalapa from April to June and was instructed to keep Scott's supply lines open along the National Road. He was later made military governor at Puebla, where his force was limited to 400 active men and nearly 2,000 sick or convalescing soldiers.

After Mexico City fell to Scott in September, Santa Anna circled around behind Scott and besieged Childs's garrison at Puebla. On September 13–14, approximately 4,000 Mexicans under Brigadier General Joaquín Rea entered Puebla. The U.S. troops were posted in a citadel, Fort Loretto, and a convent. Childs refused to surrender and fought off sporadic attacks until October 1. Reinforcements finally arrived from Veracruz after a four-week siege, and Childs was brevetted to brigadier general for his defense of the city.

After the war, Childs saw duty in Maryland and Florida. In 1852, he died from yellow fever at Fort Brooke, Florida.

For further reading: Cullum, *Biographical Register of the Officers and Graduates of the United States Military Academy from 1802 to 1867*, 1879; Frost, *The Mexican War and Its Warriors*, 1848; Oswandel, *Notes of the Mexican War*, 1885.

China

Located about 70 miles southwest of Camargo, China, Nuevo León, was a refuge and gathering place for various guerrilla units, including that of the infamous General Antonio Canales, in northern Mexico during the Mexican-American War.

U.S. scouting parties occasionally passed through China or camped there for the night. Dragoon Samuel Chamberlain remembered the town as a "filthy sewer, full of dogs, mud, vermin, and all uncleanness, a place that would make a Comanche vomit.… Our camp was filled with disgusting beggars." Violence was commonplace, and both U.S. soldiers and Mexicans were occasionally murdered. China was the headquarters for raids on U.S. patrols and supply trains. These raids killed more than 160 U.S. soldiers in February 1847. Guerrilla activity lessened after General Zachary Taylor's victory at the Battle of Buena Vista on February 23 and the shift of the fighting to Veracruz. The town was later occupied by troops from General John E. Wool's remaining Army of Occupation in northern Mexico.

For further reading: Bauer, *The Mexican War, 1846–1848,* 1974; Chamberlain, *My Confession,* 1956; Curtis, *Mexico under Fire,* 1994.

Churubusco, Battle of
(August 20, 1847)

The Battle of Churubusco was one of the most hard-fought, bitterly contested U.S. victories of the Mexican-American War. General Antonio López de Santa Anna lost nearly a third of his fighting force and, the following day, negotiated the Armistice of Tacubaya, which stopped the fighting for about two weeks.

Following the Battle of Cerro Gordo in April 1847, Major General Winfield Scott continued to advance toward Mexico City. By August 11, Scott's army had approached to within 15 miles of the capital.

Santa Anna, commanding approximately 20,000 men, made his headquarters at a well-fortified convent called San Mateo (called San Pablo by U.S. troops) at Coyoacán, five miles from Mexico City. In his front was a vast natural defense—a five-mile-wide, rocky, jagged lava field, called *el pedregal,* that limited the approach toward the capital to two roads. Not knowing whether Scott would approach from the west or the south, Santa Anna posted General Gabriel Valencia's 6,000 men at the village of Padierna, General Francisco Pérez and 3,500 men at San Angel, General Nicolás Bravo Rueda at San Antonio, and General Manuel Rincón at Churubusco. The Churubusco defenses were located about one-half mile northeast of San Mateo and protected a bridge crossing over Río Churubusco. Santa Anna's troops covered a semicircular, five-mile front and were positioned so that they could quickly assist each other.

Scott's troops arrived in the area around San Agustín on August 18 and faced the

The capture of the Tête de Pont during the Battle of Churubusco, from an undated engraving (Library of Congress)

immense southern front of the lava field. His patrols that advanced up the highway toward Churubusco from the south were fired on by Bravo's troops positioned at San Antonio. The following day, Scott and his officers discussed battle plans. His engineers, led by Robert E. Lee, discovered routes through the lava field that, with widening, would allow the passage of men, wagons, and artillery.

Scott's first concern was Valencia's force at Padierna. It was positioned on some low hills west of the small village (misidentified by the U.S. force as Contreras, the ensuing battle was given that name). Santa Anna had ordered Valencia on August 18 to pull back about two miles to San Angel and join his forces, but Valencia remained where he was. Santa Anna was so infuriated that he ordered Valencia shot on sight. Although only two miles apart, they refused to support each other for personal and political reasons. Early in the morning on August 20, Valencia was struck hard by soldiers under General Persifor Smith and General James A. Shields and driven in total panic through San Angel toward Churubusco. The assault had lasted less than half an hour.

The fleeing Mexican soldiers were chased up the road toward Churubusco by U.S. forces, some of whom were emerging from the lava field. Bravo's men from San Antonio also fell back. Santa Anna decided to concentrate his forces at Mexico City, which meant that they had to cross the bridge over Río Churubusco. Santa Anna ordered the bridge to be held at all costs. Troops were massed behind the stonework of the bridge and in the massive San Mateo Convent, which had a sweeping view of the approach to the bridge. The San Mateo force consisted of approximately 1,800 national guardsmen and 200 U.S. deserters who fought for Mexico under the colors of the San Patricio Battalion. Knowing they would be executed if captured, they grimly watched the approaching blue mass of U.S. soldiers. Santa Anna's men at Churubusco and San Mateo totalled approximately 8,000.

The first attacks on Churubusco were launched about noon on August 20. Scott uncharacteristically committed all his available men to the fight. The divisions of Generals William J. Worth and Gideon Pillow converged on the well-defended Churubusco Bridge, General David E. Twiggs attacked San Mateo, and the divisions of General James Shields and Franklin Pierce crossed a different bridge and flanked the Churubusco defenders. Steady pressure from Colonel Newman S. Clarke's and Brigadier General George Cadwalader's brigades, assisted by Colonel James Duncan's artillery, finally breached the Mexican line at the bridge. The U.S. forces then turned left to help Twiggs attack the convent. The San Patricio Battalion engaged in some of the most desperate fighting of the war. Their spirited resistance lasted for several hours, and the accuracy of their artillery forced the U.S. gunners to retreat. Many fought to the death in hand-to-hand combat, knowing that their fate, if captured, was hanging.

After three hours of fighting, the convent finally fell, and the victorious U.S. troops joined Shields and Pierce on the north side of the river. Zealous troops chased the Mexicans toward the city gates, but were turned back by heavy musket fire, which wounded Captain Philip Kearny. Mexican losses were ghastly: Santa Anna lost approximately 4,000 in killed and wounded and nearly 3,000 captured in the battles of Contreras and Churubusco. Scott's casualties were 1,053 killed and wounded, including several valuable officers.

Much to Santa Anna's relief, General Scott agreed to consider a truce the following day, which was quickly drafted and signed on August 22. Scott agreed to the Armistice of Tacubaya in hopes of meaningful peace negotiations; instead, Santa Anna violated the armistice and used the truce to improve his fortifications around Mexico City.

See also Contreras, Battle of; *Pedregal*; San Patricio Battalion.

For further reading: Alcaraz, *The Other Side*, 1850; *Churubusco en la accion militar del 20 de Agosto de 1847*, 1947; Grant, *Personal Memoirs of U. S. Grant*, 1885; Semmes, *Service Afloat and Ashore during the Mexican War*, 1851; Weems, *To Conquer a Peace*, 1974.

Citadel, Monterrey

Known to the U.S. forces as the Black Fort, the Citadel was an unfinished cathedral approximately 1,000 yards north of the city of Monterrey, Nuevo León. A formidable structure, its

30-foot-high stone walls were enclosed in a quadrangular, bastioned earthwork about 12 feet in height, and it was surrounded by an unfinished moat. The fort had a commanding view of the northern and eastern approaches to the city. General Pedro de Ampudia, commander of the Army of the North, stationed approximately 300 men with 12 mounted guns inside the fortress.

The Citadel worried General Zachary Taylor as he planned for the impending Battle of Monterrey in September 1846. He avoided it as long as possible, but its cannons inflicted high casualties during his assaults on the city from the north and east on September 21. The position was never taken by force during the Battle of Monterrey.

When the armistice between the U.S. and Mexican forces was signed on September 25, the defenders in the Black Fort finally emerged.

See also Monterrey, Battle of.

For further reading: Weems, *To Conquer a Peace*, 1974.

Clark, Meriwether Lewis

(1809–1881)

A volunteer officer in General Stephen Watts Kearny's Army of the West, Meriwether Lewis Clark marched with Kearny to Santa Fe, and later to Chihuahua with Colonel Alexander Doniphan. Clark's artillery skill during the Battle of Río Sacramento in February 1847 was a crucial contribution that led to the defeat of the superior Mexican force.

The son of the explorer William Clark, Meriwether Lewis Clark was born in Missouri. He attended the U.S. Military Academy from 1825 to 1830. Commissioned as a second lieutenant in the 6th U.S. Infantry, Clark served in the Black Hawk War. He resigned in 1833 to pursue a career as a civil engineer and later served in the Missouri legislature.

Clark volunteered for the Mexican-American War and was part of General Stephen Watts Kearny's Army of the West that was organized at Fort Leavenworth, Kansas, in the summer of 1846. A major in the Missouri Battery of Volunteer Artillery, Clark was part of Doniphan's march to Chihuahua and handled his artillery well at the Battle of Río Sacramento in February 1847. His skillful use of his guns forced the Mexicans to abandon their defensive position.

When the war ended, Clark became U.S. surveyor general for Missouri from 1848 to 1853. He later served as a Confederate officer during the Civil War and died at the age of 72 in Frankfurt, Kentucky.

See also Doniphan's March; Río Sacramento, Battle of.

For further reading: Bauer, *The Mexican War, 1846–1848*, 1974; Cullum, *Biographical Register of the Officers and Graduates of the United States Military Academy from 1802 to 1867*, 1879; Hughes, *Doniphan's Expedition, Containing an Account of the Conquest of New Mexico*, 1973.

Clay, Cassius Marcellus

(1810–1903)

A volunteer cavalry officer from Kentucky, Captain Cassius Marcellus Clay was captured with his men by Mexican cavalry at La Encarnación on January 23, 1847, during a scouting expedition. Their capture was embarrassing because they neglected to post pickets.

Born in Kentucky, Clay developed a reputation for hotheadedness at a young age. He graduated from Yale in 1832 and became a lawyer. A passionate abolitionist, he entered the Kentucky legislature in 1835. His political and military career was marred by brawls, duels, and killings and mutilation of a man's face with a bowie knife.

Although, as an abolitionist, he opposed the annexation of Texas, Clay volunteered to fight the Mexicans in 1846 because he thought a military career would help his political future. His scouting patrol was ignominiously captured by Mexican cavalry at La Encarnación on January 23, 1847, when they neglected to post pickets before falling asleep. Clay was later released and served in subsequent engagements.

Returning to Kentucky in 1848, Clay later became the governor of Kentucky and a close friend of Abraham Lincoln. After serving as foreign minister to Russia from 1861 to 1869, Clay retired to his Kentucky estate. A few weeks before his death in 1903, his increasingly unstable behavior led to a court's decision that he was insane.

See also La Encarnación.

For further reading: Johnson and Malone, *Dictionary of American Biography*, 1928–1936; Scott, *Encarnación Prisoners, Comprising an Account of the March of the Kentucky Cavalry from Louisville to the Rio Grande*, 1848.

Clay, Henry
(1777–1852)

Whig Henry Clay, who was defeated by Democrat James K. Polk in the 1844 presidential election, vehemently opposed the Mexican-American War.

A native of Virginia, Clay moved to Kentucky, where he developed a law practice. As a U.S. representative, he supported the War of 1812 and presented the Missouri Compromise in 1820. He approved of the annexation of Texas, only if it could be done "without dishonor, without war, and with the common consent of the Union, and upon just and fair terms." The most prominent Whig in the country, Clay was defeated by Polk in the 1844 U.S. presidential election.

Clay constantly attacked the Mexican-American War, calling it the "most unnecessary and horrible war." He maintained that expansionist objectives could still be realized through continued negotiation and compromise with Mexico. In addition to the tremendous cost in lives and treasury funds, Clay was concerned about the expansion of slavery into any new territory gained by the war. His favorite son, Henry, Jr., was bayoneted to death during the Battle of Buena Vista in February 1847. As the war dragged on, Clay opposed the growing "All of Mexico" movement and asked Congress to disavow an intent of seizing the entire country.

A member of the U.S. Senate from 1849 to 1852, Clay argued for moderation on the issue of slavery and predicted disunion if the sectionalism continued. Clay died of tuberculosis at the age of 75.

See also Clay, Henry, Jr.

For further reading: Clay, *The Private Correspondence of Henry Clay*, 1855; Remini, *Henry Clay*, 1991; Rogers, *The True Henry Clay*, 1902.

Clay, Henry, Jr.
(1811–1847)

Lieutenant Colonel Henry Clay, Jr., a West Point graduate and promising volunteer officer with General Zachary Taylor's Army of Occupation, was killed in action during the Battle of Buena Vista in 1847.

The son of statesman Henry Clay, Henry Clay, Jr., was born near Lexington, Kentucky. At the age of 16, he graduated from Transylvania College, where he became close friends with Jefferson Davis. Later they were classmates at the U.S. Military Academy. After travels in Europe, Clay practiced law and entered the Kentucky legislature.

Offered a commission as lieutenant colonel of the 2nd Kentucky Volunteers, Clay joined General Taylor's Army of Occupation in 1846. He fought bravely during the Battle of Buena Vista on February 23, 1847. His steady leadership helped keep Taylor's left from totally collapsing early in the battle. Wounded in the thigh, he was carried by his men up a steep ravine until he ordered them to leave him and retreat. Lying on the hill and swinging his sword, he was bayoneted to death as the Mexicans surged by. Taylor wrote that his "zeal in engaging the enemy, and the cool and steadfast courage with which [he held his] position during the day, fully realized my hopes, and caused me to feel yet more sensibly [his] untimely loss." Fellow officer Jefferson Davis of the Mississippi Rifles escorted Clay's body to Louisville, Kentucky, where Clay was buried.

See also Buena Vista, Battle of.

For further reading: Carleton, *The Battle of Buena Vista*, 1848; Frost, *The Mexican War and Its Warriors*, 1848; Lavender, *Climax at Buena Vista*, 1966.

Clifford, Nathan
(1803–1881)

As attorney general under President James K. Polk, Nathan Clifford advised Polk on military and political matters during the Mexican-American War and was involved in the ratification of the Treaty of Guadalupe Hidalgo.

Clifford, who was born in New Hampshire, studied law and was admitted to the bar in

Nathan Clifford
(Library of Congress)

1827. Three years later, he entered the political arena as a Democrat in the Maine legislature. After serving as the state's attorney general, he was elected to the House of Representatives in 1838.

Following Polk's election to the presidency, Clifford became Polk's attorney general. One of Clifford's more important roles during the Mexican-American War was as facilitator between President Polk and Secretary of State James Buchanan, who disagreed on how to conduct the war.

As peace negotiations dragged on in late 1847 and early 1848, Clifford was eager to take more Mexican territory. He argued for including the state of Tamaulipas and taking the entire country if Mexico resisted. After the Treaty of Guadalupe Hidalgo had been amended by the U.S. Senate, the changes needed to be approved by the Mexican government. Polk sent Clifford and Senator Ambrose H. Sevier (chairman of the Senate Foreign Affairs Committee) to Mexico to streamline the approval process. Clifford remained in Mexico as minister plenipotentiary to stimulate a new relationship between the two countries.

After his return to the United States in 1848, Clifford moved to Portland, Maine, and practiced law. Under President James Buchanan's administration, Clifford became a Supreme Court justice, a position he held for 23 years. A stroke left him in ill health in 1880, and he died the following year.

See also "All of Mexico" Movement; Guadalupe Hidalgo, Treaty of.

For further reading: Johnson and Malone, *Dictionary of American Biography*, 1928–1936; Pletcher, *The Diplomacy of Annexation*, 1973; Smith, *The War with Mexico*, 1919.

Coahuila y Texas

During 1689–1690, the Spanish government in the province of Coahuila extended its authority to Texas, its neighboring province to the north. This created a simmering resentment between the two states. Texas was occasionally free of Coahuila rule during the eighteenth century as local governments rose and fell.

In 1824, the Mexican Constitution united the two provinces as one state. The capital of Coahuila y Texas was established in Saltillo, and a provincial governor was selected. Texan interests were recognized by the formation of the Department of Texas, a subdivision of the Coahuila y Texas state government. The capital moved from Saltillo to Monclova in 1833. The government tried to appease the increasingly divergent interests of the Texan population, including the appointment of an Anglo-American as a superior judge. The government collapsed shortly afterward into bitter squabbling between Monclova and Saltillo factions. As arbitrator, President Antonio López de Santa Anna ordered that Monclova would remain the seat of government. The situation continued to worsen, including accusations about fraudulent land sales in Texas.

In 1835, Texas representatives voted to separate from Coahuila. Although still recognizing the Mexican Constitution of 1824, Texas established its own provincial government. The increasingly independent behavior of Texas led to the Texas Revolution and the formation of the Republic of Texas in 1836. The break between Texas and Coahuila was not officially recognized by Mexico until the end of the Mexican-American War.

For further reading: Alessio Robles, *Coahuila y Texas desde la consumación de la independencia hasta el tratado de paz de Guadalupe Hidalgo,* 1979; Bancroft, *History of the North Mexican States and Texas,* 1884–1889; Webb, *The Handbook of Texas,* 1952.

Cochori, Skirmish at
(January 30, 1848)

Cochori was the site of a skirmish between a small U.S. Navy–Marine Corp force and Mexican irregulars on January 30, 1848. The fight destroyed one of the last pockets of Mexican resistance in the Guaymas area.

A small fishing village, Cochori was a supply point for U.S. Navy vessels along the Pacific coast. Located on a shallow bay, called La Laguna, about 8 miles east of Guaymas, Indians were supplying the ships with fish and other food. A detachment of Mexicans under the command of a Captain Mendoza moved into the village to break the supply line. On January 30, 1848, Lieutenant Tunis A. M. Craven and more than 100 sailors and Marines crossed La Laguna in small boats from the USS *Dale*. They landed three miles south of Cochori, moved up the coast, surrounded the village, and launched a surprise attack. Mexican losses were 3 killed, 5 wounded, and 15 captured, including the captain. A small amount of weapons and ammunition was also confiscated.

For further reading: Bauer, *Surfboats and Horse Marines,* 1969; Craven, *A Naval Campaign in the Californias—1846–1849,* 1973.

Collado Beach

Collado Beach, a smooth sand beach a few miles south of the port city of Veracruz, was the site in March 1847 of General Winfield Scott's amphibious landing, which began his campaign for Mexico City.

Collado Beach was chosen for the landing because it was out of range of the Veracruz cannons and partially protected by Sacrificios Island, which helped shelter the transport vessels and the beach from strong winds and northers. A reconnaissance had indicated that the Mexican forces had not constructed any defenses there, despite a line of sand hills being approximately 150 yards inland from which a Mexican force could have contested Scott's landing. Only a few skirmishers met the landing parties, and by nightfall more than 10,000 U.S. troops were on the beach.

See also Veracruz, Battle of.

For further reading: Bauer, *Surfboats and Horse Marines,* 1969; Semmes, *Service Afloat and Ashore during the Mexican War,* 1851.

Collins, John L.

An experienced trader in New Mexico and Chihuahua, John L. Collins operated as a scout and interpreter for Colonel Alexander Doniphan's U.S. force that occupied El Paso and Chihuahua during 1846–1847.

Originally from Missouri, Collins was an active participant in the Santa Fe Trail trade between Santa Fe–Chihuahua and the western United States. Colonel Doniphan and his 1,100-man regiment had originally been sent to Chihuahua to join General John E. Wool's command in November 1846. However, during the march, Doniphan was informed that Wool had gone to Saltillo instead. Continuing on to Chihuahua, Doniphan occupied that city in March 1847 and had received no new orders.

On March 20, 1847, Doniphan sent Collins, an experienced trader-scout-interpreter who knew the area well, and an escort of 13 soldiers to carry correspondence cross-country to General Wool in Saltillo. Riding at night to escape detection and the heat, the party crossed deserts and mountain passes. They eventually ran out of water; on one occasion, their desperate thirst took them miles off course as they pursued a shimmering mirage. Close to complete exhaustion, they finally found water at Río Conchos.

Collins proved to be a good leader and negotiator as they passed through the villages of Saucillo, La Cruz, Mapimi, and San Sebastian. When challenged near San Sebastian by a large group of Mexicans who demanded to see their passports, Collins reportedly raised his rifle and said "These are our passports, sir, and we think they are sufficient." Collins and his men arrived on April 2 in Saltillo and reported to General Wool.

After a week's rest, Collins and his party

began their long and hazardous route back to Chihuahua on April 9, complete with fresh horses and a 26-man squadron of cavalry under Captain Albert Pike. They arrived in Chihuahua without incident on April 23, 1847.

See also Doniphan's March.

For further reading: Allsopp, *The Life Story of Albert Pike*, 1920; Brown, "The Mexican War Experiences of Albert Pike and the 'Mounted Devils' of Arkansas," 1953; Hughes, *Doniphan's Expedition, Containing an Account of the Conquest of New Mexico*, 1973; Smith, *The War with Mexico*, 1919.

Colorado

The first inhabitants of what is present-day Colorado were the Plains tribes, including the Arapaho, Cheyenne, Comanche, Kiowa, and Ute Nations. Spanish explorers from New Spain first entered the territory in the mid-1500s. The eastern part of the state, originally claimed by France in 1682, was purchased by the United States in 1803 as part of the Louisiana Purchase. The western portion of the state remained a possession of New Spain as part of the provinces of Alta California and New Mexico. When it gained independence from Spain in 1821, Mexico acquired ownership of this area.

Bent's Old Fort in southern Colorado was an important stopover and supply point for Brigadier General Stephen Watts Kearny's Army of the West when it marched into New Mexico in 1846. As per the Treaty of Guadalupe Hidalgo in 1848, Alta California and Nuevo Mexico were given to the United States at the end of the Mexican-American War. The territory of Colorado became a U.S. state in 1876.

For further reading: Bancroft, *History of Nevada, Colorado and Wyoming*, 1890.

Conner, David
(1792–1856)

One of the most able leaders in the U.S. Navy, Commodore David Conner commanded the blockade of the Mexican gulf coast and the highly successful amphibious landing of 10,000 U.S. troops at Veracruz during the Mexican-American War.

Conner, who was born in Harrisburg, Pennsylvania, was appointed a midshipman in the U.S. Navy in 1809. He was severely wounded in the hip during the War of 1812 and was required to use crutches for two years. Conner later had commands in the Pacific, West Indies, and Mediterranean. He was unquestionably one of the best commanders in the U.S. Navy at the start of the Mexican-American War.

Conner commanded naval forces (U.S. Home Squadron) in the Gulf of Mexico. In 1846, his ships blockaded port cities along the Mexican gulf coast and attacked Alvarado, Tabasco, and Tampico. Because of the shallow coastal waters and his lack of small steamers, Conner was cautious using his larger ships, and this caution frustrated President James K. Polk.

Under Conner's direction, the first U.S. amphibious landing of a large military force was a tremendous success, placing more than 10,000 men on the beach in five hours at Veracruz in March 1847. Conner was replaced on March 21 by his second in command, Matthew C. Perry. Conner had been ill, and it was a good time for Polk to install a more aggressive leader.

Conner briefly commanded the Philadelphia Naval Yard in 1850. He retired in Philadelphia and died there at the age of 64.

See also Alvarado; Navy, United States.

For further reading: Bauer, *Surfboats and Horse Marines*, 1969; Conner, *The Home Squadron under Commodore Conner in the War with Mexico*, 1896; Knox, *A History of the United States Navy*, 1936; Semmes, *Service Afloat and Ashore during the Mexican War*, 1851; Smith, *The War with Mexico*, 1919.

Contreras, Battle of
(August 20, 1847)

The 1847 Battle of Contreras (known to Mexicans as the Battle of Padierna), fought between General Winfield Scott's Army of Occupation and General Gabriel Valencia's Army of the North, lasted only approximately 20 minutes before the Mexican forces retreated in disorder.

After the fall of Veracruz and Cerro Gordo to General Scott's advancing army, General Antonio López de Santa Anna deployed his troops about five miles outside Mexico City. Most of his men were placed at San Angel,

Coyoacán, and Churubusco, a few miles from the city's gates. From north of Mexico City, Santa Anna ordered General Valencia and approximately 6,000 men from the Army of the North to occupy San Angel. Without orders, Valencia took his men three miles further south to a position just west of the Indian village of Padierna (which the U.S. forces mistook for the nearby village of Contreras). On August 18, 1847, fearing that Valencia was too exposed, Santa Anna ordered him to fall back to Coyoacán and to send his artillery to Churubusco; Valencia refused.

Valencia believed that his position in the low hills overlooking Padierna could be assaulted only via the road between San Agustín and Padierna; any efforts to flank his army would be blocked by the *pedregal*, the jagged lava field in his front and to his left.

Scott's army began to arrive at San Agustín on August 18. Careful reconnaissance by engineer Captain Robert E. Lee discovered a route through the *pedregal* that could be widened for wagons and artillery. Accepting Lee's recommendations, Scott decided to attack Valencia the following day.

Five hundred men from General Gideon Pillow's division toiled on August 19 to cut the road through the lava field that one soldier called a "raging sea of molten rock." An artillery duel developed between Valencia's 22 artillery pieces and U.S. guns under Captain John Magruder. Valencia let Pillow's forces move cautiously forward to position themselves in his front. Meanwhile, Santa Anna advanced southward from Churubusco with a large force to assist Valencia and, at dark, stopped less than two miles from Padierna.

General Persifor Smith, the commander of the 5,000 U.S. soldiers in Valencia's front, had decided to attack in the morning. A cold rainstorm swept across the hills that soaked both armies. For some unexplained reason, Santa Anna moved back toward Coyoacán, which completely demoralized Valencia's men. (Santa Anna's refusal to help Valencia is considered by many to be a result of their political and military rivalry.) The U.S. troops struck hard at daybreak on August 20, and the Battle of Contreras lasted about 20 minutes before Valencia's soldiers were running northward in full retreat.

Valencia lost approximately 700 in killed and wounded, and 813 were taken prisoner, including four generals. Learning that an infuriated Santa Anna had ordered him shot on sight, Valencia escaped through the backcountry. Smith's victorious soldiers pursued the fleeing Mexican army relentlessly toward its defenses at Churubusco, about 5 miles north along the road. Santa Anna quickly decided to send as many of his soldiers as possible to Mexico City; the Battle of Churubusco, his delaying action, was fought a few hours later.

See also Churubusco, Battle of; Valencia, Gabriel.

For further reading: Alcaraz, *The Other Side*, 1850; Brooks, *A Complete History of the Mexican War, 1846–1848*, 1849; Grant, *Personal Memoirs of U. S. Grant*, 1885; Smith, *To Mexico with Scott*, 1917.

Cooke, Philip St. George
(1809–1895)

A capable and diplomatic officer assigned to General Stephen Watts Kearny's Army of the West, Philip St. George Cooke dealt with New Mexican leaders during Kearny's occupation of New Mexico in 1846 and later led the Mormon Battalion to California during 1846–1847.

Cooke, who was born in Virginia, graduated from the U.S. Military Academy in 1827 and was assigned to the 6th U.S. Infantry. After serving in the Black Hawk War in 1832, he was appointed first lieutenant of the 1st Dragoons and fought Indians on the western frontier.

During the Mexican-American War, Cooke served with General Stephen Watts Kearny's Army of the West in New Mexico and California. With 12 men, Cooke rode ahead of Kearny from Bent's Fort to Santa Fe in the role of negotiator and peacemaker, but encountered no resistance. In Santa Fe, he held discussions with local political and military leaders, including Diego Archuleta. Cooke was made lieutenant colonel of the Mormon Battalion, when it arrived later in Santa Fe. Cooke wrote that "It was enlisted too much by families; some were too old, some feeble, and some too young; it was embarrassed by many women; it was undisciplined; it was much worn by traveling on foot." Cooke drilled the men incessantly and, leaving most of the family members behind, left Santa Fe on October 19, 1846. Accomplishing their task of opening a wagon road through the mountains of California, they arrived in San Diego on January 29, 1847.

After the war, as major of the 2nd Dragoons, Cooke operated across the western frontier, skirmished with Indians, and wrote a manual of cavalry tactics for the U.S. Army. During the Civil War, he was a Union brigadier general and saw action in the early years of the war. Cooke retired in 1873, wrote his memoirs, and died in Detroit at the age of 86.

See also Kearny's March; Mormon Battalion.

For further reading: Cooke, *The Conquest of New Mexico and California,* 1878; Cooke, *Scenes and Adventures in the Army,* 1857; Golder, "The March of the Mormon Battalion from Council Bluffs to California," 1928; Johnson and Malone, *Dictionary of American Biography,* 1928–1936; Tyler, *A Concise History of the Mormon Battalion in the Mexican War 1846–1847,* 1964.

Cooke's March

See Mormon Battalion.

Cooper, James Fenimore

(1789–1851)

An influential writer during the Mexican-American War, James Fenimore Cooper supported the war effort and believed that the U.S. government would bring fair and democratic rule to the Mexican people.

Born in New Jersey to wealthy parents, Cooper lived in Cooperstown, New York, a town founded by his father. Cooper entered Yale in 1806, but was dismissed at age 16. He began his literary career in the 1820s after a short term in the U.S. Navy. His second novel, *The Spy,* was an immediate success. *The Last of the Mohicans,* a novel published in 1826, won him international fame.

Cooper believed that the Mexican-American War was part of a worldwide mission to spread democracy. Although he favored a negotiated peace, once the war had begun he supported it enthusiastically. Cooper stated that the purpose of the war was to bring the "inestimable blessings of real liberty" to Mexico. As his career began to fade in the 1840s, he wrote the Mexican-American War novel called *Jack Tier; or the Florida Reef,* which had the theme of a benevolent U.S. government that rescued a troubled Mexico that had "suffered from ambitious rulers, and from military rule, while we have been advancing under the arts of peace, favored by a most beneficent Providence."

Cooper's last novel was *The Ways of the Hour* (1850). He remained in Cooperstown, where he died at the age of 62.

For further reading: Cooper, *The Correspondence of James Fenimore Cooper,* 1971; Cooper, *The History of the Navy of the United States of America,* 1853; Johnson and Malone, *Dictionary of American Biography,* 1928–1936.

Corpus Christi

Corpus Christi, a village along the Texas coast, was the first campsite for General Zachary Taylor's newly mobilized Army of Occupation during the winter of 1845–1846.

After President James K. Polk ordered Taylor to move his Army of Occupation from Fort Jesup, Louisiana, to Texas, Taylor transferred his men to Corpus Christi. Henry Lawrence Kinney, an early settler who had arrived there in 1832, had developed a thriving trade with the Mexicans at Matamoros. Known more by the name "Kinney's Ranch," the community on Corpus Christi Bay had about 30 houses, 100 people, evergreens, and a pastoral appearance.

Kinney's property was taken over by General Taylor when the army arrived by steamboat. Kinney was angered, but eventually came to terms with Taylor.

Taylor's first troops arrived in July 1845. Captain W. S. Henry wrote that "Kinney seems to have a government of his own here, and to be alternately the friend and foe of Mexicans, Texans, Americans, and Indians...." Captain E. Kirby Smith remembered Corpus Christi as being "the most delightful spot on the globe, cool, healthy, no insects, not a mosquito, an abundance of oysters, fish, and venison, but unfortunately no wood to cook with."

The 4,000 troops quickly erected an orderly "canvas town." With no immediate plans to move, the army created its own entertainment, such as an 800-seat theater under the direction of Captain John Magruder. Soldiers painted sets and acted in plays. Captain Ulysses S. Grant played Desdemona in Shakespeare's *Othello*. Other enjoyments were Mexican food and good fishing in the ocean. Always the entrepreneur, Kinney assisted in the publication of a weekly newspaper called *La Estrella Americana*.

As time passed, the troops became less disciplined; drinking, brawling, gambling, and deserting increased. Within six months, the population of Corpus Christi had grown to more than 2,000 residents, mostly owners of new businesses such as brothels, gambling houses, and saloons. A soldier remembered it as being the "most murderous, thieving, gambling, cutthroat, God-forsaken hole in the Lone Star State."

The winter of 1845–1846 proved to be cold and miserable. The tents were rotten and leaked, and everything was damp. Cold winds howled from the north and west. "Troops, after being drenched all day, and without fires to dry by, slept miserably at night in wet blankets on the wet ground," complained a soldier. Because firewood was scarce, campfires were usually not permitted. The drinking water was also brackish. Nearly a quarter of Taylor's army suffered from diarrhea and dysentery in the winter months.

The soldiers finally struck camp eagerly on March 8, 1946, and marched southward to the Río Grande. "Corpus Christi looked perfectly deserted," recalled Captain W. S. Henry. "The field of white canvas was no longer visible; and the camp ground looked like desolation itself...."

The site was used as an army depot until 1855. The community continued to grow, and Corpus Christi became the county seat of newly organized Nueces County in 1846. A gathering place for wagons heading west to the California gold fields, the city later became an important wool, cattle, and oil center.

See also Kinney, Henry Lawrence.

For further reading: Henry, *Campaign Sketches of the War with Mexico*, 1847; Patch, *The Concentration of General Zachary Taylor's Army at Corpus Christi, Texas*, 1962; Smith, *To Mexico with Scott*, 1917; Smith and Judah, *Chronicles of the Gringos*, 1968; Webb, *The Handbook of Texas*, 1952.

Corwin, Thomas
(1794–1865)

Thomas Corwin, a Whig senator from Ohio during the Mexican-American War, spoke out so vigorously against the conflict that he alienated antiwar members of his own party. He was later minister to Mexico.

Born in Kentucky, Corwin grew up in Ohio. He became a successful attorney and long-term member in the state's general assembly. As his political career evolved, he became a U.S. representative, the governor of Ohio, and a U.S. senator from 1844 to 1850.

As a member of the Whigs, Corwin supported Henry Clay's opposition to the Mexican-American War. Corwin insisted that the war was strictly for territorial gain, and he opposed all appropriations for more troops and funds.

On February 11, 1847, Corwin delivered a speech that condemned the war and predicted sectional problems over slavery if new territory was added. He went on to proclaim that, if he were a Mexican, he would ask the United States "Have you not room in your own country to bury your dead men? If you come into mine, we will greet you with bloody hands and welcome you to hospitable graves." This statement shocked both Whigs and Democrats alike, who attacked his "traitorous" views.

During President Millard Fillmore's administration, Corwin was secretary of the treasury. He was elected as a Republican to the House of Representatives in 1858 and opposed slavery in the new territories. During the Civil War, he was minister to Mexico. Corwin died in 1865, a few months after returning to Washington to open a law practice.

For further reading: Johnson and Malone, *Dictionary of American Biography*, 1928–1936; Morrow, *The Life and Speeches of Thomas Corwin*, 1896; Weems, *To Conquer a Peace*, 1974.

Cos, Martín Perfecto de
(1800–1854)

General Martín Perfecto de Cos commanded a small contingent of Mexican troops during the U.S. attack in 1847 on the port of Tuxpan, which he was forced to evacuate.

Cos was born in Veracruz. He joined the Spanish Army in 1820 and was quickly promoted to lieutenant. His engineering skills were applied to the construction of defenses along Mexico's gulf coast. After supporting General Antonio López de Santa Anna in overthrowing Agustín de Iturbide's administration in 1823, Cos eventually became a brigade general in the Mexican army. His troops helped suppress rebel outbreaks in Zacatecas and Monclova, but he was later captured by rebellious Texans in December 1835. He also fought at the battles of the Alamo and San Jacinto in 1836.

Cos did not have a prominent leadership role during the Mexican-American War. He commanded approximately 400 soldiers at the port of Tuxpan on the Gulf of Mexico in March 1847. At the request of the citizens who worried about the town's safety, Cos removed his troops a short distance. U.S. naval forces occupied the city after brief skirmishing with Cos, whose men soon scattered.

After the war, Cos was the well-respected commandant general of the Territory of Tehuantepec. He died in Minatitlán, Veracruz, at the age of 54.

For further reading: Bancroft, *History of the North Mexican States and Texas,* 1884–1889; Chamberlain, *My Confession,* 1956; DePalo, *The Mexican National Army, 1822–1852,* 1997; *Diccionario Porrúa,* 1995; Smith, *The War with Mexico,* 1919.

Couch, Darius
(1822–1897)

An artillery officer with the U.S. Army, First Lieutenant Darius Couch performed well during the American victories at Buena Vista and in the Veracruz–Mexico City campaign.

Darius Couch was born on a farm in New York. He graduated from the U.S. Military Academy in 1846. After receiving his commission as a second lieutenant in the 4th U.S. Artillery, he was sent to Mexico, where he spent his first few months bedridden with fevers.

Couch handled his guns well as part of Captain John M. Washington's artillery battery that was posted in the road at La Angostura (the narrows) during the Battle of Buena Vista on February 23, 1847. After serving with General Winfield Scott in the Veracruz–Mexico City campaign, Couch was promoted to first lieutenant on December 4, 1847.

Couch resigned from the army after the war and participated in expeditions to Mexico during 1853–1854 to collect zoological specimens for the Smithsonian Institute. During the Civil War, he was a brigadier general for the Union and performed well from the Battle of Fair Oaks to Bentonville in 1865. He retired to Connecticut, where he died at the age of 75.

See also Buena Vista, Battle of.

For further reading: Henry, *The Story of the Mexican War,* 1950; Johnson and Malone, *Dictionary of American Biography,* 1928–1936; Lavender, *Climax at Buena Vista,* 1966.

Court of Inquiry, Scott
(1847)

In response to subversive reports about his alleged poor leadership during the Veracruz–Mexico City campaign, Major General Winfield Scott arrested General Gideon J. Pillow, General William J. Worth, and Colonel James Duncan on insubordination charges in November 1847. President James K. Polk then relieved Scott of command and called for a court of inquiry, which cleared Scott of all misconduct charges.

Pillow, a volunteer general and close friend of Polk, had become Scott's second-ranking commander, largely through political favoritism. Pillow had not performed well at the Battle of Cerro Gordo, and Scott did not fully trust his military judgment. Other problems emerged. In a report dated August 24, 1847, Pillow took credit for the victories at the Battles of Contreras and Churubusco. He also tried to steal a Mexican cannon as a souvenir, for which he was reprimanded by Scott.

Stories that glorified Pillow's battle roles and ridiculed Scott's leadership began to appear in U.S. newspapers. The New Orleans *Delta* stated that "[A Mexican] made one terrible charge at our General [Pillow] with his lance, which the latter evaded with great promptitude and avidity, using his sword, tossed the weapon of the Mexican high in the air and then quietly blew his brains out with his revolver."

Some historians have suggested that Pillow had presidential aspirations in 1848 and was trying to increase his fame at Scott's expense. Also, if Scott could be dishonored and removed, Pillow would command the Army of Occupation. More letters appeared in different newspapers that lauded the performances of General William J. Worth and Colonel James Duncan and again attacked Scott. (Duncan later admitted writing these.) Caught in the middle and offended by Scott's comments about this "scandalous" behavior, Worth wrote to Polk and accused Scott of "arbitrary and illegal conduct, [of] malicious and gross injustice." Pillow then asked the president to dismiss Scott's court-martial charges regarding his stolen cannon.

Disgusted and infuriated, Scott ordered Pillow, Duncan, and Worth arrested for insubordination in November 1847. This action enraged Polk, who called Scott vain and "tyrannical." On February 18, 1848, Scott received notification from Secretary of War William L. Marcy that he had been relieved of command and that a court of inquiry would be convened to investigate the entire matter.

Begun in Mexico City in March 1848 and concluded in Frederick, Maryland, the court of inquiry cleared Scott of all allegations and chastised Pillow's behavior. Many believe that the court-martial damaged Scott's presidential appeal. He lost the Whig nomination to Zachary Taylor in 1848.

For further reading: Dufour, *The Mexican War, a Compact History, 1846–1848,* 1968; Elliott, *Winfield Scott,* 1937; Scott, *Memoirs of Lieutenant General Scott,* 1864; Sellers, *James K. Polk, Continentalist, 1843–1846,* 1966; Smith, *The War with Mexico,* 1919.

Couto, José Bernardo
(1803–1862)

A prominent politician in Mexico City, Couto played an important role in the negotiation and ratification of the Treaty of Guadalupe Hidalgo in 1848.

Couto was born to an affluent family in Orizaba, Veracruz. He graduated with a law degree in 1827 in Mexico City. In the 1830s and 1840s, he was a member of the *moderado* faction and the Mexican Congress. In 1845, he was briefly José Joaquín de Herrera's minister of justice.

Couto's greatest contribution during the Mexican-American War was in negotiating the Treaty of Guadalupe Hidalgo. Couto was one of the four commissioners selected by General Antonio López de Santa Anna to negotiate with U.S. envoy Nicholas P. Trist in August 1847, and his diplomatic skills helped overcome numerous obstacles. As peace commissioner, Couto convinced Trist to continue with negotiations and disobey his orders from President James K. Polk to return to Washington.

Couto realized that a treaty was imperative to prevent all of Mexico being taken by the United States. To that end, he aggressively defended the Treaty of Guadalupe Hidalgo in the spring of 1848 when certain groups opposed its ratification and wanted to continue the war. His tireless efforts during negotiation and ratification were critical to preserving Mexican sovereignty, especially in the face of the growing "All of Mexico" movement in the United States.

Couto retired from politics after the war, wrote several history books, and studied the history of painting in Mexico. He died in Mexico City in 1862.

See also "All of Mexico" Movement; Guadalupe Hidalgo, Treaty of.

For further reading: Costeloe, *The Central Republic in Mexico, 1835–1846,* 1993; *Diccionario Porrúa,* 1995; Griswold del Castillo, *The Treaty of Guadalupe Hidalgo,* 1991; Pletcher, *The Diplomacy of Annexation,* 1973.

Cross, Trueman
(ca. 1795–1846)

Colonel Trueman Cross, killed by Mexican bandits along the Río Grande in April 1846, was the first U.S. casualty of the Mexican-American War.

Cross was born in Maryland. He joined the U.S. Army in 1814. His organizational skills were quickly apparent, and he became assistant quartermaster general in 1838.

As chief quartermaster for General Zachary Taylor's Army of Occupation, Colonel Cross marched from Corpus Christi, Texas, to the Río Grande in the spring of 1846. On April 10, Cross departed the U.S. camp for a solitary ride along the river, but did not return. In case he had become lost, General Taylor ordered a cannon fired to help him find his way back. A week later, a scouting party found his blue coat in the chaparral. On April 21, the remains of Colonel Cross were discovered by a Mexican farmer. Cross had been stripped of his clothing, and his skull was crushed. His death was attributed to bandits led by Rámon Falcón.

The first U.S. casualty of the war, his flag-draped body was carried to his grave in Fort Texas on April 24 by a caisson and six horses. The proceedings were watched by hundreds of Mexicans across the river in Matamoros, who crowded the rooftops and riverbanks.

For further reading: Frost, *The Mexican War and Its Warriors*, 1848; Weems, *To Conquer a Peace*, 1974.

Cuevas, Luis Gonzago
(1800–1867)

A prominent member of the Mexican government during the Mexican-American War, Luis Gonzago Cuevas was involved in the negotiation, writing, and ratification of the Treaty of Guadalupe Hidalgo in 1848.

Cuevas was born to an affluent family in Lerma, Mexico. He attended college and became active in politics by the time he was 25 years old. He served in various foreign affairs roles, often as a foreign minister, for the Mexican government from 1826 to 1838.

While serving as minister to France in 1836, Cuevas condemned the aggressiveness of the United States and hoped that other Spain-controlled states south of Mexico would help "defend Mexico against an always threatening enemy, which with its ever monstrous greed seems a volcano ready to burst upon them."

In 1845, as Mexican minister of foreign relations under President José Joaquín de Herrera, Cuevas wrote that "Mexico has been left no choice except to fight the United States." After Herrera was overthrown by General Mariano Paredes y Arrillaga, Cuevas retired from governmental affairs. He left Mexico City for Querétaro with the Mexican Congress as General Winfield Scott prepared to occupy the capital in 1847.

An important part of the peace process, Cuevas negotiated almost daily with Nicholas P. Trist in 1848. He later wrote that "of [Trist] there remain in Mexico none but grateful and honoring recollections." Cuevas drafted certain sections of the Treaty of Guadalupe Hidalgo and later defended it before the Mexican Congress.

After the war, Cuevas retired to write a political history of Mexico. He died in Mexico City in 1867.

For further reading: Cárdenas de la Peña, *Tiempo y tarea de Luis Gonzaga Cuevas*, 1982; Cuevas, *Porvenir de México*, 1851; *Diccionario Porrúa*, 1995.

Cushing, Caleb
(1800–1879)

A well-respected lawyer and politician from Massachusetts, Caleb Cushing helped organized the 1st Massachusetts Volunteers in 1847. Accepting an appointment as brigadier general, he arrived too late in Mexico to participate in combat.

Born to a wealthy family in Massachusetts, Cushing entered Harvard University at age 13. After graduating in 1817, he taught mathematics and became a lawyer. After almost a decade in state politics, in 1834 Cushing was elected to the House of Representatives, where he served four consecutive terms. President John Tyler nominated Cushing as his secretary of the treasury, but he was rejected by the Senate. Tyler later appointed him commissioner to China.

In 1846, Cushing was one of the few northern congressmen who supported a war against Mexico. Eager to fight, he spent $12,000 of his own money to help organize and lead the 1st Massachusetts Volunteers. On April 14, 1847, he accepted a commission of brigadier general of volunteers. By the time he arrived in Mexico City in December 1847, the fighting had ended. He was not a natural military leader, and his efforts at harsh discipline alienated his troops. Cushing participated in the Scott-Worth-Pillow-Duncan court of inquiry in Mexico City during March–April 1848.

After returning to Massachusetts, Cushing became a member of the state supreme court. In 1852, he supported the presidential candidacy of Franklin Pierce and became his attorney general (1853–1857). Stating that "I have no desire to survive the overthrow of the United States," he zealously supported President Abraham Lincoln during the Civil War. After the war, he was a trusted advisor to Presidents Andrew Johnson and Ulysses S. Grant. He died from the effects of erysipelas in 1879.

See also Court of Inquiry, Scott.

For further reading: Fuess, *The Life of Caleb Cushing*, 1923; Johnson and Malone, *Dictionary of American Biography*, 1928–1936.

D

Dallas, George Mifflin
(1792–1864)

A former U.S. senator and foreign minister, George M. Dallas served as vice-president during President James K. Polk's administration and supported the Mexican-American War.

Dallas was born in Philadelphia, Pennsylvania, and received an excellent education at Princeton University. After graduating in 1810, he chose a career in law. Dallas was later drawn to local, state, and national politics, with stints as mayor of Philadelphia, U.S. senator (1831–1833), state attorney general (1833–1835), and foreign minister to Russia (1837–1839).

Presidential candidate Polk's first choice as running mate was Silas Wright, who declined the nomination. Polk then turned to Dallas. Although they disagreed on certain issues, the Polk-Dallas ticket was calculated by the Democratic Party to have broader appeal to the U.S. public.

Dallas served as the vice-president of the United States from 1845 to 1849. Polk did not rely on Dallas as much as he did other members of his cabinet, such as Secretary of State James Buchanan. Although he was a moderate, Dallas supported Polk's war plan and presided over the Senate during the Wilmot Proviso debate.

As President Franklin Pierce's foreign minister to Great Britain, Dallas was a key player in U.S.-British relations regarding Latin America from 1856 to 1861. He died in Philadelphia at the age of 72.

For further reading: Belohlavek, *George Mifflin Dallas,* 1977; Sellers, *James K. Polk, Continentalist 1843–1846,* 1966.

Dalton, Patrick
(ca. 1824–1847)

A U.S. deserter and member of the San Patricio Battalion of the Mexican Army, Irishman Patrick Dalton was executed by order of General Winfield Scott following the Battle of Chapultepec.

Dalton was born in Ireland. He immigrated to the United States and enlisted in the 2nd U.S. Infantry. A member of General Zachary Taylor's Army of Occupation in northern Mexico, he deserted from the U.S. camp at Camargo on October 23, 1846.

Dalton was commissioned a first lieutenant in the Mexican Army. He was promoted to captain and second in command of the St. Patrick's (San Patricio) Battalion—approximately 200 men, mostly deserters, under the leadership of John Reily.

The San Patricio Battalion became known as one of the hardest-fighting units in the Mexican army and was hated by the U.S. soldiers. Dalton was an able commander and was captured after a desperate, hand-to-hand fight at Churubusco on August 20, 1847. During his court-martial, he maintained that he had been captured by Mexican rancheros and that he was later taken to Santa Anna, "who asked me whether I would join the artillery or not. I told him how I had been taken and that I did not come there to be a soldier in the Mexican Army. He said he would not compel me to soldier, but at the same time told me I was in danger of my life if I proceeded further, and having no means to live, I concluded that it was better to join the army until I could get an opportunity to leave it." Conflicting testimony revealed that Dalton coerced, or physically forced, other U.S. soldiers to join the battalion.

Dalton was sentenced to death. On September 10, 1847, Dalton and 15 others, dressed in their Mexican uniforms with white sacks over their heads, stood on wagons as nooses were tightened around their necks. Teamsters drove out the wagons, and "they all, but one, died without a struggle; the exception, who was named Dalton, was literally choked to death." (Miller 1989)

See also Churubusco, Battle of; San Patricio Battalion.

For further reading: Miller, *Shamrock and Sword*, 1989.

Davis, Jefferson

(1808–1889)

Colonel Jefferson Davis, whose leadership saved the U.S. left flank during the Battle of Buena Vista in February 1847, was one of General Zachary Taylor's best volunteer officers during Taylor's campaign in northern Mexico.

Davis was born in Christian (Todd) County, Kentucky, and entered the U.S. Military Academy at age 16. He graduated in 1828 as a second lieutenant and served in the Black Hawk War. In 1835, he married Sarah Taylor, the daughter of then Colonel Zachary Taylor.

After resigning from the military in 1835 and settling in Mississippi, Davis developed a prosperous plantation. A slave owner, Davis was bitterly opposed to abolition.

Having been newly elected to the House of Representatives when the Mexican-American War was declared, Davis resigned to lead the 1st Mississippi Volunteer Regiment. Part of General Taylor's Army of Occupation in northern Mexico, Davis bravely led his troops during the Battle of Monterrey in September 1846 and helped draft the Armistice of Monterrey. With a bullet in his foot, his unflinching leadership of the "Mississippi Rifles" during the Battle of Buena Vista helped repel Mexican attacks on Taylor's crumbling left flank and ultimately contributed to the U.S. victory. The Mississippi Rifles were one of the hardest fighting and best behaved of the volunteer regiments, largely because of Davis's military background and insistence on constant drilling.

Davis returned to the United States in 1847 and served as a U.S. senator from 1847 to 1854. He condemned any restrictions on the institution of slavery. As the resourceful and innovative secretary of war under President Franklin Pierce, Davis worked to improve the army's tactical training, weaponry, and engineering capabilities. He was one of the strongest proponents for acquiring more Mexican territory through the Gadsden Purchase.

As the president of the Confederate States of America (CSA) during the Civil War, Davis failed to gain recognition for the CSA from Europe. Although Davis was sometimes a brilliant administrator and planner, he often misjudged people and frequently alienated the Confederate Congress. After the Civil War, he was imprisoned for treason by the federal government. Horace Greeley and Gerrit Smith, two abolitionists, paid his bail in 1867 to free him. His health failing, Davis retired to Mississippi, where he died in 1889.

For further reading: Carleton, *The Battle of Buena Vista*, 1848; Chance, *Jefferson Davis's Mexican War Regiment*, 1991; Cullum, *Biographical Register of the Officers and Graduates of the United States Military Academy from 1802 to 1867*, 1879; Davis, *Jefferson Davis, Ex-president of the Confederate States of America*, 1890; Johnson and Malone, *Dictionary of American Biography*, 1928–1936; McElroy, *Jefferson Davis, the Unreal and the Real*, 1937.

Davis, John

(1787–1854)

Known for his opposition to the Mexican War, Whig Senator John Davis voted against the declaration of war against Mexico and filibustered President James K. Polk's $2 million appropriations bill in 1846.

"Honest John" Davis was born in Massachusetts, and he graduated from Yale University in 1812. He settled in Worcester, Massachusetts, in 1815 to practice law. A supporter of John Quincy Adams, Davis was elected to Congress for four consecutive terms in the

1820s. After serving as the governor of Massachusetts for two years, Davis became a U.S. senator in 1835.

Opposed to the spread of slavery in any new territories, Davis was one of two senators who voted against the declaration of war with Mexico. His long speech on August 12, 1846, caused the senate session to end without the senate voting on President Polk's proposed $2 million appropriations bill and the attached Wilmot Proviso. As a result, Davis's "unseasonable loquacity" was harshly criticized.

After his term as senator, Davis retired to Worcester, where he died at the age of 67.

See also Wilmot, David.

For further reading: Johnson and Malone, *Dictionary of American Biography*, 1928–1936; Smith, *The War with Mexico*, 1919.

Dayton, Wreck of
(September 13, 1845)

The *Dayton* was a side-wheel steamboat that was used to transport the 4th U.S. Infantry from Camp Jesup, Louisiana, to Corpus Christi, Texas. Its boiler blew up on September 13, 1845, wrecking the ship, instantly killing 8, and wounding 17.

The explosion hurled passengers on the boiler deck high into the air or out into the water. Many of the wounded were seriously burned in a "shocking matter." Captain E. Kirby Smith remembered that "the explosion instantly killed two officers, Lieutenants Higgins and Berry, of the Fourth Infantry, a sergeant, and five men. Some others have since died of their wounds. Captain Crossman and Lieutenant Gordon were thrown some fifty or sixty yards from the boat, but, incredible as it may appear, were not seriously injured."

For further reading: Henry, *Campaign Sketches of the War with Mexico*, 1847; Smith, *To Mexico with Scott*, 1917.

de la Rosa, Luis
(1804–1856)

A *moderado* political activist and Mexican minister of foreign relations, Luis de la Rosa

Luis de la Rosa
(Library of Congress)

helped draft the Treaty of Guadalupe Hidalgo in 1848.

de la Rosa was born in Mineral de los Pinos, Zacatecas. He was well educated and specialized in law. His entrance into the field of politics was as a state legislator. As a *moderado*, he wrote frequent editorials and later helped depose General Antonio López de Santa Anna in 1844.

After briefly serving as minister of finance in 1845, de la Rosa joined in another political revolt—this time overthrowing General and President Mariano Paredes y Arrillaga. Unquestionably a political activist, de la Rosa almost immediately began quarreling with *puro* factions.

de la Rosa was appointed minister of foreign relations in September 1847 and helped oversee the protracted peace negotiations that resulted in the Treaty of Guadalupe Hidalgo in 1848. His concern over U.S. changes to the treaty resulted in the Protocol of Querétaro, which called for additional changes and clarifications.

Following the war, de la Rosa was minister to the United States in 1848. He was defeated in Mexico's 1851 presidential election and later assumed the familiar role of minister of foreign relations in 1855. He died in Mexico City in

1856 shortly after he had been appointed chief justice in the Mexican Supreme Court.

See also Guadalupe Hidalgo, Treaty of.

For further reading: Diccionario Porrúa, 1995; Griswold del Castillo, *The Treaty of Guadalupe Hidalgo*, 1991; Santoni, *Mexicans at Arms*, 1996.

Delaware Indians

Approximately 12 men from the Delaware Nation accompanied Colonel John C. Frémont on his expedition to California during 1845–1846 and served as scouts, hunters, and soldiers.

The Delaware Nation (Lenni-Lenape, or "Genuine People") originally lived on the lands that are now Delaware, New Jersey, New York, and Pennsylvania. In 1818, the tribe ceded its lands east of the Mississippi River to the U.S. government and moved to what is now present-day Missouri and Kansas. There they interacted with the Anglo-American fur trade that was centered in St. Louis.

By the start of his third expedition, explorer John C. Frémont had become familiar with the tribe. Frémont wrote that from the "Delaware nation twelve men had been chosen to go with me. These were known to be good hunters and brave men and two of them were chiefs, Swanok and Sagundai." Frémont intended them to work as scouts, hunters, and emissaries, although they were warlike to the other native tribes they encountered. The Delawares hunted buffalo for the 60-man expedition. One of the hunters was named Crane, who was a "good judge of country with a quick eye exercised in hunting. He was one of the men I liked to have near me," wrote Frémont. "He was usually serious and dignified even for an Indian, who are naturally grave men."

The Delawares scouted out trails and Indian encampments. Eager to fight with other Indians, they fought bravely in skirmishes and battles. Crane, Frémont's favorite scout, was killed during a skirmish with Indians at Klamath Lake. In his memoirs, Frémont frequently mentions the Delawares for their acts of courage.

See also Frémont, John C.; Klamath Indians.

For further reading: Frémont, *Memoirs of My Life*, 1886.

Dent, Frederick Tracy
(1821–1892)

Colonel Frederick Dent commanded the 6th U.S. Infantry during General Winfield Scott's Veracruz–Mexico City campaign in 1847 and was severely wounded at the Battle of El Molino del Rey.

Raised in Missouri, Dent graduated from the U.S. Military Academy in 1843. Commissioned a second lieutenant with the 6th U.S. Infantry, he served on the western frontier prior to the Mexican-American War.

Dent was active in most of the battles of Major General Winfield Scott's Veracruz–Mexico City campaign in 1847. Dent led his men in a frontal charge through heavy fire into hand-to-hand combat on September 8, 1847, during the Battle of El Molino del Rey, during which he was wounded in the leg. He received brevets to first lieutenant and colonel for his performances at the Battles of Contreras, Churubusco, and El Molino del Rey.

Dent was assigned to various posts on the western frontier after the war. A brother-in-law to General Ulysses S. Grant, he served on Grant's staff during the Civil War and also during his presidency. Dent retired from service in 1883, and died in 1892 from the effects of a stroke.

For further reading: Cullum, *Biographical Register of the Officers and Graduates of the United States Military Academy from 1802 to 1867*, 1879; Grant, *Personal Memoirs of U. S. Grant*, 1885; Johnson and Malone, *Dictionary of American Biography*, 1928–1936; Weems, *To Conquer a Peace*, 1974.

Desertion

U.S. Soldiers

Approximately 9,000 (approximately 9 percent) of the 104,556 U.S. soldiers that served during the Mexican-American War deserted. Of the 548 U.S. Marines that served, only 8 deserted. Those deserters who were recaptured were often flogged, branded, or shot.

Probably the biggest reason for desertion was the harsh treatment and discipline the soldiers received from commanding officers. This included being flogged, branded, bucked and gagged, or assigned to solitary confinement in an underground pit or to hard labor—often for relatively minor offenses. Regarding the death sentences given to two Maryland volunteers for sleeping on picket duty near Mexico City in November 1847, private J. J. Oswandel wrote "if this kind of court were held in every small division of our army, there wouldn't be many left to fight the Mexicans.... They were tried by regular officers, who, we all know, hold prejudice against the volunteers. Also sentenced was one of our men, named James B. Wilson, who, while intoxicated, took a pair of *socks*, worth fifteen cents, out of a barrel. He was tried, found guilty and sentenced to be taken to the castle of San Juan de Ulloa in irons, and there kept at hard labor, forfeit all his pay, have his head shaved, and remain confined until the termination of the present war, and then receive a dishonorable discharge from the service.... It is one of the most outrageous sentences that has ever been heard of in any civilized country."

George Ballentine, a British soldier in the army, stated that deserters are "driven to the foolish step they had taken by harsh and cruel handling. The barbarous treatment which soldiers sometimes received from ignorant and brutal officers...would seem almost incredible. I have frequently seen foolish young officers violently strike and assault soldiers on the slightest provocation. To tie them up by the wrists, as high as their hands would reach and with a gag in their mouths, was a common punishment for trivial offences." Samuel Chamberlain, a U.S. dragoon, remembered with great bitterness being hung by his thumbs for questioning his commanding officer.

The Mexican government tried to get U.S. soldiers to desert for religious reasons or economic gain. Mexican authorities hired British agents to inform U.S. troops that deserters would receive free land grants and financial assistance for bringing their families to Mexico. Higher military rank was also promised. (Fewer than 300 U.S. soldiers joined the Mexican army during the war.) Catholic soldiers of British or Irish descent received the greatest attention. Leaflets were published that proclaimed that the war was an attack by the U.S. government on the Roman Catholic Church.

General Pedro de Ampudia, commander of the Mexican Army of the North, distributed, near the U.S. camp along the Río Grande in 1846, handbills that were addressed to British soldiers:

> Know ye: That the Government of the United States is committing repeated acts of barbarous aggression against the magnanimous Mexican Nation; that the Government which exists under "the flag of the stars" is unworthy of the designation of Christian. Recollect that you were born in Great Britain; that the American Government looks with coldness upon the powerful flag of St. George, and is provoking to a rupture the warlike people to whom it belongs; President Polk boldly manifesting a desire to take possession of Oregon, as had already done of Texas. Now, then, come with all confidence to the Mexican ranks, and I guarantee to you upon my honor, good treatment, and that all your expenses shall by defrayed until your arrival in the beautiful capital of Mexico.

Mexican Soldiers

Desertion was even more of a problem for the Mexican armies. In addition to suffering harsh disciplinary measures, the Mexican soldier was usually hungry, poorly clothed, and frequently without shelter or medicine. The majority of the army consisted of conscripts from isolated rural areas; they had little interest in fighting the "norteamericanos" or in the unity of the nation in general. In fact, nationalism was poorly developed across the country because the individual provinces were more focused on their self-interests and autonomy. Finally, the conscript was poorly trained and did not have enough time to develop an esprit de corps within their regiments or confidence in their commanders. When General Antonio López de Santa Anna marched his Army of the North from San Luis Potosí toward Saltillo in January 1847, it numbered approximately 20,000 men; by the time it returned after the Battle of La Angostura (Buena Vista), an estimated 4,000 to 5,000 soldiers, or 20 to 25 percent of the fighting force, had deserted. Desertion in the Army of the East, that faced General Winfield Scott in 1847, likely had a similar rate of desertion. Probably at least 10,000 Mexican soldiers had deserted by the end of the war.

See also San Patricio Battalion.

For further reading: Alcaraz, *The Other Side*, 1850; Ballentine, *Autobiography of an English Soldier in the United States Army*, 1853; McCaffrey, *Army of Manifest Destiny*, 1992; Miller, *Shamrock and Sword*, 1989; Oswandel, *Notes of the Mexican War*, 1885; Winders, *Mr. Polk's Army*, 1997.

Diarrhea

Diarrhea was one of the most common, and the most deadly, afflictions that struck the U.S. soldier during the Mexican-American War. Virtually every soldier suffered from it to some degree, and the most serious cases were often fatal.

Actually more of a symptom than a disease, diarrhea was poorly understood by U.S. doctors. It was often a chronic condition that was never cured. Diarrhea was associated with other illnesses such as dysentery, malaria, and yellow fever and could last for months. Patients became weak from dehydration and were often fevered. Chronic diarrhea was extremely debilitating and quickly eroded a soldier's spirits.

Diarrhea was a persistent condition and difficult to treat. It arose from a variety of conditions, such as bad food, polluted water, poor camp sanitation, and lack of personal hygiene. For example, the U.S. camp at Camargo drew its drinking water from the San Juan River, which was contaminated by human and animal waste. Doctors usually treated diarrhea with opium, sulfur or lead compounds, antimony, calomel, bleeding every two or three days, or gentle emetics of torrefied rhubarb, ipecacuanha, and opium.

Diarrhea was often a fatal condition. It could so weaken a soldier that he became susceptible to a wide range of other diseases. More soldiers died of diarrhea than from yellow fever at the U.S. hospital in Veracruz in 1847. A serious outbreak struck General Winfield Scott's men at Puebla. Thousands were hospitalized with diarrhea, and up to 50 men were dying daily from the condition.

For further reading: Brown, *The Medical Department of the United States Army from 1775 to 1873*, 1873; Duncan, "A Medical History of General Zachary Taylor's Army of Occupation in Texas and Mexico, 1845–1847," 1921; Gillett, *The Army Medical Department, 1818–1865*, 1987; Robards, "The Diseases of the Army of Occupation in the Summer of 1846," 1847.

Díaz de la Vega, Rómulo
(ca. 1804–1877)

A brave and capable general in the Mexican army, Rómulo Díaz de la Vega was captured by U.S. forces at the Battle of Resaca de Guerrero (Resaca de la Palma) and later at the Battle of Cerro Gordo, both times for refusing to retreat before the enemy.

Díaz de la Vega was born in Mexico City. He joined the new Mexican army in 1822. A member of the Engineering Battalion, he directed the construction or upgrading of defenses along the Mexican coastline. He performed well during the Texas campaign and against the French at Veracruz in 1838, for which he was promoted to colonel. In 1845, he became a brigade commander in the Army of the North at Monterrey.

Known as a brave and patriotic leader, Díaz de la Vega commanded a regiment of infantry in the Army of the North under General Mariano Arista in 1846. After the U.S. army arrived on the north bank of the Río Grande, Díaz de la Vega rode forward from Matamoros to inform General William J. Worth that the Mexican government considered the U.S. army's presence an act of hostility. Shortly afterward, he led troops at the Battles of Palo Alto and Resaca de Guerrero (Resaca de la Palma) in May 1846. Captured during the Battle of Resaca de la Palma, the general refused parole and was eventually exchanged after being imprisoned in Kentucky.

In January 1847, General Díaz de la Vega, as part of the Army of the East, commanded the first line of defense from Veracruz to Corral Falso, along the National Road. His men had begun making earthworks at the National Bridge until he was ordered by General Antonio López de Santa Anna to abandon them for a stronger position. His unit was held in reserve during the Battle of Cerro Gordo in

April, and Díaz de la Vega was captured by General Winfield Scott's advancing army after refusing to retreat. He was freed in December after being imprisoned for eight months.

Díaz de la Vega remained a prominent military and political figure after the war. He was promoted to general of a division for his handling of the unrest in Yucatán in 1854 and was interim president of Mexico for about two months between the administrations of Santa Anna and Juan Álvarez. A key supporter of Emperor Maximilian in 1863, Díaz de la Vega was later imprisoned in Puebla, where he died impoverished in 1877.

For further reading: Alcaraz, *The Other Side,* 1850; *Diccionario Porrúa,* 1995; Sánchez Lamego, *Generales de ingenieros del ejército mexicano, 1821–1914,* 1952.

Dimick, Justin
(1800–1871)

A capable officer who served under Generals Zachary Taylor and Winfield Scott, Colonel Justin Dimick received two brevets for gallant conduct during the Mexican-American War. He was wounded during the Battle of Chapultepec.

Dimick was born in Connecticut. He attended the U.S. Military Academy from 1814 to 1819 and graduated eleventh in his class of 29. He taught infantry tactics at West Point, was brevetted during the Second Florida War, and served along the Canadian border.

As part of both General Taylor's and General Scott's Armies of Occupation, Dimick saw action at the Battles of Palo Alto and Resaca de la Palma in May 1846. His leadership at the Battles of Contreras and Churubusco resulted in a brevet to lieutenant colonel. He received a brevet to colonel in September 1847 after the Battle of Chapultepec, during which he was wounded. Dimick commanded the occupational troops in the district of Veracruz from 1847 to 1848 and helped oversee the deoccupation of Mexico in 1848.

After the war, Colonel Dimick served in New York, Florida, and Vermont. He retired from his position as prison administrator during the Civil War in 1863 and presided as governor of the "Soldier's Home" in Washington from 1864 to 1868. Dimick died in Philadelphia in 1871.

For further reading: Boatner, *The Civil War Dictionary,* 1959; Cullum, *Biographical Register of the Officers and Graduates of the United States Military Academy from 1802 to 1867,* 1879; Smith, *The War with Mexico,* 1919.

Dominguez, Manuel

Manuel Dominguez was a Mexican citizen and bandit who was employed as a scout and guerrilla fighter by General William J. Worth, as General Winfield Scott's Army of Occupation marched its way to Mexico City in 1847.

After General Worth's troops arrived in Puebla following the Battle of Cerro Gordo, a citizen went to Worth and stressed that Dominguez was a criminal and should be imprisoned. After arresting Dominguez, Worth offered him employment as a courier. Dominguez was immediately put to work in June 1847 and was generally well regarded by the commanding officers. He has been described as both a murdering criminal and a respectable merchant, who, after being ruined by guerrillas, turned to highway robbery.

Lieutenant Henry Judah of the 4th U.S. Infantry wrote that "This captain of robbers is a very fine-looking man with a good face and nothing indicating cruelty about it. He can command by a sign, 10,000 men on the road from Mexico to Vera Cruz; he can give you a passport which will carry you in perfect safety over the worst infested road, and has made a great deal of money by these passes given to rich merchants.… Dominguez says he never killed a man in his life and I do not believe he ever did." Others claimed witness to his attempts to murder Mexican prisoners.

Because of Dominguez's influence, the numerous bands of guerrillas and highwaymen on the National Road from Veracruz to Mexico City stopped robbing, in return for a fee. From June to early August, General Scott disbursed approximately $3,000 to local spies, much of it to Dominguez. By July, Dominguez was the leader of nearly 200 freed criminals that formed the Dominguez (Mexican) Spy Company. They served mostly as scouts and spies and kept the National Road open between the U.S. army and Veracruz. On January 6, 1848, Dominguez captured Generals Antonio Gaona and Anastasio Torrejón in a skirmish near Nopalucan.

Dominguez and his family of nine fled to New Orleans at the conclusion of the war, where they lived in poverty. Colonel Ethan A. Hitchcock appealed on Dominguez's behalf for restitution from the U.S. government, considering his loyalty to the United States and high-risk work. No funds were ever granted.

See also Dominguez's Spy Company.

For further reading: Caruso, The Mexican Spy Company, 1991; Smith and Judah, Chronicles of the Gringos, 1968.

Dominguez's Spy Company (Mexican Spy Company)

Formed by Manuel Dominguez, the Mexican Spy Company consisted of about 200 Mexican criminals hired by General William J. Worth to work as spies, scouts, and guerrilla fighters during General Winfield Scott's Veracruz–Mexico City campaign in 1847.

Mostly bandits and highwaymen, the members of the Mexican Spy Company were chosen by Manuel Dominguez. Freed from jail cells in Puebla and other nearby communities, they were formed into companies and overseen by Colonel Ethan Allen Hitchcock. Each man was paid $20 per month.

The spy company's principal duties were scouting, spying, and carrying messages. They reported activities in towns and along the National Road. Usually successful in penetrating Mexican defenses, they brought back reliable information about troop movements. Occasionally the spies fought as soldiers, as in the pitched battle with guerrillas near Puebla on August 3, 1847. They also joined U.S. troops in a skirmish two weeks later near San Agustín.

The Mexican Spy Company was hated by the Mexican populace and any captured members were immediately killed. Despite this, it was a remarkably loyal and effective unit during Scott's march from Puebla to Mexico City during August–September 1847.

For further reading: Caruso, The Mexican Spy Company, 1991; Smith and Judah, Chronicles of the Gringos, 1968.

Donelson, Andrew Jackson
(1799–1871)

As U.S. minister to the Republic of Texas during 1844–1845, Andrew Jackson Donelson promoted to Texas representatives the political and economic benefits of joining the United States. Partly because of his lobbying efforts, Texas voted on July 4, 1845, to endorse annexation.

Donelson was born in Tennessee. A nephew of Andrew Jackson, he was raised at Jackson's stately home, the "Hermitage." Donelson graduated second in his class from the U.S. Military Academy and served on Jackson's staff during the First Seminole War. He also worked for Jackson during his presidency.

Donelson was appointed U.S. minister to Texas in September 1844 by President John Tyler as a replacement for Tilghman A. Howard, who died of yellow fever. Residing in the Texas capital Washington-on-the-Brazos, Donelson had frequent contact with Duff Green, one of President James K. Polk's secret agents, and in March 1845 presented to the Texas government U.S. proposals for annexation. Influential Texan Henry Lawrence Kinney, a prominent trader and landowner, stressed to Donelson the economic benefits of making the Texas border the Río Grande instead of the Nueces River.

One of the few men who had Polk's confidence, Donelson worked with Polk's agents Charles Anderson Wickliffe and Archibald Yell to spread U.S. goodwill throughout Texas, including promises of military and economic support.

Donelson reported regularly to Secretary of State James Buchanan. On May 24, 1845, Donelson wrote that "I had secret and timely information of every movement calculated to produce delay, and was able to look without apprehension on the…extraordinary efforts of the French and British Ministers to make the execution of our proposals impossible." Donelson worked tirelessly with members of the Texas Congress and persuaded many of them that a threat of Mexican invasion existed.

Texas President Anson Jones, however, did not believe that the threat was as severe as Donelson indicated.

Jones was distrustful of the political favors promised by Donelson and of the pressure from the U.S. government to start a war with Mexico. After Texas voted to accept annexation on July 4, 1845, Donelson returned to Washington in September and briefed President Polk on the state of affairs in Texas.

Later, Donelson became minister to the Kingdom of Prussia from 1846 to 1849. During the U.S. Civil War, he refused to take up the Confederate cause. He died in Memphis in 1871.

For further reading: Caruso, *The Mexican Spy Company,* 1991; Johnson and Malone, *Dictionary of American Biography,* 1928–1936; Parton, *Life of Andrew Jackson,* 1860.

Doniphan, Alexander William
(1808–1887)

A volunteer colonel with little military training, Alexander William Doniphan was one of the most celebrated U.S. combatants of the Mexican-American War. His diplomatic and leadership skills resulted in negotiating a treaty with the Navajo Nation, winning two battles, and completing one of the longest, most arduous marches of the war.

The son of a Revolutionary War soldier, Doniphan was born in Kentucky. After moving to Missouri in 1830, he began a career in law and became a well-known attorney.

Nearly six and one half feet tall and weighing about 240 pounds, Doniphan had sandy red hair that stuck out "like porcupine quills." Doniphan commanded militia troops during the conflict between the state of Missouri and its Mormon population. He disobeyed his commanding officer's order to shoot Prophet Smith and his followers after their court-martial because it would have been cold-blooded murder. (The order was later rescinded.) Doniphan later served in the state legislature in 1836, 1840, and 1854. His sense of humor, calm demeanor, and frequent smile made him a popular militia officer and politician.

At the Missouri governor's request, Doniphan organized the 1st Regiment of Missouri Mounted Volunteers, numbering approximately 1,100 men, for the Mexican-American War. Doniphan enlisted as a private, but was quickly elected colonel, despite that there were others with more military experience in the regiment.

Traveling to Fort Leavenworth, Kansas, Doniphan's command joined General Stephen Watts Kearny's Army of the West. After entering New Mexico and occupying Santa Fe in August 1846, Doniphan helped Kearny draft a constitution for the new U.S. territory. When Kearny left for California in September, Doniphan commanded the military district of New Mexico.

Doniphan rode into the mountains and skillfully negotiated a treaty with the Navajo Nation, which was attacking New Mexican settlements. In December 1846, Doniphan and his regiment of Missourians began a grueling, three-month march from New Mexico to Chihuahua. After winning the Battles of the Brazito and Río Sacramento, they occupied the city of Chihuahua in March 1847 and then marched to Saltillo, where they were discharged.

Doniphan returned to Missouri a hero. He favored Missouri's neutrality on slavery and opposed any invasion of the state by Union or Confederate forces. Resolutely refusing to par-

Alexander W. Doniphan, ca. 1850
(Library of Congress)

ticipate in the Civil War, he settled near St. Louis to take care of his ill wife. He continued his law career and also served as a bank president.

See also Doniphan's March.

For further reading: Connelley, *Doniphan's Expedition and the Conquest of New Mexico and California*, 1907; Edwards, *A Campaign in New Mexico with Colonel Doniphan*, 1847; Hughes, *Doniphan's Expedition, Containing an Account of the Conquest of New Mexico*, 1973; Launius, *Alexander William Doniphan*, 1997.

Doniphan's March
(1846–1847)

Colonel Alexander Doniphan led his 1st Regiment of Missouri Mounted Volunteers on a grueling, 2,500-mile march from Fort Leavenworth, Kansas, to Santa Fe, El Paso, Chihuahua, and Saltillo during 1846–1847. Underequipped and with little military training, the regiment also won the Battles of Brazito and Río Sacramento.

Colonel Doniphan's 1st Missouri Mounted Volunteers arrived at Fort Leavenworth in mid-June 1846. Numbering about 900 men, they were given a rudimentary, two-week military training. Part of Brigadier General Stephen Watts Kearny's Army of the West, they moved out between June 22 and June 28.

The 500-mile march to Bent's Old Fort, Colorado, was dusty and hot, with little water along the route. Soldiers' tongues were swollen from thirst, and many men gulped water that horses refused to drink. The army camped along the Arkansas River on July 29, about 9 miles from Bent's Old Fort, where the troops rested and refitted.

In early August, they continued southward to New Mexico and were briefly part of Kearny's occupational force in Santa Fe. With more reinforcements arriving under Colonel Sterling Price, Kearny decided to send his "excess" troops under Doniphan to Chihuahua to reinforce a small command under General John E. Wool that would be leaving from San Antonio for Chihuahua in September.

Before he could leave, however, Doniphan was instructed to control the hostile Utes and Navajos, who were raiding white settlements. Doniphan sent out patrols that struggled through the harsh October–November weather to meet with Indian leaders. On November 22, at Bear Spring, or Ojo Oso, near present-day Gallup, New Mexico, Doniphan signed a peace treaty with approximately 500 Navajo. Pleased with his negotiating successes, Doniphan stopped on his way back to Santa Fe and facilitated a treaty between the Zuni and Navajo.

By mid-December, Doniphan had approximately 900 mounted men, tired and "much worse by the arduous campaign," assembled at Valverde, New Mexico Territory, on the Río Grande. Also at Valverde were anxious traders, who joined the expedition, with more than 300 wagons full of goods to be sold in Chihuahua.

Leaving for El Paso in mid-December, Doniphan decided to take a more direct route, across a 95-mile-wide desert known as the Jornada del Muerto (Journey of Death), instead of following a wide bend in the Río Grande that would take them far to the west. Although it was cold and windy, with little water and no fuel for fires, the men crossed relatively unscathed in three days.

On Christmas Day, about 30 miles from El Paso near El Brazito (the Mexicans called it Temascalitos), an island in the Río Grande, they fought off an attack by 1,200 Mexican dragoons and militia. Doniphan lost 7 men wounded; Mexican casualties were approximately 200 killed and wounded. After arriving at El Paso on December 27, Doniphan learned that Wool had abandoned his march to Chihuahua, and that the Mexicans were still prepared to defend that city. On February 1, 1847, Doniphan was reinforced with an artillery battery and 117 men.

Doniphan continued southward on February 8 with approximately 1,100 men, six artillery pieces, teamsters, traders, and more than 300 wagons. It was a punishing march to Chihuahua. Plagued by deep sands and little water, the men abandoned equipment and goods to lighten their loads. Scabbards were filled with precious water. "Horse, mule & man vied with each other in drinking out of the same puddles," wrote a veteran. After 200 miles, the army reached Laguna de Encinillas, a shallow, brackish lake. They accidentally started a prairie fire that roared to life with flames 20 feet in height. Wagons were hauled into the water and backfires built to save the supply train.

A new Mexican force decided to make a stand at hacienda Río Sacramento, about 15 miles north of Chihuahua. The Mexicans had developed a good defensive position on the banks of an arroyo, including a reinforced hacienda and connected earthworks. Doniphan daringly split his forces, used his wagons as a fort, and eventually flanked the Mexican position late in the afternoon to win the battle. Doniphan's casualties were surprisingly light—1 man was killed and 11 wounded. Mexican losses were estimated at approximately 600 killed and wounded. Doniphan marched into Chihuahua on March 2, 1847, with the band playing "Yankee Doodle."

During the city's occupation, the soldiers turned private homes into stables, and the public drinking fountain into a bathtub. Doniphan again used his diplomatic skills to arrange for the safety of the traders and merchants who wanted to stay in Chihuahua.

After finally receiving orders to proceed to Saltillo, Doniphan's army moved out on April 25, eastward through the states of Chihuahua, Durango, and Coahuila. On May 22, they passed in ragged review for General John E. Wool at Buena Vista. An observer wrote that "no two men were dressed alike. Most of them were in buckskin hunting-shirts and trousers, and many had their trousers' legs torn. Some were mounted on donkeys, some on mustang ponies, and others on mules…." (Hughes 1973) Two days later they were reviewed by General Zachary Taylor, commander of the Army of Occupation. As Taylor passed, one of the Missourians asked "Well, old man, what do you think of this crowd?" Taylor chuckled and said that it looked like they had seen hard times.

Indeed they had: Doniphan's regiment had marched more than 2,500 miles in desolate and poorly mapped terrain and fought and won two battles. The following day, Doniphan and his men marched northeastward toward the Río Grande and boarded ocean vessels on June 10 that carried them to New Orleans.

For further reading: Connelley, *Doniphan's Expedition and the Conquest of New Mexico and California*, 1907; Edwards, *A Campaign in New Mexico with Colonel Doniphan*, 1847; Hughes, *Doniphan's Expedi-*

A dramatic portrayal of U.S. dragoons engaged against Mexican infantrymen, created ca. 1846 (Library of Congress)

tion, Containing an Account of the Conquest of New Mexico, 1973; Robinson, *A Journal of the Sante Fe Expedition under Colonel Doniphan*, 1932.

Dos Amades

Little is known about this resident/soldier of Monterrey, Nuevo León. She participated in the bitter street fighting during the Battle of Monterrey in September 1846 by putting on a captain's uniform and leading a company of Mexican lancers in a mounted charge. U.S. officers referred to her as a "second Joan of Arc." She survived the battle.

For further reading: Johannsen, *To the Halls of the Montezumas*, 1985.

Dragoons

A form of U.S. light cavalry, dragoons were essentially mounted infantrymen who would fight either on horseback as cavalry or as dismounted infantrymen. Dragoons were armed with pistols, carbines, musketoons, and sabers. The Hall carbine and 1847 cavalry musketoon (a shortened percussion musket) were easier to use in the saddle than the standard infantry musket or rifle.

For further reading: Scott, *Military Dictionary*, 1968; Winders, *Mr. Polk's Army*, 1997.

Drum, Simon H.
(1807–1847)

A talented officer in the 4th U.S. Artillery, Captain Simon H. Drum was killed by heavy crossfire as he commanded his artillery pieces at Belén Gate on the outskirts of Mexico City.

Drum was born in Pennsylvania and attended the U.S. Military Academy from 1825 to 1830. He was commissioned a second lieutenant in the 4th Artillery and served in the Black Hawk War, New York, and the Florida Wars. He was promoted to captain in 1846.

Drum fought capably in all of General Winfield Scott's battles from Veracruz to Mexico City. On September 13, 1847, during the Battle of Belén Gate at Mexico City, Drum was killed by solid shot while directing artillery fire from an exposed position.

For further reading: Cullum, *Biographical Register of the Officers and Graduates of the United States Military Academy from 1802 to 1867*, 1879; Smith, *The War with Mexico*, 1919.

Du Pont, Samuel Francis
(1803–1865)

As part of the Pacific Squadron during the Mexican-American War, U.S. naval commander Samuel Francis Du Pont blockaded the Baja California coast and captured or destroyed 30 Mexican vessels.

Born in New Jersey, Samuel F. Du Pont was raised in New York, Delaware, and Pennsylvania. He was appointed a midshipman in 1815 and served in the Mediterranean, West Indies, and China.

In 1845, Du Pont commanded the frigate *Congress*, the flagship of Commodore Robert F. Stockton. The *Congress* sailed to Monterey, where Stockton assumed control of the U.S. naval forces in the Pacific. When in command of the sloop-of-war *Cyane*, Du Pont transported John C. Frémont's California Battalion to San Diego. In September 1846, Du Pont sailed to San Blas, where a landing party spiked the Mexican guns on shore. Continuing into the Gulf of California, he seized La Paz and

Samuel F. Du Pont
(Library of Congress)

attacked the port city of Guaymas. In March 1847, Du Pont dispatched a landing force at San José that marched three miles inland to rescue imprisoned U.S. soldiers. By the end of the war, Du Pont had captured or destroyed 30 Mexican vessels in the Gulf of California.

Du Pont helped organize the new U.S. Naval Academy at Annapolis following the war and developed curricula for midshipmen. During the Civil War, he commanded the South Atlantic blockading squadron. He was highly criticized for his attack on Charleston in 1863. During that attack, he lost approximately 50 vessels from his fleet, including an armored gunboat. In failing health from various tropical diseases that he had contracted over his career, he resigned and died two years later in Philadelphia.

For further reading: Bauer, *Surfboats and Horse Marines*, 1969; Du Pont, "The War with Mexico," 1882; Johnson and Malone, *Dictionary of American Biography*, 1928–1936; Meadows, *The American Occupation of La Paz*, 1955.

Duran, Augustín

Augustín Duran was one of three New Mexicans who conspired to overthrow the U.S. government in New Mexico in 1846 and assassinate Governor Charles Bent.

A resident of Santa Fe, Duran plotted with Diego Archuleta and Tomás Ortiz to overthrow the U.S. military government in New Mexico. The plot included killing Colonel Sterling Price and Governor Charles Bent. Men were recruited from surrounding areas, including Taos. Scheduled for Christmas, the plan called for small groups of men to hide in the church in Santa Fe. Peeling church bells at midnight would be the signal to capture the artillery in the plaza and kill Price and Bent. Messengers would ride out to inform waiting bands of rebels, and the wave of revolution would be carried into outlying areas. The plans were eventually leaked to Price, and Duran, Ortiz, and Archuleta barely escaped in the night on horseback.

Although the planned attack was never carried out, the Taos Rebellion erupted in January 1847, which resulted in the death of Governor Bent.

See also Taos Rebellion.

For further reading: Keleher, *Turmoil in New Mexico, 1846–1848*, 1952; Lavender, *Bent's Fort*, 1954.

E

Echeagaray, Miguel María
(1816–1891)

The able and aggressive leader of the Mexican 3rd Light Infantry, Lieutenant Colonel Miguel María Echeagaray launched an attack during the Battle of El Molino del Rey that temporarily crippled the U.S. right flank.

Lieutenant Colonel Echeagaray was born in Jalapa, Veracruz. During the Mexican-American War, he commanded the 3rd Light Infantry. While watching the Battle of El Molino del Rey from his position at nearby Chapultepec, and without orders, Echeagaray launched a hard-hitting assault that staggered the U.S. right flank. Echeagaray regained a Mexican battery that had fallen into U.S. hands after bitter hand-to-hand fighting; some of his men slit the throats of the wounded U.S. soldiers. The charge of the 3rd Light Infantry was not supported, and eventually the regiment fell back stubbornly to Chapultepec. Echeagaray fought bravely during the Battle of Chapultepec in September 1847 and coolly led his men in retreat toward San Cosmé *garita* (gate) outside Mexico City. During that retreat, he directed several rear-guard actions.

Echeagaray remained in the military after the war and commanded the garrison at Colima. Opposed to French intervention, he participated in the Mexican victory at Jiquilpan. His troops were defeated in 1865 at the city of Guzmán. He remained politically active in various administrations until about 1880. He died in Mexico City in 1891.

See also El Molino del Rey, Battle of.

For further reading: Alcaraz, *The Other Side*, 1850; *Diccionario Porrúa*, 1995; Smith, *The War with Mexico*, 1919.

El Bosque de San Domingo
See Walnut Springs.

El Brazito, Battle of
(December 25, 1846)

Fought on December 25, 1846, the Battle of El Brazito was a clash between Colonel Alexander Doniphan's 1,100-man force and 2,000 Mexicans commanded by Lieutenant Colonel Luis Vidal and Lieutenant Colonel Antonio Ponce de León. More accurately called a skirmish, the fight resulted in a U.S. victory.

The state of Chihuahua could not be properly defended by the Mexican government, which was nearly bankrupt and fighting the U.S. Army of Occupation in northern Mexico. President James K. Polk was eager to occupy Chihuahua City, an important trading center. Colonel Doniphan and approximately 1,100 men had left New Mexico in early December to march to Chihuahua. The Mexican government responded to the threat by sending a thousand muskets and ammunition to Chihuahua. Ángel Trías Álvarez, governor of Chihuahua, pulled together a makeshift army, collected more weapons, and built a cannon foundry. The 2,000-man force was a mix of volunteers, cavalry, and national guardsmen.

The men, commanded by Lieutenant Colonel Vidal, had barely started drilling when Doniphan's regiment approached El Paso del Norte (present-day Juárez, Mexico). Vidal sent his second in command, Lieutenant Colonel Ponce de León, and about 600 men forward on December 24 to locate Doniphan. Discovering the U.S. soldiers along the Río Grande across from Temascalitos Island (called El Brazito by the U.S. troops) about 30 miles from El Paso del Norte, Ponce de León immediately deployed his men in a line of battle. A single howitzer was with a small group of reserves in the rear.

Doniphan's men scrambled for weapons and formed three lines. The first U.S. volley confused the advancing Mexicans and opened gaps in their ranks. Mexican orders became confused, and the right and left flanks retreated, leaving the infantry in the center to press the attack. Ponce de León was wounded, and the Mexicans soon fled, leaving their prized howitzer to be captured by the U.S. troops. The battle had lasted about half an hour. Doniphan's loss was 7 wounded; Mexican losses were approximately 40 killed and an undetermined number of wounded.

The following day (December 26), the Mexican force entered Chihuahua and disbanded. A group of citizens from El Paso went to Doniphan and pleaded for the protection of their city and property. Later in the day, the U.S. flag was raised in the city plaza.

See also Doniphan's March.

For further reading: Armstrong, "The Brazito Battlefield," 1960; Connelley, *Doniphan's Expedition and the Conquest of New Mexico and California*, 1907; Gallaher, "The Official Report of the Battle at Temascalitos (Brazito)," 1928; Hughes, *Doniphan's Expedition, Containing an Account of the Conquest of New Mexico*, 1973.

El Embudo Pass, Skirmish at

(January 29, 1847)

The skirmish at El Embudo Pass, New Mexico, was fought between approximately 500 U.S. soldiers under Colonel Sterling Price and a combined Mexican-Indian rebel force that was positioned across the road in El Embudo Canyon. The U.S. victory continued to drive the Taos Rebellion insurgents toward Taos, where they were defeated and captured.

Colonel Price and a command of approximately 350 men were in pursuit of the rebel force that had killed several people in New Mexico in January 1847, including Charles Bent, the military governor of Santa Fe. Price had brushed aside approximately 1,500 rebels in a skirmish at La Cañada on January 24. Reinforced to a total of 480 men and several artillery pieces, Price pushed on. Five days later, his scouts reported that the reorganized rebels were positioned in El Embudo, a narrow canyon through a rugged range of hills. Price quickly deployed his men and attacked the entire rebel line. The Mexican-Indian forces soon fled through the deep snow in the mountains; several of the U.S. pursuers suffered from frostbite. The quick victory indicated that the rebels were demoralized, and many of them slipped away and rejoined their families. Price reported one man killed and another wounded; he indicated that New Mexican losses were approximately 20 killed and 60 wounded.

See also La Cañada, Battle of; Taos Rebellion.

For further reading: Keleher, *Turmoil in New Mexico, 1846–1848*, 1952; Lavender, *Bent's Fort*, 1954; McNierney, *Taos 1847*, 1980; Twitchell, *The History of the Military Occupation of the Territory of New Mexico from 1846 to 1851 by the Government of the United States*, 1909.

El Molino del Rey, Battle of

(September 8, 1847)

One of Major General Winfield Scott's costliest victories, the Battle of El Molino del Rey was meant to destroy a cannon foundry. After a loss of nearly 800 U.S. soldiers, it was discovered that the foundry did not exist. Scott was harshly criticized for his poor reconnaissance before the battle.

Major General Scott's U.S. Army of Occupation had been pushing relentlessly inward from Veracruz toward Mexico City in 1847 and had defeated General Antonio López de Santa Anna's forces at Cerro Gordo, Contreras (Padierna), and Churubusco. A truce halted any further advance from August 22 to September 7. The truce allowed both armies to draw supplies, exchange prisoners, and take care of the wounded. It also gave Santa Anna critical time to plan for the defense of the nation's capital; his violation of the armistice by constructing fortifications at Mexico City compelled Scott to end the truce and attack.

Scott's divisions were camped at Tacubaya, San Angel, Mixcoac, and San Agustín. His scouts discovered Mexican troops at El Molino del Rey (King's Mill), a group of stone buildings about two miles southwest of Mexico City. Five brigades of Mexican infantry (2nd Light, 1st Light, 10th Line, 1st Line, and 11th Line) manned a strong east-west position nearly a mile in length that was fronted by a dry ditch, earthworks, and stone buildings and walls. Half a mile toward the city from El Molino del Rey was the hilltop fortress of Chapultepec, which was also well defended with soldiers and cannon.

Scott's scouts indicated that El Molino del Rey held a cannon foundry and ammunition magazine. If El Molino del Rey and Chapultepec fell, nothing would stop the U.S. forces from surging down the causeways that led to the gates of Mexico City.

Brigadier Generals Antonio León and Joaquín Rangel commanded the national guard units on the Mexican left. General Francisco Pérez commanded approximately 1,500 troops at Casa Mata, a fortified stone structure, on the Mexican right. The center was held by Brigadier General Simeon Ramírez's brigade and some artillery. A strong cavalry force of 4,000 men under General Juan Álvarez was held in reserve about one mile to the west. Exact figures are not known, but a total force of 8,000 to 10,000 Mexican soldiers probably defended the main complex. Santa Anna had not selected an overall commander to coordinate the defense; the generals were left to decide how they would respond to a U.S. attack.

Scott's plan was to shell the enemy artillery and the buildings of El Molino del Rey, attack both flanks, and charge the center of the complex with a force of 500 handpicked men (called the "forlorn hope") under the command of Major George Wright. The assault troops—a total of approximately 3,300 men—consisted of General William J. Worth's division and Brigadier General George Cadwalader's brigade. At dawn, Worth opened the battle with a brief artillery barrage. Wright's initial charge was a success: the Mexicans were driven back by bayonet, and their artillery was captured. A Mexican called the U.S. attack one of "great courage." Before Wright's men could turn the artillery on the enemy, Mexican officers had quickly regrouped their men and counterattacked, inflicting heavy losses on the storming party and sending them in retreat. Without orders, Lieutenant Colonel Miguel María Echeagaray, a member of the 3rd Light Infantry, led a column from Chapultepec that joined in the counterattack. Eleven of 14 officers and more than half of Wright's storming party were shot down. "A fearful carnage ensued in which the struggle went on, hand-to-hand, costing the lives of the two valiant officers [General León and Colonel Lucas Balderas of the Batallón de Mina]," wrote Ramon Alcaraz. "Meanwhile the miserable, cowardly cavalry [Álvarez] remained where it was, watching the scene which it could have changed...."

By this time, the Mexican flanks were under attack by artillery and musket fire. The reserve force of Mexican cavalry finally approached, but was quickly turned back by some well-directed cannister fire from the U.S. left. The cavalry then permanently retired. Some Mexican soldiers were witnessed killing wounded Americans on the battlefield. (This led to the retaliatory killing of surrendering or wounded Mexicans during the Battle of Chapultepec.) As the Mexican defense began to crumble, knots of desperate hand-to-hand fighting erupted inside the complex. The Mexicans finally retreated stubbornly toward Chapultepec. Brigadier General Matías Peña y Barragán rallied some of these men and launched two brave but hopeless counterattacks.

The battle of El Molino del Rey was a fierce struggle that lasted about two hours. It had ended by 7:00 in the morning. The fighting decimated some units, such as the 5th U.S. Infantry that lost nearly 40 percent of its effective strength. The 1st Line Infantry Regiment was listed in Mexican reports as *dejó de existir* (wiped out). Worth's casualties, approximately 25 percent of his fighting strength, were severe—117 killed, approximately 660 wounded, and 18 missing. Mexican losses were also appalling. A U.S. estimate of the killed and wounded was 2,000, and 680 soldiers were captured. After the battle, Worth's men destroyed the fortifications; in the process, a gunpowder magazine exploded, which killed an additional 12 men. It was also discovered that a cannon foundry never existed at the site.

Instead of following up their attack, the U.S. forces regrouped and did not attack Chapultepec until September 13. On September 9, from Chapultepec's walls, a crowd of Mexican soldiers watched as the U.S. dead were buried in a long trench on the heights of Tacubaya. The Battle of El Molino del Rey had the highest number of U.S. casualties of any engagement of the war.

Contemporaries and historians have criticized Scott's decision to attack El Molino del Rey. His decision was at least partly based on erroneous information from his scouts: there was no cannon foundry, which he had wanted to destroy, and the fortifications were stronger than had been reported (including the number of artillery). Many of his officers felt that Chapultepec would have fallen the same day, and possibly Mexico City, if the U.S. army had pursued the retreating defenders of El Molino del Rey. Worth was also criticized for beginning the assault after only ten rounds of artillery fire. The Mexicans could have conceivably won the battle if their cavalry had struck the U.S. left hard at the height of the struggle, as its commander had been instructed to do by General Santa Anna.

See also Balderas, Lucas; León, Antonio; Wright, George.

For further reading: Alcaraz, *The Other Side*, 1850; Balbontín, *La invasión americana, 1846 a 1848*, 1888; Grant, *Personal Memoirs of U. S. Grant*, 1885; Hitchcock, *Fifty Years in Camp and Field*, 1909; Semmes, *The Campaign of General Scott in the Valley of Mexico*, 1852; Wallace, *General William Jenkins Worth, Monterey's Forgotten Hero*, 1953.

El Rincón del Diablo

An earthen fortification on the eastern edge of Monterrey known to the U.S. soldiers as "Devil's Corner," El Rincón del Diablo could hold 200 men and three cannon. General Zachary Taylor launched several assaults against the fort during the Battle of Monterrey in September 1846. Each assault was turned back by the accurate fire of the Mexican artillerymen. After the U.S. troops had gained nearby Fort Tenería, the soldiers and cannon were withdrawn from El Rincón del Diablo during the night of September 22 and placed in the city for the street fighting that was to erupt the following day.

See also Monterrey, Battle of.

For further reading: Alcaraz, *The Other Side*, 1850; Smith, *The War with Mexico*, 1919.

El Tomacito (Tomás Baca)

A Pueblo Indian and leader in the 1847 Taos Rebellion in New Mexico, El Tomacito (also called Tomás Baca) was captured with the rebel force at Pueblo de Taos, an Indian village north of Taos. After El Tomacito was accused of the murder of Governor Charles Bent on January 19, Colonel Sterling Price insisted that the rebels turn El Tomacito over—which they did—before Price would accept their surrender. While El Tomacito was in a guard room awaiting his trial, "a dragoon by the name of Fitzgerald…was allowed to go into the room where the Indian was confined, along with others who wanted to take a look at him. The soldier looked at the savage a few minutes, and then quick as a flash, drew a pistol and shot him in the head, killing him instantly. Fitzgerald then made his escape from the building, and succeeded in getting away out of the country." (McNierney 1980)

For further reading: Bauer, *The Mexican War, 1846–1848*, 1974; Keleher, *Turmoil in New Mexico, 1846–1848*, 1952; McNierney, *Taos 1847*, 1980.

Emerson, Ralph Waldo
(1803–1882)

A famous U.S. essayist and poet, Ralph Waldo Emerson opposed the Mexican-American War and claimed that it would lead to corruption and immorality.

Emerson was born in Boston, Massachusetts. He excelled in literature and language at Harvard University and briefly attended divinity school. His travels in Europe helped develop his metaphysical approach to nature. His career as a writer, essayist, and poet began in the 1830s. As his popularity grew, Emerson began to lecture on natural history and human society.

An adamant opponent to the Mexican-American War, Emerson frequently commented that Anglo-Americans would overrun North America not by divine will, but by "race-drive." A U.S. victory over Mexico, he claimed, would lead to corruption, degradation, and immorality. Emerson wrote that "We have a bad war, many victories—each of which converts the country into an immense chanticleer." In reference to the war, he also claimed that "most of the great results of history are brought about by discreditable means."

After the war, Emerson became an advocate for Native American and African American rights and supported the Union during the Civil War. Emerson retired in 1873 to Concord, New Hampshire, and died there from pneumonia.

For further reading: Allen, *Waldo Emerson*, 1981; Johannsen, *To the Halls of the Montezumas*, 1985; Porte, *Representative Man*, 1979.

Emory, William Hemsley

(1811–1887)

A soldier, engineer, and scientist, William Hemsley Emory served with Brigadier General Stephen W. Kearny's Army of the West during 1846–1847 and helped direct the Mexico–United States boundary survey in the 1850s.

Emory, who was born in Maryland, graduated in 1831 from the U.S. Military Academy, where he was nicknamed "Bold Emory." At first assigned to the 4th U.S. Artillery, he later joined the Topographic Engineers as a first lieutenant. Emory helped survey the Canadian–United States border between 1844 and 1846.

During the Mexican-American War, he was the chief engineer officer and acting assistant adjutant general for General Stephen Watts Kearny's Army of the West, which occupied New Mexico in 1846. Emory traveled west to California with Kearny and his 300-man column in September 1846. Emory distinguished himself at the Battles of San Pascual, San Gabriel, and Mesa and won two brevets.

Emory helped survey the boundary line between California and Mexico during 1849–1857 and was the U.S. commissioner for the Gadsden Treaty in 1854. During the Civil War, he became a Union brigadier general and served with distinction as a brigade, division, and corps commander. He retired from the military in 1876.

For further reading: Cullum, *Biographical Register of the Officers and Graduates of the United States Military Academy from 1802 to 1867*, 1879; Emory, *Notes of a Military Reconnaissance*, 1848; Goetzmann, *Army Exploration in the American West, 1803–1863*, 1959; Johnson and Malone, *Dictionary of American Biography*, 1928–1936.

Ewell, Richard Stoddert

(1817–1872)

A fiery lieutenant in the 2nd U.S. Dragoons, Richard Stoddert Ewell performed bravely during the battles of Major General Winfield Scott's Veracruz–Mexico City campaign and was one of the first soldiers to reach the gates of Mexico City on September 13, 1847.

Ewell was born in Georgetown, District of Columbia. He graduated from the U.S. Military Academy in 1840 and was commissioned a second lieutenant of dragoons. He served on the western frontier, where he quickly developed a reputation for a hot temper and eccentric speech. He was plagued by severe headaches throughout his military career.

During the Mexican-American War, Ewell was brevetted for gallantry at the Battles of Contreras and Churubusco in August 1847. After the U.S. troops overran Chapultepec on September 13, Ewell and Captain Philip Kearny aggressively pursued the fleeing Mexicans to the gates of Mexico City, where terrific musket fire stopped the advance. Kearny's arm was mangled, and Ewell had two horses shot from under him as he led the dragoons in retreat from the San Antonio *garita* (gate).

Following the war, Ewell continued his frontier duties, including battling the Apache Nation in New Mexico in 1857. He resigned from the U.S. army to join the Confederate States of America and rose to the rank of lieutenant general. One of the South's most determined fighters during the Civil War, he lost a leg at the Battle of Groveton. He retired to his farm in Tennessee, where he died of pneumonia at the age of 55.

For further reading: Cullum, *Biographical Register of the Officers and Graduates of the United States Military Academy from 1802 to 1867,* 1879; Hamlin, "Old Bald Head," 1940; Johnson and Malone, *Dictionary of American Biography,* 1928–1936.

F

Falcón, Rámon
(d. 1847)

A cunning and sometimes ruthless Mexican guerrilla, Rámon Falcón operated along the Río Grande between Texas and Mexico. He is blamed for the murder of Colonel Trueman Cross in April 1846, the first U.S. casualty of the Mexican-American War.

Falcón had clashed with Texans for years along the Texas-Mexico border. He was often hunted by Texas Ranger patrols. Falcón carried the rank of lieutenant in the La Bahía Company of the Mexican Army of the North at Matamoros, but also operated independently as a scout and guerrilla. After General Zachary Taylor and his Army of Occupation arrived on the Río Grande, they were watched intently by Mexican cavalry patrols, bands of guerrillas, and rancheros, including men led by Falcón.

After he had left camp for a recreational ride along the river, Colonel Trueman Cross, Taylor's quartermaster, was murdered on April 10, 1846. His naked body with its skull crushed was found 11 days later. Mexicans in the area claimed that Falcón had killed him. After Taylor occupied Matamoros, patrols of Texas Rangers scouted the hills and vast tracts of chaparral for Falcón and General Antonio Canales, another guerrilla leader, with no success.

In 1847, Falcón was captured near Saltillo. According to Samuel Chamberlain, a U.S. dragoon, Falcón "was arrested at last at a Fandango in Saltillo, recognized by a man he had left for dead at the Rinconada Pass, when he killed three discharged Mississippians." On the day of his execution, Falcón approached the gallows smoking a cigar. Chamberlain claimed he said "Good night, my American friends, give my love to all your wives, and I will see you again in hell." He was hanged in the Grand Plaza of Saltillo on December 19, 1847.

See also Cross, Trueman.

For further reading: Bauer, *The Mexican War, 1846–1848,* 1974; Chamberlain, *My Confession,* 1956.

Flores, José María
(1818–1866)

Captain José María Flores, with limited resources and manpower, challenged the U.S. forces that had seized California in 1846. In one of the few Mexican triumphs of the war, he forced the surrender of Los Angeles. Later, losing the Battles of San Gabriel River and La Mesa forced him to disband his army and retreat southward.

Born in Saltillo, Flores began his army career at the age of 12. He arrived in Alta California in 1842 as a Mexican captain and assistant to Governor Manuel Micheltorena. When the governor was overthrown in 1845, Flores quickly became a California partisan and worked for California's military commander, José Castro.

After Los Angeles fell to U.S. forces under Commodore Robert F. Stockton and Colonel John C. Frémont in August 1846, Flores retreated to southern California to raise an army, even though he had pledged not to fight against the United States. Within a month, he had returned with a force of approximately

500, well-armed Californios and immediately lay siege to Los Angeles and its 59-man U.S. garrison. The U.S. commander surrendered on September 29, and Flores and his victorious troops reoccupied the city.

On October 26, Flores was elected governor and military commander of California. He launched assaults on the small U.S. garrisons at San Diego, Santa Barbara, Santa Ines, and San Luis Obispo. Guerrillas harassed U.S. soldiers, and all men between 15 and 60 years of age were ordered to join the army. Suspicious Californio subordinates, who distrusted Flores because of his Mexican heritage and aggressive tactics, jailed Flores for a short time.

His imprisonment stalled the momentum of his campaign. When he was released, morale had fallen, and he struggled to keep his men together. By this time, Commodore Stockton and Brigadier General Stephen W. Kearny were marching northward from San Diego to retake Los Angeles. Flores led his force of approximately 500 men to challenge the U.S. troops, but lost the Battles of San Gabriel River (January 8, 1847) and La Mesa (January 9, 1847). The United States regained Los Angeles on January 10. With Californio resistance crushed and his men scattered, Flores rode south to Sonora with a few loyal followers. He again tried to recruit a force of 400 to 500 men, but never reentered California.

Captain Flores became the military commandant in Sonora in 1851 and evicted a party of U.S. settlers from Mexican territory along the Gila River. Opposed to French intervention, he fought French forces in Hermosillo and won the Battle of Las Avispas. He remained in political and military service at Mazatlán until his death in 1866.

See also La Mesa, Battle of; Los Angeles; San Gabriel River (Bartolo Ford), Battle of.

For further reading: Bancroft, *History of California*, 1886; *Diccionario Porrúa*, 1995; Harlow, *California Conquered*, 1982; Johannsen, *To the Halls of the Montezumas*, 1985.

Flying Artillery

One of the greatest advantages that the U.S. army enjoyed during the Mexican-American War was its Flying Artillery. These lighter, more mobile artillery pieces could be moved quickly across a battlefield and were critical to General Zachary Taylor's early victories in northern Mexico.

The Flying Artillery started as an experimental battery organized by Major Samuel Ringgold in 1838, who enlarged on the concepts of Captain Robert Anderson. The guns could be quickly moved into forward positions or across a battlefield to wherever they were most needed. The success of the Flying Artillery was largely a result of the rigorous training of artillerymen, teamsters, and horses. Sometimes riding the horses and the caisson, the men would advance at a full gallop, unlimber, fire, remount, and move. Their constant movement made it difficult for enemy gunners to sight them as a target.

The Flying Artillery often fought from exposed forward positions and targeted masses of infantry and cavalry. These artillerists were some of the bravest men in the U.S. army and frequently took heavy losses. The artillery was highly effective at the Battle of Palo Alto on May 8, 1846, and cut huge holes in the Mexican ranks from as close as 100 yards. Ringgold was mortally wounded during the fight and died three days later. The Flying Artillery continued to torment the Mexican armies throughout the rest of General Zachary Taylor's campaign in northern Mexico and throughout General Winfield Scott's Veracruz–Mexico City campaign in 1847.

See also Anderson, Robert; Palo Alto, Battle of; Ringgold, Samuel.

For further reading: Birkhimer, *Historical Sketch of the Organization, Administration, Materiél and Tactics of the Artillery, United States Army*, 1884; Dillon, *American Artillery in the Mexican War 1846–1847*, 1975; Johannsen, *To the Halls of the Montezumas*, 1985.

Ford, John Salmon
(1815–1897)

An officer in the Texas Rangers, John Salmon Ford served, principally as a scout and guerrilla fighter, under General Joseph Lane during Major General Winfield Scott's Veracruz–Mexico City campaign.

Born in South Carolina, Ford was raised in Tennessee and studied medicine. After moving to Texas to establish a medical practice, he became involved in political and military affairs in the republic.

He volunteered for the Mexican-American War and was adjutant to Colonel John C. Hays of the 2nd Regiment of the Texas Rangers. Ford participated in the hard-marching, antiguerrilla campaigns of General Joseph Lane in 1847 along the National Road, including the fight at Galaxara Pass. Ford was nicknamed "RIP" for "rest in peace," the phrase that ended the letters that he wrote to families to inform them of the deaths of soldiers.

Ford helped blaze an immigrant trail from San Antonio to El Paso in 1849 and later commanded a company of Texas Rangers in South Texas. During the Civil War, he fought as a Confederate cavalry officer. After serving two terms in the Texas Senate, he retired to San Antonio and wrote his memoirs.

For further reading: Davis, *The Texas Rangers,* 1991; Ford, *Rip Ford's Texas,* 1963; Hughes, *Rebellious Ranger,* 1964.

Forrest, French
(1796–1866)

As part of the U.S. Navy's Home Squadron, Captain French Forrest participated in the attacks on Alvarado and Tabasco in 1846 and later oversaw the landing of General Winfield Scott's 10,000-man army at Veracruz in March 1847.

Forrest, who was born in Maryland, was appointed a midshipman in the U.S. Navy in 1811. He served in the War of 1812 and was promoted to captain in 1844. He was highly regarded for being methodical, well organized, and courageous.

During the Mexican-American War, Forrest commanded the *Cumberland* and also the *Raritan,* two flagships in the U.S. Home Squadron in the Gulf of Mexico. He commanded the second division in the attack on Alvarado on October 16, 1846, and led the landing force of 200 during November 23–26 at Tabasco. His party was attacked by superior numbers on the 25th, but kept the attackers at a distance until the ships withdrew the following morning. Under his supervision as the officer in charge, General Scott's army of 10,000 men was put safely ashore at Veracruz on March 9, 1847.

Duties after the war included supervising the Washington Navy Yard and commanding the Brazil Squadron until May 1859. As a captain in the Confederate Navy in 1861, Forrest helped build the *Merrimac.* He died in Georgetown at the age of 70.

For further reading: Bauer, *Surfboats and Horse Marines,* 1969; Johnson and Malone, *Dictionary of American Biography,* 1928–1936; Knox, *A History of the United States Navy,* 1936.

Fort Brown

Built by General Zachary Taylor's men on the north bank of the Río Grande, Fort Brown, Texas, withstood a week-long artillery barrage by Mexican forces in May 1846.

When his Army of Occupation arrived on the north bank of the Río Grande in the spring of 1846, General Taylor ordered his engineers to build a fort. Originally called Fort Texas, it was constructed across the river from the Mexican village of Matamoros. Designed by engineer J. K. F. Mansfield, the fort had six bastion fronts and a perimeter of 800 yards. The thick earth walls were approximately 10 feet high, capped by a 15-foot-thick parapet, and surrounded by a deep ditch. The powder magazine was made from wooden barrels filled with sand (seven barrels thick and four barrels high), with a timber roof covered by 12 feet of sand.

Knowing that General Taylor had taken the rest of his army to his staging area at nearby Point Isabel, General Mariano Arista, commander in chief of the Mexican Army of the North, decided to lay siege to Fort Texas to bring Taylor to battle. A severe cannonading from Matamoros by General Pedro de Ampudia began at dawn on May 3, 1846.

The shelling inflicted little damage to the fort and its force of 500—men from the 7th U.S. Infantry, several artillery companies, and a contingent of female laundresses. The men occasionally returned fire and continued to build bombproofs that were formed by layers of poles and pork barrels covered with embankments of earth. During the first two days of shelling, one U.S. soldier was killed.

On May 6, Major Jacob Brown, the commander, was gruesomely wounded by a cannonball and died three days later. The command devolved to Captain Edgar Hawkins. Later in the day, Ampudia ordered the fort to surrender, which Hawkins refused to do. Soldiers cut up tents to make sandbags to repair damage to the parapets. By this time, the noise and shock of the incessant shelling was beginning to affect the nerves of the soldiers. The laundresses, especially Sarah Borginnis, known as the "Great Western," took care of the wounded.

Having surrounded the fort on all sides, Ampudia was planning to storm the fort when Arista ordered him to rejoin the army to face Taylor's approaching force. Shelling of the fort continued until May 10, when Taylor's men finally appeared, having just won the Battles of Palo Alto (May 8) and Resaca de la Palma (May 9). Nearly 3,000 shells had been fired at the fort during the week-long siege. U.S. casualties were 2 killed and 13 wounded; Mexican losses from the sporadic U.S. fire are not known.

Taylor changed the name of the fortification to Fort Brown, in honor of Major Jacob Brown. It was manned throughout the war and into the 1850s to discourage Indian raids. Abandoned by U.S. forces during the Civil War, it was occasionally occupied by Confederate forces. Fort Brown was used as late as 1914 in chasing Mexican bandits along the border and was deactivated in 1944. The city of Brownsville has grown around the fort.

See also Borginnis, Sarah; Brown, Jacob; Mansfield, Joseph King Fenno.

For further reading: Frost, *The Mexican War and Its Warriors,* 1848; Hitchcock, *Fifty Years in Camp and Field,* 1909; Webb, *The Handbook of Texas,* 1952.

Fort Jesup

Fort Jesup in southwestern Louisiana was the location where Colonel Zachary Taylor, by order of President John Tyler in 1844, assembled the Army of Observation to protect Texas from a possible invasion by Mexico.

Built in 1822 by the U.S. government along the Sabine River border between New Spain and the United States, the garrison was initially commanded by Lieutenant Colonel Zachary Taylor. Its force policed the border, helped quell slave insurrections, and maintained and improved the road networks that led to Texas.

Fort Jesup became an important staging area in July 1845, when President James K. Polk ordered Brigadier General Taylor to move his force to the Nueces River boundary between Texas and Mexico. Officially now the Army of Occupation, Taylor's forces vacated Fort Jesup and moved to Corpus Christi on the Nueces River. With the annexation of Texas in December 1845, Fort Jesup was no longer needed as a border outpost and was abandoned.

See also Army, United States.

For further reading: Hardin, *Fort Jesup—Fort Selden—Camp Sebina—Camp Salubrity,* 1933; Park Literature, Fort Jesup State Commemorative Area, Many, LA.

Fort Marcy

Built by on a small hill north of Santa Fe, New Mexico, in 1846, Fort Marcy was the garrison for Brigadier General Stephen Watts Kearny's occupational force in New Mexico. After arriving in Santa Fe in August 1846, Kearny ordered his topographic engineer, Lieutenant Jeremy F. Gilmer, to oversee the construction of the fort. The strong, irregularly shaped, earthen fort, with numerous gun placements, was designed to hold 1,000 men. Its massive, thick walls were built from adobe bricks two feet long, one foot thick, and six inches high. It was named for Secretary of War William L. Marcy.

For further reading: Henry, *The Story of the Mexican War,* 1950; Hughes, *Doniphan's Expedition, Containing an Account of the Conquest of New Mexico,* 1973.

Fort Polk

Located in present-day Cameron County, Texas, the earthen-walled Fort Polk was established at Point Isabel by Brigadier General Zachary Taylor on March 26, 1846, as a military depot. The fort was occupied from 1848 to 1850 by a company of the 4th U.S. Artillery. The buildings were dismantled in 1849, and the post abandoned the following year.

For further reading: Pierce, *A Brief History of the Lower Río Grande Valley*, 1917; Smith, *The War with Mexico*, 1919; Webb, *The Handbook of Texas*, 1952.

Fort Tenería

Fort Tenería guarded the eastern approach to the city of Monterrey, Nuevo León. The fort's center was a former commercial tannery that was reinforced by sandbags and parapets and could hold 200 men.

As described by historian Justin Smith, the fortification "consisted of two short parallel sides prolonged and drawn together in front so as to meet at a sharp angle; and the north side was similarly prolonged and drawn in toward the rear so as to protect partially the opening or throat … the parapet was completed with sand-bags made with ordinary cotton cloth; and the guns, mounted in barbette without platforms, were hard to manage on fresh dirt soaked with rain…but the redoubt was [still] a serious obstacle for infantry."

The target of several U.S. assaults during the Battle of Monterrey on September 21, 1846, the guns at Fort Tenería inflicted heavy U.S. casualties. A portion of the 4th U.S. Infantry lost nearly a third of its men in a frontal assault. The Mexicans finally evacuated Tenería and moved to more interior positions within the city.

See also Backus, Electus; Monterrey, Battle of.

For further reading: Alcaraz, *The Other Side*, 1850; Backus, "Brief Sketch of the Battle of Monterey," 1866.

Fort Texas

See Fort Brown.

Foster, John Gray
(1823–1874)

An engineer with Major General Winfield Scott's Army of Occupation in 1847, Lieutenant John Gray Foster conducted important reconnaissance work at the Battles of Cerro Gordo and El Molino del Rey, where he was seriously wounded.

Foster was born in New Hampshire. He graduated fourth in his class from the U.S. Military Academy in 1846 and was commissioned a second lieutenant in the corp of engineers.

Foster served in Major General Scott's Army of Occupation during the Mexican-American War. He helped survey and clear the flanking route that Captain Robert E. Lee had discovered prior to the Battle of Cerro Gordo in April. Foster also conducted high-risk reconnaissance work around the Mexican positions at El Molino del Rey on September 8, 1847, especially the defenses at Casa Mata. As part of the first assault, he was severely wounded, and he was brevetted twice for distinguished service by the end of the war.

Returning to West Point, Foster taught engineering from 1855 to 1857. During the Civil War, he rose to the rank of major general of volunteers and later commanded the Department of North Carolina.

For further reading: Cullum, *Biographical Register of the Officers and Graduates of the United States Military Academy from 1802 to 1867*, 1879; Trass, *From the Golden Gate to Mexico City*, 1993.

Frémont, John C.
(1813–1890)

Nicknamed the "Pathfinder," John C. Frémont became famous for his exploration of the lands of the western United States. His third expedition during 1845–1847 took him to California, where he commanded a U.S. military force that helped seize the province during the Mexican-American War.

Born out of wedlock in Savannah, Georgia, Frémont was raised in Charleston, South Carolina. Energetic and adventuresome, he impressed with his quickness and talents some influential citizens, who paid for his private education. Keenly interested in sailing, he went to sea for two years. Upon his return, he worked as a surveyor and engineer with the U.S. Topographical Corps, during which time he developed his love for wilderness exploration.

The success of his western surveys made him a national celebrity. Thomas Hart Benton, a Missouri senator and expansionist, especially took interest in Frémont's abilities. Frémont

John C. Frémont, ca. 1850
(Library of Congress)

fell in love with Benton's daughter Jessie. After they eloped in the summer of 1841, he explored Iowa Territory.

After exploring the Oregon Trail and Oregon Territory with frontiersman Kit Carson in 1842, Frémont explored the Great Basin in 1843. Against the advice of others, he pushed on through the winter passes of the Sierra Nevada. His party barely survived, and some of his men were driven crazy by frostbite. His return to Washington in the fall of 1844 made him a hero, and he was mobbed in public. His passionate descriptions of the West helped fan the public's support of Manifest Destiny.

Brevetted a captain in the U.S. army, Frémont began his third expedition in the summer of 1845 with 62 men. Guiding him to the Great Basin were Kit Carson and mountain man Joseph Walker. Although no written documentation survives to verify his claim, Frémont maintained that he had been instructed that, if he reached California and hostilities with Mexico had begun, he was to use his men as a military force.

Frémont's party arrived at Sutter's Fort in California on December 9, 1845. Frémont wandered freely and met with U.S. consul Thomas O. Larken in Monterey. Californio authorities were alarmed by Frémont's rough-looking, heavily armed group. José Castro, the military commander at Sonoma, ordered Frémont to leave. Frémont was confrontational, constructed fortifications on Hawk's Peak north of Monterey, and raised the U.S. flag in March 1846. Castro prepared to attack, but Frémont withdrew toward Oregon.

In the Upper Sacramento Valley, Frémont's party attacked an Indian village, probably the Klamath Nation. Nearly 200 natives were killed, including women and children. Led by a frenzied Kit Carson, Frémont described it as "perfect butcher," followed by two days of celebration.

On May 9, 1846, Frémont was overtaken by Lieutenant Archibald Gillespie with orders from President James Polk, Secretary of State James Buchanan, Secretary of the Navy George Bancroft, and Thomas Benton. Gillespie supposedly also delivered verbal orders that he had memorized. That evening, the camp was attacked by Indians, and three of Frémont's men were killed. Frémont's group retaliated by assaulting a village on Upper Klamath Lake, killing more than 20 Indians, and burning the village to the ground.

Worried that Castro would try to incite the native population against the United States, Frémont "resolved…to strike them a blow which would make them recognize that Castro was far and that I was near." Frémont attacked and destroyed the village of the peaceful Maidu Indians along the Sacramento River. A small group of U.S. settlers, excited by Frémont's activities, overran Sonoma in June, raised a white flag with a single red star and a grizzly bear, and skirmished with Mexican troops. Called the Bear Flaggers, they aligned themselves with Frémont. On July 7, U.S. warships arrived at Monterey and raised the U.S. flag, and Commodore Robert F. Stockton combined the Bear Flaggers and Frémont's force into the California Battalion, with Frémont as lieutenant colonel.

Stockton used some of the California Battalion in July and August 1846 to occupy Los Angeles and other cities, including San Juan Bautista, San José, and San Diego. Frémont took the rest of his men northward toward Sacramento.

After the Californios, led by José María Flores, retook Los Angeles and became a threat to U.S. authority, Frémont remained surprisingly idle as Stockton and Brigadier General Stephen W. Kearny assembled an army-navy force to seize the city. After Stockton and Kearny defeated Flores in two battles to formally enter the city on January 10, 1847, Frémont rode in casually a few days later and presented the Treaty of Cahuenga, a document that he had drafted and signed with General Andrés Pico to end the warfare in California.

Both Stockton and Kearny were angry that their subordinate had undertaken this responsibility, when they were the higher-ranking officers in charge. Stockton, however, appointed Frémont governor of California. Outraged because he outranked Frémont, Kearny complained to Washington. In March 1847, Kearny was officially appointed governor by General Winfield Scott. In June 1847, Frémont, his scientific material, and some of his men headed east to Washington with Kearny. Upon reaching Fort Leavenworth, Kansas, Kearny promptly had Frémont arrested for mutiny and insubordination.

Frémont's court-martial was held in Washington, D.C., from November 1847 to January 1848. Charged with mutiny, disobeying orders, and poor military conduct, Frémont was found guilty on all three counts and ordered dismissed from the army. Although President Polk overturned the decision, Frémont resigned.

A string of triumphs and disasters awaited Frémont in the years following the Mexican-American War. In 1848, he tried to cross the San Juan Mountains in southwestern Colorado in the winter. Ten men died, and survivors resorted to eating boiled rawhide, rope, and human remains. Later, the discovery of gold on his ranch in California made Frémont a wealthy man. In 1854, he became trapped again in the mountains in winter during a railroad survey and nearly perished.

Antislavery Republicans needed a strong candidate to challenge Democrat James Buchanan and American Party candidate Millard Fillmore in the 1856 presidential campaign, and they chose Frémont. Buchanan, however, won the election.

Controversy continued to follow Frémont as a Union general during the Civil War. In Missouri, he announced that captured Confederate guerrillas would be executed and that slaves would be freed. This stunned Lincoln, who reassigned him. As the commander of the Department of West Virginia, Frémont lost five straight battles to Stonewall Jackson. Then, in the Panic of 1873, Frémont's fortune was lost. After serving as territorial governor of Arizona from 1878 to 1883, he died from peritonitis in New York City.

See also Bear Flag Revolt; Benton, Thomas Hart; Cahuenga, Treaty of; California Battalion; Gillespie, Archibald H.; Hawk's Peak; Klamath Indians.

For further reading: Durham, *The Desert between the Mountains*, 1997; Egan, *Frémont*, 1977; Frémont, *Memoirs of My Life*, 1886; Harlow, *California Conquered*, 1982; Harris, *John C. Frémont and the Great Western Reconnaissance*, 1990; Marti, *Messenger of Destiny*, 1955; Nevins, *Frémont*, 1955; Stenberg, "Polk and Frémont, 1845–1846," 1938.

French, Samuel Gibbs
(1818–1910)

An artillery officer, Lieutenant Samuel Gibbs French was part of the 3rd U.S. Artillery. His Flying Artillery performed admirably during the Battles of Palo Alto, Resaca de la Palma, Monterrey, and Buena Vista during 1846–1847.

French was born New Jersey. He graduated fourteenth of 39 students from the U.S. Military Academy in 1843. Commissioned a second lieutenant in the 3rd U.S. Artillery, he served in various garrisons on the western frontier.

During the Mexican-American War, French was part of General Zachary Taylor's Army of Occupation along the Río Grande during 1846–1847. He assisted Major Samuel Ringgold with the Flying Artillery during the Battle of Palo Alto in May 1846. French lost four of his five gunners during the brutal street fighting at the Battle of Monterrey in September. During the Battle of Buena Vista on February 23, 1847, French was positioned to support the U.S. left flank. He was wounded in the thigh early in the morning, but refused to leave the field. His leadership helped to stabilize the crumbling left flank. Surgeons could not find the bullet, and he was confined to a cot for 40 days. The bullet was finally removed with surgery using a long steel hook, and French was sent to Washington, D.C., to recuperate.

French had a variety of assignments after the war, including being a quartermaster. Resigning from the federal service to serve as a brigadier general in the Confederacy during the Civil War, he fought capably during the Battles of Atlanta, Franklin, and Nashville. French retired to his plantation after the war and died in Florida.

For further reading: Cullum, *Biographical Register of the Officers and Graduates of the United States Military Academy from 1802 to 1867*, 1879; French, *Two Wars, an Autobiography*, 1901; Weems, *To Conquer a Peace*, 1974; Welsh, *Medical Histories of Confederate Generals*, 1995.

G

Gadsden Treaty
(1853)

The Gadsden Treaty, also known as the Treaty of La Mesilla, enabled the United States to acquire the Mesilla Valley from Mexico for $10 million in 1853. This acquisition was intended to facilitate the construction of a transcontinental railroad.

Interest in U.S. expansionism continued after the end of the Mexican-American War. The U.S. government wanted to purchase more Mexican land for the transcontinental railroad. The U.S. minister to Mexico, James Gadsden, proposed the purchase of five border states and Baja California to Mexican minister of foreign relations Manuel Díez de Bonilla. When President Antonio López de Santa Anna resisted, 2,000 U.S. troops were mobilized to the border by President Franklin Pierce to "preserve order."

Weak, needing funds, and fearing the possibility of another war with the United States, Mexico signed the Gadsden Treaty in December 1853. The treaty called for the purchase by the United States of approximately 29 million acres along the southern border of Arizona and New Mexico for $10 million. The stated area included the fertile Mesilla Valley and the towns of Tucson and Mesilla; other terms included access rights across the Isthmus of Tehuantepec. The treaty was ratified by the U.S. Senate in 1854. Although it provided Mexico with badly needed funds, the decision to sell to the United States more Mexican territory resulted in Santa Anna's overthrow in 1854.

For further reading: Falk, *Too Far North, Too Far South,* 1967; Garber, *The Gadsden Treaty,* 1959; Martínez, *Troublesome Border,* 1988.

Gaines, John Pollard
(1795–1857)

A volunteer cavalry officer from Kentucky, John Pollard Gaines was captured by Mexican troops at La Encarnación in January 1847. He later escaped and served creditably during Major General Winfield Scott's Veracruz–Mexico City campaign.

Born in Virginia, Gaines was raised in Kentucky. He served in the War of 1812. Commissioned a major in the Kentucky cavalry brigade in 1846, he was a part of General Zachary Taylor's army along the Río Grande. Gaines joined Captain Cassius M. Clay's scouting party that was sent out by Taylor to locate General Antonio López de Santa Anna's advancing army. On January 22, 1847, the scouting party spent the night at the abandoned hacienda La Encarnación and failed to post pickets. Gaines and the others awoke to find themselves surrounded by thousands of Mexican cavalry under General José Vicente Miñón. The group surrendered, and Gaines later escaped. In the Mexico City campaign, he served as aide-de-camp to General Scott and fought bravely at the Battle of El Molino del Rey on September 8, 1847.

Entering politics after the war, Gaines was elected to the Thirtieth Congress. Under President Taylor, Gaines was appointed governor of Oregon Territory from 1847 to 1849. He later lived in San Francisco, California; and Salem, Oregon.

See also La Encarnación.

For further reading: Bauer, *The Mexican War, 1846–1848*, 1974; Johnson and Malone, *Dictionary of American Biography*, 1928–1936; Scott, *Encarnación Prisoners, Comprising an Account of the March of the Kentucky Cavalry from Louisville to the Rio Grande*, 1848.

Galaxara, Skirmish at
(November 24, 1847)

After defeating a Mexican force at Matamoros on November 23, 1847, a 160-man force under General Joseph Lane began its return to Puebla the following day. His advance guard of 30 men, entering the narrow mountain pass at Galaxara, was attacked by Mexican soldiers. Colonel John C. Hays and some Texas Rangers rode to the front and were confronted by 500 Mexican lancers and guerrillas under guerrilla chief General Joaquín Rea. Lane wrote that "never did any officer act with more gallantry than did Colonel Hays.... As the enemy advanced, [he] deliberately shot two of them dead, and covered his [men's] retreat until the arrival of reinforcements." Two U.S. soldiers were killed and two wounded; Mexican losses were estimated at 50 killed and wounded. Lane continued on to Puebla without incident.

For further reading: Bauer, *The Mexican War, 1846–1848*, 1974; Webb, *The Texas Rangers in the Mexican War*, 1975.

Gaona, Antonio
(1793–1848)

A Mexican brigadier general, Antonio Gaona commanded forces at Puebla during the Mexican-American War and helped defend Mexico City in August–September 1847.

Born in Havana, Cuba, Gaona joined the Spanish army at the age of eight. He helped suppress various rebellions in Mexico until independence was won in 1821, when he joined ranks with Agustín de Iturbide. Remaining in the military, Gaona's solid conduct led to his promotion to brigade general in 1832.

Gaona was a general in the Mexican Army at the time of the Texas Revolution, and he fought at the Alamo. As the commandant of the San Juan de Ulúa fortress at Veracruz, he surrendered to a French expeditionary force in 1838. For this action he was court-martialed, but cleared.

During the Mexican-American War, Gaona commanded troops at Puebla and Perote Prison. In August 1847, as General Winfield Scott's Army of Occupation moved inland from Veracruz, Gaona was ordered to fall back and defend Mexico City, but he was not involved in the combat outside the Belén and San Cosmé *garitas* (gates). He died in the capital during the occupation by U.S. forces.

For further reading: Bancroft, *History of the North Mexican States and Texas*, 1884–1889; Carreño, *Jefes del ejército mexicano en 1847*, 1914; *Diccionario Porrúa*, 1995.

García Condé, Pedro
(1806–1851)

General García Condé had a minor role during the Mexican-American War, leading a small force at the Battle of Río Sacramento in the state of Chihuahua in 1847. His greatest accomplishment, however, was as the Mexican commissioner of the Mexico–United States boundary survey, in which capacity he saved much of the Mesilla Valley via the Bartlett-Condé Agreement.

Born in Arizpe, Sonora, García Condé joined the Spanish Army at the age of 12. Popular and well liked, he continued in the military and became minister of war in 1845 and a congressman the following year.

During the Mexican-American War, General Antonio López de Santa Anna sent García Condé to Chihuahua in 1847 to help the local troops fight Colonel Alexander Doniphan and his 1,100-man regiment. García Condé assisted Governor Ángel Trías Álvarez in organizing his makeshift force of 2,000 men. Riding northward, García Condé selected the ground to defend and constructed an extensive series of earthworks. His men broke and ran during the resulting Battle of Río Sacramento on February 28, 1847. He and Trías Álvarez retreated to Parral in the southern part of the state of Chihuahua, where they established Chihuahua's government-in-exile.

After the war, García Condé was appointed by the Mexican government in 1849 to help establish the new border with the United States. After disagreeing with U.S. surveyor John Russell Bartlett about the starting point of the survey, they compromised by signing the Bartlett-Condé Agreement. This piece of diplomatic work helped Mexico retain most of the Mesilla Valley, which would otherwise have been within the U.S. border. García Condé died in 1851 before the border survey was completed. Part of the disputed territory was later sold to the United States as the Gadsden Purchase.

See also Bartlett-Condé Agreement; Gadsden Treaty; Río Sacramento, Battle of.

For further reading: Diccionario Porrúa, 1995; Goetzmann, "The United States–Mexico Boundary Survey, 1848–1853," 1985; Martínez, *Troublesome Border*, 1988; Smith, *The War with Mexico*, 1919.

Garrison, William Lloyd
(1805–1879)

An outspoken U.S. abolitionist, William Lloyd Garrison denounced the Mexican-American War as immoral and claimed it was waged to punish Mexico for abolishing slavery.

Garrison, who was born in Massachusetts, worked in the newspaper business and later became an editor. He gave his first speech against slavery in 1829 and was one of the first to demand "immediate and complete" emancipation of slaves. Zealous to the point of alienating fellow abolitionists, he was occasionally jailed. In 1841, he called for the northern states to secede from the Union, a reactionary opinion that other abolitionists disapproved of.

Garrison was vehement in his condemnation of the annexation of Texas and the Mexican-American War. In his abolitionist journal, *The Liberator*, he occasionally published antiwar poetry, of which this excerpt from "The War for Slavery" is typical:

> If ever war was waged for basest ends,
> By means perfidious, profligate and low,
> It is the present war with Mexico,
> Which in deep guilt all other wars transcends.

Garrison frequently attacked the U.S. military for abusing Mexico, a defenseless and bankrupt nation. He also claimed that President James K. Polk was punishing Mexico for abolishing slavery in 1829. These ideas were generally regarded as unpatriotic and did little to change public opinion about the war.

Often in ill health, Garrison nevertheless toured the country campaigning against slavery after the war and wrote numerous articles, editorials, and sonnets. Always a crusader, he also fought for prohibition, women's rights, Indian rights, and the prohibition of prostitution.

For further reading: Johnson, *William Lloyd Garrison and His Times*, 1879; Johnson and Malone, *Dictionary of American Biography*, 1928–1936; Swift, *William Lloyd Garrison*, 1911.

Gillespie, Archibald H.
(ca. 1812–1873)

Lieutenant Archibald H. Gillespie carried top-secret documents from President James K. Polk to U.S. consul Thomas O. Larkin and Colonel John C. Frémont in California in 1846 and was later the military commander at Los Angeles.

A first lieutenant in the U.S. Marine Corps, Gillespie was summoned to a meeting with President James K. Polk on October 30, 1845. Polk instructed him to carry dispatches from the State Department to U.S. consul Larkin in Monterey, California, and deliver others to explorer Frémont. Polk wrote in his diary that he had "held a confidential conversation with Lieutenant Gillespie of the Marine Corps…on the subject of a secret mission on which he was about to go to California. His secret instructions and the letter to Mr. Larkin…will explain the object of his mission."

Gillespie began his journey in November 1845. Disguised as a British merchant, he sailed from New York to Veracruz, crossed overland to the port of Mazatlán, and then sailed up the Pacific coast to Monterey on the USS *Cyane*. Fearing capture, he had memorized some of the official correspondence and then burned it. He reached Monterey on April 17, 1846. After informing Larkin that he was to subvert any foreign attempts to seize California and support any Californio rebellions against Mexico, Gillespie hurried northward to Sutter's Fort to find Frémont. Gillespie finally caught up with him on the shore of Klamath Lake on May 9, 1846.

His mission accomplished, Gillespie later joined Frémont's California Battalion. Gillespie commanded the U.S. occupational forces in Los Angeles in August 1846. His severe martial laws made him an unpopular figure. Residents were overjoyed when Gillespie was forced to surrender the city to Californio rebels.

Later exchanged, Gillespie was ordered to take weapons and reinforcements in December 1846 to Brigadier General Stephen Watts Kearny, who was marching from New Mexico to San Diego. Gillespie joined Kearny on December 5, in time to be wounded during the Battle of San Pascual a few days later. He was part of the Stockton-Kearny operation that retook Los Angeles on January 10, 1847.

See also Frémont, John C.; San Pascual, Battle of.

For further reading: Bauer, *Surfboats and Horse Marines,* 1969; Caruso, *The Mexican Spy Company,* 1991; Harlow, *California Conquered,* 1982; Hussey, "The Origin of the Gillespie Mission," 1940.

Gillespie, Robert Addison
(1815–1846)

Texas Ranger Captain Robert Addison Gillespie led storming parties up the slopes of Federation Hill and Independence Hill in September 1846 during the Battle of Monterrey, in which he was mortally wounded.

A Tennessee native who moved to Texas in 1837, Gillespie and his brothers opened a mercantile business in La Grange. He served along the Texas-Mexico border under Captain John C. Hays of the Texas Rangers and received a serious lance wound in the Battle of Walker's Creek in 1844.

In 1845, Gillespie formed a company of volunteers to join General Zachary Taylor's Army of Occupation at Corpus Christi, Texas. During the Mexican-American War, Gillespie commanded a company of the First Texas Mounted Riflemen, under Colonel John C. Hays. Gillespie fought bravely in General Taylor's early battles in 1846. During the Battle of Monterrey in September 1846, he helped storm Fort El Soldado on Federation Hill on the western outskirts of the city. Gillespie is credited with being the first U.S. soldier to leap into the fort. The following day, September 22, with several hundred other men, he scaled the western face of Independence Hill in a driving rainstorm. Wounded as he entered the Mexican redoubt at dawn, he died the following day.

Gillespie was one of the more gentlemanly Texas Rangers and was well liked by Taylor and the regular army officers. His body was shipped to San Antonio for burial. Gillespie County, Texas, is named in his honor.

See also Monterrey, Battle of; Texas Rangers.

For further reading: Chamberlain, *My Confession,* 1956; Webb, *The Handbook of Texas,* 1952; Webb, *The Texas Rangers in the Mexican War,* 1975.

Gómez Farías, Valentín
(1781–1851)

Politician Valentín Gómez Farías tried ardently to establish *puro* political control of the Mexican government from about 1833 to 1850. His plan to take 15 million pesos from the Roman Catholic Church in the middle of the Mexican-American War led to the *Polkos* Revolt and his being stripped of the vice-presidency.

Gómez Farías was born in Guadalajara in 1781 to an affluent family. He attended the University of Guadalajara and graduated with a medical degree. He practiced medicine until 1820, when he entered the field of politics. In the next ten years, he held local, state, and national offices, including secretary of the treasury. By 1830, he had become the well-respected leader of the *puros* political faction (radical liberals).

Gómez Farías acted as provisional president of Mexico during 1833–1834 during the absence of President and General Antonio López de Santa Anna. Gómez Farías took this opportunity to try to limit the control the military and the Catholic Church held on the Mexican economy and to introduce educational and social reforms. His efforts at secularizing the Spanish church missions in California led to a wider rift between California and Mexico. His agenda upset many political leaders and led to widespread distrust. Worried about his own political viability, Santa Anna exiled Gómez Farías to Texas.

As the political scene shifted in the next decade, Gómez Farías returned to Mexico in 1845. Still a dedicated *puro*, he wanted to bring back the 1824 constitution and regain Texas by force. President José Joaquín Herrera rejected his proposal, and Gómez Farías tried to enlist the help of high-ranking General Mariano Paredes y Arrillaga in organizing a rebellion. When Paredes y Arrillaga succeeded in his own coup and deposed Herrera, he too rejected the *puro* overtures of Gómez Farías. Frustrated, Gómez Farías resorted to trying to overthrow Paredes and finally found support in *moderado* General Santa Anna in exile in Cuba. The Paredes administration fell in August 1846, and Gómez Farías again became vice-president to Santa Anna.

As Santa Anna led his newly formed Army of the North northward in January 1847 to fight General Zachary Taylor at La Angostura (Buena Vista), Gómez Farías introduced legislation that would take 15 million pesos from the church by forcing it to sell its property. This scheme immediately backfired, creating tremendous public and political outrage and resulting in the *Polkos* Revolt in February 1847. Organized by high-ranking citizens and militia officers, armed clashes occurred in the streets, and the government was paralyzed for nearly a month—exactly when Major General Winfield Scott placed more than 10,000 men on the beaches south of Veracruz in an uncontested landing. By the end of March, Santa Anna had returned to Mexico City, placated the church by taking only 2 million pesos, and ejected Gómez Farías as vice-president.

Refusing to concede, Gómez Farías continued to try to organize influential *puros* into fighting peace negotiations and continuing the war effort. The war-weary government and public refused to embrace his goals, and he retired from politics about 1851. He died in Mexico City at the age of 66, still bitter over the rejection of his *puro* platform.

See also Polkos Revolt; Puros.

For further reading: Costeloe, *The Central Republic in Mexico, 1835–1846*, 1993; Fowler, "Valentín Gómez Farías," 1996; Fuentes Díaz, *Valentín Gómez Farías, padre de la reforma*, 1981; Hutchinson, "Valentín Gómez Farías," 1948; Ramirez, *Mexico during the War with the United States*, 1950; Ruiz, *Triumphs and Tragedy*, 1992; Santoni, *Mexicans at Arms*, 1996.

Graham, Richard H.
(ca. 1817–1846)

A lieutenant in the 4th U.S. Infantry, Richard H. Graham fought in 1846 at the Battles of Palo Alto, Resaca de la Palma, and Monterrey. He was mortally wounded during the Battle of Monterrey and died at age 29.

Graham, who was born in Kentucky, attended the U.S. Military Academy from 1834 to 1838. Serving a short time as a second lieutenant in the 2nd Dragoons, he was later transferred to the 4th U.S. Infantry. He helped direct the removal of the Cherokee Nation to Indian territory and served along the western frontier.

Graham was part of General Zachary Taylor's Army of Occupation at Corpus Christi, Texas, during 1845–1846. He participated in the Battles of Palo Alto and Resaca de la Palma in early May 1846. In response to Taylor's anxiety at not having pontoon boats by which to cross the Río Grande, Graham and a few other soldiers swam the river on May 15, cut free some Mexican boats on the other side, and towed them to the northern bank. The boats were used to begin the transfer of the army to Matamoros on May 18.

Graham was mortally wounded during an assault during the Battle of Monterrey in September 1846. He lingered for nearly three weeks before dying on October 12.

For further reading: Cullum, *Biographical Register of the Officers and Graduates of the United States Military Academy from 1802 to 1867*, 1879; Henry, *The Story of the Mexican War*, 1950.

Grant, Ulysses S.
(1822–1885)

Although he disapproved of the Mexican-American War, Lieutenant Ulysses S. Grant served in the 4th U.S. Infantry under Generals Zachary Taylor and Winfield Scott. He was later the eighteenth president of the United States.

Grant was born in Point Pleasant, Ohio. He disliked farming and working in his father's tannery business. His love of horses and riding led him to the U.S. Military Academy, where he hoped to serve in the cavalry. After graduating as a second lieutenant in 1843, he was assigned to the 4th U.S. Infantry.

Ulysses S. Grant
(Library of Congress)

Grant strongly disapproved of the Mexican-American War. He wrote in his memoirs that it was "the most unjust war ever waged by a stronger against a weaker nation.... an instance of a republic following the bad example of European monarchies.... We were sent to provoke a fight, but it was essential that Mexico should commence it."

As part of General Taylor's Army of Occupation, Grant spent the winter of 1845–1846 at Corpus Christi, Texas. He performed capably during the Battles of Palo Alto and Resaca de la Palma in May 1846. During the Battle of Monterrey, he led his regiment on horseback in a frontal assault and later rode through the enemy-held streets to obtain ammunition. Grant was similar to Taylor in some ways, such as his disheveled dress, quiet demeanor, and battlefield calm.

Detached from Taylor's army in 1847, Grant participated in General Scott's Veracruz–Mexico City campaign. Grant was in the thickest of the fighting at the Battle of El Molino del Rey. He was cited for bravery during the attack at the gates of Mexico City. By the end of the war, he had been promoted to first lieutenant with a brevet to captain.

Service after the war included military posts in New York and Michigan. He resigned in 1854 and was unsuccessful in a variety of business ventures. In 1861, Lincoln made him a brigadier general of Union troops. Grant developed a reputation as being one of the North's best fighters, winning important battles in the western theater. He became the supreme commander of the Army of the Potomac in 1864 and never retreated for the rest of the war. Not always a creative strategist, he was criticized for the high casualties his army suffered.

Grant won the 1868 presidential election against Horatio Seymour and Horace Greeley. Scandals and corruption checkered his administration, usually by trusted friends he had appointed. After his presidency, he toured the world and settled in New York. Deeply in debt and suffering from throat cancer, he began to write his memoirs. Grant finished *Personal Memoirs of U. S. Grant* in July 1885 and died a few days later. The book was very successful, and his widow Julia lived comfortably from the royalties for the rest of her life.

For further reading: Catton, *U. S. Grant and the American Military Tradition*, 1954; Grant, *Personal Memoirs of U. S. Grant*, 1885; Weems, *To Conquer a Peace*, 1974.

Gray, Andrew Belcher

(1820–1862)

An experienced surveyor, Andrew Belcher Gray was appointed to the joint Mexico–United States boundary commission established by the Treaty of Guadalupe Hidalgo and helped survey the new border.

Born and raised in Virginia, Gray excelled in mathematics and studied surveying. Surveying projects included the Mississippi Delta, the United States–Texas border (1839–1840), Lake Superior, and the San Diego area of California.

After the Mexican-American War, Gray was appointed in 1850 as chief surveyor and member of the joint commission established by the Treaty of Guadalupe Hidalgo to survey the new United States–Mexico border. In 1853, he surveyed the line for the Southern Pacific Railroad from Texas to California. He argued so bitterly with commissioner John R. Bartlett over the Bartlett-Condé Agreement that Gray was eventually replaced by W. H. Emory.

Joining the Confederate army in 1861, Gray became chief engineer overseeing the fortification of strongholds along the Mississippi River. He was killed in 1862 by a sharpshooter's bullet at Fort Pillow, Tennessee.

For further reading: Goetzmann, *Army Exploration in the American West, 1803–1863*, 1959; Webb, *The Handbook of Texas*, 1952.

Gray, Mabry B.

(1817–1848)

Captain Mabry B. Gray was a resourceful Texas Ranger who scouted and chased guerrillas for General Zachary Taylor during the Mexican-American War. He was well known for his acts of violence against Mexican citizens.

Gray was born in South Carolina and moved to Texas in 1835. Nicknamed "Mustang" for reputedly roping and taming a mustang after losing his horse during a buffalo hunt, he enlisted in the Texas Army in 1836.

Gray was hated by Mexicans for his raids along the Nueces River and Río Grande—Mexican citizens were murdered, homes burned, and livestock seized. At the outbreak of the Mexican-American War, Gray joined Samuel H. Walker's First Texas Mounted Riflemen. After his men were sent home in the fall of 1846, Gray returned to Mexico with his own company (the "Mustangers") and was given the task of keeping the roads around Monterrey clear of guerrillas. Again renown for his random killing, Gray was apparently responsible for the massacre at Guadalupe Rancho. While in Camargo he became seriously ill and died (probably of cholera). Gray is buried along the Río Grande, near Río Grande City, in an unmarked grave.

For further reading: Chamberlain, *My Confession*, 1956; Smith, *Chili Con Carne*, 1857; Webb, *The Handbook of Texas*, 1952.

Green, Duff

(1791–1875)

An agent in Great Britain and Texas for President John Tyler, Duff Green reported frequently to Tyler on the condition of Mexican-Texan affairs and lobbied to Texan leaders for a war with Mexico.

Green, who was born in Kentucky, fought in the War of 1812, studied medicine, and was also a surveyor and attorney. He moved to Missouri in the 1820s, founded a Democratic newspaper, and entered state politics. Green started another newspaper in Washington, D.C., in 1825 that championed Andrew Jackson. Serving as a U.S. envoy to Great Britain under President Tyler, Green used his diplomatic skills to collect information on British intentions regarding Texas.

Green believed that a war with Mexico was critical to acquiring new territory for slavery. He wrote to Secretary of State John C. Calhoun in 1844 that "a war with Mexico will cost us nothing and [will] reinstate us in the estimation of other nations."

Green traveled to Galveston, Texas, as Tyler's envoy and secret agent in September 1844. He reported that Mexico was adamant about not selling New Mexico and California. Green even proposed using the "Indians of the United States and Texas in the invasion of Mexico [to] revolutionize the country from the Río Grande to the Pacific under the flag of Texas." This alarmed both Mexico and Texas. Green spent much of his time trying to organize a group that would seize the northern states of Mexico for the benefit of Texas. Texan President Anson Jones rejected this scheme, and Green threatened to start a revolution in Texas, a threat for which he later apologized. By 1845, Green had become a Texas citizen and was continuing to plot with Henry L. Kinney, an influential trader and politician at Corpus Christi.

The "Green Affair" had exposed the keen U.S. interest in having Texas start a war with Mexico, an idea that had not been previously discussed with Texan leaders. This irritated some Texans such as Anson Jones, who became more interested in a negotiated peace with Mexico or continuing as an independent republic.

After the Mexican-American War, Green was an agent for the United States in making payment to Mexico according to the Treaty of Guadalupe Hidalgo. Later, he became involved in a number of different businesses, including canal and railroad building. A supporter of the

South, he operated iron works for the Confederacy during the Civil War and consulted with President Jefferson Davis on foreign affairs. Green helped coordinate the reconstruction of the South after the war ended.

For further reading: Caruso, *The Mexican Spy Company*, 1991; Green, *Facts and Suggestions, Biographical, Historical, Financial, and Political*, 1866; Hietala, *Manifest Design*, 1985; Johnson and Malone, *Dictionary of American Biography*, 1928–1936.

Guadalupe Hidalgo, Treaty of
(1848)

Signed on February 2, 1848, the Treaty of Guadalupe Hidalgo ended the Mexican-American War and granted the United States nearly half of the Republic of Mexico. It is still a binding agreement and is occasionally introduced as evidence in court cases today.

After months of negotiation, largely between U.S. representative Nicholas P. Trist and Mexican commissioners Luis G. Cuevas, José Bernardo Couto, and Miguel Atristain, the treaty was signed at the village of Guadalupe Hidalgo near Mexico City on February 2, 1848. After some modifications, it was ratified by both governments. It recognized U.S. ownership of Texas with a southern border of the Río Grande, Upper California (including the port of San Diego), and New Mexico. Mexico was to receive a cash payment of $15 million, and the outstanding claim of $3 million against Mexico by U.S. citizens would be dropped. The ceded territory later became the present-day states of California, Nevada, Arizona, New Mexico, Utah, western and southern portions of Colorado, and small parts of Wyoming, Nebraska, and Oklahoma.

Many prominent Mexicans objecting to these terms included Melchor Ocampo, governor of Michoacán, journalist Ponciano Arriaga, General Mariano Paredes y Arrillaga, and José María Cuevas, a lawyer who gave an impassioned speech before the Mexican Congress. Many *puros* favored continuing the war and disapproved of the treaty negotiated by the *moderado* leaders. An "All of Mexico" movement was gaining momentum in the United States, and the Mexican commissioners feared that more territory would be lost if the war continued. (In fact, Trist angered President James K. Polk by refusing to return as ordered toward the end of 1847. Polk had decided to demand more territory, and it is possible that Trist's insistence on working out a treaty saved Mexican sovereignty.)

Although Mexico surrendered more than 500,000 square miles of territory, it lost less than 1 percent of its citizens. Any Mexican citizen in the conquered lands had the right to remain a Mexican citizen or to become a U.S. citizen. Property, liberty, and religion were to be protected. Only approximately 2,000 Mexicans chose not to become U.S. citizens. The new Mexican Americans were frequently victimized by marauding U.S. citizens (especially in the goldfields of California), and the protection of their culture, religion, and property was rarely enforced by U.S. authorities for decades after the war.

Numerous violations of the treaty have occurred since 1848. The United States has repeatedly violated the treaty's provision for the peaceful settlement of future disputes (Article 21) and ignored other provisions during military or political interventions in Mexico. The treaty's validity continues to be examined today in courts of law, especially regarding the rights of Mexican Americans. In the 1990s, Indians and Chicanos have been using the treaty to seek compensation for various grievances, especially regarding immigration issues.

See also Couto, José Bernardo; Cuevas, Luis Gonzago; Trist, Nicholas Philip.

For further reading: Chacon Gómez, "The Intended and Actual Effects of Article VIII of the Treaty of Guadalupe Hidalgo," 1966; Griswold del Castillo, *The Treaty of Guadalupe Hidalgo*, 1991; Hammond, *The Treaty of Guadalupe Hidalgo, 1848*, 1949; Klein, *The Making of the Treaty of Guadalupe Hidalgo, on February 2, 1848*, 1905; Peña Reyes, *Algunos documentos sobre el tratado de Guadalupe y la situación de México durante la invasión americana*, 1930; Pletcher, *The Diplomacy of Annexation*, 1973; Reeves, "The Treaty of Guadalupe Hidalgo," 1905; Ruiz, *Triumphs and Tragedy*, 1992.

Guaymas, Battle of
(October 20, 1847)

Guaymas, a port in the Gulf of California, was blockaded by the U.S. Pacific Squadron during

1847–1848. It was occupied by U.S. forces after the city was heavily shelled and surrendered on October 20, 1847.

A port city along the Gulf of California coast in the state of Sonora y Sinaloa (Occidental), Guaymas was the focus of a blockade by the U.S. Pacific Squadron. On October 17, 1847, the *Portsmouth* and *Congress* anchored offshore. On October 19, Captain Elie A. F. La Vallette of the *Congress* demanded the surrender of the town. Colonel Antonio Campuzano, the commander of the 400-man garrison at Guaymas, refused.

The naval vessels offered to hold their fire for two hours so that women and children could be evacuated. Campuzano then asked for five hours, which was granted. After five hours, it was nearly dark, so the U.S. attack was postponed until morning.

Campuzano withdrew his forces in the middle of the night to Bocachicacampo, about four miles up the coast. The U.S. vessels bombarded Guaymas for about an hour on the morning of the 20th, launching nearly 500 shells. Several homes were destroyed, and one citizen was killed. The town quickly surrendered. U.S. Marines occupied it in the afternoon and raised the U.S. flag. The following day, the Marines destroyed the Mexican fortifications. The presence of the U.S. Navy effectively shut Guaymas down for the duration of the war. Light skirmishing with Campuzano's nearby forces did, however, occasionally erupt.

Landing parties from the USS *Dale* between November 1847 and April 1848 raided Mexican camps along the coast near Guaymas, and most of Campuzano's men were captured or deserted. On November 17, a 67-man landing force was attacked by 250 Mexicans at the fort on Casal Blanca Hill, seriously wounding the commanding officer. The siege was broken by artillery fire from the USS *Dale*, which inflicted a few Mexican casualties and drove the remaining Mexicans away. By this time, Campuzano's small force was thoroughly demoralized and undersupplied, and desertion greatly reduced his numbers. By the end of the war, every home or building in Guaymas had been damaged during the blockade.

See also Bocachicacampo, Skirmish at; Campuzano, Antonio.

For further reading: Bauer, *Surfboats and Horse Marines*, 1969; Craven, *A Naval Campaign in the Californias—1846–1849*, 1973; Knox, *A History of the United States Navy*, 1936.

Guerrilla Warfare

Guerrilla warfare, or hit-and-run attacks on small parties of U.S. soldiers and supply trains, was a frequent Mexican tactic during the Mexican-American War. Although bothersome, its impact was not great enough to alter the course of major campaigns. In fact, the indiscriminate abuse of Mexican citizens by the guerrillas and the harsh retaliatory measures by aggravated U.S. commanders greatly reduced the Mexican public's support of guerrilla units.

Guerrilla warfare was an accepted part of Mexican heritage in the nineteenth century and had been important during Mexico's fight for independence from Spain and in subsequent revolutions. Guerrillas favored attacks on small groups, unwary individuals, and supply trains. Usually mounted and heavily armed with daggers, sabers, lances, pistols, rifles, and lassos, guerrillas ranged through the mountains and lowlands along a network of paths, passes, and trails. After an attack, they frequently scattered across the countryside to regroup at a later time. U.S. soldiers feared the guerrilla's expert use of the lasso; victims were frequently pulled from their horses and dragged to death through the chaparral.

Also called rancheros or "hawks of the chaparral," most guerrillas were expert horsemen and wore tough rawhide chaps to protect their legs on narrow trails through the thorny chaparral. Guerrillas robbed and murdered Mexican citizens as well and were often more interested in personal gain than in defeating an enemy. Guerrillas frequently killed prisoners and wounded soldiers. Despite their treacherous reputation, guerrillas received the support of the Mexican population for shelter, food, and supplies. The harsh antiguerrilla tactics of the Texas Rangers and General Joseph Lane, for example, reduced the population's willingness to cooperate with the guerrillas, which reduced their effectiveness.

Noted guerrilla leaders Rámon Falcón and

Mexican guerrillas carry lances into battle, ca. 1848. (Library of Congress)

Antonio Canales (the "Chaparral Fox") cautiously harassed the army of General Zachary Taylor along the Río Grande in the summer of 1846. Falcón was blamed for killing Trueman Cross, the first U.S. casualty of the war. Both Canales and Falcón were familiar to the Texas Rangers, who had fought them for years along the Texas border. As Taylor moved from Matamoros to Monterrey in September, his longer supply lines became more attractive targets to guerrilla bands and harder for Taylor to defend. A large group of guerrillas and irregular Mexican cavalry under General José Urrea infested the Monterrey-Camargo road.

Attacks became more frequent. In February 1847, Generals Canales and Urrea plundered a wagon train near Ramos and killed 50 teamsters. Another group was attacked at Marin. The brutal attacks reduced wagon traffic; those that dared to travel were guarded by heavily armed troops. On March 7, a wagon train destined for Camargo was ambushed—17 soldiers were killed and 40 wagons captured. Canales claimed that his force killed a total of 161 U.S. soldiers in the month of February. Taylor began to strike back with the Texas Rangers. They quickly began to kill Mexicans, including 24 at Rancho Guadalupe in retaliation for the attack at Ramos. Indiscriminate looting and killing became commonplace by both sides near Saltillo and Camargo. Canales reportedly tortured and mutilated Mexicans who aided U.S. forces, including cutting off the ears of a woman who warned a U.S. officer of his approach.

As General Winfield Scott's army advanced toward Mexico City from Veracruz in April 1847, the Mexican Congress considered arming 50,000 men with lances, daggers, and machetes to carry on guerrilla warfare. On April 21, General José Mariano Salas called for volunteers to form a "guerrilla corp with which to attack and destroy the invaders in every manner imaginable." Their motto was "war without pity, unto death." Scott announced that he would penalize communities and town leaders for nearby guerrilla actions.

During Scott's march, guerrillas harassed the rear of the army and the wagon trains. Single shots by sharpshooters fighting from trees and dense chaparral regularly claimed U.S. lives, with the shooter vanishing into the desolate countryside.

Prominent guerrilla leaders Celestino Domeco de Jarauta and Juan Aburto, commanded guerrilla forces up to 1,500 in number. In one attack on Scott's rear, they captured 10 wagons stocked with supplies. On April 24, after the Battle of Cerro Gordo, Scott wrote that "Mexico has no longer an army.... Yet we cannot, at once, advance in force. We are obliged to look to the rear.... Deep sand, disease and bands of exasperating rancheros constitute difficulties.... Our cavalry is already meager, and, from escorting, becoming daily more so."

Small parties of soldiers who strayed from camp were always at risk. J. J. Oswandel wrote on May 2, 1847, that two "men were lassoed around their necks and dragged on the ground for some distance at full speed. After which the guerillas killed them with their *vanallos* (spears)." Captain Samuel H. Walker arrived in late May to begin counterattacks on guerrillas. Meanwhile, along Mexico's gulf coast, guerrillas preyed on the small occupational forces that Commodores Matthew C. Perry and David E. Conner had left behind in captured cities. On May 29, 1847, Perry wrote to the secretary of the navy requesting more marines to fight the annoying guerrillas around Tampico and Alvarado.

Guerrilla attacks on wagon trains became more frequent along the Veracruz-Jalapa road in June. Pitched fights between guerrillas under Jarauta and U.S. forces occurred at Las Vigas and La Hoya, where Walker killed or wounded 50 Mexicans. Marching from Veracruz in July to reinforce Scott at Puebla, General Franklin Pierce's brigade was attacked five or six times by guerrillas. U.S. losses in June and July along the Veracruz-Puebla road were about 200 killed and wounded and numerous wagons, animals, and supplies captured. General John E. Wool in northern Mexico announced that he would execute all captured guerrillas.

Guerrilla attacks on U.S. troops continued from August through November near Mier, Agua Fria, Ramos, and Saltillo and on the National Road between Veracruz and Mexico City. The violence began to degenerate into attacking Mexicans and stealing from families and churches. A command of 1,000 men under Major Folliot T. Lally lost 100 soldiers on the National Road; another force of 200 men suffered 40 casualties. In December, Secretary of War William L. Marcy permitted the army to seize the property of those civilians who aided or harbored guerrillas. Heavy fines on communities were also imposed.

Once Scott's men were concentrated near Mexico City in August–September 1847, traveling the National Road became a high-risk gauntlet. Sixty-four wagons and a 1,000-man escort left Veracruz on August 6 and arrived after losing 92 killed and wounded. Guerrilla attacks began to wane when Juan Aburto died from a fever, and a regiment of Texas Rangers arrived and began killing and burning. Guerrilla activity occurred in Mexico City as well: U.S. soldiers were frequently found murdered in the streets.

Scott ordered Brigadier General David E. Twiggs to clear the National Road of guerrillas. The U.S. soldiers often won the cooperation of the local populace, including informants who supplied information about guerrilla encampments and raiding plans. Stationed at Puebla, General Lane was one of the most aggressive guerrilla fighters. His 1,500-man force and artillery inflicted heavy losses and property damage to guerrilla bases at Atlixco and Tlaxcala. In December 1847, commanding the remnants of Taylor's army in northern Mexico, General Wool proclaimed that Mexican towns would be held responsible for guerrilla attacks and were expected to hunt down and turn over the "brigands."

Guerrilla activities also disrupted U.S. naval operations along the Pacific coast. Many residents of Baja California were discontent with offshore blockades by the Pacific fleet. A guerrilla rebellion was launched around Mulejé, Comondu, and San Anita under the command of Captain Manuel Pineda; his men drove back a landing party from the USS *Dale* near Guaymas in October 1847. Other attacks, inflicting minor losses, struck La Paz and San José del Cabo in November. Pineda was successful in penetrating San José del Cabo in

March 1848 and laid siege to its 72-man occupational force for about two weeks. The U.S. forces began to launch well-armed inland strikes that seriously wounded Pineda's rebel camps. Most of the guerrillas had surrendered or scattered by the end of April 1848. The last skirmish of the Mexican-American War at Agua Fria on June 4, 1848, was between a band of guerrillas and a detachment of U.S. dragoons.

See also Aburto, Juan; Agua Fria, Skirmish at; Atlixco, Skirmish at; Canales Rosillo, Antonio; Falcón, Rámon; Gray, Mabry B.; Jarauta, Celestino Domeco de; La Hoya, Skirmish at; Lane, Joseph; Ramos; Urrea, José; Walker, Samuel H.

For further reading: Alcaraz, *The Other Side*, 1850; Chamberlain, *My Confession*, 1956; Johannsen, *To the Halls of the Montezumas*, 1985; Ramirez, *Mexico during the War with the United States*, 1950; Smith, *The War with Mexico*, 1919; Webb, *The Texas Rangers in the Mexican War*, 1975.

H

Hall, Willard Preble
(1820–1882)

An attorney and soldier in Colonel Alexander W. Doniphan's First Regiment of Missouri Mounted Volunteers, Willard Preble Hall helped draft a new set of civil laws for New Mexico in 1846.

Hall was born in 1820 in Virginia and graduated from Yale College in 1839. He moved to Missouri the following year to practice law and became the circuit attorney in St. Joseph.

When the Mexican-American War began, Hall enlisted as a private in the volunteer Missouri regiment commanded by Colonel Doniphan. Marching with Brigadier General Stephen W. Kearny's Army of the West to Santa Fe, New Mexico, Hall and Doniphan drafted a code of civil laws for the new U.S. territory. The code remained in effect until 1891, a testimony to its quality.

Having been elected to the U.S. Congress during the march, Hall was discharged to serve in the House of Representatives from 1847 to 1853. He was also Missouri's governor during 1864–1865. After his governorship ended, he returned to St. Joseph, where he farmed and practiced law.

For further reading: Official Manual of the State of Missouri, 1964.

Halleck, Henry Wager
(1815–1872)

First Lieutenant Henry Wager Halleck served as a military engineer in Upper and Lower California during the Mexican-American War and oversaw the construction of defenses at Mazatlán.

Born in rural New York, Halleck disliked working on the family farm and craved an education. He ran away and lived with his grandfather, who placed him in school. Halleck later graduated third of 32 students from the U.S. Military Academy in 1839 and was commissioned a second lieutenant of engineers.

During the Mexican-American War, as a first lieutenant, Halleck was ordered to Monterey, California. His trip on the transport vessel *Lexington* around Cape Horn took nearly seven months. He served in various administrative and military-political positions in California and designed the fortifications for the U.S. navy occupational force at Mazatlán, where he was also lieutenant governor, in November 1847. For "gallant conduct in affairs with the enemy on the 19th and 20th of November 1846, and for meritorious services in California" (Cullum 1879), he was brevetted a captain on May 1, 1847. Halleck resigned in 1854 to write books about engineering and military policy.

Known as being disciplined and sometimes overly critical, Halleck was given the command of the Department of the Missouri during the Civil War, which he transformed into an efficient organization. In 1862, he became Lincoln's military advisor and served as both general in chief and chief of staff of the Union Army. He died in Louisville, Kentucky.

For further reading: Ambrose, Halleck, 1962; Bauer, Surfboats and Horse Marines, 1969; Cullum, Biographical Register of the Officers and Graduates of the United

States Military Academy from 1802 to 1867, 1879; Halleck, The Mexican War in Baja California, 1977.

Halls of the Montezumas, Mexico City

A battle cry and patriotic headline for the U.S. army during the Mexican-American War, "To the Halls of the Montezumas!," can still be heard today in its paraphrase in the U.S. Marine Corps fight song.

The slogan, used in newspaper headlines across the United States and frequently in speeches on the senate floor, refers to Moctezuma I and II (sometimes spelled Motechuzoma or Montezuma), two great Aztec leaders in the 1400s and early 1500s. Under the guidance of Moctezuma II, the Aztec empire had reached its zenith by the time the Spanish arrived as conquerors. Moctezuma was eventually killed and the Aztec empire was crushed under the forces of Hernán Cortés. Cortés then built the magnificent National Palace, the capital of New Spain, directly on top of the ruins of Moctezuma's palace, reportedly to capture the spiritual power of the site. Thus, Mexico City's National Palace was referred to as the "Halls of the Montezumas" by the U.S. soldiers and press.

For further reading: Bancroft, *The History of Mexico*, 1966; Weaver, *The Aztecs, Maya, and Their Predecessors*, 1972.

Hamer, Thomas Lyon
(1800–1846)

A staunch Democrat, General Thomas Lyon Hamer was one of General Zachary Taylor's better volunteer generals in northern Mexico. He died from a fever-related disease in 1846.

Born in Pennsylvania, Hamer was raised in New York and finally settled in Ohio. Enterprising and dedicated, he financed his own education and became a lawyer. After serving in the state legislature, he served three terms as a Democrat in the U.S. House of Representatives from 1832 to 1838.

A loyal Democrat, Hamer vigorously supported the Mexican-American War and joined an Ohio volunteer regiment as a private. President James K. Polk, however, commissioned him a brigadier general in July 1846.

Hamer and his men arrived at Camargo to join Major General Taylor's Army of Occupation. Hamer ably led his regiment in its assault on Purisima Bridge during the Battle of Monterrey in September 1846 and occupied Fort Tenería after it had fallen. Hamer became divisional commander when General William O. Butler was recovering from wounds he received during the battle. While stationed at Monterrey, Hamer developed a fever, which progressively worsened, and he died on December 2, 1846. The Ohio legislature sent a delegation to bring his body home.

Hamer had been a popular and resourceful officer, and Taylor lamented, "I have lost the balance wheel of my volunteer army."

See also Monterrey, Battle of.

For further reading: Giddings, *Sketches of the Campaign in Northern Mexico, in Eighteen Hundred Forty-six and Seven*, 1853; Winders, *Mr. Polk's Army*, 1997.

Hannegan, Edward Allen
(1807–1859)

Senator Edward Allen Hannegan was an expansionist and keen supporter of President James K. Polk and the Mexican-American War. At one point, he favored seizing the entire Republic of Mexico.

Born in Ohio and raised in Kentucky, Hannegan later moved to Indiana, where he became a lawyer. During 1833–1837, he was a member of the U.S. House of Representatives, and he served in the Senate from 1843 to 1849. An excellent orator, he championed the expansionist platform, including fighting Great Britain for all of Oregon and overrunning Mexico. Although he wanted the riches of Mexican territory, Hannegan stated that "Mexico and the United States are peopled by two distinct and utterly unhomogeneous races.... [The Mexicans] are utterly unfit for the blessings and restraints of rational liberty."

Hannegan briefly served as U.S. envoy to Prussia before he retired to St. Louis in 1850, where he died at the age of 52.

For further reading: Shepherd, *A Biographical Directory of the Indiana General Assembly*, 1980.

Hardee, William Joseph

(1815–1873)

A capable officer in the U.S. 2nd Dragoons, William Joseph Hardee fought with both Generals Zachary Taylor and Winfield Scott during the Mexican-American War. Hardee was one of the first U.S. prisoners of war when he was captured at the skirmish of Carricitos Ranch.

Hardee, who was born in Georgia, graduated from the U.S. Military Academy in 1838 as a second lieutenant in the 2nd Dragoons. He was promoted to captain in 1844 and studied cavalry operations in Europe.

During the Mexican-American War, Hardee served under Generals Taylor and Scott. He was second in command to Captain Seth B. Thornton when their scouting patrol was captured by Mexican cavalry at Carricitos Ranch in April 1846.

Hardee was later exchanged. He was bedridden in Camargo with dysentery in July and August, but joined his regiment before the Battle of Monterrey. As part of Scott's Army of Occupation, Hardee was present during the Veracruz–Mexico City campaign. Promoted twice for bravery, he emerged from the war as a lieutenant colonel.

Hardee authored *Rifle and Light Infantry Tactics*, which became a standard army textbook, and was later the commandant at the U.S. Military Academy. In 1861, he joined the Confederacy as a brigadier general, serving mostly with the Army of Tennessee. He fought well at the Battles of Shiloh, Perryville, Murfreesboro, and Atlanta. Hardee settled in Alabama after the war and died in Wytheville, Virginia, at age 58.

For further reading: Cullum, *Biographical Register of the Officers and Graduates of the United States Military Academy from 1802 to 1867*, 1879; Hughes, *General William J. Hardee*, 1965.

Hardin, John J.

(1810–1847)

Colonel John J. Hardin commanded the 1st Regiment of Illinois Volunteers. He was killed in action at the Battle of Buena Vista on February 23, 1847.

Hardin, who was born in Kentucky, became a lawyer. After serving in the Black Hawk War, he moved to Illinois. In 1837, he and Abraham Lincoln were the premiere Whig leaders in the state. Hardin's popularity continued to grow, and he was elected to the U.S. Congress in 1843.

At the outbreak of the Mexican-American War, Hardin was elected colonel of the 1st Regiment of Illinois Volunteers. He joined General John E. Wool's Army of the Center at San Antonio and marched toward Chihuahua and then joined General Zachary Taylor's Army of Occupation near Saltillo.

During the Battle of Buena Vista, Hardin was posted on the left flank of the U.S. line with the Indiana and Kentucky volunteer regiments. He ordered a mixed group of Kentucky and Illinois soldiers forward in a charge, only to be surprised by a mass of Mexican infantry that suddenly appeared from a deep ravine. The volunteers grappled hand to hand with the soldiers under the command of General Francisco Pérez. Hardin took the flag from the Hidalgo Battalion color-bearer and soon fell wounded. Hardin and several other officers remained behind until they were killed to protect their retreating men.

See also Buena Vista, Battle of.

For further reading: Engelmann, "The Second Illinois in the Mexican War," 1934.

Harney, William Selby

(1800–1889)

William S. Harney commanded the 2nd U.S. Dragoons during the Mexican-American War and served in northern Mexico and Major General Winfield Scott's Veracruz–Mexico City campaign.

Harney was born in Tennessee. He joined the army in 1818 as a second lieutenant of the First U.S. Infantry. In 1836, he was made lieutenant colonel of the 2nd Dragoons and was brevetted to colonel during the Second Seminole War. He was promoted to colonel of the 2nd Dragoons in 1846.

By this time, Harney had developed a reputation for being hard-edged and impulsive. He was criticized for summarily executing native prisoners during the Second Seminole War and was accused of beating a slave to death in Missouri (for which he was acquitted).

Harney frequently quarreled with his commanding officers. He led an unauthorized cavalry expedition from San Antonio in 1846, which resulted in his arrest by General John E. Wool. Major General Scott, unhappy with Harney as the leader of the cavalry, ordered him to turn the command over to a subordinate. Harney refused, and the resulting court-martial found him guilty of disobedience. After taking his case to Washington, he was reinstated by Secretary of War William L. Marcy.

Harney showed courageous leadership throughout the Veracruz–Mexico City campaign in 1847. He engaged a larger force of Mexican lancers during the siege of Veracruz. Other important tasks included scouting in advance of Scott's army. In the Battle of Cerro Gordo on April 18, Harney charged up the heights of El Telégrafo at the head of a brigade in the face of destructive fire. For this, he was brevetted brigadier general. He also fought at the Battles of Contreras and Churubusco. When the U.S. flag was raised over Chapultepec on September 13, he executed 30 U.S. deserters from the San Patricio Battalion, including a prisoner who was already dying from his wounds.

Harney's military work continued on the western frontier after the war and included the Battle of Sand Hill against the Sioux Nation. Because of the courteousness that he showed to Confederate troops under Sterling Price in Missouri, he was regarded as a Confederate sympathizer and never had an important command during the Civil War. He retired in 1863 to Mississippi and died in Orlando, Florida.

For further reading: Chamberlain, *My Confession*, 1956; Reavis, *The Life and Military Services of General William Selby Harney*, 1878.

Hawk's Peak

In his first, outwardly hostile act against the Mexican government in California, Captain John C. Frémont ordered his men to build a log defense on the summit of Hawk's Peak, near San Juan Bautista, in March 1846.

Frémont and approximately 60 men entered California in December 1845. After he promised the Mexican government that he would winter in the San Joaquín Valley, Frémont and his group wandered freely. In February 1846, they had moved south through Santa Cruz and Monterey. The heavily armed, hostile-looking group alarmed the Californios, and Mexican authorities were suspicious of their intentions.

On March 5, 1846, Frémont received a message from José Castro, the commandant general, to withdraw immediately. Manuel Castro, the prefect at Monterey, wrote to Frémont that "I have learnt with surprise that you, against the laws of the authorities of Mexico, have introduced yourself into the towns of this Departmental district under my charge with an armed force under a commission which must have been given you by your government only to survey its own proper lands. In consequence, this Prefectura now orders that you will immediately on receipt of this without any pretext return with your people out of the limits of this territory. If not this office will take the necessary measures."

Frémont, never one for being told what to do, instead took his men to the highest part of the Gavilan Mountains and occupied one of the wooded summits. His men busily felled trees and built a stout, log breastwork, from which they flew the U.S. flag. On the following day, they watched the Californio forces gathering at San Juan Bautista as U.S. envoy Thomas O. Larkin's efforts at mediation were dismissed by Castro.

On March 8, General Castro assembled approximately 400 men to drive Frémont from their district. After having spent three days in the Gavilan Mountains, and having received copies of the official correspondence between Larkin and Mexican officials and Secretary of State James Buchanan, Frémont decided to withdraw. Leaving his campfires burning, his men slipped out from their log fortress the night of March 9–March 10, 1846. Frémont taunted Castro by moving northward only a few miles a day, but eventually entered Oregon Territory.

See also Castro, José María; Frémont, John C.

For further reading: Frémont, *Memoirs of My Life*, 1886; Harlow, *California Conquered*, 1982; Nevins, *Frémont*, 1955.

Hays, John Coffee

(1817–1883)

A soldier and surveyor, John (Jack) Coffee Hays led two regiments of Texas volunteers during the Mexican-American War and was renown as a scout and guerrilla fighter.

Hays was born in Tennessee. He began surveying at the age of 15 and worked in Mississippi. In 1836, Hays moved to Texas, where he joined the Texas Rangers and participated in warfare against Comanches and Mexicans along the Río Grande and Nueces River. In 1842, he was promoted to major for gallantry in opposing Mexican raids on San Antonio.

Of slight build and modest personality, "his face was sun-browned; his cheeks gaunt; and his dark hair and dark eyes gave a shade of melancholy to his features.... His small size—he being only about five feet eight—made him appear more like a boy than a man." (Webb 1975)

Hays recruited the 1st Regiment of Mounted Texas Volunteers, mostly fierce-looking frontiersmen and Indian fighters, and joined General Zachary Taylor in May 1846 along the Río Grande. Hays conducted important scouting and reconnaissance work during Taylor's march from Matamoros toward Monterrey. He performed bravely at the Battle of Monterrey in September 1846. His men defeated a company of Mexican lancers in the opening cavalry clash on September 21, and Hays personally led the early morning storming party that crept up the steep side of Independence Hill the following day and drove the Mexican defenders from the top. His unit then returned to Texas.

By July of 1847, Hays had formed another regiment, which was sent to help Major General Winfield Scott disperse guerrillas around Puebla and Mexico City. Hays arrived at Veracruz in October and marched with the brigade of General Joseph Lane. Hays quickly led his men in harsh attacks on guerrilla bases between Veracruz and Mexico City. These attacks included ransacking and burning private homes.

Discharged in 1848, Hays emigrated the following year to California, where he served as sheriff of San Francisco County. In 1853, he became the surveyor general of California. Later successful in real estate, he died an invalid at his home near Piedmont, California.

See also Monterrey, Battle of.

For further reading: Brackett, *General Lane's Brigade in Central Mexico,* 1854; Greer, *Colonel Jack Hayes,* 1987; Webb, *The Texas Rangers in the Mexican War,* 1975.

John Coffee Hays
(Library of Congress)

Hébert, Paul Octave

(1818–1880)

An engineer and soldier, Paul Octave Hébert served in Major General Winfield Scott's Army of Occupation in 1847 and fought bravely at the Battles of El Molino del Rey and Chapultepec.

Hébert was born in Louisiana, and he graduated first in his class from the U.S. Military Academy in 1840. He was commissioned second lieutenant in the Corps of Engineers and later resigned to pursue civic engineering.

Hébert left his job as chief engineer for the state of Louisiana to join the U.S. army. Commissioned a lieutenant colonel in the 14th U.S. Infantry, Hébert was part of General Franklin Pierce's brigade in the Veracruz–Mexico City campaign in 1847. Hébert's cool leadership during the Battle of El Molino del Rey won a personal congratulations from General Scott and a brevet to colonel. Hébert also led troops during the storming of Chapultepec, and defeated a group of lancers who attempted to turn the U.S. flank.

After the war, Hébert retired to his plantation in Louisiana and was elected state governor in 1852. As a brigadier general for the Confederacy, Hébert commanded the Department of Texas and the subdistrict of North Louisiana. He resumed his engineering career when the war ended and died of cancer at the age of 62.

For further reading: Cullum, *Biographical Register of the Officers and Graduates of the United States Military Academy from 1802 to 1867,* 1879.

Henderson, James Pinckney
(1808–1858)

James Pinckney Henderson was the first governor of Texas and commanded Texas volunteers during the Mexican-American War. He was cited for gallantry during the Battle of Monterrey in 1846.

Henderson, who was born in North Carolina, was educated as a lawyer. Drawn to the military, he became a colonel of militia. He marched a company of men to fight in the Texas Revolution, but the war had ended before they arrived. Henderson was appointed attorney general of the republic in 1836, and later he became secretary of state. He helped execute a treaty of recognition between France and Texas in 1839. When Texas became a state in 1845, Henderson was elected its first governor.

At the outset of the Mexican-American War, Henderson took command of four Texas regiments and became a brigadier general of volunteers. He was cited for his gallant leadership in September 1846 during the Battle of Monterrey, in which his men seized the western approaches to the city. General Zachary Taylor appointed him to a commission that negotiated the surrender of the city and the Armistice of Monterrey.

After the war, Henderson resumed his law practice and became an elected U.S. senator in 1855. He died in Washington, D.C., at age 50.

For further reading: Johnson and Malone, *Dictionary of American Biography,* 1928–1936; Morris, "James Pinckney Henderson," 1931; Winchester, *James Pinckney Henderson,* 1971.

Henrie, Daniel Drake

A scout and interpreter for General John E. Wool, Daniel Drake Henrie was captured at La Encarnación in January 1847 and later escaped and returned to Wool's camp.

Little is known about the early life of Henrie. Born in Ohio, he moved to Texas in the early 1830s and participated in the Texas Revolution.

Henrie was part of the Mier Expedition that was captured by General Pedro de Ampudia in 1842. Imprisoned at Perote Castle near Puebla, Henrie and six other U.S. citizens made a daring escape and returned to Texas.

Four years later, Henrie joined the U.S. Army of the Center in San Antonio as a scout, guide, and translator. He accompanied General Wool's army from San Antonio to Saltillo. In early January 1847, he was part of a scouting party that was captured by Mexican cavalry at the hacienda La Encarnación.

As the prisoners were taken south, Major John P. Gaines allowed Henrie, as a wounded man, to ride his horse, and Gaines walked beside him. Henrie soon bolted from the procession and outrode the cavalrymen who pursued him. According to trooper Samuel Chamberlain, Henrie became lost and suffered greatly from lack of food and water until he was found by some of Wool's troopers. Henrie was later sent to carry messages to Washington, but was severely wounded by guerrillas near Seralvo.

See also La Encarnación; Mier Expedition.

For further reading: Chamberlain, *My Confession,* 1956; Frost, *The Mexican War and Its Warriors,* 1848; Johannsen, *To the Halls of the Montezumas,* 1985.

Heredia, José Antonio de
(ca. 1800–ca. 1870)

General José Antonio de Heredia was the supreme commander of the makeshift troops that were assembled in Chihuahua to fight Colonel Alexander Doniphan and his regiment at the Battle of Río Sacramento in 1847.

Heredia, who was born in Chilpancingo, joined the Spanish Army at the age of 15. After participating in several skirmishes with armed rebels, he joined the forces of Agustín de Iturbide in 1821. Heredia was the governor and military commandant of the state of Durango in 1844.

When war was declared, General Heredia was sent to Chihuahua to help the local forces defend themselves against an approaching U.S. force under the leadership of Colonel Doniphan. The Mexican force lost the Battle of Río Sacramento to Doniphan's regiment in February 1847; Heredia was summoned to a court of inquiry in Mexico City, but was cleared of charges of misconduct.

Heredia remained in Durango after the war and chased raiding Indians. His support and leadership resulted in the foundation of the first public library system in Durango. Having aligned himself with Emperor Maximilian in the 1860s, Heredia was imprisoned for two years at the end of the French Intervention. He died in Mexico City.

See also Río Sacramento, Battle of.

For further reading: Diccionario Porrúa, 1995.

Herrera, José Joaquín de
(1792–1854)

Soldier and politician, José Joaquín de Herrera served as president of the Republic of Mexico in 1845, during which time he tried to negotiate a settlement with the United States to avoid war, and in 1848 after the Treaty of Guadalupe Hidalgo.

Herrera, who was born in Jalapa, joined the Spanish army at a young age and saw action in a number of skirmishes with revolutionary factions. Joining forces with Agustín de Iturbide, Herrera quickly became a brigadier general in the Mexican army. He helped depose Iturbide in 1824 and served in important government positions under subsequent presidents for nearly 20 years.

Herrera became the interim leader of Mexico when President Antonio López de Santa Anna was overthrown in 1844. When he was elected on August 1, 1845, Herrera inherited a country that was politically and economically falling apart. He tried to prevent the annexation of Texas by recognizing its independence on the condition that it would not join the United States. Herrera also knew that Mexico did not have the strength to win a war with its hostile neighbor. As a *moderado*, when this failed, he agreed to discuss peace terms with a U.S. envoy. This enraged an already discontent and frustrated public, and his administration was short-lived: General Mariano Paredes y Arrillaga took over the presidency in December 1845.

In 1848, Herrera served as a peace commissioner during the negotiation of the Treaty of Guadalupe Hidalgo. Called upon by Mexicans to lead the country after the war ended, Herrera accepted the presidency in June 1848. As he did in his first administration, he inherited a number of problems, including meager funds, a disillusioned public, and various hot spots of rebellion. Leaving office in 1851, Herrera died in Tacubaya at the age of 62.

For further reading: Cotner, The Military and Political Career of José Joaquín de Herrera, 1792–1854, 1949; DePalo, The Mexican National Army, 1822–1852, 1997; Ramirez, Mexico during the War with the United States, 1950.

Hill, Daniel Harvey
(1821–1889)

An artillery officer, Daniel Harvy Hill served capably under Generals Zachary Taylor and Winfield Scott during the Mexican-American War and was brevetted twice for gallantry.

Hill was born in South Carolina. He graduated from the U.S. Military Academy in 1842 and was stationed at various garrisons on the northern and western frontiers.

Hill served under both Generals Taylor and Scott during the Mexican-American War and led troops during the bitter street fighting in Monterrey in September 1846. During Scott's Veracruz–Mexico City campaign in 1847, Hill was brevetted to captain for his role in the Battle of Churubusco and to major for his leadership during the storming of Chapultepec.

Hill later taught mathematics at Washington College in Virginia. As a major general in the Confederate army during the Civil War, he fought skillfully during a number of battles. After the war, he was president of the University of Arkansas.

For further reading: Cullum, Biographical Register of

the Officers and Graduates of the United States Military Academy from 1802 to 1867, 1879.

Hitchcock, Ethan Allen
(1798–1870)

One of the more highly regarded officers in General Zachary Taylor's army, Ethan Allen Hitchcock was chosen by General Winfield Scott to be his inspector general during his Veracruz–Mexico City campaign in 1847.

Hitchcock, grandson of Revolutionary War hero Ethan Allen, was born in Vermont. He graduated from the U.S. Military Academy in 1817. Promoted to captain in 1824, he saw service in Wisconsin, Florida, and the northwestern frontier from 1833 to 1840. Given the command of the 3rd U.S. Infantry in 1842 as a lieutenant colonel, he molded it into one of the best units in the army.

During the Mexican-American War, Hitchcock served under General Taylor in 1846 and was the inspector general for Major General Scott in 1847. Hitchcock was sick much of the time, and on the march he rode in an ox wagon on a bed set upon boxes of ammunition. Hitchcock helped organize and administrate the Mexican Spy Company under outlaw Manuel Dominguez. Hitchcock advised Scott on a variety of issues and helped organize the details for the occupation of Mexico City.

After the war, Hitchcock commanded the Military Division of the Pacific. During the Civil War, he had largely an administrative role and coordinated prisoner-of-war exchanges. He retired to South Carolina and Georgia, where he wrote books on a variety of topics.

For further reading: Caruso, *The Mexican Spy Company,* 1991; Hitchcock, *Fifty Years in Camp and Field,* 1909; Weems, *To Conquer a Peace,* 1974.

Holzinger, Sebastián

Of German nationality, Lieutenant Sebastián Holzinger was a member of the Mexican Marines. During the siege of Veracruz in March 1847, Holzinger commanded the defenders of Fort Santa Barbara, one of the city's artillery posts. When a U.S. shell snapped off part of the fort's flagpole on March 24, Holzinger and another soldier climbed the exposed wall and nailed the Mexican colors back to the flagstaff. A second well-aimed shot struck the wall just below the flag, burying the two soldiers in rubble. They escaped, and their bold act was applauded by the U.S. gunners. Captain John H. Aulick, the U.S. commander during the artillery duel, was so impressed by Holzinger's act that he mentioned it in his official report.

For further reading: Bauer, *The Mexican War, 1846–1848,* 1974.

Hooker, Joseph
(1814–1879)

A talented staff officer who served in both General Zachary Taylor's and General Winfield Scott's armies during 1846–1847, Joseph Hooker was one of the few officers to receive three or more brevets during the war.

Hooker, who was born in Massachusetts, graduated twenty-ninth of 50 from the U.S. Military Academy in 1837. He served in the Second Seminole War and on the western frontier. A member of the 1st U.S. Artillery in the Mexican-American War, he later served on the

Ethan Allen Hitchcock
(Library of Congress)

staffs of Generals Persifor F. Smith, Thomas Hamer, William O. Butler, and Gideon J. Pillow. Hooker saw action with Taylor in northern Mexico in 1846 and with Scott from Veracruz to Mexico City in 1847. Hooker received his first brevet to captain for gallantry at the Battle of Monterrey. During Scott's march, he was brevetted major for leading a charge across the National Bridge and lieutenant colonel for his actions during the Battle of Chapultepec.

Hooker resigned from the army in 1853 and took up farming in California. His early years as a brigadier general for the Union during the Civil War were quite successful—he earned the nickname "Fighting Joe" and was promoted to the commander of the Army of the Potomac in 1863. At this level, however, he became overly cautious and was defeated by Generals Robert E. Lee and Stonewall Jackson at Chancellorsville. He was later moved to the western theater.

For further reading: Cullum, *Biographical Register of the Officers and Graduates of the United States Military Academy from 1802 to 1867,* 1879; Hebert, *Fighting Joe Hooker,* 1944.

Houston, Samuel
(1793–1863)

The first president of the Republic of Texas, Sam Houston was enthusiastic about the Mexican-American War, and he vigorously supported it as a U.S. senator during 1846–1847.

Born in Virginia and raised in Tennessee, Houston ran away from home when he was 15 and was adopted into the Cherokee Nation. He later served with General Andrew Jackson in the Creek Indian Wars in Alabama, where he was severely wounded. In the 1820s, Houston began his political career and became the governor of Tennessee. He moved to Texas in 1829.

A key military and political figure during the Texas Revolution in 1836, Houston's leadership of the army resulted in the U.S. victory at San Jacinto, the capture of General Antonio López de Santa Anna, and the Treaties of Velasco. Houston served from 1836 to 1838 as the first president of the new Republic of Texas and again from 1841 to 1844.

Although not an active participant in the Mexican-American War, Houston strongly supported it. Wanting to stay with his family, he declined a military appointment from President James K. Polk and disagreed with him about military strategy. Houston argued for more property concessions in the Treaty of Guadalupe Hidalgo and refused to vote on the treaty in the U.S. Senate in 1848.

A long-term U.S. senator (1846–1859), Houston was a Unionist and refused to support the secession of Texas, which led to his removal as governor. Houston retired and died in Huntsville, Texas.

For further reading: Campbell, *Sam Houston and the American Southwest,* 1993; Williams and Barker, *The Writings of Sam Houston, 1813–1863,* 1938–1943.

Huamantla, Battle of
(October 9, 1847)

The Battle of Huamantla was the last major conflict of the Mexican-American War around Mexico City and was marked by widespread murder, pillaging, and rape in the town of Huamantla following the battle.

After General Winfield Scott had seized Veracruz in 1847 and pushed his army westward along the National Road toward Mexico City, U.S. reinforcements continued to arrive in Veracruz.

Following the fall of Mexico City in September 1847, General Antonio López de Santa Anna escaped with remnants of his army. Refusing to surrender, he skirted eastward and attacked the small U.S. garrison at Puebla. Gaining word that reinforcements under Brigadier General Joseph Lane were approaching from Veracruz, Santa Anna removed most of his men from Puebla and planned to ambush Lane near Huamantla, where Santa Anna concealed his force.

Lane's 2,500 men marched to Jalapa, where they were joined by 1,000 men under Major F. T. Lally. Lane then marched his 3,500 men toward Puebla to break the siege. En route, Lane learned about Santa Anna's presence at Huamantla and moved quickly to attack him.

On October 9, 1847, Texas Ranger Captain Samuel H. Walker and four companies of cavalry were in advance of Lane's infantry. About three miles from Huamantla they caught sight of a large body of green-clad lancers, and Walker ordered a charge. Pursuing the fleeing horsemen into town, Walker's men were met by heavy musket and artillery fire. Riding among the guns, Walker beheaded a Mexican officer who was preparing to fire a cannon. Walker's command was shattered by the crossfire, and Walker fell, mortally wounded, from his horse. The U.S. survivors took shelter in a church until Lane's infantry arrived and drove the Mexicans toward Querétaro. U.S. losses were 13 killed and 11 wounded; Mexican losses were estimated between 50 and 100 killed, wounded, and missing.

Infuriated by the death of Walker, Lane ordered his men to "avenge the death of the gallant Walker... and take all we could lay hands on," remembered Lieutenant William D. Wilkins of the 15th U.S. Infantry. Liquor stores were "liberated" first, and the men quickly became drunk. "Old women and girls were stripped of their clothing—and many suffered still greater outrages." Dozens of citizens were murdered, women raped, and homes looted and burned.

Two hundred soldiers were too drunk to march afterward. Wilkins wrote that "It gave me a lamentable view of human nature, stripped of all disguise and free from all restraint, and made [me] for the first time, ashamed of my country."

The Battle of Huamantla was the last major conflict of the Veracruz–Mexico City campaign, although sporadic guerrilla skirmishes continued until June 1848. Six days after Huamantla, Santa Anna resigned command of the Mexican army.

See also Lane, Joseph; Walker, Samuel H.

For further reading: Alcaraz, *The Other Side*, 1850; Brackett, *General Lane's Brigade in Central Mexico*, 1854; Oswandel, *Notes of the Mexican War*, 1885; Smith and Judah, *Chronicles of the Gringos*, 1968.

Huger, Benjamin

(1805–1877)

Artillery officer and chief of ordnance Benjamin Huger was one of the few U.S. officers who were brevetted three or more times during the Mexican-American War.

Huger was born in South Carolina. He graduated eighth of 37 from the U.S. Military Academy in 1825 and was commissioned a second lieutenant of artillery.

During the Mexican-American War, Huger was chief of ordnance for General Winfield Scott's Army of Occupation in 1847. Huger helped place and fire the batteries during the siege of Veracruz, for which he was brevetted to major; his expert leadership and gunnery skills during the Battles of El Molino del Rey and Chapultepec resulted in brevets to lieutenant colonel and colonel, respectively. After the fall of Mexico City, Huger was bedridden with respiratory illnesses and rheumatism.

As a general for the Confederacy during the Civil War, Huger's actions on the battlefield were criticized by his superiors and the Confederate Congress. He later returned to being an inspector of artillery and ordnance. After the Civil War, he retired to Virginia and South Carolina.

For further reading: Cullum, *Biographical Register of the Officers and Graduates of the United States Military Academy from 1802 to 1867*, 1879; Rhoades, *Scapegoat General*, 1985.

Hughes, John Joseph

(1797–1864)

A bishop in the Catholic Church, John Joseph Hughes counseled President James K. Polk about the use of Catholic chaplains in the U.S. army during the Mexican-American War.

Hughes was born in Ireland and educated in Pennsylvania and Maryland. He enjoyed defending the Catholic religion and became a well-known and skillful orator.

In 1846, Hughes was called to Washington to discuss with President Polk the appointment of army chaplains and Polk's concerns that the Mexican public feared for their religious freedom. Hughes declined an appointment to the U.S. army when Polk would not give him the full rank of envoy. He recommended that Polk discuss finding suitable chaplains with Reverend Peter Verhaegen of Georgetown College. Fathers Antony Rey and John McElroy, two Georgetown priests, later served as chaplains in General Zachary Taylor's Army of Occupation along the Río Grande in 1846.

Hughes went on to fight for famine relief, emancipation, and other reforms. He later became a personal agent for President Abraham Lincoln in Europe during the Civil War.

See also Catholic Church, Mexico.

For further reading: Hassard, *The Life of Reverend John Hughes*, 1866.

Hunt, Henry Jackson
(1819–1889)

An officer in the 2nd U.S. Artillery, Henry Jackson Hunt was a steady and capable leader in the battles of Major General Winfield Scott's 1847 campaign, especially at San Cosmé gate outside Mexico City.

Jackson was born in Detroit, Michigan. He graduated from the U.S. Military Academy in 1839 and joined the 2nd U.S. Artillery. Jackson displayed excellent leadership in the battles of General Winfield Scott's 1847 Veracruz–Mexico City campaign. He is best remembered for his handling of a two-gun battery at the San Cosmé *garita* of Mexico City on September 13, 1847. Firing from an exposed position in the street, Hunt lost five of his eight gunners as his battery was swept by musket fire. Wounded twice, Hunt received two brevets during the war.

Serving on an artillery board, Hunt helped modernize artillery tactics in the 1850s. Appointed a Union general during the Civil War, he was praised for his artillery fire at Malvern Hill, Antietam, and Gettysburg. Hunt remained with the artillery until he retired in 1883. He died in Washington, D.C., six years later.

For further reading: Cullum, *Biographical Register of the Officers and Graduates of the United States Military Academy from 1802 to 1867*, 1879; Dillon, *American Artillery in the Mexican War 1846–1847*, 1975; Fitz Gerald, *In Memorium: General Henry Jackson Hunt*, 1889.

Hunter, Charles G.
(1813–1873)

Lieutenant Charles G. Hunter became famous in the U.S. press as the officer responsible for the 1847 occupation of Alvarado, a port city that the U.S. Navy had failed twice before to capture.

Born in Newport, Rhode Island, Hunter was appointed as a midshipman in the U.S. Navy in 1835. He was promoted to lieutenant in 1841 and in 1846 was given command of the *Scourge*.

After General Winfield Scott landed his Army of Occupation at Veracruz in March 1847, he decided to seize the city of Alvarado and use it as a supply center. Lieutenant Hunter commanded the steamer *Scourge*, which sailed for the Alvarado River to await the arrival of Brigadier General John A. Quitman's occupational force that was marching overland from Veracruz. On March 31, after the *Scourge* fired a few shells toward the city, local citizens informed Hunter that the Mexican forces had evacuated the night before.

Taking the initiative, Hunter occupied the town and raised the U.S. flag. Leaving six men to defend Alvarado, he continued upriver, burned or captured other Mexican vessels, and occupied the village of Tlacotalpán on April 1.

Hunter's premature occupation of Alvarado angered General Scott and Commodore Matthew C. Perry. Having planned a surprise attack by land, Scott and Perry believed that Hunter's actions prompted the Mexicans to burn their supplies and scatter their horses and livestock. Perry court-martialed Hunter, who was reprimanded and dismissed from the squadron. Perry was roundly criticized for this harsh punishment, and "Alvarado" Hunter became a hero in the U.S. press. Although Hunter may have exceeded his orders, it is possible that they were not clear; it is also possible that Perry's reaction was because he had wanted to be the first to take the city, a port that the U.S. Navy had twice failed to take.

During the Civil War, Hunter commanded the Union steamer *Montgomery* in the Gulf of Mexico. His overly aggressive pursuit of a British blockade runner into Cuban waters led to his dismissal from the U.S. Navy. Hunter retired to Rhode Island, and he and his family drowned in a shipwreck in 1873.

See also Alvarado; Veracruz.

For further reading: Bauer, *Surfboats and Horse Marines*, 1969; Griffis, *Matthew Calbraith Perry*, 1890; Morison, *"Old Bruin" Commodore Matthew Calbraith Perry*, 1967.

I

Ide, William Brown

(1796–1852)

A U.S. settler in California, William Brown Ide helped organize in June 1846 the Bear Flag Revolt, which declared California free from Mexican rule.

Ide, who was born in Massachusetts, was a Mormon who eventually settled in the upper Sacramento Valley, near Sutter's Fort.

As one of the leaders of the Bear Flaggers, Ide helped organize the capture of Sonoma by his group of 30 to 40 rebellious U.S. settlers in June 1846. The Bear Flaggers also imprisoned several prominent citizens, including Mariano Vallejo, at Sutter's Fort. Ide declared Sonoma free of Mexican rule and raised the flag of the Bear Flag Republic. He later joined John C. Frémont's California Battalion as a private.

In 1847, Ide became a surveyor for the Northern Department of California. After the Mexican-American War, he held the position of county judge and justice of the peace in Colusi County. Stricken with smallpox, he died in Monroeville.

See also Bear Flag Revolt.

For further reading: Rogers, *William Brown Ide,* 1962.

Immortal 14

The Immortal 14 were 14 Whigs in the U.S. House of Representatives who voted against President James K. Polk's war bill on May 11, 1846.

After Democratic President Polk received word of the April 1846 skirmish at Carricitos Ranch on the north side of the Río Grande, he quickly drafted a war message that claimed that Mexico had spilled U.S. blood on U.S. soil. The war bill, maintaining that Mexico had started a war with the United States, called for money and soldiers.

The U.S. House of Representatives overwhelmingly supported the war effort by a vote of 173 to 14 on May 11. The 14 opponents—all antislavery Whigs from eastern or New England states—believed that the war was immoral and was being waged to gain new territory for slavery. Led by John Quincy Adams, the Immortal 14 consistently voted against all efforts to support the war.

See also Adams, John Quincy.

For further reading: Schroeder, *Mr. Polk's War,* 1973.

Indians

Members of Indian tribes that had already been suppressed served as soldiers and scouts in both the U.S. and Mexican armies. The lack of a strong military presence in New Mexico, Chihuahua, and Sonora during the Mexican-American War resulted in continual raiding by western tribes.

The presence of warring Indians helped Mexico shape its initial foreign policy with the United States regarding Texas. Mexico welcomed U.S. settlers into Texas to reduce the frequency and severity of Indian attacks on Mexican citizens south of the Río Grande. It was hoped that a prosperous population of U.S. settlers would satiate Indian raiders and keep them from raiding deeper into Mexico's interior.

A small number of Native Americans, mostly from eastern tribes, served in the U.S. Army during the Mexican-American War. Approximately one dozen Delaware Indians accompanied John C. Frémont's California campaign during 1846–1847 and served as scouts and hunters. Frémont's men frequently fought the Klamath Nation in Oregon, burning villages and killing a number of men, women, and children. Approximately 50 Shawnee and Delaware Indian scouts accompanied Brigadier General Stephen W. Kearny's Army of the West to Santa Fe, New Mexico. Pueblo Indians, most notably El Tomacito, were involved in the Taos Rebellion in New Mexico in 1847.

The Mexican Army consisted of many Indian and Indian-Spanish soldiers from eastern and central Mexico, often from isolated, rural communities. Because of the number of different dialects, communication among soldiers, and soldiers and officers, was often impaired. The Mexican Army frequently foraged for food on the march and often relied on Indian fields and stores.

While the U.S. and Mexican armies were locked in struggle during the Mexican-American War, the western tribes, especially the Comanche, Apache, and Navajo, continued to raid white settlements in northern Mexico and Texas. Attacks increased in New Mexico and Chihuahua and became so troublesome that Brigadier General Kearny ordered Colonel Alexander Doniphan to negotiate a treaty with the warring Navajo in New Mexico. Doniphan managed to assemble nearly 500 warriors and chiefs, many of whom signed the Treaty of Ojo Oso in 1846. (The treaty, however, did not reduce raiding.)

After the war, both the U.S. and Mexican governments had more resources to undertake long-term containment policies. The state of Chihuahua, for example, continued to hire people, such as U.S. bounty hunter James Kirker, to kill Apaches. The bounty hunters were paid by the number of scalps they collected.

The U.S. campaign against the western tribes, especially the Apache, is well known.

See also Delaware Indians; El Tomacito; Kirker, James; Klamath Indians; Ojo Oso.

For further reading: DePalo, *The Mexican National Army, 1822–1852*, 1997; Hale, *Mexican Liberalism in the Age of Mora, 1821–1853*, 1968; Hefter, *El soldado mexicano*, 1958; Richardson, *The Comanche Barrier*, 1933; Smith, "Indians in American-Mexican Relations before the War of 1846," 1963; Trennert, *Alternative to Extinction*, 1975.

Ingraham, Duncan N.
(1802–1891)

A commander in the U.S. Navy's Home Squadron in the Gulf of Mexico, Duncan N. Ingraham participated in blockading activities, including expeditions at Tabasco and Alvarado, along Mexico's east coast during 1847–1848.

Ingraham was born in Massachusetts. He joined the U.S. Navy as a midshipman at the age of nine and served in the War of 1812. By 1838, his rank had risen to commander.

During the Mexican-American War, Ingraham was attached to the U.S. Home Squadron, which patrolled the Gulf of Mexico. He assisted Commodore David Conner during the seizure of Tampico. Ingraham and Commander Josiah Tattnall negotiated with town leaders regarding the surrender. As commander of the USS *Somers*, Ingraham supervised expeditions up the Tabasco and Alvarado Rivers.

After the war, Ingraham saw duty in the Mediterranean and Europe. In 1861, he resigned to join the Confederate navy and commanded naval forces along the coast of South Carolina. He retired to Charleston after the war and died at age 89.

For further reading: Bauer, *Surfboats and Horse Marines*, 1969; Bradlee, *A Forgotten Chapter in Our Naval History*, 1923; Knox, *A History of the United States Navy*, 1936.

J

Jackson, Andrew
(1767–1845)

An ardent Democrat and expansionist, President Andrew Jackson worked toward the separation of Texas from Mexico, its subsequent annexation into the United States, and the purchase of New Mexico and California from Mexico. He was also largely responsible for the nomination of James K. Polk as Democratic candidate in the 1844 presidential election.

Born in North Carolina to Scots-Irish immigrants, Andrew Jackson was a poor student. Fiercely independent, he fought in the American Revolution as a militiaman at age 13. Jackson was injured by a saber blow when, as a prisoner of war, he refused to clean the boots of a British officer in 1781, and he later nearly died of smallpox.

After becoming an attorney, Jackson moved to Tennessee, where he developed a reputation for enjoying a good fight. He became famous for his defense of New Orleans during the War of 1812. A Democrat and expansionist, Jackson lost a very close presidential race to John Quincy Adams in 1824 and then defeated him soundly in 1828. Jackson was president for two terms (1829–1837) and favored moving native populations west of the Mississippi River and controlling Texas, New Mexico, California, and Oregon Territory. President Jackson was responsible for the removal of the Cherokee Nation from Georgia to Oklahoma along the Trail of Tears.

The growing discontent in Texas in the 1830s was supported by the Jackson administration. Jackson continually tried to annex Texas and purchase additional Mexican lands. He advised President John Tyler and key Texans such as Sam Houston regarding the importance of annexing Texas and limiting British influence in Texas, California, and Oregon. Jackson's influence helped bring Texas into the Union, which was the major cause of the Mexican-American War. Jackson's voice was crucial in the selection of James K. Polk as the Democratic 1844 presidential candidate, who supported the annexation of Texas. Although ill with tuberculosis, Jackson continued to focus his energies during 1844–1845 on annexation until he died at his home in Tennessee in June 1845.

For further reading: Bassett, *The Life of Andrew Jackson,* 1967; Remini, *Andrew Jackson and the Course of American Democracy, 1833–1845,* 1984.

Jackson, Samuel

A seaman on the USS *St. Mary's* during the 1846 blockade of Mexico's gulf coast, Samuel Jackson was hung in September for striking a commanding officer.

The U.S. Navy's Home Squadron blockaded Mexico's eastern ports during 1846–1847. Blockade duty was boring and monotonous and usually consisted of being at anchor within view of a port or sailing back and forth along the same course, patrolling for Mexican vessels. In addition, food and water supplies on board were usually contaminated.

On the USS *St. Mary's,* an incident occurred and seaman Samuel Jackson was charged with striking a commanding officer and using mutinous language. Wanting to deter any other breakdowns in discipline, Commodore David Conner ordered Jackson to be executed. On September 17, 1846, a yellow flag was raised and the crew assembled. After the charges were read, Jackson was immediately hanged. The severity of the punishment shocked sailors and officers alike.

For further reading: Bauer, Surfboats and Horse Marines, 1969.

Jackson, Thomas Jonathan ("Stonewall")
(1824–1863)

An artillery officer in Major General Winfield Scott's Army of Occupation, Lieutenant Thomas Jonathan Jackson served capably in all the battles of the Veracruz–Mexico City campaign in 1847.

Born in Virginia, Jackson was raised by an uncle and sent to the U.S. Military Academy. Jackson graduated in 1846 as a lieutenant, and fought briefly against the Seminoles in Florida before being sent to Mexico.

Landing at Veracruz as part of Major General Scott's Army of Occupation in 1847, Jackson served with the 1st U.S. Artillery. He was cited for gallantry in nearly every battle that Scott fought from Veracruz to Mexico City, won two brevets, and had become a brevet major within 18 months of graduating from West Point. He is most remembered for holding advanced positions during the Battles of Contreras and San Cosmé *garita* (gate) and calmly directing his batteries under heavy enemy fire. For this, he was personally recognized by Scott.

Jackson joined the Confederacy as a brigadier general, and quickly became General Robert E. Lee's most trusted subordinate. He was wounded in 1863 during the Battle of Chancellorsville and died of pneumonia after his arm was amputated. Jackson earned the nickname "Stonewall" at the First Battle of Bull Run, and his infantry was called the "foot cavalry" because of their record-setting marches.

For further reading: Cook, *The Family and Early Life of Stonewall Jackson*, 1924; Cullum, *Biographical Register of the Officers and Graduates of the United States Military Academy from 1802 to 1867*, 1879; Dabney, *The Life and Campaigns of Lieutenant-General Thomas J. Jackson*, 1866; Robertson, *Stonewall Jackson*, 1997.

Jalapa

The picturesque capital city of the state of Veracruz, Jalapa was the staging area for the formation of the Army of the East in 1847. It was occupied for several months after the Battle of Cerro Gordo by Major General Winfield Scott's Army of Occupation.

After Scott's army had landed at Veracruz in March 1847, General Antonio López de Santa Anna scratched together the Army of the East, which was assembled at Jalapa under Major General Valentín Canalizo. After Santa Anna and Canalizo were defeated at the Battle of Cerro Gordo in April and retreated toward Mexico City, Jalapa was occupied by Scott's victorious forces.

Nestled in highlands above the gulf coast, Jalapa was about 100 miles east of Mexico City, Scott's final destination. Jalapa's population of about 5,000 was fairly affluent, and private homes were built of stone with large bay windows. Gardens added splashes of color throughout the city, and guitar music could frequently be heard. The surrounding hills were rich in well-maintained orange plantations, and textile factories thrived in the city.

Lieutenant Raphael Semmes noted that Jalapa "as it first strikes the beholder…is beautiful and picturesque in the extreme. I cannot describe it better than by comparing it to a delicate mosaic set in a massive frame of emerald. It sat embowered among the hills, in a wilderness of shrubbery, amid which the tall and graceful palm, with its feathery foliage, was conspicuous."

The main streets were lined with hotels, shops, and farmers selling fruits and vegetables. The Mexican men generally dressed in white cotton cloth with fanciful belts in which "machetes, or large knives used for the cutting of sugar-cane, were frequently stuck…giving the wearer an air of barbarian ferocity," reported Semmes.

Intent on good relations with the townspeople, Scott quartered his regular troops in town and his volunteers in the country. The streets were crowded with U.S. soldiers and Mexicans. The U.S. soldiers found the citizens friendly and flocked to the community bathhouses. Scott's army was stricken with illness (especially diarrhea) during its stay, and the hospitals were overcrowded. George Ballentine recalled that "sick men, some of whom were wounded, and others wasted to skeletons with diarrhea, and in the last stages of illness, lay on a thin piece of matting or a dirty doubled-up blanket on the cold and hard brick floor.... Nearly all of them were infested with vermin. Their diet was bread and coffee...."

Anxious to move on before the rainy season arrived, Scott moved most of the army ahead to Puebla. Lieutenant Colonel Thomas Childs was appointed military governor of Jalapa and assigned an occupational force of about 1,000 men.

For further reading: Ballentine, *Autobiography of an English Soldier in the United States Army*, 1853; Semmes, *Service Afloat and Ashore during the Mexican War*, 1851; Siemans, *Between the Summit and the Sea*, 1990.

Jarauta, Celestino Domeco de
(1814–1848)

A Spanish priest turned guerrilla, Padre Celestino Domeco de Jarauta harassed Major General Winfield Scott's Army of Occupation as it marched along the National Road in 1847.

Born in Spain, Jarauta became a Catholic priest and fought in Spain's First Carlist War (1833–1839). He later traveled to Cuba and then settled in Veracruz, where he was one of the most popular clergy.

Flamboyant and clever, Jarauta formed a guerrilla force to harass Scott's supply lines along the National Road, especially between Cerro Gordo and Puebla. Jarauta and his men were sheltered and supplied by Mexican sympathizers who lived along the route. A report in the London *Times* stated that "A Spanish priest, named Jarauta, has given unexpected energy to these bands, and distinguished himself personally on various occasions. The clerical and military characters do not seem to be considered incompatible either in Spain or here."

An excellent horseman, Jarauta led up to 1,500 men in quick-hitting guerrilla attacks on U.S. columns and wagon trains. His men committed various atrocities against U.S. soldiers and travelers and Mexicans alike. Although the antiguerrilla tactics of General Scott and Brigadier General Joseph Lane reduced his effectiveness, Jarauta was never captured by U.S. troops. When Scott and his men formally entered Mexico City on September 14, Jarauta led several attacks on U.S. troops in the city's streets. He still remained at large in February 1848 after the Treaty of Guadalupe had been signed.

In May 1848, Jarauta joined General Mariano Paredes y Arrillaga in a revolt, which began in the city of Aguascalientes, against the Mexican government. Jarauta and 50 men seized the military garrison at Lagos de Moreno on June 1. The revolt was suppressed by the end of July, and Jarauta was captured near Guanajuato. When informed that he was to be executed, he asked for 24 hours to write to his mother in Spain. His request was denied, and he was killed by five gunshots in the back.

See also Guerrilla Warfare.

For further reading: Diccionario Porrúa, 1995; Roa Bárcena, *Recuerdos de la invasión norte-americana*, 1947.

Jarero, José María
(1801–1867)

Brigadier General José María Jarero, as part of the Army of the East, anchored the Mexican right flank during the Battle of Cerro Gordo in April 1847 and repulsed the attack of Brigadier General Gideon J. Pillow.

Jarero was born in Jalapa in the state of Veracruz. He joined the Spanish army at the age of 15 and participated in the suppression of various rebellions. He later joined forces with Agustín de Iturbide. In 1832, Jarero had become brigade general in the Mexican army and commanded military forces at Veracruz.

Jarero became a commander in the Army of the East, a makeshift force that General Antonio López de Santa Anna assembled to fight the invasion of General Winfield Scott's Army of Occupation at Veracruz. Jarero's brigade anchored the right flank of the Mexican position at the Battle of Cerro Gordo in April 1847. Although most of the battle occurred around the Mexican left, his men poured a destructive fire into General Gideon J. Pillow's late assault on his position. Jarero surrendered to U.S. forces during the battle.

After the war, Jarero served as commandant general at Querétaro and Puebla. He died at age 66 in Mexico City.

For further reading: Alcaraz, *The Other Side*, 1850; Carreño, *Jefes del ejército mexicano en 1847*, 1914; DePalo, *The Mexican National Army, 1822–1852*, 1997; *Diccionario Porrúa*, 1995.

Jesup, Thomas Sidney
(1788–1860)

As quartermaster for the U.S. Army, Thomas Sidney Jesup was responsible for supplying the armies of Generals Zachary Taylor, Winfield Scott, John E. Wool, and Stephen W. Kearny during the Mexican-American War.

Jesup, who was born in Virginia, entered the U.S. army in 1808 and served during the War of 1812. He was brevetted to lieutenant colonel for gallantry during the Battle of Lundy's Lane, where he was severely wounded. In 1818, he was appointed brigadier general and quartermaster general by President James Monroe. Jesup said that his job was to ensure an "ample and efficient system of supply, to give the utmost facility and effect to the movements and operations of the Army, and to enforce a strict accountability on the part of all officers and agents charged with monies and supplies." Jesup founded an efficient quartermaster department that utilized a variety of business concepts. Many of the operating procedures were integrated *Army Regulations* and are essentially unchanged today. Jesup was also supreme commander of all the U.S. forces during the Second Seminole War in 1837.

During the Mexican-American War, Jesup devoted his energies to supplying the U.S. soldiers. He procured ships, boats, wagons, and animals in large numbers and went to the field himself to improve the supply system. Jesup received little cooperation from field generals regarding advance notification of their supply needs. The U.S. army was not prepared to go to war in 1846, and Jesup constantly struggled with meager reserves, a growing army, and a limited budget. Returning from the field, he recommended packaging changes, which would minimize damage, and weight restrictions for pack mules. Because there was no system of quality control, some of the hundreds of contractors Jesup dealt with supplied inferior products that were less costly to make. Jesup was also resourceful; for example, when no money was available for buying tents, he purchased ordinary muslin to provide at least some shelter.

Although Jesup was frequently chastised or censured by angry field commanders, most historians believe he did a remarkable job outfitting a large U.S. force on foreign soil, especially considering his budget limitations. Jesup struggled to maintain the efficiency of his department during severe budget cuts in the 1850s. His health failing, he died from a stroke in Washington, D.C., in his forty-second year as quartermaster general. Fort Jesup, Louisiana, was named in his honor.

For further reading: Kiefer, *Maligned General*, 1979; Rodenbaugh, *The Army of the United States*, 1896; Smith and Judah, *Chronicles of the Gringos*, 1968; Winders, *Mr. Polk's Army*, 1997.

Johnston, Albert Sidney
(1803–1862)

An officer in General Zachary Taylor's Army of Occupation, Albert Sidney Johnston led a regiment of volunteer Texas infantrymen in 1846.

Johnston, who was born in Kentucky, excelled at mathematics and Latin at Transylvania University. He graduated eighth of 41 from the U.S. Military Academy in 1826 and was commissioned a second lieutenant in the 6th U.S. Infantry. After retiring from the army, he farmed in Missouri and then moved to Texas. He became commander of the Texas army in 1837; the following year, he was the secretary of war for the republic.

Johnston volunteered as a member of the "First Regiment of Foot Riflemen of Texas" and was elected its colonel. The regiment joined General Taylor's Army of Occupation along the Río Grande in 1846. Taylor was so impressed by its military bearing that he gave Johnston command of the U.S. staging area at Camargo. Johnston later became the inspector general for General William O. Butler's division and capably led troops during the Battle of Monterrey in 1846.

After the war, Johnston served with the U.S. army in Texas and along the western frontier, fighting Indians. He joined the Confederacy as a brigadier general and lost a series of battles in Tennessee and Mississippi. A bullet severed an artery in his leg at the Battle of Shiloh in 1862, and he bled to death.

For further reading: Johnston, *The Life of General Albert Sidney Johnston,* 1878; Roland, *Albert Sidney Johnston,* 1964.

Johnston, Joseph Eggleston
(1807–1891)

An infantry officer and engineer with Major General Winfield Scott's Army of Occupation in 1847, Joseph Eggleston Johnston was wounded five times during the Veracruz–Mexico City Campaign. He was one of the few U.S. officers who were awarded three or more brevets during the war.

Johnston was born in Virginia. He graduated thirteenth of 46 students from the U.S. Military Academy in 1829. Commissioned a second lieutenant in the 4th U.S. Artillery, he resigned in 1837 to become a civil engineer. He later joined the Topographic Engineers as a first lieutenant.

Johnston served under General Scott during the Mexican-American War. In 1847, Johnston was appointed lieutenant colonel of the Regiment of Voltigeurs and was wounded twice near Cerro Gordo. He recovered, but fell with three more wounds while he was leading an assaulting column at Chapultepec. By the end of the war, Johnston had won three brevets.

As a Confederate brigadier general, Johnston displayed excellent leadership in the early years of the Civil War and was wounded twice during the Battle of Seven Pines. His forces in North Carolina were some of the last Confederates to surrender at the end of the war. In 1878, Johnston was elected to Congress and later served as the commissioner of railroads.

For further reading: Govan, *A Different Valor,* 1956; Johnston, *A Narrative of Military Operations,* 1995.

Jones, Anson
(1798–1858)

Physician Anson Jones served during the Texas Revolution and was the last president of the Republic of Texas before it was annexed by the United States in 1845.

Jones, who was born in Massachusetts, studied medicine, taught school, and traveled overseas before settling down in 1833 as a doctor in Brazoria, Texas. In 1836, he served as the physician for the revolutionary army under Sam Houston and fought as a private in the Battle of San Jacinto.

His various political posts included the Texas Congress, Texas minister to Washington, and the Texas Senate. In 1841, President Sam Houston made Jones his secretary of state. Three years later, with Houston's encouragement, Jones was elected president of the Republic of Texas.

Much of his term was spent dealing with winning foreign recognition of the Republic of Texas. Not convinced that annexation to the United States was the best path to follow, Jones listened carefully to British agents and worked hard at establishing a good relationship with Mexico. Jones was wary of U.S. agents such as Andrew Jackson Donelson and Duff Green, whose intent was to start a war between Mexico and Texas. Despite offering two proposals to the Texas convention about Mexican recognition of Texas, the convention voted overwhelmingly on July 4, 1845, to join the United States. Jones later wrote that "war with the United States and Mexico was inevitable, only because the United States had predetermined it should be so; and solely for that reason."

As the last president of the Republic of Texas, Jones left office in February 1846. Disappointed at not being elected to the U.S. Senate in 1857, he shot and killed himself in Houston.

See also Donelson, Andrew Jackson; Green, Duff.

For further reading: Caruso, *The Mexican Spy Compa-*

Jornada del Muerto

Colonel Alexander Doniphan and his regiment of Missouri volunteers crossed this desolate stretch of desert in New Mexico during their march from Valverde, New Mexico, to Chihuahua during 1846–1847.

Doniphan's command left Valverde, New Mexico, on December 14, 1846. Marching southward, his destination was El Paso, and then Chihuahua. In an effort to shorten the march, rather than following the Río Grande along a wide bend to the west, Doniphan decided to cross the Jornada del Muerto (Journey of Death), a sun-baked, arid desert valley—a more direct, but much less hospitable, route.

The landscape over this 100-mile stretch was windswept desert, barren rock, scattered sagebrush, and one muddy water hole. Strong winds blew constantly, and it was bitterly cold. With no firewood, the soldiers sometimes set fire to the occasional patch of dry grass for momentary warmth. After three days, Doniphan's men had crossed the desert.

The Jornada del Muerto lies east of the stretch of Interstate 25 between Soccoro and Truth or Consequences, New Mexico.

See also Doniphan's March.

For further reading: Connelley, *Doniphan's Expedition and the Conquest of New Mexico and California*, 1907; Hughes, *Doniphan's Expedition, Containing an Account of the Conquest of New Mexico*, 1973.

Juvera, Julián
(1784–1860)

A Mexican cavalry general during the Mexican-American War, Julián Juvera fought at the Battles of La Angostura (Buena Vista) and El Molino del Rey.

Juvera was born in Atitaliquia. He joined the Spanish army at a young age and fought against several rebellions. He continued in the Mexican army after independence in 1821 and rose steadily in rank.

Serving as a cavalry general, Juvera led his horsemen in advance of General Antonio López de Santa Anna's Army of the North as it marched from San Luis Potosí to La Angostura. Juvera's brigade fought on the Mexican right during the ensuing battle on February 23, 1847.

Later a part of the Army of the East, Juvera's forces were part of the cavalry division led by General Juan Álvarez. The cavalry failed to attack the vulnerable U.S. left flank during the Battle of El Molino del Rey on September 8. An attack could have possibly changed the outcome of that hard-fought battle. Álvarez is generally blamed for the failure, although he accused Juvera and others of not following his order to charge.

After the war, Juvera remained in the military as commander of the army at Querétaro and later became its governor. He died there at the age of 76.

For further reading: Alcaraz, *The Other Side*, 1850; Balbontín, *La invasión americana, 1846 a 1848*, 1888; Roa Bárcena, *Recuerdos de la invasión norteamericana*, 1947.

K

Kearny, Philip
(1814–1862)

Brevet Major Philip Kearny served in the 1st U.S. Dragoons during the Mexican-American War and lost an arm as a result of a cavalry charge toward the San Antonio *garita* (gate) in Mexico City.

Born in New York City, Kearny was raised by his grandfather. A keen rider and lover of horses, he was appointed a second lieutenant in the 1st U.S. Dragoons (commanded by Stephen Watts Kearny, his uncle). Kearny studied cavalry tactics in Europe and saw action in Algiers in 1840.

During the Mexican-American War, Kearny became Major General Winfield Scott's bodyguard on the advance from Veracruz to Mexico City in 1847. He is most remembered for recklessly leading a squadron of dragoons into heavy fire at the outskirts of Mexico City, where his left arm was so badly shattered that it had to be amputated. He was later promoted to major for the act.

Following the war, Kearny traveled to Europe. He fought with the French cavalry and was awarded the Cross of the Legion of Honor for his valorous conduct. During the Civil War, he was commissioned a Union brigadier general. Kearny preferred to do his own reconnaissance and was shot from his horse and killed at the Battle of Chantilly in 1862.

General Scott once called him "the bravest man I ever knew, and a perfect soldier."

For further reading: De Peyster, *The Personal and Military History of Philip Kearny,* 1869; Kearny, *General Philip Kearny, Battle Soldier of Five Wars,* 1937.

Kearny, Stephen Watts
(1794–1848)

Brigadier General Stephen Watts Kearny commanded the U.S. Army of the West during its 1846 march from Fort Leavenworth, Kansas, to Santa Fe, New Mexico. He later took a small force to California and participated in the battles that led to the reoccupation of Los Angeles in January 1847.

Kearny was born in New York City. He joined the U.S. army during the War of 1812. As commander of the 1st U.S. Dragoons, he

Stephen W. Kearny
(Library of Congress)

served at frontier posts for nearly 25 years before the onset of the Mexican-American War.

In May 1846, Kearny was given the command of the Army of the West. His job was to march to Santa Fe, secure the occupation of New Mexico, and then move on to California. In June, he was appointed brigadier general, and he quickly assembled and trained his largely volunteer army of 1,660 men.

After briefly resting at Bent's Old Fort, Colorado, Kearny entered Santa Fe unopposed on August 18. En route, he had stopped and proclaimed the U.S. desire for peace to curious New Mexican citizens who gathered in the villages through which he passed. At Bent's Fort, Kearny announced that he entered New Mexico with the "object of seeking union and to ameliorate the condition of its inhabitants...." At Las Vegas, New Mexico, he climbed on to a rooftop to guarantee that not a "pepper, nor an onion, will be taken by my troops without pay." He also pledged to protect New Mexicans from raiding Indians and to hang anyone "found in arms against me."

As the military governor of New Mexico, Kearny absolved New Mexicans of their allegiance to Mexico. Eager to win the support of New Mexicans, he tried to be tactful and respectful, attended Mass, and put on a ball to which both U.S. citizens and New Mexicans were invited. With the help of soldier lawyers Alexander W. Doniphan and Willard P. Hall, Kearny made certain that a working civic government was in place before taking 300 dragoons and marching for California on September 25, 1846.

On December 6, Kearny attacked a superior force of Californios at the Indian village of San Pascual, where he lost a third of his command and was wounded by a lance. Reinforcements arrived from Commodore Robert F. Stockton, and Kearny's force marched on to San Diego.

The united force of Stockton and Kearny won the Battles of San Gabriel River and La Mesa and seized Los Angeles in January 1847. Kearny and Stockton argued bitterly about seniority and overall command, and John C. Frémont, who had been appointed civil governor by Stockton, refused to give up the position to Kearny. Eventually, Kearny's authority was reaffirmed by new orders from Washington. Shortly afterward, Kearny and Frémont returned eastward, and Kearny had Frémont court-martialed for insubordination. Although Frémont was found guilty in the bitter proceedings, Kearny emerged with a somewhat tarnished reputation.

Kearny was later civil governor of Veracruz and Mexico City in 1847 and brevetted to major general. Seriously weakened by malaria, he died shortly after his return to St. Louis in 1848.

See also Frémont, John C.; Kearny's March; La Mesa, Battle of; San Gabriel River (Bartolo Ford), Battle of; San Pascual, Battle of.

For further reading: Clarke, *Stephen Watts Kearny, Soldier of the West*, 1961; Lavender, *Bent's Fort*, 1954; McNierney, *Taos 1847*, 1980.

Kearny's March

(1846)

Commanding the Army of the West, Brigadier General Stephen Watts Kearny marched from Fort Leavenworth, Kansas, to Santa Fe, New Mexico, during June–August 1846. He later took a 100-man expedition to San Diego, California, during September–December 1846.

From Fort Leavenworth to Santa Fe

President James K. Polk was eager to occupy New Mexico and California in the first months of the Mexican-American War. He ordered soon-to-be Brigadier General Kearny to organize and lead the Army of the West. The men were assembled and trained at Fort Leavenworth, Kansas, in June 1846. The force consisted of 300 soldiers from Kearny's 1st U.S. Dragoons, approximately 900 men from Colonel Alexander Doniphan's First Regiment of Missouri Mounted Volunteers, and a 250-man artillery battery. There were also approximately 300 other volunteers, 50 Delaware and Shawnee Indian scouts, and a Spanish-speaking Roman Catholic priest. Polk wanted to occupy New Mexico and demonstrate to the New Mexican population the strength and generosity of the United States and its respect for Catholicism.

The lead elements of Kearny's army left Fort Leavenworth on June 5, 1846. After riding across desolate terrain for nearly 700 miles and being plagued by insects, heat, and thirst, the men arrived at Bent's Old Fort, a trading post along the Arkansas River (near the present-day location of Las Animas, Colorado). Kearny rested his men for a few days and received two more regiments of dragoons that had been sent from Fort Leavenworth. Kearny also received word that approximately 1,000 men under Colonel Sterling Price were being assembled and would set out shortly to join him. The Mormon Battalion—500 religious refugees from Illinois who were bound for California—enlisted in June and would also march to Santa Fe.

In New Mexico, Kearny proclaimed at Las Vegas, Tecolote, and San Miguel that he and his men would liberate New Mexico from the unjust rule of Mexico and protect property and religious freedom. He announced that he and his men were "among [them] as friends—not as enemies; as protectors—not as conquerors; for [their] benefit—not [their] injury." Kearny's scouts reported that opposition was strongest at Taos and Santa Fe. Expecting combat at Apache Canyon, Kearny learned that the rebels under Manuel Armijo and Diego Archuleta had fled. Kearny's men marched unopposed into Santa Fe in mid-August and raised the U.S. flag.

Santa Fe's citizens greeted the U.S. troops warmly, and city officials pledged allegiance to the United States. Pueblo chieftains met with Kearny on August 18. His troops constructed Fort Marcy on a prominent hill approximately 600 yards from the governor's adobe palace. Satisfied that Santa Fe and New Mexico were secured, Kearny took 300 men and rode west for California on September 25, 1846. The remaining portion of his army was commanded by Colonel Doniphan, and reinforcements under Colonel Price and the Mormon Battalion eventually arrived in Santa Fe. Knowing that a garrison that size was not needed to maintain peace in New Mexico, Kearny ordered Doniphan and his men to march to Chihuahua.

From Santa Fe to California

After leaving Santa Fe, Kearny rode southward through Socorro and Valverde before turning west along the Gila River. At Socorro, he met frontiersman Kit Carson, who informed him that California was under the control of Commodore Robert F. Stockton. Kearny then decided to send approximately 200 men back and convinced Carson to guide his remaining 100-man column through the dry, mountainous country. Winding their way along the Gila River, they rested for two days in Tucson before continuing westward across the desolate deserts of southern California.

December 5 brought the arrival of navy Lieutenant Archibald H. Gillespie and 39 men, who planned to escort Kearny to San Diego. The following day, Kearny's men clashed with Californio rebels under the command of Captain Andrés Pico at the Battle of San Pascual. Rashly leading a charge at the urging of Kit Carson, Kearny was surprised by a Californio counterattack that killed 18 and wounded 13, including Kearny and Gillespie. Retreating to a small hill, the U.S. forces were kept under siege by Pico's men until a U.S. Navy relief force arrived from San Diego. Kearny's ragged command finally entered San Diego on December 12, 1846.

See also Apache Canyon; Archuleta, Diego; Armijo, Manuel; Bent's Old Fort; Carson, Christopher ("Kit"); Doniphan's March; Kearny, Stephen Watts; San Pascual, Battle of.

For further reading: Clarke, *Stephen Watts Kearny, Soldier of the West*, 1961; Cooke, *The Conquest of New Mexico and California*, 1878; Hughes, *Doniphan's Expedition, Containing an Account of the Conquest of New Mexico*, 1973; Lavender, *Bent's Fort*, 1954; McNierney, *Taos 1847*, 1980.

Kendall, George Wilkins
(1809–1867)

Often called the first "modern" war correspondent, George Wilkins Kendall traveled with the U.S. armies in Mexico and kept the U.S. public informed about the Mexican-American War with his stories in the New Orleans *Picayune*.

Kendall, who was born in New Hampshire, worked in the printing/newspaper business as a journalist and editor. In the early 1830s, he was employed by Horace Greeley in New York City. In 1837, Kendall cofounded the first daily newspaper in New Orleans called the *Picayune*.

As a member of the Santa Fe expedition in 1841, Kendall was captured by Governor Manuel Armijo and marched to Mexico City and there imprisoned. After his release and return to the United States, Kendall editorialized about the necessity of war with Mexico. Reporting from the field, he rode with the Texas Rangers, witnessed battles, and actually captured a cavalry banner during the Battle of Monterrey. A volunteer aid to General William J. Worth, Kendall witnessed most of the battles of Major General Winfield Scott's Veracruz–Mexico City campaign. Kendall was wounded in the knee during the storming of Chapultepec in September 1847. After the fall of Mexico City, the *Picayune* published his detailed coverage of the peace negotiations.

Kendall traveled to Europe after the war and later retired to a Texas ranch. He died at the age of 58.

For further reading: Copeland, *Kendall of the Picayune*, 1943.

Henry Lawrence Kinney
(Library of Congress)

Kinney, Henry Lawrence
(1814–1862)

A Texas rancher and land speculator, Henry Lawrence Kinney was a prominent resident of the Corpus Christi area and served General Zachary Taylor's Army of Occupation as a supplier and scout.

Kinney, who was born in Pennsylvania, farmed in Illinois before moving to Texas in 1838. He began ranching and trading with Matamoros on a large scale in 1841 near Corpus Christi, a community that he helped establish. Kinney was periodically raided by Comanches and had an army of 40 to 50 men to defend his property.

In 1845, Kinney became a senator in the Texas Congress. After having discussions with General Mariano Arista later that year, Kinney informed Texas President Anson Jones that he thought peace negotiations between Texas and Mexico were possible.

Kinney was delighted by the appearance of the U.S. army at Corpus Christi in the fall of 1845. He made immense profits supplying the army with beef and equipment, and he fostered relationships with the commanders. As a staff member of James Pinckney Henderson, Kinney traveled with the army and acted as a quartermaster, securing beef cattle, mules, and other forms of transportation, often using his network of Mexican trading partners. Captain W. S. Henry recalled that Kinney was very efficient and had "perfect knowledge of the Mexican character."

Kinney exposed himself to enemy fire as a volunteer aide-de-camp during the Battle of Monterrey in September 1846. In 1847, he served as General Winfield Scott's beef contractor at Veracruz. Kinney actually purchased a large head of cattle, horses, and mules from General Antonio López de Santa Anna's agent, but delivery was hampered by incessant guerrilla raids.

After the war, Kinney returned to Corpus Christi and traded around the world. He was elected to the state senate in 1849. In 1854, he attempted to establish a colony in Nicaragua, but the enterprise failed. Opposed to the Confederate status of Texas at the beginning of the Civil War, Kinney went to Matamoros and was killed there in 1862.

See also Chapita.

For further reading: Caruso, *The Mexican Spy Company*, 1991; Henry, *Campaign Sketches of the War with*

Mexico, 1847; Smith and Judah, *Chronicles of the Gringos*, 1968; Webb, *The Handbook of Texas*, 1952.

Kinney's Ranch

See Corpus Christi; Kinney, Henry Lawrence.

Kirker, James
(1793–1853)

A notorious bounty hunter, James Kirker joined Colonel Alexander Doniphan's regiment of Missouri volunteers as a guide and interpreter on their march from El Paso to Chihuahua during January–March 1847.

Kirker, who was born in Ireland, emigrated to New York City in 1810 and the western frontier in 1822. Kirker worked as a trapper and guarded ore trains from the Santa Rita copper mines. In 1835, he received a license to trade with the Apaches; two years later he began to hunt them professionally for the state of Chihuahua. Kirker's men were paid $40 for every male scalp and $20 for scalps of women and children.

Living in El Paso during Colonel Doniphan's occupation of the city in December 1846, Kirker volunteered to join his regiment as a guide for the rest of his march. Doniphan accepted his services. Kirker was sent forward to scout the Mexican position at Río Sacramento, and he later participated in the battle.

After the war, Kirker continued to hunt Indians and fought the Ute Nation in 1848. Resuming trading, he traveled frequently between St. Louis and California. Kirker died at Oak Springs, California, at the age of 62.

For further reading: Hughes, *Doniphan's Expedition, Containing an Account of the Conquest of New Mexico*, 1973; Lavender, *Bent's Fort*, 1954; McGaw, *Savage Scene*, 1972.

Klamath Indians

Colonel John C. Frémont fought several skirmishes with the Klamath Nation in Oregon Territory in 1846.

Having left California in the spring of 1846 after confronting forces under military commandant José Castro, Frémont's expedition moved northward into Oregon Territory. Frémont and 12 men were camped along the shore of Klamath Lake in southeastern Oregon when Lieutenant Archibald H. Gillespie arrived on May 9, 1846, carrying dispatches from Thomas Hart Benton and Secretary of State James Buchanan.

That night was one of the few nights Frémont failed to post sentries. A party of 15 to 20 Klamath warriors crept up on the camp and killed two of his men. Kit Carson awoke to the sound of an axe being driven into one of the men's heads. The Klamaths then charged across the open ground and Crane, Frémont's favorite Delaware scout, was killed. Frémont's losses were three killed and one wounded. In the morning, they found the body of a dead chief. Frémont recalled that Carson "knocked his head to pieces" with an axe. The dead were packed on mules and on the way back to the main camp were buried in a shallow grave. Frémont named Denny's Creek and Crane Creek for his two fallen scouts.

The Delaware scouts mourned the loss of their men. When Frémont and his men rode out of the main camp the following morning, the Delawares crept back on foot and remained hidden in thick brush. Shortly afterward, several Klamath ventured into the abandoned campsite and were killed by the vengeful Delawares. Frémont later came upon the main Klamath village and immediately attacked. Fourteen Indians were killed, the rush-and-willow huts burned, and drying fish and scaffolds destroyed.

See also Delaware Indians; Frémont, John C.

For further reading: Frémont, *Memoirs of My Life*, 1886.

L

La Angostura, Battle of

See Buena Vista, Battle of.

La Cañada, Battle of

(January 24, 1847)

La Cañada was the first battle between the New Mexican forces of the Taos Rebellion and a U.S. force under the command of Colonel Sterling Price.

When Colonel Price, the U.S. military commander in Santa Fe, learned of the murder of military governor Charles Bent and other Anglo-American and New Mexican citizens in Taos, New Mexico, in January 1847, he quickly assembled a force of 353 men and four howitzers. His force left Santa Fe for Taos on January 23.

The following day, Price encountered a force of nearly 1,500 New Mexican rebels at La Cañada, about 20 miles north of Santa Fe. Commanded by Jesus Tafoya, Pablo Chavez, and Pablo Montoya, the skittish rebels held a defensive position in the hills above the town or in adobe houses. Price left some soldiers to protect the wagons and attacked and disbanded the rebels. The rebels also tried a flanking maneuver to attack the trains, but were chased into the hills. New Mexican losses were 36 killed and 45 captured; Price lost 2 killed and 7 wounded.

Price remained at La Cañada for another two days and was reinforced by another company of 2nd Missouri volunteers. His force numbered 479 men when he marched from the village and arrived in Taos on February 2, 1847.

See also Taos Rebellion.

For further reading: Lavender, *Bent's Fort*, 1954; McNierney, *Taos 1847*, 1980.

La Encarnación

La Encarnación, Coahuila, was an important stopover point and water source for Mexican and U.S. troops marching on the road between San Luis Potosí and Saltillo.

La Encarnación was an abandoned hacienda located between San Luis Potosí (General Antonio López de Santa Anna's staging area) and Saltillo (General Zachary Taylor's staging area). A minor skirmish erupted there in early January 1847 between a scouting party of Texas Rangers and a patrol of Mexican cavalry. Eager to confirm the rumored advance of Santa Anna's army, General William O. Butler sent out more scouting patrols. A 50-man detachment of Arkansas cavalry under Major Solon Borland occupied the hacienda on January 19. Another patrol under Major John P. Gaines and Captain Cassius M. Clay (both Kentucky cavalrymen) also arrived at La Encarnación and joined forces with Borland.

Typical of the unmilitary behavior of volunteers, the men went to sleep the night of January 22 without posting pickets. They awoke to find themselves surrounded by thousands of Mexican lancers under General José Vicente Miñón. The 71 men were forced to surrender. As they were marched south, scout and interpreter Daniel Drake Henrie escaped on a fleet horse and reported the incident to General Butler.

A U.S. patrol skirmished with Mexican cavalry near La Encarnación on February 16. By the 19th, Santa Anna's weary army had arrived at the hacienda and sprawled across the plain. Santa Anna reviewed his forces the following day; 15,142 men were ready for combat. Learning of the U.S. presence at Agua Nueva, Santa Anna hurriedly pressed on. After its defeat at the Battle of La Angostura (Buena Vista) on February 23, the demoralized Mexican army streamed back through La Encarnación on its retreat southward.

On March 1, a U.S. scouting party discovered 222 badly wounded Mexicans crowded into La Encarnación's chapel. The air inside was so foul-smelling that some U.S. soldiers were amazed that the wounded were still alive. La Encarnación then served as a field hospital for the wounded Mexican soldiers until they recovered.

See also Army, Mexico; Borland, Solon; Clay, Cassius Marcellus; Gaines, John Pollard; Henrie, Daniel Drake.

For further reading: Alcaraz, *The Other Side*, 1850; Cutrer, *Ben McCulloch and the Frontier Military Tradition*, 1993; Scott, *Encarnación Prisoners, Comprising an Account of the March of the Kentucky Cavalry from Louisville to the Rio Grande*, 1848.

La Hoya, Skirmish at
(June 20, 1847)

Captain Samuel H. Walker and 30 cavalrymen attacked a guerrilla band of nearly 700 men under Padre Celestino Domeco de Jarauta at Las Vigas, near Jalapa, on June 20, 1847. Walker was eventually reinforced by five companies of Pennsylvania volunteers under Colonel Francis M. Wynkoop. Mexican casualties were approximately 50 killed or wounded; no U.S. losses were reported. The U.S. soldiers captured a number of guerrilla flags, including one depicting a skull and crossbones with the words "No Quarters."

See also Guerrilla Warfare; Jarauta, Celestino Domeco de; Walker, Samuel H.

For further reading: Bauer, *The Mexican War, 1846–1848*, 1974; Oswandel, *Notes of the Mexican War*, 1885; Spurlin, "Ranger Walker in the Mexican War," 1971.

La Mesa, Battle of
(January 9, 1847)

Also called the Battle of Los Angeles, the Battle of La Mesa was the last significant armed conflict between U.S. and Californio forces in California. Four days later, the Treaty of Cahuenga was signed.

Determined to win Los Angeles back from Californio forces, a combined army-navy force under Brigadier General Stephen W. Kearny and Commodore Robert F. Stockton marched northward from San Diego. They fought the Californios under Captain José María Flores at the Battle of San Gabriel River on January 8, 1847, and drove them from the heights overlooking the river.

On the following day, the 600-man U.S. force advanced cautiously across a broad mesa toward Los Angeles. The flanks of the small army were guarded by horsemen and scouting parties. After traveling about 6 miles, the U.S. force came upon Flores's defensive line (500 to 600 men) along a deep ravine, anchored with several artillery pieces.

The U.S. troops continued to advance. Stockton instructed his men to lie down when they saw the flash of the cannon and to resume the march after the cannonballs had passed. Stockton began to return the artillery fire.

As the Californios began to form a horseshoe-shaped line to envelop the U.S. position, Stockton ordered his men to form a square, into which they moved the wagons and artillery. The U.S. soldiers continued to march toward Los Angeles. Several Californio mounted charges were attempted, but were turned away by the heavy musket fire. Excellent horsemen, the Californios stripped the dead horses of saddles and bridles, and picked up their dead and wounded, without dismounting. This slow-moving march/battle lasted about two and one-half hours. U.S. losses were one killed and five wounded; Californio losses were one killed and five to ten wounded. Stockton continued to advance in a square formation and camped a few miles from Los Angeles that night.

See also San Gabriel River (Bartolo Ford), Battle of.

For further reading: Emory, *Notes of a Military Reconnaissance*, 1848; Griffin, *A Doctor Comes to California*, 1943; Harlow, *California Conquered*, 1982.

La Mesilla, Treaty of

See Gadsden Treaty.

La Paz

A city along the Baja California coastline, La Paz was blockaded and occupied by U.S. naval forces during 1846–1848.

The capital of Baja California, La Paz was a pearl-fishing village along the Gulf of California. The village consisted of approximately 500 residents living in flat-topped adobe homes. The target of a blockade by the U.S. Pacific Fleet, its harbor was invaded by the USS *Cyane* under Commander Samuel F. Du Pont in September 1846. Du Pont seized nine small Mexican vessels and discussed neutrality issues with the state government.

A new blockade was launched in 1847. The USS *Portsmouth* anchored offshore on April 13. La Paz agreed to surrender terms that included keeping the civil government intact and granting Baja Californians the rights of U.S. citizens. This friendly capitulation angered many patriots, and in mid-February a group of rebels formed under Captain Manuel Pineda.

In May, Brigadier General Stephen W. Kearny ordered Lieutenant Colonel Henry S. Burton and two companies of New York volunteers to La Paz. Sailing on the storeship *Lexington*, they arrived on July 21. Approximately 3,000 feet from the beach, they jumped into the 4-foot-deep water and waded to shore. Burton built a fort on a rise that overlooked the town and harbor, and his forces patrolled the streets.

Captain Pineda and 120 men assaulted La Paz on November 11, but were turned back by U.S. artillery fire. Another attack on November 17 was also repulsed. The two attacks resulted in one U.S. soldier killed and two wounded; approximately ten Mexicans were killed and wounded.

Reinforced to a total of 350 men, Pineda attacked the town again on November 27 and began a siege that lasted until December 8, when the USS *Cyane* again arrived in the harbor. U.S. casualties were one killed and three wounded; Pineda lost about 17 killed and wounded. During February–March 1848, Burton used La Paz as his base for launching raids on guerrilla camps at San Antonio and Todos Santos. Despite these attacks, Pineda remained active in the area.

The U.S. force was evacuated from La Paz in September 1848. Approximately 300 people, many of them prominent families, who had collaborated with the U.S. occupiers also left the village.

For further reading: Bauer, *Surfboats and Horse Marines*, 1969; Meadows, *The American Occupation of La Paz*, 1955.

Lamy, Jean Baptiste
(1814–1888)

Jean Baptiste Lamy was a Catholic priest who came to New Mexico Territory in 1850 to reorganize its Catholic churches and make them conform to the traditional practices of the Roman Catholic Church.

Lamy, who was born and ordained in France, emigrated to the United States as a Catholic priest. He worked as a missionary in Ohio in 1839. In 1850, he was appointed vicar apostolic to reorganize the Catholic Church in New Mexico after the Mexican-American War. Three years later, he was bishop of the huge diocese of Santa Fe, which covered a large portion of New Mexico Territory.

Frequently described as rigid and dictatorial by other clergymen, Lamy did not embrace New Mexican Catholic traditions. He imposed his own strict interpretation of Catholicism, such as an insistence on tithing. His administration was interpreted by New Mexicans as violating the religious freedom that they had been promised by General Stephen Watts Kearny and the U.S. government.

In his diocese, Lamy clashed with most of the New Mexican clergy, the more rebellious of whom he excommunicated. Lamy also tried to suppress the Penitente brotherhood, which had always operated independently of the church. Lamy brought more priests from Europe and built more schools and churches. He retired in Santa Fe in 1885 and died three years later.

For further reading: Horgan, *Lamy of Santa Fe*, 1975; Meier and Rivera, *Dictionary of Mexican American History*, 1981.

Landero Bauza, José Juan
(1802–1869)

General Landero Bauza commanded Mexican forces during Major General Winfield Scott's siege of Veracruz in March 1847.

Landero Bauza was born in Veracruz. He studied for the ministry before entering the Mexican army shortly after Mexico's independence in 1821. He remained a prominent military and political figure in Veracruz. He fought the French in 1838 and was made a brigadier general in 1843 during the administration of General Antonio López de Santa Anna.

Landero Bauza welcomed the return of Santa Anna from exile in August 1846, and he commanded the Mexican troops at Veracruz during Major General Winfield Scott's assault on the city in March 1847. Ordered to hold the city at all costs, he finally surrendered after nearly a four-week siege. Santa Anna quickly imprisoned him in Perote Castle, where he remained until he was released by Scott's army.

After the war, Landero Bauza remained in the military at Veracruz and fought against the French intervention. He died in Veracruz at the age of 67.

For further reading: Alcaraz, *The Other Side,* 1850; *Diccionario Porrúa,* 1995.

Lane, Joseph
(1801–1881)

A volunteer brigadier general, Joseph Lane was best known for his relentless antiguerrilla maneuvers along the National Road during Major General Winfield Scott's Veracruz–Mexico City campaign.

Lane was born in North Carolina and later moved to Indiana, where he was a farmer and businessman. Drawn to politics, he entered the state legislature and served in the U.S. Senate from 1844 to 1846.

Lane resigned from the Senate at the outbreak of the Mexican-American War and became the colonel of the 2nd Indiana Volunteers. President James K. Polk soon appointed him a brigadier general. Lane led his brigade unevenly during the Battle of Buena Vista in February 1847 and was wounded. After leaving General Zachary Taylor's army to join Major General Scott on the road to Mexico City, Lane and his men saved the besieged U.S. garrison at Puebla and relentlessly hunted down guerrillas. After winning the Battle of Huamantla in October 1847, Lane deliberately turned his troops loose to murder, rape, and burn in one of the ugliest incidents of the war. Despite this act, he emerged as a U.S. hero and was brevetted to major general.

President Polk appointed Lane governor of Oregon Territory in 1848. In the 1850s, Lane served four terms in the state legislature and later as U.S. senator. After losing the 1860 election as vice-president for candidate John C. Breckenridge, Lane retired to his farm in Oregon.

For further reading: Brackett, *General Lane's Brigade in Central Mexico,* 1854; Frost, *The Mexican War and Its Warriors,* 1848; Kelly, *The Career of Joseph Lane, Frontier Politician,* 1952; Oswandel, *Notes of the Mexican War,* 1885.

Larkin, Thomas Oliver
(1802–1858)

As U.S. consul to California at Monterey from 1843 to 1848, Thomas O. Larkin monitored foreign interest in California and the shifting political climate, and he facilitated the relationship between U.S. forces and Californio military and political leaders.

Larkin was born in Massachusetts. He lived briefly in North Carolina before moving to California in 1832. Settling in Monterey, he became a successful businessman and developed a good rapport with Mexican traders. Accepting the role of U.S. consul in 1843, Larkin helped U.S. settlers in California and promoted business relations with the United States.

As the conflict between the United States and Mexico brewed during 1845–1846, Larkin became a confidential agent to President James K. Polk from 1846 to 1848 and a naval agent from 1847 to 1849. In full support of U.S. ownership of California, Larkin tracked the dealings of British and French agents with the Californio government. President Polk, by secret dispatch dated October 17, 1845, appointed Larkin "confidential agent in California" to convince Californios to reject French and British interests and to "arouse in their bosoms that love of liberty and independence so natural to the American Continent." Polk also warned that "in the contest between Mexico and California we can take no part, unless the former should commence hostilities against the United States." In 1846, Larkin continuously proposed to the Californio government the benefits that separation from Mexico would bring. He also acted an as intermediary between John C. Frémont's forces and Californio officials in 1846.

Larkin continued to manage his business interests in California after the war and died in 1858 at the age of 56.

For further reading: Hague and Langum, *Thomas O. Larkin,* 1990; Hammond, *The Larkin Papers,* 1951–1962; Harlow, *California Conquered,* 1982.

Robert E. Lee
(Library of Congress)

Lee, Robert Edward
(1807–1870)

Major General Winfield Scott depended on engineer Robert Edward Lee for detailed reconnaissance reports on Mexican defensive positions during Scott's Veracruz–Mexico City campaign of 1847.

Lee was born in Virginia. His father, "Lighthorse" Harry Lee, was a distinguished cavalry officer in the American Revolution. Displaying excellent mathematical abilities, Lee graduated from the U.S. Military Academy in 1829 second in his class. Lee was commissioned a second lieutenant of engineers and conducted surveying work along the Mississippi and Missouri Rivers.

During the Mexican-American War, Lee was first attached to General John E. Wool's Army of the Center. After arriving at Saltillo, Lee conducted extensive reconnaissance work prior to the Battle of Buena Vista in February 1847. Lee was transferred to Major General Scott's Army of Occupation that landed at Veracruz in March. Lee personally located the heavy land batteries for the bombardment of the city. The victory at Cerro Gordo in April was largely because of a route Lee discovered that enabled the U.S. forces to maneuver and turn the Mexican left flank. He also managed to pick out pathways through the supposedly impenetrable *pedregal* (lava field) for infantry and artillery that surprised the Mexican commanders at the Battle of Contreras. During the Battle of Churubusco, he helped position artillery batteries under heavy fire and was slightly wounded. By the time the battle was over, Lee had been on his feet for 36 straight hours. Scott called the crossing of the lava field "the greatest feat of physical and moral courage performed by any individual, in my knowledge, pending the campaign...." By the end of the war, Lee had received three brevets for gallantry.

Later a commandant at the U.S. Military Academy, Lee had never commanded more than four squadrons of cavalry in the field prior to the Civil War. In 1862, Lee took command of the Army of Northern Virginia as its general and won a series of important battles before his narrow defeat at Gettysburg in 1863. Lee's forces could not withstand General Ulysses S. Grant's larger and better-equipped Army of the Potomac, and Lee surrendered to Grant in April 1865, thus ending the Civil War.

Lee's health was compromised by a heart condition, and he died at his home in Virginia at the age of 61.

For further reading: Freeman, *R. E. Lee,* 1934; Thomas, *Robert E. Lee,* 1995.

León, Antonio
(1794–1847)

A brigadier general in the Mexican army, Antonio León was killed in action during the Battle of El Molino del Rey in September 1847.

León, who was born in Huajuapam, joined the revolutionary forces at age 17. After Mexico gained independence from Spain in 1821, León became a member of the Mexican army. He later served as the military commander of Oaxaca and a member of the Mexican Congress. In the late 1830s and early 1840s, he suppressed various revolutions against the government, especially in Chiapas. He remained an important political and military figure and became a brigade general in 1843.

As part of General Antonio López de Santa Anna's Army of the East, General León's brigade fought at the Battle of Cerro Gordo in April 1847. He led his men courageously during the Battle of El Molino del Rey, where he was killed in action on September 8. Ramon Alcaraz wrote that "General Leon, moving serene and unmindful, passing in the midst of a shower of balls…received a severe wound and fell, terminating his career."

See also El Molino del Rey, Battle of.

Antonio León
(Library of Congress)

For further reading: Alcaraz, The Other Side, 1850; Carreño, Jefes del ejército mexicano en 1847, 1914; Diccionario Porrúa, 1995.

Lincoln, Abraham
(1809–1865)

As a young congressman during the Mexican-American War, Abraham Lincoln vigorously opposed the conflict, to the point of being called a traitor.

Born in Kentucky and later raised in Indiana and Illinois, Lincoln was educated in local schools. He served in the Black Hawk War in 1832 and was elected to the state legislature in 1834. Lincoln moved to Springfield, Illinois, in 1837 to open a law office.

Lincoln served as a Whig in Congress during the Mexican-American War. He had not originally opposed the war while campaigning as a candidate; but when the Whigs denounced President James K. Polk for starting an unjust war, Lincoln concurred. On December 22, 1847, during the Thirtieth Congress, Lincoln introduced a series of resolutions that demanded that Polk present "all the facts with which to establish whether the particular spot of soil on which the blood of our *citizens* was so shed, was, or was not, *our own soil*." Lincoln challenged Polk to prove his claims, "but if he can not or will not do this—if on any pretense or no pretense he shall refuse or omit it—than I shall be fully convinced of what I more than suspect already—that he is deeply conscious of being in the wrong." Polk never responded to Lincoln's challenge.

In January 1848, Lincoln questioned Polk's motives for the war, especially in the context of protracted peace negotiations. Lincoln approved of the antislavery Wilmot Proviso. Although he voted to grant supplies to sustain the war, Lincoln's pro-Mexican stance was seen by many as unpatriotic. Because of this, many of his constituents referred to him as a traitor, and he was not reelected.

In 1860, Lincoln was elected the sixteenth president of the United States on an antislavery platform, which led to the secession of 11 states that became the Confederate States of America. Lincoln then guided the Union through four bloody years of the Civil War.

The president was shot by John Wilkes Booth on April 14, 1865, and died the following day.

For further reading: Donald, *Lincoln,* 1995; Ruiz, *Triumphs and Tragedy,* 1992; Thomas, *Abraham Lincoln,* 1952.

Lombardini, Manuel María
(1802–1853)

A close ally of General Antonio López de Santa Anna, General Manuel María Lombardini commanded a division during the Battle of La Angostura (Buena Vista) and later helped defend Chapultepec and Mexico City.

Lombardini joined the Spanish army at the age of 12. He remained in the military after Mexican independence from Spain and became an ally of General Santa Anna in the 1830s. A brigadier general by 1834, Lombardini fought in the Texas Revolution in 1836 and against the French at Veracruz two years later.

One of Santa Anna's favorite generals, Lombardini commanded a division posted at Veracruz when war with the United States erupted in 1846. After the early Mexican disasters at Palo Alto, Resaca de Guerrero (Resaca de la Palma), and Monterrey, he joined Santa Anna's new Army of the North at San Luis Potosí. On February 23, 1847, at the Battle of La Angostura (Buena Vista), Lombardini bravely led a frontal assault on the U.S. left flank and was wounded. The performance of Lombardini's troops impressed their U.S. adversaries: "No troops in the world ever showed more reckless valor than did this division of Lombardini, exposed to double charges of canister," wrote Samuel Chamberlain of the 2nd Dragoons. Lombardini's advance prompted the collapse of the U.S. left flank in the early stages of the battle.

As General Winfield Scott's Army of Occupation was closing in on Mexico City from Veracruz in August 1847, Lombardini commanded the defenses of Mexico City, including the stubborn rear-guard action he directed at Belén *garita* (gate) after the fall of Chapultepec.

Lombardini remained in the army after the war and led troops against various uprisings. He served as a provisional president for three months in 1853 until Santa Anna took office. Lombardini died at age 51 while commanding the troops in the Federal District.

For further reading: Carreño, *Jefes del ejército mexicano en 1847,* 1914; Chamberlain, *My Confession,* 1956; DePalo, *The Mexican National Army, 1822–1852,* 1997; Lavender, *Climax at Buena Vista,* 1966.

Longstreet, James
(1821–1904)

A capable infantry lieutenant, James Longstreet served with Generals Zachary Taylor and Winfield Scott and was wounded during the Battle of Chapultepec in September 1847.

Born in South Carolina, Longstreet was raised in Alabama and Georgia. Graduating near the bottom of his class from the U.S. Military Academy in 1842, he was commissioned a second lieutenant in the 4th U.S. Infantry. Longstreet was posted in Missouri, Louisiana, and Florida during 1842–1846.

During the Mexican-American War, Longstreet was part of General Taylor's Army of Occupation during 1846–1847 and was later attached to Major General Scott's Veracruz–Mexico City campaign in 1847. Longstreet commanded troops during the Battles of Palo Alto and Resaca de la Palma in May 1846 and during the bitter street fighting in Monterrey in September. He was wounded in the thigh while carrying the regimental colors during the Battle of Chapultepec in September 1847. Longstreet was cared for in a private home in Mexico City. By the time the war was over, he had received two brevets.

Longstreet resigned from the U.S. army in 1861 to join the Confederate army. Although he tended to be cautious and deliberate, he became one of General Robert E. Lee's favorite generals. After the war, Longstreet held various governmental positions, including postmaster and railroad commissioner, until his death at age 83.

For further reading: Cullum, *Biographical Register of the Officers and Graduates of the United States Military Academy from 1802 to 1867,* 1879; Eckenrode, *James Longstreet,* 1936; Longstreet, *From Manassas to Appomattox,* 1896.

Loreto

A small port community in Baja California, Loreto was occupied by a naval force from the

USS *Dale* on October 5, 1847. Commander Thomas O. Selfridge landed approximately 100 sailors and U.S. Marines, who searched the town. They stayed in the village only one day, long enough to confiscate three cannons, lances, and one musket.

For further reading: Bauer, *Surfboats and Horse Marines*, 1969.

Loring, William Wing
(1818–1886)

Commander of the U.S. Mounted Rifles regiment during the Mexican-American War, Major William Wing Loring was severely wounded during the Battle of Chapultepec in September 1847.

Loring was born in North Carolina and raised in Florida. After fighting the Seminoles in Florida, he was given the rank of second lieutenant. He later became a lawyer and a member of the state legislature in Florida.

Promoted to major in 1847, Loring commanded the U.S. Mounted Rifles during Major General Winfield Scott's Veracruz–Mexico City campaign in 1847. After faltering at Cerro Gordo, Loring led his regiment capably at the Battle of Contreras and lost an arm in the Battle of Chapultepec. By October 1847, he had received two brevets and was ordered home to recuperate from his amputation surgery.

Loring later battled Indians in Oregon and Texas before joining the Confederacy as a brigadier general. He served in both eastern and western theaters and fought well at the Tennessee battles of Nashville and Franklin. When the Civil War ended, he joined the Egyptian army (1869–1879), in which he was highly decorated. Loring died of pneumonia at the age of 68 in New York City.

For further reading: French, *Two Wars, an Autobiography*, 1901; Smith, *The War with Mexico*, 1919; Wessels, *Born to Be a Soldier*, 1971.

Los Angeles

The village of Los Angeles, California, became the site of one of the few Mexican victories of the Mexican-American War when its U.S. force surrendered to Californio rebels led by José María Flores in 1846.

Commodore Robert F. Stockton, determined to capture Los Angeles, marched from Santa Barbara on August 11, 1846, with a force of 360 sailors. Approximately 90 men were armed with muskets; the others carried carbines, sidearms, swords, and boarding pikes. They marched northward along the coast in a square, which shielded their livestock, wagons, and artillery. Californio military leader José Castro and Governor Pío de Jesús Pico abandoned their force of rebels in Los Angeles and fled south to the state of Sonora. The remnants of the rebel army, including Captain José María Flores and Captain Andrés Pico, surrendered the city to Stockton on August 14, and were paroled.

Stockton promised the citizens of Los Angeles that a civilian government would eventually be installed. When Stockton left, he made John C. Frémont the governor of California and Archibald H. Gillespie, the commander of the occupation force at Los Angeles, the secretary of California. Stockton's capture of Los Angeles was the first time in U.S. military history that a naval force conducted an extensive operation on land.

Gillespie was not well received by the Californios. He was arrogant and tactless, and his 48 men were rude and often drunk. Their ill treatment of the local population led to a growing hostility that erupted in skirmishing and small arms fire on September 20, 1846. The insurgency spread, and soon most of the town's 1,500 citizens had formed a rebel force, under Captain Flores, intent on overthrowing Gillespie. Under siege and out of water, Gillespie surrendered on September 29. Allowed to keep their sidearms, Gillespie and his men boarded the U.S. merchant ship *Vandalia* in San Pedro Harbor on October 4.

Using Los Angeles as his headquarters, Flores drove out or captured the small U.S. garrisons at Santa Barbara and San Diego. Low on ammunition and supplies, Flores decided to mount a guerrilla campaign to keep U.S. forces away from Los Angeles.

After learning of Gillespie's surrender, Stockton put together a joint navy-army force of approximately 600 men with Brigadier General Stephen W. Kearny. Together they marched 140 miles from San Diego toward Los Angeles and defeated Flores's small force at the Battle of San Gabriel on January 8, 1847.

The following day, a few miles from Los Angeles, they again routed Flores at the Battle of La Mesa and occupied the city of Los Angeles on January 10. La Mesa ended the organized Californio resistance in Upper California, and Los Angeles remained in U.S. control for the duration of the war.

See also Flores, José María; Gillespie, Archibald H.; Stockton, Robert Field.

For further reading: Bauer, *Surfboats and Horse Marines*, 1969; Grivas, *Military Governments in California, 1846–1850*, 1963; Harlow, *California Conquered*, 1982.

Lowell, James Russell
(1819–1891)

A U.S. humorist and satirist, James Russell Lowell was an outspoken critic of the Mexican-American War. He argued that it was being fought to extend slavery.

Lowell was born in Cambridge, Massachusetts. He graduated from Harvard University in 1838 with a special interest in poetry and literature. He worked as an editor and often wrote satirical, political commentary.

Lowell published the *Bigelow Papers* in 1848, which criticized the U.S. government and its conduct of the Mexican-American War, especially in the context of extending slavery to new territory. Lowell wrote that the war was being waged to make "bigger pens to cram with slaves." In the *Bigelow Papers*, a fictional volunteer soldier complained that

> Ez fer war, I call it murder—
> There you hev it plain an' flat;
> They may talk o' Freedom's airy
> Tell they're pupple in the face—
> It's a grand gret cemetary
> Fer the barthrights of our race;
> They just want this Californy
> So's to lug new slave-states in
> To abuse ye, an' to scorn ye,
> An' to plunder ye like sin.

After the Mexican-American War, Lowell traveled overseas, was a professor at Harvard, and edited the *Atlantic Monthly*. During the Civil War, he became an editor with the *North American Review*. He died at the age of 72.

For further reading: Heymann, *American Aristocracy*, 1980; Johannsen, *To the Halls of the Montezumas*, 1985; Lowell, *The Writings of James Russell Lowell*, 1890; Scudder, *James Russell Lowell*, 1901.

M

Mackenzie, Alexander Slidell
(1803–1848)

During the Mexican-American War, Alexander Slidell Mackenzie met with exiled Mexican dictator Antonio López de Santa Anna in Havana, Cuba, and also served as a U.S. naval commander at Veracruz and Tabasco.

Mackenzie, who was born in Scotland and raised in New York, joined the navy as midshipman at the age of 12. After sailing the Pacific and fighting pirates, he wrote popular books about his travels and also biographies of U.S. naval commanders.

In May 1846, President James K. Polk, after conferring with Alexander J. Atocha, asked Mackenzie to visit exiled Mexican leader General Santa Anna in Havana, Cuba. Mackenzie arrived on July 5 and met with Santa Anna two days later. Mackenzie told him that, if he regained power and sought peace, the United States would suspend military operations and that terms would essentially consist of a negotiated price for claims and territory, including New Mexico and California. Mackenzie returned to Polk with Santa Anna's assurance that he would negotiate a settlement. After U.S. ships allowed Santa Anna through the blockade at Veracruz in August, Santa Anna quickly escalated the war effort.

During the Mexican-American War, Mackenzie acted as an envoy and interpreter for the U.S. Navy at the siege of Veracruz and commanded artillery during the second attack on Tabasco.

Retiring from federal service to New York City, Mackenzie continued to write books until he died in 1848.

See also Atocha, Alexander J.

For further reading: Bauer, *Surfboats and Horse Marines*, 1969; Emmons, *The Navy of the United States*, 1853; Polk, *The Diary of James K. Polk*, 1910.

Magoffin, James Wiley
(1799–1868)

James Magoffin was a successful New Mexico trader who traveled with Brigadier General Stephen W. Kearny's Army of the West in 1846 as an envoy and interpreter.

Magoffin was born in Kentucky. He moved to Texas and became a successful trader with Mexico. In 1825, he was appointed U.S. consul at Saltillo, where he was highly regarded by Mexican citizens.

After marrying a local woman and living 14 years in Chihuahua, he moved to Missouri, where his wife suddenly died. In 1845, Senator Thomas H. Benton introduced Magoffin to President James K. Polk. Polk was so impressed by him that he hired Magoffin as a scout, interpreter, and envoy to assist Kearny's Army of the West in subjugating New Mexico.

As Kearny neared Santa Fe in August 1846, Magoffin rode ahead and discussed matters with Governor Manuel Armijo. Armijo then abandoned his army and defensive position at Apache Canyon, and Kearny seized New Mexico without any casualties. Magoffin was apparently under the impression that Polk wanted only the eastern half of New Mexico, which Texas had long claimed. Either acting on his own or under secret orders from Polk, Magoffin suggested to Diego Archuleta, Armijo's second in command, that he could govern the western half of New Mexico. This was accepted by Archuleta, only to be overturned by Kearny when he decided to claim all of New Mexico and march to California.

Kearny then ordered Magoffin to join General John E. Wool in Chihuahua to help him as an envoy and negotiator. (Wool never arrived because he was ordered to go to Saltillo instead.) Although he was well liked in Chihuahua and had married a Chihuahuan, the Mexican forces imprisoned him in Chihuahua and Durango jails for almost a year. He reputedly supplied his jailers with hundreds of bottles of champagne, which helped save him from being executed.

In 1849, Magoffin received $30,000 from the U.S. government as compensation for his expenses and losses during the war. He founded the small town of Magoffinsville, which is now part of El Paso, Texas. He died in San Antonio at the age of 69.

See also Apache Canyon; Archuleta, Diego; Armijo, Manuel; Kearny's March.

For further reading: Keleher, *Turmoil in New Mexico, 1846–1848*, 1952; Lavender, *Bent's Fort*, 1954; Magoffin, *Down the Santa Fe Trail and into Mexico*, 1926.

Magruder, John Bankhead
(1810–1871)

An artillery officer in the Army of Occupation, John Bankhead Magruder served under Major General Winfield Scott in the battles of the Veracruz–Mexico City campaign of 1847.

Magruder was born in Virginia. He graduated from the U.S. Military Academy in 1830 as a second lieutenant of infantry and later transferred to the artillery. He fought Seminole Indians in Florida and was stationed in Texas. In 1836, he was promoted to first lieutenant.

During the Mexican-American War, Magruder commanded the light artillery attached to General Gideon J. Pillow's division. Magruder's expert artillery fire helped break the Mexican defenses at the Battle of Cerro Gordo in April. He advanced his field battery "nearly a mile without cover over that almost impassable ground" to duel with Mexican batteries during the Battle of Contreras. After the victory at Chapultepec, he took his battery down the San Cosmé causeway in pursuit of the retreating enemy. Considered restless and hot-tempered, he was brevetted twice for "gallant and meritorious conduct" and wounded twice by grapeshot.

Magruder joined the Confederate army as a colonel in 1861, but was rapidly promoted to general. Although he performed well in some battles, in others he was slow to react and questioned orders. General Robert E. Lee transferred Magruder to the Department of Texas. Refusing parole at the end of the war, he rode into Mexico and became a major general under Emperor Maximilian. Magruder finally settled in Houston, where he died at the age of 61.

For further reading: Cullum, *Biographical Register of the Officers and Graduates of the United States Military Academy from 1802 to 1867*, 1879; Settles, "The Military Career of John Bankhead Magruder," 1972.

Manifest Destiny

Manifest Destiny was the concept that Euro-Americans were, by God's design, intended to occupy the entire North American continent and transform native peoples with the Euro-American progressive political, economical, and social systems.

Soon after the Revolutionary War, U.S. citizens began to look to western lands for natural resources and as a place for their growing population to settle. During his first inaugural address in 1801, Thomas Jefferson referred to a vast territory that would provide "room enough for our descendents to the thousandth and ten thousandth generation." Interest in the West was fueled by the Louisiana Purchase and explorations by Zebulon Pike, Meriwether Lewis, and William Clark.

In the early 1800s, the population west of the Appalachian Mountains had grown twice as quickly as in the original 13 colonies. Henry David Thoreau wrote "Eastward I go only by force, but westward I go free. Mankind progresses from East to West."

Hundreds of thousands of Europeans continued to emigrate to the United States in the 1840s, creating a constant pressure and restlessness. The once abundant natural resources, such as wild game, began to dwindle. Native American tribes were displaced to far-removed reservations. Euro-Americans began to see themselves as superior to native cultures, including Mexicans. More radical proponents of expansion believed that God intended the Euro-Americans to bring democratic government, and its social, religious, and economic stability, to "underdeveloped" cultures—hence they were "destined" to perform this role.

In 1821, Mexico stretched from the Sabine River to the Pacific Ocean, from 15 degrees North latitude to 42 degrees North latitude—more than 1.6 million square miles. Presidents John Quincy Adams (1825–1829) and Andrew Jackson (1829–1837) tried repeatedly to purchase Texas from Mexico. Jackson hoped that the United States would someday expand over "all Spanish North America," including the lush lands of California. As the momentum of Manifest Destiny grew, more U.S. citizens began to view Mexicans as inferior, with an almost immoral culture that needed a firm hand to guide it toward the benefits of a U.S.-style democracy. The United States was also worried that California and possibly all of Mexico, both weakened by internal conflict and empty treasuries, would be overrun by the British.

New York journalist John L. O'Sullivan first used the term "Manifest Destiny" in an 1845 *Democratic Review* article about annexing Texas. Manifest Destiny became a popular phrase, headline, and rallying cry before and during the Mexican-American War.

Opponents of Manifest Destiny feared that new territory would exacerbate slavery issues or lead to war with other nations such as Great Britain, which had an interest in Oregon and California. Others favored peaceful negotiation rather than occupation and annexation. Thomas Hart Benton, an ardent expansionist, believed that U.S. citizens needed to be informed about the West through expeditions and mapping parties to better embrace Manifest Destiny.

The Mexican-American War fulfilled the U.S. dream of owning New Mexico and California and being a country that extended "from sea to shining sea." Manifest Destiny remained a popular concept in the late nineteenth century and was applied to U.S. interests in South America and Cuba.

For further reading: Brack, *Mexico Views Manifest Destiny, 1821–1846*, 1975; Garrison, *Westward Extension*, 1906; Graebner, *Empire on the Pacific*, 1955; Hietala, *Manifest Destiny*, 1985; Merk, *Manifest Destiny and Mission*, 1995; Merk, *The Monroe Doctrine and American Expansionism, 1843–1849*, 1966; Pratt, "The Origins of 'Manifest Destiny,'" 1927; Ruiz, *The Mexican War*, 1963.

Mansfield, Joseph King Fenno
(1803–1862)

An engineer with General Zachary Taylor's Army of Occupation along the Río Grande, Joseph King Fenno Mansfield designed Fort Brown (Fort Texas), conducted reconnaissance, received three brevets, and was wounded once.

Mansfield, who was born in Connecticut, graduated from the U.S. Military Academy in 1822. Commissioned a second lieutenant in the Corps of Engineers, he supervised the construction of coastal defenses in the southeastern United States until the Mexican-American War.

During the war, he was chief engineer for General Taylor's Army of Occupation along the Río Grande. Mansfield designed and constructed Fort Texas (Fort Brown) on the north bank of the river and took part in its defense. At Monterrey, he conducted the preliminary reconnaissance on which the battle plan was based and led one of the attacking columns. Mansfield also performed reconnaissance and placed troops during the Battle of Buena Vista. For gallant and distinguished service at Fort Brown, he was brevetted to major; and for Monterrey and Buena Vista, brevetted to lieutenant colonel and colonel.

In 1853, at the request of Secretary of War Jefferson Davis, Mansfield was promoted to colonel and inspector-general of the U.S. army. Joining the Union Army as a brigadier general in the Civil War, he commanded the 12th Corp of the Army of the Potomac. In 1862, two days before the Battle of Antietam, he was mortally wounded conducting reconnaissance near the Confederate position.

See also Fort Brown.

For further reading: Gould, *Joseph K. F. Mansfield*, 1895.

Marcy, William Learned
(1786–1857)

As President James K. Polk's secretary of war, William Learned Marcy helped develop military strategies during the Mexican-American War and convinced Polk to accept the Treaty of Guadalupe Hidalgo.

Marcy was born in Massachusetts and graduated from Brown University. After serving in the War of 1812, he settled in New York and became an attorney. Marcy became politically connected with New York Governor De Witt Clinton, Martin Van Buren, Rufus King, and other influential New York leaders. During 1829–1838, Marcy served variously as a state supreme court justice, U.S. senator, and three-term governor. During 1840–1842, as part of the Mexican Claims Commission under President Van Buren, he secured for the U.S. claimants an award of approximately $2.5 million.

In 1845, he became Polk's secretary of war. Marcy's end-of-the-year report that called for expanding the size of the army was rejected by Congress. Within six months, U.S. and Mexican armies were battling along the Río Grande, and Congress declared war and voted to muster in 50,000 more men.

Marcy frequently advised and consulted with President Polk and Major General Winfield Scott on military matters during the Mexican-American War. His other responsibilities included working with the Committees on Military Affairs and juggling the influx of requests for commissions. Marcy believed that an attack on Mexico City via Veracruz was more practical than striking overland from northern Mexico, and he was instrumental in making Scott's Veracruz–Mexico City campaign in 1847 a reality. When Polk, incensed at negotiator Nicholas P. Trist's refusal to break off negotiations as ordered, considered rejecting the Treaty of Guadalupe Hidalgo, Marcy convinced him otherwise.

Under President Franklin Pierce, Marcy served as secretary of state. He negotiated more than 20 treaties, including the Gadsden Treaty with Mexico in 1853. Marcy died suddenly in Ballston, New York, at the age of 71.

For further reading: Polk, *The Diary of James K. Polk*, 1910; Spencer, *The Victor and the Spoils*, 1959.

William L. Marcy
(Library of Congress)

Marshall, Thomas
(1793–1853)

Brigadier General Thomas Marshall is most remembered for opening top-secret orders addressed to General Zachary Taylor and being partly responsible for those orders falling into the hands of General Antonio López de Santa Anna.

Marshall, who was born and raised in Kentucky, served in the War of 1812. He was later a long-term member of the state legislature and served a term as Speaker of the House.

President James K. Polk appointed Marshall, a loyal Democrat, brigadier general of Kentucky volunteers in 1846. Marshall was stationed at Camargo until December, when he was ordered to Monterrey. While stationed at Monterrey, Marshall opened secret orders addressed to Taylor that detailed the plans for attacking Veracruz. He then sent them on to Taylor at Victoria in January 1847, but the courier was murdered by guerrillas and the message was delivered to General Santa Anna at San Luis Potosí. Major General Winfield Scott was infuriated at Marshall for opening the secret orders and reading them aloud and then sending the courier with an inadequate guard to Taylor. Many historians believe that Santa Anna was prompted, after learning of Scott's plans to take half of Taylor's army, to launch his assault on Taylor at La Angostura (Buena Vista).

Marshall returned to Kentucky in 1848 to resume his political career. He was murdered in 1853.

For further reading: French, *Two Wars, an Autobiography*, 1901; Scott, *Memoirs of Lieutenant General Scott*, 1864.

Martinez, Antonio José
(1793–1867)

Father Antonio José Martinez opposed the U.S. occupation of New Mexico during the Mexican-American War and fought the efforts of Jean Baptiste Lamy to change the New Mexican Catholic Church.

Martinez was born in Abiquiu on the upper Río Grande to an affluent, politically powerful family. He moved to Durango and became an ordained priest in 1822. Four years later, he was sent to the Taos parish, where he built schools and taught. Martinez argued that celibacy was contrary to the nature of the Catholic Church and had several concubines. Martinez also challenged the legality of Charles Bent's large land grants from Governor Manuel Armijo.

Before the Mexican-American War, Martinez opposed the steady influx of U.S. settlers into New Mexico and their control on New Mexico trade. He especially opposed Armijo's land grants to powerful U.S. settlers or pro-U.S. New Mexicans.

Martinez wanted to fight the military invasion of New Mexico. Although there is no evidence, Padre Martínez was likely involved in the Taos Rebellion in 1847, which resulted in the murder of Governor Charles Bent and other U.S. settlers in the Taos area. After the war, Martinez accepted the U.S. government and was a long-standing member of the territorial legislature.

Martinez dedicated himself to the preservation of New Mexican culture after the war. He quarreled frequently with new bishop Jean Baptiste Lamy and his attempts to change the New Mexican Catholic Church. Martinez resisted the practice of tithing and the assignment of new, mostly European priests, who were decidedly anti–New Mexican, at the expense of New Mexican clergy.

Lamy finally excommunicated the troublesome priest in 1857. Still immensely popular, Martinez led his own church until his death in Taos in 1867.

See also Lamy, Jean Baptiste; Taos Rebellion.

For further reading: Francis, "Padre Martínez," 1956; Sanchéz, *Memories of Antonio José Martínez*, 1978.

Mason, Richard Barnes
(1797–1850)

Colonel Richard Barnes Mason of the 1st U.S. Dragoons served as military governor of California during 1847–1849 and drafted a civil code for the territory.

Mason, who was born in Virginia, joined the U.S. 8th Infantry as a second lieutenant in 1817. He served with Zachary Taylor during the Black Hawk War in Wisconsin in 1832 and was promoted to colonel of the 1st U.S. Dragoons in 1846.

Mason arrived in California in February 1847 with orders from Washington that upheld Brigadier General Stephen W. Kearny's authority over military governor John C. Frémont, who had been appointed by Commodore Robert F. Stockton. In May 1847, Kearny relinquished his short-lived position as governor of California to Mason, who was authorized to establish a temporary civil government.

Mason's department created a code of laws for California, but did not enact them because Mason had not received congressional approval. He was relieved as governor in 1849. Mason returned to Missouri at the headquarters of the 1st U.S. Dragoons and died there the following year.

See also Frémont, John C.

For further reading: Harlow, *California Conquered*, 1982; Hunt, *California and Californians*, 1926.

Matamoros

The city of Matamoros, Tamaulipas, located on the Río Grande, was an important staging area for Mexican and U.S. forces during the Mexican-American War, especially during the early battles of General Zachary Taylor's 1846 campaign in northern Mexico.

Founded in 1782 on the south bank of the Río Grande in Tamaulipas, a few miles from the Gulf of Mexico, Matamoros was an important trading center. Lucrative but highly dangerous contraband trading occurred between Matamoros and points in Texas, especially the ranch of H. L. Kinney at Corpus Christi.

Matamoros was a gathering place for soldiers, traders, robbers, and guerrillas who worked along the Río Grande. It was also a main garrison for troops of Mexico's Army of the North, including far-ranging cavalry under General José Urrea. Several expeditions were planned against the city during the Texas Revolution in 1835 and 1836, but were either aborted or routed by Mexican forces. U.S. prisoners were frequently jailed in the city's prison. When one group of U.S. prisoners was ordered to be shot, sympathetic Mexicans appealed to General Antonio López de Santa Anna and promised to raise $20,000 if the prisoners could receive a reprieve. When Nicolás Bravo became the commanding officer in 1837, the men were released.

The 1846 Matamoros population of nearly 20,000 lived in small wooden and brick houses. The city's fortifications consisted of scattered breastworks and redoubts on all sides. As the threat of war along the border increased, the military population continued to grow, including a battalion of sappers, four infantry regiments, the Tampico marines, a cavalry regiment, and several other battalions, auxiliaries, and national guard units. Curious citizens thronged the rooftops to watch General Taylor's Army of Occupation set up camp and build Fort Texas (Fort Brown) on the other bank. U.S. soldiers were equally fascinated with Matamoros, especially the women bathing nude in the river, and a small number of U.S. soldiers deserted by swimming the Río Grande.

Matamoros was occupied by Taylor's forces in May 1846 after the Battles of Palo Alto and Resaca de la Palma. The town and its inhabitants were treated roughly by the U.S. army, especially the volunteer units. For the duration of the war, Matamoros remained occupied by various U.S. forces, who were subjected to occasional attacks by Mexican patrols and guerrilla units. The last U.S. soldiers left the city on August 9, 1848.

For further reading: Alcaraz, *The Other Side*, 1850; Smith, *To Mexico with Scott*, 1917; Thorp, *Our Army on the Rio Grande*, 1846; Webb, *The Handbook of Texas*, 1952.

Mazatlán

A port city on Mexico's Pacific coast, Mazatlán, Sinaloa, was occupied by elements of the U.S. Navy's Pacific Squadron during 1847–1848.

The busiest port on the west coast of Mexico, and second in size to Veracruz, Mazatlán was targeted by the U.S. Pacific fleet during the Mexican-American War. U.S. warships *Independence, Congress,* and *Cyane* left San José del Cabo on November 8, 1847, and arrived at Mazatlán two days later. Mazatlán's garrison of 560 Mexican soldiers commanded by Colonel Rafael Téllez withdrew inland to Palos Prietos when the U.S. ships dropped anchor in the harbor.

The following day, a small force led by Captain Elie A. F. La Vallette went ashore to demand surrender. Within four hours, 730 naval personnel had landed, raised the U.S. flag, and fired a 21-gun salute. Mexican army equipment and supplies were collected and burned.

Commodore W. Branford Shubrick installed La Vallette as military governor and gave him 400 men. Lieutenant Henry W. Halleck of the U.S. Army Corp of Engineers designed fortifications in the town for the naval troops. La Vallette allowed all goods to be freely exported, assured religious freedom, forbade the sale of liquor to U.S. sailors, and promised not to interfere with the town's usual activities.

On November 14, Téllez moved closer to Mazatlán and sent out cavalry patrols. The Mexicans collided with a U.S. patrol in a dawn skirmish near Urias that resulted in one U.S. soldier killed and 20 wounded; Mexican casualties were four deaths and an unknown number wounded. Night skirmishes erupted in mid-December in the countryside around Mazatlán, including at Palos Prietos.

By February 1848, the U.S. fort was completed and could accommodate 500 men and artillery. By this time, Mexican resistance had been reduced to only a few minor raids and guerrilla actions.

For further reading: Bauer, *Surfboats and Horse Marines,* 1969; Knox, *A History of the United States Navy,* 1936; Rowan, "Recollections of the Mexican War," 1888.

McClellan, George Brinton

(1826–1885)

An engineer with the Army of Occupation, George Brinton McClellan served under Generals Zachary Taylor and Winfield Scott during the Mexican-American War and was brevetted twice for gallantry.

McClellan, who was born in Philadelphia, graduated from the U.S. Military Academy in 1842 as a second lieutenant and engineer. He was part of a company of sappers and miners that arrived in Matamoros in 1846. In January 1847, he marched with a detachment to Tampico and supervised improvements to roads and bridges. Later part of General Scott's Army of Occupation, he landed with the first troops at Veracruz in March 1847. McClellan was brevetted to first lieutenant for gallantry at Contreras and Churubusco and to captain for his leadership during the Battle of Chapultepec.

Following the war, McClellan taught engineering at the U.S. Military Academy and traveled to Europe to study foreign army procedures.

A major general during the Civil War, McClellan did an excellent job of training and outfitting the Army of the Potomac, but he was a slow and overly cautious commander and was relieved of his command by President Lincoln in 1862. McClellan lost the 1864 presidential election. He was later governor of New Jersey and died there in 1885.

For further reading: McClellan, *McClellan's Own Story,* 1887; McClellan, *The Mexican War Diary of General George B. McClellan,* 1917; Myers, *General George Brinton McClellan,* 1934; Sears, *George B. McClellan,* 1988.

McCulloch, Ben

(1811–1862)

Texas Ranger Ben McCulloch conducted scouting operations for U.S. General Zachary Taylor in 1846–1847. His discovery of the location of General Antonio López de Santa Anna's army just prior to the Battle of Buena Vista allowed Taylor to withdraw to a better defensive position.

Born in Tennessee, McCulloch was raised in Alabama and Tennessee and worked in the logging industry. A friend of Davy Crockett, McCulloch went to Texas to join the revolution and commanded two artillery pieces during the Battle of San Jacinto.

McCulloch took up surveying in Gonzales in 1838 and later joined the Texas Rangers. As a ranger, he became a skilled Indian fighter and scout and skirmished with Mexican forces along the Río Grande border.

During the Mexican-American War, McCulloch raised a company of mounted men who served under Colonel John C. Hays's 1st Regiment of Texas Mounted Volunteers. McCulloch quickly became General Zachary Taylor's favorite scout, and McCulloch and his Spy Company ranged far in advance of the army. Operating individually or in small parties, and often dressed as Mexicans, they conducted a variety of activities, including scouting for Mexican troops, passable roads, and sources of food and water and breaking up guerrilla operations.

During the Battle of Monterrey in September 1846, McCulloch led his men in the dangerous storming of Federation and Independence Hills and seizing the batteries at the top. On the night of February 20, 1847, McCulloch, dressed as a Mexican, slipped into General Antonio López de Santa Anna's encampment at La Encarnación. McCulloch climbed a small hill, estimated the size of the army from the burning campfires, and raced back to inform Taylor that Santa Anna was 15 miles away. This timely warning allowed Taylor to withdraw to better defensive ground at Buena Vista. McCulloch's mounted rangers helped protect the U.S. left and rear during the battle.

McCulloch emerged from the war as a major. In the 1850s, he served as a marshal in Sacramento and Texas and helped mediate the difficulties between the Mormons and U.S. government in Utah. As a colonel in the Texas army, he received the surrender of federal troops in Texas shortly after secession.

Appointed a brigadier general in the Confederate army during the Civil War, McCulloch was killed at Pea Ridge in 1862 while scouting the federal position.

See also Buena Vista, Battle of; Monterrey, Battle of; Texas Rangers.

For further reading: Cutrer, *Ben McCulloch and the Frontier Military Tradition*, 1993; Davis, *The Texas Rangers*, 1991; Frost, *The Mexican War and Its Warriors*, 1848; Rose, *The Life and Services of General Ben McCulloch*, 1888.

McCulloch Spy Company

See McCulloch, Ben.

McElroy, John
(1782–1877)

Father John McElroy was one of two Catholic priests who were attached to General Zachary Taylor's Army of Occupation on the Río Grande in 1846. In addition to tending the sick and wounded, McElroy tried to convince the local populace that the war was not being waged against their Catholic religion.

McElroy was born in Ireland and emigrated to the United States in 1803. Drawn to the ministry and ordained in 1817, he was active in building churches, orphanages, and schools throughout the eastern United States. Having a tall and dominating presence, McElroy soon had a reputation as a forceful preacher and retreat master. Later a pastor in Georgetown, he became close friends with Bishop John Hughes.

In 1846, probably at the suggestion of Hughes, the U.S. government asked McElroy to serve as a chaplain to U.S. soldiers during the Mexican-American War. McElroy and another Georgetown pastor, Antony Rey, left Washington on June 2, 1846. McElroy served in Taylor's army on the Río Grande with considerable success. Soldiers liked him, and his interactions with Mexican citizens promoted their belief in the army's goodwill toward Catholicism. Stationed in Matamoros, McElroy tended the sick and wounded, held services, and baptized soldiers who were near death. "There were in the city five different buildings occupied as hospitals, in which...I [visited] each ward and each bed," he remembered. McElroy also taught Mexican children in school for four hours a day.

McElroy later traveled to Boston, where he became rector of the largest Catholic Church in the area. Archbishop John J. Hughes called for him on his deathbed. Near the end of his long life, McElroy was the world's oldest living Jesuit. Blind in his later years, he died in Maryland at the age of 95.

See also Hughes, John Joseph; Rey, Antony.

For further reading: McElroy, "Chaplains for the Mexican War—1846," 1886–1887; Wynne, "Memoir of the Rev. Antony Rey, S.J.," 1847.

Meade, George Gordon
(1815–1872)

A topographical engineer, George Gordon Meade served in the Mexican-American War under Generals Zachary Taylor and Winfield Scott and performed valuable reconnaissance work.

Meade was born in Spain. He received his early education in Washington, D.C., and attended the U.S. Military Academy from 1831 to 1835. Attached to the 3rd U.S. Artillery, he fought the Seminoles in Florida and was greatly weakened by fever. Meade resigned and undertook surveying along the U.S.-Mexico border in 1840. Two years later, he rejoined the army as a second lieutenant in the Topographical Engineers.

As part of General Taylor's Army of Occupation, Meade arrived in Corpus Christi in September 1845. In preparation for Taylor's advance toward Matamoros in the spring of 1846, Meade scouted territory from Corpus Christi and the Nueces River to the Río Grande. Meade was concerned by the soft soil, bad roads, and the concealing qualities of the high chaparral.

Meade fought at the Battles of Palo Alto and Resaca de la Palma in May 1846 and was brevetted to first lieutenant for daring reconnaissance work during the Battle of Monterrey in September. In 1847, he was transferred to Major General Scott's Army and participated in the battles of the Veracruz–Mexico City campaign.

Returning to the United States, Meade again fought the Seminoles in Florida during 1848–1849. He later built coastal defenses and lighthouses. In the Civil War, he was appointed a brigadier general of volunteers in 1861 and was seriously wounded at the Battle of Glendale, Virginia. His leadership of the Union army at Gettysburg resulted in an important victory.

Meade retired to pursue business interests, but the wound he received at the Battle of Glendale led to his death at the age of 57.

For further reading: Cleaves, *Meade of Gettysburg,* 1960; Cullum, *Biographical Register of the Officers and Graduates of the United States Military Academy from 1802 to 1867,* 1879; Meade, *Life and Letters of George Gordon Meade, Major General, United States Army,* 1913.

Medical Practices, Mexico

The Mexican armies during the Mexican-American War lacked skilled physicians, medical supplies, and ancillary needs such as assistants, ambulance wagons and animals, and tents.

In August 1836, a Military Health Corps was established. On February 12, 1846, it was enlarged and attached to the regular army. It consisted of approximately 160 officer physicians and ambulance companies that consisted of eight men for every 100 soldiers. Medics were trained by the doctors to handle the wounded. Ambulance tents were marked with a white pennant, and a "Hospital" bugle call alerted doctors to conditions at the front. When the bugle called "Open Fire," the attendants assembled their mule-mounted stretchers, and medics moved along the battle line to help the wounded.

Mexican doctors helped Mexican and U.S. soldiers alike. A medical surgeon wrote that "besides the wounded of our division, 17 enemy soldiers were aided, and one captain whose left arm had to be amputated...." (Hefter 1958) Some Mexican surgeons were quite skilled, and several were credited with saving the life of General John A. Quitman, who was seriously wounded during the Battle of Cerro Gordo in April 1847. George Ballentine recalled that "Mexican surgeons made their appearance and proceeded with much apparent skill to dress and bandage the wounds of their unfortunate countrymen. They were assisted by our surgeons, after they had cared for their own wounded...."

All medical officers carried medical equipment. The medical wagons carried rolled bandages, folded bandages, compresses, thread, silk, fracture boards, adhesive plaster, lime chloride, needles, pins, and cotton. Drugs included Jalapa powder, sulphate of soda, leaves, castor oil, emetic, ipecacuanha, calomel, corrosive sublimate, quinine, liquid ammonia, bicarbonate of soda, camphor, devil's stone, opium extract, nitric salt, crystal lead acetate, gum arabic powder, licorice extract, citric acid, mercury plaster, mercury salve, cantharis flakes, belladonna extract, and sodium chloride. Because of limited funds and the lack of a quartermaster supply system, the Health Corps frequently lacked the necessary medicines to treat their sick and wounded.

The Mexican army was inefficient in managing casualties and setting up field hospitals. The wounded were moved over long distances, usually with the retreating army, in carts hauled by oxen or mules. The grievously wounded were often left on the battlefield to die, to make room for those soldiers with lesser wounds who were more likely to recover and fight again.

The large caliber and low velocity of the musket balls inflicted horrible, gaping wounds and frequently dragged in filthy bits of cloth and uniform. The spread of infection was not understood, and gangrene was common. Soldiers frequently died from amputations, and those with stomach wounds were susceptible to peritonitis. Field hospitals were overcrowded and filthy. Many of the Mexican wounded suffered shattered limbs inflicted by the U.S. artillery. George Ballentine saw a wounded man who kept "the flies off by means of a palmetto leaf in his mouth, both arms having been torn off at the shoulder joints." Another observed that the conditions were so bad in Mexican hospitals in Jalapa that "impelled by the urgency of the situation, [the wounded] leave the hospitals and perish in the open country, where the ground is strewn with corpses."

As the war continued, medical aid for the armies was even more reduced. General Antonio López de Santa Anna's 20,000-man Army of the North that marched northward from San Luis Potosí in January 1847 had only 26 medical officers and 35 assistants. After the Battle of La Angostura (Buena Vista), Santa Anna left many of his wounded on the field to be cared for by U.S. doctors.

Because of the lack of stationary field hospitals, the constant influx of new conscripts, high desertion rates, the low number of doctors, and lack of record keeping, the effects of disease on Mexican soldiers in not accurately known. It is likely that they suffered less from those "regional" illnesses, such as yellow fever or malaria, to which they had a certain immunity. However, diseases and conditions, such as cholera, typhoid fever, diarrhea, dysentery, and smallpox, that are caused by polluted water, contaminated or spoiled food, and poor hygiene were probably as serious in the Mexican army as they were in the U.S. army.

For further reading: Ballentine, *Autobiography of an English Soldier in the United States Army*, 1853; DePalo, *The Mexican National Army, 1822–1852*, 1997; Hefter, *El soldado mexicano*, 1958; Ramirez, *Mexico during the War with the United States*, 1950.

Medical Practices, United States

The U.S. army during the Mexican-American War was understaffed with medical personnel and often lacked important medicines, such as quinine and smallpox vaccine. Compared with the Mexican army, the U.S. army was better supplied with medicines, tents, and other equipment because of its quartermaster department.

The skills of the army doctor in the mid–nineteenth century varied greatly. Doctors who had unsuccessful private practices often joined the army. Congress allowed three doctors per regiment of regulars (approximately 1,000 men), but only two per volunteer regiment. Volunteers also tended to have inferior doctors who were not adapted to the rigors of the field. Despite the urging of Surgeon General Thomas Lawson, army medical staff was not expanded until February 1847, when two surgeons and 12 assistants were added. Even with these additions, the army medical department remained understaffed and overworked, and doctors were frequently sick or broken down from overexhaustion.

Shipping delays and guerrilla attacks on wagon trains interrupted the flow of medical supplies from New York and St. Louis. Some medicines, such as smallpox vaccine, were hard to preserve in the heat. Quinine was a popular drug for a number of illnesses and was used up quickly in the field. The army had only a few spring wagons or civilian ambulances. The wounded generally had an excruciating ride in rough-jolting army wagons.

The army's medical department was not prepared for the Mexican-American War. In addition to not having enough doctors, few able-bodied men were spared for hospital duty. Thus, hospitals were often tended by the sick themselves or cooks and nurses. Also, the best supplies, including tables and kitchen facilities, went with the army to the front.

Disease killed more than three-quarters of the U.S. soldiers who died during the war. Yellow fever (black vomit), dysentery, and diarrhea were the leading killers, followed by malaria, measles, smallpox, typhoid fever, venereal disease, pneumonia, and rheumatism. The regular U.S. soldier was vaccinated against smallpox; most of the volunteers were not. Alcoholism was also a serious problem. The medical profession in the mid–nineteenth century did not understand the transmission of most diseases; for example, doctors were just beginning to consider mosquitos as carriers of malaria and yellow fever.

Regulars were more used to arduous conditions than were the volunteers, many of whom came from farms and had never been exposed to diseases. Volunteers quickly fell ill.

A satirical cartoon, created ca. 1846, comments on how frequently U.S. surgeons used amputation to treat wounded Mexican soldiers. (Library of Congress)

Some companies lost half their men to disease and debility in the first few months of the campaign. Conditions that contributed to poor health were exposure to the elements, contaminated drinking water and food, careless cooking habits, and poor personal hygiene.

Veteran soldiers were more careful about what they ate and followed the examples of the Mexicans. Soldiers who ate just bread, meat, and beans and avoided the plentiful fresh fruits and vegetables (often on the advice of physicians) usually developed scurvy. Surgeon Charles S. Tripler wrote that the "use of fresh provisions exclusively no doubt occasion disturbance of the digestive organs & swells the number of our cases of diarrhea. The improvident use of the fruits of the climate occasions many cases and is a great impediment in the way of convalescence." Colonel Samuel R. Curtis remembered that "hundreds pass down the [Río Grande] daily on their way home, having [been attacked] by incurable disease. They will many of them return home to their families emaciated, sick, and unable to toil. They are the wounded soldiers who have met the pestilential foes of the South; and as much deserve the honor and care of their country as though the fatal shaft had been composed of lead."

Psychiatric casualties, broken bones from accidents, and gunshot, bayonet, shrapnel, and artillery wounds were the typical cases generated from the battlefield. If a bullet was close to the surface of the skin, it was extracted with forceps. Amputation was the only major surgery, and the stump was cauterized with hot tar. Anesthesia was used only briefly in Veracruz toward the end of the war; usually patients drank whiskey or chewed on a lead bullet during amputation surgery. Psychiatric problems often struck the physicians themselves; at least one suffered a complete mental breakdown. One soldier wrote that "Nothing can exceed the devotion of our medical officers; they are literally fatigued to death."

As mentioned, skills of the surgeons varied. Surgeons rarely washed their hands, saws, or swabs between patients. It was nearly impossible to remove all the foreign matter, bullet shards, and bone fragments in a gunshot wound, which usually suppurated. Antiseptics were not available. Stubborn infections often appeared after an amputation. If they continued, or the stump became gangrenous, the limb would be amputated again at a higher point. Some soldiers underwent three amputations and often were so weak that they died. "Apparently the most trifling wounds require an unusual time for healing...." wrote Dr. Nathan S. Jarvis.

The Medical Department established hospitals at cities such as Camargo, Veracruz, Corpus Christi, Mier, Cerralvo, Monterrey, Matamoros, Point Isabel, Saltillo, and Jalapa—along the routes that the army traveled. The hospitals were drastically understaffed. More than 1,500 soldiers died in the hospital at Camargo. Many soldiers, especially at Veracruz, had a greater fear of hospitalization than of dying on the battlefield. Milton Jamieson, of the 5th Regiment of Ohio Volunteers, recalled that "I hope never again to behold such horrid, ghastly and shocking pictures of humanity.... Diseases of all kinds were prevailing there.... Some were bearing the pains of their diseases with fortitude, some were screaming, some were praying to God to release them from their miseries, and others were raving maniacs.... Some were so reduced in flesh that they looked more like walking skeletons.... They died at the rate of eight or ten per day."

Another deadly side effect from illness resulted on the march: Sick soldiers who could not keep up were forced to rest on the roadside. Exhausted, delirious, or sleeping, they were easy victims for the bands of guerrillas that constantly trailed the army.

For further reading: Ashburn, *A History of the Medical Department of the United States Army*, 1911; Gillett, *The Army Medical Department, 1818–1865*, 1987; Miller, *Shamrock and Sword*, 1989; Smith and Judah, *Chronicles of the Gringos*, 1968; Winders, *Mr. Polk's Army*, 1997.

Mejía, Francisco
(1822–1901)

General Francisco Mejía was a capable senior military commander in the Mexican army who fought in many of the important battles in northern Mexico and around Mexico City.

Mejía, who was born in Ixtapan, joined the Spanish army at a young age. After participating in the suppression of various uprisings, he joined Agustín de Iturbide's revolutionary forces in 1821. He remained in the Mexican army and served in northern Mexico in the early 1840s. He disobeyed the orders of General Nicolás Bravo when he refused to execute members of the Mier Expedition. He remained the commander of the Mexican forces at Matamoros and occasionally launched raids into Texas.

As General Zachary Taylor's Army of Occupation marched toward the Río Grande from Corpus Christi, General Mejía rode northward with a small column and tried to deceive Taylor into thinking he was facing a much larger Mexican force at Arroyo Colorado. The ruse failed to halt Taylor's march, and Mejía returned to Matamoros and improved its defenses. He was shortly superseded as commander of the Army of the North by Generals Mariano Arista and Pedro de Ampudia.

As the second-ranking commander at Monterrey, Mejía helped plan the defense of the city and fought in the ensuing battle in September. As part of the reorganized Army of the North under General Antonio López de Santa Anna, Mejía marched northward from San Luis Potosí and helped fight Taylor at the Battle of La Angostura in February 1847. Mejía's infantry brigade suffered heavy losses during the Battle of Contreras in August.

Mejía remained a highly respected military figure after the war and commanded districts in Durango and San Luis Potosí in the early 1850s.

For further reading: Carreño, *Jefes del ejército mexicano en 1847*, 1914; DePalo, *The Mexican National Army, 1822–1852*, 1997.

Mervine, William
(1791–1868)

Captain William Mervine served in the U.S. Pacific Squadron during the Mexican-American War and raised the U.S. flag over Monterey in 1846.

Mervine was born in Philadelphia. He was appointed a midshipman in 1809 and was wounded during the War of 1812. His naval career took him to the Mediterranean and the West Indies. He was promoted to captain in 1841.

During the Mexican-American War, Mervine commanded two ships that were part of the Pacific Squadron, the *Cyane* during 1845–1846 and the *Savannah* during 1846–1847. On July 7, 1846, he took possession of Monterey, California, and served as its military commander. In October, he commanded a landing party that skirmished with Mexicans near Los Angeles.

Mervine became the commander of the Pacific Squadron after the war. During the Civil War, he commanded the Gulf Blockading Squadron that patrolled the Atlantic from Key West to Galveston. Mervine retired as a rear admiral and died at age 77 in New York.

For further reading: Bauer, *Surfboats and Horse Marines*, 1969; Knox, *A History of the United States Navy*, 1936.

Mexico

Mexico experienced more than 30 political administrations in its first 25 years of existence as an independent country. Its numerous economic and political problems made it ill prepared to fight a war with the United States.

The earliest native populations in Mexico included the Olmec, Zapotec, Mayan, Toltec, and Aztec tribes. The Aztecs dominated the other native groups in the 1400s. The Aztec capital, Tenochtitlán, was an intricately designed city of 100,000 people.

The Spaniards came to Mexico's shores in 1517. The Aztec emperor Moctezuma resisted the Spaniards, who later joined with the oppressed tribes to seize the capital and capture Moctezuma. Bitter fighting between 1519 and 1521 killed thousands of Aztecs and almost completely destroyed the capital city. Hernán Cortés then became the ruler of New Spain and built the elegant National Palace on the ruins of Moctezuma's palace. The resultant dictatorial regime in New Spain was dominated by Spanish leaders, who installed the Roman Catholic Church, and great efforts were made to convert the native peoples to Catholicism.

Most natives had severely restricted rights, and Africans were imported to work as slaves. A caste system developed in which the most powerful and privileged citizens were Spanish-born people. Creoles (people of Spanish ancestry born in New Spain) held unimportant government or church posts. Mestizos (mixed white and Indian ancestry) were farmers and laborers. Indians were generally impoverished. From approximately 1810 to 1820, a series of bloody and short-lived revolts erupted between Spanish troops and rebel forces. Inspired by the successful revolutions in the United States and France and with liberal changes in the Spanish government in 1820, the leadership of revolutionaries Agustín de Iturbide and Vicente Guerrero helped Mexico win its independence from Spain in 1821 with little bloodshed.

The following years brought a series of short-lived governments as different political/social groups fought for control of the country. Mexico became polarized by the centralists (conservatives), who wanted to keep the old Spanish ways, and the federalists (liberals), who sought a democratic republic. Iturbide was deposed as emperor by Antonio López de Santa Anna in 1823. In 1824, a federalist constitution was adopted, and Guadalupe Victoria was elected as the republic's first president.

Santa Anna remained a dominant political figure over the next 20 years as power struggles continued to disrupt the new republic. In 1832, Santa Anna was elected president as a liberal. When the conservatives rebelled against the new policies, Santa Anna became a conservative, seized power as a dictator, abolished the constitution, and established a centralist government. Santa Anna's downfall came after he personally led the Mexican army against Texan rebels in 1836, lost to Sam Houston, and surrendered Texas via the Treaties of Velasco. Santa Anna was then exiled to Cuba.

The period between 1821 and 1846 was marked by frequent rebellions, invasions by Spain and France, and more than 30 presidents and provisional presidents. Although Mexico City seemed to be in an almost constant state of turmoil, the effects were rarely discerned in the outlying, rural communities. The uncertainties of governmental policies led to a stagnation in economic development and a growing national debt. The liberals split into *puro* and *moderado* factions, which further complicated political matters. Thus, Mexico was a country that was ill prepared to enter the war with the United States in 1846.

See also Halls of the Montezumas, Mexico City; Moderados; Puros.
For further reading: Alamán, *Historia de Méjico desde los primeros movimientos que prepararon su independencia en el año de 1808 hasta la época presente*, 1850; Bancroft, *The History of Mexico*, 1966; Callcott,

Church and State in Mexico, 1926; Costeloe, *The Central Republic in Mexico, 1835–1846*, 1993; Cotner and Castañeda, *Essays in Mexican History*, 1958; Hale, *Mexican Liberalism in the Age of Mora, 1821–1853*, 1968.

Mexico City

Mexico City was founded in approximately 1520 on the ruins of the Aztec capital Tenochtitlán. By the time of the Mexican-American War, Mexico City's population had grown to 200,000.

Broad avenues lined with trees ran through the city toward the great central plaza. Built in the ornate, Spanish style, the National Palace, museums, and elegant cathedrals dominated the core of the city. Lining the streets were two-story houses built from stone, with exteriors painted in white, orange, blue, red, or pale green. Courtyards, gardens, fountains, gambling houses, and cockpits were in abundance. Thousands of carriages traveled the promenade, and streets were lined with vendors selling goods and produce. Many of the republic's wealthiest families and businessmen resided in the city. The vast surrounding suburbs, where the poorer, lower-class population lived, were littered, dirty, and in disrepair.

"On descending by a winding road [from the mountains] into the great valley of Mexico, you can see some of the prettiest views that human eye can see.... In the centre is the city of Mexico, with its immense towers and cupolas, and religious monuments.... On the right, about five or six miles from the city, lies the beautiful Lake Tezueco, full of wild ducks and floating gardens," wrote J. J. Oswandel. The giant Catholic cathedral attracted thousands of people from all social classes. Stationed in Mexico City in 1847, Oswandel remembered that "It being Christmas there were great sights to be seen in the Cathedral. The whole building was illuminated with five thousand wax lights. They had an image of our Saviour in a cradle and were rocking it like a child, singing verses, etc., and the organ playing to its utmost extent. The ceremonies were grand and the building was crowded with all classes of people."

For further reading: Alcaraz, *The Other Side*, 1850; Gayón, *La ocupación yanqui de la Ciudad de México*, 1997; Oswandel, *Notes of the Mexican War*, 1885.

General Winfield Scott and his troops march into Mexico City. This portrayal first appeared in George Kendall's *War between the United States and Mexico*, 1851. (Library of Congress)

Mexico City, Battle of
(September 13–14, 1847)

The capital of Mexico, and its largest city, Mexico City was the object of Major General Winfield Scott's advance from Veracruz in March 1847. After the Battles of Cerro Gordo, Contreras, Churubusco, El Molino del Rey, and Chapultepec, the city fell to the U.S. Army of Occupation on September 14, 1847.

By September 1847, the Mexican forces, having lost the fiercely contested Battle of El Molino del Rey on September 8, 1847, were in a desperate situation. The remnants of General Antonio López de Santa Anna's army had taken up position at Chapultepec and the City of Mexico. Scott's army was less than two miles from the capital city, and Santa Anna was in despair.

Scott decided to attack Chapultepec and then advance on Mexico City from the south and west. The open ground in front of the city was impassable marsh and swamp. Thus, any advance would be restricted to the narrow causeways that entered the city at its northwest and southwest corners. Scott selected attack paths along the La Verónica and Belén causeways. La Verónica followed an aqueduct that ran two miles in a northeasterly direction, and then turned east toward the northwestern *garita* (gate) of San Cosmé. The Belén causeway ran almost due east to the southwestern Belén *garita*. The *garitas* were solid, square buildings that served as tollgates. Belén *garita* was also defended by the massive stone Ciudadela (Citadel) fortress.

The attack on Chapultepec began at dawn on September 13, and by 9:30 A.M. the formidable defenses had been overrun by U.S. troops. As the defeated Mexicans streamed back to Mexico City, Generals John A. Quitman and William J. Worth ordered their divisions to advance down the causeways. Scott ordered two brigades to support Worth and one to support Quitman. Scott and his staff followed Worth. Engineer and scout Robert E. Lee, after three days of no sleep, collapsed and fell from his horse.

General David E. Twiggs and his men demonstrated all day at San Antonio Abad *garita*, two miles south of Belén *garita*. This forced a large portion of the city's soldiers to remain in their position and not reinforce the fighting at San Cosmé and Belén *garitas*.

The U.S. soldiers advanced cautiously along the aqueduct, taking shelter behind its arches. Pockets of Mexican defenders made spirited stands, only to be pushed back, sometimes at the point of the bayonet. Brief Mexican counterattacks were led by Generals Joaquín Rangel, Matías de la Peña y Barragán, and Anastasio Torrejón.

Part of the San Cosmé causeway was lined with well-built houses that were filled with sharpshooters. Using picks and crowbars, the infantry dug through the walls of the houses on both sides of the causeways and fought the Mexicans hand to hand. The U.S. advance was still hampered by severe fire from Mexican batteries farther up the road. Lieutenant Henry Hunt moved forward through the Mexcian fire with his single artillery piece. He quickly lost five of his eight gunners as he fought to within a few yards of the enemy's breastworks. The Mexicans still resisted stubbornly, and by 5:00 P.M. Rangel had been severely wounded. Disheartened by the loss of Rangel, the Mexican defense finally gave way at the point of U.S. bayonets.

Santa Anna, mobilizing troops and artillery from other parts of the city, personally directed the defense at Belén *garita*. Quitman had gone through the gate but stopped when he saw the heavily armed buildings of the Ciudadela and Belén prison. The resistance at Belén *garita* was led by Brigadier General Andrés Terrés and approximately 200 infantrymen from the Morelia Battalion. Their furious counterattack drove Quitman back until the Mexicans ran out of ammunition and withdrew to the Ciudadela with 70 survivors. Resupplied, they maintained a heavy fire, which wounded several U.S. officers, including P. G. T. Beauregard, Earl Van Dorn, and Zealous B. Tower. The musket fire was so intense that Lieutenant Fitz John Porter lost 27 of his 30 men. Several other counterattacks were launched from the Ciudadela, and by nightfall nearly all of Quitman's officers had been shot.

By nightfall, however, both Worth and Quitman were in possession of the *garitas*. Despite his courageous leadership, Terrés was blamed by Santa Anna for the fall of Mexico City. That night, with U.S. forces camped in the shadows of the city, Santa Anna held a junta. Although he still had approximately 10,000 scattered troops, the cause seemed hopeless. City leaders feared that continued fighting would kill thousands of civilians. Santa Anna evacuated his army from the city and marched to the northern suburb of Guadalupe Hidalgo by 1:00 A.M. City officials then met with Worth and Scott regarding terms of surrender, which Scott refused to consider.

The following morning, Scott ordered Worth and Quitman to advance with caution toward the center of the city. Quitman was greeted by a white flag and reached the Grand Plaza at 7:00 A.M. He entered the National Palace, raised the U.S. flag, drove away looters, and placed a guard of U.S. Marines. Generals Scott and Worth advanced into the city in full dress uniform at approximately 8:00 A.M. from the northwestern corner of the city with regimental bands playing "Yankee Doodle."

Quitman's entrance into the palace had annoyed Scott, whom Beauregard wrote as seeming "considerably vexed at our temerity and success." Nevertheless, Scott appointed Quitman military governor of the city. The streets were crowded with civilians waving white handkerchiefs. "The various streets poured forth their thousands of spectators, and the balconies and house-tops were filled beside," wrote Raphael Semmes.

Shortly afterward, from the rooftops musket fire erupted, seriously wounding Lieutenant Colonel John Garland. Brisk sniping continued over the next 24 hours and killed a number of U.S. soldiers. Many of the snipers were some of the 30,000 convicts that the Mexican army had freed from prisons as they had retreated. Scott wrote that "this unlawful war lasted more than twenty-four hours, in spite of the exertions of the municipal authorities, and was not put down until we had lost many men." Scott had approximately 6,000 soldiers in a city of nearly 200,000 citizens. The U.S. troops retaliated with artillery fire on houses from which firing occurred. "In some cases whole blocks were destroyed and a great number of men, women and children killed and wounded," wrote Mexican historian Ramon Alcaraz.

Most of the shooting stopped by September 16, but murders were common at night. Scott organized a 500-man military police force, which worked with Mexican police to halt the violence on both sides.

See also Chapultepec, Battle of; Terrés, Andrés.

For further reading: Alcaraz, *The Other Side*, 1850; Lewis, *Captain Sam Grant*, 1950; Rea, *Apuntes históricos sobre los acontecimientos notables de la guerra entre México y los Estados Unidos del norte*, 1945; Semmes, *Service Afloat and Ashore during the Mexican War*, 1851; Smith and Judah, *Chronicles of the Gringos*, 1968; Wessels, *Born to Be a Soldier*, 1971.

Mier Expedition
(1842)

A small Mexican town on the Río Grande border near present-day Roma Los Saenz, Texas, Mier was the target of a Texan attack in 1842. The mistreatment of Texan prisoners taken during this expedition led to greater mistrust and hatred by Texans for Mexico.

In response to General Adrian Woll and his Mexican troops occupying San Antonio and killing Anglo-Texans, Texas president Sam Houston called for volunteers to go to San Antonio in September 1842. After the mission was terminated near Guerrero, along the Río Grande, 262 Texans were pinned down in buildings on the outskirts of Mier by approximately 1,000 Mexican troops under Generals Pedro de Ampudia and Antonio Canales. The Texans surrendered on December 26 when they were promised that they would be treated honorably as prisoners of war and not be shipped to Mexico. Ampudia promptly marched his prisoners on foot to Matamoros and then on toward Mexico City.

Near Saltillo the Texans plotted and attempted an escape that resulted in approximately ten Mexican casualties; the Texans fled into a barren and waterless region and were recaptured. On March 25, 1843, at hacienda del Salado, 17 soldiers were selected for execution by randomly drawing beans from an earthen pot filled with 159 white beans and 17 black beans. Those who drew black beans were killed by firing squads. Another soldier was executed a month later by Santa Anna's order. The prisoners worked as road gangs and were imprisoned in Perote Castle in September 1843. A few prisoners, including Samuel H.

Walker, escaped to freedom by tunneling under the castle walls. On September 16, 1844, Santa Anna released the remaining 107 Texans.

For further reading: Bancroft, *History of the North Mexican States and Texas,* 1884–1889; Day, *Black Beans and Goose Quills,* 1970; Green, *Journey of the Texian Expedition against Mier,* 1845; Hayes, *Soldiers of Misfortune,* 1990.

Miñón, José Vicente
(1802–1878)

A cavalry general during the Mexican-American War, José Vicente Miñón captured a U.S. scouting party at La Encarnación and was later blamed by General Antonio López de Santa Anna for the loss of the Battle at La Angostura (Buena Vista).

Miñón's family emigrated to Mexico from Cádiz, Spain, shortly after Miñón was born. Miñón served in the Spanish army before he joined forces with Agustín de Iturbide's revolutionary army in 1821.

Miñón commanded a cavalry brigade in General Santa Anna's Army of the North. Marching in advance of the army, Miñón's cavalry captured a U.S. scouting party at La Encarnación in January 1847. Before the Battle of La Angostura (Buena Vista) commenced on February 23, Santa Anna planned for Miñón's brigade to circle the right flank of General Zachary Taylor's Army of Occupation and descend on its rear; General Julián Juvera's brigade would sweep around the left flank and join forces with Miñón. Juvera succeeded in reaching the U.S. army's rear at hacienda Buena Vista, but Miñón never appeared and Juvera was forced back. Had Miñón arrived as planned, the joint cavalry force could have turned the narrow Mexican loss into a victory.

Santa Anna was incensed at Miñón's poor performance and held him responsible for the failed flank attack. According to Samuel Chamberlain, a U.S. dragoon, Miñón delayed his assault for several hours while he kept a tryst with his lover, Caroline Porter, in an upstairs room at Arispe's Mill about five miles from Saltillo. He later made an ineffective attack on Saltillo that was easily turned back by a U.S. artillery battery. As the defeated Mexican army retreated southward, Santa Anna arrested Miñón at Matehuala.

After the war, Miñón commanded garrisons at Querétaro and Oaxaca and participated in quelling various rebellions. Miñón later supported the French intervention. He died in Mexico City at the age of 76.

See also Buena Vista, Battle of; Porter, Caroline.

For further reading: Carleton, *The Battle of Buena Vista,* 1848; Chamberlain, *My Confession,* 1956; DePalo, *The Mexican National Army, 1822–1852,* 1997; *Diccionario Porrúa,* 1995; Lavender, *Climax at Buena Vista,* 1966; Santoni, *Mexicans at Arms,* 1996.

Moderados

A subfaction of the liberal political group in Mexico, *moderados* favored the gradual implementation of liberal reforms, such as reducing the power of the Roman Catholic Church.

The liberal faction, or the federalists, in Mexican politics favored a democratic government that gave individual states greater control over their own affairs and also protected free speech and press. In the 1840s, the liberals began to split into two groups: those favoring radical reforms were called *puros*; those favoring gradual changes were called *moderados*. *Moderados* believed that massive *puro* reforms would lead to political instability; instead the *moderados* favored a gradual reduction in the powers and privileges of the Roman Catholic Church and Mexican army. During Herrera's administration of 1844–1845, the *moderados* sought a negotiated settlement rather than war with the United States.

In 1847, the conflicts between *puros* and *moderados* continued to escalate. Both groups had their own militia. When *puro* Vice-President Valentín Gómez Farías attempted to take 15 million pesos from the Catholic Church to finance the war effort, *moderados* helped instigate the *Polkos* Revolt. *Moderados* also participated in the Treaty of Guadalupe Hidalgo negotiations during 1847–1848. *Moderado-puro* conflicts continued into the 1860s, when most *moderados* supported French Emperor Maximilian.

See also Polkos Revolt; *Puros*.

For further reading: Costeloe, "The Mexican Church and the Rebellion of the Polkos," 1966; Hale, *Mexican Liberalism in the Age of Mora, 1821–1853,* 1968;

Ramirez, *Mexico during the War with the United States*, 1950; Santoni, *Mexicans at Arms*, 1996.

Molino del Rey, Battle of

See El Molino del Rey, Battle of

Monclova

Located in the province of Coahuila, the city of Monclova was occupied by General John E. Wool's Army of the Center in the fall of 1846.

Founded in 1647 by Antonio de Balcárcel, Monclova became the capital of the joint state Coahuila y Texas in 1833. Located between a line of mountains and a fertile valley, its water came from fresh creeks that ran from springs high in the hills. "The valley is filled with fields of sugar, cotton, wheat and corn," wrote Josiah Gregg in the nineteenth century. The population of the city and its outlying areas was approximately 8,000. Local businesses included cotton, cattle, sheep, horses, and mining. Gregg went on to marvel that the city is "better built, and has more indications of wealth, refinement, etc., than any town we have met with [in] Mexico."

General Wool, on his way from San Antonio to occupy Chihuahua with his Army of the West, entered Monclova unopposed on October 29, 1846. Because of the armistice that General Zachary Taylor signed after the Battle of Monterrey, Wool was required to stay at Monclova for nearly 4 weeks. Camped about a mile from the city, his men rested and resupplied. The U.S. troops were generally well-received by the Mexican citizens. On November 24, Wool continued his march toward Parras and left four companies of infantry to guard the supplies and wagons he left behind as a depot.

For further reading: Baylies, *A Narrative of Major General Wool's Campaign in Mexico*, 1851; Engelmann, *The Second Illinois in the Mexican War*, 1934.

Monroe Doctrine (1823)

Presented by President James Monroe and Secretary of State John Quincy Adams in December 1823 to the U.S. Congress, the Monroe Doctrine was a foreign policy that recognized the independence and sovereignty of the new Latin American countries, including Mexico, that had been formerly under Spanish rule, and it pledged noninterference in their internal affairs. It also called for the noncolonization of North America by European nations.

The principles of the Monroe Doctrine became secondary during the expansionist years of the United States in the 1830s and 1840s. Although the annexation of Texas and the Mexican-American War appeared to be in direct conflict with the Monroe Doctrine, President James K. Polk argued that Texas was a republic and free of Mexican rule when it was annexed by the United States in 1845. He further claimed that by annexing Texas the United States was preventing Great Britain and France from colonizing the republic.

See also Adams, John Quincy.

For further reading: May, *The Making of the Monroe Doctrine*, 1992.

Monterey

The capital of California during the Mexican-American War, the port city of Monterey was occupied by U.S. naval forces in July 1846 and proclaimed part of the United States.

Founded in 1770, Monterey was the capital of California. It became an important trading port in the early 1800s. The small but thriving town consisted mostly of one-story, white adobe buildings surrounded by expanses of green grasslands with herds of horses and cattle. Majestic mountains rose in the distance, and the port had an excellent harbor. Monterey was home to U.S. businessman and consul Thomas O. Larkin, who had fostered congenial relationships with Mexican and Californio leaders.

In 1846, warlike activities had broken out between U.S. explorer John C. Frémont and his frontiersmen in northern California at Sonoma. Shortly afterward, war was declared between the United States and Mexico.

The *Cyane*, *Levant*, and *Savannah*, ships from the U.S. Navy's Pacific Squadron, gathered outside Monterey's harbor. On July 7, 1846, Captain William Mervine of the *Cyane* and a small force entered the city and demanded its surrender. Captain Mariano Silva, the military commandant, responded that he did not have the authority to surrender the town. Mervine left and returned with a landing party of 235 sailors and marines. He announced that California had become part of the United States and raised the U.S. flag while a military band paraded through the streets. Captain Mervine became the military commander of the city, imposed martial law, and forbade the sale of liquor. He put his 300 men to work building fortifications, including a blockhouse called Fort Mervine that held three cannon. Monterey remained under U.S. control for the rest of the war.

See also Mervine, William.

For further reading: Bauer, *Surfboats and Horse Marines*, 1969; Harlow, *California Conquered*, 1982; Rowan, "Recollections of the Mexican War," 1888; Sherman, *The Life of the Late Rear Admiral John Drake Sloat*, 1902.

Monterrey, Armistice of
(1846)

The Battle of Monterrey in September 1846 was the third major conflict of the Mexican-American War and resulted in a costly U.S. victory. A generous armistice between General Pedro de Ampudia and General Zachary Taylor resulted in the departure of the Mexican army with its arms from the city and the establishment of a line across which the U.S. troops could not pursue for two months. President James K. Polk believed that Taylor could have ended the war if he had insisted on the unconditional surrender of Ampudia's men.

Following the Battle of Monterrey (September 21–23, 1846), General Ampudia requested General Taylor's approval for the safe withdrawal of his army, equipment, and baggage. Taylor refused, but he later met with Ampudia and agreed to a three-officer team from each army to work out the details of an armistice. Taylor was represented by General William J. Worth, General James Pinkney Henderson, and Colonel Jefferson Davis; Ampudia was represented by General José María Ortega, General Tomás Requena, and Don Manuel M. Llano, the governor of the province Nuevo León. The discussions became heated. Late on September 24, Taylor agreed to very generous terms because "of the gallant defense of the town, and the fact of a recent change of government in Mexico [the ascension of President and General Antonio López de Santa Anna, whom Polk allowed to enter Mexico less than two months ago] believed to be favorable to the interests of peace."

The Mexicans were required to surrender the city, public property, defenses, artillery, and ammunition; in return, Ampudia's men would retain their arms and accouterments, including a few artillery pieces and ammunition. Furthermore, within a week's time, the Mexicans would withdraw from the battered city to a line about 40 miles from Monterrey beyond which Taylor could not move for two months. The following day, September 25, the Mexican soldiers fired an 8-gun salute as their flag was taken down; the U.S. soldiers fired a 28-gun salute as the U.S. flag was raised.

President Polk was infuriated by the armistice. He believed that Taylor should have captured the entire army, which could have ended the war. Taylor believed that his orders were to facilitate peace and that the armistice was a respectful way to give the new government an opportunity to consider a peace settlement. After receiving the news of the armistice, Polk immediately ordered Taylor to terminate the truce, which he did on November 13, 1846. Although Ampudia lost the Battle of Monterrey, the armistice was a tremendous victory for the Mexican army, which gained precious time to regroup. The armistice quite possibly allowed the Mexicans to fight for their country for another year.

See also Monterrey, Battle of; Tacubaya, Armistice of.

For further reading: Alcaraz, *The Other Side*, 1850; Bauer, *Zachary Taylor*, 1985; Taylor, *Letters of Zachary Taylor from the Battlefields of the Mexican War*, 1908.

Monterrey, Battle of
(September 21–23, 1846)

The Battle of Monterrey in northern Mexico was General Zachary Taylor's third consecutive victory against the Army of the North, but

General William Worth and his troops move into position under the guns of the enemy on the morning of September 21, 1846, as they prepare for the Battle of Monterrey. (Library of Congress)

his uneven leadership resulted in high casualties (about 9 percent of his fighting force).

Following the Battles of Palo Alto and Resaca de la Palma in May 1846 along the Río Grande, the defeated Army of the North retreated southward to Linares in late May. General Taylor and his Army of Occupation seized Matamoros and then moved up the Río Grande and occupied Camargo in July. From Linares, General Mariano Arista ordered a battalion of engineers and sappers to fortify the city of Monterrey, capital of Nuevo León and Taylor's most likely target. The rest of the Army of the North moved out on July 9, 1846.

An attractive city with well-built stone houses, Monterrey lay in a fertile valley beside a majestic range of mountains. The city had a beautiful plaza graced with gardens, trees, and a fountain. The clear waters of the Santa Catarina River bordered the city to the south. The engineers fortified an unfinished cathedral just north of the city, a tannery called La Tenería, and other forts and entrenchments that guarded the western and eastern approaches.

Arista was removed from command and succeeded by Brigadier General Francisco Mejía. A debilitating illness forced Mejía to temporarily relinquish command to General Tomás Requena, who marched the army to Monterrey in July. General Pedro de Ampudia, the new general in chief, arrived in early August with more men and ammunition, bringing his army to a total of nearly 7,000 men and 32 pieces of artillery.

On August 10, Taylor sent Captain Ben McCulloch of the Texas Rangers forward to scout the roads leading to Monterrey. Taylor was eager to leave Camargo, where nearly a third of his 15,000-man army had fallen ill. Taylor's first 6,000 men, half of whom were regulars, moved out on August 19; the rest were not mobilized until the first week of September. By September 19, Taylor had approached to within three miles of Monterrey and camped in a 100-acre grove of trees with clear-running water that they called "Walnut Springs" (Bosque de San Domingo).

The roads that led into Monterrey from the north and east were protected by the fortified walls of the Ciudadela (Citadel), an unfinished cathedral about 1,000 yards north of the city. The U.S. forces called it the "Black Fort." The road from the south crossed a stream at the fortified bridge La Purisima. The eastern approach to the city was also protected by forts called La Tenería (a stone building and parapet reinforced with sandbags) and el Rincón del Diablo, or "Devil's Corner." Westward from the city, the road to Saltillo passed between two rugged hills—Loma Independencia (Independence Hill) to the north and Loma Federación (Federation Hill) to the south. Both were crowned with artillery redoubts, and the lower slope of Independence Hill was also protected by the abandoned Obispado, or "Bishop's Palace." The western slope was nearly vertical. Inside the city, the houses were loopholed for muskets, and rooftops had parapets. As formidable as the defenses were, they were too far apart to support each other.

On the afternoon of September 20, Taylor divided his forces: General William J. Worth's command (2,000 men) would assault the western end of the city, and Taylor would strike from the east. Worth camped west of the city just out of range of the Mexican guns on the hills. A severe rainstorm made it a cold and sleepless night. The following day, September 21, Colonel John C. Hays's Texas cavalry, behind skirmishers under Lieutenant Colonel Charles F. Smith, were attacked by Mexican lancers under the command of Lieutenant Colonel Juan Nájera. After some fierce hand-to-hand fighting, the Mexicans retreated after suffering approximately 100 casualties, including the death of Nájera; Hays lost approximately 12 men.

U.S. soldiers then waded the Santa Catarina River under heavy fire and steadily scaled the rocky slope of Federation Hill. The storming party of 300 (half regulars and half volunteer Texans) were commanded by Smith. Later reinforced by the 7th Infantry and 5th Infantry, they drove the defenders from the heights and turned the Mexican battery on Independence Hill. Another storm resulted in a wet, cold night.

On the east side, Taylor's troops assaulted the city at approximately 10:00 A.M. on September 21. The 1st and 3rd U.S. Infantry and the Baltimore-Washington Volunteers, led by Lieutenant Colonel John Garland across an open plain, suffered heavy casualties from the artillery at the Black Fort and Fort Tenería.

The city of Monterrey, Mexico, during its occupation by U.S. troops (Library of Congress)

Captain Braxton Bragg's field battery managed to advance into the city's streets, but the lime and dust from the Mexican shells exploding into the adobe buildings blinded them, and they fell back. Not hearing the order to retreat, approximately 50 U.S. soldiers under Captain Electus Backus of the 1st U.S. Infantry were left behind in a building to the rear of Fort Tenería and maintained an annoying, constant fire at the Mexican defenders.

Piecemeal attacks by the 4th U.S. Infantry and the Ohio Volunteers were also turned back by intense fire from blockaded houses and the Purisima bridge. Troops led by Colonel Jefferson Davis managed to find a less exposed route toward Fort Tenería and, assisted by the heavy fire from Backus, were finally able to overrun the fort. (Nearly a quarter of Taylor's losses for the day occurred in front of Fort Tenería.) Another Ohio charge penetrated the city, but was driven back. A Mexican counterattack surprised the retreating troops, and approximately 50 soldiers were lanced. By nightfall, Taylor had lost nearly 400 men and gained only Fort Tenería.

At 3:00 A.M. on September 22, in the darkness and rain, Lieutenant Colonel Thomas Childs and approximately 500 men began to climb the steep rock face of Independence Hill on the west side of the city. At dawn, a few feet from the summit, they were discovered by the Mexican gunners in the redoubt. The Mexicans retreated after bitter hand-to-hand fighting. Another 50 U.S. soldiers managed to haul a dismantled howitzer to the top, reassemble it, and deliver a destructive fire on Obispado below. A Mexican counterattack failed, and soon the U.S. troops swarmed through the blasted gate of the palace and turned the abandoned Mexican guns on the fleeing soldiers. Disheartened, Ampudia concentrated his forces in the Great Plaza and the cathedral. Taylor's men on the east side were not engaged on the 22nd.

On September 23, Taylor cautiously advanced and occupied the abandoned defenses, including el Rincón del Diablo. Worth resumed his attack from the west, blasting the town with artillery and advancing to its edge. Sprays of grape and canister were fired down the streets. U.S. soldiers with picks and crowbars breached walls of barricaded homes and cautiously advanced. Detonating six-pound shells with short fuses to kill the Mexicans on the ground floor, they would then rush upstairs to challenge the enemy on the rooftops. Taylor rejected the governor's plea for a truce to withdraw women and children. Worth shelled the interior of the city the entire night.

At 3:00 A.M. on September 24, Ampudia proposed to surrender the city and withdraw, taking with him all his personnel and equipment. Taylor refused, but met with Ampudia in the afternoon to authorize commissioners—Generals José María Ortega and Tomás Requena and Don Manuel Llano, governor of Nuevo León, and Generals William J. Worth and James Pinckney Henderson and Colonel Jefferson Davis—to work out the details of an armistice. It was finally agreed that Ampudia would surrender the town and its munitions, the Mexican forces would retain their arms and accouterments, and the Mexican army would retire within seven days beyond the line drawn through Rinconada Pass and Linares (40 miles beyond Monterrey), beyond which Taylor's army could not advance for 8 weeks.

The following day, the Mexican flag came down to an 8-gun salute from its own battery, and the U.S. flag was raised to a 28-gun salute. The U.S. troops marched in with bands playing "Yankee Doodle."

Taylor was roundly criticized for the armistice's generous terms, which he said were justified because of the "gallant defense of the town, and the fact of a recent change of government in Mexico, believed to be favorable to the interests of peace." (On July 31, a revolution had deposed General-President Mariano Paredes y Arrillaga and installed General José Mariano Salas as provisional president until the arrival of General Antonio López de Santa Anna about one month later.)

U.S. losses were approximately 500 killed and wounded; Ampudia lost approximately 370. The city was strewn with wreckage and bloated corpses. Taylor's army remained at Monterrey for approximately six weeks, resting and refitting. General Worth was appointed the acting governor of the city. Monterrey remained an important staging area throughout the rest of 1846 and 1847.

See also Backus, Electus; Hays, John Coffee; Monterrey, Armistice of; Walnut Springs.

For further reading: Alcaraz, *The Other Side,* 1850; Anderson, *An Artillery Officer in the Mexican War, 1846–1847,* 1911; Balbontín, "The Siege of Monterrey," 1887; Dana, *Monterrey Is Ours!,* 1990; Grant, *Personal Memoirs of U. S. Grant,* 1885; Kenly, *Memoirs of a Maryland Volunteer,* 1873.

Mora, Skirmish at
(January 25, 1847)

Eight U.S. citizens were killed at the village of Mora, New Mexico, during the Taos Revolt in 1847. U.S. forces later killed 25 rebels and destroyed the town.

In the wake of the killings of U.S. citizens in Taos and Arroyo Hondo by New Mexican rebels in January 1847 (Taos Revolt), a group of insurgents killed eight Americans with a caravan at the village of Mora. On January 25, a force of 80 U.S. soldiers marched to Mora from Las Vegas to suppress the insurrection. They immediately attacked the town, where the rebels had taken up positions in barricaded buildings. Not having artillery, the U.S. soldiers broke down doors and engaged in hand-to-hand combat. The commanding officer, Captain I. R. Hendley, was killed. U.S. losses were one killed and three wounded; the rebels lost 25 killed and 17 captured. The remainder of the rebel force took shelter in a church, and the U.S. soldiers marched back to Las Vegas.

Another detachment from Santa Fe arrived at Mora with an artillery piece and proceeded to destroy the town. Most of the rebels had already fled, but several prisoners were taken who led the U.S. soldiers to the graves of the eight U.S. settlers who had been killed in the initial uprising.

See also Arroyo Hondo, Skirmish at; Taos Rebellion.

For further reading: Keleher, *Turmoil in New Mexico, 1846–1848,* 1952; Lavender, *Bent's Fort,* 1954; McNierney, *Taos 1847,* 1980.

Mora y Villamil, Ignacio
(1791–1870)

A general of engineers, Ignacio Mora y Villamil was one of General Antonio López de Santa Anna's favorite officers and supervised the construction of defenses at Chapultepec and Mexico City in 1847.

Mora y Villamil was born in Mexico City. He joined the Spanish army as a young man. After Mexico gained its independence, Mora y Villamil was appointed commander of the Corps of Engineers and designed a plan of defense for the new republic.

During the Mexican-American War, General Santa Anna elevated Mora y Villamil to general of the Corp of Engineers in the fall of 1846. Mora y Villamil led the remains of the Army of the North in April 1847 to Cerro Gordo, where it was decimated in the ensuing battle. In August 1847, he oversaw the construction of defenses at Chapultepec and Tacubaya. On September 13, he participated in the Battle of Chapultepec, during which he was captured. Mora y Villamil assisted General Benito Quijana during the negotiation of the Armistice of Tacubaya. He also helped defend Mexico City, and was involved in the peace negotiations that followed the occupation of the capital.

Following the war, Mora y Villamil remained in the military, wrote engineering books, and served as vice-president of the Society of Mexican Geography and Statistics from 1854 to 1857. After supporting the French intervention, he died in Mexico City at the age of 79.

For further reading: Carreño, *Jefes del ejército mexicano en 1847,* 1914; DePalo, *The Mexican National Army, 1822–1852,* 1997; Smith, *The War with Mexico,* 1919.

Mormon Battalion

A group of approximately 500 Mormon soldiers, the Mormon Battalion marched from Fort Leavenworth, Kansas, to Santa Fe, New Mexico, in 1846. They later blazed a wagon road from Santa Fe through the mountains to San Diego, California, during 1846–1847.

In June 1846, President James K. Polk called for the enlistment of 500 Mormons from Iowa Territory to fight in the Mexican-American War. The volunteers, accompanied by a group of nearly 100 women and children, left Fort Leavenworth on July 21, 1846. Under the leadership of Philip St. George Cooke, the battalion marched for Santa Fe via Bent's Fort, Colorado.

After the Mormons crossed the Arkansas River, Brigadier General Stephen W. Kearny, who was in charge of the military affairs in New Mexico, decided to send them to blaze a wagon road to California. Most of the women and family members and several sick soldiers were left behind at a log town near Fort Pueblo, where they were welcomed by a small group of Mormons who had wintered there. On November 9, Cooke requested 60 days' worth of rations from the quartermaster at Bent's Fort.

The men then marched on to Santa Fe and continued west along the Río Grande and San Pedro Rivers. On December 16, they entered Tucson and confiscated 2,000 bushels of wheat that belonged to the Mexican government. Continuing the march along the Gila River, the soldiers helped the weary animals pull the wagons through deep sand west of Tucson. After scouting the San Bernardino Mountains, they found a gap that was too narrow, by approximately a foot, to allow the passage of wagons; the rock on both sides was chipped away by hand for weeks until the canyon was wide enough to accommodate wagons.

Rations were eventually exhausted, and the men resorted to eating boiled hides from the sheepskin pads under the pack saddles. Shoes were worn out, and many men were almost barefoot or wore ox-hide shoes as the wagon teams died from exhaustion. The Mormon Battalion arrived in San Diego at the end of January 1847, having traveled about 2,000 miles.

The Mormon Battalion was discharged in July 1847 at Los Angeles. Many of them traveled to Salt Lake City; others stayed and mined gold at Sutter's Mill to bring back to the Mormon community in Utah.

See also Cooke, Philip St. George.

For further reading: Lavender, *Bent's Fort*, 1954; McCaffrey, *Army of Manifest Destiny*, 1992; Tyler, *A Concise History of the Mormon Battalion in the Mexican War 1846–1847*, 1964.

Mule Hill

Following the Battle of San Pascual, Brigadier General Stephen W. Kearny and approximately 100 men were trapped on Mule Hill, California, by Californio forces under Captain Andrés Pico from December 7 to December 10, 1846.

After occupying New Mexico in August of 1846, Brigadier General Kearny left most of his Army of the West at Santa Fe and traveled west toward San Diego with approximately 100 dragoons. After being surprised in the Battle of San Pascual on December 6, 1846, Kearny was concerned about the strength of the Californio rebels under Captain Andrés Pico. Kearny had lost one-third of his strength, their provisions were nearly gone, and most of the animals were dead. The wounded were strapped to rough litters, made from willow poles, that dragged on the ground.

Kearny marched westward the following day and drove a small Californio force from a rocky height near the San Bernardo ranch of Joseph Snook. The weary soldiers set up camp, arranged defenses, collected water, and slaughtered mules for food.

The night of December 8, frontiersman Kit Carson, Lieutenant Edward Beale, and an Indian guide named Andrés volunteered to go to San Diego to bring back reinforcements. After creeping on their bellies through the Californio defenses undetected, the barefoot men hurried to San Diego, about 40 miles away. One of Kearny's wounded men died and was buried on Mule Hill that night.

In the middle of the night on December 10, 180 sailors under the command of Lieutenant Andrew Gray marched into Kearny's camp. Pico's force suddenly withdrew. After four days on Mule Hill, Kearny's group marched westward toward San Diego and ransacked a rancho along the way.

See also San Pascual, Battle of.

For further reading: Bonsal, *Edward Fitzgerald Beale, a Pioneer in the Path of Empire, 1822–1903*, 1912; Carter, "Dear Old Kit," 1990; Clarke, *Stephen Watts Kearny, Soldier of the West*, 1961; Harlow, *California Conquered*, 1982.

Mulejé, Skirmish at
(October 1, 1846)

A small skirmish at the Gulf of California port Mulejé was fought between a U.S. naval landing force from the USS *Dale* and approximately 200 Mexican soldiers under Captain Manuel Pineda.

Hearing that 200 armed Mexicans had left Guaymas for Mulejé in September 1846, Commander Thomas O. Selfridge and the USS *Dale* sailed from La Paz toward this small port city on the Gulf of California. Arriving on September 30 and flying British colors, the landing party was turned back by a hostile Mexican force. Shortly afterward, Lieutenant T. A. Craven and 50 men in four boats rowed to the Mexican schooner *Magdalen* and towed it back to the *Dale*. The ship had already been stripped by the Mexicans, so the U.S. sailors burned it.

On October 1, Selfridge demanded the surrender of the village and its pledge of neutrality. Captain Manuel Pineda, the local commander, responded that "this port...with its valiant soldiers who have their instructions, will defend itself, and they will maintain their arms until the last drop of blood has been shed."

The *Dale* opened fire and landed a party of 17 U.S. Marines and 57 sailors. After a brisk skirmish, the U.S. troops retreated with two wounded men, and Pineda abandoned his defenses. After returning to the *Dale* that night, the U.S. force left the following day.

This action could be considered a Mexican victory because Selfridge had failed to eliminate the Mexican resistance, and the landing incited more Baja Californios to join Pineda's force.

For further reading: Bauer, *Surfboats and Horse Marines*, 1969; Rowan, "Recollections of the Mexican War," 1888.

Munroe, John
(ca. 1795–1861)

Chief of artillery for General Zachary Taylor's Army of Occupation during the Mexican-American War, Major John Munroe was brevetted for gallantry at the Battles of Monterrey and Buena Vista.

Munroe, who was born in Scotland, attended the U.S. Military Academy from 1812 to 1814 and was assigned to the 3rd Light Artillery. He fought in the Black Hawk War, against Seminoles in Florida, and later taught tactics at the academy.

A major in the 2nd U.S. Artillery when the Mexican-American War began, Munroe was part of General Taylor's Army of Occupation at Corpus Christi in 1845. As Taylor's chief of artillery, Munroe remained at Point Isabel (Fort Polk) to defend the army's supply base when Taylor battled the Mexican Army of the North at Palo Alto and Resaca de la Palma in May 1846.

Munroe was brevetted to lieutenant colonel for his performance at the Battle of Monterrey. His command of troops and artillery helped stabilize the crumbling U.S. left flank during the Battle of Buena Vista and resulted in a brevet to colonel. He remained Taylor's artillery chief until November 25, 1847.

After the war, Munroe served as the military governor of New Mexico at Santa Fe and later was assigned to Florida. He died in New Jersey during a leave of absence on April 26, 1861.

For further reading: Carleton, *The Battle of Buena Vista*, 1848; Cullum, *Biographical Register of the Officers and Graduates of the United States Military Academy from 1802 to 1867*, 1879; Dillon, *American Artillery in the Mexican War 1846–1847*, 1975.

N

National Road

The National Road connected the city of Veracruz to Mexico City and was the route by which Major General Winfield Scott marched during his campaign of 1847. Mostly paved, the highway passed through Cerro Gordo, Jalapa, Perote, and Puebla. It served as a busy supply line between the U.S. garrison/supply base at Veracruz and Scott's troops on their march to Mexico City. U.S. reinforcements and wagon trains continually moved along the road, which was plagued by guerrilla units that found shelter in the rugged countryside.

For further reading: Alcaraz, *The Other Side*, 1850.

Navajos

See Ojo Oso.

Navy, Mexico

At the beginning of the Mexican-American War, Mexico's navy consisted of fewer than a dozen small vessels, most of which were captured or destroyed. The lack of a strong naval presence allowed the U.S. Navy to control the sea lanes, blockade the coast, and move men and material freely.

Mexico did not have an effective naval force to combat U.S. Navy ships during the Mexican-American War. Mexico's navy consisted of 16 vessels—11 schooners, 3 brigs, and 2 steamers. Most of the ships were purchased from Great Britain or the United States. The two British-built steamers, the *Montezuma* and the *Guadaloupe*, were repossessed by British manufacturers in May 1846 after the Mexican government defaulted on their contracts; the rest were destroyed or seized by U.S. forces and were never a major factor in combat.

On June 26, 1846, President Mariano Paredes y Arrillaga tried to stimulate privateering by pledging to foreign captains and vessels commissions and protection of the assets they seized. In the fall, Mexican agents flooded the West Indies, Britain, France, and Spain with commissions. A few Spanish vessels attempted to hunt U.S. ships, but many feared the retaliation of the U.S. government. A Spanish felucca, *El Unico*, is the only commissioned privateer that is known to have seized a U.S. ship. After seizing the U.S. ship *Carmelita* and taking it to Barcelona, the crew of *El Unico* was imprisoned for piracy, and the U.S. ship was released.

Mexico's navy vessels were stationed at Guaymas, Alvarado, Tampico, Acapulco, and the Yucatán. Several ships helped defend Alvarado against an invasion by Commodore David Conner and the U.S. Home Squadron in October 1846. That invasion included the deliberate sinking of three vessels to block the channel. Other vessels were burned to keep them from being captured by occupational forces. The fate of each of the Mexican navy's ships is as follows:

Aguila. A 130-ton schooner with seven

guns was sunk in the Alvarado River in April 1847.

Anahuac. A 105-ton schooner with one gun, this Mexican-built vessel was destroyed at Guaymas on October 7, 1846.

Guadaloupe. A powerful 775-ton steamer with six guns, the *Guadaloupe*, built in Great Britain, was repossessed by William Laird and Sons because of the Mexican government's failure to pay for it.

Guerrero. A one-gun, 49-ton schooner, this vessel was scuttled in the Alvarado River in April 1847.

Isabel. Seized by U.S. naval forces at Tampico on November 14, 1846, this 74-ton schooner was reoutfitted for the U.S. Navy and named USS *Falcon*.

Libertad. This 89-ton schooner was captured in the Yucatán and sunk in the Alvarado River in April 1847.

Mexicano. This 208-ton brig with 16 guns was captured in the Yucatán and sunk in the Alvarado River in April 1847.

Montezuma. The biggest and most powerful ship in the Mexican navy, this 1,111-ton steamer was built in Great Britain and mounted with eight guns. It was repossessed by the British contractor in May 1846 because of lack of payment.

Morelos. Captured and destroyed in the Alvarado River in April 1847, the *Morelos* was a 59-ton schooner with one gun.

Pueblano. Captured at Tampico on November 14, 1846, this 74-ton schooner became the USS *Tampico*.

Queretana. A small schooner, the *Queretana* was sunk in the Alvarado River in April 1847.

Sonorense. This 27-ton schooner was destroyed at Guaymas on October 7, 1846.

Union. Captured at Tampico on November 14, 1846, this 74-ton schooner became the USS *Union*.

Veracruzano Libre. A 174-ton brig with nine cannon, the *Veracruzano Libre* was destroyed in the Alvarado River in April 1847.

Victoria. This 49-ton schooner was destroyed in the Alvarado River in April 1847.

Zempoalteca. A six-gun brig that was seized in the Yucatán, the *Zempoalteca* was sunk in the Alvarado River in April 1847.

For further reading: Bauer, *Surfboats and Horse Marines*, 1969; Bonilla, *Historia marítima de México*, 1962; Scheina, "The Forgotten Fleet," 1970.

Navy, United States

The U.S. Navy dominated the Mexican coastline during the Mexican-American War. Principal duties included blockading, chasing privateers, and supporting army operations, especially the landing of General Winfield Scott's 10,000-man Army of Occupation at Veracruz in March 1847.

Knowing Mexico did not have a navy that could contest the U.S. fleet, President James K. Polk and Secretary of the Navy George Bancroft wanted the U.S. Navy to patrol and blockade Mexico's coastlines, run down privateers, and support land operations.

The Pacific Squadron was led by Commodore John D. Sloat and later Commodore Robert F. Stockton. It blockaded ports and landed squadrons of sailors and marines to seize ports and cooperate with U.S. army commanders, such as Brigadier General Stephen W. Kearny and Colonel John C. Frémont. The Home Squadron was led by Commodore David E. Conner and his second in command Commodore Matthew C. Perry. It blockaded Mexico's gulf coast, occupied port cities, conducted operations up major rivers, and supported army land operations.

On August 10, 1846, President Polk authorized the U.S. Navy to increase its strength from 7,500 men to 10,000 men for the duration of the war. Few volunteers came forward, and total strength never exceeded 8,000 men. In fact, some naval vessels did not participate in the war because they could not be manned.

One of the biggest problems for the Home Squadron was being nearly 1,000 miles from the main base at Pensacola. Unprepared for war, it did not have enough supplies for the blockading ships. A lack of coal for steamers left many of them anchored offshore, inactive. In addition to blockade duty and some small-scale engagements, the Home Squadron supported the landing of more than 10,000 U.S. army troops on Collado Beach south of Veracruz in March 1847. This landing, the beginning of Major General Scott's Veracruz–Mexico City campaign, was the first major amphibious landing in U.S. history, and it was well planned and well executed by the naval commanders. Navy personnel ferried troops ashore and nearly destroyed Veracruz with

A typical camp kitchen in the U.S. Army of Occupation, as depicted in John Frost's *Pictorial History of Mexico and the Mexican War*, 1849 (Library of Congress)

their accurate shelling. Antón Lizardo became the main base of the Home Squadron, about 12 miles south of Veracruz.

The Home Squadron committed one of the first warlike acts of either side on April 17, 1846, when, at the request of General Zachary Taylor, it blockaded the mouth of the Río Grande. The blockade drove away Mexican ships carrying supplies for the Army of the North at Matamoros. At this point, the Skirmish at Carricitos Ranch had not been fought, and the two countries had yet to declare war. General Pedro de Ampudia protested the blockade, but the mouth of the Río Grande remained closed.

Blockade duty was tedious. It consisted of cruising constantly back and forth in front of a port and rarely involved chasing a vessel trying to escape through the blockade. Many sailors were struck by scurvy and dysentery because fresh fruit was impossible to get along the hostile coast. Ships also lacked adequate supplies of fresh water.

Mexico's coastal cities were well protected by reefs, sandbars, and treacherous shallows, which kept the cities safe from sloops of war. Mexican ports Soto la Marina, Tampico, Tuxpan, Alvarado, and Tabasco lay up shallow-mouthed rivers, where some of the Mexican navy's vessels were anchored. Conner pleaded for smaller, light-draft vessels that could navigate these rivers. Two small side-wheel vessels (*Vixen* and *Spitfire*) and three schooners (*Bonita*, *Petrel*, and *Reefer*) that were being built for the Mexican navy in New York were purchased by Bancroft. Openly criticized by the U.S. press for its lack of military accomplishments, the naval blockade cost Mexico at least half a million dollars in lost revenues.

Eastern Operations
(Gulf of Mexico, Home Squadron)

May 7, 1846. When General Taylor left the supply base at Point Isabel to engage the Mexican army at Palo Alto, 500 sailors and marines under Captain F. H. Gregory from the Home Squadron went ashore to protect the base. They remained until May 13.

May 18, 1846. Two hundred men from the *Potomac* and *Cumberland* under Captain J. H. Aulick occupied Barrita, Mexico. This force also went up the Río Grande and helped occupy Matamoros after the Battle of Resaca de la Palma.

June 8, 14–15, 1846. The sloop *St. Mary's*, under the command of J. L. Saunders, attacked Tampico and Mexican troops who were constructing new defenses.

August 7, 1846. Under the command of Commodores David E. Conner and Matthew C. Perry, the *Mississippi, Princeton, Potomac, Cumberland, Reefer, Bonito, Petrel, Falmouth,* and *Somers* attempted to seize the port city of Alvarado. Bad weather forced them to withdraw. The brig-of-war *Truxton* ran aground on a reef near Tuxpan and sank. Most of the crew surrendered; six others escaped in a small boat into the open sea, captured a small Mexican ship, and sailed to Antón Lizardo.

October 15, 1846. Commodores Conner and Perry attempted again to capture Alvarado with the *Vixen, Bonito, Reefer, McLane, Nonata, Petrel, Forward,* and *Mississippi*. Some of the ships ran aground in the shallow water. The return fire from Mexican batteries along the shore inflicted minor damage. Again Conner and Perry withdrew.

October 16–November 1, 1846. Commodore Perry and Commander J. R. Sands launched an attack against Frontera and Tabasco with the *Vixen, Bonito, Reefer, Nonata, McLane,* and *Forward*. The towns were defended by General Nicolás Bravo, but eventually captured after some brief skirmishing. U.S. losses were three killed and three wounded. Also during this time, a small group of sailors boarded the Mexican merchant brig *Creole,* anchored beside the walls of San Juan de Ulúa at Veracruz, and burned it.

November 10–December 13, 1846. Tampico and Panuco were attacked by the *Mississippi, Princeton, Spitfire, Vixen, St. Mary's, Porpoise, Petrel,* and numerous smaller vessels. Although defended by coastal fortifications and cannon, the Mexican troops had withdrawn from Tampico the night before and destroyed their weapons and supplies. The city was occupied by a force of sailors and marines, and three gunboats were seized. Commander Josiah Tattnall later captured Panuco.

December 8, 1846. While chasing a Mexican vessel, the U.S. brig *Somers* was struck by a heavy norther, capsized, and sank in ten minutes. More than half of the 79-man crew drowned. Many of the survivors were saved by English, French, and Spanish ships of war, lying at Sacrificios Island, that sent out small boats in the gale to bring back the men. "The brig was filling very fast, and her masts and yards lying flat upon the surface of the sea…," wrote Raphael Semmes. "The severest gale I ever experienced, in any part of the world…. It blew for three days and nights. As the waves would strike the vessel, every timber and plank in her would tremble and quiver as though she were being shaken to pieces."

December 17–27, 1846. Commodore Perry and Commander J. R. Sands captured Laguna de los Terminos without opposition. The flotilla was comprised of the *Mississippi, Vixen, Bonito,* and *Petrel*. Sands was appointed military governor.

March 9–29, 1847. The Home Squadron landed more than 10,000 army troops on Collado Beach, a few miles south of Veracruz, in the largest amphibious landing in history at that time. The *Spitfire, Vixen, Bonito, Reefer, Petrel, Falcon, Tampico, Raritan, Potomac, Albany, St. Mary's, Princeton, Petrita,* and *Porpoise,* under Commanders J. Tattnall, J. R. Sands, J. L. Saunders, and F. Engle, shelled the city of Veracruz and the fortress San Juan de Ulúa. Navy personnel insisted on moving and manning the heavy guns from the ships to the shore. U.S. navy losses were seven killed and eight wounded.

April 1, 1847. The *Scourge,* under the command of Lieutenant Colonel G. Hunter, captured the town of Alvarado without resistance.

April 2, 1847. Under the command of Commodore Perry, the *Mississippi, Reefer, Spitfire, Bonito, Petrel, Vixen, Tampico,* and *Falcon* helped seize Alvarado, in cooperation with infantry marched overland by General John A. Quitman.

April 13–18, 1847. Once Alvarado was securely fortified, U.S. naval forces moved upriver to pursue retreating Mexican forces. Commander Tattnall took the *Spitfire, Petrita,* and *Reefer* to occupy Tlacotalpán. Six U.S. seamen were wounded in skirmishing with Mexican riflemen hidden in the chaparral along the banks.

April 18, 1847. Led by Commodore Perry, the *Mississippi, Spitfire, Vixen, Scourge, Bonito,*

Petrel, Reefer, and smaller steamers and barges attacked Tuxpan. The town was well defended by three forts and approximately 600 men under General Perfecto de Cos. The Mexican batteries swept the U.S. ships with grape and canister. U.S. guns returned the fire, and eventually the forts were taken. A landing force occupied the town and wrecked its defenses and artillery. U.S. losses were 14 killed and wounded.

June 16, 1847. Perry launched a second attack against Tabasco with the *Scorpion, Spitfire, Scourge, Vixen, Stromboli, Vesuvius, Aetna, Washington,* and *Bonito.* After occupying the town, the 1,200-man force destroyed the earthen fortifications. Eight U.S. sailors were wounded during the skirmish.

July 1847. The Home Squadron suffered a severe outbreak of yellow fever that crippled the squadron for the rest of the summer. Worst on the *Mississippi,* Perry sent the ship to Florida to have it fumigated and whitewashed. At one point during the epidemic, only one physician was serving seven ships. The epidemic began to lessen by the end of September. The *Vixen* was sterilized by releasing steam into the holds, which also killed rats and roaches.

Western Operations (Pacific Ocean, Pacific Squadron)

July 7, 1846. Vessels commanded by Commodore John D. Sloat, Commander Samuel F. Du Pont, and Commander H. W. Page arrived at Monterey, California. A landing party of U.S. Marines and seamen under Captain W. Mervine occupied the city and raised the U.S. flag.

July 9, 1846. The sloop *Portsmouth,* commanded by Commander John B. Montgomery, seized the bay of San Francisco without opposition. A landing party under Lieutenant Joseph Warren Revere seized Sonoma.

July 29, 1846. Forces from Commander Du Pont's sloop *Cyane* occupied the port of San Diego.

August 6, 1846. Commanded by Commodore Robert F. Stockton, troops from the USS *Congress* occupied the town of San Pedro.

August 13, 1846. Los Angeles was occupied by forces under the command of Commodore Stockton and Colonel John C. Frémont. The U.S. flag was raised without opposition.

January 8, 1847. A joint naval-army force of approximately 700 men under Commodore Stockton and Brigadier General Stephen W. Kearny, after marching northward from San Diego toward Los Angeles, engaged a smaller force of Californio rebels under Captain José María Flores at the Battle of San Gabriel River. U.S. losses were one killed and nine wounded in the two-hour fight.

January 9, 1847. The Stockton-Kearny force skirmished with the army of Captain Flores at the Battle of La Mesa, a few miles from Los Angeles. U.S. losses were one killed and five wounded. The Californios retreated, and the U.S. forces occupied Los Angeles the following day.

March 30, 1847. Commanded by Montgomery, with a landing party of 140 men from the sloop *Portsmouth* occupied San José and raised the U.S. flag.

April 3, 1847. Montgomery and the crew from the Portsmouth occupied San Lucas.

April 14, 1847. The USS *Portsmouth* occupied La Paz.

October 1, 1847. Under Commander T. O. Selfridge, the sloop of war *Dale* attacked the town of Mulejé and dispersed a force of 150 Mexicans under Captain Manuel Pineda. A landing party briefly occupied the city.

October 20, 1847. The USS *Congress* and USS *Portsmouth* shelled the port village of Guaymas and drove away a 250-man force under Colonel Antonio Campuzano.

November 1–7, 1847. A U.S. naval force attacked a small Mexican force at Todos Santos, killing eight.

November 11, 1847. Under the command of Commodore W. B. Shubrick, sailors on board the *Independence, Congress, Cyane,* and *Erie* attacked and occupied the town of Mazatlán.

November 17, 1847. A Mexican force was routed at Guaymas by a naval force under Lieutenant W. T. Smith.

November 19, 1847. Naval forces under Lieutenant C. Heywood dispersed Mexican troops at San José and occupied the town.

November 20, 1847. Lieutenant G. S. Sheldon and his naval brigade fought a brisk skirmish at Urias, in which 21 of his 94-man force were killed or wounded.

January 12, 1848. The *Lexington*, in command of Lieutenant T. Bailey, attacked San Blas and destroyed its fortifications.

January 30, 1848. A naval brigade from the USS *Dale* under the command of Lieutenant T. A. M. Craven attacked a small Mexican force at the town of Cochori. Nine Mexicans were killed or wounded, and six prisoners were taken.

February 15, 1848. A landing force of 102 men under Commander Samuel F. Du Pont from the *Cyane* landed at San José to reinforce the besieged occupation force under Lieutenant Heywood. Four U.S. seamen were wounded.

March 24, 1848. Commander Du Pont's naval force from the *Cyane* skirmished with Mexican troops at Santanita.

April 9, 1848. A naval brigade from the USS *Dale* under Lieutenant F. Stanley attacked Guaymas. They marched 12 miles inland, spiked three cannon, and skirmished with Mexicans on the way back. Two U.S. seamen were wounded.

> *See also* Alvarado; Cochori, Skirmish at; Guaymas, Battle of; La Mesa, Battle of; Los Angeles; Monterey; Muleje, Skirmish at; San Gabriel River (Bartolo Ford), Battle of; *Somers*, USS; Tabasco, Battles of; Tampico; *Truxtun*, USS; Tuxpan; Veracruz, Battle of.
>
> *For further reading:* Bauer, *Surfboats and Horse Marines*, 1969; Cooper, *The History of the Navy of the United States of America*, 1853; Craven, *A Naval Campaign in the Californias—1846–1849*, 1973; Downey, *The Cruise of the* Portsmouth, 1958; Du Pont, "The War with Mexico," 1882; Jones, "The Pacific Squadron and the Conquest of California," 1966; Knox, *A History of the United States Navy*, 1936; Morison, *"Old Bruin" Commodore Matthew Calbraith Perry*, 1967; Neeser, *A Statistical and Chronological History of the United States Navy*, 1909; Parker, *Recollections of a Naval Officer*, 1883; Rowan, "Recollections of the Mexican War," 1888; Semmes, *Service Afloat and Ashore during the Mexican War*, 1851.

Nevada

Present-day Nevada was largely the east-central portion of Alta California, which was ceded to the United States at the end of the Mexican-American War according to the Treaty of Guadalupe Hidalgo.

The native nations that populated this portion of Alta California were the Pueblo, Mohave, Paiute, Shoshoni, and Washoe. Francisco Garces, a Spanish missionary, was probably the first European to enter Nevada in the mid-1700s. Spain surrendered ownership to Mexico in 1821, and fur traders and trappers began to explore the area during 1825–1830.

In 1830, the Old Spanish Trail connected Santa Fe to Los Angeles, thus making Nevada more accessible. Joseph Walker blazed another trail along the Humboldt River to California in 1833. Much of the Utah-Nevada Great Basin was explored by John C. Frémont during 1843–1845, and Nevada became U.S. territory after the Mexican-American War according to the terms of the Treaty of Guadalupe Hidalgo. Nevada became a state in 1864.

> *For further reading:* Bancroft, *History of Nevada, Colorado and Wyoming*, 1890.

New Mexico

What is present-day New Mexico was largely the Mexican province of New Mexico during the Mexican-American War. The province of New Mexico was ceded to the United States according to the Treaty of Guadalupe Hidalgo in 1848.

The earliest native people in New Mexico were the Anasazi (Pueblo) Nation. The Navajo, Apache, Utes, and Comanches later moved into the area. Spanish expeditions were launched in the mid-1500s under Francisco Vasquez de Coronado, who claimed the land for Spain. Santa Fe, founded in 1610, was one of the first Spanish colonies, and Roman Catholic missionaries attempted to convert the Indians to Christianity. After years of conflict, many of the native people were finally suppressed by Spanish forces.

U.S. trappers began to frequent New Mexico in the early 1800s, and Spanish authorities evicted or imprisoned them. In 1821, Mexico won its independence from Spain, and New Mexico became a province of the new republic. A booming trade along the Santa Fe Trail connected Santa Fe and New Mexico to the United States economically, and New Mexicans grew dependent on U.S. trade.

In 1837, the New Mexicans and Indians in New Mexico rebelled, executed the Mexican governor, and seized the governor's palace in Santa Fe. Shortly afterward, General Manuel Armijo became the new dictator. Mexican forces remained in New Mexico and skirmished periodically with armed Texans.

During the Mexican-American War, New Mexico was occupied by forces under Brigadier General Stephen Watts Kearny. He entered Santa Fe in August 1846, established a military government, and was generally welcomed by New Mexicans. The Taos Revolt in January 1847, which resulted in the death of military governor Charles Bent, was suppressed by Kearny's men in Santa Fe.

The United States took possession of New Mexico according to the terms of the Treaty of Guadalupe Hidalgo (1848). The province of New Mexico consisted of what is today New Mexico and parts of Arizona, Colorado, Texas, Utah, Nebraska, and Oklahoma. The southwestern corner of New Mexico was enlarged through territory gained according to the 1853 Gadsden Purchase. New Mexico became a territory in 1853 and the forty-seventh state in 1912.

See also Armijo, Manuel; Gadsden Treaty; Taos Rebellion.

For further reading: Bancroft, *History of Arizona and New Mexico 1530–1888*, 1889; Beck, *New Mexico*, 1962; Cutts, *The Conquest of California and New Mexico by the Forces of the United States in the Years 1846 and 1847*, 1847.

Niños Héroes

During the Battle of Chapultepec on September 13, 1847, a small group of teenaged military cadets helped defend its walls during the U.S. assault. Six cadets were killed and three wounded in the bitter hand-to-hand fighting.

The fortifications on Chapultepec Hill outside Mexico City consisted of a castle and the Colegio Militar (military college), where young cadets trained for the Mexican military.

Chapultepec, the last line of defense between Major General Winfield Scott's Army of Occupation and the gates of Mexico City, was defended by 1,000 troops and the cadets from the military academy. General Nicolás Bravo, the commander, ordered the boys to leave, but a few remained to fight.

Scott launched his attack on the hill on September 13, 1847. U.S. soldiers raised ladders, scaled the walls, and entered hand-to-hand combat with the Mexican defenders. Reputedly some of the last defenders were the cadets—6 were killed, 3 wounded, and 37 taken prisoner during the struggle. Rather than surrendering, cadet Fernando Montes de Oca is said to have wrapped himself in the Mexican flag and thrown himself to his death from the castle wall. Other accounts have him running along the wall with the Mexican colors when he was shot and killed and fell with the flag from the wall. Other cadets who died were Juan de la Barrera, Francisco Márquez, Agustín Melgar, Juan Scutia, and Vicente Suárez Ferrer. These six cadets are known as the *Niños Héroes*, or the "Heroic Children."

Their remains were discovered at the base of the hill in 1947 and were reinterred at the base of an impressive stone monument ten years later. Every evening, the Colegio Militar holds a retreat ceremony in their honor.

See also Chapultepec, Battle of.

For further reading: Carreño, *El Colégio Militar de Chapultepec, 1847–1947*, 1972; DePalo, *The Mexican National Army, 1822–1852*, 1997; Echánove Trujillo, *Juan Crisóstomo Cano, héroe de Chapultepec*, 1947; Sánchez Lamego, *El Colegio Militar y la defensa de Chapultepec en Septiembre de 1847*, 1947.

Nueces River

The area between the Nueces River and the Río Grande was disputed territory between Texas and Mexico. Mexico recognized the Nueces River, which emptied into the Atlantic Ocean at Corpus Christi, as the southern and western boundary of Texas after it won its independence. Texas, however, maintained that its southern boundary was the Río Grande. The difference nearly doubled the territory. The United States also recognized the Río Grande as the border of Texas when it annexed the republic in 1845. Because the United States refused to acknowledge the Nueces River boundary, Mexico maintained that the United States had unjustly taken a large amount of Mexican territory (the western half of present-day Texas, the eastern third of New Mexico, and parts of Colorado and Oklahoma. The issue was resolved at the end of the Mexican-American War, when the disputed territory was given to the United States according to the 1848 Treaty of Guadalupe Hidalgo.

For further reading: Bancroft, *History of the North Mexican States and Texas*, 1884–1889; Smith, *The Annexation of Texas*, 1911.

O

O'Brien, John Paul Jones
(ca. 1818–1850)

An artillery officer with General Zachary Taylor's Army of Occupation during 1846–1847, Lieutenant John Paul Jones O'Brien used his artillery from an advanced position and helped stabilize the crumbling U.S. left flank during the Battle of Buena Vista.

O'Brien, who was born in Pennsylvania, attended the U.S. Military Academy from 1832 to 1836. Commissioned a second lieutenant in the 4th U.S. Artillery, he fought the Seminole Indians in the Second Florida War.

During the Mexican-American War, O'Brien served as a staff officer, assistant quartermaster, and artillery officer. He commanded a section of Captain John M. Washington's battery during the Battle of Buena Vista in February 1847. O'Brien's guns anchored the U.S. left flank, which was composed of volunteer Kentucky, Indiana, and Arkansas brigades.

The hard attack by General Antonio López de Santa Anna's troops began to collapse the U.S. line. O'Brien advanced his guns to within 50 yards of the Mexican advance and opened fire with canister, rocks, and stones. His artillery cut large gaps through the advancing Mexicans. As his men were being charged by troops with bayonets, O'Brien ordered one last charge. "The lanyards were not pulled until the foe had hold of the wheels of the carriages....the head of the column fell as if struck by lightning, but the survivors rushed on and the deserted guns were theirs," commented dragoon Samuel Chamberlain.

O'Brien, wounded, and a few of his men managed to fall back safely. His battery had slowed down the Mexican advance long enough for General John E. Wool to regroup part of the left flank. O'Brien was brevetted to major for his gallant conduct during the battle.

O'Brien also served as quartermaster at Camargo and after the war had an administrative position in Florida. He died in Texas at the age of 32.

See also Buena Vista, Battle of.

For further reading: Chamberlain, *My Confession*, 1956; Cullum, *Biographical Register of the Officers and Graduates of the United States Military Academy from 1802 to 1867*, 1879; Dillon, *American Artillery in the Mexican War 1846–1847*, 1975.

Ojo Oso

Also known as Bear Spring, Ojo Oso, New Mexico, was the site of a treaty signing in 1846 between representatives of the Navajo Nation and Colonel Alexander W. Doniphan of the Army of the West.

After Brigadier General Stephen W. Kearny occupied Santa Fe in August 1846 with his Army of the West, he became informed about the depredations committed against New Mexicans by raiding Apaches and Navajos. As the new protector of New Mexican rights, Kearny sent messengers into Navajo country to summon native leaders to a council in Santa Fe. To the few who came, he announced that New Mexico was now part of the United States and that raids would not be tolerated. The Navajos continued to attack New Mexicans, and Kearny dispatched armed patrols to discourage them. Kearny departed Santa Fe for California in September 1846 and left dealing with the Indians to his second in command, Colonel Alexander W. Doniphan.

A practical and resourceful officer, Doniphan left Santa Fe on October 26 with 300 men and rode into the mountains to find the Navajo. Deep snows slowed the march. Doniphan planned to have a council with Indian leaders at Ojo Oso (Bear Spring), a few miles from present-day Gallup, New Mexico. After visiting a number of villages, Doniphan collected approximately 500 Navajos, many of them chiefs forced at bayonet, to come to the council.

Doniphan stressed to the Indians that they would be killed if they continued to attack New Mexicans. Sarcilla Largo, a bold young chief, said that he was pleased to learn the views of the U.S. soldiers and admired their ambition, but that he hated Mexicans. The chiefs gave speeches all day on November 21.

The following day, Doniphan explained that the United States had taken possession of New Mexico and that the New Mexicans were now U.S. citizens, protected by the laws of the United States. Sarcilla Largo objected: "Americans! You have a strange cause of war against the Navajos. We have waged war against the New Mexicans for several years. We have plundered their villages and killed many of their people, and made many prisoners. We had just cause for all this. You have lately commenced a war against the same people. You are powerful. You have great guns and many brave soldiers. You have therefore conquered them, the very thing we have been attempting to do for so many years. You now turn upon us for attempting to do what you have done yourselves. We cannot see why you have cause or quarrel with us for fighting the New Mexicans...."

The short, five-paragraph treaty was signed on November 22, 1846. Chiefs included Sarcilla Largo, Caballada de Mucho, Alexandro, Sandoval, Kiatanito, José Largo, Narbona, Sagunda, Pedro José Manuelito, Tapio, Savoietta Garcia, and Archuletté, who each signed the document by touching a forefinger to a pen as the pen was drawn to make a cross on the paper. U.S. signatures were Alexander Doniphan, Congreve Jackson, and William Gilpin. Doniphan distributed presents, including hundreds of cattle and sheep. The Indians gave the soldiers blankets.

Feeling confident, Doniphan stopped at Zuni Pueblo to try to mediate the Zuni war with the Navajo. After arguing for three days and nights, with Doniphan as the arbitrator, they signed a treaty on November 26, 1846. Within days, however, the Navajo and Zuni were fighting, and the Navajo continued their raids on New Mexican settlements.

See also Doniphan, Alexander William.

For further reading: Goetzmann, Army Exploration in the American West, 1803–1863, 1959; Hughes, Doniphan's Expedition, Containing an Account of the Conquest of New Mexico, 1973; Keleher, Turmoil in New Mexico, 1846–1848, 1952.

Olompali, Skirmish at
(June 23, 1846)

A minor engagement, the Skirmish at Olompali in Upper California was fought between a small force of Bear Flaggers and a 70-man Californio group led by Juan Padilla.

After arriving in California in December 1845, John C. Frémont and his force of armed men refused to obey Mexican directives. Emboldened by Frémont's warlike presence, a group of U.S. settlers revolted against Mexican rule at Sonoma. Calling themselves the Bear Flaggers, they seized prisoners, scrapped with Mexican troops, and declared California a republic. Meanwhile, General Manuel Castro called for volunteer troops to suppress the rebellion.

A detachment of Bear Flaggers from Sonoma rode to the Russian River to get supplies in mid-June 1846. En route, they were ambushed, and several were taken prisoner. On June 23, 17 to 18 men under Henry L. Ford left Sonoma to rescue the prisoners. At Olompali Rancho, they collided with a Californio force of approximately 70 men led by Juan Padilla. The Californios attacked in a mounted charge, and several were killed or wounded on both sides. The U.S. prisoners escaped, and Ford and his men returned to Sonoma.

See also Bear Flag Revolt,; Frémont, John C.

For further reading: Harlow, California Conquered, 1982.

Ortega, José María
(1793–1871)

An artillery commander and infantry general, José María Ortega capably led troops at the Battles of Monterrey and La Angostura (Buena Vista) during the Mexican-American War and was one of the commissioners of the Armistice of Monterrey.

Ortega, who was born in Mexico City, became a member of the Spanish army at the age of 16. He participated in the suppression of various rebellions and later joined the revolutionary forces of Agustín de Iturbide in 1821. In the Mexican army, he became an artillery officer and later a brigade general.

At the beginning of the Mexican-American War, Ortega commanded troops at Nuevo León. He participated in the Battle of Monterrey in September 1846 and helped negotiate the armistice at the end of the battle. As part of General Antonio López de Santa Anna's Army of the North at San Luis Potosí in 1847, Ortega's division marched northward to battle General Zachary Taylor at La Angostura (Buena Vista) in February. Ortega's division suffered heavy casualties in the fight.

Ortega remained a high-ranking figure in the Mexican military after the war and commanded the district of Jalisco. He died in Mexico City at the age of 78.

For further reading: Balbontín, "The Battle of Angostura (Buena Vista)," 1894; Carreño, *Jefes del ejército mexicano en 1847,* 1914.

Ortiz, Tomás

Revolutionary Tomás Ortiz was one of the first New Mexicans to organize a rebellion against the U.S. occupational government in New Mexico in 1847.

Brigadier General Stephen W. Kearny and his Army of the West occupied Santa Fe, New Mexico, in August 1846. After Kearny and his second in command, Colonel Alexander W. Doniphan, left on other missions, command devolved to Colonel Sterling Price. By this time, the behavior of the occupational troops had begun to deteriorate.

Diego Archuleta, Augustín Duran, and Tomás Ortiz, three local citizens, began to plot a rebellion that would overthrow the U.S. government in New Mexico. Plans included killing Price and military governor Charles Bent, but Bent and others learned of the plot. U.S. soldiers searched the home of Ortiz, but he lay flat on his balcony and was not detected. Reportedly dressed as a peasant girl, he escaped from Santa Fe on horseback.

See also Taos Rebellion.

For further reading: Keleher, *Turmoil in New Mexico, 1846–1848,* 1952; Lavender, *Bent's Fort,* 1954; McNierney, *Taos 1847,* 1980.

P

Padierna, Battle of
See Contreras, Battle of.

Palo Alto, Battle of
(May 8, 1846)

The opening battle between Mexican and U.S. forces in what shortly thereafter became the Mexican-American War, Palo Alto was a U.S. victory largely through the effective use of General Zachary Taylor's artillery.

By the end of April 1846, Mexican and U.S. armies faced each other across the Río Grande near Matamoros. Taylor's forces were at Fort Texas and the Point Isabel supply base on the north side of the river; the Mexicans were gathered at Matamoros.

Mexican cavalry had crossed the Río Grande above and below Fort Texas. General Anastasio Torrejón attacked a U.S. patrol under Captain Seth Thornton at Carricitos Ranch and also a camp of Texas Rangers. Torrejón's men later screened the crossing of approximately 4,000 infantry under General Mariano Arista about 13 miles below Fort Texas on April 30. Arista wanted to cut Taylor's army off from its supply base at Point Isabel, but Arista had only two boats by which to ferry his troops, and this considerably delayed his crossing.

Learning of the Mexican activity and worried about protecting Point Isabel, Taylor left a small force at Fort Texas and force-marched to Point Isabel on May 1, arriving the following day after covering approximately 30 miles in 20 hours. Taylor's weary men immediately began to fortify the meager defenses of Fort Polk at Point Isabel. By the time Taylor had passed, Arista had crossed his men and occupied the road between Taylor and Fort Texas. Arista sent General Pedro de Ampudia to besiege Fort Texas with a cannon barrage, which began at dawn on May 3.

After receiving a report from Texas Ranger Samuel Walker, who had slipped through the Mexican forces to confer with Major Jacob Brown, the commander at Fort Texas, Taylor moved out in the afternoon of May 7 with approximately 2,200 men, artillery, and 200 wagons. Knowing that Taylor was approaching, Arista recalled Ampudia's men to join the pending battle.

Arista deployed his 4,000-man army across the road on an open grassy plain. The Mexican line was formed by midmorning on May 8. Interspersed between Arista's infantry regiments were artillery batteries. The extreme left was anchored by Torrejón's cavalry in a swampy thicket, and more cavalry was held in reserve behind the line in a tall stand of timber. General Arista rode along the line as the bands played and the colors and pennants fluttered in the breeze.

Taylor marched the final 12 miles in the morning. The day had became very hot as the U.S. troops came within a mile of the brightly colored Mexican army and gleaming lances and other weapons. Sitting sideways on his horse and spitting tobacco, Taylor casually deployed his infantry and artillery; his dragoons were held in reserve with the supply wagons. Arista allowed two U.S. scouts to ride to within 100 yards of his position and examine his line through field glasses. U.S. soldiers refilled their canteens from nearby ponds.

Approximately 2:30 P.M., Taylor began his advance. The Mexican gunners began firing from a range of 700 yards. The copper cannonballs simply rolled through the tall grass, and the men jumped over them. Taylor's artillery, 10 to 20 yards in advance of the infantry, began firing at the dense mass of Mexican soldiers. Mexican gunners tried to knock out Taylor's batteries. Captain Ulysses S. Grant recalled that the exploding U.S. shells "cut away through their ranks making a perfect road, but they would close up the interval without showing signs of retreat." The fire from Major Samuel Ringgold's Flying Artillery inflicted terrible losses on the Mexican left.

A charge by Torrejón attempted to sweep around Taylor's right flank and strike the rear and supply wagons. The Mexican cavalrymen were slowed by the boggy ground, which allowed the U.S. 3rd and 5th Infantry Regiments time to run to the rear and challenge the attack. Torrejón tried to position two field pieces, but the accurate and constant fire of Ringgold's artillery forced them back.

Despite the deadly effectiveness of the U.S. artillery, the Mexican troops held firm—Taylor reported that they were the "theme of comment and admiration." The Mexican left was beginning to break under the heavy fire. A grass fire developed on Taylor's left, and thick, blinding smoke covered the battlefield. Most of the firing stopped for approximately one hour. "The fire began to spread," wrote Ramon Alcaraz. "Its sinister splendor illuminated the camp…and in which now were heard heartrending groans of our wounded. As most of these were [wounded] from cannon-shot, they were horribly mutilated."

During this interval, both Arista and Taylor adjusted the positions of their lines. Taylor tried to turn the Mexican left with Lieutenant Colonel Charles May's dragoons, but the Mexican fire drove them back. Mexican battery fire killed Major Ringgold and forced the U.S. 4th Infantry to retreat. As the Mexicans began an assault on the U.S. left flank, Captain James Duncan's light field batteries unleashed an unexpected enfilading fire that broke the attack.

Cannonading by both sides continued until dusk. The Mexican cavalry was turned back in a final charge, which began a general retreat on the Mexican right flank. The rest of the line fell back in good order to the edge of the woods. Taylor did not pursue because it was near nightfall. Search parties from both sides impartially brought in the wounded during the night. Surgeons amputated limbs long into the night.

The Mexican army was demoralized by the unexpected strength of the U.S. army, their deadly artillery, the frightful casualties, and the ineffectual leadership of their own generals. (Some soldiers even believed that Arista had wanted to lose to the U.S. army and was guilty of treason.) The battle was largely an artillery fight that was tactically a U.S. victory because Taylor had not retreated; strategically it was more of a draw because Arista still blocked the road to Fort Texas. The effective use of the U.S. Flying Artillery, including firing at masses of men instead of at enemy artillery batteries, made the difference in the fight. Taylor's casualties were approximately 55 killed, wounded, and missing; Arista's, approximately 400, an indication of the artillery advantage that the United States had.

A volunteer soldier described the Mexican position on the battlefield a few months afterward as being a line of scattered bones and rags—many of the dead had not been buried.

The battlefield became a National Historic Site in June 1992. Recent archaeological surveys have identified major portions of the Mexican line through the recovery of buttons, badges, and other equipage.

See also Blake, Jacob E.; Carricitos Ranch, Skirmish at; Flying Artillery; Fort Brown; Point Isabel; Ringgold, Samuel.

For further reading: Alcaraz, *The Other Side*, 1850; Baxter and Killen, *A Study of the Palo Alto Battleground, Cameron County, Texas*, 1976; Duncan, "The Artillery in the Mexican War, Reports of Captain James Duncan," 1908; Grant, *Personal Memoirs of U. S. Grant*, 1885; Haecker, *A Thunder of Cannon*, 1994.

Pánuco

Located approximately 50 miles upriver from the port of Tampico, Pánuco, Veracruz, was seized by U.S. naval forces from the Home Squadron on November 18, 1846.

Before the fall of Tampico to U.S. naval forces under Commodore David E. Conner in November 1846, Mexican forces and private citizens evacuated the city and went upriver, taking equipment and ammunition for the Mexican army. On November 18, Commander Josiah Tattnall, in command of the *Spitfire* and *Petrel*, sailed up Río Pánuco in pursuit. The following day, his force arrived at the town of Pánuco, where his men located and destroyed a cache of military equipment, cannon, cannonballs, and gunpowder.

See also Tampico.

For further reading: Bauer, *Surfboats and Horse Marines*, 1969; Smith, *The War with Mexico*, 1919.

Paredes y Arrillaga, Mariano
(1797–1849)

A prominent military and political figure in Mexican history, General Mariano Paredes y Arrillaga was involved in several political rebellions, including his own coup that installed him as the president of Mexico on January 1, 1846. Paredes y Arrillaga favored war with the United States and disapproved of the Treaty of Guadalupe Hidalgo.

Paredes y Arrillaga was born in Mexico City. He joined the Spanish army at the age of 15 and quickly became an officer. He participated in suppressing various uprisings until 1821, when he joined the revolutionary forces of Agustín de Iturbide. Paredes y Arrillaga helped overthrow Iturbide in 1823. In the Mexican army, Paredes y Arrillaga became a brigade general and launched a rebellion that toppled President Anastasio Bustamante. Paredes y Arrillaga also helped install, and then depose, presidents Antonio López de Santa Anna and José Joaquín Herrera.

Frustrated with Herrera's *moderado* attempts at a compromised settlement with the United States in 1845, Paredes y Arrillaga took over the government on January 1, 1846. His political and military allies included Lucas Alamán, Nicholás Bravo, and Gabriel Valencia. Paredes y Arrillaga soon pledged a "defensive war" against the United States and hoped for European assistance with the war effort.

Paredes y Arrillaga's warlike attitude was popular with the public until the military losses and casualties began to mount and the treasury approached bankruptcy. His administration was terminated in August 1846, and he was exiled to Europe, where he continued to try to interest countries in taking over Mexico.

Having returned by 1848, Paredes y Arrillaga vehemently opposed the Treaty of Guadalupe and urged the continuation of the war. He conspired with military troops in the city of Aguascalientes and, with the help of Spanish priest and guerrilla Celestino Domeco de Jarauta, launched a revolt in May 1848. His troops seized Lagos de Moreno and, later, Guanajuato. Forces loyal to new president José Joaquín Herrera, after seven weeks of pursuit and skirmishing, finally ended the insurrection. Paredes y Arrillaga escaped and remained hidden in a Mexico City convent, until he died the following year at age 52.

See also War Message, Mariano Paredes y Arrillaga.

For further reading: Costeloe, *The Central Republic in Mexico,1835–1846*, 1993; Paredes y Arrillaga, *Últimas comunicaciones entre el gobierno mexicano y el enviado extraordinario y ministro plenipotenciario nombrado por de los Estados Unidos sobre la cuestión de Tejas*, 1846; Robertson, "The Military and Political Career of Mariano Paredes y Arrillaga," 1955.

Mariano Paredes y Arrillaga, ca. 1848
(Library of Congress)

Parras

This thriving community, approximately 100 miles west of Saltillo, was occupied in December 1846 by the Army of the Center under Brigadier General John E. Wool.

Parras, Coahuila, located on a plain at the base of a high mountain front, was a city of approximately 5,000 inhabitants. More affluent than many Mexican communities, Parras held a number of aristocratic and wealthy families. It was well known for its pure air, clear streams, excellent climate, and fields and orchards where "pears, grapes, pomgranats [sic], olives and melons of all kinds grow in abundance and of the best quality," recalled Samuel Chamberlain, U.S. dragoon. "Wheat, corn, oats and barley fields cover the plains while the wine and Brandy is famed all over Mexico. The City contains a Citadel and is usually garrisoned by some three hundred men as a protection against Lipans and Comanches.... The women of the place possess more than their share of beauty."

General Wool's Army of the Center, marching from Monclova toward Chihuahua, occupied the town on December 5, 1846. His men were reasonably well behaved and were well treated by the citizens. Wool purchased large amounts of flour, bread, and grain from local merchants, and his army left Parras on December 17 to reinforce General William J. Worth at Saltillo.

After General Taylor left the Army of Occupation in November 1847, Wool reoccupied Parras until the end of the war.

For further reading: Chamberlain, *My Confession*, 1956; Smith, *The War with Mexico*, 1919.

Parrodi, Anastasio
(1805–1867)

General Anastasio Parrodi served as the military commandant of the state of Tamaulipas during the Mexican-American War and fought during the Battles of La Angostura and Padierna in 1847.

Parrodi, who was born in Havana, Cuba, emigrated to Mexico and joined the Mexican army. By 1846, he had become the military commandant of Tamaulipas.

During the Mexican-American War, the port of Tampico in Tamaulipas became the target of U.S. warships in the Gulf of Mexico. Parrodi busied his command with improving the city's defenses until he was ordered to abandon the city by General Antonio López de Santa Anna. Taking as much army equipment as possible, Parrodi abandoned or destroyed the rest when he left the city on October 27, 1846. He later commanded troops in the Army of the North at the 1847 Battles of La Angostura (Buena Vista) and Padierna (Contreras), where he was wounded.

Parrodi's postwar years included serving as governor of Jalisco and Tamaulipas and as military commander of Coahuila. He died in Mexico City at the age of 62.

For further reading: Alcaraz, *The Other Side*, 1850; *Diccionario Porrúa*, 1995; Roa Bárcena, *Recuerdos de la invasión norte-americana*, 1947.

Parrott, William S.
(1798–1863)

A U.S. agent in Mexico City, William S. Parrott kept President James K. Polk informed about the political climate in Mexico from 1845 to 1848.

Parrott was born in Virginia and raised in Tennessee. He fought during the War of 1812 and was wounded in the leg. In 1822, he moved to Mexico City, where he opened several successful businesses. As U.S. consul to Mexico from 1834 to 1836, Parrott dealt with Mexican leaders and assisted U.S. citizens. Regarded as rough and somewhat tactless, and at times dishonest, Parrott was driven into debt by Mexican lawsuits, and he left the country.

In March 1845, President Polk sent Parrott to Mexico to discern Mexican opinions regarding issues such as the annexation of Texas. Parrott wrote that he was "very precise in stating, that the government of the United States could never recognize in Mexico the right to claim an indemnity for the annexation of Texas to the American Union; but that, in a treaty of limits, for the sake of peace and good neighborhood, the United States would, no doubt, be disposed…to meet Mexico…in negotiation."

Despite Parrott's congenial efforts to socialize with Mexican congressmen, the Mexican government did not want to deal with him; he then became the assistant of U.S. envoy John Slidell. Parrott interacted with other U.S. agents on a regular basis in Mexico City and remained there in an official capacity until 1848.

After the war, he served in an administrative position for the U.S. Navy and died in Pennsylvania at the age of 65.

For further reading: Caruso, *The Mexican Spy Company*, 1991; Farrabee, "William Stuart Parrott, Businessman and Diplomat in Mexico," 1944; Pletcher, *The Diplomacy of Annexation*, 1973.

Patterson, Robert
(1792–1881)

A high-ranking volunteer general in the U.S. Army of Occupation, Robert Patterson served along the Río Grande and later at Veracruz and Cerro Gordo in 1847.

Patterson was born in Ireland. Later moving to Pennsylvania, he began his military career in the War of 1812 and commanded units of state militia.

A loyal Democrat, Patterson was appointed a major general of volunteers by President James K. Polk. Attached first to General Zachary Taylor's Army of Occupation along the Río Grande in 1846, Patterson later joined the army of Major General Winfield Scott for the Veracruz–Mexico City campaign in 1847. Patterson participated in the Battles of Veracruz and Cerro Gordo in the spring of 1847. Scott wrote that at Cerro Gordo Patterson was so ill "that it was almost madness to think of leaving his bed…he astonished his command by riding in among them immediately previous to the attack, and was received by a simultaneous shout, from three or four thousand voices.… He was so weak he could scarcely manage the animal he rode." Patterson returned to the United States to bring back new reinforcements. He arrived at Veracruz in October and arrived in Mexico City the following month.

After the war, Patterson returned to his political career and cotton mills in Pennsylvania. He served as a major general of volunteers in 1861 during the Civil War, but was removed from command after the First Battle of Mannassas. He died in 1881 at the age of 89.

For further reading: Frost, *The Mexican War and Its Warriors*, 1848.

Pedregal

The *pedregal* (stony place) was a vast area of rocky, solidified lava that protected the approaches to Churubusco. Captain Robert E. Lee discovered routes through the lava rock that helped Major General Winfield Scott's army win the Battles of Contreras and Churubusco in August 1847.

The *pedregal* was an oval-shaped expanse of lithified lava, roughly five miles by three miles, that obstructed General Scott's army as it neared Mexico City in August 1847. The town of San Agustín was on its southern side. From San Agustín, one road swung north around the lava field through San Antonio to Churubusco on the northern side; the other road went west for two miles to Padierna and then turned north and passed through San Geronimo and San Angel. From San Angel, it turned east through Coyoacán to Churubusco.

This fifteen-square-mile area of treacherous land was freuqently described by U.S. soldiers as looking like a rough sea that had been instantly transformed into stone. The rocks were hot, black, and jagged. The Mexicans thought that the *pedregal* was unpenetrable and that the U.S. army could advance only down the two main roads. Yet during his reconnaissance prior to the Battles of Contreras and Churubusco, engineer Captain Lee discovered narrow passageways through the rock that would allow the passage of troops and, with some construction work, artillery.

A work force of 500 men labored in the lava field on August 19, 1847, prying away rocks from the walls of the passageways. Although they heard the U.S. troops working, the Mexicans were surprised when streams of blue-clad soldiers poured through the rock walls during the assaults on Padierna (Battle of Contreras) and Churubusco on August 20. Navigating the *pedregal* allowed Scott's men to flank the Mexican positions, which led to their collapse and retreat.

See also Lee, Robert Edward.

For further reading: Freeman, *R. E. Lee,* 1934; Hitchcock, *Fifty Years in Camp and Field,* 1909; Semmes, *Service Afloat and Ashore during the Mexican War,* 1851.

Pemberton, John Clifford

(1814–1881)

An aide to General William J. Worth, John C. Pemberton saw action in most of the major battles of the Mexican-American War and was wounded twice during the assault on Mexico City.

Pemberton was born in Philadelphia. He attended the U.S. Military Academy from 1833 to 1837 and was commissioned a second lieutenant in the 4th U.S. Artillery Regiment. He fought in the Second Seminole War and saw service along the Canadian border.

During the Mexican-American War, Pemberton was an aide-de-camp to General William J. Worth and saw action at the Battles of Palo Alto, Resaca de la Palma, Monterrey, Veracruz, Cerro Gordo, Churubusco, El Molino del Rey, Chapultepec, and Mexico City. He was wounded twice in the fighting that swirled around San Cosmé *garita* (gate) outside the city on September 13, 1847. Pemberton also assisted in the organization of the occupational government. By the end of the war, he had been brevetted to captain and major.

In the 1850s, Pemberton served on the western frontier. During the Civil War, he was a major general for the Confederacy and defended Vicksburg in 1863. He retired to Philadelphia after the war, where he died at age 67.

For further reading: Ballard, *Pemberton, a Biography,* 1991; Cullum, *Biographical Register of the Officers and Graduates of the United States Military Academy from 1802 to 1867,* 1879; Dillon, *American Artillery in the Mexican War 1846–1847,* 1975; Pemberton, *Pemberton,* 1987.

Peña y Barragán, Matías de la

(ca. 1798–1850)

General Matías de la Peña y Barragán helped launch the *Polkos* Revolt against the liberal government in 1847 and later fought capably at El Molino del Rey, Chapultepec, and Mexico City.

Peña y Barragán, who was born in Mexico City, received a good education overseas before he joined the Mexican army. Well regarded by military officials, he became a brigade general in 1840 and suppressed various rebellions against the government.

Furious at Vice President Valentín Gómez Farías's order in January 1847 to strip the Roman Catholic Church of 15 million pesos, Peña y Barragán launched a conservative rebellion (the *Polkos* Revolt) that included street fighting between armed militia units. His revolt succeeded in the removal of Gómez Farías from office and a restructured arrangement with the church for 2 million pesos.

Shortly afterward, Peña y Barragán joined the Army of the East to challenge the advance of Major General Winfield Scott's Army of Occupation from Veracruz. Peña y Barragán bravely led troops in two counterattacks against U.S. forces at the Battle of El Molino del Rey and organized some of the stiff resistance that faced U.S. troops as they surged toward San Cosmé *garita* (gate) outside Mexico City on September 13. As part of Santa Anna's junta, Peña y Barragán voted to evacuate the city.

He remained in the military until 1850, when he died as the military commandant in Jalapa.

For further reading: Alcaraz, *The Other Side,* 1850; *Diccionario Porrúa,* 1995.

Peña y Peña, Manuel de la

(1789–1850)

A lawyer, politician, and judge, Manuel de la Peña y Peña served twice as minister of foreign relations, tried to stimulate a negotiated settlement with the United States before the Mexican-American War erupted, and later endorsed the Treaty of Guadalupe Hidalgo.

Born near Mexico City to an affluent family, Peña y Peña became a lawyer and later a politician. In 1837, he held the post of Minister of Justice and Ecclesiastical Affairs under President Anastasio Bustamante. One of the more learned and respected men in Mexican politics and a *moderado*, Peña y Peña helped draft the 1843 constitution.

As minister of foreign relations under President José Joaquín Herrera in 1845, he tried to facilitate negotiations between Mexico and the United States regarding Texas, but diplomatic relations eventually broke down between Peña y Peña and U.S. envoy John Black. During the Mexican-American War, he remained active in political affairs and served as a member of the supreme court.

Aged and in poor health, Peña y Peña became involved in the treaty negotiations after the fall of Mexico City as provisional president Pedro María Anaya's minister of foreign relations. Peña y Peña endorsed the Treaty of Guadalupe Hidalgo in front of the Mexican Congress in May 1848 and urged its ratification.

After the war, he served briefly as governor of the state of Mexico before he died at the age of 61 in Mexico City.

For further reading: Alcaraz, *The Other Side,* 1850; *Diccionario Porrúa,* 1995; Pletcher, *The Diplomacy of Annexation,* 1973; Ramirez, *Mexico during the War with the United States,* 1950; Robinson, *The View from Chapultepec,* 1989.

Pérez, Francisco
(ca. 1810–1864)

General Francisco Pérez bravely led troops during the Battle of La Angostura (Buena Vista) in 1847 and the battles of Major General Winfield Scott's Veracruz–Mexico City campaign.

Pérez, who was born in Tulancingo, joined the Mexican army after independence had been won from Spain. He served in Texas and the Yucatán before he was promoted to general in 1846.

As part of General Antonio López de Santa Anna's Army of the North, Pérez launched several attacks during the Battle of La Angostura (Buena Vista) in February 1847. Later assigned to the Army of the East, Pérez fought valiantly in several battles against Major General Winfield Scott's advancing Army of Occupation. He commanded the Casa Mata complex during the Battle of El Molino del Rey and inflicted heavy casualties upon the assaulting U.S. columns. Pérez fought in the subsequent battles that led to Mexico City and advised Santa Anna to evacuate the city. Santa Anna left the night of September 13 with a portion of the army and appointed Pérez the second general in chief.

Pérez remained a popular political and military figure after the war. His positions included governor of Puebla and army general. He fought against the French intervention in the early 1860s and died in Tulancingo at the age of 54.

For further reading: Roa Bárcena, *Recuerdos de la invasión norte-americana,* 1947; Smith, *The War with Mexico,* 1919.

Perote Castle

Perote Castle, located on the outskirts of the village of Perote, Veracruz, was a stone-walled citadel that served as a fortress and prison during the Mexican-American War.

An impressive structure, Perote Castle was built by the Spanish government in the 1770s to guard trade routes and protect treasure and goods. Called the Castle Prison by Mexicans, its dark dungeons confined the Texan prisoners from the Mier Expedition, political prisoners, and Mexican officers in disfavor with General Antonio López de Santa Anna during the Mexican-American War.

During General Winfield Scott's Veracruz–Mexico City campaign in 1847, General William J. Worth's division occupied Perote Castle on April 22. Mexican defenders under General Valentín Canalizo had fled a few days before, leaving behind cannon and muskets, U.S. prisoners, and Generals José Juan Landero and Juan Morales, who had been imprisoned for surrendering Veracruz

J. J. Oswandel, of the 1st Regiment of Pennsylvania Volunteers, stated that "this castle is a grand, but gloomy, pile of the best stonemasonry, situated in a beautiful level valley between two mountains, and about one mile from the town of Perote." The walls, built from massive black volcanic rocks, were more than 8 feet thick and rose 60 feet from the bottom of the moat. Ramparts were 70 feet in width and could accommodate 100 pieces of artillery. "It is considered by engineers to be one of the best constructed castles in the world," wrote Oswandel.

For further reading: McGrath and Hawkins, "Perote Fort—Where Texans Were Imprisoned," 1944–1945; Oswandel, *Notes of the Mexican War,* 1885; Smith and Judah, *Chronicles of the Gringos,* 1968.

Perry, Matthew Calbraith
(1794–1858)

Commodore Matthew C. Perry commanded the U.S. Home Squadron in the Gulf of Mexico during the Mexican-American War, captured several ports, and supported the landing of Major General Winfield Scott's Army of Occupation at Veracruz in March 1847.

Perry, who was born in Rhode Island, enlisted in the U.S. Navy at age 15. After various maritime duties, he commanded his first ship in 1830. He originated the apprentice system for the education of seamen, and, as a captain during 1839–1840, directed the first naval school for gunnery. In 1843, he commanded the African Squadron, which protected the settlement of black Americans in Africa.

During the Mexican-American War, Perry was second in command, and later commander in chief, of the U.S. Home Squadron along the east coast of Mexico. His vessels blockaded Mexican ports, chased down privateers, and conducted expeditions up waterways. U.S. Navy patrols captured Frontera, Tabasco, and Laguna and destroyed supplies destined for the Mexican army. In 1847, Perry commanded the navy forces that landed Scott's Army of Occupation south of Veracruz in March and that shelled the city into submission. Perry continued to occupy ports, including Tuxpan, along the gulf coast and negotiated a promise of neutrality from the rebellious province of Yucatán.

After the war, Perry helped supervise the construction of mail steamships. His negotiation of a treaty with Japan in 1854 began an important U.S.-Japanese trade that led to Japan's rapid industrialization. Perry died in New York City at the age of 64.

See also Tabasco, Battles of; Tuxpan; Veracruz, Battle of.

For further reading: Barrows, *The Great Commodore,* 1935; Bauer, *Surfboats and Horse Marines,* 1969; Griffis, *Matthew Calbraith Perry,* 1890; Morison, *"Old Bruin" Commodore Matthew Calbraith Perry,* 1967.

Matthew C. Perry
(Library of Congress)

Petrita, USS

Commodore David E. Conner and Major General Winfield Scott, before the invasion of Veracruz in 1847, decided to make a joint reconnaissance of potential landing sites for Scott's 10,000-man army. On March 6, they boarded the small steamer *Petrita*. Other high-ranking officers on board included Generals William J. Worth, Robert Patterson, David E. Twiggs, and Gideon J. Pillow, Captains Robert E. Lee and Joseph E. Johnston, Lieutenants Pierre G. T. Beauregard and George G. Meade, and other staff.

As the ship sailed north from Collado Beach toward Veracruz, it was fired on by the heavy guns of Fort San Juan de Ulúa. The first shell sailed over the steamer, and the second fell short. The third burst high over the top and rained debris on the ship. The USS *Petrita* finally turned out of range after about ten shells had been fired.

Several officers considered the tour to be a very high risk. E. A. Hitchcock wrote that "We were in a ridiculous position…in danger with no adequate object, without means of defense, with all our officers of rank on board. If a chance shot had struck our engines we should have cut a pretty figure."

For further reading: Bauer, *Surfboats and Horse Marines*, 1969; Hitchcock, *Fifty Years in Camp and Field*, 1909.

Pico, Andrés
(1810–1876)

An enterprising Californio officer during the Mexican-American War, Captain Andrés Pico scored one of the few Mexican victories during the war when he defeated Brigadier General Stephen W. Kearny at the Battle of Pascual in 1846.

Pico, who was born in San Diego to an affluent family, was a prominent local politician and soldier. Opposed to the U.S. intervention in California in 1846, he commanded approximately 100 horsemen, mostly lancers, who defeated Brigadier General Kearny's 100-man force at the Battle of San Pascual on December 6, 1846. Kearny lost nearly a third of his force in killed and wounded and was under siege by Pico at Mule Hill until reinforcements arrived from San Diego. Pico later fought with Captain José María Flores against U.S. forces at San Gabriel River and La Mesa in January 1847. Flores turned command over to Pico after La Mesa, and Pico signed the Treaty of Cahuenga a few days later.

Pico's business and political success, including operating a gold mine, managing ranches, and serving in the California legislature, continued after the war. He died at the age of 66.

See also Cahuenga, Treaty of; San Pascual, Battle of.

For further reading: Harlow, *California Conquered*, 1982; Rosenus, *General M. G. Vallejo and the Advent of the Americans*, 1995.

Pico, Pío de Jesús
(1801–1894)

The governor of California at the onset of the Mexican-American War, Pío de Jesús Pico

Pío Pico
(Library of Congress)

organized the early resistance to the U.S. invasion, but later fled to Mexico.

Born at Mission San Gabriel, Pico became an enterprising, successful businessman in Los Angeles in the 1820s. Later, he served in the territorial legislature as governor and as civilian administrator at Mission San Luis Rey. In March 1845, after Mexican governor Manuel Micheltorena was overthrown, Pico again became governor. Based in Los Angeles, he appointed José Castro as military commander at Monterey.

Pico opposed the U.S. intervention in California during the Mexican-American War and disapproved of the actions of John C. Frémont and his men. Pico had frequent discussions with U.S. consul Thomas O. Larkin regarding U.S. intentions in California and spearheaded the initial resistance to U.S. troops, including ordering in July 1846 the conscription of all men between the ages of 15 and 60. As few came forward, he quickly became discouraged and left Los Angeles to go to Baja California and Sonora. The Californio struggle was then carried on by Captain José María Flores.

After the war ended, Pico returned to California as a rancher, but was one of many Californios who lost their lands in court. He remained active in Los Angeles politics and built and operated a large hotel called the Pico House. His business later failed, and he died destitute at the age of 93.

See also Frémont, John C.

For further reading: Harlow, *California Conquered*, 1982; Meier and Rivera, *Dictionary of Mexican American History*, 1981; Rosenus, *General M. G. Vallejo and the Advent of the Americans*, 1995.

Pierce, Franklin
(1804–1869)

A volunteer brigadier general during the Mexican-American War, Franklin Pierce was injured near Contreras before he could participate in combat and was later unjustly accused of cowardice. He later became president of the United States.

The son of a Revolutionary War veteran, Pierce was born in New Hampshire and attended several New England academies. An excellent student, he became a lawyer. A political career followed, including terms in the New Hampshire legislature and the U.S. House of Representatives and Senate. In 1842, Pierce returned to New Hampshire to practice law.

When the Mexican-American War began, Pierce volunteered as a private, but was not called to serve. President James K. Polk offered him the position of attorney general, but he refused. On February 15, 1847, a congressional bill was passed that increased the size of the army. Pierce was appointed a colonel and later was promoted to brigadier general by Polk. Pierce organized and equipped his own brigade, which sailed for Veracruz in May 1847. Pierce and his 2,500 men arrived in June, and his first task was collecting nearly 2,000 wild mules to haul their supplies. He then led his force over 150 miles of the guerrilla-infested National Road to join Major General Winfield Scott's army at Puebla on August 6.

Pierce was positioning his men for a frontal assault on the Mexican position at the beginning of the Battle of Contreras on August 19, when his horse fell. Pierce's left knee was severely twisted and the pain was so intense that he lost consciousness. Having heard some men accuse him of cowardice, he insisted on participating in the Battle of Churubusco the following day, only again to injure his knee and faint from pain. He insisted on remaining on the field so he would not be called a coward.

Scott appointed Pierce and two other brigadier generals to work out the details of the Truce of Tacubaya after the Battle of Churubusco. Still desperate for combat, Pierce was bedridden during the Battle of Chapultepec with dysentery. After three months of garrison duty in Mexico City, Pierce left in December 1847 after a farewell dinner with General Scott.

Pierce won the Democratic presidential nomination in 1852 and defeated Scott by an electoral vote of 254 to 42 to become the fourteenth U.S. president (1853–1857). Pierce recommended the purchase of Hawaii and finalized the Gadsden Purchase (1853) that settled the boundary conflict with Mexico.

Pierce and his wife traveled extensively after he left the presidency. He died in Concord, New Hampshire, at the age of 65.

For further reading: Frost, *The Mexican War and Its Warriors*, 1848; Nichols, *Franklin Pierce*, 1931; Scott, *Memoirs of Lieutenant General Scott*, 1864.

Pike, Albert
(1809–1891)

A capable Arkansas cavalry officer, Captain Albert Pike commanded a regiment of cavalry during Brigadier General Zachary Taylor's campaign in northern Mexico during 1846–1847.

Pike was born in Massachusetts. He traveled to St. Louis and Santa Fe in the 1830s as an adventurer and writer and later settled in Arkansas as a newspaper writer. He then studied to become an attorney.

Pike volunteered for the Mexican-American War and commanded a cavalry brigade that he had recruited. He was openly critical of Colonel Archibald Yell's Arkansas "Ransackers," the 1st Arkansas Volunteer Cavalry, and the two officers feuded constantly. Pike conducted reconnaissance missions for Generals Zachary Taylor and John E. Wool in northern Mexico and escorted a squadron of Alexander Doniphan's men back to Chihuahua from Saltillo. During the Battle of Buena Vista in February 1847, Pike's Arkansas squadron, stationed in the rear of the U.S. battle line, helped turn away a flank attack by the Mexican cavalry.

Pike joined the Confederacy as a brigadier general and commanded Indian regiments at the Battle of Pea Ridge in Arkansas. He resumed his career as a lawyer and writer in New York, Canada, and Washington, D.C., where he died at the age of 82.

For further reading: Allsopp, The Life Story of Albert Pike, 1920; Brown, "The Mexican War Experiences of Albert Pike and the 'Mounted Devils of Arkansas,'" 1953; Duncan, *Reluctant General*, 1961; Hughes, *Doniphan's Expedition, Containing an Account of the Conquest of New Mexico*, 1973.

Pillow, Gideon Johnson
(1806–1878)

One of the highest-ranking U.S. volunteer generals during the Mexican-American War, Gideon J. Pillow was highly criticized for his poor performance at the Battle of Cerro Gordo and for his slanderous attacks on his commander, Major General Winfield Scott, in the U.S. newspapers.

Born in Tennessee, Pillow graduated from the University of Nashville. As a lawyer, he partnered with future president James K. Polk. A loyal and influential Democrat, Pillow also dabbled in politics.

Although unquestionably brave, Pillow was often described by other officers as vain, ambitious, quarrelsome, and a poor tactical commander. Appointed a brigadier general of volunteers in 1846 by President Polk, Pillow did not see combat under General Zachary Taylor in 1846 and sharply criticized his commander, the first of several such occurrences. Later transferred to Major General Scott's Army of Occupation, Pillow botched his attack on the Mexican right during the Battle of Cerro Gordo in April 1847 and suffered heavy casualties. (He himself was wounded.) He was promoted to major general and was second only to Scott in rank. Commanding a division, he fought capably at Contreras, Churubusco, and Chapultepec, where he was wounded again.

Scott reprimanded Pillow for trying to steal a Mexican cannon as a war trophy and planned a court-martial. Angry at Scott for not recognizing his performance in battle and by not involving him in peace negotiations, Pillow began to author articles in U.S. newspapers that minimized Scott's role in recent victories and elevated his own participation. Pillow also appealed directly to his good friend President Polk. Exasperated, Scott had Pillow arrested. Shortly thereafter, Polk suspended Scott and conducted a court of inquiry that went on for months in Mexico City and Washington, D.C. Although Pillow was chastised for insubordination, he was cleared of all charges.

Upon his return to the United States, Pillow helped nominate Franklin Pierce for the presidency in 1852. Pillow's uneven, often-criticized military leadership continued during the Civil War, during which he was a Confederate general. He later practiced law in Memphis and died in Helena, Arkansas.

See also Cerro Gordo, Battle of; Court of Inquiry, Scott.

For further reading: Frost, *The Mexican War and Its Warriors*, 1848; Hughes and Stonesifer, *The Life and Wars of Gideon J. Pillow*, 1993.

Point Isabel

Point Isabel became the first staging area for General Zachary Taylor's Army of Occupation along the Río Grande in 1846.

Having been stationed at Corpus Christi during the winter of 1845–1846, Taylor received orders from President James K. Polk on February 4, 1846, to move to "a position on or near the east bank of the Rio Del Norte." Taylor selected Point Isabel in Brazo Santiago. Taking most of his men on an overland route along a rough trail used by traders and smugglers, the army arrived at Point Isabel on March 24 and brought with it 300 wagons and carts and thousands of animals. The quartermasters, engineers, and artillery arrived at Point Isabel by ship.

The tiny village of Frontón on Point Isabel had been abandoned, and some of the buildings had been burned. Taylor quickly transformed it into a busy supply depot that was active throughout the Mexican-American War. Earthen fortifications, named Fort Polk, were raised to better protect the site from Mexican attack. Fort Polk was occasionally manned by navy personnel from the U.S. Home Squadron. A steady stream of new volunteers arrived by boat, and veterans whose enlistments had expired or who were wounded or sick waited for ships to take them home. By 1848, private businessmen had erected warehouses, hotels, and a post office.

For further reading: Chance, *Jefferson Davis's Mexican War Regiment*, 1991; Curtis, *Mexico under Fire*, 1994; Winders, *Mr. Polk's Army*, 1997.

Polk, James Knox
(1795–1849)

The eleventh president of the United States, expansionist James K. Polk was eager to acquire New Mexico and California from Mexico. He deftly steered the United States into war with Mexico in 1846 and personally supervised U.S. operations, from dispersing secret agents to appointing generals and devising military strategy.

Born on a farm near Pineville, North Carolina, Polk was a sickly child and endured high-risk surgery to remove gallstones. The surgery was successful, and his energy returned. After graduating from the University of North Carolina in 1818 at the top of his class, he studied law in Tennessee. With the support of Andrew Jackson, he entered the Tennessee legislature. By 1825, he was a member of the U.S. House of Representatives and was later governor of Tennessee. Polk was an ardent expansionist and envisioned the United States extending to the Pacific Ocean.

Polk was renown for his ambition, tireless energy, and dedication to politics. This resulted in little time for social life. "I cannot lose half a day just to go and dine," Polk once commented.

On a platform of westward expansion, Polk won the presidential race against Whig Henry Clay. Not yet 50 years of age when he was inaugurated in 1845, Polk was the youngest president in the history of the United States. In his State of the Union message, he was quick to condemn Mexico for its wrongs against the United States.

Polk liked to do many things himself. "I prefer to supervise the whole operations of the

James K. Polk
(Library of Congress)

Government myself rather than entrust the public business to subordinates, and this makes my duties very great," he once wrote. His wife Sarah was his personal secretary.

Polk was determined to acquire Texas, New Mexico, and California, whether by peaceful settlement or war. He dispersed secret agents to Texas to sway popular opinion toward the United States and to disrupt British designs on Texas. Polk wanted Texas to invade the disputed border area between the Nueces River and the Río Grande to start a war with Mexico, in which the United States would offer unlimited support. Efforts to arrive at a peaceful settlement with Mexico regarding Texas, New Mexico, and California continued to deteriorate, especially after Texas accepted annexation.

Upon receiving word of the Skirmish at Carricitos Ranch along the Río Grande in April 1846, Polk addressed Congress on May 11 that "Mexico has passed the boundary of the United States, has invaded our territory, and shed American blood upon the American soil." War was declared two days later.

Although he had no military training, Polk maintained strict control over the larger strategies of the U.S. army and navy. Recognizing Mexico's many weaknesses, including lack of funds, a poorly supplied military, and rebellious northern states, Polk developed a four-pronged campaign: defeat the Mexican army in northern Mexico, occupy Chihuahua and New Mexico, seize California, and blockade both Mexican coasts. Although he worked closely with the War Department, Secretary of War William Marcy, and Secretary of the Navy George Bancroft, Polk insisted in reviewing all decisions, including logistical matters.

After discussions with Alexander J. Atocha, an ally of exiled Mexican leader Antonio López de Santa Anna, Polk was convinced that Santa Anna, if allowed to return through the U.S. blockade to Mexico, would begin earnest peace negotiations with the United States. Polk allowed Santa Anna to land at Veracruz in August 1846. Despite his assurances to U.S. envoy Alexander Slidell Mackenzie that he would pursue peace, Santa Anna quickly escalated the war fervor once he reached Mexico City. Allowing one of Mexico's most influential leaders back into Mexico, and thus into its presidency, may have considerably extended the war.

Polk devised legislation that authorized more troops and funds to help end the war and the appointment of more generals (many of whom were loyal Democrats that Polk rewarded with volunteer appointments). Growing impatient with General Zachary Taylor's lack of speed (including his Armistice of Monterrey and refusal to attack Mexico City), Polk reluctantly turned to Major General Winfield Scott to command an inland march on Mexico City from Veracruz. Polk was equally irritated by Scott's Armistice of Tacubaya.

After Mexico City had finally fallen and peace negotiations had stalled, Polk was eager to dictate new terms that would call for additional territory, and he ordered negotiator Nicholas P. Trist to return to Washington. Trist refused and concluded the Treaty of Guadalupe Hidalgo in February 1848. Angry at Trist's insubordination, Polk nonetheless accepted the treaty and Mexico's cession of New Mexico and California to the United States.

Polk refused to run for a second term. Shortly after he left the presidency he was stricken with cholera and died in Nashville at the age of 54. His aggressive, expansionist administration had acquired more than one million square miles of new territory and expanded the United States to the Pacific shore.

See also War Address, James K. Polk.

For further reading: Bergeron, *The Presidency of James K. Polk*, 1987; Caruso, *The Mexican Spy Company*, 1991; Chase, *History of the Polk Administration*, 1850; Horn, "Trends in Historical Interpretation," 1965; McCormac, *James K. Polk*, 1965; Polk, *The Diary of James K. Polk*, 1910; Sellers, *James K. Polk, Continentalist, 1843–1846*, 1966.

Polkos Revolt (1847)

The *Polkos* Revolt during February–March 1847 was led by high-ranking *moderados* whose goal was to reverse the January 11 decree by Vice-President Valentín Gómez Farías that planned to strip the Roman Catholic Church of 15 million pesos to fund the war effort.

With President and General Antonio López de Santa Anna leading the Army of the North to fight General Zachary Taylor at the Battle of La Angostura (Buena Vista), *puro* Vice-President Valentín Gómez Farías had free political rein. On January 11, he decreed that Roman Catholic Church property would be sold to raise 15 million pesos to fund the Mexican-American War.

This policy outraged *moderado* leaders such as General José Mariano Salas and Pedro María Anaya. The *moderados*, many of them from affluent families in Mexico City, plotted to overthrow Gómez Farías. This group became known as the *polkos* (presumably because, as the wealthy elite, they frequently danced the polka at social and political parties). Several militia units were recruited to the *polkos* cause.

The revolt erupted on February 27, 1847, and continued for nearly a month. Skirmishing occurred in the streets between armed *puro* and *moderado* militias. Unfortunately for Mexico, this civil unrest in the capital city paralyzed the Mexican government just as General Winfield Scott began his uncontested landing of 10,000 troops at Veracruz in early March. Freshly defeated at La Angostura, Santa Anna returned to Mexico City, removed Gómez Farías, and negotiated a donation of 2 million pesos from the church instead of seizing assets worth 15 million pesos. This work delayed Santa Anna from planning a military strategy to deal with Scott's army.

See also Gómez Farías, Valentín; *Moderados*; *Puros*.

For further reading: Alcaraz, *The Other Side*, 1850; Costeloe, "The Mexican Church and the Rebellion of the Polkos," 1966; Ramirez, *Mexico during the War with the United States*, 1950.

Porter, Caroline

A U.S. manager at the Arispe Cotton Mills near Saltillo, Caroline Porter was a mistress of Mexican general José Vicente Miñón. Their two-hour tryst on the morning of February 23, 1847, reputedly delayed his attack on the rear of the U.S. army at the Battle of Buena Vista.

The Arispe Cotton Mills was a successful cotton factory a few miles from Saltillo. According to U.S. dragoon Samuel Chamberlain, Porter, from Lowell, Massachusetts, had come to Mexico three years before to teach Mexican women how to weave cotton cloth. That enterprise was short-lived, but Porter remained to manage the facility. In 1845, she and General Miñón developed an amorous relationship when he commanded the military district at Saltillo.

On February 23, 1847, the day of the Battle of Buena Vista, Miñón and his cavalry brigade had been sent by General Antonio López de Santa Anna to attack the rear of the U.S. army under General Zachary Taylor at Saltillo. Miñón halted to reform his troops at Arispe Cotton Mills, where he was reunited with Porter and stepped inside the building. His troops became impatient, and Miñón emerged an hour or so later. He led his brigade to Saltillo, where it made two feeble attacks and was turned back by an artillery battery. After rejoining Santa Anna's defeated army on its way back to San Luis Potosí, Miñón was arrested by Santa Anna, who blamed Miñón's late and uninspired attack for the defeat.

Chamberlain went on to write that both U.S. and Mexican officers believed that, if Miñón had struck the U.S. army's rear early in the day, the battle could have been a Mexican victory. Porter later claimed credit for the U.S. triumph by conducting a "most patriotic and praiseworthy act." Chamberlain maintained that "the laws of compensation that put General Taylor in the White House should have placed Miss Porter there as the Lady."

For further reading: Chamberlain, *My Confession*, 1956.

Posada y Garduño, Manuel

An archbishop in the Roman Catholic Church in Mexico City, Manuel Posada y Garduño prayed with huge public crowds for Mexican victory and negotiated with Major General Winfield Scott for the release of Mexican prisoners.

As General Scott's Army of Occupation approached Mexico City in August 1847, patriotic archbishop Posada y Garduño exhorted the public to defend the city. His public masses before huge crowds in the city prayed for Mexican victory and warned of the ruin of the Catholic faith:

> With foreign domination, if such an abominable misfortune occurs, you will see altars erected against altars, and sects and dissident communions formed, which secretly and openly will make cruel and incessant war on our sacred, uniquely true religion.... If the invaders triumph and subjugate us, ultimately they will try to eradicate us and carry off to their country, as an object our credulity and fanaticism, or of speculation, our image of Our Lady of Guadalupe. The result: they will have robbed from us that precious gift from Heaven, that lodestone of Mexican hearts, that precious object of our worship and hope.

Learning of the planned execution of the captured members of the San Patricio Battalion, Posada y Garduño met with Scott in an attempt to save their lives. His influence may have resulted in Scott's commuting some of the death sentences of the San Patricio prisoners.

During the occupation of Mexico City, the archbishop met with Scott regarding the parole of Mexican prisoners of war. Scott later agreed to release prisoners if the archbishop would refuse absolution to those who violated their word of honor or if the archbishop promised the oath of the church that the men would not take up arms again. This was agreed to, and, a few days before Christmas, Scott released approximately 500 Mexican prisoners of war. Each man was given a paper signed by the archbishop that pledged that they would not rejoin the Mexican army.

For further reading: Callcott, *Church and State in Mexico,* 1926; Miller, *Shamrock and Sword,* 1989.

Price, Sterling (1809–1867)

A volunteer colonel from Missouri in General Stephen W. Kearny's Army of the West, Sterling Price was the commanding officer during the Taos Revolt in New Mexico in 1847.

Born and raised in Virginia, Sterling Price later moved to Missouri. He became involved in state and national politics, including serving as a Democrat in the U.S. House of Representatives.

Volunteering for the Mexican-American War, he became colonel of the 2nd Regiment of Missouri Volunteers. Attached to Brigadier General Kearny's Army of the West, his regiment marched from Fort Leavenworth, Kansas, to Santa Fe, New Mexico, during August–October 1846. After Kearny and Colonel Alexander Doniphan left on different missions, Price became the commander of the occupational forces in New Mexico. His slack discipline resulted in disorderly troops, which increased resentment by the local citizens. In January 1847, a band of rebels killed Governor Charles Bent and six others during the Taos Revolt. Price moved quickly. With a small force of 300 to 500 men, he pursued the poorly organized, 1,500-man rebel force relentlessly. After winning several skirmishes, he trapped them at Pueblo de Taos, where 150 were killed in a sharp fight. The leaders of the insurrection were promptly hanged.

Price continued to chase small guerrilla bands across New Mexico with squadrons of his Missouri cavalry in 1847. Chaffing for action, the following year he occupied the city of Chihuahua. Without orders, and after the Treaty of Guadalupe Hidalgo had been signed, Price skirmished with Mexican troops at Santa Cruz de Rosales. The victory resulted in a sharp reprimand from Secretary of War William Marcy, who ordered Price to return to his base at El Paso.

Resuming his political career after the war, Price served as governor of Missouri. His leadership as a Confederate major general during the Civil War was often criticized. He refused to surrender and escaped to Mexico, where he served briefly under Emperor Maximilian. He died in St. Louis from cholera in 1867.

See also Santa Cruz de Rosales, Battle of; Taos Rebellion.

For further reading: McNierney, *Taos 1847,* 1980; Shalhope, *Sterling Price,* 1971; Twitchell, *The Conquest of Santa Fe 1846,* 1967.

Puebla

A prominent city on the National Road between Veracruz and Mexico City, Puebla, Veracruz, was occupied by U.S. troops from May 1847 until the end of the Mexican-American War.

After the Battle of Cerro Gordo in April 1847, Major General Winfield Scott sent General William J. Worth's division ahead to Puebla, a town of approximately 70,000 people, on the National Road. U.S. soldiers were struck by the beauty of the city—the many spires and domes, gardens, orchards, and lively music. Raphael Semmes recalled that "from the cultivated fields you come at once among the compactly built dwellings. The streets are broad, and were swarming with the multitude as far as the eye could reach—the cross streets too were filled in every direction, indeed, I am sure I never before saw half so many people together. Our little army of four thousand was completely lost in the crowds that pressed around us, examining us pretty much as they would the animals in a menagerie.... A great many priests [in black robes] were moving about among the throng or sitting on the balconies with the ladies.... The city is kept exceedingly clean—the streets which are all admirably paved with square blocks of granite look as if they were not only swept, but scoured."

Worth arrived in Puebla on May 15; Scott, a

few weeks later. Scott had wanted to take Mexico City by June, before the rainy season began. After losing approximately 3,700 soldiers at Puebla who returned to Veracruz because their enlistments had ended, Scott's reduced army consisted of approximately 7,100 men, many of whom were in the hospital suffering from diarrhea and dysentery. Even though they were greeted warmly by the citizens, U.S. soldiers were occasionally stabbed or murdered on the streets, as were Mexicans. Having received reinforcements from Veracruz, Scott mobilized the lead elements of his army for Mexico City on August 5. A garrison force of approximately 400 men under Colonel Thomas Childs was left behind to occupy the city.

For further reading: McCaffrey, *Army of Manifest Destiny*, 1992; Semmes, *Service Afloat and Ashore during the Mexican War*, 1851.

Puebla, Siege of

(September–October 1847)

The U.S. garrison force at Puebla was besieged by Mexican forces under the command of Generals Joaquín Rea and Antonio López de Santa Anna during September–October 1847.

Colonel Thomas Childs and 400 men were ordered to remain in Puebla as an occupation force when Major General Winfield Scott's Army of Occupation moved out on August 5, 1847. Hundreds of sick or convalescing soldiers remained in the army's field hospitals in the city.

Childs and his men quickly became targets for the guerrilla bands that prowled the National Road. Mexican General Rea soon appeared with approximately 2,000 cavalrymen to challenge the U.S. force. On August 26, guerrillas stole approximately 700 mules from a nearby corral. A small party of wagon masters, teamsters, army followers, and a few soldiers—approximately 32 men—rode out in pursuit. Ambushed by the cavalry, only 10 men returned. A Mexican came into the U.S. camp the next day with 13 mutilated U.S. corpses in a cart.

Rea's cavalry cut off the water supply to the U.S. fortifications and delivered an annoying sniper fire. A siege began on September 13, and "the enemy augmented [its] numbers daily, and daily the firing was increased," wrote Childs. Within ten days, General Santa Anna arrived after the loss of Mexico City with a battered remnant of the Army of the East, swelling the Mexican numbers to approximately 4,000.

Childs refused Santa Anna's surrender demand on September 25, but Santa Anna's plans to retake Puebla were ruined when Brigadier General Joseph Lane arrived with more than 1,000 reinforcements after a forced march from Veracruz. The siege ended on October 12 with the retreat of the Mexican forces. Total U.S. casualties were 94 killed and wounded.

See also Childs, Thomas; Lane, Joseph; Puebla.

For further reading: Alcaraz, *The Other Side*, 1850; Frost, *The Mexican War and Its Warriors*, 1848; Oswandel, *Notes of the Mexican War*, 1885; Semmes, *Service Afloat and Ashore during the Mexican War*, 1851.

Pueblo de Taos, Skirmish at

(February 4, 1847)

This 1847 skirmish near Taos between a 700-man rebel force and Missouri troops under Colonel Sterling Price ended the Taos Revolt in New Mexico.

After military governor Charles Bent and six other U.S. settlers were murdered in Taos to start the Taos Rebellion in January 1847, Colonel Sterling Price mobilized his Missouri volunteers from Santa Fe to subdue the New Mexican rebels. Easily defeating the skittish rebels at La Cañada and El Emboda, he followed them to the large adobe structure at Pueblo de Taos, about two miles from Taos. The two tallest buildings were seven stories high. Almost 300 rooms were enclosed within the thick adobe walls.

Price arrived on the evening of February 3 and attacked the 700 rebels the following morning. The U.S. forces launched artillery and ground assaults, and the cautious fighting continued all day. The pueblo surrendered the following day when all the "women issued from the fort [pueblo], each bearing a white flag." (McNierney 1980)

The surrender terms called for the rebels to

turn over El Tomacito, the Pueblo Indian blamed for the killing of Charles Bent. (Pablo Chavis, another one of the leaders, had been killed in the fighting.) U.S. losses were 7 killed and 45 wounded; Mexican losses were approximately 150 killed, and an unknown number of wounded.

The rebel leaders were sentenced to hang, and ropes and lariats were collected. "The ropes, by reason of size and stiffness despite the soaping given them, were adjusted with difficulty," recalled an observer The condemned stood on a wagon under a large tree limb and bid each other "adios." The wagon was pulled away. As the bodies dangled "the hands of two came together, which they held with a firm grasp until the muscles loosened in death." (McNierney 1980)

See also El Tomacito (Tomás Baca).

For further reading: Grant, *When Old Trails Were New,* 1934; McNierney, *Taos 1847,* 1980; Twitchell, *The History of the Military Occupation of the Territory of New Mexico from 1846 to 1851 by the Government of the United States,* 1909.

Puros

A faction of the liberal political group in Mexico, *puros* believed in a democratic constitution and reduction of the power of the Roman Catholic Church and the Mexican military.

Liberals (federalists) in Mexico supported Mexico's 1821 constitution, free speech, free religion, and less control by the Catholic Church and the Mexican army on social and political matters. Liberals were split into two factions: the *puros,* who favored immediate reforms, and the *moderados,* who preferred gradual changes in government.

The *puros* (pure ones) opposed the great wealth of the church, its vast landholdings, and the special privileges enjoyed by the clergy. In fact, Catholicism was the only religion allowed in Mexico. The *puros* also wanted to reduce the influence of the Mexican military on governmental affairs, including political appointments.

Puros clashed with *moderados* regarding affairs with the United States. *Moderados* favored an agreement, not war, with the United States regarding Texas. The more radical *puros* supported the war effort. *Puro* leader Valentín Gómez Farías, as vice-president to General Antonio López de Santa Anna, supported the war effort and tried to force 15 million pesos in funding from the Catholic Church in 1847. This radical, strong-arm tactic resulted in the *Polkos* Revolt, which removed Gómez Farías from power.

Many *puros* wanted to continue the war and opposed the Treaty of Guadalupe Hidalgo, which ended the Mexican-American War in 1848. The *moderado-puro* conflict continued to result in political turmoil well into the next decade.

See also Gómez Farías, Valentín; *Polkos* Revolt.

For further reading: Costeloe, "The Mexican Church and the Rebellion of the Polkos," 1966; Hale, *Mexican Liberalism in the Age of Mora, 1821–1853,* 1968; Ramirez, *Mexico during the War with the United States,* 1950; Santoni, *Mexicans at Arms,* 1996.

Q

Quartermaster Departments

The U.S. armies held a great advantage over the Mexican armies in that they were supplied by a relatively well funded government, a hardworking quartermaster department, and an unrestricted naval fleet that transported men, equipment, ammunition, and food.

Mexico

The Mexican government was nearly bankrupt at the beginning of the Mexican-American War and could not afford to adequately clothe and supply its fighting men. What little supply system it had was poorly organized, and staging areas were not maintained and supplied throughout the war. Equipment was typically carried by mules or oxen-drawn carts. The Mexican troops, especially its thousands of *soldaderas* (camp followers), often foraged in the countryside that they passed through. The Mexican army paid for food and supplies with unredeemable drafts, which made the citizens unwilling to part with their goods. The troops were frequently hungry and mutinous, and U.S. naval blockades quickly eliminated shipping food and equipment by water routes.

United States

The United States had the political stability and industrial capacity to equip, mobilize, and sustain its armies in the field. Its steamships, river systems, and railroads were capable of delivering supplies to staging areas, such as New Orleans.

The quartermaster general was Thomas S. Jesup, who was energetic and dedicated to the cause of supplying the U.S. army. The Subsistence Department bought food and stored it at depots such as San Antonio, Brazos Island, Camargo, Tampico, Santa Fe, and Monterey. The Ordnance Department supplied weapons and ammunition.

As many advantages as the U.S. army already held over its Mexican counterpart, Jesup wrote that the war "found us entirely unprepared in men, as well as in the means of equipment and movement." Jesup ordered huge requisitions for horses, mules, wagons, steamships, and other boats. Despite these efforts, the men in the field cursed the quartermaster department. In August 1846, Brigadier General John A. Quitman wrote that the "quarter-master's department is wretchedly managed. The medical department worse. There are here no horse-shoes or nails...and, though we have 6,000 men, there are no medicines...."

Bickering escalated between Jesup and field commanders. Contractors, recognizing the urgent demand, charged more money and often delivered shoddy goods. Equipment often arrived broken because of poor packaging and handling. Meat was often so spoiled that it would stick to the plank it was thrown against. There was no question that it was a ragtag-looking army in need of shoes, shirts, and pants. Inspector General Ethan Allen Hitchcock commented that the "army dress appears to be continually diverging from the prescribed patterns" and that it was often difficult to identify officers from their uniforms.

The Quartermaster Department had little reliable intelligence about the country, climate, conditions, and elevations to make decisions in Washington. When was the rainy season? When did yellow fever strike? Jesup received few answers from the many questionnaires he sent to commanders in the field.

A concern about being adequately supplied was one of the main reasons General Zachary Taylor did not want to strike out for Mexico City from Monterrey during 1846–1847. If he committed to that march, he would be doubling the length of his supply line, which would make it that much more vulnerable to guerrilla raids. "The task of beating the enemy is among the least difficult which we encounter," he wrote. "The great question of supplies necessarily controls all the operations in a country like this."

Despite the complaints from the field, there were many accomplishments. Among them were a line of communications via steamboats, arduous long marches that were well-enough supplied to be successful, and a well-executed amphibious landing of 10,000 men at Veracruz. The lack of supplies and support never hindered the army to the point of not being able to move or running out of ammunition; however, greater funding and a more efficient supply system would have increased the overall health of the army by having better food, clothing, shelter, and medicines.

See also Jesup, Thomas Sidney.

For further reading: DePalo, *The Mexican National Army, 1822–1852,* 1997; Ganoe, *The History of the United States Army,* 1964; Kieffer, *Maligned General,* 1979; McCaffrey, *Army of Manifest Destiny,* 1992; Winders, *Mr. Polk's Army,* 1997.

Quijano, Benito

(1800–1865)

Mexican General Benito Quijano helped negotiate the Armistice of Tacubaya in August 1847 and the Treaty of Guadalupe Hidalgo during 1847–1848.

Born in Mérida in the Yucatán, Quijano joined the Spanish army at the age of 12. He fought various uprisings, including that of Agustín de Iturbide in 1821. After Mexican independence was achieved, he was the assistant governor and military commander at Veracruz. He later served as the military commander in Tamaulipas.

Quijano was one of several Mexican generals who met with U.S. representatives to negotiate an armistice after the Battle of Churubusco in August 1847. The armistice was used by General Antonio López de Santa Anna to improve the defenses around Mexico City. Quijano was also involved in the 1847–1848 negotiations that resulted in the Treaty of Guadalupe Hidalgo.

After the war, Quijano was involved in several political coups. In 1863, he became the governor of the state of Yucatán. He helped found Club Mexicano in New York City and was a political envoy of Mexican revolutionary Benito Juárez. Quijano died in New York at the age of 65.

See also Tacubaya, Armistice of.

For further reading: Alcaraz, *The Other Side,* 1850; Carreño, *Jefes del ejército mexicano en 1847,* 1914; *Diccionario Porrúa,* 1995.

Quitman, John Anthony

(1799–1858)

Brigadier General John Anthony Quitman was one of the U.S. army's best volunteer generals and served creditably in Major General Winfield Scott's Veracruz–Mexico City campaign in 1847.

Quitman, who was born in New York, taught English at Mount Airy College in Pennsylvania. Later a lawyer, he settled in Mississippi and participated in state politics. He later was commander of the Mississippi militia.

During the Mexican-American War, he was commissioned a brigadier general of volunteers under General Zachary Taylor in northern Mexico. He led his brigade capably at the Battle of Monterrey in September 1846 and later occupied Victoria.

Transferred to Major General Winfield Scott for his Veracruz–Mexico City campaign, Quitman landed with the Army of Occupation at Veracruz in March 1847. He mobilized his troops overland to help the U.S. Navy occupy Alvarado. Polk commissioned Quitman a

John A. Quitman (Library of Congress)

major general in April. Quitman served as one of Scott's commissioners in negotiating the Armistice of Tacubaya following the Battle of Churubusco in August 1847. His division stormed the castle walls at Chapultepec on September 13 and later pursued the retreating

Mexicans along the Belén causeway to the Belén *garita* (gate) outside Mexico City, where his unit suffered severe casualties. Annoyed that Quitman had pressed the attack against such a formidable position, Scott nonetheless told Quitman's men that they had "gone through fire and come out steel."

Quitman's command was the first to enter Mexico City upon its surrender on September 14, 1847, and Scott appointed him governor of the city. Quitman worked closely with city officials on actions, including establishing military police, to curb the frequent murders on both sides during the occupation. He was also the first president of the Aztec Club in Mexico City.

A believer in owning all of Mexico, Quitman upon his return to Washington delivered to President James K. Polk a detailed plan for the permanent occupation of Mexico. Quitman later served as governor of Mississippi and cast an expansionist eye toward Cuba. He died at his home in Mississippi in 1858, three years after being elected to the U.S. Congress.

For further reading: Clairborne, *Life and Correspondence of John A. Quitman,* 1860; Frost, *The Mexican War and Its Warriors,* 1848; May, *John A. Quitman,* 1985.

R

Ramos

A small village near Monterrey, Ramos, Nuevo León, was the site of a grisly guerrilla attack on a wagon train. The attack led to widespread retaliatory violence by the Texas Rangers.

Located on the road between Camargo and Monterrey, the village of Ramos was frequently a support base for large bands of guerrillas operating in the area. As Taylor advanced toward Monterrey in September 1846, he sent Captain Ben McCulloch's Texas Rangers to scout ahead. On September 14, McCulloch's 35-man force encountered 200 Mexican cavalry in Ramos. The cavalry scattered in the face of an attack by McCulloch.

On February 22, 1847, approximately five miles from Ramos, a procession of 110 wagons, 300 pack mules, and 34 soldiers were attacked by a large cavalry/guerrilla force under the commands of General José Urrea and Antonio Canales. Approximately 50 of the teamsters were killed, and many of the supplies were seized. Some of the victims were reportedly tortured or mutilated. A number of the wagons were burned, and exploding ammunition killed several guerrillas.

Retaliation was quick. On March 28, a squadron of Texas Rangers rode into Rancho Guadalupe near Ramos and killed 24 civilians suspected of supporting the guerrillas. Ramos was later burned by Texas Rangers under Captain "Mustang" Gray. Josiah Gregg recalled that it was once "a beautiful little village of 500 souls or more...but now reduced to ashes, without a soul remaining." He went on to say that the "Mexicans on this route still speak [of Gray] with horror."

Another retaliatory hunt in April led a detachment of Texas Rangers under Major Michael Chavallie to Hacienda del Patos. According to Samuel Chamberlain, a drunken ranger tore down a large wooden crucifix from the church, dragged it behind his horse, and trampled the aged priest who resisted him. The outraged witnesses captured the ranger and nearly whipped him to death before his comrades "charged on the mass with bowie knife and revolver, sparing neither age or sex in their terrible fury." The flogged ranger begged to be shot, so the "Ranger Captain put a bullet through the brain of the wretch."

For further reading: Chamberlain, *My Confession,* 1956; Webb, *The Texas Rangers in the Mexican War,* 1975.

Rancho Dominguez, Skirmish at
(October 8, 1846)

A U.S. force of approximately 260 men, intent on seizing Los Angeles, were driven back by a 100-man Californio force under José Carrillo in October 1846.

Having received the news that the U.S. garrison under Archibald H. Gillespie at Los Angeles had surrendered in September 1846 to a force of Californio rebels, Commodore Robert F. Stockton ordered Captain William Mervine and the *Savannah* to sail to San Pedro.

Mervine arrived on October 6 and conferred with the exiled Gillespie and his men, still on board the *Vandalia* in San Pedro's harbor. Within 24 hours, Mervine's 225 men and Gillespie's small command were marching northward to retake Los Angeles. En route they skirmished with Californios at Rancho Palos Verdes and marched across flat plains of wild mustard that reached 8 feet in height. That night they camped at Rancho Dominguez in present-day North Long Beach. Skirmish fire continued throughout the night.

Mervine's force resumed the march at daylight on October 8. After one hour, they encountered approximately 100 mounted rebels with one artillery piece under the command of José Antonio Carrillo. Mervine formed his men in a square and charged, but suffered casualties from the Mexican cannon. After two more charges, he retreated. Four of his ten wounded died and were buried on an island in San Pedro Harbor, now known as Deadmen's Island (Isla de los Muertos).

For further reading: Bauer, *Surfboats and Horse Marines*, 1969.

Rancho El Pasa, Skirmish at

See San José del Pozo, Skirmish at.

Rangel, Joaquín
(1803–1874)

Mexican general Joaquín Rangel helped lead the Army of the East in the battles against Major General Winfield Scott's army during the Veracruz–Mexico City campaign of 1847.

Rangel, who was born in Mexico City to a prominent family, joined the Mexican Army at the age of 20. His support of General Antonio López de Santa Anna led to increasingly prominent military and political roles, including general and chief of artillery in 1844. Implicated in an unsuccessful coup in 1845 to overthrow President José Joaquín Herrera, Rangel was briefly imprisoned before the outbreak of the Mexican-American War.

Santa Anna ordered Rangel to take command of the remains of the Army of the East after the Battle of Cerro Gordo in April 1847. Rangel's troops fought well at the Battle of El Molino del Rey. Rangel was involved in organizing the defense of Mexico City, and he fought at Chapultepec and led troops during the fighting on September 13 at San Cosmé *garita* (gate), where he was gravely wounded.

Rangel remained a prominent military and political figure after the war. He served as a national congressman and became a brigadier general. He died in Cacahuatal de San Pablo at the age of 71.

For further reading: Alcaraz, *The Other Side*, 1850; Costeloe, *The Central Republic in Mexico, 1835–1846*, 1993; *Diccionario Porrúa*, 1995; Ramirez, *Mexico during the War with the United States*, 1950.

Rea, Joaquín
(ca. 1791–1850)

General Joaquín Rea commanded a guerrilla cavalry force of approximately 2,000 men in and around the state of Puebla. He clashed with elements of General Winfield Scott's Army of Occupation during 1847–1848.

Rea was born in Spain. He moved to Mexico as a young man and joined in the revolution for independence. He later became a successful businessman in Acapulco and joined with General Nicolás Bravo in several political coups.

During the Mexican-American War, Rea was a noted guerrilla commander. His mounted "irregular" cavalry operated in Puebla along the National Road and tormented elements of Scott's Army of Occupation as it approached Mexico City. Rea's men raided wagon trains and new regiments of volunteers marching inland from Veracruz. His 2,000 cavalrymen began a siege of the U.S. garrison at Puebla that lasted nearly a month before U.S. reinforcements arrived. Rea retreated to Atlixco, where he was attacked by troops under Brigadier General Joseph Lane. Rea launched a few other minor guerrilla operations before his force disintegrated, mostly from desertion, in early 1848.

Rea was killed at the age of 59 during a political uprising in Tecuanapa in the state of Guerrero.

For further reading: Brackett, *General Lane's Brigade in Central Mexico*, 1854; *Diccionario Porrúa*, 1995; Oswandel, *Notes of the Mexican War*, 1885.

Reily (Reilly, Riley, O'Reilly), John

An Irish immigrant and U.S. army deserter, John Reily formed the Saint Patrick (San Patricio) Battalion of the Mexican army. He fought courageously against U.S. forces until he was captured at the Battle of Churubusco in 1847.

Reily was born in County Galway, Ireland. He served in the British army in Canada and worked in Michigan from 1843 to 1845. He enlisted as a private in Company K, 5th U.S. Infantry, in September 1845. After General Zachary Taylor's Army of Occupation arrived at the Río Grande in the spring of 1846, he swam the river presumably to attend mass at Matamoros and never returned.

He soon joined the Mexican army as a lieutenant and quickly formed a company of 48 fellow Irish deserters into the Saint Patrick (San Patricio) Battalion, with its own distinctive shamrock flag. Reily recruited more than 150 men for the battalion.

The San Patricios became an important part of the Mexican army and one of its most reliable fighting units. They fought bravely under Reily's leadership at the Battles of Monterrey, La Angostura (Buena Vista), Cerro Gordo, and Churubusco. After La Angostura, Reily was awarded the Angostura Cross of Honor for valor and promoted to captain. He often circulated among U.S. prisoners to encourage them to join his battalion.

After fighting ferociously at the Battle of Churubusco in August 1847, Reily and 69 other San Patricios were captured by General Winfield Scott's troops. During his court-martial, Reily claimed that he was captured and forced to serve in the Mexican army, and he presented four character witnesses. Reily and 67 of his men were found guilty of desertion and sentenced to be hanged. Notable Mexicans, including the archbishop of Mexico, appealed to Scott to spare their lives, especially Reily's. Scott canceled Reily's death sentence because he had deserted before the U.S. Congress declared war against Mexico.

Reily was sentenced to 59 lashes, branding, and imprisonment. Most U.S. soldiers were dismayed by the light sentence, especially since Reily's artillerymen had inflicted severe U.S. losses. Captain George Davis witnessed the lashing and wrote that "why those thus punished did not die under such punishment was a marvel to me. Their backs had the appearance of a pounded piece of raw beef." Two two-inch "D" (deserter) brands were burned into Reily's cheeks.

Reily was released on September 5, 1848. He rejoined the Mexican infantry and was stationed at Veracruz. Reily remained with the army until the summer of 1850, when he was honorably discharged. Most accounts indicate that he returned to Ireland.

After the war, he wrote, "I have had the honour of fighting in all the battles that Mexico has had with the United States and by my good conduct and hard fighting, I have attained the rank of Major.... A more hospitable or friendly people than the better or upper class of Mexicans there exists not on the face of the earth."

See also Desertion; San Patricio Battalion.

For further reading: Baker, "The St. Patricks Fought for Their Skins, and Mexico," 1978; Downey, "Tragic Story of the San Patricio Battalion," 1955; Krueger, *Saint Patrick's Battalion*, 1960; Miller, *Shamrock and Sword*, 1989; Wallace, "The Battalion of Saint Patrick in the Mexican War," 1950; Wynn, *The San Patricio Soldiers*, 1984.

Rejón, Manuel Crecencio
(1799–1849)

An influential politician, Manuel Crecencio Rejón helped General Antonio López de Santa Anna regain the presidency in 1846 and served as his minister of foreign affairs. Rejón vigorously opposed the Treaty of Guadalupe Hidalgo.

Rejón who was born in the Yucatán to a prominent family, earned a degree in philosophy at the age of 19. An ardent *puro*, he quickly became active in politics, joined the Mexican Congress, and helped draft Mexico's 1824 constitution. He voiced opposition to the expansionist policies of the United States. As a *puro*, Rejón favored more political independence for the Mexican states and was a major figure in the civil unrest in the Yucatán Peninsula.

Rejón served as minister of foreign relations in 1844 under Santa Anna before the administration collapsed and they were exiled to Cuba. In Cuba, with the help of Santa Anna and Valentín Gómez Farías, Rejón plotted Santa Anna's return to the presidency in 1846. Rejón became a top advisor to Santa Anna and Gómez Farías and served also as minister of foreign relations.

Despite the tremendous destruction and loss of life during the Mexican-American War, Rejón condemned the Treaty of Guadalupe Hidalgo and wanted to continue to fight. Recognizing the advantage the United States had in controlling both oceans during the war, Rejón lobbied for a stronger Mexican navy. He died in Mexico City at the age of 50.

For further reading: Diccionario Porrúa, 1995; Ramirez, *Mexico during the War with the United States*, 1950; Robinson, *The View from Chapultepec*, 1989; Santoni, *Mexicans at Arms*, 1996.

Reno, Jesse L.

(1823–1862)

Lieutenant Jesse L. Reno commanded the experimental Howitzer and Rocket Company during Scott's Veracruz–Mexico City campaign in 1847. Reno's lightweight howitzers were used effectively during the Battles of Cerro Gordo, Contreras, and Churubusco.

Born in Virginia and raised in Pennsylvania, Reno graduated from the U.S. Military Academy as a second lieutenant of ordnance in 1846. He joined Major General Winfield Scott's Army of Occupation that landed at Veracruz in 1847.

Although he was part of the ordnance department, Reno served with the artillery. He commanded the Howitzer and Rocket Company, an experimental unit that used mountain pack howitzers and fired Hale's rockets. He fought in all the engagements along the National Road that culminated in the fall of Mexico City in September 1847. Reno was brevetted to first lieutenant for gallant and meritorious service during the Battle of Cerro Gordo and later to captain for his actions at the Battle of Chapultepec.

After the war, Reno taught mathematics at the U.S. Military Academy and was the chief ordnance officer for Albert Sidney Johnston's Utah campaign. Reno was commissioned a Union brigadier general of volunteers in the Civil War in 1861. He was killed leading his men during the Battle of South Mountain in 1862. Reno, Nevada, is named in his honor.

See also Rockets.

For further reading: Cullum, *Biographical Register of the Officers and Graduates of the United States Military Academy from 1802 to 1867*, 1879; Dillon, *American Artillery in the Mexican War 1846–1847*, 1975.

Repatriation

At the end of the Mexican-American War, the Mexican government assisted its citizens who wished to move from the lands turned over to the United States to the remaining half of Mexico, or to repatriate.

Although a number of repatriation agents were ordered to California, New Mexico, and Texas in 1848, only New Mexico was visited. Father Ramón Ortiz arrived in April 1849 and traveled through most of the villages and communities in New Mexico. He offered land and agricultural equipment to any New Mexicans who were willing to relocate. The U.S. occupational government, worried that Ortiz might incite a rebellion, ordered him to conduct his activities from Santa Fe, where his program could be monitored more closely. Mexico complained to the United States that this unfairly blocked its efforts to repatriate its citizens. Another effort at repatriation was made after the Gadsden Treaty was signed in 1853.

For further reading: Meier and Rivera, *Dictionary of Mexican American History*, 1981.

Resaca de la Palma, Battle of

(May 9, 1846)

Fought on May 9, 1846, the Battle of Resaca de la Palma was a definitive victory for General Zachary Taylor and wrecked the Army of the North under General Mariano Arista.

On May 8, 1846, in the first battle of the Mexican-American War, General Taylor's Army of Occupation defeated General Arista's Army of the North at Palo Alto. At dawn on May 9, the Mexican army retreated southward toward the Río Grande. Amid a dense tangle of chaparral and trees in the hills and swampy ravines *(resacas)*, Arista chose a defensive position at Resaca de la Guerrero. (U.S. troops called it Resaca de la Palma.) Arista positioned his men at a 10-foot-deep, 200-foot-wide ravine that bristled with chaparral and thorny scrub.

Arista's ammunition supply was low from the previous day's battle. The morale of his men was also low, and infantry gossip accused Arista of being a traitor who would sacrifice his army for economic or political gain in the United States. Believing that Taylor would not attack his position, Arista ordered the army to unload the wagons, unhitch the mules, and establish camp. Once his tent was erected, he began to write reports and letters.

Most of Arista's men were in the ravine to take advantage of its cover and to minimize the deadly effects of the U.S. artillery. His line was centered on the road that passed through the ravine. The cavalry was held in reserve in the rear, the artillery was positioned behind the ravine, and skirmishers hid in the chaparral.

As Taylor's men ate breakfast, Taylor called a council of war with his senior officers. Although seven of ten recommended no action, Taylor decided to cautiously advance. Leaving his wagons behind in an entrenched position and protected by artillery, U.S. soldiers moved out about noon down the hot, dusty road. Skirmish fire soon erupted as they reached the Mexican position.

As more U.S. soldiers arrived on the battlefield, the U.S. troops drew Mexican fire to expose the location of Mexican artillery batteries. The 5th and part of the 4th U.S. Infantry entered the thorny chaparral to the left of the road; the rest of the 4th and the 3rd U.S. Infantry plunged in on the right. As the firing between the hidden skirmishers began to increase, Arista remained in his tent.

The chaparral was nearly impenetrable, and the order of the U.S. regiments quickly broke down as they fought their way through the chaparral toward Resaca de la Guerrero. The U.S. troops eventually pushed the Mexican skirmishers back to the *resaca*, but could not advance further because of the shelling from the Mexican battery. Hand-to-hand fighting broke out as U.S. soldiers approached the edge of the ravine. Taylor ordered Brevet Major Charles May's squadron of 2nd Dragoons to charge the battery. Although they succeeded in taking the position with heavy losses, no infantry support followed, and the dragoons retreated with prisoners, including General Rómulo Díaz de la Vega.

Incensed that May could not hold the position, Taylor sent the 5th and 8th U.S. Infantry through heavy fire across the ravine to seize the artillery. This successful attack drove back the Mexican right flank, which began to crumble. About this time, Captain Robert C. Buchanan and part of the 4th U.S. Infantry found a trail through the chaparral that flanked the Mexican left; the 4th Infantry's sudden fire caused the left to break, and soon the Mexican army was in full retreat. Arista, suddenly realizing that the skirmishing had turned into a full-fledged battle, led a cavalry charge to the front, but could not reverse his fleeing troops. The panicked soldiers trampled each other and threw themselves into the Río Grande. Many were shot or drowned. After the battle, General Díaz de la Vega admitted "If I had had with me yesterday $100,000 in silver, I would have bet the whole of it that no 10,000 men on earth could drive us from our position."

Taylor pursued the Mexicans with dragoons, some infantry, and an artillery battery. A number of Mexican stragglers were captured, and the U.S. army camped that night on the north bank of the Río Grande. The artillery at Fort Texas shelled the Mexican survivors as they streamed into Matamoros. The U.S. army captured an impressive amount of artillery, ammunition, small arms, mules, horses, oxen, and carts from Arista's army.

On May 11, the two armies exchanged prisoners and the wounded. The Mexican army left Matamoros on May 17, destroying the supplies it couldn't carry, and Taylor occupied the city the following day. At Rancho de la Venada, Arista had left 400 wounded soldiers who had received no medical care. Afraid that they would be killed or tortured by the "norteamericanos," some crawled out of the hospitals to follow the army.

Taylor's casualties were approximately 121 killed and wounded; Mexican numbers vary, but are close to 700 killed, wounded, or missing.

Construction in 1967 unearthed near the battlefield a number of mass burial sites of Mexican soldiers. The skeletal remains show evidence of battle injuries such as bullet wounds and cuts from sabers or bayonets. Female remains, most likely of wives and camp followers who were killed in the fighting, were also in the mass graves.

See also Palo Alto, Battle of.

For further reading: Alcaraz, *The Other Side,* 1850; Grant, *Personal Memoirs of U. S. Grant,* 1885; Haecker, *A Thunder of Cannon,* 1994; Henry, *Campaign Sketches of the War with Mexico,* 1847; Taylor, *Letters of Zachary Taylor from the Battlefields of the Mexican War,* 1908.

Rey, Antony
(d. 1847)

Antony Rey was one of two Catholic priests assigned to Zachary Taylor's Army of Occupation along the Río Grande during 1846–1847. President James K. Polk wanted Catholic priests in the army to show the Mexican populace that the United States was not anti-Catholic.

A Catholic priest in Georgetown, Virginia, Rey met with President Polk in 1846 and agreed to join General Taylor's army in northern Mexico. Polk's objective was to show the Mexican populace that the U.S. government was not fighting a war against Catholicism. In the company of fellow priest John McElroy, also of Georgetown College, Rey arrived in Matamoros in the summer of 1846. After tending to the spiritual needs of the U.S. soldiers in Matamoros, especially the sick and wounded, and visiting with Mexican clergy and citizens, Rey traveled with the army to Camargo. He was troubled that soldiers were dying so quickly from disease that they were not "receiving the last Sacraments." Rey was murdered by Mexican guerrillas in January 1847 as he traveled back to Matamoros.

See also Hughes, John Joseph; McElroy, John.

For further reading: Honeywell, *Chaplains of the United States Army,* 1958; McElroy, "Chaplains for the Mexican War—1846," 1887; Wynne, "Memoir of the Rev. Antony Rey, S.J.," 1847.

Reynolds, John Fulton
(1820–1863)

A talented artillery officer, John Fulton Reynolds was brevetted twice for gallantry in General Zachary Taylor's 1846–1847 campaign in northern Mexico.

Reynolds, who was born in Pennsylvania, graduated twenty-sixth of 52 from the U.S. Military Academy in 1841. Appointed a second lieutenant in the 3rd U.S. Artillery, he saw service in South Carolina and Florida.

As part of General Zachary Taylor's Army of Occupation along the Río Grande in 1846, Reynolds was assigned to help defend Fort Texas, which was later held under siege by Mexican forces under General Pedro de Ampudia. In 1847, Reynolds was promoted to first lieutenant. He received a brevet to captain for his leadership in the bitter street fighting during the Battle of Monterrey. At the Battle of Buena Vista, his courage and artillery skills, for which he won a brevet to major, helped repel the Mexican attack on the U.S. rear.

Most of Reynolds's postwar years were spent on the western frontier. At the start of the Civil War, he was the commandant of the U.S. Military Academy. A major general in the Civil War, he was killed by a sharpshooter's bullet at Gettysburg.

For further reading: Cullum, *Biographical Register of the Officers and Graduates of the United States Military Academy from 1802 to 1867,* 1879; Dillon, *American Artillery in the Mexican War 1846–1847,* 1975; Lavender, *Climax at Buena Vista,* 1966; Nichols, *Toward Gettysburg,* 1988.

Reynosa

A small community in Nuevo León, Reynosa was the headquarters for a scouting party of Texas Rangers during June–July 1846. The rangers committed various outrages against the citizens during their two-week stay.

As General Zachary Taylor began to advance his army from Matamoros toward Monterrey in the summer of 1846, he relied on his companies of Texas Rangers for vital scouting information. Captain Ben McCulloch and 40 rangers moved out on the afternoon of June 12, 1846, to find the location of the Mexican army and the best route to take for wagons, artillery, and foraging.

Avoiding the main roads, McCulloch went cross-country and skirmished regularly with guerrilla units, including men led by the notorious Rámon Falcón. The rangers marched night and day, slept in downpours, and suffered greatly from the heat and lack of water. McCulloch seized the Monterrey mail and took letters of military interest. The squadron spent two days tracking McCulloch's old border nemesis Antonio Canales, the "Chaparral Fox," with no success. McCulloch reported to Taylor that the Mexican army had left Linares for Monterrey and that the road to Linares was inadequate for artillery.

Arriving in Reynosa on June 23, the rangers camped there until July 9. McCulloch's men were relatively idle, which led to a high incidence of depredations against the community. The "outrages committed by the Texas volunteers on the Mexicans & others," wrote Taylor on June 30, "I have not the power to remedy it, or apply the corrective, I fear they are a lawless set."

For further reading: Webb, *The Texas Rangers in the Mexican War,* 1975.

Richey, John A.
(1825–1847)

A messenger who carried top-secret orders to General Zachary Taylor from General Winfield Scott, John A. Richey was murdered en route by guerrillas who delivered the orders to General Antonio López de Santa Anna.

General Scott, having been ordered by President James K. Polk to take approximately half of General Taylor's men from northern Mexico and attack Veracruz, traveled up the Río Grande to deliver the news to Taylor in January 1847. When he arrived at Camargo, he found that Taylor had advanced to occupy the town of Victoria. On January 3, Scott explained the invasion plan in detail in a top-secret dispatch addressed to Taylor.

The dispatch was forwarded to Monterrey, where it was opened and read aloud by Brigadier General Thomas Marshall. The dispatch was then resealed and given to Lieutenant John A. Richey to deliver to Taylor at Victoria. Protected by a guard of only ten dragoons, Richey was lassoed by guerrillas on January 13 and dragged to death through the chaparral near the town of Villa Gran. Recognizing the importance of Scott's letter, the guerrillas delivered it to General Santa Anna. It is probable that Santa Anna, then aware of Taylor's reduced strength, planned to rush north and defeat him with an overwhelming force near Saltillo (Buena Vista) and then turn and strike Scott with his victorious army.

See also Marshall, Thomas.

For further reading: Webb, *The Texas Rangers in the Mexican War,* 1975.

Ridgely, Randolph
(1814–1846)

An artillery officer with General Zachary Taylor's army in northern Mexico, Randolph Ridgely skillfully commanded his guns in the Battles of Palo Alto, Resaca de la Palma, and Monterrey before he died in an accident in October 1846.

Ridgely was born in Maryland. He graduated from the U.S. Military Academy in 1837 and joined the Flying Artillery under Major Samuel Ringgold.

During the Mexican-American War, the 3rd U.S. Artillery was part of General Taylor's Army of Occupation in 1846. Commanded by Ridgely, these guns guarded the U.S. army's right flank during the Battle of Palo Alto on May 8 and defeated a Mexican cavalry attack. Taylor wrote that Ridgely deserved "special notice for the gallant and efficient manner in which [he] maneuvered and served [his] battery." After the death of Ringgold from wounds received during that battle, Ridgely led Ringgold's artillery company during the Battle of Resaca de la Palma the following day. Ridgely declined a brevet promotion in favor of a staff appointment. He later commanded his artillery from exposed positions during the street fighting in Monterrey in September and helped shell the Mexican headquarters in the central plaza.

While on a pleasure ride in the city in October, his horse stumbled, throwing Ridgely onto the stone street. Ridgely went into a coma and died without regaining consciousness. A popular officer, "his funeral at Monterrey was attended by all the officers of the army, and in solemn and dignified pomp as well as in size, has rarely been equalled."

For further reading: Cullum, *Biographical Register of*

the Officers and Graduates of the United States Military Academy from 1802 to 1867, 1879; Dillon, *American Artillery in the Mexican War 1846–1847,* 1975; Frost, *The Mexican War and Its Warriors,* 1848; Heitman, *Historical Register and Dictionary of the United States Army,* 1903.

Riley, Bennet
(1787–1853)

The commander of the 2nd U.S. Infantry during General Winfield Scott's Veracruz–Mexico City campaign in 1847, Bennet Riley was brevetted to brigadier general for his capable leadership at Cerro Gordo, Churubusco, and Chapultepec.

Riley, who was born in Maryland, joined the U.S. Army during the War of 1812. Subsequently he spent much of his time on the western frontier and protected trading caravans along the Santa Fe Trail. He was brevetted to colonel for his actions during the Second Seminole War in Florida.

During the Mexican-American War, Riley was part of Major General Scott's Veracruz–Mexico City campaign in 1847 and was brevetted after the Battle of Cerro Gordo. Selected to lead an assault on the Mexican flank at the Battle of Contreras, Riley's force overran the Mexican position. By December 1847, Riley had been brevetted to brigadier general and contributed to the military operations in Mexico City.

Following the war, Riley held military appointments in Louisiana, Missouri, and California, where he helped draft the first constitution and lobbied for admission to the Union. Suffering from cancer, he died in Buffalo, New York, at the age of 66.

For further reading: Cullum, *Biographical Register of the Officers and Graduates of the United States Military Academy from 1802 to 1867,* 1879; Frost, *The Mexican War and Its Warriors,* 1848.

Rincón, Manuel E.
(1784–1849)

As the second in command of Mexico's Army of the East, General Manuel E. Rincón led troops against Major General Winfield Scott's invading U.S. army in 1847. Rincón fought well at Churubusco and helped organize the defense of Mexico City.

Rincón was born in Perote, Veracruz. He joined forces with Agustín de Iturbide to help gain independence from Spain in 1821. He became an officer in the Mexican army and attained the rank of division general by 1837. He also served as governor of Veracruz. His troops suppressed various rebellions and helped fight an invasion by the French in 1838.

Rincón was named second in command of the Army of the East in 1847 by General Antonio López de Santa Anna. Although in poor health, Rincón fought against General Scott and the Army of Occupation during Scott's Veracruz–Mexico City campaign in 1847. The Rincón-led troops at the convent at Churubusco delivered some of the fiercest resistance that U.S. troops faced during the war. Rincón was also involved in the peace negotiations that resulted in the Treaty of Guadalupe Hidalgo in 1848.

After the war, Rincón lived in Mexico City and published poetry. He died in 1849 at the age of 65.

For further reading: Alcaraz, *The Other Side,* 1850; Carreño, *Jefes del ejército mexicano en 1847,* 1914; DePalo, *The Mexican National Army, 1822–1852,* 1997; *Diccionario Porrúa,* 1995; Roa Bárcena, *Recuerdos de la invasión norte-americana,* 1947.

Ringgold, Samuel
(1800–1846)

U.S. Major Samuel Ringgold helped develop the Flying Artillery. His well-trained 3rd U.S. Artillery was instrumental in winning the Battle of Palo Alto, the opening battle of the soon-to-be-declared war.

Ringgold was born in Washington, D.C. In 1818, he graduated from the U.S. Military Academy as a second lieutenant. He was promoted to major in 1838 for his service in the Second Seminole War.

Attached to Brigadier General Zachary Taylor's Army of Occupation along the Río Grande in 1846, Ringgold's 3rd U.S. Artillery operated the Flying Artillery—lightweight, mobile field pieces that could be moved easily during battle. The Flying Artillery had never been tested in combat.

The Battle of Palo Alto on May 8, 1846, was

Major Samuel Ringgold is mortally wounded during the Battle of Palo Alto, May 8, 1846. (Library of Congress)

essentially an artillery duel: Ringgold's lightweight guns and skilled artillerymen fired eight shells for every Mexican cannonball and inflicted heavy casualties in the Mexican ranks. While leading his battery from a forward position, Ringgold was hit by a cannonball that "struck the middle of his right thigh, passed through it, and through the shoulders of his horse, and came out through the left thigh," wrote John Frost. Ringgold lingered for two days before dying on May 10.

See also Flying Artillery.

For further reading: Cullum, *Biographical Register of the Officers and Graduates of the United States Military Academy from 1802 to 1867*, 1879; Dillon, *American Artillery in the Mexican War 1846–1847*, 1975; Frost, *The Mexican War and Its Warriors*, 1848.

Río Calaboso, Skirmish at
(July 12, 1847)

Mexican troops attacked a U.S. column from Tampico at Río Calaboso, killed or wounded more than 10 percent of the force, and compelled it to return to Tampico.

Following the occupation of Tampico, a 126-man force under Colonel L. G. De Russey was ordered to Huejutla to free U.S. prisoners who had been captured at La Encarnación in January 1847. The command left Tampico on July 8. On July 12, De Russey encountered a strong force of Mexican troops and was forced back to the town of Tantuyac after heavy skirmishing. Having run out of ammunition for his light artillery piece, he found gunpowder and lead balls in the town. Champagne bottles were packed with powder and balls to be used as shells, and sand was used for packing. Returning to Tampico through several ambushes and under constant sniper fire, De Russey lost 19 men killed or wounded.

For further reading: Scott, *Encarnación Prisoners, Comprising an Account of the March of the Kentucky Cavalry from Louisville to the Río Grande*, 1848.

Río Colorado

Two U.S. trappers were killed by an angry mob at the village of Río Colorado during the Taos Rebellion in January 1847.

The killing of New Mexico military governor Charles Bent and other U.S. settlers in early January 1847 was the beginning of the Taos Rebellion. Acts of violence quickly spread to outlying communities. At Río Colorado, a small Mexican settlement near Taos, U.S. trappers Mark Head and William Harwood had just ridden into town when news of the rebellion arrived. Caught in an angry crowd, the men were robbed of their belongings and shot in the back. The bodies were later scalped, stripped, and mutilated. This is one of the incidents that led Colonel Sterling Price to retaliate against the rebel force in January and February 1847.

See also Taos Rebellion.

For further reading: McNierney, *Taos 1847,* 1980.

Río Grande

Known to Mexicans as the Río del Norte, the Río Grande was not an important boundary until the Texas Revolution in 1836 and later during the Mexican-American War.

The Río Grande, from its headwaters in the northwestern part of the Mexican province of New Mexico, wound southward into Chihuahua and then turned southeastward toward the Gulf of Mexico. The river served as a partial border between the provinces of Coahuila and Texas before it flowed through Tamaulipas. The northern border of Tamaulipas, below Texas, was the Nueces River.

After Texas won its independence from Mexico in 1836, Texas maintained that its southern border was the Río Grande, not the Nueces River. According to Mexico, the Texan insistence that the Río Grande was its southern border was unlawful, because the river enclosed the northern third of Tamaulipas. This disputed area became the source of great agitation between Mexico and the Republic of Texas, and the disagreement eventually led to the escalation of border violence.

The United States also recognized the Río Grande as the southern border of Texas when it was annexed in 1845, which further alienated Mexico. Mexico viewed General Zachary Taylor's march from Corpus Christi (at the mouth of the Nueces River) to the northern bank of the Río Grande as an act of hostile aggression across what was rightfully Mexican territory. The United States, however, insisted that the land between the Nueces River and Río Grande was now part of the United States. As the two armies gathered along the banks of the Río Grande near Matamoros, a skirmish at Carricitos Ranch north of the river resulted in U.S. casualties. Shortly afterward, President James K. Polk announced that Mexico had killed U.S. citizens on U.S. soil, and Congress quickly declared war in May 1846.

The Treaty of Guadalupe Hidalgo, signed in 1848, officially declared the boundary between the United States and Mexico as being the Río Grande from the Gulf of Mexico to El Paso del Norte (present-day Juárez, Mexico), before it turned west toward the Gila River.

For further reading: Bancroft, *History of the North Mexican States and Texas,* 1884–1889; Griswold del Castillo, *The Treaty of Guadalupe Hidalgo,* 1991; Pletcher, *The Diplomacy of Annexation,* 1973.

Río Sacramento, Battle of

(February 28, 1847)

Fought between Colonel Alexander Doniphan's command and a 2,500-man Chihuahuan force led by General José Antonio de Heredia, the Battle of Río Sacramento was a resounding U.S. victory that resulted in the occupation of Chihuahua.

Brigadier General Stephen W. Kearny, after occupying New Mexico in August 1846, sent Colonel Alexander W. Doniphan and approximately 1,000 men southward to occupy Chihuahua. After winning the brief battle of El Brazito in December 1846, Doniphan occupied El Paso del Norte.

After their loss at El Brazito, the small Chihuahuan force, led by General José A. Heredia, General Pedro García Condé, and Governor Ángel Trías Álvarez, chose to confront Doniphan's 1st Regiment of Missouri Mounted Volunteers at the hacienda Río Sacramento, about 15 miles from Chihuahua, and on the main road. The road passed through a narrow opening in the surrounding hills, and it was here that the Mexicans built a series of fortifications. The Mexican force totalled approximately 2,500 men, including 119 artillerymen with ten cannons. Most of the troops were national guardsmen or local militia. Heredia believed that his left flank was protected by a deep arroyo that the U.S. force would not be able to cross. Heredia was confident that the main attack would be confined to the main road.

The Mexicans were relatively well armed and had been trained for the past two months. Heredia posted his men in front of their defenses. When Doniphan approached about 1:30 P.M., he promptly sent much of his army across the nearly vertically walled, 50-foot-deep arroyo to attack the Mexican left flank. The enterprising soldiers quickly built a dirt ramp to help them cross the arroyo and then struck the Mexican flank. The U.S. artillery scared the Mexicans and opened gaps in their ranks, and the Mexicans quickly fell back to their entrenchments. Orders became confused. A brave infantry charge, led by national guard officer Pedro Horcacitas, was quickly turned back with heavy losses. Hand-to-hand fighting also erupted during a series of short, poorly supported counterattacks launched by both sides.

By sundown, the Mexican forces were in full retreat, leaving their dead and wounded behind, along with their arms and artillery. Doniphan lost 12 men killed or wounded; Mexican losses were approximately 169 killed, 300 wounded, and 79 taken prisoner.

The U.S. army marched victoriously into Chihuahua on March 2, 1847, with the army band playing "Yankee Doodle."

See also Doniphan's March; García Condé, Pedro; Heredia, José Antonio de; Trías Álvarez, Ángel.

For further reading: Alcaraz, *The Other Side*, 1850; Connelley, *Doniphan's Expedition and the Conquest of New Mexico and California*, 1907; Hughes, *Doniphan's Expedition, Containing an Account of the Conquest of New Mexico*, 1973.

Roberts, William
(d. 1847)

An assistant surgeon with the U.S. 5th Infantry, William Roberts ran forward to lead a company into battle at El Molino del Rey in 1847 and was mortally wounded.

Little is known about the early life of Roberts. As an assistant surgeon with the U.S. 5th Infantry, he established his medical position in a slight hollow in the rear of his regiment during the Battle of El Molino del Rey on September 8, 1847. During the advance, Second Lieutenant C. S. Hamilton, commander of Company I, U.S. 5th Infantry, fell with a severe wound. According to Colonel J. Lugenbeel,

> Surgeon Roberts ran to him from the rear, and, after examining his wounds, started forward to the line of battle. I called to him to go back, but he pointed to Hamilton's company and ran on. When next I saw him he was lying on the field with the wound in his forehead, which afterwards caused his death. Lieutenant Hamilton informed me that Surgeon Roberts sent him to the rear and then went forward to take command of his company, as it was without an officer. At Churubusco he had attempted the same thing, but I was near enough to see him and sent him to the rear.

Roberts was taken to a field hospital at the Bishop's Palace. After lingering for over a month, he died on October 13, 1847.

For further reading: Ashburn, *A History of the Medical Department of the United States Army*, 1911; Duncan, "Medical History of General Scott's Campaign to the City of Mexico in 1847," 1920.

Robidoux, Antoine
(1794–1860)

Frontiersman and trader Antoine Robidoux served as General Stephen W. Kearny's guide and interpreter during his march to New Mexico and California in 1846.

Robidoux, who was born in Mississippi, followed the fur trade to St. Louis and later moved to Santa Fe in 1823. After spending 20 years in the western mountains, he returned to Missouri in 1844.

Recruited as a guide and interpreter, Robidoux accompanied Brigadier General Kearny's Army of the West from Fort Leavenworth, Kansas, to Santa Fe, New Mexico, in 1846. Well liked by the New Mexicans,

Robidoux stood at Kearny's side and translated into Spanish Kearny's speeches to the New Mexicans who gathered to listen at communities such as Las Vegas and Santa Fe. Robidoux also translated the rules of the new occupational government that were drafted shortly after the army occupied Santa Fe in August.

Robidoux left with Kearny from Santa Fe in September for California with a small force of dragoons. Robidoux received a painful lance wound during the Battle of San Pascual in December 1846.

See also San Pascual, Battle of.

For further reading: Cooke, *The Conquest of New Mexico and California,* 1878; Coy, *The Battle of San Pasqual,* 1921; Hughes, *Doniphan's Expedition, Containing an Account of the Conquest of New Mexico,* 1973; Wallace, *Antoine Robidoux, 1794–1860,* 1953.

Rockets

In addition to the British Congreve rocket, rockets invented by U.S. rocketeer William Hale were occasionally used by ordnance personnel during the Mexican-American War. Rockets were fired at the Battles of Veracruz, Cerro Gordo, and Contreras during General Winfield Scott's Veracruz–Mexico City campaign in 1847.

Because they were infrequently used, rockets were not a significant part of the artillery's role in the war. Used by the Howitzer and Rocket Company, the rocket's range was approximately 2,200 yards. Mexican soldiers found them frightening. Overseen in the field by Major George Henry Talcott and Captain Jesse Reno, the rockets had both solid and explosive heads. An inadequate guidance system made the rockets fairly inaccurate, although they did prove effective in close-up work, such as attacking buildings and gates.

See also Reno, Jesse L.

For further reading: Dillon, *American Artillery in the Mexican War 1846–1847,* 1975.

Rogers, R. Clay

While stationed on the USS *Somers* off the port city of Veracruz in December 1846, past midshipman R. Clay Rogers and several others landed on the beach at night to try to locate and destroy a reported powder magazine.

Surprised by a Mexican patrol, Rogers was captured and imprisoned at Veracruz and later moved to Perote Castle. As Major General Winfield Scott's army advanced down the National Road from Cerro Gordo in April, Rogers was taken to Mexico City. Mexican authorities claimed that he had been captured in disguise and was therefore a spy; the U.S. navy insisted that he had been captured in full uniform. President James K. Polk promised to retaliate if Rogers was punished as a spy. Although Rogers was not tried as a spy, the Mexican authorities refused to parole him.

As ordered by President Polk, Commodore Robert F. Perry selected Lieutenant Raphael Semmes to go to Mexico City and investigate the case of Rogers. Scott had also told Mexican soldiers he paroled that, if Rogers was harmed, Scott would equally harm a Mexican officer. As it turned out, Rogers was comfortably on parole in the city of Mexico, as an honorable prisoner of war.

For further reading: Bauer, *Surfboats and Horse Marines,* 1969; Semmes, *Service Afloat and Ashore during the Mexican War,* 1851.

S

Saint Joseph's Island

Located off the Texas coast in Aransas Bay, St. Joseph's Island is about 21 miles long and 5 miles wide. Its white sand beaches and rolling sand dunes greeted Zachary Taylor's soldiers when they first arrived at Corpus Christi. The infantry was delighted to land on the island after three weeks of sailing from New Orleans. Dangerous shoals and flats in the bay forced Taylor to first land his Army of Occupation on the island in July 1845. The men were then ferried across to Corpus Christi. The island was a stepping stone for five days until all of Taylor's troops were across.

For further reading: Webb, *The Handbook of Texas*, 1952.

Salas, José Mariano
(1797–1867)

A competent general and short-term provisional president, José Mariano Salas helped bring Antonio López de Santa Anna back to power in 1846 and later commanded troops in the Army of the East.

Salas, who was born in Mexico City, joined the Spanish army at the age of 16. He later aligned himself with the revolutionary forces of Agustín de Iturbide in 1821. Salas gained higher military positions and led troops during the Battle of the Alamo in 1836.

A loyal disciple of Santa Anna, Salas was commander in chief of the Mexican army in 1844, until Santa Anna was deposed and exiled. Salas continued to be an influential leader during the political turmoil between 1844 and 1846. After supporting the coup that toppled José Joaquín Herrera and installed Mariano Paredes y Arrillaga as president, Salas later worked to overthrow Paredes and bring Santa Anna back from exile.

As the top-ranking officer in Mexico City, Salas and Valentín Gómez Farías ran the government after Paredes was removed in August 1846. Salas brought back the 1824 constitution and acted as provisional president until December, when Santa Anna resumed office.

Eager to contribute to the war effort, Salas called for the formation of "Guerrillas of Vengence" to harass Major General Winfield Scott's Army of Occupation as it moved from Veracruz toward Mexico City in 1847. Salas was second in command at the Battle of Padierna (Contreras) and tried to rally the defeated soldiers as they streamed northward toward Churubusco, but he was captured.

After the war, Salas resumed military responsibilities, and was appointed president of the war tribunal. He plotted with the French to invade Mexico and was an advisor to Emperor Maximilian. Salas died in the village of Guadalupe at the age of 70.

For further reading: *Diccionario Porrúa*, 1995; Ramirez, *Mexico during the War with the United States*, 1950.

Saltillo

An important city in Coahuila, Saltillo was occupied by General Zachary Taylor's army

A mounted U.S. soldier in front of a church in Saltillo, pictured in one of the few photographs from the Mexican War (Beinecke Rare Book and Manuscript Library, Yale University)

during Taylor's campaign in northern Mexico and served as an important supply base in 1847.

Saltillo was founded in 1586. It was the capital of the joint state Coahuila y Texas during 1824–1833, before the seat of government was moved to Monclova. The city of 14,000 residents was occupied by General Zachary Taylor's Army of Occupation from November 1846 to July 1848.

U.S. officer W. S. Henry wrote,

> ...this is a larger town than Monterrey, containing 14,000 inhabitants, but is not so well built. The building material is clay formed into square blocks and hardened in the sun. The Cathedral is a gorgeous affair, the altarpiece is more than thirty feet in height by twenty-five in breadth, and is composed of pillars, wreaths, mouldings, etc., heavily gilded.... Cock fighting is quite the rage.... I rode into a cock pit, and you may imagine my astonishment when I beheld the old priest presiding, receiving the bets, and heeling the chickens, as putting on the iron spurs or slashers is technically called....

A place of commerce, Saltillo was well known for its cotton factory, mills, fruit orchards, and agricultural fields. The adobe houses, often two stories high, were painted white, and fountains and gardens graced the city's plazas and well-paved streets. The Mexican citizens were generally friendly to the U.S. forces, although U.S. soldiers were occasionally murdered in the city, and guerrillas prowled the surrounding countryside. Some U.S. soldiers married Saltillo women.

Saltillo remained an important U.S. military base for the duration of the Mexican War. Both Mexican and U.S. wounded were treated after the Battle of Buena Vista in February 1847 in Santiago Cathedral, which still stands today.

For further reading: Bancroft, *History of the North Mexican States and Texas,* 1884–1889; Cuéllar Valdés, *Historia de la ciudad de Saltillo,* 1982; Henry, *Campaign Sketches of the War with Mexico,* 1847.

San Antonio, Skirmish at
(March 25, 1848)

The Skirmish at San Antonio, between U.S. naval personnel and Mexican forces in the La Paz–San José–San Antonio area, helped break the last guerrilla resistance along the Gulf of California in 1848.

Nearly two months after the Treaty of Guadalupe was signed, a U.S. landing party launched an attack against the camp of Captain Manuel Pineda at San Antonio, Baja California. Pineda's small force of regulars and guerrillas had harassed the U.S. occupational forces at Guaymas and San José along the Baja coastline. Pineda was resourceful and cunning and used his forces effectively in low-risk attacks on U.S. soldiers.

On March 25, 1848, 33 New York volunteers under the command of Captain Seymour G. Steele left La Paz and attacked Pineda near San Antonio. The raid was a success in that some U.S. prisoners held by Pineda were released. Also, Pineda was severely wounded, and three Mexicans were captured. The Mexican force dispersed a short time afterward.

For further reading: Bauer, *Surfboats and Horse Marines,* 1969.

San Francisco

The village of San Francisco, California, was occupied by U.S. naval forces under Commander John B. Montgomery on July 8, 1846.

After Commodore John D. Sloat of the U.S. Pacific Squadron occupied Monterey, California, on July 7, 1846, he instructed Commander Montgomery of the USS *Portsmouth* to seize San Francisco. Montgomery received the order the following day.

Montgomery had translated into Spanish Sloat's proclamation that California was now part of the United States. Montgomery and 70 men went ashore at Clark's Point in dress uniforms and marched to the customhouse in what is now Portsmouth Square in present-day San Francisco. Watched by approximately 40 curious inhabitants, Montgomery read aloud that the U.S. naval force would not rule oppressively. The U.S. flag was raised, and a 21-gun salute was fired from the USS *Portsmouth* anchored offshore.

After inspecting the Presidio and Battery San Joaquín, Montgomery ordered another battery to be built on Telegraph Hill, which commanded the harbor. Fourteen U.S. Marines under Lieutenant Henry B. Watson were detached as a garrison force.

For further reading: Bauer, *Surfboats and Horse Marines,* 1969; Downey, *The Cruise of the Portsmouth,* 1958; Harlow, *California Conquered,* 1982.

San Gabriel River (Bartolo Ford), Battle of
(January 8, 1847)

Fought between the U.S. joint army-navy force under Commodore Robert F. Stockton and Californio rebels led by José María Flores, this U.S. victory opened the way for the U.S. reoccupation of Los Angeles in January 1847.

Having easily occupied New Mexico, Brigadier General Stephen Watts Kearny and 300 dragoons from his Army of the West marched for California on September 25, 1846, to join forces with Commodore Stockton. After some surprising hardships (including 31 soldiers killed or wounded at the battle of San Pascual), Kearny's force arrived in San Diego on December 11.

Both Kearny and Stockton were eager to march northward and retake Los Angeles, which had fallen earlier to Californio forces under Flores. Stockton's sailors took quickly to infantry training under the watchful eye of Kearny. Satisfied with the combined army-navy force, Kearny and Stockton moved out on December 29 with 607 men armed with muskets, boarding pikes, and six artillery pieces. Supplies were kept to a minimum and consisted of a few wagons, mules, and cattle.

A message received during the march from Flores that called for an armistice was summarily rejected by Stockton. On January 8, 1847, the U.S. force had reached the San Gabriel River, about 12 miles south of Los Angeles. Stockton's scouts had discovered that Flores had his men in place for an ambush at their intended crossing point of La Jabonería Ford. Learning this, Stockton ordered his men to cross further upstream at Bartolo Ford; Flores quickly mounted his 450-man army and deployed them on a low ridge about 600 yards beyond the ford before the U.S. force arrived. The morale of the Californios was low because they were poorly armed, outnumbered, and wedged between John C. Frémont's California Battalion to the north and Stockton-Kearny to the south. Also, Flores's four poorly supplied artillery pieces offered little tactical advantage.

The U.S. troops formed a hollow square formation, advanced skirmishers, and began to cross the shallow river. Flores launched piecemeal cavalry attacks with no success against the slowly advancing enemy. The Californio cannons were ineffective. Flores's men began to fall from accurate artillery fire that was directed by Stockton. Within two hours, the U.S. force had scattered the rebels and gained the ridge by the late afternoon, where they camped that night. Many of the Californios deserted in the darkness and went home; a few returned to the battlefield and fired sporadically at the U.S. camp during the night. The following day, the U.S. force brushed aside a lackluster attack during the Battle of La Mesa as they closed in on Los Angeles, which they occupied on January 10.

Total U.S. casualties during the Battle of San Gabriel were between 11 and 13 killed and wounded; Californio losses were about the same. The U.S. victory effectively ended the rebellion in California. A few days later, the Treaty of Cahuenga was signed, which ended Californio resistance to U.S. rule.

See also Cahuenga, Treaty of; Flores, José María; Kearny, Stephen Watts; La Mesa, Battle of; Stockton, Robert Field.

For further reading: Harlow, *California Conquered*, 1982.

San José del Cabo

From November 1847 to March 1848, Mexicans under Captain Manuel Pineda and U.S. naval forces and struggled for control over the port of San José del Cabo on the Gulf of California.

U.S. Navy Lieutenant Henry A. Wise described this Baja California port as standing "in a pretty valley, with red, sterile mountains topping around it. One broad street courses between two rows of cane and mud-built dwellings, thatched with straws.... At the upper end of the avenue, standing on a slight, though abrupt, elevation from the valley behind, was the cuartel [barracks]...."

As part of the blockade by the U.S. Pacific Squadron, the bay of San José del Cabo was occupied by the *Congress, Independence,* and *Cyane* on October 29, 1847. Commodore W. B. Shubrick was concerned about rumors of rebellion elsewhere along the coast, especially at Todos Santos and La Paz. Shubrick left 24 men under Lieutenant Charles Heywood as a garrison force at San José del Cabo, along with a month's worth of supplies, on November 8. Heywood's men occupied an old mission in town.

The supreme commander of the Mexican resistance in the area was Captain Manuel Pineda. He dispatched 150 men under Vicente Mejía of the Mexican Navy to San José del Cabo. Ordered on November 19 by Mejía to surrender, Heywood refused. Mejía attacked that night, but was repulsed with a loss of approximately 2 killed and 3 wounded; three U.S. seamen were also wounded. Another attack the following night ended with similar results. The siege finally ended when U.S. sailors and supplies, including two artillery pieces, arrived on November 26 on the *Southampton*. The rebels rejoined Pineda, who was planning an attack on La Paz.

When the U.S. warships left San José del Cabo in January 1848, a garrison force of approximately 60 men remained behind. Pineda immediately moved his entire army into the area, and approximately 50 women and children took refuge in the U.S. garrison. The U.S. troops began to suffer from reduced supplies, especially food and water. Pineda captured a foraging party on January 22, 1848, which officially began the second siege of the city.

In full view of the garrison, the town was occupied by Pineda's men from January 22 to February 14. The Mexicans kept up a steady sniper fire. Because of limited ammunition, the U.S. sailors did not return the fire. Heywood launched three attacks/forays into the town on February 6 and 7 for supplies, losing one man killed and several wounded. On February 11, a sniper's bullet killed another sailor.

Pineda seized control of the well and built a breastwork to defend it. Desperate for water, Heywood's men tried to dig a well, but with no success.

Much to Heywood's relief, the USS *Cyane* was sighted on February 14. Within hours, Commander Samuel F. Du Pont and 102 men landed approximately three miles from San José del Cabo and skirmished toward the city. Joining Heywood, they reoccupied the city.

Pineda withdrew to San José Viejo and later to Santa Anita. On March 24, a U.S. force attacked Santa Anita, but Pineda's men had already retreated to Santiago.

For further reading: Bauer, *Surfboats and Horse Marines*, 1969; Knox, *A History of the United States Navy*, 1936.

San José del Pozo, Skirmish at
(May 13, 1847)

A rare example of Mexican citizens and U.S. soldiers fighting together side by side during the Mexican-American War, U.S. troops helped Mexican ranchers defeat an Apache raiding party.

Located approximately 25 miles from Parras, Coahuila, Rancho San José del Pozo was run by approximately 50 Mexican citizens. As Colonel Alexander W. Doniphan's 1,000-man command marched from Chihuahua to Saltillo, his advance guard camped at Parras. Learning that a Lipan Apache raiding party, returning from a raid farther south, had entered the valley, the owner of the hacienda rode hard to Parras and offered the advance U.S. guard horses as gifts if it would help defend the hacienda. Captain John Reid and approximately 20 men volunteered and rode all night.

Shortly after they arrived in the morning, the Lipans descended on the hacienda. After an hour's fighting, the Indians retreated, having lost approximately a dozen men. In addition to 13 Mexican women and children who were being taken north as prisoners, the Mexicans recovered 250 head of stolen animals. Josiah Gregg commented that "this is certainly a novel warfare: fighting and defending the same people at the same time."

For further reading: Gregg, *Diary and Letters of Josiah Gregg*, 1944.

San Juan, Skirmish at
(July 30, 1847)

Located about 5 miles north of Ojo de Agua near the National Road, a 300-man Mexican infantry-guerrilla force at this tiny village was attacked and routed by approximately 90 U.S. troops.

Ordered by General Persifor F. Smith to wipe out a band of Mexican troops and guerrillas at San Juan de los Llaños, Captain Charles F. Ruff and approximately 90 mounted riflemen left Puebla and arrived at San Juan on July 30. Leaving 24 men with the horses, Ruff divided his force into three squadrons and attacked the town. Approximately 200 infantry and 100 guerrillas had taken shelter in buildings in the center of town. Ruff's men fought from house to house and eventually trapped the Mexicans in a church. The Mexicans surrendered after suffering losses of approximately 43 killed and 54 wounded; one U.S. soldier was wounded during the fight. Ruff captured an abundance of weapons, ammunition, and supplies.

For further reading: Brackett, *General Lane's Brigade in Central Mexico*, 1854; Hughes, *Rebellious Ranger*, 1964.

San Juan de Ulúa

A massive stone fortress built on a reef, San Juan de Ulúa defended the Atlantic approach to the city of Veracruz.

Located on the Gallega Reef off the port city of Veracruz, San Juan de Ulúa was not built until the late eighteenth century. The stone fort was in the shape of a large quadrangle with a bastion at each corner. The southernmost bastion had a raised platform that gave the defenders command of the adjacent area of the fort and allowed them to fire over their own exterior parapets. A formidable structure, the fortress could hold more than 1,000 soldiers and 135 heavy guns.

On March 6, 1847, the gunners from San Juan de Ulúa nearly sank the USS *Petrita*, which carried Major General Winfield Scott and his entire senior staff. Respectful of the fort, Scott landed his troops a few miles south of Veracruz, out of range of San Juan de Ulúa's guns. The fort was shelled by U.S. ships later that month during the siege of Veracruz, but little damage resulted.

For further reading: Bauer, *Surfboats and Horse Marines*, 1969.

San Luis Potosí

San Luis Potosí, the capital city of the province of San Luis Potosí, was an important staging area for General Antonio López de Santa Anna's Army of the North in 1847.

Located approximately 200 miles northwest of Mexico City, San Luis Potosí was founded in the late sixteenth century. The town prospered from the development of silver mines in the nearby San Pedro Mountains. At an elevation of 6,300 feet, it was known for its good water and climate. Many of the handsome colonial churches, convents, monasteries, theaters, and larger structures were built with blocks of granite. The brightly colored domes of the churches could be seen from some distance away. The population of 30,000 in 1846 enjoyed a fairly prosperous economy.

San Luis Potosí was the scene of frenzied military buildup after the arrival of General Santa Anna in August 1846. The remains of the Army of the North were assembled at San Luis Potosí in preparation for the advance on General Zachary Taylor's forces near Saltillo. Various state militias, guardsmen units, and raw recruits from aggressive conscription efforts flowed into the city. Supplies (although meager) were stockpiled, and the troops were drilled constantly on the plain outside the city. Several well-supplied guerrilla groups were also headquartered at San Luis Potosí.

In addition to outfitting a new army, Mexican military leaders improved San Luis Potosí's defenses in the fall of 1846 in case Taylor decided to advance on Mexico City from Monterrey via San Luis Potosí. The construction of defenses was supervised by one of Mexico's best military engineers, General Ignacio Mora y Villamil. The improved fortifications and the presence of a growing Mexican army were two of the reasons that Taylor was reluctant to advance on Mexico City.

For further reading: Gregg, *Diary and Letters of Josiah Gregg,* 1944; Muro, *Historia de la San Luis Potosí,* 1910; Valázquez, *Historia de la San Luis Potosí,* 1982.

San Pascual, Battle of
(December 6, 1846)

In one of the few Mexican victories of the Mexican-American War, General Stephen W. Kearny's small force of dragoons was defeated at the Battle of San Pascual by Californio rebels under Major Andrés Pico.

After occupying Santa Fe in August 1846 and establishing a military government for New Mexico, Brigadier General Kearny and approximately 100 dragoons headed west for San Diego. Near dawn on December 6, outside the Indian village of San Pascual, Kearny encountered approximately 75 Californio rebels led by Major Pico. Assured by his guide Kit Carson that they would flee, Kearny attacked.

After an initial collision, the Californios, all expert horsemen armed with crude lances, fled down the road. Well ahead of their pursuers, Pico split his men, turned, and charged the surprised, straggling U.S. dragoons. In short order, the deadly Californio lances had killed approximately 18 and wounded 15 of Kearny's men, nearly a third of his force; Mexican losses were approximately 15 killed and wounded.

Shocked by the loss, and suffering from a painful lance wound in the groin, Kearny retired his men to Mule Hill. Pico kept them trapped on the hill for three days until a U.S. naval force reinforced them from San Diego.

See also Beale, Edward Fitzgerald; Carson, Christopher ("Kit"); Mule Hill; Pico, Andrés.

For further reading: Colton, *Three Years in California,* 1850; Cooke, *The Conquest of New Mexico and California,* 1878; Coy, *The Battle of San Pasqual,* 1921; Griffin, *A Doctor Comes to California,* 1943; Harlow, *California Conquered,* 1982; Todd, *The Battles of San Pasqual,* 1925.

San Patricio Battalion

Organized by Irishman and U.S. army deserter John Reily, the San Patricio Battalion was a group largely of U.S. deserters that became one of the hardest-fighting units in the Mexican army.

Best described as a soldier of fortune, Reily

served in the British army in Canada before deserting to the U.S. army in 1845. Shortly after arriving at the Río Grande as part of General Zachary Taylor's Army of Occupation in the spring of 1846, he swam the river and enlisted in the Mexican army.

Quickly rising to the rank of major (later brevet colonel), Reily organized the San Patricio (Saint Patrick) Battalion. He personally recruited more than 150 men, most of them Irish or other foreign-born deserters from the U.S. army. Reily even designed the battalion's distinctive shamrock flag.

The San Patricio Battalion was commanded by Lieutenant Colonel Francisco Schafino, Florida-born Major Francisco Rosendo Moreno, and Major José María Calderón during the Mexican-American War. The battalion was variously called the Irish Volunteers, Colorados, Red Guards (because of the reddish hues of the many Irishmen), and San Patricio Guards.

The San Patricios were trained as an artillery unit and fought at Monterrey, Buena Vista, and Cerro Gordo. A San Luis Potosí newspaper wrote that "these brave men, who have abandoned one of the most unjust of causes for the purpose of defending the territory of their adopted country, will find in the Mexicans a frank and loyal heart, open and hospitable; and besides, a just and ample recompense for their merited services."

During the Battle of Angostura (Buena Vista) on February 23, 1847, the San Patricios fought well with clumsy, antiquated artillery pieces. Over one-third of the 80-man force was killed or wounded. Converted to infantry in June, they were attached to the Army of the East, which faced the advance of Major General Winfield Scott toward Mexico City and fought at Cerro Gordo.

During the Battle of Churubusco in August, the battalion held the convent for nearly two hours after the rest of the Mexican forces had fallen back. Reily's men were fighting with a desperation born from the fact that they knew they would be hanged if captured by U.S. forces. After three hours of bitter fighting, nearly 50 had been killed or wounded.

Seventy of the San Patricios, including Reily, were captured. After a court-martial, 50 were sentenced to be hanged; the others received severe lashings and were branded with the letter "D" (deserter) on the cheek. Most of the U.S. soldiers were outraged that Reily received the lightest sentence: 59 lashes and a "D" on each cheek. Sixteen San Patricios were hanged on September 9, 1847, at San Angel. Another four were hanged on the following day at Mixcoac. On September 13, the day Chapultepec was to be stormed, "a gallows was erected on a rising piece of ground…in full view of the attack on the castle." The last 30 victims stood on wagons with nooses around their necks. When the U.S. flag was raised over the castle walls, the wagons were drawn.

After the Treaty of Guadalupe Hidalgo was signed in 1848, the San Patricio Battalion still functioned as a distinct military unit that served at Querétaro, Mexico City, and Guadalupe Hidalgo. After some San Patricios aligned themselves with General Mariano Paredes y Arrillaga's revolt in May 1848, the Mexican government became suspicious of their loyalty and discharged the unit in August 1848. Several returned to Great Britain.

The San Patricios are still revered as heroes of the Mexican-American War. A plaque at the execution site in San Angel reads "In Memory of the Irish Soldiers of the Heroic San Patricio Battalion, Martyrs Who Gave Their Lives for the Cause of Mexico during the Unjust American Invasion of 1847." Public ceremonies are held on St. Patrick's Day in their honor.

See also Desertion; Reily (Reilly, Riley, O'Reilly), John.

For further reading: Baker, "The St. Patricks Fought for Their Skins, and Mexico," 1978; Downey, "Tragic Story of the San Patricio Battalion," 1955; Hopkins, "The San Patricio Battalion in the Mexican War", 1913; Krueger, *Saint Patrick's Battalion,* 1960; Miller, *Shamrock and Sword,* 1989; Wallace, "The Battalion of Saint Patrick in the Mexican War," 1950.

Sands, Joshua Ratoon

(1795–1883)

A senior U.S. naval officer during the Mexican-American War, Commander Joshua Ratoon Sands participated in most of the operations against the Mexican gulf coast during 1846–1847.

Sands, who was born in Brooklyn, New

York, joined the navy in 1812 and served in the War of 1812. He saw service in the Mediterranean.

During the Mexican-American War, Sands commanded the small steamship *Vixen* as part of the U.S. Home Squadron along the gulf coast of Mexico. He was involved in most of the naval operations during 1846–1847, including Alvarado, Tabasco, Tampico, Tuxpan, and Laguna. The *Vixen* was the only ship that managed to penetrate the shallow harbor during the second attack on Alvarado in October 1846, and Sands was reluctant to abandon the attack as ordered by Commodore David Conner. Sands served as the military governor at Laguna until the siege of Veracruz, during which he carried out reconnaissance close to the fortress San Juan del Ulúa.

Sands held a variety of assignments after the war, including ones in Brazil and Nicaragua. He retired as a captain in 1861 and died in Baltimore, Maryland.

For further reading: Bauer, *Surfboats and Horse Marines*, 1969; Knox, *A History of the United States Navy*, 1936.

Santa Anna, Antonio López de
(1794–1876)

One of Mexico's most influential leaders of all time, President and General Antonio López de Santa Anna directed the Mexican government and military from September 1846 to September 1847, when Mexico City was seized by General Winfield Scott.

Born in Jalapa to a middle-class family, Santa Anna received little schooling before he joined the Spanish Army in 1810 as a cadet. As a soldier, he helped suppress Indian tribes, public uprisings against the Roman Catholic Church, and Mexican and U.S. settler uprisings in Texas. His bravery led to recognition and promotions. As did many other officers in the Spanish army, Santa Anna embraced the revolution of Agustín de Iturbide, which resulted in independence from Spain in 1821. Soon afterward, Santa Anna was promoted to brigadier general and supported the overthrow of Iturbide.

In 1829, Santa Anna gained widespread recognition by raising and commanding a

Antonio López de Santa Anna
(Library of Congress)

2,000-man army that defeated a Spanish expeditionary force in 1829 at Tampico. His success at Tampico resulted in his election as the (liberal) president of Mexico in 1833, with Valentín Gómez Farías as vice-president. By 1834, mostly for reasons of self-preservation, he adopted a centralist platform, exiled his vice-president, shut down Congress, and declared himself dictator. In 1836, Santa Anna replaced the constitution with the "Seven Laws," which eliminated self-rule in the states of Mexico and lengthened his term to eight years. As dictator, he spent much of his time acquiring vast land holdings around Veracruz.

Santa Anna continued to rule with a heavy hand, repressing rebellious cultures in the Yucatán and Tabasco. In 1836, with an army of 6,000 men, he defeated Texan rebels at the Alamo and Goliad, but was badly beaten by Sam Houston at the Battle of San Jacinto, where he displayed poor tactical judgment and a keen interest in self-preservation. He ultimately signed the Treaties of Velasco, which granted Texas its freedom from Mexico. A few months after his return to Mexico in 1837, Anastasio Bustamante had been chosen as president by the centralist regime, and Santa Anna retired to his hacienda at Veracruz.

In 1838, Santa Anna was called upon to expel a French force at Veracruz; during the skirmish, he was wounded by a cannonball, and his left leg was amputated below the knee. The bone was not properly cut, and he lived with pain for the rest of his life. Back in favor, and with the help of Generals Mariano Paredes y Arrillaga and Gabriel Valencia, Santa Anna regained the presidency in 1843. His severed leg was disinterred from his estate at Veracruz and, in a formal military procession, escorted in an urn to the cemetery of Santa Paula, where it was placed in a vault.

In 1844, Santa Anna ordered a levy of 30,000 new troops. Under his leadership, the country was nearly bankrupt through the misuse of government funds. Santa Anna's preoccupation with regaining Texas was not embraced by other Mexican leaders. The political and military arenas grew increasingly unstable, and uprisings increased. After he left Mexico City to deal with a revolt by former ally Paredes y Arrillaga, Mexico City rioted, and Santa Anna's severed limb was dragged through the streets. Santa Anna was captured in disguise and imprisoned at Perote Castle until he was exiled to Cuba for life in May 1845.

After discussions between President James K. Polk and Alexander J. Atocha in 1846, and Commander Alexander Slidell Mackenzie and Santa Anna himself in Cuba, Polk allowed Santa Anna to pass through the U.S. naval blockade to Veracruz in August 1846. Polk had been assured that Santa Anna would easily regain the presidency and then seek a negotiated peace. Santa Anna's return at Veracruz was marked by celebratory cannon discharges and fireworks. In September, he rode into Mexico City in an elegant carriage bedecked with tricolored ribbons with Valentín Gómez Farías by his side.

Mexico felt momentarily redeemed and hopeful with the return of Santa Anna as president. Up to this point, the war with the United States had gone badly—General Taylor had won three straight battles, inflicted terrible losses on the Army of the North, and controlled northern Mexico. While Vice-President Gómez Farías ran the day-to-day government, Santa Anna, with his usual energies (and wanton waste of funds), reorganized the Army of the North into a 20,000-man army with which he planned to destroy Taylor.

After leaving cheering crowds in San Luis Potosí in late January 1847, Santa Anna returned with his broken army two months later, having lost the close Battle of La Angostura (Buena Vista) and over half the strength of his army. By the time he returned to Mexico City, it was wracked by civil unrest and the *Polkos* Revolt, and a U.S. army under Major General Winfield Scott had landed without the loss of a single man at Veracruz. To face Scott, Santa Anna rushed to organize the makeshift Army of the East, which he personally led during the bloody defeats that led to the fall of Mexico City in September 1847.

Santa Anna resigned as president of Mexico on September 16, 1847. After surrendering to U.S. forces at Puebla, he voluntarily exiled himself in 1848 to Venezuela, where he lived in a comfortable hacienda and enjoyed his favorite hobby of cockfighting.

Mexico, again adrift and leaderless in 1853, asked the aged dictator to return, which he did. Santa Anna quickly sold the Mesilla Valley to the United States for $10 million (Gadsden Treaty) to generate badly needed revenue. Overthrown by the liberals in 1855, he left for Havana, Cuba. Allowed to return to Mexico City in 1874, he died there at the age of 82.

See also Atocha, Alexander J.; Gómez Farías, Valentín; Mackenzie, Alexander Slidell.

For further reading: Calderón de la Barca, *Life in Mexico*, 1982; Callcott, *Santa Anna*, 1936; Costeloe, *The Central Republic in Mexico, 1835–1846*, 1993; Hanighen, *Santa Anna*, 1934; Jones, *Santa Anna*, 1968; Olivera and Crete, *Life in Mexico under Santa Anna, 1822–1855*, 1991; Ruiz, *The Mexican War*, 1963; Santa Anna, *The Eagle*, 1967; Santa Anna, "Letters of General Antonio López de Santa Anna Relating to the War between the United States and Mexico, 1846–1848," 1920; Trueba, *Santa Anna*, 1958; Valadés, *Santa Anna y la guerra de Texas*, 1935.

Santa Clara, Battle of

(January 2, 1847)

Discontented Californios led by Francisco Sánchez skirmished with a U.S. force under Captain Ward Marston at Santa Clara, California. An agreement was reached a few days later that ended organized Californio resistance in northern California.

Most Mexican citizens near San Francisco accepted the U.S. occupation that was announced to them in July 1846 by Commander John B. Montgomery. As the occupation of California wore on, local ranches began to be exploited by a group of foreigners led by Prussian immigrant Carlos María Weber, who had dubious ties to the U.S. military. Although he rarely had orders to do so, Weber seized property, weapons, horses, and cattle under the explanation that they were to be used for operations in southern California.

The victimized *rancheros* (ranchers) appealed to the U.S. government for intervention, but with no success. Raiding became more frequent in October and November, and civilians were beaten on the streets. Although Weber had some authorization to supply John C. Frémont's California Battalion with horses, the depredations continued into December, long after Frémont had left.

One of the most victimized ranchers, Francisco Sánchez, sought the support of other ranchers in challenging Weber's attacks. Eager to negotiate instead of fight, the ranchers captured a small group of U.S. soldiers as hostages and took them to the old Mission Santa Clara. In response, a U.S. expeditionary force consisting of 101 U.S. Marines, sailors, and local militia, commanded by U.S. Marine Captain Ward Marston, left San Francisco on December 29, 1846, for Santa Clara.

On January 2, 1847, the forces of Marston and Sánchez clashed at the Battle of Santa Clara. The two forces surprised each other about seven miles from the mission. Approximately 100 Californio *rancheros* deployed on horseback across an open plain. The U.S. force opened fire with grape and shot from its artillery battery, which killed four and wounded five Californios; skirmish fire from the Californios wounded two U.S. personnel. The rebels then scattered into the Santa Cruz Mountains.

The following day, Marston and his officers met with Francisco Sánchez and José de la Cruz Sánchez and discussed their grievances. On January 7, 1847, it was agreed that the Californios would surrender their hostages and cannon; in return, California property would be respected, or paid for in full if taken, and the stolen horses returned. Amnesty was also ensured to all those who had participated in the rebellion. Although a formal agreement was never signed, it was honored by both sides and sufficient to end the conflict in northern California.

For further reading: Bauer, *Surfboats and Horse Marines,* 1969; Regnery, *The Battle of Santa Clara,* 1978.

Santa Cruz de Rosales, Battle of
(March 16, 1848)

In this last battle of the Mexican-American War, Brigadier General Sterling Price, without orders and after the signing of the Treaty of Guadalupe Hidalgo, defeated a Mexican force under Governor Ángel Trías Álvarez at Santa Cruz de Rosales.

As part of Brigadier General Stephen W. Kearny's Army of the West, Colonel Price commanded the U.S. occupational forces in the province of New Mexico from December 1846 until the end of the war. After suppressing the Taos Rebellion in January 1847, the rest of the year was spent serving dull garrison duty and chasing marauding Indians and guerrillas.

Eager for combat and acknowledgment, when the newly brevetted brigadier general heard that a large Mexican force was advancing on El Paso del Norte (today Juárez, Mexico), Price mobilized his men and arrived there on February 23, only to find the rumor false. Still looking for a fight, Price pushed on toward Chihuahua City. He received a message from Governor Trías Álvarez that the Treaty of Guadalupe Hidalgo had been signed and the war was over. Unconvinced, Price and his troops marched into Chihuahua City on March 7. Trías Álvarez and his army of 800 men had retreated about 60 miles southeastward to Santa Cruz de Rosales.

Price carried on the pursuit and arrived at Santa Cruz on March 9. Again, Trías Álvarez insisted that the treaty had been signed. After waiting a week for a confirmation of peace that never arrived, Price bombarded the city with artillery and charged the town. Trías Álvarez put up a stiff resistance during the house-to-house fighting, but surrendered after taking approximately 100 casualties; Price lost 23 killed and wounded of his 665-man force. Eleven citizens were killed during the battle.

An irritated Secretary of War William L. Marcy ordered Price to return El Paso and for restitution to be paid to Chihuahua and Santa Cruz de Rosales for Price's illegal actions.

See also Price, Sterling; Trías Álvarez, Ángel.

For further reading: Johnston, *Marching with the Army of the West*, 1936; Shalhope, *Sterling Price*, 1971; Smith and Judah, *Chronicles of the Gringos*, 1968; Roa Bárcena, *Recuerdos de la invasión norteamericana*, 1947.

Santa Fe

A bustling trading center with the United States, Santa Fe, New Mexico, was occupied by Brigadier General Stephen W. Kearny's Army of the West during 1846–1848.

The capital of New Mexico, Santa Fe by 1740 had become a trading center between Chihuahuan merchants and French traders in the Mississippi Valley. Trading with Missouri began in 1821 along the Santa Fe Trail. This new trade route brought in a large amount of manufactured goods; provided an important market for mules, woolen blankets, and silver; and generated income in the form of customs duties for the province. As important a community as Santa Fe was, one U.S. observer described it as "an irregular cluster of low, flat roofed, mud built, dirty houses" that looked more like a "prairie-dog village than a capital." (Lavender 1954)

In 1846, Santa Fe was occupied by Brigadier General Kearny's Army of the West. Kearny worked hard at developing a good relationship with New Mexicans in Santa Fe. The Santa Feans were always discontent with Mexican rule, and their economic dependence on U.S. trade made them much more willing to accept the U.S. occupation. The discipline of the U.S. troops in Santa Fe began to deteriorate in late 1846 and led to widespread resentment among the citizens. Rebels met in the city to plan the murders of military governor Charles Bent and military commander Colonel Sterling Price, which led to the Taos Revolt.

Santa Fe remained the seat of the U.S. occupational government during 1846–1848, from which U.S. troops suppressed the Taos Revolt and other small-scale guerrilla uprisings in 1847.

By 1850, trade along the Santa Fe Trail was worth approximately $5 million annually, and trade continued to grow through the 1880s. After the Mexican-American War, Santa Fe became a political and cultural center, especially after its railroad connections were completed in 1879.

For further reading: Lavender, *Bent's Fort*, 1954; McNierney, *Taos Revolt*, 1980; Noble, *Santa Fe: History of an Ancient City*, 1989.

Scott, Winfield
(1786–1866)

The most senior commander in the U.S. army during the Mexican-American War, Major General Winfield Scott commanded the Army of Occupation during the Veracruz–Mexico City campaign in 1847. His success on the battlefield led to his presidential nomination in 1852.

Scott, who was born in Virginia, enlisted in the U.S. Army in 1808. He led his troops capably during the War of 1812 and became a brigadier general by 1814. Known as an aggressive fighter, he was severely wounded in a charge at the Battle of Lundy's Lane on July 25, 1814. Scott also served in the 1832 Black Hawk War and fought the Seminole Indians in Florida in 1836. Not afraid to disagree with his superiors, Scott was court-martialed by Andrew Jackson during the Florida campaign, but was fully exonerated. Scott was respected for his good negotiating and mediating skills.

As the Mexican-American War approached, Scott was the commander in chief of the U.S. army and nearly 60 years old. He recommended Zachary Taylor as commander of the Army of Occupation that was to invade northern Mexico. Knowing Taylor's disinterest in communicating from the field, Scott assigned him, as his adjutant general, Major W. W. S. Bliss, one of the most capable administrative officers in the army. Although Taylor was winning battles, both Scott and President James K. Polk were frustrated by the lack of speed of Taylor's small army. Polk and Scott decided to open a

Winfield Scott
(Library of Congress)

new front at Veracruz and march inland to occupy Mexico City.

On November 23, 1846, Scott was ordered to take approximately half of Taylor's men, sail to Veracruz, and seize the city. When Scott arrived at Camargo to discuss the plan with Taylor, he discovered that Taylor had moved ahead to Victoria. He took most of Taylor's regular troops anyway and, by March 9, 1847, had flawlessly landed a 10,000-man army at

Collado Beach near Veracruz. After a brutal siege and artillery barrage, Veracruz fell with 20 U.S. casualties. Determined to miss the yellow fever season, Scott rushed his troops westward on April 8 toward Mexico City.

Scott's army won all the battles it faced on the way to Mexico City: Cerro Gordo, Contreras, Churubusco, El Molino del Rey, and Chapultepec. On September 14, 1847, Scott entered the National Palace in Mexico City. One of the more humane military leaders of his day, Scott firmly believed in a disciplined army that respected Mexican citizens and their property. He refused an order from Secretary of War William L. Marcy to take provisions from citizens without paying for them. Consequently, his men were often supplied along the way by grateful citizens. His staff worked closely with Mexican officials in Mexico City to establish a military police force to reduce the frequent murders in the city. In fact, Mexicans were so impressed by his magnanimity that a delegation urged him to become Mexico's next dictator.

A group of subordinates, led by Scott's second in command Gideon J. Pillow, began to undermine Scott's reputation for leadership in the Veracruz–Mexico City campaign in the U.S. press. Pillow had aspirations to be the commander in chief and possibly a candidate in the next presidential campaign. Exasperated, Scott had Pillow arrested. President Polk, who never liked Scott and now viewed the Whig war hero as a presidential threat, suspended Scott and convened a court of inquiry to investigate the entire matter. Scott was exonerated, and Pillow received a slight reprimand for his subversive behavior.

Scott lost the 1848 Whig presidential nomination to fellow general Zachary Taylor. Scott gained the nomination in 1852, but was defeated in the presidential race by Franklin Pierce.

Scott helped mediate problems with Great Britain in the Pacific Northwest in 1859 and organized and trained Union troops to defend Washington, D.C., in the first year of the Civil War. After retiring at age 76, he traveled to the U.S. Military Academy, where he died in 1866.

See also Court of Inquiry, Scott; Tacubaya, Armistice of.

For further reading: Castañeda, "Relations of General Scott with Santa Anna," 1949; Eisenhower, *Agent of Destiny*, 1997; Elliott, *Winfield Scott*, 1937; Grant, *Personal Memoirs of U. S. Grant*, 1885; Hitchcock, *Fifty Years in Camp and Field*, 1909; Mansfield, *Life of General Winfield Scott*, 1851; Scott, *Memoirs of Lieutenant General Scott*, 1864; Smith, *Old Fuss and Feathers*, 1937; Smith, *To Mexico with Scott*, 1917.

Semmes, Raphael

(1809–1877)

A U.S. naval lieutenant, Raphael Semmes served in the U.S. Home Squadron during the Mexican-American War, participated in blockade duty and the Veracruz invasion, and marched with General Winfield Scott to Mexico City.

Semmes was born in Maryland. Both of his parents died in his early childhood, and he was raised by an uncle in Georgetown. At age 17, he joined the U.S. Navy and served in the Mediterranean, South America, and the West Indies. From 1837 to 1846, he surveyed the U.S. coast along the Gulf of Mexico.

As part of the U.S. Home Squadron during the Mexican-American War, Semmes commanded the brig *Somers* during the blockade of the east coast of Mexico. The ship was sunk

Raphael Semmes
(Library of Congress)

by a sudden tropical squall in December and half the crew drowned. As a flag lieutenant with Commodore David Conner, Semmes helped coordinate the naval artillery that bombarded Veracruz in March 1847. Semmes also participated in the naval expedition against Tuxpan and marched to Mexico City with General Scott. As a volunteer aide to General William J. Worth, Semmes was cited several times for gallantry.

During the Civil War, Semmes joined the Confederate navy. He went to sea as a commerce raider and developed a reputation as a clever hunter of U.S. ships in the Caribbean, West Indies, and Atlantic. Commissioned a rear admiral in the South and called a pirate in the North, Semmes commanded the CSS *Alabama* and is credited with capturing or sinking more than 80 ships. After the Civil War, Semmes retired in Mobile, Alabama, and wrote military books.

See also Rogers, R. Clay; *Somers*, USS.

For further reading: Meriwether, *Raphael Semmes*, 1913. Semmes, *Service Afloat and Ashore during the Mexican War*, 1851.

Sequalteplan, Skirmish at
(February 25, 1848)

The Skirmish at Sequalteplan in the late fall of 1847 was one of many attempts by Brigadier General Joseph Lane to eradicate guerrilla commands after the fall of Mexico City.

Attacks by Mexican guerrillas continued to be a problem for U.S. troops after the fall of Mexico City in September 1847. Guerrilla bands swept down on supply trains and columns of soldiers on the National Road between Veracruz and Mexico City.

General Joseph Lane and 400 men, including 250 Texans, left Mexico City on February 17 in search of a guerrilla force under Padre Celestino Domeco de Jarauta. Jarauta's men scattered just before Lane descended on the village of Tulancingo. Undaunted, Lane pushed his men on relentlessly to Sequalteplan. Led by Texan John C. Hays and Lane, the U.S. troops charged the village at dawn on February 25. Close-up fighting erupted in the streets. An undetermined number of Mexicans were killed or captured in the chapel; Jarauta, however, escaped.

See also Jarauta, Celestino Domeco de.

For further reading: Brackett, *General Lane's Brigade in Central Mexico*, 1854; Davis, *The Texas Rangers*, 1991; Greer, *Colonel Jack Hayes*, 1987; Webb, *The Texas Rangers in the Mexican War*, 1975.

Sevier, Ambrose Hundley
(1801–1848)

A Democratic expansionist and chairman of the Foreign Relations Committee, Ambrose Hundley Sevier helped ratify the Treaty of Guadalupe Hidalgo in 1848.

Sevier was born in Tennessee. He moved to Arkansas and, after becoming a lawyer, he served in the state legislature and later as both a U.S. senator and representative.

An expansionist, Sevier voted for U.S. recognition of Texas and later for its annexation in 1844. During the Mexican-American War, he was chairman of the Foreign Relations Committee. Sevier introduced and pushed through Congress the "3 Million Dollar Bill," which called for more money for peace negotiations. After the Treaty of Guadalupe Hidalgo was amended by the U.S. Senate, President James K. Polk asked Sevier to accompany Nathan Clifford to Mexico to help expedite Mexican ratification. Sevier fell seriously ill, and, upon his return to the United States, died in Little Rock at the age of 47.

For further reading: Polk, *The Diary of James E. Polk*, 1910.

Sherman, Thomas West
(1813–1879)

A brevet major in the 3rd U.S. Artillery, Thomas West Sherman performed capably in General Zachary Taylor's northern Mexico operations and General Winfield Scott's Veracruz–Mexico City campaign.

Sherman, who was born in Rhode Island, was a man of determination. He walked from Rhode Island to Washington, D.C., to beseech President Andrew Jackson for an appointment to the U.S. Military Academy. Sherman graduated from West Point in 1836 as a second lieutenant in the 3rd U.S. Artillery and fought the Seminole Indians in Florida.

Sherman served in General Zachary Taylor's Army of Occupation along the Río Grande during 1846–1847 and fought at Fort Brown and Monterrey. Sherman was brevetted to major for his actions that helped defend the threatened U.S. left flank and rear during the Battle of Buena Vista in February 1847. He later served capably during Major General Scott's Veracruz–Mexico City campaign in 1847.

A Union brigadier general during the Civil War, Sherman was wounded and his leg was amputated after the Battle of Port Hudson in 1863. Sherman retired in 1870 to Rhode Island, where he died at the age of 66.

For further reading: Cullum, *Biographical Register of the Officers and Graduates of the United States Military Academy from 1802 to 1867*, 1879; Dillon, *American Artillery in the Mexican War 1846–1847*, 1975.

Shields, James

(1806–1879)

James Shields
(Library of Congress)

One of the U.S. army's more capable and unassuming volunteer generals, James Shields served under Generals John E. Wool, Zachary Taylor, and Winfield Scott and was severely wounded twice during the Veracruz–Mexico City campaign.

Sheilds, who was born in Ireland, sailed to the United States in 1822. The ship sank off the Canada coast, and he was one of only three survivors. He made his living as a teacher and a lawyer in Minnesota and Illinois before he entered the Illinois state legislature in 1836. As state auditor, he challenged Abraham Lincoln to a duel. Shields became an Illinois Supreme Court justice in 1843.

During the Mexican-American War, Shields was commissioned a brigadier general of Illinois volunteers on July 1, 1846. He marched with his unruly Illinois men as part of the Army of the Center under Brigadier General Wool and later served with General Taylor. Transferred to Major General Scott's army, Shields was believed to be mortally wounded after the Battle of Cerro Gordo, but was saved by the expert work of several Mexican surgeons. He was brevetted to major general for his actions at Cerro Gordo. Although criticized for not leading his men into heavy fire during the Battle of Churubusco, he led them courageously at the Battle of Chapultepec, during which he was seriously wounded in the arm. He convalesced in Mexico City until July 1848, when he returned to Illinois.

After a brief term as governor of Oregon, Sheilds served in the U.S. Senate from 1849 to 1855. Shields had moved to Mazatlán, Mexico, to undertake a mining operation when the Civil War began. He returned to be commissioned a Union brigadier general of volunteers and fought well at Winchester and Port Republic. Shields served as U.S. senator from Illinois, Missouri, and Minnesota before dying at age 73.

For further reading: Condon, *The Life of Major-General James Shields*, 1900.

Shubrick, William Branford

(1790–1874)

A commodore in the U.S. Navy, William Branford Shubrick commanded the U.S. Pacific Squadron during the Mexican-American War. His oversaw the blockade and invasion of Mazatlán.

Shubrick was born in South Carolina. He entered the U.S. Navy as a midshipman in 1806 and saw duty around the world, including the Mediterranean and West Indies. He also fought in the War of 1812.

During the Mexican-American War, Shubrick sailed on the *Independence* to relieve Commodore John Drake Sloat of the command of the Pacific Squadron. The shuffling of leaders continued. When Commodore James Biddle arrived in Monterey in January 1847, Shubrick oversaw the Mazatlán blockade from April to June, when he was recalled to California to resume the command of the Pacific Squadron. Along the Pacific coast Shubrick continued blockading actions, including a hazardous night landing of 600 men at Mazatlán in November. His forces continued to systematically occupy coastal towns along the Gulf of California and skirmish with small Mexican forces.

After the war, Shubrick became the head of the Philadelphia naval yard in 1849. He commanded a flotilla and 2,500 men who went to Paraguay in 1858 to mediate trading problems. Nearly blind, he retired a rear admiral in 1862.

For further reading: Bauer, *Surfboats and Horse Marines*, 1969; Knox, *A History of the United States Navy*, 1936.

Slavery

Slavery was a hotly debated topic during the Mexican-American War. Northerners denounced the war as an effort to gain territory for the expansion of slavery.

The enslavement of Africans was a divisive issue in the United States in the 1840s. At the risk of sounding unpatriotic and treasonous, abolitionists denounced the war effort as evil and immoral. Southerners championed Manifest Destiny and the need for expansion and wanted any new territories to be open to slavery. Mexico, on the other hand, had abolished slavery.

The fervor over the slavery issue peaked in August 1846 with the Wilmot Proviso. Authored by Pennsylvania representative David Wilmot, the amendment to an appropriations bill declared that "neither slavery nor involuntary servitude shall ever exist in any part" of any Mexican territory acquired by the Mexican-American War. The Wilmot Proviso narrowly passed in the U.S. House of Representatives, but was defeated in the Senate. Although many southerners believed that slavery could not be used beyond Texas because of the poor agricultural climate of northern Mexico, they fought every effort to restrict slavery as an institution and regarded the Wilmot Proviso as an insult to southern states.

Mexico had hoped that the political issue of slavery, combined with other distractions such as the possibility of war with Great Britain over Oregon, would derail President James K. Polk's war efforts. Mexicans were considered by many U.S. citizens to be an inferior race incapable of meaningful self-leadership. Aware of U.S. attitudes about slavery and the U.S. relocation policy regarding Native Americans, some Mexicans feared similar treatment if subjugated by the U.S. government.

African American slaves and servants who attended white officers in the U.S. army frequently ran away in Mexico, where their freedom was recognized and they were relatively well treated.

See also Abolitionists; African Americans; Immortal 14; Wilmot, David.

For further reading: Filler, *The Crusade against Slavery 1830–1860*, 1960; Merk, *Slavery and the Annexation of Texas*, 1972; Sewell, *Ballots for Freedom*, 1976.

Slidell, John
(1793–1871)

In December 1845, President James K. Polk sent John Slidell as a U.S. envoy to Mexico City to negotiate the purchase of New Mexico and California. Slidell was not received, and he returned to the United States in April 1846.

Slidell was born in New York. He was a Spanish scholar from Columbia University who moved to New Orleans in 1819 to open a law practice. After his mercantile business failed, he entered politics and became a U.S. congressman in 1845.

After U.S. consul John Black informed President Polk that Mexico was willing to negotiate regarding U.S. damage claims and offers to purchase New Mexico and Califor-

John Slidell
(Library of Congress)

nia, Polk sent Slidell to Mexico City as U.S. minister extraordinary and plenipotentiary. Black and Mexican Minister of Foreign Affairs Manuel de la Peña y Peña had failed to clarify the issues to be discussed, and Mexico wanted to negotiate only the border problems with Texas. Slidell was authorized to recognize only the Río Grande as the southern border of Texas.

After Slidell arrived on December 6, 1845, José Joaquín de Herrera's government refused to see him over the minor point that it had not agreed to meet with a minister plenipotentiary. The insulting treatment of Slidell further aggravated Polk. Meanwhile, Herrera's administration was eventually overthrown by the more warlike Mariano Paredes y Arrillaga at the end of the year.

In January 1847, convinced by Slidell that a peaceful settlement was unlikely, Polk ordered Taylor to move his army from Corpus Christi to the Río Grande, a move that eventually resulted in a declaration of war against the Republic of Mexico in May.

Slidell continued in politics after the war. He managed the presidential campaign of James Buchanan in 1856. During the Civil War, he represented the Confederate States of America in France, where he died in 1871.

For further reading: Cotner, *The Military and Political Career of José Joaquín de Herrera, 1792–1854*, 1949; DePalo, *The Mexican National Army, 1822–1852*, 1997; Pletcher, *The Diplomacy of Annexation*, 1973; Ramirez, *Mexico during the War with the United States*, 1950; Sears, *John Slidell*, 1925.

Sloat, John Drake
(1781–1867)

Commodore John D. Sloat commanded the U.S. Navy Pacific Squadron during the Mexican-American War from May to July 1846 and landed troops at Monterey.

Born and raised in New York, Sloat became a midshipman 1800. He served in the West Indies, War of 1812, and the Pacific. In 1844, Sloat commanded the U.S. Pacific Squadron. Anchored at Mazatlán from November 1845 to June 1846, he received instructions from Secretary of the Navy George Bancroft to occupy San Francisco and blockade the Pacific coast if war was declared with Mexico.

In June 1846, after receiving word of the Skirmish at Carricitos Ranch along the Río Grande, Sloat mobilized his fleet for California. After arriving in Monterey on July 2 and meeting with U.S. consul Thomas O. Larkin, he landed a detachment of seamen and marines under Captain William Mervine five days later. The force raised the U.S. flag and declared California a part of the United States.

Shortly afterward, Sloat directed the occupation of San Francisco, Santa Barbara, and other northern coastal towns. Because of ill health, he was relieved of the command of the Pacific Squadron by Commodore Robert F. Stockton on July 29, 1846. Sloat had served as California's first U.S. military governor for about three weeks.

From 1848 to 1855, Sloat supervised the construction and repair of coastal defenses. He retired in 1866, and died in New York City.

For further reading: Bauer, *Surfboats and Horse Marines*, 1969; Harlow, *California Conquered*, 1982; Knox, *A History of the United States Navy*, 1936; Sherman, *The Life of the Late Rear Admiral John Drake Sloat*, 1902.

Smallpox

Although regular U.S. troops were vaccinated against smallpox, epidemics struck volunteer troops at Mier, Monterrey, and Camargo during the Mexican-American War.

Smallpox, a highly contagious viral infection, was a serious health problem for U.S. troops in Mexico. Smallpox was introduced to North America by some of the earliest European immigrants. Symptoms included fever, aches, and a rash or "pox" on the face that rapidly spread. Approximately 20 percent of all victims died from the disease; survivors were scarred or sometimes blinded.

Smallpox was somewhat understood by medical science in the 1800s, and a vaccine had been developed. Soldiers in the regular army were vaccinated for smallpox; the many volunteer troops were not. Consequently, outbreaks of smallpox were mostly among the volunteer regiments, and victims were typically quarantined. U.S. camps at Mier and Monterrey were struck by smallpox during the winter of 1847–1848, and additional outbreaks occurred in the Camargo camps. Vaccinations in camp helped limit the spread of the disease.

Some soldiers caught smallpox from local citizens, and it is likely that the disease also affected the Mexican army.

For further reading: Gillett, *The Army Medical Department, 1818–1865*, 1987; Smith and Judah, *Chronicles of the Gringos*, 1968.

Smith, Persifor Frazer

(1798–1858)

One of the U.S. army's more capable volunteer officers, Persifor Frazer Smith fought in both northern Mexico and the Veracruz–Mexico City campaign. He also served as the military governor of Mexico City.

Smith, who was born in Philadelphia, studied law in New Jersey and later moved to New Orleans. After commanding a battalion of militia, he raised a regiment of soldiers to fight in the Second Seminole War. He later became a judge in New Orleans.

During the Mexican-American War, Smith was commissioned colonel in the U.S. Mounted Rifles in 1846. Attached to General Zachary Taylor's Army of Occupation, Smith helped lead the bold attacks on Independence and Federation Hills during the Battle of Monterrey in September 1846. For this he was highly commended. Later attached to Major General Winfield Scott's army, Smith participated in the siege of Veracruz. During the siege, he was defeated in a skirmish near Vergara by a Mexican force that had advanced to harass the U.S. troops.

Smith led troops in most of Scott's battles during the Veracruz–Mexico City campaign. His performance at the Battle of Contreras resulted in a recommendation for brevet to major general. Scott's trust in Smith's abilities was evident by Smith's prominent role in negotiating the Armistice of Tacubaya and ending the hostilities in Mexico City. Smith was also appointed governor of the capital in October 1847. U.S. negotiator Nicholas P. Trist called him "one of the most beautifully balanced characters that I have ever known."

Unlike many volunteer officers, Smith remained in the U.S. army after the war and retired as a brigadier general in 1856. He died two years later at the age of 60.

For further reading: Frost, *The Mexican War and Its Warriors*, 1848; Johnson and Malone, *Dictionary of American Biography*, 1928–1936; Scott, *Memoirs of Lieutenant General Scott*, 1864.

Soldado River, Skirmish at

(April 9, 1848)

The minor Skirmish at Soldado River between guerrilla forces and a U.S. naval landing party near Guaymas, in Sonora y Sinaloa, was one of the last armed conflicts of the Mexican-American War.

On April 9, 1848, a U.S. naval landing party under Lieutenant Fabius Stanly of the USS *Dale* disembarked at the mouth of the Soldado River, near Guaymas, along the Gulf of California. Stanly's mission was to destroy three Mexican artillery pieces reported to be in the area. After marching 12 miles inland and spiking the cannon, the party was ambushed by guerrillas during its return. Two U.S. sailors were wounded. U.S. reports indicated that the Mexicans suffered one killed and three wounded.

For further reading: Bauer, *Surfboats and Horse Marines*, 1969; Craven, *A Naval Campaign in the Californias—1846–1849*, 1973.

Somers, USS

A U.S. brig in the Home Squadron, the USS *Somers* participated in blockading activities until it was sunk in a gale in December 1846.

Commanded by Lieutenant Raphael Semmes, the USS *Somers* was part of the Home Squadron's naval blockade of Mexico's gulf coast in 1846. After Semmes had failed to keep the Mexican schooner *Criolla* from penetrating the blockade, he approached Veracruz (where the *Criolla* was docked beside the steep walls of the fortress San Juan de Ulúa) on November 26 and launched a small boat with seven men under the command of Lieutenant James Parker. They boarded the ship and captured the crew. Concerned guards shouted down from the fort's walls, but Parker replied in excellent Spanish that he was putting some disorderly men in chains. The U.S. sailors quickly set fire to the *Criolla* and returned to the *Somers* with seven prisoners. (Semmes learned later that the *Criolla* was a spy ship that had been authorized by Commodore David Conner to pass unmolested through the blockade.)

On December 8, 1846, while chasing a blockade runner, the *Somers* was caught by a sudden norther and capsized. The ship sank in about ten minutes, and more than half of the 79-man crew drowned. Many of the survivors were saved by English, French, and Spanish warships that were lying at Sacrificios Island near Veracruz and that sent out small boats in the gale to bring back the men. "The brig was filling very fast, and her masts and yards [were] lying flat upon the surface of the sea...." wrote Semmes. "The severest gale I ever experienced, in any part of the world...blew for three days and nights. As the waves would strike the vessel, every timber and plank in her would tremble and quiver as though she were being shaken to pieces."

For further reading: Semmes, *Service Afloat and Ashore during the Mexican War*, 1851.

Stevens, Isaac Ingalls
(1818–1862)

A lieutenant of engineers, Isaac Ingalls Stevens performed various engineering and reconnaissance missions during Major General Winfield Scott's Veracruz–Mexico City campaign in 1847.

Stevens was born on a farm in Massachusetts. He graduated first in his class from the U.S. Military Academy in 1839. Commissioned a second lieutenant of engineers, he supervised the construction of defenses along the New England coast.

During the Mexican-American War, Stevens served as adjutant engineer on General Scott's staff during the Veracruz–Mexico City campaign in 1847. Stevens's daring leadership and reconnaissance at the Battles of Contreras, Churubusco, and Chapultepec resulted in brevets to captain and major. Stevens was wounded during the capture of Mexico City on September 13, 1847.

In 1849, Stevens resumed work on coastal fortifications, and his book, *Campaigns of the Río Grande and of Mexico*, was published in 1851. President Franklin Pierce appointed Stevens governor of Washington Territory in 1853. A major general with the Union Army, Stevens was killed at the Battle of Chantilly in 1862.

For further reading: Cullum, *Biographical Register of the Officers and Graduates of the United States Military Academy from 1802 to 1867*, 1879; Stevens, *The Life of Isaac Ingalls Stevens*, 1901; Stevens, *Campaigns of the Río Grande and of Mexico*, 1851.

Stockton, Robert Field
(1795–1866)

Commodore Robert Field Stockton was the energetic and enterprising commander of the U.S. Pacific Squadron during much of the Mexican-American War. With a relatively small naval force, he occupied southern California, fought two battles, and broke the Californio resistance by early 1847.

Born in New Jersey, Stockton went to college at the age of 13 and excelled in mathematics. Joining the navy as a midshipman in 1811, he participated in the War of 1812 and

Robert F. Stockton, 1840
(Library of Congress)

missions in the Mediterranean and off the coasts of Africa and France. Stockton had a special interest in steamships and commanded the steamer *Princeton* from 1843 to 1845. President John Tyler selected Stockton to personally carry the proposal for annexation to Texas in 1845.

In October 1845, Stockton was ordered to proceed to the Pacific in the *Congress* and reinforce the Pacific Squadron. On July 15, 1846, he arrived in Monterey, California, where he relieved Commodore John D. Sloat as commander of the squadron. Eager to take control of U.S. operations in California, Stockton assumed command of the land operations, including enrolling Colonel John C. Frémont's California Battalion into the U.S. army, and proceeded to occupy the ports of southern California. By August 17, he had orchestrated the occupation of Los Angeles by a joint army-navy force and raised the U.S. flag there. Further, he proclaimed California a part of the United States and made himself governor of the new civil and military government.

Stockton continued to blockade the southern California coast. After learning that the scant occupation force at Los Angeles had surrendered to Californio rebels in October, he began to plan a campaign to retake the city. In January 1847, a combined navy-army force under Stockton and Brigadier General Stephen W. Kearny won the small-scale Battles of San Gabriel and La Mesa, reoccupied Los Angeles, and ended the Californio resistance in California by the end of the month. Stockton and Kearny squabbled incessantly about control of the military government in California. Kearny eventually won control by order of Washington.

Stockton resigned from the navy in 1850 and became a U.S. senator for two years (1851–1853). While in office, he introduced a bill that called for the prohibition of flogging as a punishment in the U.S. navy. Retiring to Princeton, New Jersey, he died there at the age of 71.

See also Frémont, John C.; Kearney, Stephen Watts; Los Angeles.

For further reading: Bauer, *Surfboats and Horse Marines*, 1969; Bayard, *A Sketch of the Life of Commodore Robert F. Stockton*, 1856; Harlow, *California Conquered*, 1982; Neeser, *A Statistical and Chronological History of the United States Navy*, 1909.

Storms, Jane McManus
(1807–1878)

A journalist and secret agent for President James K. Polk, Jane McManus Storms conducted covert operations with Moses Y. Beach in Mexico during the Mexican-American War.

Storms, who was born in New York State, received a formal education at a female academy in Troy, New York. She escaped a troubled marriage and secured a land grant in Texas in 1832. Her business plans failed, and she then moved to New York City and wrote editorials and commentary for the city's newspapers. She became a regular contributor to Beach's New York *Sun*.

Impressed by her work and pro-expansion views, Beach employed her as his Washington, D.C., correspondent in 1845. President James K. Polk, eager to deploy more secret agents in Mexico to spread pro-U.S. sentiment and keep him informed about new political developments, convinced Beach and Storms, who was fluent in Spanish, to travel to Mexico under British aliases.

Beach and Storms, circulating among high-ranking politicians and clergy, suggested new ideas for a peaceful settlement of the war. From December 1846 to March 1847, Storms, under the name Montgomery, wrote numerous articles for the *Sun* regarding developments in Mexico. However, the onset of the *Polkos* Revolt prompted the return of General Antonio López de Santa Anna. Aware of their mission and suspecting that they were at least in part responsible for the revolt, Santa Anna put out notices for their arrest. Beach and Storms split up, and both eventually arrived in Veracruz during General Winfield Scott's attack on the city.

After the war, Storms married William L. Cazneau and settled in Texas. She continued her clandestine activities, mostly in Caribbean countries, for Presidents Franklin Pierce, James Buchanan, and Andrew Johnson. A prolific writer, she published eight books before drowning in a shipwreck in the Caribbean.

See also Beach, Moses Y.

For further reading: Beach, "A Secret Mission to Mexico," 1879; Caruso, *The Mexican Spy Company*, 1991; May, "Plenipotentiary in Petticoats," 1987; Nelson, "Mission to Mexico—Moses Y. Beach, Secret Agent," 1975.

Surfboats

Surfboats were specially designed, flat-bottomed boats with six-man rowing crews that transported more than 10,000 soldiers from U.S. warships to Collado Beach south of Veracruz on March 9, 1847.

For his invasion of Veracruz in March 1847, Major General Winfield Scott was in special need of smaller craft that would transport his men from the warships of the U.S. Navy's Home Squadron across the shallow waters to Collado Beach. Designed by Lieutenant George M. Totten, surfboats met this need and were the first amphibious landing craft ever built by the U.S. Navy.

Constructed by the Quartermaster Department near Philadelphia, the surfboats were double-ended, broad-beamed, and flat-bottomed. The frames were made from white oak. The largest boat was approximately 40 feet in length and could hold approximately 50 men; the smallest was approximately 35 feet in length and could hold 35 men. Built in three sizes so they could be stacked during transport, the surfboats were shipped from Philadelphia to the Gulf of Mexico.

The U.S. Navy ordered 141 surfboats at a cost of $795 per boat Only about half of the boats were constructed and shipped in time to be used during the amphibious landing on March 9, 1847. Manned by a skipper, coxswain, and six oarsmen, the surfboats successfully landed more than 10,000 men on Collado Beach by the end of the day.

See also Veracruz, Battle of.

For further reading: Bauer, *Surfboats and Horse Marines*, 1969; Knox, *A History of the United States Navy*, 1936.

Sutter, John Augustus
(1803–1880)

A Swiss immigrant who arrived in California via the United States, John A. Sutter owned vast tracts of land in northern California near Sonoma. His walled complex, called Sutter's Fort, was a staging area for the Bear Flag Revolt and Colonel John C. Frémont's California expedition in 1846.

John A. Sutter
(Library of Congress)

Sutter's Fort in California, ca. 1847 (Library of Congress)

Sutter arrived in the United States in 1834 from Switzerland. He worked his way west from New York City via St. Louis, Santa Fe, and Oregon before he reached San Francisco Bay in 1839. Sutter received permission from the Mexican government to establish a colony in northern California.

Sutter began to build Sutter's Fort at the junction of the American and Sacramento Rivers on August 16, 1839. Many acres were cleared that were converted to agricultural fields, orchards, and vineyards. Sutter worked hard at establishing a good relationship with the Mexican government and the neighboring Californios. In 1841, he was awarded Mexican citizenship and granted a larger tract of land, upon which he built a stately dwelling. Sutter's Fort became a gathering place for Anglo-American settlers in the Sacramento Valley.

Colonel Frémont seized Sutter's Fort in June 1846 as he collaborated with the Bear Flaggers. He later released Sutter's Fort after his California Battalion entered the service of the U.S. army.

Sutter helped draft the state constitution after the Mexican-American War. After gold was discovered on his vast land holdings in 1848, the California Gold Rush that followed ruined his assets and land holdings. By 1852, he was virtually bankrupt. In 1871, Sutter was in Washington, D.C., presenting claims to the U.S. government for his lost holdings. He was not successful, and he died in Washington at the age of 76.

For further reading: Dana, *Sutter of California*, 1938. Schoonover, *The Life and Times of General John A. Sutter*, 1895; Sutter, *The Diary of Johann August Sutter*, 1932; Zollinger, *Sutter*, 1967.

Sutter's Fort

See Sutter, John Augustus.

Tabasco, Battles of
(October 25, 1846; July 16, 1847)

Located in the state of Tabasco, the town of Tabasco was the target of two U.S. naval raids during the Mexican-American War.

Anxious to conduct a successful naval operation after the double failure at Alvarado, Commodore Matthew C. Perry proposed seizing Tabasco. Taking the *Mississippi, Vixen, McLane, Reefer, Bonita, Nonata,* and *Forward,* Perry left Veracruz on October 15, 1846. After sailing through heavy storms, they reached the mouth of the Tabasco River five days later.

The town of Tabasco is located 72 miles up the Tabasco River; at the mouth of the river is the village of Frontera. Because the Mexican military believed the shallow waters would prohibit any attacking naval expedition, Frontera had only minimal defenses. Mexican forces under Lieutenant Colonel Juan Bautista Traconis at Tabasco consisted of 300 men, who manned four guns at Fort Acachapan.

On October 22, *Vixen* was anchored at Frontera. Perry's force had captured the Mexican schooner *Laura Virginia* and the steamers *Petrita* and *Tabasqueña.* Perry left an occupational force to hold Frontera, with the support of the *Mississippi* and the *McLane* anchored in deeper water. He and the rest of the flotilla then sailed upriver to Tabasco.

On October 25, they approached Fort Acachapan. Upon seeing the U.S. ships, the Mexican defenders fled. By noon the guns were spiked. The quiet town of Tabasco was occupied by a U.S. landing party under Captain French Forrest, and six Mexican vessels were seized. Traconis, however, refused to surrender. At nightfall Perry's men reboarded their ships, and Traconis's men slipped back into town and deployed behind defensible positions.

Mexican sharpshooters fired on the U.S. vessels on the morning of October 26. Perry was reluctant to return the fire for fear of hurting civilians. Perry agreed to a cease-fire at the request of foreign merchants in the city, who were afraid their merchandise would be ruined. During the cease-fire, Lieutenant Charles W. Morris was killed by musket fire. Enraged, Perry shelled the city for half an hour. U.S. losses were two killed, two wounded, and two drowned; five Mexican soldiers and four civilians were killed. The city quickly surrendered.

On the return trip, Perry burned the *Alvarado* after it ran aground; the brig *Rentville* and the sloop *Campeche* were burned at Frontera. The *Petrita* and *Laura Virginia* were entered into U.S. service; the *Laura Virginia* was renamed *Morris* in honor of Lieutenant Morris.

Perry returned to Tabasco the following year. Supplies to General Antonio López de Santa Anna's army continued to flow through Tabasco. Its defenses had also been strengthened. Obstructive pilings had been driven into the riverbed, La Colmena breastwork defended treacherous Devil's Bend, Fort Acachapan had been strengthened, and Fort La Independencia and Fort Iturbide had also been built. The 900-man Mexican force was commanded by General Domingo Echeagaray.

On June 14, 1847, Perry's flotilla, consisting of the *Scorpion, Vesuvius, Washington, Spitfire,*

More than 1,000 U.S. seamen and Marines land under the command of Commodore Matthew C. Perry, beginning the attack on Tabasco. (Library of Congress)

Stromboli, Bonita, Scourge, Etna, Vixen, and a host of smaller boats moved up the river past Frontera. Perry's force totaled about 1,200 men and seven artillery pieces. Constant sounding of the river channel greatly slowed the procession. Local Indians in a canoe warned them about sharpshooters hiding in the chaparral, and minor skirmishing occurred as the ships moved upriver.

A lieutenant in a reconnaissance party was seriously wounded by heavy musket fire as he examined the pilings in the river. Perry promptly landed his naval brigade and artillery in ten minutes' time and swept the surrounding chaparral with grape and musket fire. With Perry in the lead, the naval force was marching down the road to Tabasco within half an hour, the artillerists pulling their guns by hand.

When they reached Fort Acachapan, commanded by Colonel Claro Hidalgo and about 600 men, Perry fired a few artillery shots and charged the fort. The Mexicans quickly retreated. Meanwhile, the ships in the river blasted the log pilings loose with kegs of gunpowder.

The *Scorpion* forced its way through the hot fire from Forts La Independencia and Iturbide and then attacked the unprotected portions from behind. The Mexicans again fled.

By June 16, U.S. warships were again anchored at Tabasco, and the town was occupied by naval troops. Guerrilla sniper fire continued from the chaparral. Perry remained until June 22, destroying military supplies and fortifications. U.S. casualties were 5 wounded; Mexican losses were 30 killed and wounded. Commander Gersham J. Van Brunt remained in Tabasco as military governor, with the *Spitfire, Scourge*, and *Etna*. Although river expeditions farther upstream and landing parties attacked and scattered pockets of guerrillas in June and July, guerrilla strikes remained a problem.

Perry did not want to hold Tabasco at the "expense of many valuable lives." In addition, nearly one-third of his force was sick with yellow fever. After one sailor was killed and three others wounded in a guerrilla fight on July 21, Perry ordered the evacuation of Tabasco the following day. By strengthening the U.S.

defenses at Frontera, Perry cut off all trade from Tabasco without having to permanently occupy the town.

See also Perry, Matthew Calbraith.

For further reading: Barrows, *The Great Commodore*, 1935; Bauer, *Surfboats and Horse Marines*, 1969; Knox, *A History of the United States Navy*, 1936.

Tacubaya

A small village near Mexico City, Tacubaya was the site of negotiations between Mexican and U.S. leaders that resulted in the Armistice of Tacubaya after the Battle of Churubusco.

Located on a gentle hillside a few miles from Mexico City, Tacubaya was described by Raphael Semmes as being "a pleasant little village, containing about 1,500 inhabitants, and is kind of a watering-place in the neighborhood of the capital. Many of the city merchants have extensive villas here with highly cultivated gardens, luxurious baths, etc."

The village was occupied by various portions of Major General Winfield Scott's Army of Occupation from August 1847 until the end of the war. Scott took one of the most beautiful palaces as his personal headquarters.

For further reading: Bauer, *The Mexican War*, 1974; Semmes, *Service Afloat and Ashore*, 1851.

Tacubaya, Armistice of
(1847)

After Churubusco had fallen to Major General Winfield Scott's army on August 20, 1847, at the request of General Antonio López de Santa Anna a truce was negotiated between representatives of the two armies to pursue peace talks. The chief result was Santa Anna's violation of the treaty to strengthen the defenses of Mexico City against the impending U.S. attack.

The Battles of Contreras and Churubusco outside Mexico City in August 1847 had been bloody affairs. Santa Anna's forces had retired toward Mexico City. Fearful that Scott would overrun the capital, Santa Anna sent two members of the British consul to negotiate a truce on his behalf with General Scott on the evening of August 20. (Scott had established his headquarters at the village of Tacubaya.) Scott was willing to consider the idea—his troops were worn out and had suffered heavy casualties in the recent fighting and needed to rest. The following day Mexican representatives appealed for a yearlong truce to entertain peace proposals from U.S. President James K. Polk's negotiator Nicholas P. Trist. Scott flatly rejected the proposal, but wrote that he was "willing to sign, on reasonable terms, a short armistice."

Santa Anna quickly agreed, and on August 22, Mexican Generals Ignacio Mora y Villamil and Benito Quijano met with Generals John A. Quitman, Persifor F. Smith, and Franklin Pierce at Tacubaya to draft the armistice. The resultant legal document became effective on August 24 within 78 miles of Mexico City "for the purpose of enabling the government of Mexico to take under consideration the propositions which the commissioner for the President of the United States has to make." Either party could cancel on a 48-hour notification. Other terms included bans on building or improving fortifications and on receiving reinforcements, weapons, or ammunition. Prisoners could be exchanged, and army supplies such as rations could be received.

Both Scott and Trist believed the armistice was a good way to show respect toward the fallen Mexican government, to facilitate a peaceful settlement, and to avoid more bloodshed (the U.S. army had lost nearly 15 percent of its fighting force at Churubusco, and Mexico City was well fortified). Lieutenant P. G. T. Beauregard wrote that "no reconnaissance was permitted by the general-in-chief, although it was a notorious fact that the enemy was violating it day and night."

Scott's soldiers were disappointed and angry at being stopped within full view of Mexico City. Many saw it as a Mexican ploy to gain time to fortify the capital. Captain Roswell S. Ripley later wrote emphatically that the armistice cost the U.S. army the loss of 1,652 men (the casualties from the future battles of El Molino del Rey, Chapultepec, and Mexico City). The armistice had forbidden the U.S. army from moving forward to seize Chapultepec, which would have quickly led to the capitulation of the Mexican capital. Exasperated at the Mexican violations and the lack of progress during daily peace talks, Scott ended the armistice on September 6.

As with the armistice that General Zachary Taylor had signed at Monterrey the previous year, President Polk was bitterly disappointed with Scott's armistice. Many historians feel that had Scott immediately advanced on the capital after Churubusco, the lives of many U.S. soldiers would have been saved; instead Santa Anna used the two-week period to fortify his defenses, which were later overrun in the bloody battles of El Molino del Rey and Chapultepec and in the fighting at the gates of Mexico City. General Cadmus Wilcox wrote that "no cities were sacked, no domain plundered. Scott's act in halting his troops after the battle of Churubusco at the gates of the City of Mexico, and, instead of imposing humiliating terms, inviting the Mexicans to listen to propositions of peace, is without parallel in military annals."

See also Churubusco, Battle of; Monterrey, Armistice of; Trist, Nicholas Philip.

For further reading: Alcaraz, *The Other Side,* 1850; Scott, *Memoirs of Lieutenant General Scott,* 1864; Smith, *To Mexico with Scott,* 1917.

Tampico

Tampico, one of Mexico's best ports, was occupied by U.S. naval forces in November 1846 after its Mexican garrison had been withdrawn by the order of General Antonio López de Santa Anna.

Tampico lies about five miles inland from the Gulf of Mexico, along Río Pánuco. The city's fortifications had been built under the direction of General Anastasio Parrodi, the military commander of the state of Tamaulipas. By October 1846, Parrodi's force totalled about 1,000 men.

As General Antonio López de Santa Anna prepared his army at San Luis Potosí for his campaign against General Zachary Taylor, he ordered the garrison at Tampico to abandon the city and join his force. General Parrodi, who objected to the order, reluctantly moved his men out on October 27. Loading their ships with as much gear and munitions as possible, the Mexican soldiers retreated up the Río Pánuco. Dismayed by Parrodi's delay, Santa Anna replaced him with General José Urrea.

The abandonment of Tampico fit well with U.S. invasion plans. When they received word from Tampico resident Anna Chase that the Mexicans had left, U.S. naval forces took possession of the port on November 14, 1846. Five Mexican schooners were captured, three of which were reoutfitted and became part of the U.S. Navy.

Commander Josiah Tattnall sailed up Río Pánuco on November 18 to the town of Pánuco. Arriving the next day, he occupied the town, pitched ammunition into the river, and dug up and destroyed nine buried cannon. He returned to Tampico on November 21.

Meanwhile, Urrea's men continued their struggle westward through the mountains, carrying their cannon by hand. On December 25, the weary soldiers entered Tula. They joined Santa Anna's new Army of the North in January 1847 as it marched northward to find Taylor.

See also Chase, Anna McClarmonde; Parrodi, Anastasio.

For further reading: Bauer, *Surfboats and Horse Marines,* 1969; Knox, *A History of the United States Navy,* 1936; Meyer and Sherman, *The Course of Mexican History,* 1995; Neeser, *A Statistical and Chronological History of the United States Navy,* 1909.

Taos Rebellion

(January–February 1847)

The Taos Rebellion, a violent struggle by about 1,500 New Mexican and Indian rebels against the U.S. military government in New Mexico in January and February 1847, was suppressed by Colonel Sterling Price.

Located in a fertile valley about 70 miles north of Santa Fe, Taos at the time of the rebellion was a town of about 5,000 in the Mexican state of New Mexico. Most of the homes were modest adobe buildings covered with white coats of gypsum. Taos was an important trading center in the 1840s, and Chihuahuans, Anglo-American trappers, New Mexicans, Navajos, Utes, and Comanches all brought goods to the town for sale. Locally grown wheat was used to make the famous "Taos Lightning" liquor.

Brigadier General Stephen W. Kearny and his Army of the West occupied Santa Fe in August 1846. Under his leadership, the U.S. troops were relatively well behaved, and a good relationship developed with the New Mexicans. After Kearny left, however, the behavior of the bored U.S. army deteriorated rapidly, first under Colonel Alexander Doniphan and later under Colonel Sterling Price. Drunken brawls and violations against the public became commonplace.

The New Mexicans became increasingly distressed, and prominent leaders such as Diego Archuleta and Tomás Ortiz began to plot an overthrow of the U.S. government in New Mexico in December 1846, including the assassination of Price and acting Governor Charles Bent. A mob of Mexicans and Indians, led by Pablo Montoya and El Tomacito, surged through the streets of Taos on January 19, 1847. Charles Bent was brutally killed in front of his wife and children on that night, as were the town sheriff and *prefecto*. Eager to kill U.S. citizens or pro-U.S. New Mexicans, the crowd carried Bent's severed head through the streets. Mexican women married to Caucasian men, worried about the safety of their children, darkened their children's skin and hair. The wave of violence spread to the towns of Mora and Arroyo Hondo, where 15 more American traders and settlers were murdered.

Mobilizing a force of about 500 men, Colonel Sterling Price moved out from Santa Fe on January 23. After fighting skirmishes at La Cañada and El Embudo Pass, he cornered the insurgents at Taos Pueblo, a large, walled adobe structure and church a few miles north of Taos, on February 4. Price killed 150 rebels before they surrendered. A smaller U.S. force from Las Vegas under Captain Israel Hendley attacked rebels at Mora and destroyed the village.

After a quick trial, two judges who had lost friends or family during the revolt repeatedly announced the death penalty for 16 of the rebel leaders. They were hanged on February 7 from an improvised gallows in the plaza, using borrowed lariats and tether ropes.

See also Arroyo Hondo, Skirmish at; Bent, Charles; El Embudo Pass, Skirmish at; El Tomacito (Tomás Baca); La Cañada, Battle of; Mora, Skirmish at; Price, Sterling; Pueblo de Taos, Skirmish at.

For further reading: Bancroft, *History of Arizona and New Mexico 1530–1888*, 1889; Cooke, *The Conquest of New Mexico and California*, 1878; Grant, *When Old Trails Were New*, 1934; Keleher, *Turmoil in New Mexico,1846–1848*, 1952; McNierney, *Taos 1847*, 1980; Twitchell, *The History of the Military Occupation of the Territory of New Mexico from 1846 to 1851 by the Government of the United States*, 1909.

Tattnall, Josiah
(1795–1871)

The commander of the U.S. Navy Home Squadron's Mosquito Flotilla, Josiah Tattnall participated in most of the naval actions along the Mexican gulf coast in 1846–1848.

Born in Georgia, Tattnall was orphaned at the age of nine and raised by his grandfather in London, England. In 1812, he joined the U.S. navy and fought in the War of 1812. Mapping expeditions took him to Florida, Texas, and Mexico in the 1830s. In 1837, on the *Pioneer*, he transported General Antonio López de Santa Anna (who had been taken prisoner by the Texans during the Battle of San Jacinto in 1836) to Veracruz.

During the Mexican-American War, Tattnall participated in most of the U.S. Navy Home Squadron's operations along the gulf coast of Mexico. He was in charge of the Mosquito Flotilla, with the *Spitfire* as his flagship. The smaller ships in his command participated in most of the river expeditions that occupied port cities, such as Tampico and Pánuco. Tattnall boldly bombarded Fort San Juan de Ulúa during the siege of Veracruz in March 1847. Tattnall was wounded in the arm during the capture of Tuxpan in April 1848.

Tattnall returned from Mexico in poor health. Nevertheless, after the war he led several diplomatic missions to China and the Mediterranean. During the Civil War he commanded the Confederate ironclad vessel *Virginia* (formerly the *Merrimac*) during its battle with the USS *Monitor*. Tattnall died in Georgia at age 76.

For further reading: Bauer, *Surfboats and Horse Marines*, 1969; Jones, *The Life and Services of Commander Josiah Tattnall*, 1878; Knox, *A History of the United States Navy*, 1936.

Taylor, Zachary
(1784–1850)

The first general of the U.S. Army of Occupation, Brigadier General Zachary Taylor scored the first four victories of the Mexican-American War: Palo Alto, Resaca de la Palma, Monterrey, and Buena Vista. An immensely popular figure, he was elected U.S. president in 1849.

Taylor was born in Virginia and later moved with his parents to Kentucky. He joined the U.S. army in 1808 as a first lieutenant and served in the Black Hawk War (1832). His aggressive leadership during the Second Seminole War (1837–1840) won him the nickname "Old Rough and Ready." He was brevetted brigadier general for leading 1,100 men through a waist-deep swamp to flank the enemy position.

Zachary Taylor, 1847 (Library of Congress)

In 1845, at age 61, Colonel Taylor commanded the 6th U.S. Infantry. At the urging of Andrew Jackson, President James K. Polk selected Taylor to lead the Army of Observation, an army assembled to protect Texas against Mexican aggression. About 2,000 troops gathered at Fort Jesup, Louisiana, just across the Sabine River from Texas. Taylor was known as a determined and fearless leader, but not the best tactician or communicator. General Winfield Scott, the supreme commander of the U.S. Army, wrote that Taylor was "slow of thought, of hesitancy in speech and unused to the pen." To counteract these traits, he assigned Taylor the articulate staff officer Captain William Bliss to ensure accurate, routine correspondence.

Stories that demonstrate Taylor's self-effacing, homespun demeanor abound. He was well liked by his men because he generally won his battles, and he often looked as disheveled as they did. For example, during the Second Florida War he often sat contentedly outside his tent in nongeneral dress and occasionally was mistaken for an orderly. During a grand review of the army at Camargo in August 1846, an observer noted that Taylor, "clad in plain undress, was conspicuous in the glittering group" of generals and staff officers. Unlike some generals, he led at the front and put himself at risk during battle, which was also respected by his men. Taylor trusted his subordinates and seldom intervened in their decisions during combat.

In mid-1845, Taylor moved his Army of Occupation to Corpus Christi, Texas, where it spent a hard winter along the gulf coast. In March 1846, he received orders to march to the Río Grande. Taylor suffered in the heat along with his troops, his face red, cracked, and peeling from sunburn. Elements of Taylor's army quickly clashed with Mexican cavalry, and on May 8 and May 9, his men defeated the Mexican Army of the North at the Battles of Palo Alto and Resaca de la Palma. In typical fashion, Taylor sat comfortably astride his horse, chewing tobacco, in an exposed position near the front. He was quickly promoted to major general.

In September 1846, after a difficult fight, Monterrey fell to Taylor's victorious army. Here his tactical weaknesses became apparent. He had not developed an overall battle strategy, and his attacks on the east side of the city were poorly coordinated and resulted in high casualties. He suffered President Polk's wrath after he signed the Armistice of Monterrey, which allowed the Mexican army to withdraw.

Both Polk and Secretary of War William L. Marcy were anxious for Taylor to advance on Mexico City from Monterrey. Taylor resisted, citing difficulties in supplying his army. This further irritated Polk. Major General Winfield Scott was then sent to the Río Grande to take the better half of Taylor's troops and open a new front at Veracruz. On January 27, 1847, Taylor wrote "I am constrained to believe that I no longer possess the confidence of the government. I can only regret that the President did not think proper, while withdrawing so large a portion of my command, to relieve me from a position where I can no longer serve the country with that assurance of confidence and support so indispensable to success."

When General Antonio López de Santa Anna discovered Taylor was at half-strength, he pushed his 20,000-man Army of the North relentlessly northward from San Luis Potosí in January–February 1847 to crush Taylor. Taylor's force numbered about 5,000 men, many of them untested volunteers. Arriving late on the Buena Vista battlefield on February 23, 1847, Taylor found that the Mexican army had already crumpled the U.S. left flank. After Major Bliss reported to him that the army was "whipped," Taylor answered "I know it, but the volunteers don't know it. Let them alone, we'll see what they do." Rallies on the left and rear stalled Mexican flank attacks, and by nightfall the Mexicans had retreated. Taylor and General John E. Wool hugged each other in relief.

With the focus of the war now the Veracruz–Mexico City campaign, Taylor's army occupied its various supply bases and chased guerrillas. Returning to the United States in November 1847, Taylor found himself welcomed as a hero. Convinced by the Whig party to be its presidential candidate, Taylor won the election against Democrat Lewis Cass to become the twelfth president of the United States in 1849.

Taylor's friendly, unassuming manner did not change in the White House. He wore baggy, comfortable suits, greeted guests outside the White House, and went on morning walks along Washington streets. His Mexican War horse, "Old Whitey," grazed on the White House lawn. Although he owned slaves, he opposed the extension of slavery into the new western territories. Before he could deal with the divisive slavery issue and the flurry of bills that resulted in the Compromise of 1850, Taylor suddenly became ill, and he died four days later.

See also Bliss, William; Monterrey, Armistice of; Wool, John Ellis.

For further reading: Bauer, *Zachary Taylor*, 1985; Dyer, *Zachary Taylor*, 1946; Fry, *A Life of Zachary Taylor*, 1848; Hamilton, *Zachary Taylor*, 1951; Howard, *General Taylor*, 1892; Hoyt, *Zachary Taylor*, 1966; McKinley, *Old Rough and Ready*, 1946; Montgomery, *The Life of Major-General Zachary Taylor*, 1847; Nichols, *Zach Taylor's Little Army*, 1963; Taylor, *Letters of Zachary Taylor*, 1908.

Téllez, Rafael

Lieutenant Colonel Rafael Téllez led small-scale resistance against U.S. naval forces at Mazatlán along the Gulf of California coast in 1847–1848.

Rafael Téllez commanded Mexican forces at Mazatlán, Sinaloa, during the Mexican-American War. Although anxious to combat U.S. naval forces, the Mexican government did not have supplies, weapons, or men to devote to the smaller-scale operations of the U.S. Navy along the Gulf of California coast.

Téllez embarked on his own campaign that included recruiting troops and guerrillas and attempting to establish his own military government. In fact, in September 1847, he dispersed the city's own forces at Mazatlán and occupied the city. His posturing and demonstration did not deter Commodore W. B. Shubrick from advancing on Mazatlán, and Téllez quickly withdrew to Palo Prietos.

With a strong U.S. presence at Mazatlán, Téllez lost a number of his men to desertion. He continued to launch annoying guerrilla attacks in the area until he was driven out in January 1848.

See also Mazatlán.

For further reading: Alcaraz, *The Other Side*, 1850; Bauer, *Surfboats and Horse Marines*, 1969; Knox, *A History of the United States Navy*, 1936.

Temascalitos, Battle of

See El Brazito, Battle of.

Tenería, La

See Fort Tenería.

Terrés, Andrés
(1777–1850)

General Andrés Terrés commanded the Mexican defense at Garita Belén outside Mexico City on September 13, 1847. Although he was censured and arrested after the battle by General Antonio López de Santa Anna, most accounts indicate that his leadership was commendable.

Terrés, who was born in Barcelona, Spain, joined the artillery in the Spanish army and saw action in various European campaigns. He was later shipped to New Spain to help fight the movement for independence. Terrés remained in Mexico and later was admitted to the ranks of the Mexican army. He was promoted to general by 1842.

Terrés fought bravely during the defense of Garita Belén on the outskirts of Mexico City. On September 13, after the fall of Chapultepec, General Santa Anna positioned Terrés and about 400 infantrymen at Garita Belén. As the U.S. troops surged down the causeway toward the gate, a large portion of the defenders fled. After heavy fighting, and discovering that his artillery ammunition was defective, he withdrew to the nearby Ciudadela, from which he maintained a destructive fire on the U.S. soldiers. Despite Terrés's valiant defense and high casualties, Santa Anna insisted on blaming him directly for the fall of Mexico City, struck him with a whip, and placed him under arrest.

After the war a court of inquiry absolved Terrés of all charges. In 1853, President Santa Anna restored his rank and granted him a military pension.

For further reading: Alcaraz, *The Other Side,* 1850; Roa Bárcena, *Recuerdos de la invasión norte-americana,* 1947.

Texas

The annexation of Texas by the United States in 1845 led to severed diplomatic relations with Mexico because Mexico did not recognize the Treaties of Velasco, which granted Texas its independence, or the Río Grande border that was claimed by Texas.

Originally a province of New Spain and later the Republic of Mexico, Texas bordered the western United States. The Adams-Onís Treaty of 1819 between the United States and Spain fixed the boundary between Texas and the United States as the Sabine and Red Rivers.

After the fall of the Agustín de Iturbide administration in 1823, Texas was joined with its neighbor, Coahuila, to form the state of Coahuila y Texas the following year. The region was sparsely settled and ravaged by Indian raids, and the Mexican government, anxious to establish colonies, encouraged U.S. emigration. With the permission of the Mexican government, Stephen F. Austin brought about 300 Catholic families to Texas. Incentives for American settlers included cheap land and a seven-year exemption from paying Mexican taxes.

Many of the later arrivals were not Catholic, and they refused to learn Spanish. Concerned about the lack of cultural assimilation, Mexico began to restrict immigration in 1830. By 1835, there were about 30,000 immigrants from the United States and fewer than 8,000 Mexicans in Texas.

Most of the American colonists remained loyal to the United States and refused to be assimilated. The first uprising by rebellious settlers was in 1825, when a group seized Nacogdoches. More resistance led to armed confrontations between settlers and Mexican troops. The fight with U.S. settlers culminated in the 1836 Texas Revolution. Mexican president General Antonio López de Santa Anna marched into Texas from San Luis Potosí with a 6,000-man army that crushed the Texans at the Alamo in San Antonio; he later executed more than 350 Texan prisoners at Goliad.

Santa Anna's brutal policies enraged Anglo-American Texans, who united under General Sam Houston to defeat Santa Anna at the Battle of San Jacinto. The resulting Treaties of Velasco granted Texas its independence from Mexico. The newly created Republic of Texas consisted of present-day Texas and parts of present-day Oklahoma, Colorado, Wyoming, New Mexico, and Mexico.

The Mexican government refused to recognize the treaties, although most foreign nations considered Texas a republic. Texas insisted that its southern boundary was the Río Grande; Mexico maintained it was the Nueces River, which had been the original border between Texas and Coahuila. Border raids continued to inflict casualties and damage to Texan property as Mexico continued to simmer over the border issue.

Most Texans favored annexation by the United States, although Texan President Anson Jones persistently attempted to persuade Mexico to recognize Texas's independence. U.S. President John Tyler sent agents into Texas to sway Texan opinion toward the United States and away from both Great Britain and Mexico. They also emphasized the threat of an invasion from Mexico. After much debate, Texas (to its Río Grande boundary) was annexed by the United States, becoming the 28th state on December 29, 1845.

Dismayed and angered, Mexico immediately severed diplomatic relations with the United States. The resulting Mexican-American War, and the Treaty of Guadalupe Hidalgo, finally eliminated all Mexican claims to Texas.

For further reading: Bancroft, *History of the North Mexican States and Texas,* 1884–1889; Binkley, *The Expansionist Movement in Texas,* 1925; Chipman, *Spanish Texas,* 1992; Foote, *Texas and the Texans,* 1935; Hardin, *Texian Iliad,* 1994; Hogan, *The Texas Republic,* 1946; Marshall, "The Southwestern Boundary of Texas," 1911; Nackman, *A Nation within a Nation,* 1975; Nance, *Attack and Counterattack,* 1964; Pletcher, *The Diplomacy of Annexation,* 1973; Richardson, *Texas,* 1958.

Texas Rangers

A fierce group of mounted Texan volunteers during the Mexican-American War, the Texas

A heavily armed Texas Ranger, from an engraving that first appeared in John Frost's *Pictorial History of Mexico and the Mexican War,* 1849 (Library of Congress)

Rangers provided valuable services as scouts and guerrilla fighters. They also committed frequent atrocities against the Mexican populace.

The first rangers on the Texas frontier were formed by Stephen F. Austin in the early 1800s to protect American settlers along the Brazos River from raids by Indians and Mexican bandits. The Texas Rangers were formally organized in 1835, and the force grew rapidly in size after 1836.

Rangers were experienced outdoorsmen who adapted some of the fighting methods of the Comanches, one of their most desperate enemies. Typically armed with rifles, pistols, revolvers, lariats, and Bowie knives, the rangers patrolled the 1,000-mile-long border with Mexico. They quickly developed a reputation for lightning-quick actions and vigilante-style justice.

Anxious to fight Mexico during the Mexican-American War, the 1st and 2nd Regiments of Texas Mounted Volunteers (formerly "Rangers") were led by famous men such as Ben McCulloch, Samuel H. Walker (responsible for arming many of the Rangers with Colt revolvers), George T. Wood, and John Coffee Hays. Attached to General Zachary Taylor's army in northern Mexico, the Texans were indispensable as scouts, couriers, and fighters. They quickly developed a reputation for committing atrocities against Mexican civilians, who were terrified of them. The Rangers were called "Diablo Tejanos" ("devil Texans") and looked the part: most of them were tall and bearded, heavily armed, and wildly dressed, occasionally with bloodstained buckskin shirts.

During the Battle of Monterrey in September 1846, the Rangers defeated a Mexican cavalry charge that opened the battle on the western outskirts of the city. They later scaled the steep, rocky face of Independence Hill at three o'clock in the morning during a rainstorm to drive the Mexican defenders from the top. Taylor wrote that "the mounted men from Texas have scarcely made one expedition without unwarrantably killing a Mexican…. There is scarcely a form of crime that has not been reported to me as committed by them." Overall about 1,300 Rangers served in the war. Many of them were discharged in October 1846 at the expiration of their three-month terms.

Captain McCulloch voluntarily returned to help Taylor for a six-month term on January 31, 1847. He performed scouting duties and located General Antonio López de Santa Anna's camp at La Encarnación before the Battle of Buena Vista. He slipped into the Mexican camp at night, climbed a small hill, counted campfires, and returned undetected to report to Taylor the following day. His information allowed Taylor just enough time to retreat from Agua Nueva to a better defensive position near Buena Vista.

General Winfield Scott was plagued by guerrillas during his Veracruz–Mexico City campaign in 1847. U.S. soldiers under the command of Samuel H. Walker kept the roads open and chased guerrillas from their mountain hideouts. The death of Walker during the Battle of Huamantla in 1847 resulted in the vengeful troops committing one of the worst atrocities of the war.

The Texas Rangers continued to patrol the Texas border after the war and during the Civil War. In 1874, they were commissioned as peace officers to fight the rampant frontier violence in Texas. From 1874 to 1918, they succeeded in establishing law and order to even the most remote portions of Texas. The Texas Rangers remain in operation today.

See also Ford, John Salmon; Hays, John Coffee; Huamantla, Battle of; Monterrey, Battle of; Walker, Samuel H.

For further reading: Davis, *The Texas Rangers*, 1991; Samora, *Gunpowder Justice: A Reassessment of the Texas Rangers*, 1979; Sterling, *Trails and Trials of a Texas Ranger*, 1968; Webb, *The Texas Rangers: A Century of Frontier Defense*, 1965.

Thoreau, Henry David
(1817–1862)

A prominent U.S. writer and naturalist, Henry David Thoreau opposed the Mexican-American War and argued against it in his writings.

Thoreau was born in Massachusetts, and his love of the wilderness started at a very early age. After he graduated from Harvard University, he taught school and emphasized nature field trips. In 1845, he moved to the shores of Walden Pond, where he lived and wrote until 1847.

As an act of demonstration against the impending conflict with Mexico, Thoreau refused to pay a poll tax in 1845. He was later arrested and jailed. Thoreau maintained that the Mexican-American War was being waged to propagate slavery. In *Civil Disobedience* (1849), he wrote,

> In other words, when a sixth of the population of a nation which has undertaken to be the refuge of liberty are slaves, and a whole country is unjustly overrun and conquered by a

foreign army, and subjected to military law, I think that it is not too soon for honest men to rebel and revolutionize. What makes this duty the more urgent is the fact that the country so overrun is not our own, but ours is the invading army.... This people must cease to hold slaves, and to make war on Mexico, though it cost them their existence as a people.

After the war, Thoreau developed a close friendship with fellow author Ralph Waldo Emerson. Thoreau's famous *Walden, or Life in the Woods* was published in 1854. He adamantly supported abolitionist John Brown in 1859. Suffering from tuberculosis, he lived his last few years as a semi-invalid. Too weak to hold a book, he died at age 45.

For further reading: Harding, *The Days of Henry David Thoreau*, 1970; Sanborn, *The Life of Henry David Thoreau*, 1917; Thoreau, *Civil Disobedience and Other Essays*, 1993.

Thornton, Seth B.
(d. 1847)

Lieutenant Seth B. Thornton of the 2nd U.S. Dragoons was captured by General Anastasio Torrejón at the Skirmish of Carricitos Ranch in April 1846. Dragoon casualties from the fight prompted President James K. Polk to call for a war against Mexico.

After General Zachary Taylor's Army of Occupation arrived on the Río Grande in 1846, Thornton and a squadron of 56 men rode out on a patrol April 25. Led by a Mexican named Chapita, they had gone about 20 miles before Chapita insisted the Mexicans were quite near, and refused to go further. Chapita returned to the camp.

Thornton pushed on to the abandoned Carricitos Ranch, where his men were trapped by a large group of cavalry under General Anastasio Torrejón. The dragoons tried to fight their way out, but they soon surrendered after losing 11 killed and 6 wounded. Shortly afterward a Mexican cart bearing a wounded dragoon arrived in Taylor's camp. Thornton and the other survivors were marched to Matamoros and were later exchanged.

On August 15, 1847, while escorting some engineers near the fortifications at Churubusco, Thornton was killed by an exploding artillery shell.

See also Carricitos Ranch, Skirmish at; Chapita.

For further reading: Alcaraz, *The Other Side*, 1850; Cullum, *Biographical Register of the Officers and Graduates of the United States Military Academy from 1802 to 1867*, 1879; Smith, *To Mexico with Scott*, 1917.

Tilghman, Lloyd
(1816–1863)

An engineer, Lieutenant Lloyd Tilghman performed engineering, reconnaissance, and artillery duties under General Zachary Taylor and General Winfield Scott during the Mexican-American War.

Tilghman, who was born near Clairborne, Maryland, graduated from the U.S. Military Academy in 1836. After briefly serving in the 1st U.S. Dragoons, he resigned to become a civil engineer.

Tilghman reenlisted for the Mexican-American War. As part of General Zachary Taylor's Army of Occupation, he helped build Fort Texas (later Fort Brown). He and Lieutenant Jacob E. Blake rode forward before the Battle of Palo Alto in May 1846 and scouted the Mexican line from 100 yards away with field glasses, looking for artillery hidden in the tall prairie grass. In a chivalrous gesture, General Mariano Arista did not allow his troops to fire on the two scouts. Tilghman also served as aide-de-camp to Brigadier General David E. Twiggs. He performed capably as captain of the Maryland and D.C. Regiment of Volunteer Artillery in 1847–1848.

After the war Tilghman was employed as a construction engineer on railroad projects in the South. He later became a brigadier general for the Confederacy during the Civil War and was killed in action at Champion's Hill in 1863 while positioning artillery.

See also Blake, Jacob E.; Palo Alto, Battle of.

For further reading: Cullum, *Biographical Register of the Officers and Graduates of the United States Military Academy from 1802 to 1867*, 1879; Henry, *Campaign Sketches of the War with Mexico*, 1847.

Todos Santos, Skirmish at
(March 28, 1848)

As part of the U.S. occupational force at La Paz along the Gulf of California, Lieutenant Colonel Henry S. Burton and 217 New York volunteers left La Paz on March 28, 1848, for the village of Todos Santos, a base for guerrilla Mauricio Castro. On March 31, they attacked the Mexican camp and dispersed the guerrilla force after a 30-minute fight. Ten Mexicans were killed or wounded. The rest were captured by U.S. patrols. The skirmish ended the fighting in Baja California.

For further reading: Bauer, *Surfboats and Horse Marines*, 1969.

Tornel y Mendivil, José María
(1789–1853)

General José María Tornel y Mendivil was an active member of the Mexican Army during the war with the United States and worked closely with General Antonio López de Santa Anna during the Veracruz–Mexico City campaign.

Born in Orizaba, Veracruz, Tornel y Mendivil was educated in Mexico City. He joined the revolutionary forces that fought against the Spanish government. After independence was won, he served closely in various positions with Presidents Guadalupe Victoria, Vicente Guerrero, and Antonio López de Santa Anna. From 1829 to 1831, Tornel y Mendivil served as plenipotentiary minister to the United States and worked hard to minimize conflict between Mexico and the U.S. government, which at that time was led by Andrew Jackson.

After the rebellion of General Mariano Paredes y Arrillaga in December 1845 that toppled the government of José Joaquín de Herrerra, Tornel y Mendivil, who had supported the rebellion, became the new secretary of war. A close ally of Santa Anna, he frequently advised Santa Anna during the Mexican-American War and urged him to command the Army of the East. Santa Anna appointed Tornel y Mendivil governor of the Federal District, and Tornel y Mendivil remained a trusted aide, advisor, and liaison throughout the Veracruz–Mexico City campaign in 1847. As part of the junta in Mexico City on the night of September 13, Tornel y Mendivil helped Santa Anna decide to withdraw his forces from the city.

Tornel y Mendivil continued to be an important political and military figure after the war. He wrote several history books and plays and promoted education. The active minister of war in 1853, he died at age 64 in Mexico City.

For further reading: Alcaraz, *The Other Side*, 1850; *Diccionario Porrúa*, 1995.

Torrejón, Anastasio
(ca. 1802–ca. 1861)

One of the more capable Mexican generals during the Mexican-American War, Anastasio Torrejón commanded the Mexican cavalry during the northern Mexico and Veracruz–Mexico City battles.

Born in the Llanos de Apan, Torrejón joined the Spanish army at age 14. He participated in various campaigns against rebel groups fighting for independence from Spain. In 1823, he aligned himself with Antonio López de Santa Anna in the overthrow of Agustín de Iturbide. Torrejón was part of fellow general Mariano Paredes y Arrillaga's revolt that deposed President José Joaquín Herrera in 1845.

By the outbreak of the Mexican-American War, Torrejón was one of the most highly regarded officers in the Mexican army. As a brigadier general of cavalry he was attached to General Mariano Arista's Army of the North at Matamoros and conducted reconnaissance patrols. His men surprised a squadron of U.S. cavalry under Lieutenant Seth B. Thornton at Carricitos Ranch on April 25 in the first armed fight in the war. This was the skirmish that compelled President James K. Polk to claim that American blood had been spilled on American soil.

A faithful supporter of Santa Anna, Torrejón was apparently in good standing with his commander throughout the war. Torrejón commanded his cavalry at the Battles of Palo Alto, Resaca de Guerrero (Resaca de la Palma), Monterrey, and La Angostura (Buena Vista), where his cavalry attack on the U.S. left flank nearly won the battle. His cavalry suffered heavy losses at the Battle of Padierna (Contreras) in August 1847; they also fought outside Mexico City at Garita San Cosmé. He was captured toward the end of the war by General Winfield Scott's Dominguez Spy Company after a skirmish with guerrilla forces near Mexico City.

After the war Torrejón remained in the military and served as the commandant general of Michoacán.

See also Carricitos Ranch, Skirmish at.

For further reading: Alcaraz, *The Other Side,* 1850; Carreño, *Jefes del ejército mexicano en 1847,* 1914.

Tower, Zealous Bates
(1819–1900)

An engineer with General Winfield Scott's Army of Occupation in 1847, Tower performed dangerous reconnaissance missions and was one of the few officers to receive three or more brevets during the Mexican-American War.

Tower, who was born in Massachusetts, graduated from the U.S. Military Academy in 1841. He was commissioned a second lieutenant in the Corps of Engineers and supervised the building of fortifications in Virginia.

During the Mexican-American War, Tower served as an engineer with Major General Winfield Scott's Army of Occupation. He performed dangerous reconnaissance missions in front of Mexican positions and commanded troops in battle. During the Battle of Chapultepec in September 1847, he was wounded in the head while leading a storming column through heavy fire. By the end of the war, he had been brevetted three times to the rank of major.

After the war Tower continued to construct coastal defenses. As a brigadier general of volunteers for the Union, he fought in the Battle of Cedar Mountain and in the second Battle of Bull Run, during which he was badly wounded. In 1864, he became the superintendent at the U.S. Military Academy, and he also supervised the construction of Union defenses in Tennessee. Tower retired in 1883 to Massachusetts.

For further reading: Cullum, *Biographical Register of the Officers and Graduates of the United States Military Academy from 1802 to 1867,* 1879.

Transcontinental Treaty
(1819)

The United States agreed, according to the terms of the 1819 Transcontinental Treaty, to surrender all rights to what became the lands of the Republic of Mexico in 1821, including Texas. This conflicted with the U.S. expansionism in the 1840s.

The 1819 treaty between the United States and Spain (the Adams-Onís Treaty) defined the boundaries between the United States and New Spain (later Mexico). Article III stated that

> The boundary line between the two countries, west of the Mississippi, shall begin on the Gulph of Mexico, at the mouth of the river Sabine, in the sea, continuing north, along the western bank of that river, to the 32d degree of latitude; thence, by a line due north, to the degree of latitude where it strikes the Rio Roxo of Nachitoches, or Red River; then following the course of Rio Roxo westward to the degree of longitude 100 west from London and 23 from Washington; then, crossing the said Red River, and running thence by a line due north, to the river Arkansas; thence, following the course of the southern bank of the Arkansas, to its source, in latitude 42 north; and thence, by that parallel of latitude, to the South Sea....
>
> The two high contracting parties agree to cede and renounce all their rights, claims, and pretensions, to the territories described by the said line, that is to say: The United States hereby cede to His Catholic Majesty, and renounce forever, all their rights, claims and pretensions, to the territories lying west and south of the above-described line; and in like manner, His Catholic Majesty cedes to the said United States

all his rights, claims, and pretensions to any territories east and north of the said line, and for himself, his heirs, and successor, renounces all claim to the said territories forever....

Signed by John Quincy Adams, the United States plenipotentiary, this treaty surrendered all U.S. rights to, and any possible U.S. ownership of, the lands of New Spain. When Mexico won independence from Spain in 1821, the lands west and south of this border became part of the Republic of Mexico. The document clearly states that the border between the United States and Texas was the Sabine River, and this was the legal basis by which Mexico claimed sovereignty over this territory. The United States maintained that since the province of Texas had seceded from Mexico and was recognized as an independent republic, it was no longer Mexican territory. However, the treaty states that any U.S. claim to the territory is renounced "forever."

For further reading: Brooks, *Diplomacy and the Borderlands*, 1939.

Treaties

See Cahuenga, Treaty of; Gadsden Treaty; Guadalupe Hidalgo, Treaty of; Transcontinental Treaty.

Trías Álvarez, Ángel
(1809–1867)

The affluent governor of the state of Chihuahua, Ángel Trías Álvarez commanded troops against the invasion of Colonel Alexander Doniphan in 1847 and Brigadier General Sterling Price in 1848.

Ángel Trías Álvarez was born in Chihuahua City to an affluent family. Educated in Europe, he returned and became involved in the state's military and political affairs. A popular citizen and large landowner, he became governor in 1845.

The governor frequently appealed to the Mexican government for military assistance and supplies, but little was provided. As the 1,100-man expedition of Colonel Alexander Doniphan approached in February 1847, Trías Álvarez was determined to organize an army to fight Doniphan. Using his own wealth, he quickly assembled and outfitted a 2,000-man army. A foundry was built to cast new cannon. Additional troops arrived under the command of Brigadier General José A. Heredia. After losing the Battle of Río Sacramento, Trías Álvarez withdrew his state government to Parral. In an effort to regain his capital, Trías Álvarez went to Mexico City to see General Antonio López de Santa Anna about money and supplies for reinforcements; he eventually found Santa Anna at Cerro Gordo and fought during the battle there. Trías returned to Parral with no promises from Santa Anna.

After the Treaty of Guadalupe Hidalgo had been signed in February 1848, Brigadier General Sterling Price invaded Chihuahua. Despite Trías Álvarez's face-to-face insistence with Price that a treaty had been signed, Price seized Chihuahua City. Again Trías Álvarez retreated to Santa Cruz de Rosales, where his small force was defeated during a daylong battle with Price on March 16, 1848. Captured as a prisoner of war, the governor was released when Price was ordered to withdraw by Secretary of War William L. Marcy.

Trías Álvarez remained in Chihuahua for the rest of his life and was a well respected and influential politician. He commanded state troops during the tense negotiations regarding the Mesilla Valley in 1853. He died in Chihuahua City at the age of 58.

See also Chihuahua; Price, Sterling; Río Sacramento, Battle of; Santa Cruz de Rosales, Battle of.

For further reading: Bieber, *Marching with the Army of the West 1846–1848*, 1936; Chamberlain, *My Confession*, 1956; *Diccionario Porrúa de historia, biografía y geografía de México*, 1995.

Trist, Nicholas Philip
(1800–1874)

Nicholas P. Trist helped negotiate the Treaty of Guadalupe Hidalgo in 1847–1848. Signed on February 2, 1848, the treaty ended the Mexican-American War.

Trist, who was born in Virginia, studied law and attended the U.S. Military Academy. He

Nicholas Philip Trist
(Library of Congress)

later served in the U.S. State Department and as a secretary to President Andrew Jackson. From 1833 to 1841, he was the U.S. consul in Havana, Cuba. He later rejoined the State Department, and Secretary of State James Buchanan recommended his appointment as the U.S. envoy to negotiate peace with Mexico in 1847.

Departing for Mexico on April 15, Trist was authorized to secure New Mexico, California, and the right of passage across the Isthmus of Tehuantepec and to offer no more than $20 million as compensation. Trist arrived at Veracruz in May and traveled with Major General Winfield Scott's army as it approached Mexico City. Peace negotiations began in September 1847, following the Battle of Churubusco. An impasse was quickly reached, and the talks were abandoned on September 6.

President James K. Polk recalled Trist on October 2. He wanted to change the terms to include more Mexican territory (Baja California and Tampico) and worried that Trist's extended presence might give Mexico the impression that the United States was desperate for a peace settlement. Trist, however, knew that the war would drag on if he did not succeed with a treaty and that the entire Republic of Mexico might be overrun. Knowing that the *puros* wanted to continue the war, Trist also feared a shutdown in negotiations would strengthen the *puro* position. Remarkably, Trist defied Polk's order and remained in Mexico City to successfully conclude the Treaty of Guadalupe Hidalgo in February 1848.

Polk was incensed by the treaty, but because it met his territorial objectives and had public support, he was forced to accept it. Trist returned to the United States to work as a paymaster and postmaster. He died in Washington at age 74.

See also Guadalupe Hidalgo, Treaty of.

For further reading: Drexler, *Guilty of Making Peace*, 1991; Fuller, *The Movement for the Acquisition of All Mexico,1846–1848*, 1936; Griswold del Castillo, *The Treaty of Guadalupe Hidalgo*, 1991; Mahin, *Olive Branch and Sword*, 1997; Pletcher, *The Diplomacy of Annexation*, 1973.

Truxtun, USS

The USS *Truxtun* ran aground near Tampico in August 1846, and its crew was captured by Mexican troops. The ship was later burned by U.S. forces.

On August 12, 1846, Commodore David E. Conner of the U.S. Navy Home Squadron ordered the *Truxtun* to Tampico. On August 14, during a strong gale, it was driven upon Tuxpan Reef. Its commander, Edward W. Carpender, was ordered to surrender by General Antonio Rosas. Carpender refused and dispatched Lieutenant Ortway H. Berryman in one of its cutters to Antón Lizardo for help. Meanwhile, Carpender surrendered.

Lieutenant Berryman was picked up by the *St. Mary's*, and as soon as Conner was informed of the *Truxton's* plight he sent the *Princeton* and the *Falmouth* to her aid. A boarding party on August 21 discovered the ship was bilged, and almost everything had been salvaged by the Mexicans. The sailors then set fire to the ship. In October, the crew of the *Truxton* was exchanged for General Rafael de la Vega and other officers who had been captured by General Zachary Taylor's army during the Battle of Resaca de la Palma.

For further reading: Bauer, *Surfboats and Horse Marines*, 1969.

Turley's Mill

See Arroyo Hondo, Skirmish at.

Tuxpan

The river port of Tuxpan in the state of Veracruz was occupied by a U.S. naval force under Commodore Matthew C. Perry in April 1847. The town of Tuxpan is located along the Tuxpan River, about six miles upstream from its mouth on the Mexican gulf coast.

Commodore Matthew C. Perry of the U.S. Home Squadron decided to attack the city in April 1847. A squadron of U.S. ships arrived at the mouth of the Tuxpan River on April 17 carrying a 1,500-man landing party. Boat parties carefully sounded the notoriously shallow channel. On board the *Spitfire, Vixen, Scourge, Bonita, Petrel, Reefer,* and about 30 barges, the invasion force crossed the bar and steamed upriver.

About three miles upstream atop a 60-foot-high hill, La Peña—a small fort with three guns—guarded the approach to Tuxpan. Farther upstream was La Palmasola, a two-cannon battery. Two guns also crowned Hospital Hill on the outskirts of Tuxpan. The defenses were manned by about 350 soldiers under General Martín Perfecto de Cos.

Perry's flotilla drew the fire of La Peña on April 18. A landing party soon captured the fort without any resistance. Sniper fire from the thick chaparral along the banks wounded Commander Josiah Tattnall and three other officers. La Palmasola also fell after a brief exchange of shots, as did Hospital Hill late in the afternoon. Tuxpan was occupied that night, but continued skirmishing resulted in U.S. casualties of two killed and nine wounded. An expedition sailed upriver the following day and seized several small ships and destroyed military equipment and munitions. When Perry left on April 22, the *Albany* and *Reefer* remained behind to guard the mouth of the Tuxpan River.

See also Cos, Martín Perfecto de; Perry, Matthew Calbraith; Tattnall, Josiah.

For further reading: Bauer, *Surfboats and Horse Marines,* 1969; Morison, *"Old Bruin" Commodore Matthew Calbraith Perry,* 1967; Semmes, *Service Afloat and Ashore during the Mexican War,* 1851.

Twiggs, David Emanuel
(1790–1862)

Brigadier General David E. Twiggs led U.S. troops during most of the battles in northern Mexico and the Veracruz–Mexico City campaign. His cool leadership helped General Zachary Taylor win the Battles of Palo Alto and Resaca de la Palma in May 1846, which gave the U.S. army tremendous confidence and momentum.

The son of an American Revolutionary general, David E. Twiggs was born in Georgia. He saw action as an officer in the 8th U.S. Infantry during the War of 1812 and against the Seminoles in Florida. Later he became the colonel of the 2nd U.S. Dragoons. Twiggs was nicknamed "Old Davy" and was well known for his quick temper and curtness.

When the Mexican-American War began, Twiggs was part of General Zachary Taylor's Army of Occupation. Taylor quickly grew tired of the squabbling between Twiggs and brevet Brigadier General William J. Worth, whose regular-army rank was junior to Twiggs. Twiggs's sound leadership as Taylor's second in command during the pivotal battles of Palo

David E. Twiggs
(Library of Congress)

Alto and Resaca de la Palma in May 1846 won him a promotion to brigadier general on June 30, 1846.

After Taylor's northern campaign stalled following the Battle of Monterrey, Twiggs's division was assigned to General Winfield Scott's army that landed at Veracruz on March 9, 1847. Twiggs's men led the vanguard of the army as it advanced into Mexico's interior along the National Road. Twiggs pushed his men relentlessly, to the point where the road was dotted with soldiers who had collapsed from the heat. His impetuous streak showed when he nearly charged General Antonio López de Santa Anna's fortified position at Cerro Gordo before the rest of the army arrived. After capably leading the attack during the Battle of Cerro Gordo on April 17, Twiggs did not have a prominent role in the subsequent battles that led to the occupation of Mexico City. He was later a member of the court of inquiry that investigated charges against his old nemesis General Worth, and he also served as military governor of Veracruz from December 1847 to March 1848.

Following the war, Twiggs held a variety of frontier commands. As commander of the Department of Texas, he surrendered his soldiers and supplies to Texas colonel General Ben McCulloch in Texas at the beginning of the Civil War, which led to his dismissal from the U.S. Army. He became a major general for the Confederacy afterward, but he was too old for field duty. He died in Georgia in 1862.

See also Cerro Gordo, Battle of; Palo Alto, Battle of; Resaca de la Palma, Battle of; Worth, William Jenkins.

For further reading: Frost, *The Mexican War and Its Warriors*, 1848.

Tyler, John
(1790–1862)

The tenth president of the United States, John Tyler worked diligently at annexing Texas. On his last day in office, he sent Texas a Congress-approved offer of annexation, which was accepted four months later during President James K. Polk's administration.

Tyler, who was born in Virginia, graduated from the College of William and Mary at age 17. After studying law, he entered Virginia politics. Tyler served as a congressman in Washington, D.C., from 1816 to 1821 and was elected governor of Virginia in 1825. Tyler became vice-president when William Henry Harrison won the presidential race in 1840. Harrison's premature death in 1841 made Tyler the tenth president of the United States.

Tyler's protracted quarrels with the U.S. Congress led to his nickname "Old Veto." Initially, Tyler was hesitant about annexing Texas because of the slavery issue. Yet also concerned about British and French interest in Texas, Tyler later tried to acquire the republic. Captain John C. Frémont explored extensively during his administration, which added to the growing expansionist mood of the country. Led by Henry Clay and Martin Van Buren, the first attempt to annex Texas was rejected by the U.S. Senate in 1844.

Later that year Tyler sent Duff Green to Mexico to negotiate the purchase of Texas, California, and New Mexico. Mexico adamantly refused. In September, Tyler appointed Green U.S. consul to Texas at Galveston. Anxious to annex Texas before James K. Polk took office in 1845, Tyler sent other representatives to Texas and Mexico City and continued to advocate annexation before the U.S. Congress. On February 27, 1845, the Senate passed the annexation bill. On March 3, his last day in office, Tyler sent the annexation plan to the Republic of Texas (which was accepted in July 1845).

Tyler's other presidential accomplishments included reorganizing the U.S. Navy and founding the National Weather Bureau. After his presidency he retired to his Virginia plantation. Tyler briefly served in the Confederate Congress during the Civil War before he died at age 72.

See also Donelson, Andrew Jackson; Green, Duff.

For further reading: Caruso, *The Mexican Spy Company*, 1991; Peterson, *The Presidencies of William Henry Harrison and John Tyler*, 1989; Smith, *The Annexation of Texas*, 1911; Tyler, *The Letters and Times of the Tylers*, 1885.

U

Urrea, José
(1797–1849)

A Mexican general during the Mexican-American War, José Urrea commanded regular cavalry and guerrilla troops during General Zachary Taylor's campaign in northern Mexico.

Raised in the state of Durango, Urrea joined the Spanish army at age 11. He participated in the suppression of revolutions against the Spanish government until 1821, when he joined the forces of Agustín de Iturbide. In 1835, he was elected governor of Durango and appointed brigadier general. During the Texan Revolution, as ordered by General Antonio López de Santa Anna, he advanced to Matamoros in 1836 and entered Texas. He performed well in the Battle of Agua Dulce Creek and the Battle of Coleto Creek, during which he captured nearly 300 Texans under James W. Fannin. Despite Urrea's protestations, General Santa Anna ordered that the prisoners be shot (for which Urrea was frequently blamed). After the Texas Revolution, Urrea held military positions at Matamoros and Sonora, where he controlled the local government.

During the Mexican-American War, Urrea served as a cavalry general. In command of an ever-changing cavalry-guerrilla force of several thousand soldiers, Urrea tormented U.S. patrols and wagon trains along General Zachary Taylor's supply routes. In February 1847, his men brutally attacked a wagon train near Ramos; several teamsters were reportedly tortured and mutilated. Urrea later took his men to San Luis Potosí and continued to launch guerrilla raids, mostly in the province of Tamaulipas.

After the war Urrea was named commandant general of Sonora. He was in the process of writing his memoirs when he died at the age of 52.

See also Ramos.

For further reading: Alcaraz, *The Other Side*, 1850; Bancroft, *History of the North Mexican States and Texas*, 1884–1889; Chamberlain, *My Confession*, 1956; *Diccionario Porrúa de historia, biografía y geografía de México*, 1995; Roa Bárcena, *Recuerdos de la invasión norte-americana*, 1947; Ruiz, *Triumphs and Tragedy*, 1992.

Utah

Present-day Utah was originally part of the Mexican provinces of Alta California, Sonora y Sinaloa, and New Mexico, which were ceded to the United States at the end of the Mexican-American War.

Some of the earliest inhabitants of the area of present-day Utah were native tribes such as the Gosiute, Paiute, Shoshoni, and Ute. One of the last sections of North America to be explored by Europeans, Utah was first visited by Spanish Franciscan monks in 1776. American and Canadian fur traders began to enter the area from the north and east in the early 1800s. This part of Alta California, Sonora y Sinaloa, and New Mexico belonged to the Republic of Mexico after it gained independence from Spain in 1821.

As southern Utah was crossed by travelers going from Santa Fe to Los Angeles in the 1830s, more Americans settled in the area. The first large group of permanent settlers, Mormons led by Joseph Smith, arrived in 1847. Utah was given to the United States according to the terms of the Treaty of Guadalupe Hidalgo in 1848, and the territory of Utah became the forty fifth U.S. state in 1896.

For further reading: Peterson, *Utah,* 1977; Poll, *Utah's History,* 1978.

V

Valencia, Gabriel
(1799–1848)

A prominent Mexican general, Gabriel Valencia quarreled with General Antonio López de Santa Anna and was disgraced at the Battle of Padierna (Contreras) in August 1847.

Valencia, who was born in Mexico City, joined the Spanish army as a youth. After fighting various insurrections against the Spanish government, he joined the forces of Agustín de Iturbide in 1821. Continuing in the Mexican army, Valencia was soon a brigadier general and ally of General Antonio López de Santa Anna. Santa Anna and Valencia continued to work together to gain political advantage, including participating in the overthrow of President Anastasio Bustamante in 1841. Valencia also helped depose President José Joaquín Herrera in 1845 and aligned himself with new president Mariano Paredes y Arrillaga.

Valencia was stationed at San Luis Potosí in 1847, and he argued with Santa Anna about attacking General Zachary Taylor's army in northern Mexico. Santa Anna instead ordered Valencia and his Army of the North to join the Army of the East in attempting to stop General Winfield Scott's advance from Mexico City. Settling at Padierna against Santa Anna's wishes, Valencia then refused to obey Santa Anna's orders to pull back toward Churubusco. On the eve of the Battle of Padierna (Contreras), Santa Anna had advanced reinforcements toward Valencia, only to withdraw them. The following day, August 20, Valencia's force was wrecked in a battle that lasted less than 30 minutes. Santa Anna's refusal to help Valencia has been interpreted by some as an effort to disgrace Valencia with an embarrassing and costly loss. After the battle, Santa Anna issued orders to have Valencia shot on sight. Valencia retreated through the backcountry to safety.

Valencia died in Mexico City in 1848, shortly after the Treaty of Guadalupe Hidalgo had been signed. U.S. soldier J. J. Oswandel recalled that "his death has caused a gloom and great mourning among the gentle portion of the community. At San Angel all the church bells tolled in sorrow at his death.... It is a well-known fact that if Gen. Santa Anna, with his twelve thousand troops who were in reserve, had supported. Gen. Valencia at the battle of Contreras...our army would not so easy have gotten into the city of Mexico...."

For further reading: Alcaraz, *The Other Side*, 1850; Costeloe, *The Central Republic in Mexico, 1835–1846*, 1993; DePalo, *The Mexican National Army, 1822–1852*, 1997; Oswandel, *Notes of the Mexican War*, 1885.

Vallejo, Mariano Guadalupe
(1808–1890)

One of the most prominent citizens in northern California, Vallejo was captured during the Bear Flag Revolt in 1846. He was later active in the U.S. military government that was established in 1847–1848.

Born in Monterey to Mexican parents, Vallejo was raised in an affluent family. He attended a military academy in California and commanded forces in 1829 that suppressed an

283

Indian rebellion. Vallejo also helped the Mexican government secularize the Franciscan missions, and in the process he acquired vast property holdings. He was also elected to the territorial legislature.

In the 1840s, Vallejo was supportive of the possible takeover of California by the United States. One of Sonoma's most prominent citizens, he was seized by the unruly Bear Flaggers in 1846 and was imprisoned at Sutter's Fort for two months under the watchful eye of Captain John C. Frémont. His incarceration was largely symbolic, and he was well treated. After the U.S. government in California was established in 1847, he served on the legislative council. Brigadier General and temporary Governor Stephen W. Kearny also made him an Indian agent.

In 1849, Vallejo was elected to the constitutional convention and California's first senate. He fought for nearly a decade to save his land grants, but they were eventually lost to squatters and speculators. He did, however, receive a payment of nearly $50,000 for damages. When he died in 1890, he owned only a tiny portion of his once vast landholdings.

See also Bear Flag Revolt.

For further reading: McKittrick, *Vallejo, Son of California*, 1944; Rosenus, *General M. G. Vallejo and the Advent of the Americans*, 1995.

Van Dorn, Earl
(1820–1863)

A U.S. infantry officer, Earl Van Dorn was frequently cited for gallantry during his Mexican-American War service, and he was brevetted twice for his actions at Monterrey and Contreras.

Van Dorn was born in Mississippi. Although his father wanted him to receive a formal education, Van Dorn instead appealed to President Andrew Jackson for an appointment to the U.S. Military Academy, from which he graduated in 1842. He fought Indians in Florida before becoming part of General Zachary Taylor's Army of Occupation at Corpus Christi, Texas, in 1845.

In 1846, the Army of Occupation moved to the Río Grande. Assigned to the 7th U.S. Infantry, Van Dorn rescued a fallen U.S. flag in front of Fort Brown during the fighting there in May. His bravery and leadership were frequently noted by his commanding officers. Van Dorn helped lead the attack that drove the Mexican defenders from Federation Hill during the Battle of Monterrey in September 1846, which helped secure the western approach to the city.

Transferred to Major General Winfield Scott's army that landed at Veracruz in 1847, Van Dorn led forces that assaulted El Telégrafo during the Battle of Cerro Gordo in April. He was commended by General Scott and was brevetted to captain. His accomplishments during the Battles of Contreras and Chapultepec won him a brevet to major. During the intense fighting at Garita Belén outside Mexico City on September 13, he was wounded in the foot.

Returning to the United States, Van Dorn fought Indians on the western frontier and was wounded four times by arrows during a fight with Comanches in 1858. Van Dorn joined the Confederacy during the Civil War as a brigadier general. He was murdered in Tennessee in 1863 by a jealous husband who accused him of having an affair with his wife.

For further reading: Cullum, *Biographical Register of the Officers and Graduates of the United States Military Academy from 1802 to 1867*, 1879; Hartje, *Van Dorn*, 1967.

Vázquez, Ciriaco
(1794–1847)

General Ciriaco Vázquez commanded a brigade of infantry in the Army of the North and the Army of the East during the Mexican-American War. He was killed in action at the Battle of Cerro Gordo in April 1847.

Vázquez, who was born in Veracruz, joined a Spanish infantry regiment at age 15. He fought various revolutionary forces until independence in 1821, when he joined the new Mexican army. His leadership in driving a Spanish invasion force from Tampico resulted in a promotion to brigade general. He was also the commandant general at Veracruz and Jalapa.

At the onset of the Mexican-American War, Vázquez commanded a division of troops that

Ciriaco Vázquez
(Library of Congress)

guarded the region around Tamaulipas. After the fall of Veracruz to General Winfield Scott in March 1847, Vázquez and his brigade marched quickly to join the Army of the East being assembled to defend Cerro Gordo. Entrenched on the summit of El Telégrafo, his men at first offered a determined resistance to the U.S. attack on their position on April 18, 1847. Vázquez was killed in the midst of the fighting as he tried to rally his troops.

See also Cerro Gordo, Battle of.

For further reading: Alcaraz, *The Other Side*, 1850; *Diccionario Porrúa de historia, biografía y geografía de México*, 1995; Roa Bárcena, *Recuerdos de la invasión norte-americana*, 1947.

Veracruz

Veracruz, in the state of Veracruz, was the best port city along Mexico's gulf coast. Connected to Mexico City by the National Road, it was the starting point of Major General Winfield Scott's 1847 campaign for Mexico City.

An attractive city on the edge of the Gulf of Mexico, Veracruz was the deepest port along the gulf. A reef of sand and rock, known as Gallega, stood about 1,500 feet away to the northeast. Upon it was built the castle San Juan de Ulúa, a formidable structure that bristled with cannon from its 60-foot-high walls.

Many of the homes and buildings of Veracruz were built from massive sandstone blocks. Above the walls that enclosed the city in a hexagonal shape could be seen glittering cupolas, church spires, and domes. The walls were mounted with batteries that guarded the approaches and could enfilade the deep ditch that surrounded the outer wall. April through October was the rainy season, which brought the dreaded *vomito*, or yellow fever. When the city was infected, all business and trade stopped until the epidemic passed.

Blockading ships from the U.S. Home Squadron were frequently seen close by in 1846–1847. After Veracruz was shelled into submission by General Winfield Scott in March 1847, it became a busy U.S. military base. Commodore Matthew C. Perry's headquarters were in the city. The harbor was crowded with vessels bringing soldiers and supplies. Coal was stored at San Juan de Ulúa, and new wharves, sheds, and buildings were constructed. The city was garrisoned by the 1st U.S. infantry and two companies of volunteers, whose job was to keep the U.S. soldiers at the waterfront and out of the city. Veracruz was also the site of a large field hospital in 1847–1848.

See also Veracruz, Battle of.

For further reading: Alcaraz, *The Other Side*, 1850; Bauer, *Surfboats and Horse Marines*, 1969; Semmes, *Service Afloat and Ashore during the Mexican War*, 1851; Trens, *Historia de Veracruz*, 1947–1950.

Veracruz, Battle of
(March 9–29, 1847)

After the amphibious landing of 10,000 men and artillery under the command of Major General Winfield Scott, the city of Veracruz was shelled into submission during a 21-day siege. From Veracruz, Scott launched his inland advance along the National Road to take Mexico City five months later.

Dismayed by the slow progress of the war in northern Mexico and by General Zachary Taylor's reluctance to strike overland for Mexico City from Monterrey, President James K. Polk authorized the opening of another front:

Veracruz. Major General Scott, the senior commander of the U.S. Army, was chosen to lead the advance. Sailing in January 1847 from New Orleans to Camargo on the Río Grande, Scott took the better portion of Taylor's idle Army of Occupation and ventured down the gulf coast for Veracruz.

Scott had put considerable care into planning the landing of his 10,000-man army. Only half of the specially designed surfboats he had ordered for transporting his soldiers had arrived, but it was imperative he land his army, organize, and move out before the rainy season, and its rampant yellow fever, began in April (Mexican leaders were confident the *vomito* would incapacitate the army enough that an expert defense could be planned).

Scott had chosen to land his troops at Collado Beach, a few miles south and out of range of the city's defenses and artillery, and sheltered by Sacrificios Island. The first major sea invasion in U.S. military history went very smoothly on March 9. About 100 vessels landed more than 12,000 soldiers and tons of equipment by midnight. An observer wrote of the spectacle, "the tall ships of war sailing leisurely along under their topsails, their decks thronged in every part with dense masses of troops whose bright muskets and bayonets were flashing in the sunbeams; the jingle of spurs and sabres; the bands of music playing; the hum of the multitude rising up like the murmors [sic] of the distant ocean; the small steamers plying about, their decks crowded with anxious spectators; the long line of surfboats towing astern of the ships." (Bauer 1969)

Scott wanted no more than 100 casualties in taking the city. As his men moved toward Veracruz they found the approaches had been planted with prickly pears, trenches, and sharpened stakes to slow their advance. On March 10, Scott began to encircle the city with his forces and shut off the water supply to the city. The heavy guns from the warships were hauled by hand across the deep sand under the guidance of engineers, such as Captain Robert E. Lee. It took nearly two weeks to place all the guns.

Scott's ultimatum to surrender was rejected by the Mexican commanders on March 22. He then began to use the land batteries, and those on the U.S. warships, to shell the city. Lee recalled painfully that "the shells thrown from our battery were constant and regular discharges, so beautiful in their flight and so destructive in their fall. It was awful! My heart bled for the inhabitants. The soldiers I did not care so much for, but it was terrible to think of the women and children." Houses were shattered, field hospitals at the Church of San Francisco and Santo Domingo were destroyed, and corpses littered the streets.

After the second day of shelling, Scott refused a plea to allow women, children, and noncombatants to leave the city. The shelling continued night and day. On March 26, the acting commander, General José Juan Landero, asked Scott for terms. A temporary truce was called. Commissioners from both sides agreed on treaty terms on March 29. The city had been demolished by nearly 7,000 shells, and hundreds of civilians, including many women and children, had been killed. The bombardment drew criticism from Mexico, Europe, and the United States as being cruel and inhumane. Mexican losses are estimated as high as 1,100 military and civilian deaths; Scott lost only 68 killed and wounded.

The Mexican army marched out of Veracruz on March 29. Pennsylvania soldier J. J. Oswandel recalled,

> At 10 o'clock, A.M., the Mexicans blew their trumpets announcing their coming, and all eyes were then cast toward the Mexicans. It was a beautiful sight to see the Mexican army with their drums, fifes and bands of music playing and their flags flying in the air, marching out of their doomed city, which they have so bravely and gallantly defended to the last hour.
>
> As they marched, we could see them now and then look back to Vera Cruz, kiss and wave their hands and bidding it good-bye, when they came to a halt opposite the flag-staff. The Mexican officers then came to Gen. Scott's headquarters, who was surrounded in full uniform, by his staff Commissioners, and Commodores [Matthew C.] Perry and [Josiah] Tattnall, and their staff officers. After greeting one another,

some conversation took place in regard to the stipulation and agreement. After this the signal was given for the Mexican soldiers to stack their arms, or muskets, cartridge boxes, belts, and other munitions and implements of war, after which they were let go to their homes.

Some showed signs that they were glad to get rid of their arms, and seemed to lay them down cheerfully, while others slammed their muskets and accoutrements down on the ground with an oath and anger. One fellow could be seen taking the flag off the pole and hiding it away in his bosom…and he swore by the great God of the Universe, that he would for ever protect it, stand by and defend it from falling into the hands of the enemy. He was let keep it. He was so rejoiced over it that he cried like a child.

The whole number of prisoners were nearly six thousand soldiers. They were all well uniformed and drilled…[The surrender] was one of the grandest sights and spectacles that I have ever seen. Yet I tell you it was hard to see the poor women with their small children strapped upon their mother's back, and with what little clothing they could carry, toddling along with the Mexican soldiers.

Everything passed off quietly; no insulting remarks or fun was made towards the Mexicans as they passed out, we looked upon them as a conquered foe, who have fought for their firesides and property, the same as we would have done if attacked by a foreign foe.…

See also Collado Beach; *Petrita*, USS; San Juan de Ulúa; Veracruz; Yellow Fever.

For further reading: Alcaraz, *The Other Side*, 1850; Bauer, *Surfboats and Horse Marines*, 1969; Elliott, *Winfield Scott*, 1937; Knox, *A History of the United States Navy*, 1936; Morison, *"Old Bruin" Commodore Matthew Calbraith Perry*, 1967; Oswandel, *Notes of the Mexican War*, 1885; Semmes, *Service Afloat and Ashore during the Mexican War*, 1851; Trens, *Historia de Veracruz*, 1947–1950.

Vomito

See Yellow Fever.

W

Walker, Robert John
(1801–1869)

Robert J. Walker served as President James K. Polk's secretary of the treasury during the Mexican-American War. An ardent expansionist, he argued for overrunning all of Mexico.

Walker was born in Pennsylvania in 1801. He graduated first in his class from the University of Pennsylvania in 1819. A lawyer and politician, he supported Andrew Jackson. In 1826, he moved to Mississippi and invested in plantations and real estate. Walker served in the U.S. Senate from 1836 to 1845, and he supported western expansion, the annexation of Texas, and the Mexican-American War. Walker, as the head of the Democratic campaign convention in 1844, also helped James K. Polk secure the presidential nomination.

President Polk made Walker his secretary of the treasury. Walker enthusiastically accepted this role and helped finance the Mexican-American War through increased duties and fees on imported and exported goods and through numerous loans. However, because the tax base was not increased, the national debt soared. In 1847, as the war dragged on at higher and higher cost, Walker emphasized taking all of Mexico. In 1848 he also discussed with Polk the possibilities of annexing the Yucatán peninsula and of purchasing Cuba from Spain for $100 million.

In 1856 he actively campaigned for President James Buchanan. The following year Buchanan appointed Walker governor of Kansas Territory, where he opposed slavery until he resigned from this post about a year later. Still an ardent expansionist, Walker was a U.S. envoy in Russia during the negotiations for Alaska, and he died in 1869 with the unfulfilled dream of adding Nova Scotia to the United States.

See also "All of Mexico" Movement.

For further reading: Dodd, *Robert J. Walker, Imperialist,* 1914; Shenton, *Robert John Walker, a Politician from Jackson to Lincoln,* 1961.

Walker, Samuel H.
(1817–1847)

Samuel H. Walker led a regiment of Texas Rangers during the Mexican-American War. He was instrumental in outfitting the rangers with Colt revolvers, which gave them a tremendous advantage in close-quarters fighting.

Walker, who was born in Maryland, went to Texas in 1842. As a member of the ill-fated Mier Expedition in December 1842 during the Texan revolution, he was imprisoned in Castle Perote, but he tunneled under the massive stone walls and managed to escape to Texas. The harsh treatment of the Texan prisoners embittered Walker toward Mexico. In 1844, he joined the Texas Rangers under John C. Hays, and he fought Indians and Mexican bandits.

Anxious to fight in the Mexican-American War, Walker organized a company of rangers who joined Jack Hays's 1st Regiment of Texas Mounted Volunteers. As part of General Zachary Taylor's army on the Río Grande in April 1846, Walker and his men scouted and fought at the Battles of Palo Alto, Resaca de la Palma, and Monterrey. When Taylor needed to know the situation at Fort Texas before the Battle of Palo Alto in May 1846, Walker alone penetrated the Mexican lines around the fort the night of May 4, scaled the wall, and passed on instructions from Taylor to the fort's commander. He then reported back to Taylor in the morning.

At Monterrey, the Texans bravely stormed the heights of Independence and Federation Hills on the western outskirts of the city. Walker also showed General William J. Worth's men the cunning "Texan way" of fighting from house to house, which minimized casualties during the bitter street fighting that followed. Although Taylor appreciated the bravery and scouting abilities of this "tried frontier soldier," he was aghast at the atrocities his unruly rangers committed.

After the Texas Rangers disbanded at the end of September 1846, Walker traveled to New York to visit gun designer Samuel Colt. He made suggestions for changes in the Colt revolver, which resulted in the popular "Walker Colt" models. Walker returned to Mexico in 1847. Appointed captain of the U.S. Mounted Rifles, Walker joined Major General Winfield Scott's army as it moved from Veracruz toward Mexico City along the National Road. Walker's Rifles arrived in Perote on May 25, 1847. Ironically, he and his men were quartered in Perote Castle, where he had been imprisoned five years before. Walker quickly developed a reputation for ruthless fighting. Pennsylvania soldier J. J. Oswandel wrote that "should Capt. Walker come across the guerrillas, God help them, for he seldom brings in prisoners. The Captain and most all of his men are very prejudiced and embittered against every guerrilla in the country."

On October 9, 1847, Walker was part of an 1,800-man force sent by General Joseph Lane to strike General Antonio López de Santa Anna's small force at Huamantla. After charging a group of Mexican cavalry in the streets of the town, Walker was shot through the head and chest, "foremost in the advance." His death unleashed the worst atrocity committed against Mexican citizens during the Mexican-American War when soldiers, with the approval of General Joseph Lane, engaged in rampant looting, burning, murder, and rape.

See also Huamantla, Battle of; Monterrey, Battle of; Texas Rangers.

For further reading: Adler, *The Texas Rangers*, 1979; Brackett, *General Lane's Brigade in Central Mexico*, 1854; Davis, *The Texas Rangers*, 1991; Ford, *Rip Ford's Texas*, 1963; Oates, "Los Diablos Tejanos," 1972; Oswandel, *Notes of the Mexican War*, 1885; Spurlin, "Ranger Walker in the Mexican War," 1971; Webb, *The Texas Rangers in the Mexican War*, 1975.

Walnut Springs

Walnut Springs was a campsite for General Zachary Taylor's Army of Occupation during the Battle of Monterrey in September 1846. It was also used as a staging area for subsequent operations in northern Mexico.

As Taylor approached the outskirts of Monterrey from the north on September 19, 1846, he chose an attractive wooded area with several clear-running springs as the campsite for his army. Tall oak and pecan trees (but no walnut) provided welcome shade and firewood. General John A. Quitman wrote that "my tent is near a beautiful spring gushing out of rocks. Live oaks and ebony trees hang over it. Before me in full view at the distance of about ten miles is…the Sierra Madre."

The campiste was used by American forces during the remainder of the campaign in northern Mexico. Hundreds of U.S. dead were buried in a cemetery in the grove after the Battle of Monterrey. Although some of the bodies were reinterred in the United States, many remain in the cemetery, which is now buried beneath modern-day Monterrey.

For further reading: Henry, *Campaign Sketches of the War with Mexcio*, 1847; Smith and Judah, *Chronicles of the Gringos*, 1968.

War Address, James K. Polk

After receiving word on May 9, 1846, from General Zachary Taylor about the Skirmish at Carricitos Ranch and U.S. casualties, President Polk spent the next day writing his War Address. It claimed that Mexico had "shed American blood upon the American soil." His message was read to the U.S. Congress on May

11, 1846, and called for war against Mexico. Later that afternoon, the House of Representatives voted 173 to 14 for war; the following day, the Senate voted 40 to 2 in favor of war with Mexico. An except from Polk's War Address follows.

Washington, May 11, 1846

To the Senate and House of Representatives:

The existing state of the relations between the United States and Mexico renders it proper that I should bring the subject to the consideration of Congress. In my message at the commencement of your present session the state of these relations, the causes which led to the suspension of diplomatic intercourse between the two countries in March, 1845, and the long-continued and unredressed wrongs and injuries committed by the Mexican Government on citizens of the United States in their persons and property were briefly set forth....

The strong desire to establish peace with Mexico on liberal and honorable terms, and the readiness of this Government to regulate and adjust our boundary and other causes of difference with that power on such fair and equitable principles as would lead to permanent relations of the most friendly nature, induced me in September last to seek the reopening of diplomatic relations between the two countries. Every measure adopted on our part had for its object the furtherance of these desired results. In communicating to Congress a succinct statement of the injuries which we had suffered from Mexico, and which have been accumulating during a period of more than twenty years, every expression that could tend to inflame the people of Mexico or defeat or delay a pacific result was carefully avoided. An envoy of the United States repaired to Mexico with full powers to adjust every existing difference. But those present on the Mexican soil by agreement between the two Governments, invested with full powers, and bearing evidence of the most friendly dispositions, his mission has been unavailing. The Mexican Government not only refused to receive him or listen to his propositions, but after a long-continued series of menaces have at last invaded our territory and shed the blood of our fellow-citizens on our own soil...

The Army moved from Corpus Christi on the 11th of March, and on the 28th of that month arrived on the left bank of the Del Norte opposite to Matamoros, where it encamped on a commanding position, which has since been strengthened by the erection of fieldworks. A depot has also been established at Point Isabel, near the Brazos Santiago, 30 miles in rear of the encampment. The selection of his position was necessarily confided to the judgement of the general in command.

The Mexican forces at Matamoros assumed a belligerent attitude, and on the 12th of April General Ampudia, then in command, notified General Taylor to break up his camp within twenty-four hours and to retire beyond the Nueces River, and in the event of his failure to comply with these demands announced that arms, and arms alone, must decide the question. But no open act of hostility was committed until the 24th of April. On that day General Arista, who had succeeded to the command of the Mexican forces, communicated to General Taylor that "he considered hostilities commenced and should prosecute them." A party of dragoons of 63 men and officers were on the same day dispatched from the American camp up the Rio del [Bravo] Norte, on its left bank, to ascertain whether the Mexican troops had crossed or were preparing to cross the river, "became engaged with a large body of these troops, and after a short affair, in which some 16 were killed and wounded, appear to have surrounded and compelled to surrender."

The grievous wrongs perpetrated by Mexico upon our citizens through a long period of years remained unredressed, and solemn treaties pledging her public faith for this redress have been disregarded. A government either unable or unwilling to enforce the execution of such treaties fails to perform one of its plainest duties.

Our commerce with Mexico has been almost annihilated. It was formerly highly beneficial to both nations, but our merchants have been deterred from prosecuting it by the system of outrage and extortion which the Mexican authorities have pursued against them, whilst their appeals through their own Government for indemnity have been made in vain. Our forbearance has gone to such an extreme as to be mistaken in its character. Had we acted with vigor in repelling the insults and redressing the injuries inflicted by Mexico at the commencement, we should doubtless have escaped all the difficulties in which we are now involved....

The cup of forbearance has been exhausted even before the recent information from the frontier of the Del Norte. But now, after reiterated menaces, Mexico has passed the boundary of the United States, has invaded our territory and shed American blood upon the American soil. She has proclaimed that hostilities have commenced, and that the two nations are now at war.

As war exists, and notwithstanding all our efforts to avoid it, exists by the act of Mexico herself, we are called upon by every considering of duty and patriotism to vindicate with decision the honor, the rights, and in the interests of our country....

In further vindication of our rights and defense of our territory, I invoke the prompt action of Congress to recognize the existence of the war, and to place at the disposition of the Executive the means of prosecuting the war with vigor, and thus hastening the restoration of peace. To this end I recommend that authority should be given to call into public service a large body of volunteers to serve for not less than six or twelve months unless sooner discharged. A volunteer force is beyond question more efficient than any other description of citizen soldiers, and it is not to be doubted that a number far beyond that required would readily rush to the field upon the call of their country. I further recommend that a liberal provision be made for sustaining our entire military force and furnishing it with supplies and munitions of war....

War Message, Mariano Paredes y Arrillaga

After General Zachary Taylor's Army of Occupation arrived on the north bank of the Río Grande in April 1846, Mexican President and General Mariano Paredes y Arrillaga issued his War Message on April 23. Paredes declared that Mexican troops would defend Mexican territory in a "defensive war" against the United States, and began to strengthen the Mexcian army at Matamoros, along the Río Grande. Paredes y Arrillaga's War Message follows.

Mexico City, April 23, 1846

At the time Mr. Slidell presented himself, the troops of the United States occupied our territory; their squadrons threatened our ports, and they prepared to occupy the peninsula of the Californias, of which the question of the Oregon [country] with England is only a preliminary. Mr. Slidell was not received, because the dignity of the nation repelled this new insult. Meanwhile the army of the United States encamped at Corpus Christi and occupied the Isla de Padre; following this, they then moved to the point Santo Isabel, and their standard of the stars and stripes waved on the right bank of the Rio Bravo del Norte, opposite the city of Matamoros, blockading that river with their vessels of war. The village of Laredo was surprised by a party of their troops, and a small party of our men, reconnoitering there, were disarmed. Hostilities, then, have been commenced by the United States of North America, beginning new conquests upon the frontier territories of the departments [states] of Tamaulipas and Nuevo Leon, and progressing at such a rate that troops of the same United States threaten Monterey in Upper California. No one can doubt which of the two republics is responsible for this war: a war which any sense of equity and justice, and respect for the rights and laws of civilized nations, might have avoided.

I have commanded the General-in-chief of our forces on the northern frontier to repel all hostilities offered to us, which is actual war against any power making war on us, and call upon the God of battles; He will preserve the valor of our troops, the unquestionable right to our territory, and the honor of those arms which are used only in defense of justice. Our general will govern himself by the established usages of civilized warfare. With orders from me to prevent, if possible, the effusion of blood, he will intimate to the General-in-chief of the American troops that he shall return to the other side of the Rio de las Nueces, the ancient limits of Texas. Those nations interested in preserving the peace of so many years, and who may be injured in their commercial relations with the Mexican republic, will perceive the hard alternative to which they are reduced, by the politic invasion of the United States, and they (the nations) must succumb or defend their existence thus compromised. I solemnly announce that I do not declare war against the United States of America, because it pertains to the august Congress of the nation, and not to the Executive, to settle definitely the reparation which so many aggressions demand.

But the defense of the Mexican territory, which the United States troops invade, is an urgent necessity, and my responsibility would be immense before the nation if I did not give commands to repel those forces who act like enemies, and I have so commanded. From this day commences a defensive war, and those points of our territory which are invaded or attacked will be energetically defended.

See also Paredes y Arrillaga, Mariano; Río Grande; Texas.

For further reading: McAfee and Robinson, *Origins of the Mexican War*, 1982.

Washington, John Macrea
(1797–1853)

Lieutenant Colonel John M. Washington commanded the artillery on the U.S. right flank during the 1847 Battle of Buena Vista. His steady performance kept the entire U.S. line from breaking at the height of the battle.

Washington, who was born in Virginia, attended the U.S. Military Academy from 1814 to 1817. Commissioned a third lieutenant of artillery, he fought Seminole Indians in Florida and later taught artillery tactics. He fought in Florida again during the Second Seminole War.

As an officer in the 4th U.S. Artillery attached to General John E. Wool's Army of the Center, he marched from San Antonio to Saltillo in 1846. Preparing for the assault of General Antonio López de Santa Anna's army at Buena Vista, Washington's light battery of eight guns was placed in the road at La Angostura (the narrows). His guns anchored the U.S. right flank. During the battle he repelled several strong Mexican attacks and helped save the U.S. position by holding fast as the left flank fell back in disorder. His cool leadership resulted in a brevet to lieutenant colonel. Later in 1847 Washington served as the temporary governor of Saltillo, a position he also held in New Mexico in 1848–1849.

Passengers on the steamer *San Francisco* when it was caught in a violent storm near the mouth of the Delaware River in 1853, Washington and 180 other men from the 3rd U.S. Artillery were swept overboard and drowned.

See also Buena Vista, Battle of.

For further reading: Cullum, *Biographical Register of the Officers and Graduates of the United States Military Academy from 1802 to 1867*, 1879; Dillon, *American Artillery in the Mexican War 1846–1847*, 1975.

Weapons, Mexico

The weapons of the Mexican soldiers were typically smoothbore flintlock muskets, pistols, sabers and shorter swords, lances, and antiquated cannon. Mexican weaponry was older and less reliable than U.S. weapons, especially the older, heavier cannon and its ammunition.

Mexico, which did not own an operating armory, purchased its weapons from European dealers. Most infantrymen were outfitted with older .753-caliber, smoothbore flintlock muskets from the 1830s. The British Tower-type smoothbore musket, which the British government no longer favored, was purchased in large quantities at discount prices. Called the "Brown Bess," its range was less than 100 yards. A lesser number of 1838-style British Baker rifles were also used, but, because they were expensive and of better quality, they were saved for the elite troops and sharpshooters. After the Battle of Cerro Gordo, George Ballentine commented that "we found the road strewed with the muskets and bayonets which the Mexicans had thrown away in their hasty retreat. All of these muskets were of British manufacture and had the *Tower* mark on their locks. They were old and worn out, having evidently been condemned as unserviceable in the British army and then sold to the Mexicans at a low price.... After examining a few of them I came to the conclusion that for efficient service one of our muskets was equal to at least three of them."

The variable quality and style of muskets created a host of problems for the Mexican soldiers, especially in matching ammunition. During the Battle of Churubusco in August 1847, the Mexican soldiers were infuriated by the fact that their lead balls were too large and frequently jammed in the musket barrel. Because of inferior powder, they were also forced to overcharge their rifles, and the resulting kick made them fire high. The British Paget flintlock carbine, and the *escopeta*, an old-fashioned, Napoleonic variety of blunderbuss, were also used by cavalrymen.

Cavalrymen were equipped with lances, sabers, and carbines. In the hands of an experienced horseman the lance was a formidable weapon. In addition to the four cutting edges of the eight-inch blade, a flag at the tip was meant to frighten the enemy's horse. Lancers were some of the most highly regarded units in the Mexican army, and their attacks had great shock value.

Mexican artillerymen fired the antiquated Griveaubal cannon of different calibers, for which there was limited ammunition. Mexican cannoneers, especially in the beginning of the war, favored the use of solid shot in trying to knock out opposing batteries (in comparison, the U.S. artillery strategy was to destroy groups of soldiers). Toward the end of the war, during U.S. General Winfield Scott's march to Mexico City and Colonel Alexander Doniphan's march to Chihuahua, some cannons were cast in local foundries. Although the artillerists were well trained, the cannon were often defective. Uneven or inferior gunpowder overshot projectiles or made them fall dangerously short. The artillery was drawn by civilian carts and drivers, or often hauled by mules—the Mexican army did not have professional teamsters.

For further reading: Ballentine, *Autobiography of an English Soldier*, 1853; DePalo, *The Mexican National Army, 1822–1852*, 1997; Haecker, *A Thunder of Cannon*, 1994; Hefter, *El soldado mexicano*, 1958.

Weapons, United States

The weapons of the U.S. soldiers in the Mexican-American War included muskets and rifles, pistols, Colt revolvers, bayonets and swords, and artillery pieces. The high quality and reliability of the U.S. weapons, and the mobility of the Flying Artillery, gave the U.S. soldiers a distinct advantage over their Mexican counterparts.

The .69-caliber, smoothbore flintlock musket was standard issue for the U.S. soldier. It had an effective range of about 100 yards. About ten different models were used during the war, the most famous being the 1822 model. Some troops also carried the Hall breech-loading flintlock rifle or the Model 1841 percussion musket (also called the "Mississippi rifle"). Relatively few men carried percussion rifles. Many officers carried double-barreled shotguns for close combat. Dragoons also occasionally were armed with breech-loading Hall carbines with a shorter barrel.

Standard sidearms were flintlock or percussion smoothbore pistols that were inaccurate beyond a range of 10 or 15 yards. Other troops, most notably officers and Texas Rangers, carried the more expensive Colt revolver. The Hartford *Courant* reported that "each arm is calculated to hold six charges, which may be fired in as many seconds, and again reloaded as quickly as an ordinary fire arm. The regiment of the United States Mounted Rifles, for whom a thousand of these arms have been made…can fire a volley of six thousand balls into an enemy's ranks, without loading, and afterwards load and fire at the rate of six thousand charges per minute." The Colt, of course, was effective only in close quarters, such as colliding cavalry charges or hand-to-hand combat. Other weapons included swords, bayonets, and Bowie knives.

The biggest U.S. weapons advantage was its artillery. U.S. guns fired cannonballs, shells (explosive charge with fuse), spherical case (container with lead balls and explosives), and canister (tin can filled with 27 lead balls packed in sawdust). Canister was effective up to about 300 yards. The artillery consisted of long-barreled cannon, howitzers (short-barreled, lightweight guns), and mortars of various weights, cast from iron or bronze. The highly trained and disciplined Flying Artillery units could fire every 10 or 15 seconds, more than five times faster than Mexican artillery. Used mostly to inflict casualties, the Flying Artillery moved rapidly to where it was most needed on the battlefield, and usually created gaping holes in the enemy lines.

See also Flying Artillery.

For further reading: Birkhimer, *Historical Sketch of the Organization, Administration, Materiél and Tactics of the Artillery*, 1884; Dillon, *American Artillery in the Mexican War 1846–1847*, 1975; Haecker, *A Thunder of Cannon*, 1994; McCaffrey, *Army of Manifest Destiny*, 1992; Smith and Judah, *Chronicles of the Gringos*, 1968; Winders, *Mr. Polk's Army*, 1997.

Webster, Daniel
(1782–1852)

A U.S. senator and secretary of state, Daniel Webster adamantly opposed slavery, the annexation of Texas, and the Mexican-American War.

Born in New Hampshire, Webster showed his intellectual gifts at a young age. After graduating from Dartmouth College he studied law. In 1819 he opposed the admission of Missouri as a slave state. An excellent orator and lawyer, he was elected to the U.S. Senate in 1827. As U.S. secretary of state from 1841 to 1843, he disapproved of President John Tyler's efforts to annex Texas. In 1842 he negotiated the Webster-Ashburton Treaty that established the Canada-Maine border.

Webster denounced the Mexican-American War as a vehicle for expanding slavery. Once it was under way, however, he voted in favor of supplying men and materials to bring a swift conclusion. Webster introduced resolutions that prohibited the dismemberment of Mexico, but these were defeated. The Wilmot Proviso drew his support.

Webster's presidential aspirations faded when the Whig Party selected Zachary Taylor in 1847 as its candidate. He later served as secretary of state under President Millard Fillmore. In failing health, Webster retired to Massachusetts, where he died from cirrhosis in 1852.

For further reading: Bartlett, *Daniel Webster*, 1978; Van Tyne, *The Letters of Daniel Webster*, 1902.

Whitman, Walt
(1819–1892)

Writer, editor, and poet, Walt Whitman supported Manifest Destiny and the Mexican-

American War. His pro-war editorials were published in a number of newspapers and literary magazines from 1846 to 1848.

Whitman, who was born in New York, worked in a newspaper print room at the age of 11. In the 1830s he taught school and wrote poetry and verse. From 1841 to 1848 he was frequently published in major literary magazines, such as the *Democratic Review*. In 1846, as editor of a Democratic newspaper in Brooklyn, he frequently editorialized about social reform, including the abolition of slavery.

As a Democrat, however, Whitman supported Manifest Destiny and the Mexican-American War. On May 11, 1846, he wrote that "Mexico must be thoroughly chastised!... We have reached a point in our intercourse with that country, when prompt and effectual demonstrations of force are enjoined upon us by every dictate of right and policy." In a July editorial he wrote "We love to indulge in thoughts of the future extent and power of this Republic—because with its increase is the increase of human happiness and liberty.... What has miserable, inefficient Mexico—with her superstition, her burlesque upon freedom, her actual tyranny by the few over the many—what has she to do with the great mission of peopling the New World with a noble race? Be it ours, to achieve that mission! Be it ours to roll down all of the upstart leaven of old despotism, that comes our way!"

Whitman continued to work for different journals and newspapers in New York, and in 1855 he published *Leaves of Grass*, a book of 12 poems. During the Civil War he helped care for sick and wounded soldiers in Union hospitals, mostly around Washington, D.C. He stayed in the capital until 1873, when he suffered a stroke of paralysis. He died at his brother's home in New Jersey in 1892.

For further reading: Carpenter, *Days with Walt Whitman*, 1921; Johannsen, *To the Halls of the Montezumas*, 1985; Zweig, *Walt Whitman*, 1984.

Wickliffe, Charles Anderson

(1788–1869)

As one of President James K. Polk's secret agents in Texas in 1845, Charles Wickliffe tried to subvert British and French influence on the Texan government and foster a pro-U.S. attitude in Texan leaders.

Wickliffe, who was born in Kentucky, became an attorney and served in state politics and as a member in the U.S. House of Representatives. In 1841 he was appointed postmaster-general by President John Tyler.

Wickliffe was selected by President Polk in 1845 to be his confidential agent to counteract British and French efforts in Texas and to foster goodwill toward the United States. He reported regularly to Secretary of State James Buchanan. Wickliffe traveled across Texas, speaking at annexationist meetings and promising federal funds for roads, harbors, and policing the frontier. Some historians believe his secret orders were to compel Texas to seize the disputed territory west of the Nueces River, thus creating a war with Mexico that the United States could then enter. Wickliffe also met regularly with Commodore Robert F. Stockton to discuss plans and orders from Polk and Buchanan.

In 1849 Wickliffe returned to state politics in Kentucky; he was elected to the U.S. House of Representatives in 1861. While living in Washington he was thrown from a carriage and was crippled for life. Wickliffe died at the age of 81.

For further reading: Caruso, *The Mexican Spy Company*, 1991; Pletcher, *The Diplomacy of Annexation*, 1973; Price, *Origins of the War with Mexico*, 1967; Smith, *The Annexation of Texas*, 1911.

Wilmot, David

(1814–1868)

Congressman David Wilmot in 1846 drafted the Wilmot Proviso, which was an attachment to a Polk-sponsored appropriations bill that called for all new territory gained from Mexico to be free from slavery.

Born in Pennsylvania, Wilmot went to school in Pennsylvania and New York. He was admitted to the bar in 1834 and was later drawn to politics. An ardent Jacksonian, he served in Congress from 1845 to 1851.

Wilmot was anxious to neutralize the influence of the South in federal policymaking. An opponent of slavery, he feared that slavery would be permitted in new lands gained from Mexico during the war with the United States.

When President James K. Polk asked Congress for $2 million in 1846 for peace purposes, Wilmot (with the help of Jacob Brinkerhoff from Ohio) offered a proviso that called for the prohibition of slavery in any territory acquired through the use of the appropriated funds. Called the Wilmot Proviso, it stated that "provided, that, as an express and fundamental condition to the acquisition of any territory from the Republic of Mexico by the United States…neither slavery nor involuntary servitude shall ever exist in any part of said territory."

The proviso immediately divided the parties along sectional lines. It was a relief for Democrats who favored expansion but did not want to be considered proslavery. Southern Whigs joined Polk Democrats in an effort to defeat it. The proviso passed narrowly in the House of Representatives and was defeated in the Senate. The proviso was attached repeatedly by northerners to other bills in 1847, which were also rejected.

Wilmot served as a judge in Pennsylvania from 1851 to 1861, and he was a founder of the Republican Party. Lincoln offered him a cabinet position in 1861, which he declined in favor of a seat in the U.S. Senate. He died in 1868.

For further reading: Going, *David Wilmot*, 1924; Morrison, *Democratic Politics and Sectionalism*, 1967.

Wilmot Proviso

See Wilmot, David.

Women, Mexico

Thousands of women followed the Mexican army and performed domestic duties, including cooking, washing, collecting firewood, and taking care of the sick and wounded.

Female servants in the Mexican army were called *soldaderas*. Revolutionary groups before independence had long welcomed women as fighters. The presence of women in the army, both as helpers and in combat, was much more accepted in the Mexican military than in the U.S. military. In 1841 an observer of General Antonio López de Santa Anna's army noted "various masculine women with serapes or mangas, and large straw hats tied down with colored handkerchiefs, mounted on mules or horses.… Indian women trotted on foot in the rear, carrying their husbands' boots and clothes." Their duties included carrying large bundles of clothing and supplies, or firewood, and foraging miles from the army for food and water. On Santa Anna's march from San Luis Potosí to La Angostura in January to February 1847, he ordered his men to carry only a few personal effects. Wives and sweethearts, often barefoot, followed the army, carrying personal belongings and firewood on their backs for their camps at night.

Soldaderas fought side by side with the Mexican soldiers. Women operated Mexican cannons at the Battle of El Brazito, women's bodies were found among the Mexican casualties at Cerro Gordo, and female remains were discovered in a mass grave of Mexican soldiers at Resaca de la Guerrera (Resaca de la Palma). Female guerrillas attacked U.S. soldiers on the streets of Mexico City after the capital fell in September 1847. Dos Amades, a female citizen, led a company of Mexican lancers in a daring charge against the U.S. soldiers at the Battle of Monterrey. María Josefa Zozayat (the "Heroine of Monterrey"), a young woman, selflessly aided wounded U.S. and Mexican soldiers during the battle until she was killed by gunfire.

Maria de Jesús Dosamantes was one of the few female soldiers in uniform. About 25 years of age, she had personal orders from General Pedro de Ampudia that introduced her as wanting to "enter the ranks of the brave to fight…at the most dangerous part of the front." Josefa Castelar, a female citizen of Huamantla, was the only person who remained to fire a cannon on approaching U.S. troops. The townspeople briefly rallied around her until intense U.S. artillery fire drove them back. Loreto Encinas de Aviles smuggled arms, supplies, and information to Mexican forces during the defense of Guaymas in Baja California.

Mexican women who lived near U.S. army camps often helped the U.S. soldiers or became wives or mistresses. According to Samuel Chamberlain, "The position of the 'Yankedos' [women who lived with U.S. soldiers] now that their protectors were leaving

Sarah Borginnis provides care for U.S. troops during the siege of Fort Brown. This image served as the title page for *Incidents and Sufferings in the Mexican War,* 1847. (Corbis-Bettmann)

the country, [was not] a pleasant one. Their fate was truely fearful, and they suffered the worst outrages from the returned Mexican Soldierey." Chamberlain noted that 23 women who had lived with U.S. servicemen in Saltillo were tortured and killed by members of General Manuel Lombardini's division when it occupied Saltillo at the end of the war.

See also Army, Mexico; Dos Amades; Zozaya, María Josefa.

For further reading: Chamberlain, *My Confession,* 1956; DePalo, *The Mexican National Army,* 1997; Johannsen, *To the Halls of the Montezumas,* 1985; Salas, *Soldaderas in the Mexican Military,* 1990.

Women, United States

The relatively few women who traveled with the U.S. army performed support roles as laundresses, nurses, cooks, rarely as teamsters, and very rarely as soldiers. Some officers traveled with their wives. Other women served as spies and journalists.

A few women tried to join the regiments disguised as men, mostly to follow a lover. If her story is to be believed, Eliza Allen Billings volunteered as a soldier and was wounded during the Battle of Cerro Gordo. Others were discovered at enlistment centers and turned away.

Army laundresses accompanied most of the regiments, usually wives of enlisted men. Their duties were many, including cooking, washing clothes, and taking care of the sick and wounded. Officially enlisted, they were issued rations and bedding and occasionally were provided weapons. The laundresses frequently traveled at the rear of the army with the wagon train, which was vulnerable to attack by guerrillas. The most famous laundress was Sarah Borginnis (known as the "Great Western"), who took care of the 7th U.S. Infantry during the siege of Fort Texas, and who traveled with her regiment on the march. "Dutch Mary," a laundress with the 2nd Illinois Infantry, was cheered for bringing two camp kettles of coffee to the regiment in the midst of the Battle of Buena Vista in February 1847.

Anna McClarmonde Chase and Jane McManus Storms acted as spies and secret agents during the Mexican-American War. Chase, known as the "Heroine of Tampico," provided military intelligence to the U.S. navy offshore in November 1846. Storms, in the company of Moses Y. Beach, plotted with U.S. agents in Mexico City and Veracruz, tried to convince influential Mexicans of the benefits of surrender, and wrote numerous patriotic letters to U.S. newspapers.

See also Billings, Eliza Allen; Borginnis, Sarah; Chase, Anna McClarmonde; Storms, Jane McManus.

For further reading: Chamberlain, *My Confession,* 1956; Johannsen, *To the Halls of the Montezumas,* 1985; Winders, *Mr. Polk's Army,* 1997.

Wool, John Ellis
(1784–1869)

A rigid disciplinarian who was unpopular with his troops, General John E. Wool served with General Zachary Taylor in northern Mexico and led the U.S. army at the Battle of Buena Vista in 1847.

Born in New York and orphaned at age four, Wool was raised by his grandfather. He joined the army during the War of 1812 and was severely wounded. In 1826 he was given the brevet rank of brigadier general for ten

John Ellis Wool
(Library of Congress)

General John E. Wool (first horsemen left of center) and his staff in Saltillo, pictured in one of the few photographs from the Mexican War (Beinecke Rare Book and Manuscript Library, Yale University)

years of faithful service. In 1836–1837 he assisted Winfield Scott in relocating the Cherokee Nation to Oklahoma Territory.

With the beginning of the Mexican War in 1846, Wool supervised the recruitment of over 10,000 volunteer soldiers from Kentucky, Tennessee, Ohio, Indiana, Illinois, and Mississippi. On August 14 he arrived in San Antonio to march the Army of the Center to Chihuahua, Mexico. A renowned disciplinarian, Wool constantly trained his 1,400 men until he had enough supplies to move out on September 26. After occupying Monclova, he changed course and arrived in the Saltillo area in December, after traveling over 900 miles.

In February 1847, when he learned General Antonio López de Santa Anna's army was about 15 miles away, Wool and Taylor retreated from Agua Nueva to a site Wool selected: La Angostura (the narrows). He deployed the Army of Occupation on the hills and ridges overlooking the road from Agua Nueva. Wool commanded much of the ensuing Battle of Buena Vista, which resulted in a narrow U.S. victory. When the war moved south to Major General Winfield Scott's Veracruz–Mexico City campaign, Wool and Taylor remained in Saltillo, suppressing guerrilla raids and their own soldiers' depredations. When Taylor returned to the United States in November 1847, Wool assumed full command of the army and created a military government that attempted to restore order and structure to civilian life, such as reopening schools.

Between 1854 and 1857 Wool commanded the Department of the Pacific and battled warring Indians. During the Civil War he commanded the Department of the East before retiring in 1863. Wool died at the age of 85 in Troy, New York.

See also Army, United States; Buena Vista, Battle of; Wool's Chihuahua Expedition.

For further reading: Baylies, *A Narrative of Major General Wool's Campaign in Mexico,* 1851; Carleton, *The Battle of Buena Vista,* 1848; Hinton, *The Military Career of John Ellis Wool,* 1960.

Wool's Chihuahua Expedition

(1846)

General John E. Wool marched his Army of the Center from San Antonio, Texas, through Monclova and Parras to Saltillo in the fall of 1846. Originally destined for Chihuahua, he abandoned that plan when he was ordered to Saltillo to combat a possible assault by General Antonio López de Santa Anna.

In addition to General Zachary Taylor's 1846 campaign in northern Mexico and the occupation of New Mexico by General Stephen W. Kearny's Army of the West, President Polk wanted to occupy the Mexican city of Chihuahua. Chihuahua was the largest city near New Mexico and had economic ties to St. Louis. On June 11, 1846, Wool received orders to take charge of the Chihuahua Expedition. His force consisted of the 1st and 2nd Illinois Infantry Regiments, one regiment of Arkansas cavalry, and a few regular troops.

Wool assembled his Army of the Center at San Antonio from about mid-July to mid-September. Wool was exasperated with the volunteers, who resisted being trained. In particular was Colonel Archibald Yell's regiment of unruly Arkansas cavalry. In total, his army consisted of about 1,400 men (including a six-gun field battery under Captain John M. Washington) and 120 supply wagons.

Still undersupplied but determined to leave, Wool's lead elements moved out on September 23. By October 8, they had reached the Río Grande, having marched 164 miles in two weeks. At the border, Wool instructed his men to treat Mexican civilians with respect and to pay for any goods taken. Splashing across the river near present-day Eagle Pass, Texas, they marched toward Chihuahua via Parras, where they were joined by Brigadier General James Shields and a small group of soldiers that had come upriver from Camargo.

Continuing on, the army was welcomed at San Fernando de Rosas and Santa Rosa and occupied Monclova on October 29. Wool made the governor's palace his headquarters, and supplies intended for the Mexican army were confiscated. Because of General Zachary Taylor's Armistice of Monterrey, Wool was forced to stay in Monclova for 27 days. Soldiers, especially the volunteers, became undisciplined, and others fell sick.

Wool's scouts told him there was little water along the rest of the route to Chihuahua and that the city's soldiers had gone to San Luis Potosí to join General Santa Anna. Wool wrote to Taylor: "What is to be gained by going to Chihuahua? For aught I can learn, all that we shall find to conquer is distance...."

On November 18, Wool received orders to remain at Monclova and abandon the march to Chihuahua. Wool pleaded again to move, citing that the inaction from remaining "in my present position one moment longer than it is absolutely necessary...is exceedingly injurious to volunteers." Camp life had become unbearably tedious and hostile. Taylor's orders to move to Parras were received on November 26.

A grateful Wool departed Monclova at an energetic pace and covered about 200 miles in 12 days. On December 5, they reached Parras, a pastoral community of 5,000 inhabitants that welcomed the U.S. soldiers. On December 17, Wool received an urgent message from Brigadier General William J. Worth, stationed at Saltillo, that Santa Anna's army was fast approaching from San Luis Potosí. Wool mobilized his men within two hours, and in four days they reached Agua Nueva after a grueling forced march. The rumor of Santa Anna's advance proved to be false, and on December 21 Wool's Army of the Center marched into Saltillo and joined Taylor's Army of Occupation.

See also Monclova; Parras; Wool, John Ellis.

For further reading: Baylies, *A Narrative of Major General Wool's Campaign,* 1851; Hinton, *The Military Career of John Ellis Wool,* 1960.

Worth, William Jenkins

(1794–1849)

General William Jenkins Worth commanded troops during General Zachary Taylor's campaign in northern Mexico and General Winfield Scott's Veracruz–Mexico City campaign. He was well known for his quarrelsome actions with Colonel David E. Twiggs.

New York native William Worth joined the U.S. Army during the War of 1812. He was severely wounded at the Battle of Lundy's

Lane and required a year of bed rest to recover fully. He became the colonel of the 8th U.S. Infantry in 1838, and when given command of the army in Florida during the Second Seminole War, he brought the conflict to its conclusion.

Brevetted brigadier general for his service in Florida, Worth joined General Zachary Taylor's Army of Occupation in 1845 and immediately quarreled with Taylor about seniority. Worth maintained that he should be second in command over Colonel David E. Twiggs because of his brigadier general brevet, although Twiggs outranked him according to regular rank. President Polk ruled in favor of Twiggs, and Worth petulantly resigned. After learning of the Battles of Palo Alto and Resaca de la Palma in May 1846, he returned to the Army of Occupation.

Given the task of attacking Monterrey from the west, Worth's division gained the well-defended heights outside the city, which ultimately led to the U.S. victory a few days later. Worth was soon brevetted to major general and appointed military governor of Monterrey.

Later attached to Major General Winfield Scott's Army of Occupation, Worth's division was the first to land at Veracruz on March 9, 1847. As the first wave of surfboats approached, Worth raced ahead in a small gig and jumped out in water up to his armpits to be the first U.S. soldier on the beach. After the city had fallen and Worth became its military governor, he was outraged when Scott assigned Twiggs to lead the army up the National Road from Veracruz. This event marked the beginning of a progressive deterioration in the relationship between Scott and Worth. They continued to quarrel during the remaining battles of the Veracruz–Mexico City campaign. Worth's men performed well under heavy fire during the Battles of El Molino del Rey and Churubusco.

Worth's self-centered behavior detracted from his military accomplishments. Worth became involved in a power struggle between Scott and General Gideon J. Pillow and Colonel James Duncan, which ultimately resulted in all of them being relieved of duty and investigated by a court of inquiry. The court eventually realized that Worth's involvement was secondary, and he was cleared of all charges. Worth oversaw the deoccupation of Mexico City in June 1848.

After the war Worth was placed in command of the Department of Texas, where he died from cholera at age 55.

See also Court of Inquiry, Scott; Monterrey, Battle of.

For further reading: Bauer, *Surfboats and Horse Marines,* 1969; Hitchcock, *Fifty Years in Camp and Field,* 1909; Wallace, *General William Jenkins Worth,* 1953; Winders, *Mr. Polk's Army,* 1997.

Wright, George
(1803–1865)

During the Battle of El Molino del Rey, Major George Wright commanded the "forlorn hope," a handpicked party of 500 men that stormed the Mexican position on September 8, 1847.

Wright was born in Vermont and graduated from the U.S. Military Academy in 1822. Assigned to the 3rd U.S. Infantry in 1822, he served along the Canadian border and in the Second Seminole War.

As part of General Winfield Scott's Army of Occupation in 1847, Wright was brevetted to lieutenant colonel for his leadership at the Battles of Contreras and Churubusco. After the Mexican defenses had been scouted at El Molino del Rey, Wright was chosen to lead a handpicked group of 500 soldiers against the well-protected position (the storming party was called a "forlorn hope"). Captain E. K. Smith brooded that "tomorrow will be a day of slaughter."

At dawn, after a brief artillery barrage, Wright's men charged the stone foundry at El Molino del Rey. Within five minutes, more than half of the party had been shot down, including 11 of the 14 officers. Wright, who was severely wounded, was later brevetted to colonel.

In 1855, Wright commanded the 9th U.S. Infantry and fought Indians on the western frontier. In 1865, on his way to his new headquarters at the Department of the Columbia, his steamer sank off the coast of Oregon and he drowned.

See also El Molino del Rey, Battle of.

For further reading: Cullum, *Biographical Register of the Officers and Graduates of the United States Military Academy from 1802 to 1867,* 1879; Smith, *To Mexico with Scott,* 1917; Weems, *To Conquer a Peace,* 1974.

Y

Yell, Archibald
(1797–1847)

Colonel Archibald Yell was the commander of the undisciplined 1st Arkansas Volunteer Cavalry during the Mexican-American War. He was killed in action during the Battle of Buena Vista in 1847.

Born in North Carolina, Yell was raised in Tennessee. He served with Andrew Jackson during the War of 1812 and the Indian conflicts in Florida. His friendship with Jackson led to a number of governmental appointments. Yell moved to Arkansas in 1831 to open a law practice and later became a district judge. His tenure in state politics, including four years as governor, won him a seat in Congress in 1845.

President James K. Polk selected Yell to be one of his secret agents in Texas. He left for Texas in March 1845 with instructions from Secretary of State James Buchanan and Polk. Yell worked with Andrew Jackson Donelson to deliver the annexation plan to Texas and to spread U.S. goodwill. Yell returned to Washington in May 1845.

When the Mexican-American War began in 1846, Yell resigned his seat in Congress and became the colonel of the 1st Arkansas Volunteer Cavalry. Yell was one of the most undisciplined officers in the army, and his refusal to follow military protocol frustrated Generals John E. Wool and Zachary Taylor. His men frequently committed atrocities and came to be known as the "Arkansas Ransackers." They were responsible for the slayings at Catana, one of the worst atrocities of the war. During the Battle of Buena Vista on February 23, 1847, Yell was killed by a Mexican lancer as he tried to rally troops on the U.S. left flank for a charge. Polk wrote that "I deeply deplore his loss. He was a brave and good man, and among the best friends I had on earth, and had been so for 25 years."

See also Catana, Massacre at.

For further reading: Caruso, *The Mexican Spy Company,* 1991; Chamberlain, *My Confession,* 1956; Hughes, *Archibald Yell,* 1988.

Yellow Fever

Yellow fever was dreaded by the U.S. troops in Mexico. One of the most painful of afflictions, it was also one of the deadliest. On average, 28 percent of all yellow fever victims died.

Also called black vomit, *vomito,* and yellow jack, yellow fever was one of the diseases most feared by the U.S. soldiers in Mexico. Although dysentery and diarrhea occurred more frequently, yellow fever had the highest mortality rate. Mexicans regarded the disease, which was common in low-lying coastal areas, as one of their natural defenses. Ulysses S. Grant confessed that he was "ten to one more afraid of [yellow fever] than the Mexicans." Symptoms included terrible headaches, high fever, extreme pain in the lower back and limbs, constipation, and vomiting. The skin turned yellow, and internal bleeding darkened the vomit to a blackish color (*vómito negro*). A blackened tongue was typical in the second week of infection. "It is remarkable," wrote Raphael Semmes, "that the natives of Vera Cruz do not suffer from this disease; and that those who have had it once, need not fear it a second time. Thus we see that the eastern coast of Mexico has as powerful a defender in the *vomito*."

After occupying the city of Veracruz in March 1847, General Winfield Scott left before his army was fully assembled and supplied to avoid the onset of the rainy season and the yellow fever it brought. Even so, almost all of Scott's men who landed and came through Veracruz contracted yellow fever to some degree. From April through September 1847, about 28 percent of all yellow fever patients at the Veracruz field hospital died; in some months the figure approached 70 percent. Doctors prescribed quinine, mercurials, warm mustard baths, and camphorated ammonia mixtures.

See also Medical Practices, United States.

For further reading: Gillett, *The Army Medical Department, 1818–1865,* 1987; McCaffrey, *Army of Manifest Destiny,* 1992; Semmes, *Service Afloat and Ashore during the Mexican War,* 1851; Smith and Judah, *Chronicles of the Gringos,* 1968.

Yucatán

The U.S. Navy supported the pro-U.S. revolutionary government in the Mexican state of Yucatán and supplied weapons and ammunition in their fight against Mayan uprisings in 1847–1848.

The principal port of Carmen had been seized by the U.S. Navy in 1846 to strangle the smuggling between Yucatán and the rest of Mexico. A pro-U.S. party took over the government in Yucatán in January 1847 and revolted against Mexico. Rumors abounded about possible Maya Indian uprisings that could threaten the new government. On September 7, 1847, Commander Henry Adams on the *John Adams* arrived at Campeche and conferred with U.S. Consul John F. McGregor. McGregor indicated that the Mayan factions had stabilized and that the province would remain neutral. Despite that assurance, Commodore Matthew C. Perry kept the occupational force in Carmen. He also visited the garrisons at Carmen and Campeche in November 1847.

A Mayan revolt erupted in January 1848, and Perry quickly returned with five vessels in March. The Mayan revolutionaries controlled a large portion of the state's interior, and Governor Santiago Mendez requested military aid. Perry supplied the Yucatán ports with muskets and ammunition to help quell the rebellion. Most of the fighting had subsided by August 1848.

For further reading: Bauer, *Surfboats and Horse Marines,* 1969; Knox, *A History of the United States Navy,* 1936; Reed, *The Caste War of the Yucatán,* 1964.

Zozaya, María Josefa
(d. 1846)

María Josefa Zozaya cared for Mexican and U.S. wounded on the Monterrey battlefield until she was killed by sporadic musket fire.

A Mexican camp follower or possibly a local citizen, María Josefa Zozaya braved musket fire to help wounded soldiers during the Battle of Monterrey in September 1846. According to U.S. soldier Lieutenant Edmund Bradford, "some two or three hundred yards from the fort, I saw a Mexican female carrying water and food to the wounded men of both armies. I saw her lift the head of one poor fellow, give him water, and then take her handkerchief from her own head and bind up his wounds; attending one or two others in the same way, she went back for more food and water. As she was returning I heard the crack of one or two guns, and she, poor good creature fell; after a few struggles all was still—she was dead."

She was buried the next day by U.S. soldiers under "showers of grape and round shot." Called the "Maid of Monterrey" or the "Heroine Martyr of Monterrey," she was the subject of many songs, one of which contained the following lines:

> Far greater than the wise or brave,
> Far happier than the fair and gay,
> Was she, who found a martyr's grave
> On that red field of Monterrey.

For further reading: Johannsen, *To the Halls of the Montezumas*, 1985; Salas, *Soldaderas in the Mexican Military*, 1990.

Chronology

1830 After repeated efforts by the United States from 1825 to 1829 to purchase Texas and with new attempts by newly elected President Andrew Jackson, Mexico was concerned about the security of its northern states, especially Texas, New Mexico, and California. These areas were sparsely settled, contained rebellious citizens who cared little for the Mexican government, and were difficult to control. In 1830, laws were passed that required passports for entrance into Mexico from the north. In an attempt to stop the U.S. colonization of Texas, Mexico refused to allow slaves to be brought into Texas. Mexico was a proud country that would not sell its territory or allow its laws to be ignored by U.S. immigrants. Many U.S. leaders viewed the Mexican position as arrogant and unreasonable, especially in its refusing to sell its northern states.

1836 Spain, after leaving Mexico 15 years before, finally recognized Mexico as an independent country. On March 1, at Washington-on-the-Brazos, U.S. settlers in Texas drafted a declaration of independence of Texas from Mexico, and the declaration was openly supported by the U.S. government. In March, General Santa Anna had crushed rebel resistance at the Alamo in San Antonio and also at Goliad, where he ordered the execution of more than 300 prisoners because he classified them as pirates. Texas won its independence from Mexico when General Antonio López de Santa Anna's forces were defeated by a U.S. force under Sam Houston at the Battle of San Jacinto on April 21, 1836. When Santa Anna was captured after the battle, he was forced to sign the Treaties of Velasco, which defined the southern boundary of the Republic of Texas as the Río Grande. After the Treaties of Velasco, President and General Santa Anna was deposed and exiled to Cuba. The new Mexican government refused to acknowledge the treaties or the independence of Texas. In California, unhappy Mexican citizens revolted against the central government, thus creating more political turmoil.

1837 The United States, Great Britain, France, and other European countries recognized Texas as an independent nation. In August, Texas made its first formal request for annexation, which was denied by President Martin Van Buren because he felt its inclusion in the United States would intensify the slavery debate and worsen the relationship between Texas and Mexico.

1839–1841 The United States lodged claims against Mexico for damage to the property of U.S. citizens. An international board of arbitration, headed by the King of Prussia, ruled that Mexico should pay the United States $2 million for compensatory damages. The Mexican government suggested a payment plan of 20 installments. An armed Texan expedition against Santa Fe failed, and the Texans were taken to Mexico as prisoners.

1842 Santa Anna returned from exile and became the dictator of Mexico. In March, a Mexican force under Santa Anna skirmished with Texans at San Antonio and near the Nueces River. Santa Anna later attacked San Antonio again and occupied the city.

1843 The United States accepted a Mexican proposal to pay restitution in 20 installments. After making the first three payments, the Mexican government ran out of money. Santa Anna stepped up border warfare in Texas. Mexican troops were sent to California to restore law and order. In addition, all U.S. citizens were ordered to leave California and the other northern Mexican states. The lucrative trading between St. Louis and Santa Fe came to a halt. Increasingly aggravated by the actions of the United States, Mexico warned that making Texas part of the United States would be considered an act of war. With France and Britain actively courting Texas, the U.S. interest in annexing Texas became more focused, regardless of previous treaty commitments, because an alignment of Texas with Britain or France was regarded as a threat to U.S. security in North America.

1844 Efforts by the United States to annex Texas resulted in the drafting of an offer of annexation that was rejected after much debate on the U.S. Senate floor. James K. Polk was elected president on a platform of annexing Texas. Alarmed by the aggressiveness of the new U.S. president, Mexico became even more resistant to U.S. interests in Texas, New Mexico, and California. Polk made it clear that, if the U.S. annexed Texas, its southern border would be the Río Grande; Mexico recognized the province's southern border as the Nueces River. Mexico feared that it would lose Texas and this additional Mexican land.

January 1845 Surrounded by growing national discontent, Mexican President Santa Anna was deposed and exiled again. He was replaced by José Joaquín Herrera. The aggressive and warlike General Mariano Paredes y Arrillaga became the chief of the Mexican army.

February 1845 Mexican troops were driven out of California by native insurgents, who recognized Pío Pico as governor and José Castro as the commanding general. President John Tyler continued to push hard for a joint resolution from the U.S. Congress calling for the annexation of Texas.

March 1845 On March 1, three days before the end of his administration, President Tyler signed the joint resolution of the U.S. Congress that offered annexation of Texas as a state. Polk was inaugurated as president on March 4. At the end of March, Mexico withdrew its minister from the United States and broke diplomatic relations. Expecting Texas to join the Union, President Polk ordered General Zachary Taylor to pull together a force at Fort Jesup, Louisiana. Called the Army of Observation, its job was to protect the new state of Texas if war erupted with Mexico.

June 1845 After months of preparation, John C. Frémont and his 62-man force moved out from Boon's Creek in eastern Kansas en route to Bent's Old Fort. This was the beginning of his third expedition to explore the Great Basin and parts of the western frontier.

July 1845 Texas agreed to become part of the United States on July 4. Taylor's Army of Observation was mobilized to Corpus Christi, Texas, to defend this new state's border from possible Mexican attacks. Commodore David E. Conner was ordered to assemble the U.S. Home Squadron flotilla and patrol the waters of the Gulf of Mexico around important Mexico cities.

October 1845 On October 15, the Herrera government agreed to receive a U.S. representative to discuss territorial issues—if the U.S. fleet withdrew from Mexican waters. As instructed by the Polk administration, Conner removed his ships, which had been centered on Veracruz. Thomas O. Larkin, the U.S. envoy in California, was directed to interfere with any attempts by any nations to seize California. Under Commodore John D. Sloat, the U.S. naval fleet in the Pacific was ordered to be ready for action. Taylor's army remained at Corpus Christi, awaiting developments on its front.

December 1845 Talks between the United States and Mexico were slow and finally broke down when U.S. minister John Slidell was rejected by the Herrera administration. Captain Frémont's expedition arrived at Sutter's Fort on the Sacramento River in California. On the last day of the year, Herrera was deposed in a political coup orchestrated by his military chief, General Mariano Paredes y Arrillaga.

January 1846 Paredes y Arrillaga took the oath as the new president of Mexico. He announced that Mexico owned all of Texas up to the Sabine River and would defend it if necessary. On January 13, President Polk ordered General Taylor to advance to the Río Grande. Commodore Conner was directed to take his fleet back to Veracruz. Meanwhile, Captain Frémont marched his small expeditionary force to Monterey, California.

March 1846 By the end of March, Taylor's men (now the Army of Occupation) had left their camp at Corpus Christi and built a fort (Fort Texas, later named Fort Brown) on the north side of the Río Grande across from Matamoros, Mexico. Matamoros was defended by a growing number of Mexican soldiers under General Francisco Mejía. Mexico felt that this movement by the U.S. army had deeply invaded Mexican soil because the only Texas-U.S. border it recognized was the Sabine River. Never received by the Herrera or Paredes y Arrillaga governments, U.S. diplomat John Slidell finally returned to the United States. Frémont fought against Californios under Castro at Monterey and later at Gavilan Peak. Frémont finally withdrew and left for Oregon Territory.

April 1846 President Paredes y Arrillaga proclaimed a defensive war against the United States. General Pedro de Ampudia took over command of the Mexican forces at Matamoros (the Army of the North) and demanded Taylor's withdrawal. When Taylor refused, Ampudia indicated that a state of war existed between the two countries. Taylor requested a U.S. naval blockade across the mouth of the Río Grande to restrict shipping upriver to Matamoros. On April 17, after traveling for six months by ship around South America, U.S. Marine Corp officer Archibald Gillespie arrived in Monterey, California, with secret instructions from President Polk for envoy Larkin and Captain Frémont. He left shortly afterward to try to intercept Frémont in Oregon. On April 24, a Mexican cavalry force under General Anastasio Torrejón crossed the Río Grande above Matamoros; the following day, they ambushed Captain Seth Thornton and a small party of U.S. soldiers. Sixteen of the 63 men were killed or wounded, and the others were captured.

May 1846 Mexican forces under General Ampudia lay siege to Fort Texas. Returning to Fort Texas from their supply base at Point Isabel on May 8, Taylor's army was met by Ampudia's army at the Battle of Palo Alto, the first large-scale military action and a U.S. victory. The following day, with Ampudia holding a stronger defensive position, Taylor's troops drove them in retreat at the Battle of Resaca de la Palma. Although outnumbered, Taylor's army won these battles because of better leadership and better weapons, but especially because of more skilled use of artillery. The battered Mexican army withdrew to Matamoros.

Upon learning about the Thornton skirmish, President Polk quickly drafted a war message that claimed that Mexico had "shed American blood upon the American soil" and that a state of war existed with Mexico. Congress concurred, and the United States officially declared war on Mexico on May 13. The Mexican army finally retreated southward from Matamoros on May 17 and 18. Taylor crossed the Río Grande and occupied Matamoros. Lieutenant Gillespie finally overtook Frémont in Oregon on May 9 and delivered his correspondence from President Polk; Frémont then turned back to return to California.

President Polk, the commander in chief, and with no military background, began to orchestrate the military and naval operations against Mexico. His plan was two fold: to send Brigadier General Stephen Watts Kearny and an armed force (the Army of the West) westward to occupy New Mexico and California and to send Taylor's men across the Río Grande into Mexico to secure the northern provinces. Polk also ordered a naval blockade along the Mexican gulf coast. Knowing that it would be difficult for Mexico to defend itself, Polk hoped that these actions would result in rapid victories that would force the Mexican government to concede New Mexico and California, the lands that he wanted.

June 1846 Taylor sent Brigadier General John E. Wool and 300 men to occupy the Mexican state of Chihuahua. Taylor's staff spent all of June training and incorporating 3-month, 6-month, and 12-month volunteers that had arrived in their camp. From Fort Leavenworth, Kansas, Kearny began his long march to Santa Fe on June 5. Frémont, back in California, helped incite the Bear Flag Revolt, whose leaders declared California an independent republic free from Mexico.

July 1846 The Mexican Congress officially declared war against the United States. Taylor moved deeper into Mexico by marching from Matamoros and occupying the city of Camargo. The U.S. Navy's Pacific Squadron, under Commodores John D. Sloat and Robert F. Stockton, became active along the Pacific coast, occupied Monterey, and raised the U.S. flag.

August 1846 Inner turmoil in Mexico resulted in the overthrow of President Paredes y

Arrillaga; the new revolutionary government was headed by José Mariano Salas, a supporter of the exiled Santa Anna. The Home Squadron's attempt to take the gulf port of Alvarado failed; the Pacific fleet faired better and quickly occupied the city of Los Angeles in California. After having nearly a third of his army stricken by illness at Camargo, Taylor eagerly moved out on August 19 toward Monterrey. Having encountered little resistance, Kearny's Army of the West entered New Mexico, declared it part of the United States, and occupied the city of Santa Fe.

Polk's military strategies were influenced by assurances from Colonel A. J. Atocha, a friend of exiled Santa Anna, that, if Santa Anna regained leadership of Mexico and the United States showed a strong military force, the Mexican government would peacefully cede its northern territory to the United States. Meetings between U.S. agents and Santa Anna in Havana, Cuba, confirmed this intent. As per Polk's instructions, Commodore Conner's Home Squadron allowed Santa Anna to pass through its blockade and land at Veracruz on August 16. Hoping that Santa Anna would negotiate for peace, Polk sought a $2 million appropriation from Congress, but it was turned down. The Wilmot Proviso, which called for the prohibition of slavery in any new lands acquired by the United States, was hotly debated in Congress and also defeated. The new government in Mexico City organized itself and eagerly awaited the appearance of Santa Anna.

September 1846 Santa Anna entered Mexico City on September 14 amid much celebration and became commander in chief of the Mexican army. The army, which had retreated from Matamoros to Monterrey and upgraded that city's defenses, engaged Taylor in the hard-fought Battle of Monterrey during September 20–24. Taylor finally won, and the two armies agreed to a temporary, eight-week armistice. This enraged President Polk, who felt that Taylor should have crushed the weakened Mexican army and ended the war. General Wool, after receiving and training volunteers, departed San Antonio for Chihuahua. The struggle in California continued with uprisings against the U.S. occupational forces. U.S. soldiers surrendered at Los Angeles. The Californian insurgents formed a new revolutionary government in California that was to last until January 1847. Having secured New Mexico, Kearny left an occupational force there and marched westward from Santa Fe toward San Diego with a force of dragoons. Volunteer reinforcements commanded by Colonel Sterling Price arrived in Santa Fe by the end of the month. In only two weeks, Santa Anna had scratched together a poorly outfitted army and moved north on September 28 toward San Luis Potosí.

October 1846 Polk ordered Taylor to terminate the armistice with the Mexican army and resume the campaign. The U.S. Navy stepped up its operations along the gulf coast and again failed in an attempt to seize the port city of Alvarado; it did, however, occupy several towns along the Tabasco River. Attempts by U.S. forces to retake Los Angeles were defeated by the Californians after some stiff skirmishing. General Wool continued his march toward Chihuahua and had occupied the town of Monclova by the end of the month. Santa Anna began to reassemble the Army of the North at San Luis Potosí.

November 1846 Taylor notified Santa Anna on November 13 that the armistice had been terminated. Marching deeper into Mexico, Taylor occupied Saltillo on November 16. With word of a large force under Santa Anna in Taylor's front, Wool abandoned his march to Chihuahua and redirected his march to rejoin Taylor at Saltillo. Colonel Alexander Doniphan, one of the officers left behind by Kearny in New Mexico, drafted and signed a treaty with the Navajo Nation. Polk, not satisfied with Taylor's progress and impatient to end the war, decided to open up another front: land a force along the beaches of Veracruz under Major General Winfield Scott and march west to seize Mexico City, the capital.

December 1846 The nation's confidence in Santa Anna was shown by his election as the new president. The United States was becoming war weary, and the Whig party regularly denounced the war. Taylor's men continued their slow march southward, their target being the city of Victoria. Scott, eager to get his invasion under way and authorized by Polk to take some of Taylor's regiments, went to Camargo hoping to find General Taylor; Taylor had left earlier for Victoria. Worried about an impending attack from Santa Anna, General Wool drove his men on a forced march across the desert to reinforce Taylor's army at Saltillo. Kearny's men were bloodied by Major Andrés Pico's Californio forces at the Battle of San Pascual in California on December 6. Only through the timely arrival of reinforcements (a force of sailors sent out by Commodore Stockton) did Kearny escape his plight and reach San Diego.

Unaware that Chihuahua was no longer General Wool's destination, Colonel Doniphan and his Missouri Brigade left Valverde, New Mexico, on December 12 for the long, arduous march to Chihuahua (as ordered by Kearny). On December 25, Doniphan's men defeated a force of Mexicans at the Battle of El Brazito and a few days later occupied El Paso. U.S. naval forces in California occupied Laguna, and a combined navy-army force under Commodore Stockton and General Kearny marched northward from San Diego to retake Los Angeles.

January 1847 Desperate for funds, the Mexican Congress and Acting President Valentín Gómez Farías approved a law that allowed the government to seize Catholic Church property to fund the war effort. On January 4, Taylor entered Victoria and sent some of his troops on to Tampico. Scott, still in Camargo, took elements of Taylor's army to participate in the Veracruz invasion. His explanatory letter to Taylor was captured by Mexican guerrillas and forwarded to Santa Anna, who thus became aware of Scott's plans. Santa Anna, with a new and poorly equipped army of approximately 20,000 men, marched northward from his base at San Luis Potosí to fight Taylor's depleted forces. The Californians, after early victories against U.S. forces, were defeated by the combined force of Stockton-Kearny at the Battle of San Gabriel River on January 8. Two days later, Stockton reoccupied Los Angeles. The Treaty of Cahuenga, which secured California as U.S. territory, was signed by Frémont and Californian representatives on January 13. The Mormon Battalion, which had been marching westward from St. Louis following Kearny since July 1846, arrived in San Diego.

February 1847 Gómez Farías's decision to strip the church of its property resulted in the *Polkos* Revolt in Mexico City; the revolt targeted Gómez Farías and his allies. By mid-month, Taylor's army had advanced beyond Saltillo to the small community of Agua Nueva. When he became aware of Santa Anna's advance from the south, he pulled back to a better defensive position just south of the hacienda Buena Vista. The bloody Battle of Buena Vista raged on February 22 and 23. It was a hard-fought contest that was narrowly a U.S. victory. General Scott and his newly acquired forces left the Río Grande on February 15 to begin the Veracruz expedition. Insurgent uprisings in New Mexico were crushed by Colonel Price's Missourians and ended with the surrender of Taos. Doniphan's march resumed from El Paso to Chihuahua, and he defeated poorly led Chihuahuan forces at the Battle of Río Sacramento on February 28.

March 1847 The *Polkos* Revolt ended in Mexico City with Santa Anna's inauguration as president, his dismissal of Gómez Farías, and his more generous terms regarding seizure of church funds. The dominant U.S. activity was the landing of nearly 10,000 U.S. soldiers at Veracruz and the destructive siege of the city. After incessant shelling and the deaths of hundreds of civilians, Veracruz surrendered on March 29 and was occupied by Scott's forces. Doniphan's men finally arrived at Chihuahua, and San Jose and San Lucas in Lower California were occupied by the U.S. naval forces.

April 1847 Although the Mexican Congress granted the government virtually unrestricted authority to conduct the war, it did not allow it to negotiate for peace. Gómez Farías was officially expelled as vice-president, and Pedro María Anaya was elected interim president because Santa Anna was in the field. Anxious to leave Veracruz before the yellow fever season began, Scott's men marched inland along the paved National Road and defeated Santa Anna's makeshift army at the Battle of Cerro Gordo on April 18. Commodore Matthew C. Perry, now in command of the Home Squadron, occupied the port city of Tuxpan along the gulf. A portion of Brigadier General William J. Worth's command occupied the Castle of Perote near Puebla. The Pacific fleet continued to lock up Mexico's Pacific coast and garrisoned the community of La Paz.

May–June 1847 This period was relatively quiet. Santa Anna returned to the office of the presidency, and Scott's U.S. forces were reorganized as thousands of volunteers were sent home and new regiments were received. Generals Worth and Scott joined forces at Puebla on May 29. Naval operations continued along the gulf coastline of Mexico.

July 1847 Scott's army continued to grow and received reinforcements led by Gideon Pillow at Puebla on July 8. A U.S. column, sent from Tampico to release American prisoners at Huejutla, was turned back by a Mexican force at Río Calaboso.

August 1847 After marching inland from Veracruz, Franklin Pierce's 2,500-man volunteer force joined Scott's army at Puebla. After finally organizing and training his army to his liking, Scott advanced his army toward Mexico City and fought the Battles of Contreras (Padierna) and Churubusco on August 19 and 20, respectively. After these defeats, the Armistice of Tacubaya was signed on August 24 to promote peace negotiations.

September 1847 After negotiations broke down, the bloody Battle of El Molino del Rey, another U.S. victory, was fought on September 8. Unstoppable, the U.S. forces stormed Chapultepec on September 13 and fought desperately at the San Cosmé and Belén gates at the edge of the city. The following day, the triumphant U.S. forces entered Mexico City. Mexican forces lay siege to the U.S. garrison that Scott left behind at Puebla on September 14. Two days later, Santa Anna renounced his presidency, which was filled by Manuel Peña y Peña.

October 1847 The Mexican government was temporarily seated in Querétaro and ordered Santa Anna removed as commander in chief of the Mexican army. The large-scale fighting had ended; skirmishes occurred at Huamantla and Atlixco. The Mexican forces that threatened the U.S. garrison at Puebla were driven away, and the Pacific Squadron occupied the port city of Guaymas.

November 1847 The disheartened Mexican Congress in Querétaro elected Pedro María Anaya as interim president, and he appointed commissioners to negotiate a treaty with the United States. Angry with their attempts to undermine his leadership, General Scott relieved Generals Worth and Pillow of their commands. After General Taylor left his army in northern Mexico to return to the United States, General Wool became its commander.

December 1847–January 1848 A large number of new troops arrived in Mexico to replace the battle-weary veterans and to act as an occupation force. U.S. envoy Nicholas Trist led the team of U.S. commissioners that negotiated peace terms with the Mexican representatives. Peña y Peña became the acting president of Mexico after Anaya's interim term ended. A group of U.S. sailors that had been under siege at San José, California, were rescued by another naval force. Irritated by the bickering between General Scott and Generals Worth and Pillow, President Polk relieved Scott of command and ordered a court of inquiry to investigate the matter.

February 1848 On February 2, the U.S. and Mexican peace commissioners signed the Treaty of Guadalupe Hidalgo. General William O. Butler assumed the command of Scott's army after Scott was relieved. President Polk submitted the Treaty of Guadalupe Hidalgo for ratification to the U.S. Senate on February 23; a military armistice went into effect a few days later.

March 1848 Unaware of the armistice, Price and his men occupied Santa Cruz de Rosales in the state of Chihuahua. The Treaty of Guadalupe Hidalgo was accepted by the U.S. Senate with some modifications. The last shots of the war were fired during a minor skirmish at Todos Santos in Lower California on March 30.

May 1848 On May 25, the Mexican government accepted the revised Treaty of Guadalupe Hidalgo, which went into effect five days later. The Mexican-American War was officially over.

Selected References

References in English

Adams, John Q. *The Diary of John Quincy Adams.* Edited by Allan Nevins. New York: Longmans, Green and Company, 1928.

Adler, Larry. *The Texas Rangers.* New York: McKay, 1979.

Alcaraz, Ramon. *The Other Side: Notes for the History of the War between Mexico and the United States.* Translated and edited by Albert C. Ramsey. New York: John Wiley, 1850.

Aldrich, M. A. *History of the United States Marine Corps.* Boston: Henry L. Shepard and Company, 1875.

Allen, G. W. *Waldo Emerson: A Biography.* New York: Viking, 1981.

Allie, Stephen J. *All He Could Carry: U.S. Army Infantry Equipment, 1839–1910.* Fort Leavenworth, KS: Frontier Army Museum, 1991.

Allsopp, Frederick W. *The Life Story of Albert Pike.* Little Rock, AR: Parker-Harper, 1920.

Altman, Ida, and James Lockhart, eds. *Provinces of Early Mexico: Variants of Spanish American Regional Evolution.* Los Angeles: University of California, Latin American Center, 1976.

Ambrose, Stephen. *Halleck: Lincoln's Chief of Staff.* Baton Rouge: Louisiana State University Press, 1962.

An Album of American Battle Art, 1775–1918. Washington, DC: U.S. Government Printing Office, 1947.

Anderson, Robert. *An Artillery Officer in the Mexican War, 1846–1847: Letters of Robert Anderson.* Edited by E. A. Lawton. New York: G. P. Putnam's Sons, 1911.

Archer, Christon. *The Bourbon Army in Mexico, 1760–1810.* Albuquerque: University of New Mexico Press, 1977.

Armstrong, Andrew. "The Brazito Battlefield." *New Mexico Historical Review* 35 (January 1960): 63–74.

Arrom, Silvia Marina. *The Women of Mexico City, 1790–1857.* Stanford, CA: Stanford University Press, 1985.

Asbury, S. E. "The Private Journal of Juan Nepomuceno Almonte, February 1–April 16, 1836." *Southwestern Historical Quarterly* 48 (1944): 10–32.

Ashburn, P. M. *A History of the Medical Department of the United States Army.* Boston: Houghton Mifflin, 1911.

Backus, Electus. "Brief Sketch of the Battle of Monterey." *Dawson's Historical Magazine* 10(7) (1866): 207–213, 255–257.

Baker, B. Kimball. "The St. Patricks Fought for Their Skins, and Mexico." *Smithsonian* 8(12) (1978): 94–101.

Baker, George T. "Mexico City and the War with the United States: A Study in the Politics of Military Occupation." Ph.D. dissertation. Durham, NC: Duke University, 1970.

Balbontín, Manuel. "The Battle of Angostura (Buena Vista)." Translated by F. H. Hardie. *United States Cavalry Journal* 7(5) (June 1894): 125–154.

———. "The Siege of Monterey." *Journal of the Military Service Institute of the United States* 8 (1887): 325–354.

Ballard, Michael B. *Pemberton, a Biography.* Jackson: University Press of Mississippi, 1991.

Ballentine, George. *Autobiography of an English Soldier in the United States Army.* New York: Stringer and Townsend, 1853.

Bancroft, Hubert H. *History of Arizona and New Mexico 1530–1888.* San Francisco: The History Company, 1889.

———. *History of California.* San Francisco: The History Company, 1886.

———. *The History of Mexico.* Santa Barbara, CA: Wallace Hebbard, 1966.

———. *History of Nevada, Colorado and Wyoming.* San Francisco: The History Company, 1890.

———. *History of the North Mexican States and Texas.* San Francisco: The History Company, 1884–1889.

Barbour, Philip N. *Journals of the Late Brevet Major Philip Norbourne Barbour, Captain in the 3rd Regiment, United States Infantry, and His Wife Martha Isabella Hopkins Barbour, Written during the War with Mexico, 1846*. Edited by Rhoda Van Bibber Tanner Doubleday. New York: G. P. Putnam's Sons, 1936.

Barker, Eugene C. *Mexico and Texas, 1821–1835*. Dallas: Turner, 1928.

———. "President Jackson and the Texas Revolution." *American Historical Review* 12 (July 1907): 788–809.

Barrows, Edward M. *The Great Commodore: The Exploits of Matthew Calbraith Perry*. Indianapolis, IN: Bobbs-Merrill, 1935.

Bartlett, I. H. *John C. Calhoun: A Biography*. New York: W. W. Norton, 1993.

———. *Daniel Webster*. New York: W. W. Norton, 1978.

Bartlett, J. R. *Personal Narrative of the Explorations and Incidents in Texas, New Mexico, California, Sonora, and Chihuahua*. New York: D. Appleton, 1854.

Barton, Henry W. *Texas Volunteers in the Mexican War*. Waco, TX: Texian Press, 1970.

Bassett, J. S. *The Life of Andrew Jackson*. Hamden, CT: Archon Books, 1967.

Bauer, K. Jack. "The Battles on the Rio Grande: Palo Alto and Resaca de la Palma, 8–9 May 1846." In *America's First Battles, 1776–1965*. Edited by Charles E. Heller and William A. Stofft. Lawrence: University Press of Kansas, 1986.

———. *The Mexican War, 1846–1848*. New York: Macmillan, 1974.

———. *Surfboats and Horse Marines: U.S. Naval Operations in the Mexican War*. Annapolis, MD: U.S. Naval Institute, 1969.

———. "United States Naval Operations during the Mexican War." Ph.D. dissertation. Bloomington: Indiana University, 1953.

———. *Zachary Taylor: Soldier, Planter, Statesman of the Old Southwest*. Baton Rouge: Louisiana State University Press, 1985.

Baxter, Edward P., and Kay L. Killen. *A Study of the Palo Alto Battleground, Cameron County, Texas*. College Station: Texas A&M University, 1976.

Bayard, S. J. *A Sketch of the Life of Commodore Robert F. Stockton*. New York: Derby and Jackson, 1856.

Baylies, Francis. *A Narrative of Major General Wool's Campaign in Mexico*. Albany, NY: Little, 1851.

Bazant, Jan. *A Concise History of Mexico from Hidalgo to Cárdenas, 1805–1940*. Cambridge, England: Cambridge University Press, 1977.

Beach, Moses S. "A Secret Mission to Mexico." *Scribner's Monthly* 17(2) (1878): 299–300; 18(1) (1879): 136–140.

Beauregard, P. G. T. *With Beauregard in Mexico*. Edited by T. Harry Williams. Baton Rouge: Louisiana State University Press, 1956.

Beck, Warren A. *New Mexico: A History of Four Centuries*. Norman: University of Oklahoma Press, 1962.

Belohlavek, J. M. *George Mifflin Dallas: Jacksonian Patrician*. University Park: Pennsylvania State University Press, 1977.

Bemis, S. F. *John Quincy Adams and the Union*. New York: Alfred A. Knopf, 1970.

Bender, A. B. "Frontier Defense in the Territory of New Mexico, 1846–1853." *New Mexico Historical Review* 9 (July 1934): 249–274.

Bennett, James A. *Forts and Forays or a Dragoon in New Mexico, 1850–1856*. Edited by C. E. Brooks and F. D. Reeve. Albuquerque: University of New Mexico Press, 1948.

Benton, Thomas Hart. *Thirty Years' View: or A History of the Working of the American Government for Thirty Years, from 1820 to 1850*. New York: Appleton, 1856.

Berge, Dennis E., ed. and trans. *Considerations on the Political and Social Situation of the Mexican Republic: 1847*. Southwestern Studies Monograph 45. El Paso: Texas Western Press, 1975.

———. "Mexican Response to United States Expansion: 1841–1848." Ph.D. dissertation. Berkeley: University of California, 1965.

Bergeron, Paul H. *The Presidency of James K. Polk*. Lawrence: University Press of Kansas, 1987.

Bethell, Leslie, ed. *Spanish America after Independence, c. 1820–c. 1870*. Cambridge, England: Cambridge University Press, 1987.

Bieber, Ralph P., ed. *Marching with the Army of the West 1846–1848*. Glendale, CA: Clark, 1936.

Bigelow, John. *Memoir of the Life and Public Service of John Charles Frémont*. New York: Derby and Jackson, 1856.

Bill, Alfred Hoyt. *Rehearsal for Conflict, the War with Mexico, 1846–1848*. New York: Alfred A. Knopf, 1947.

Billings, Eliza Allen. *The Female Volunteer, or the Life and Wonderful Adventures of Miss Eliza Allen, a Young Lady of Eastport, Maine*. Cincinnati, OH: H. M. Rulon, 1851.

Billington, Ray Allen. *The Far Western Frontier, 1830–1860.* Albuquerque: University of New Mexico Press, 1956.

Binkley, William C. *The Expansionist Movement in Texas.* Berkeley: University of California Press, 1925.

Birkhimer, William E. *Historical Sketch of the Organization, Administration, Materiél and Tactics of the Artillery, United States Army.* Washington, DC: James J. Chapman, 1884.

Blackwood, Emma Jerome. *To Mexico with Scott.* Cambridge, England: Cambridge University Press, 1917.

Blied, Benjamin J. "Catholic Aspects of the Mexican War, 1846–1848." *Social Justice Review* 40(11) (March 1948): 367–371.

Bliss, Robert S. "The Journal of Robert S. Bliss with the Mormon Battalion." *Utah Historical Quarterly* 4 (July–October 1931): 67–96, 110–128.

Bloom, John Porter. "With the American Army into Mexico." Ph.D. dissertation. Atlanta, GA: Emory University, 1956.

Boatner, Mark M., III. *The Civil War Dictionary.* New York: David McKay Company, 1959.

Bodson, Robert L. "A Description of the United States Occupation of Mexico as Reported by American Newspapers Published in Vera Cruz, Puebla, and Mexico City; September 14, 1847, to July 31, 1848." Ph.D. dissertation. Muncie, IN: Ball State University, 1970.

Bonsal, Stephen. *Edward Fitzgerald Beale, a Pioneer in the Path of Empire, 1822–1903.* New York: G. P. Putnam's Sons, 1912.

Borah, Woodrow. "Race and Class in Mexico." *Pacific Historical Review* 22 (1954): 331–342.

Bourne, E. G. "The Proposed Absorption of Mexico, 1847–1848." *Annual Report of the American Historical Association for 1900.* Vol. 1, 155–169. Washington, DC: U.S. Government Printing Office, 1901.

———. "The United States and Mexico, 1847–1848." *American Historical Review* 5(3) (April 1900): 491–502.

Brack, Gene M. *Mexico Views Manifest Destiny, 1821–1846: An Essay on the Origins of the Mexican War.* Albuquerque: University of New Mexico Press, 1975.

Brackett, Albert G. *General Lane's Brigade in Central Mexico.* Cincinnati. OH: H. W. Derby, 1854.

Bradlee, F. B. C. *A Forgotten Chapter in Our Naval History: A Sketch of the Career of Duncan Nathaniel Ingraham.* Salem, MA: Essex Institute, 1923.

Brady, Cyrus T. *The Conquest of the Southwest.* New York: D. Appleton and Company, 1905.

Brent, Robert A. "Nicholas Trist: A Biography." Ph.D. dissertation. Charlottesville: University of Virginia Press, 1950.

———. "Nicholas Trist and the Treaty of Guadalupe Hidalgo." *Southwestern Historical Quarterly* 57(4) (April 1954): 217–234.

Brewerton, G. D. *Overland with Kit Carson: A Narrative of the Old Spanish Trail in '48.* Lincoln: University of Nebraska Press, 1993.

Brinckerhoff, Sidney B., and Odie B. Faulk. *Lancers for the King: A Study of the Frontier Military System of Northern New Spain, with a Translation of the Royal Regulations of 1772.* Phoenix: Arizona Historical Foundation, 1965.

Brooks, N. C. *A Complete History of the Mexican War, 1846–1848.* Baltimore: Hutchinson and Seebold, 1849.

Brooks, P. C. *Diplomacy and the Borderlands: The Adams-Onís Treaty of 1819.* Berkeley: University of California Press, 1939.

Brown, Harvey E., comp. *The Medical Department of the United States Army from 1775 to 1873.* Washington, DC: Surgeon General's Office, 1873.

Brown, Walter Lee. *A Life of Albert Pike.* Fayetteville: University of Arkansas Press, 1997.

———. "The Mexican War Experiences of Albert Pike and the 'Mounted Devils' of Arkansas." *Arkansas Historical Quarterly* 12(4) (Winter 1953): 301–315.

Bryant, Edwin. *What I Saw in California.* Launceton, Tasmania: Henry Dowling, 1848.

Calderón de la Barca, Frances Erskine. *Life in Mexico.* Berkeley and Los Angeles: University of California Press, 1982.

Calhoun, John C. *The Papers of John C. Calhoun.* Edited by Robert L. Meriwether and W. Edwin Hemphill. Columbia: University of South Carolina Press, 1959.

Callahan, J. M. *American Foreign Policy in Mexican Relations.* New York: Macmillan, 1932.

Callcott, Wilfrid H. *Church and State in Mexico.* Durham, NC: Duke University Press, 1926.

———. *Santa Anna: The Story of an Enigma That*

Once Was Mexico. Norman: University of Oklahoma Press, 1936.

Camp, Roderic A. *Mexican Political Biographies, 1884–1935.* Austin: University of Texas Press, 1991.

Campbell, R. B. *Sam Houston and the American Southwest.* New York: HarperCollins, 1993.

Capers, Gerald M. *John C. Calhoun, Opportunist: A Reappraisal.* Gainesville: University of Florida Press, 1960.

Carleton, James Henry. *The Battle of Buena Vista.* New York: Harper and Brothers, 1848.

Carpenter, E. *Days with Walt Whitman.* New York: Macmillan, 1921.

Carson, Kit. *Kit Carson's Own Story of His Life.* Edited by Blanche C. Grant. Taos, NM: Kit Carson Memorial Foundation, 1955.

Carter, H. L. *"Dear Old Kit": The Historical Christopher Carson.* Norman: University of Oklahoma Press, 1990.

Caruso, A. Brooke. *The Mexican Spy Company. United States Covert Operations in Mexico, 1845–1848.* Jefferson, NC: McFarland, 1991.

Cashion, Peggy. "Women and the Mexican War." M.A. thesis. Arlington: University of Texas, 1990.

Castañeda, Carlos E., trans. and ed. *The Mexican Side of the Texas Revolution.* Dallas: P. L. Turner, 1928.

———. "Relations of General Scott with Santa Anna." *Hispanic American Historical Review* 39 (November 1949): 455–473.

Catton, Bruce. *U. S. Grant and the American Military Tradition.* Boston: Little, Brown, 1954.

Caughey, John W. *California.* New York: Prentice-Hall, 1970.

Chacon Gómez, Fernando. "The Intended and Actual Effects of Article VIII of the Treaty of Guadalupe Hidalgo: Mexican Treaty Rights under International and Domestic Law." Ph.D. dissertation. Ann Arbor: University of Michigan, 1966.

Chalfant, William Y. *Dangerous Passage: The Santa Fe Trail and the Mexican War.* Norman: University of Oklahoma Press, 1994.

Chamberlain, Samuel E. *My Confession. The Recollections of a Rogue.* New York: Harper & Brothers, 1956.

Chambers, William Nisbet. *Old Bullion Benton, Senator from the New West.* Boston: Little, Brown, 1956.

Chance, Joseph E. *Jefferson Davis's Mexican War Regiment.* Jackson: University Press of Mississippi, 1991.

Chaney, Homer Campbell, Jr. "The Mexican–United States War as Seen by Mexican Intellectuals, 1846–1959." Ph.D. dissertation. Stanford, CA: Stanford University, 1959.

Chapman, Helen. *The News from Brownsville: Helen Chapman's Letters from the Texas Military Frontier, 1848–1852.* Austin: Texas State Historical Association, 1992.

Chapman, William. "Letters from the Seat of War—Mexico (1846–47)." *Green Bay Historical Bulletin* 4(4) (July–August 1928): 1–24.

Chase, Lucien B. *History of the Polk Administration.* New York: G. P. Putnam, 1850.

Chipman, Donald. *Spanish Texas, 1519–1821.* Austin: University of Texas Press, 1992.

Chitwood, Oliver Perry. *John Tyler Champion of the Old South.* New York: D. Appleton-Century, 1939.

Clairborne, J. F. H. *Life and Correspondence of John A. Quitman.* New York: Harper & Brothers, 1860.

Clark, Amasa G. *Reminiscences of a Centenarian, as Told by Amasa Gleason Clark, Veteran of the Mexican War, to Cora Tope Clark.* Edited by J. Marvin Hunter. San Antonio, TX: Naylor, 1972.

Clark, Edward H., et al. *A Century of American Medicine, 1776–1876.* Brinklow, MD: Old Hickory Bookshop, 1876.

Clark, Francis D. *The First Regiment of New York Volunteers.* New York: George S. Evans and Company, 1882.

Clarke, Benton Champ. *John Quincy Adams.* Boston: Little, Brown, 1932.

Clarke, Dwight L. *Stephen Watts Kearny, Soldier of the West.* Norman: University of Oklahoma Press, 1961.

Clay, Henry. *The Private Correspondence of Henry Clay.* Edited by Calvin Colton. New York: A. S. Barnes, 1855.

Cleaves, Freeman. *Meade of Gettysburg.* Norman: University of Oklahoma Press, 1960.

Cleland, Robert G. *From Wilderness to Empire: A History of California.* New York: Alfred A. Knopf, 1970.

Clendenen, Clarence C. *Blood on the Border: The United States Army and the Mexican Irregulars.* New York: Macmillan, 1969.

Clifford, Philip Greely. *Nathan Clifford, Democrat (1803–1881)*. New York: G. P. Putnam's Sons, 1922.

Cline, Howard F. *The United States and Mexico*. Cambridge, England: Cambridge University Press, 1953.

Coffman, E. M. *The Old Army: A Portrait of the American Army in Peace Time, 1784–1898*. New York: Oxford University Press, 1986.

Coit, Margaret L. *John C. Calhoun. American Portrait*. Boston: Houghton Mifflin, 1950.

Collins, Francis. "Journal of Francis Collins, an Artillery Officer in the Mexican War." *Quarterly Publications of the Historical and Philosophical Society of Ohio* 10 (April–July 1915): 35–109.

Collins, John R. "The Mexican War: A Study in Fragmentation." *Journal of the West* 11 (April 1972): 225–234.

Colton, Walter. *Three Years in California*. New York: Barnes, 1850.

Condon, William H. *The Life of Major-General James Shields. Hero of Three Wars and Senator from Three States*. Chicago: Blakely, 1900.

Connelley, William E. *Doniphan's Expedition and the Conquest of New Mexico and California*. Topeka, KS: Self-published, 1907.

Conner, Philip. *The Home Squadron under Commodore Conner in the War with Mexico*. Philadelphia: n.p., 1896.

Connor, Seymour V., and Odie B. Faulk. *North America Divided. The Mexican War, 1846–1848*. New York: Oxford University Press, 1971.

Cook, R. B. *The Family and Early Life of Stonewall Jackson*. Richmond, VA: Old Dominion Press, 1924.

Cook, Zo S. "Mexican War Reminiscences." *Alabama Historical Quarterly* 20 (1957): 435–460.

Cooke, Philip St. George. *The Conquest of New Mexico and California*. New York: G. P. Putnam's Sons, 1878.

———. *Scenes and Adventures in the Army; Or Romance of Military Life*. Philadelphia: Lindsey and Blakiston, 1857.

Cooper, James Fenimore. *The Correspondence of James Fenimore Cooper*. Freeport, NY: Books for Libraries Press, 1971.

———. *The History of the Navy of the United States of America*. New York: Appleton and Company, 1853.

Copeland, Fayette. *Kendall of the Picayune*. Norman: University of Oklahoma Press, 1943.

Costeloe, Michael P. *The Central Republic in Mexico, 1835–1846: Hombres de Bien in the Age of Santa Anna*. New York: Oxford University Press, 1993.

———. "The Mexican Church and the Rebellion of the Polkos." *Hispanic American Historical Review* 46 (May 1966): 170–178.

Cotner, Thomas E. *The Military and Political Career of José Joaquín de Herrera, 1792–1854*. Austin: University of Texas Press, 1949.

Cotner, Thomas E., and Carlos E. Castañeda, eds. *Essays in Mexican History*. Austin, TX: Institute of Latin American Studies, 1958.

Coy, Owen C. *The Battle of San Pasqual. A Report of the California Historical Survey with General Reference to Its Location*. Sacramento: California State Printing Office, 1921.

Cralle, Richard K. *The Works of John C. Calhoun*. New York: D. Appleton and Company, 1854–1861.

Craven, Tunis A. M. *A Naval Campaign in the Californias—1846–1849: The Journal of Lieutenant Tunis Augustus Macdonough Craven, U.S.N. United States Sloop of War Dale*. San Francisco: Book Club of California, 1973.

Crimmins, Martin Lalor. "First Stages of the Mexican War." *Journal of the Army Ordnance Association* 15 (1935): 222–225.

Crosby, H. W. *Antigua California*. Albuquerque, NM: University of New Mexico Press, 1994.

Cullum, George W. *Biographical Register of the Officers and Graduates of the United States Military Academy from 1802 to 1867*. New York: Miller and Company, 1879.

Cuncliffe, Marcus. *Soldiers & Civilians: The Martial Spirit in America, 1775–1865*. Second edition. Boston: Little, Brown, 1968.

Current, R. N. *John C. Calhoun*. New York: Washington Square Press, 1963.

Curtis, S. R. *Mexico under Fire: Being the Diary of Samuel Ryan Curtis, 3rd Ohio Volunteer Regiment, during the American Military Occupation of Northern Mexico, 1846–47*. Edited by Joseph E. Chance. Fort Worth: Texas Christian University Press, 1994.

Cutrer, Thomas W. *Ben McCulloch and the Frontier Military Tradition*. Chapel Hill: University of North Carolina Press, 1993.

Cuttings, Elizabeth. *Jefferson Davis, Political*

Soldier. New York: Dodd, Mead, 1930.

Cutts, James Madison. *The Conquest of California and New Mexico by the Forces of the United States in the Years 1846 and 1847.* Philadelphia: Carey and Hart, 1847.

Dabney, R. L. *The Life and Campaigns of Lieutenant-General Thomas J. Jackson.* New York: Blelock and Company, 1866.

Dana, J. *Sutter of California.* New York: Halcyon House, 1938.

Dana, Napoleon J. T. *Monterrey Is Ours!: The Mexican War Letters of Lieutenant Dana, 1845–1847.* Edited by Robert H. Ferrell. Lexington: University of Kentucky Press, 1990.

Davis, G. T. M. *Autobiography of the Late Colonel George T. M. Davis.* New York: Jenkins and McGowan, 1891.

Davis, John L. *The Texas Rangers: Images and Incidents.* San Antonio: University of Texas Institute of Texan Cultures, 1991.

Davis, Varina Howell. *Jefferson Davis, Ex-president of the Confederate States of America: A Memoir by His Wife.* New York: Belford Company, 1890.

Day, James M. *Black Beans & Goose Quills: Literature of the Texan Mier Expedition.* Waco, TX: Texian Press, 1970.

De la Pena, Jose Enrique. *With Santa Anna in Texas.* Edited and translated by Carmen Perry. 1836. Reprint. College Station: Texas A&M University Press, 1975.

De Leon, Arnoldo. *They Called Them Greasers.* Austin: University of Texas, 1983.

De Peyster, J. W. *The Personal and Military History of Philip Kearny.* New York: Rice and Gage, 1869.

De Shields, James T. *Border Wars of Texas.* Tioga, TX: Herald Company, 1912.

DePalo, William A. *The Mexican National Army, 1822–1852.* Albuquerque: University of New Mexico Press, 1997.

———. *Praetorians and Patriots: The Mexican National Army.* Ph.D. dissertation. Albuquerque: University of New Mexico, 1994.

DeVoto, Bernard. *The Year of Decision, 1846.* Boston: Little, Brown, 1943.

Díaz de Castillo, Bernal. *The Discovery and Conquest of Mexico.* Translated by A. P. Maudslay. New York: Farrar, Straus, and Cudahy, 1956.

Dillon, Lester R., Jr. *American Artillery in the Mexican War 1846–1847.* Austin, TX: Presidial, 1975.

Dodd, W. E. *Robert J. Walker, Imperialist.* Chicago: Chicago Literary Club, 1914.

———. "The West and the War with Mexico." *Journal of the Illinois State Historical Society* 5 (July 1912): 159–172.

Donald, David. *Lincoln.* New York: Simon & Schuster, 1995.

Dowdey, Clifford. *Lee.* Boston: Little, Brown, 1965.

Downey, F. D. *Cannonade, Great Artillery Actions of History, the Famous Cannons and the Master Gunners.* Garden City, NJ: Doubleday, 1966.

———. "Tragic Story of the San Patricio Battalion." *American Heritage* 6 (1955): 20–23.

Downey, Joseph T. *The Cruise of the* Portsmouth. New Haven, CT: Yale University Press, 1958.

Drexler, R. W. *Guilty of Making Peace: A Biography of Nicholas P. Trist.* Lanham, MD: University Press of America, 1991.

Driver, Leo. "Carillo's Flying Artillery: The Battle of San Pedro." *California Historical Society Quarterly* 35 (June 1956): 97–117.

Du Pont, Samuel F. *Extracts from Private Journal-Letters of Captain S. F. Dupont, While in Command of the* Cyane *during the War with Mexico, 1846–1848.* Wilmington, DE: Ferris Brothers, 1885.

———. "The War with Mexico: The Cruise of the U.S. Ship *Cyane* during the Years 1845–1848, from the Papers of Her Commander." *U.S. Naval Institute Proceedings* 8 (1882): 419–437.

Duffus, Robert L. *The Santa Fe Trail.* New York: Longmans, Green and Company, 1930.

Dufour, Charles L. *The Mexican War, a Compact History, 1846–1848.* New York: Hawthorn, 1968.

Duncan, James. "The Artillery in the Mexican War, Reports of Captain James Duncan, 2nd U.S. Artillery...Battles of Palo Alto and Resaca de la Palma." *Journal of the United States Artillery* 29 (May–June 1908): 313–316.

Duncan, Louis C. "Medical History of General Scott's Campaign to the City of Mexico in 1847." *Military Surgeon: Journal of the Association of Military Surgeons of the United States* 47(4) (1920): 436–470; 47(5) (1920): 596–609.

———. "A Medical History of General Zachary

Taylor's Army of Occupation in Texas and Mexico, 1845–1847." *Military Surgeon: Journal of the Association of Military Surgeons of the United States* 48 (1921): 76–104.

Duncan, Robert L. *Reluctant General: The Life and Times of Albert Pike.* New York: Dutton, 1961.

Dunlay, T. W. "Indian Allies in the Armies of New Spain and the United States." *New Mexico Historical Review* 56 (July 1981): 239–258.

Dupuy, R. Ernest. *Men of West Point: The First 150 Years of the United States Military Academy.* New York: W. Sloane, 1951.

Dupuy, R. Ernest, and Trevor N. Dupuy. *Military Heritage of America.* New York: McGraw-Hill, 1956.

Durham, M. S. *The Desert between the Mountains.* New York: Henry Holt, 1997.

Duvall, Marius. *A Navy Surgeon in California, 1846–1847: The Journal of Marius Duvall.* San Francisco: John Howell, 1957.

Dyer, Brainerd. *Zachary Taylor.* New York: Barnes and Noble, 1946.

Eckenrode, H. J. *James Longstreet, Lee's War Horse.* Chapel Hill: University of North Carolina Press, 1936.

"Editorial: Sickness in the U.S. Army in Mexico." *New Orleans Medical and Surgical Journal* 4 (1847–1848): 138–141.

Edwards, Frank S. *A Campaign in New Mexico with Colonel Doniphan.* Philadelphia: Carey and Hart, 1847.

Egan, Ferol. *Frémont: Explorer for a Restless Nation.* New York: Doubleday, 1977.

Eisenhower, John S. D. *Agent of Destiny: The Life and Times of General Winfield Scott.* New York: Free Press, 1997.

———. *So Far from God: The U.S. War with Mexico, 1846–1848.* New York: Random House, 1989.

Elderkin, J. D. *Biographical Sketches and Anecdotes of a Soldier of Three Wars, as Written by Himself.* Detroit: Record Printing Company, 1899.

Elliott, Charles W. *Winfield Scott: The Soldier and the Man.* New York: Macmillan, 1937.

Elliot, J. F. "The Great Western: Sarah Bowman, Mother and Mistress to the U.S. Army." *Journal of Arizona History* 30 (Spring 1989): 30–39.

Ellsworth, C. S. "The American Churches and the Mexican War." *American Historical Review* 45 (January 1940): 301–346.

Emmons, George Fox. *The Navy of the United States.* Washington, DC: Gideon and Company, 1853.

Emory, W. H. *Notes of a Military Reconnaissance.* New York: H. Long and Brother, 1848.

Engelmann, Otto B., ed. "The Second Illinois in the Mexican War. Mexican War Letters of Adolph Engelmann, 1846–1847." *Journal of the Illinois State Historical Society* 26 (January 1934): 357–452.

Estergreen, Marion. *The Real Kit Carson.* Taos, NM: Kit Carson Memorial Foundation, 1955.

Falk, O. B. *Too Far North, Too Far South.* Los Angeles: Western Lore Press, 1967.

Farnham, Thomas J. "Nicholas Trist and James Freaner and the Mission to Mexico." *Arizona and the West* 2(3) (Autumn 1969): 247–260.

Farrabee, Ethel. "William Stuart Parrott, Businessman and Diplomat in Mexico." M.A. thesis. Austin: University of Texas, 1944.

Faulk, Odie, and J. A. Stout, eds. *The Mexican War: Changing Interpretations.* Chicago: Swallow Press, 1973.

Ferguson, Henry N. *The Port of Brownsville, a Maritime History of the Rio Grande Valley.* Brownsville, TX: Springman-King, 1976.

Ficklin, J. R. "Was Texas Included in the Louisiana Purchase?" *Publications of the Southern Historical Association* 5 (September 1901): 351–387.

Filler, Louis. *The Crusade against Slavery 1830–1860.* New York: Harper & Row, 1960.

Fitz Gerald, David. *In Memorium: General Henry Jackson Hunt.* n.p., 1889.

Foote, Henry Stuart. *Texas and the Texans; or, Advance of the Anglo-Americans to the Southwest Including a History of Leading Events in Mexico, from the Conquest of Fernando Cortes to the Termination of the Texas Revolution.* Austin: University of Texas Press, 1935.

Ford, John Salmon. *Rip Ford's Texas.* Austin: University of Texas Press, 1963.

Fowler, Will. "Valentín Gómez Farías: Perceptions of Radicalism in Independent Mexico, 1821–1847." *Bulletin of Latin American Research* 15(1) (1996): 39–62.

Francis, E. K. "Padre Martínez: A New Mexico Myth." *New Mexico Historical Review* 31(4) (October 1956): 265–289.

Freeman, Douglas Southall. *R. E. Lee.* New York:

Scribner's, 1934.
Frémont, John C. *Memoirs of My Life*. Chicago: Belford Clarke, 1886.
———. *Narratives of Exploration and Adventure*. New York: Longmans, Green and Company, 1956.
French, Samuel G. *Two Wars, an Autobiography*. Nashville, TN: Confederate Veteran, 1901.
Frost, John. *The History of Mexico and Its Wars*. New Orleans, LA: Hawkins, 1882.
———. *The Mexican War and Its Warriors; Comprising a Complete History of All the Operations of the American Armies in Mexico: With Biographical Sketches and Anecdotes of the Most Distinguished Officers in the Regular Army and Volunteer Force*. New Haven, CT: Mansfield, 1848.
———. *Pictorial History of Mexico and the Mexican War*. Philadelphia: Thorne, Cowperthwait and Company, 1849.
Fry, J. R. *A Life of Zachary Taylor, Comprising a Narrative of Events Connected with His Professional Career*. Philadelphia: Grigg, Elliot and Company, 1848.
Fuess, Claude M. *The Life of Caleb Cushing*. New York: Harcourt Brace and Company, 1923.
Fuller, John Douglas. *The Movement for the Acquisition of All Mexico, 1846–1848*. Baltimore: Johns Hopkins Press, 1936.
———. "The Slavery Question and the Move to Acquire Mexico, 1846–1848." *Mississippi Valley Historical Review* 21 (June 1934): 31–48.
Fulton, Maurice, and Paul Horgan, eds. *New Mexico's Own Chronicle*. Dallas: B. Upshaw, 1937.
Furber, George C. *The Twelve Month Volunteer*. Cincinnati, OH: James, 1848.
Gaddy, Jerry J., ed. *Texas in Revolt: Contemporary Newspaper Accounts of the Texas Revolution*. Fort Collins, CO: Old Army Press, 1973.
Galarza, Ernesto. *The Roman Catholic Church as a Factor in the Political and Social History of Mexico*. Sacramento, CA: Capital Press, 1928.
Gallaher, F. M., trans. "The Official Report of the Battle at Temascalitos (Brazito)." *New Mexico Historical Review* 3(4) (1928): 385–389.
Gambrell, Herbert. *Anson Jones: The Last President of Texas*. Austin: University of Texas, 1964.
Ganoe, W. A. *The History of the United States Army*. Ashton, MD: Lundberg, 1964.
Garber, Paul. *The Gadsden Treaty*. Gloucester, MA: Peter Smith, 1959.
Gardiner, C. Harvey, ed. *The Literary Memoranda of William Hickling Prescott*. Norman: University of Oklahoma Press, 1961.
Garrison, George P., ed. "Diplomatic Correspondence of the Republic of Texas." Vol. 2, parts 2 and 3. *Annual Report of the American Historical Association for the Year 1908*. Washington, DC: U.S. Government Printing Office, 1911.
———. *Westward Extension*. New York: Harper & Row, 1906.
Gerhard, Peter. "Baja California in the Mexican War." *Pacific Historical Review* 14 (November 1945): 418–424.
———. *A Guide to the Historical Geography of New Spain*. Cambridge, England: Cambridge University Press, 1972.
Gettys, Warner E. *Corpus Christi—A History and Guide*. Corpus Christi, TX: Caller Times, 1942.
Gibson, George R. *Journal of a Soldier under Kearny and Doniphan*. Edited by Ralph B. Beiber. Glendale, CA: Clarke, 1936.
Giddings, Luther. *Sketches of the Campaign in Northern Mexico, in Eighteen Hundred Forty-six and Seven*. New York: G. P. Putnam's Sons, 1853.
Giffin, Helen S. "The California Battalion's Route to Los Angeles." *Journal of the West* 5 (April 1966): 207–224.
Gillett, Mary C. *The Army Medical Department, 1818–1865*. Washington, DC: Center of Military History, United States Army, 1987.
———. "Thomas Lawson, Second Surgeon General of the U.S. Army: A Character Sketch." *Prologue* 14 (1982): 16–24.
Gilliam, Albert M. *Travels in Mexico during the Years 1843 and 44*. Aberdeen: George Clark and Son, 1847.
Goetzmann, W. H. *Army Exploration in the American West, 1803–1863*. Lincoln: University of Nebraska Press, 1959.
———. "The United States–Mexico Boundary Survey, 1848–1853." *Southwestern Historical Quarterly* 62(2) (October 1985): 164–190.
Going, Charles B. *David Wilmot. Free Soiler*. New York: D. Appleton, 1924.
Golder, Frank Alfred, ed. "The March of the Mormon Battalion from Council Bluffs to California." Taken from *The Journal of Henry Standage*. New York: The Century Company,

1928.

Goodman, Thelma P., ed. *Official Manual of the State of Missouri*. Jefferson City, MO: Von Hoffmann Press, 1964.

Goodrich, James W. "Revolt at Mora, 1847." *New Mexico Historical Review* 47 (1) (1972): 49–60.

Goodwin, Cardinal. *John Charles Frémont. An Explanation of His Career*. Stanford, CA: Stanford University Press, 1930.

Gordon, George H. "The Battles of Contreras and Churubusco." *Papers of the Military Historical Society of Massachusetts* 13 (1913): 561–598.

———. "Battles of Molino del Rey and Chapultepec." *Papers of the Military Historical Society of Massachusetts* 13 (1913): 601–613.

Gould, J. M. *Joseph F. K. Mansfield*. Portland, ME: S. Barry, 1895.

Govan, G. E. *A Different Valor: The Story of General Joseph E. Johnston*. Indianapolis, IN: Bobbs-Merrill, 1956.

Graebner, Norman. *Empire on the Pacific: A Study in American Continental Expansion*. 1955. Reprint. Santa Barbara, CA: ABC-CLIO, 1983.

———, ed. *Manifest Destiny*. Indianapolis, IN: Bobbs-Merrill, 1948.

Grant, Blanche C. *When Old Trails Were New: The Story of Taos*. New York: Press of the Pioneers, 1934.

Grant, U. S. *Personal Memoirs of U. S. Grant*. Cleveland and New York: Webster and Company, 1885.

Green, Duff. *Facts and Suggestions, Biographical, Historical, Financial, and Political*. New York: C. S. Wescott, 1866.

Green, Stanley C. *The Mexican Republic: The First Decade, 1823–1832*. Pittsburgh, PA: University of Pittsburgh Press, 1987.

Green, Thomas J. *Journey of the Texian Expedition against Mier*. New York: G. P. Putnam, 1845.

Greer, James K. *Colonel Jack Hayes: Texas Frontier Leader and California Builder*. College Station: Texas A&M University Press, 1987.

Gregg, Josiah. *Diary and Letters of Josiah Gregg: Excursions in Mexico and California, 1847–1850*. Edited by Maurice Fulton. Norman: University of Oklahoma Press, 1944.

Gregg, Kate L. *The Road to Santa Fe: The Journal and Diaries of George Champlin Sibley*. Albuquerque: University of New Mexico Press, 1952.

Griffin, John S. *A Doctor Comes to California: The Diary of John S. Griffin, Assistant Surgeon with Kearny's Dragons, 1846–1847*. California Historical Society, 1943.

Griffis, W. E. *Matthew Calbraith Perry. A Typical American Naval Officer*. Boston: Houghton Mifflin, 1890.

Griggs, George. *History of the Mesilla Valley, or the Gadsden Purchase, Known in Mexico as the Treaty of Mesilla*. Mesilla, NM: George Griggs, 1930.

Grinnel, G. B. *Bent's Old Fort*. Topeka: Kansas State Historical Society, 1923.

Griswold del Castillo, Richard. *The Treaty of Guadalupe Hidalgo: A Legacy of Conflict*. Norman: University of Oklahoma Press, 1991.

Grivas, Theodore. *Military Governments in California, 1846–1850; with a Chapter on Their Prior Use in Louisiana, Florida, and New Mexico*. Glendale, CA: Arthur H. Clark, 1963.

Grove, Frank W. *Medals of Mexico, 1821–1971*. Vol. 2. San Antonio, TX: Almanzar's Coins, 1972.

Guardino, Peter. *Peasants, Politics, and the Formation of Mexico's National State: Guerrero, 1800–1857*. Stanford, CA: Stanford University Press, 1996.

Guild, Thelma S., and Harvey L. Carter. *Kit Carson: A Pattern for Heroes*. Lincoln: University of Nebraska Press, 1984.

Hackenburg, R. W. *Pennsylvania in the War with Mexico: The Volunteer Regiments*. Shippensburg, PA: White Mane, 1992.

Haecker, Charles M. *A Thunder of Cannon: Archeology of the Mexican-American War Battlefield of Palo Alto*. Santa Fe, NM: National Park Service, 1994.

Hagan, K. J., and W. R. Roberts, eds. *Against All Enemies: Interpretations of American Military History from Colonial Times to the Present*. Westport, CT: Greenwood Press, 1986.

Hague, J., and D. L. Langum. *Thomas O. Larkin: A Life of Patriotism and Profit in Old California*. Norman: University of Oklahoma Press, 1990.

Hale, Charles A. *Mexican Liberalism in the Age of Mora, 1821–1853*. New Haven, CT: Yale University Press, 1968.

———. "The War with the United States and the

Johnson, Allen, and Dumas Malone, eds. *Dictionary of American Biography*. New York: Charles Scribner's Sons, 1928–1936.

Johnson, John J. *The Military and Society in Latin America*. Stanford, CA: Stanford University Press, 1964.

Johnson, O. *William Lloyd Garrison and His Times*. Boston: B. B. Russell, 1879.

Johnson, Robert Erwin. *Thence Round Cape Horn*. Annapolis, MD: U.S. Naval Institute, 1963.

Johnston, Joseph E. *A Narrative of Military Operations*. Harrisburg, PA: The Archive Society, 1995.

Johnston, W. P. *The Life of General Albert Sidney Johnston*. New York: D. Appleton and Company, 1878.

Jones, Anson. *Memoranda and Official Correspondence Relating to the Republic of Texas*. New York: Arno Press, 1973.

Jones, Charles C., Jr. *The Life and Services of Commodore Josiah Tattnall*. Savannah, GA: n.p., 1878.

Jones, O. L. "The Pacific Squadron and the Conquest of California." *Journal of the West* 5 (April 1966): 187–202.

———. *Santa Anna*. New York: Twayne Publishers, 1968.

Jones, Robert R., ed. "The Mexican War Diary of James Lawson Kemper." *Virginia Magazine of History and Biography* 74 (1966): 387–428.

Jones, William J. *Life and Letters of Robert Edward Lee*. New York: Neale, 1906.

Jordan, H. D. "A Politician of Expansion: Robert J. Walker." *Mississippi Valley Historical Review* 19 (December 1932): 362–381.

Katcher, Phillip R. *The Mexican-American War, 1846-1848*. London: Osprey, 1976.

Katz, Friedrich, ed. *Riot, Rebellion, and Revolution: Rural Social Conflict in Mexico*. Princeton, NJ: Princeton University Press, 1968.

Kearny, Thomas. *General Philip Kearny, Battle Soldier of Five Wars*. New York: G. P. Putnam's Sons, 1937.

———. "The Mexican War and the Conquest of California." *California Historical Society Quarterly* 8 (September 1929): 251–261.

Keleher, William A. *Turmoil in New Mexico, 1846–1848*. Santa Fe, NM: Rydal Press, 1952.

Kelly, M. Margaret Jean. *The Career of Joseph Lane, Frontier Politician*. Washington, DC: Catholic University Press, 1952.

Kelsey, H. *Juan Rodríguez Cabrillo*. San Marino, CA: Huntington Library, 1986.

Kelsey, Rayner W. "The United States Consulate in California." *Academy of Pacific Coast History* 1(5) (1910).

Kenly, John R. *Memoirs of a Maryland Volunteer*. Philadelphia: J. B. Lippincott, 1873.

Kiefer, C. L. *Maligned General*. San Rafael, CA: Presidio Press, 1979.

Kirkham, Ralph W. *The Mexican War Journal and Letters of Ralph W. Kirkham*. Edited by Robert Ryal Miller. College Station: Texas A&M University Press, 1991.

Klein, Julius. *The Making of the Treaty of Guadalupe Hidalgo, on February 2, 1848*. Berkeley: University of California Press, 1905.

Klein, Philip S. *President James Buchanan: A Biography*. University Park: Pennsylvania State University Press, 1962.

Knox, D. W. *A History of the United States Navy*. New York: G. P. Putnam's Sons, 1936.

Kohl, C. C. *Claims as a Cause of the Mexican War*. New York: New York University, 1914.

Krueger, Carl. *Saint Patrick's Battalion*. New York: Dutton and Company, 1960.

Kurtz, Wilbur G. "The First Regiment of Georgia Volunteers in the Mexican War." *Georgia Historical Quarterly* 27 (December 1943): 301–323.

Ladd, Horatio O. *History of the War with Mexico*. New York: Dodd, Mead, 1883.

Lamar, Howard. *The Far Southwest, 1846-1912: A Territorial History*. New Haven, CT: Yale University Press, 1966.

———, ed. *The Reader's Encyclopedia of the American West*. New York: Crowell, 1977.

Lambert, Paul F. "The Movement for the Acquisition of All Mexico." *Journal of the West* 11 (April 1972): 317–327.

Lander, E. M. *Reluctant Imperialists: Calhoun, the South Carolinians, and the Mexican War*. Baton Rouge: Louisiana State University Press, 1980.

Lane, Henry S. "The Mexican War Journal of Henry S. Lane." Edited by Graham A. Barringer. *Indiana Magazine of History* 53(4) (1957): 383–434.

Lane, W. B. "The United States Cavalry in the Mexican War." *Journal of the United States Cavalry Association* 3(11) (December 1890): 388–408.

Launius, R. D. *Alexander William Doniphan: Portrait of a Missouri Moderate.* Columbia: University of Missouri Press, 1997.

Lavender, David. *Bent's Fort.* Lincoln: University of Nebraska Press, 1954.

———. *Climax at Buena Vista: The American Campaigns in Northeastern Mexico, 1847–48.* New York: J. B. Lippincott, 1966.

Lee, Robert E., Jr. *Recollections and Letters of General Robert E. Lee.* New York: Doubleday, 1904.

Lewis, Lloyd. *Captain Sam Grant.* Boston: Little, Brown, 1950.

Lewis, Oscar. "California in 1846: Described in Letters from Thomas O. Larkin." In *The United States Conquest of California.* New York: Arno Press, 1976.

———. *Sutter's Fort.* Englewood Cliffs, NJ: Prentice-Hall, 1966.

Long, Jeff. *Duel of Eagles: The Mexican and U.S. Fight for the Alamo.* New York: William Morrow, 1990.

Longstreet, James. *From Manassas to Appomattox.* Philadelphia: J. B. Lippincott, 1896.

Love, Thomas N. "Remarks on Some of the Diseases Which Prevailed in the 2d Reg. Mississippi Rifles, for the First Six Months of Its Service." *New Orleans Medical and Surgical Journal* 5 (1848–1849): 3–13.

Lowell, James Russell. *The Writings of James Russell Lowell.* Boston: Houghton Mifflin, 1890.

Lyons, James Gilborne. "The Heroine Martyr of Monterey." *American Quarterly Register* 2 (June 1849): 483–484.

Magner, James A. *Men of Mexico.* Milwaukee, WI: Bruce, 1942.

Magoffin, Susan. *Down the Santa Fe Trail and into Mexico: The Diary of Susan Shelby Magoffin, 1846–1857.* Edited by Stella M. Drumm. New Haven, CT: Yale University, 1926.

Mahin, Dean B. *Olive Branch and Sword: The United States and Mexico, 1845–1848.* Jefferson, NC: McFarland, 1997.

Mahoney, Tom. "50 Hanged and 11 Branded: The Story of the San Patricio Battalion." *Southwest Review* 32 (1947): 373–377.

Manning, William R., ed. *Diplomatic Correspondence of the United States: Inter-American Affairs, 1831–1860.* Washington, DC: Carnegie Endowment for International Peace, 1932–1939.

———. *Early Diplomatic Relations between the United States and Mexico.* Baltimore: Johns Hopkins Press, 1916.

Mansfield, Edward D. *Life of General Winfield Scott.* New York: Barnes and Company, 1851.

———. *The Mexican War.* New York: Barnes, 1852.

———. *The Mexican War: A History of Its Origins and a Detailed Account of the Victories Which Terminated in the Surrender of the Capital, with the Official Dispatches of the Generals.* New York: Barnes and Company, 1848.

Marichal, Carlos. *A Century of Debt Crisis in Latin America: From Independence to the Great Depression.* Princeton, NJ: Princeton University Press, 1989.

Marshall, Thomas M. *A History of the Western Boundary of the Louisiana Purchase, 1819–1841.* Berkeley: University of California Press, 1914.

———. "The Southwestern Boundary of Texas, 1821–1840." *Southwestern Historical Quarterly* 14 (April 1911): 273–293.

Marti, Werner H. *Messenger of Destiny. The California Adventures, 1846-1847 of Archibald H. Gillespie, U.S. Marine Corps.* San Francisco: John Howell, 1955.

Martínez, O. J. *Troublesome Border.* Tucson: University of Arizona, 1988.

Matthews, H. L., ed. *The United States and Latin America.* Englewood Cliffs, NJ: Prentice-Hall, 1963.

Mattison, Ray H. "Early Spanish and Mexican Settlements in Arizona." *New Mexico Historical Review* 21 (October 1946): 273–327.

May, E. R. *The Making of the Monroe Doctrine.* Cambridge, MA: Harvard University Press, 1975.

May, Robert E. "Invisible Men: Blacks and the U.S. Army in the Mexican War." *The Historian* 49 (August 1987): 463–477.

———. *John A. Quitman: Old South Crusader.* Baton Rouge: Louisiana State University Press, 1985.

———. "Pleniopotentiary in Petticoats: Jane M. Cazneau and American Foreign Policy in the Mid-Nineteenth Centuury." In *Women and American Foreign Policy: Lobbyists, Critics, and Insiders.* Edited by E. P. Crapol. New York: Greenwood Press, 1987.

Mayer, Brantz. *Mexico as It Was and as It Is.* Third revised edition. Philadelphia: G. B.

Zieber and Company, 1847.

McAfee, Ward. "Reconsideration of the Origins of the Mexican-American War." *Southern California Quarterly* 62 (Spring 1980): 49–65.

McAfee, Ward M., and J. Cordell Robinson. *Origins of the Mexican War: A Documentary Source Book.* Salisbury, NC: Documentary Publications, 1982.

McCaffrey, James M. *Army of Manifest Destiny: The American Soldier in the Mexican War, 1846–1848.* New York: New York University Press, 1992.

McClellan, George B. *McClellan's Own Story.* New York: C. L. Webster, 1887.

———. *The Mexican War Diary of General George B. McClellan.* Edited by W. S. Myers. Princeton, NJ: Princeton University Press, 1917.

McCormac, Eugene I. *James K. Polk: A Political Biography.* New York: Russell & Russell, 1965.

McCormick, Robert B. "The San Patricio Deserters in the Mexican War." *The Americas* 8 (October 1951): 131–142.

McCoy, Charles A. *Polk and the Presidency.* Austin: University of Texas Press, 1960.

McDonald, Archie, ed. *The Mexican War: Crisis for American Democracy.* Lexington, KY: D. C. Heath, 1969.

McElroy, John. "Chaplains for the Mexican War—1846." *The Woodstock Letters* 15 (1886): 198–202; 16 (1887): 33–39.

McElroy, Robert. *Jefferson Davis, the Unreal and the Real.* New York: Harper & Brothers, 1937.

McEniry, Blanche M. *American Catholics in the War with Mexico.* Washington, DC: Catholic University of America, 1937.

McGaw, W. C. *Savage Scene: The Life and Times of James Kirker, Frontier King.* New York: Hastings House, 1972.

McGrath, J. J., and Wallace Hawkins. "Perote Fort—Where Texans Were Imprisoned." *Southwestern Historical Quarterly* 48 (1944–1945).

McKinley, Silas Bent. *Old Rough and Ready. The Life and Times of Zachary Taylor.* New York: Vanguard Press, 1946.

McKinney, Francis F. *Education in Violence: The Life of George H. Thomas and the Army of the Cumberland.* Detroit: Wayne State University Press, 1961.

McKittrick, M. M. *Vallejo, Son of California.* Portland, OR: Binford and Mort, 1944.

McNaughton, Marian R. "James Walker—Combat Artist of Two American Wars." *Military Collector and Historian* 9 (Summer 1957): 31–35.

McNierney, Michael, ed. *Taos 1847: The Revolt in Contemporary Accounts.* Boulder, CO: Johnson Publishing, 1980.

McNitt, Frank. "Navajo Campaigns and the Occupation of New Mexico, 1847–1848." *New Mexico Historical Review* 43 (July 1968): 173–194.

McWhinney, Grady, and Sue McWhinney, eds. *To Mexico with Taylor and Scott, 1845–1847.* Waltham, MA: Blaisdell, 1969.

Meade, George Gordon. *Life and Letters of George Gordon Meade, Major General, United States Army.* New York: Charles Scribner's Sons, 1913.

Meadows, Don. *The American Occupation of La Paz.* Los Angeles: Glen Dawson, 1955.

Mecham, J. L. *Church and State in Latin America.* Chapel Hill: University of North Carolina Press, 1934.

———. "The Origins of Federalism in Mexico." *Hispanic American Historical Review* 17 (May 1938): 164–182.

Meier, M. S., and Feliciano Rivera. *Dictionary of Mexican American History.* Westport, CT: Greenwood Press, 1981.

Meigs, William M. *The Life of Thomas Hart Benton.* Philadelphia: J. B. Lippincott, 1904.

Meriwether, Colyner. *Raphael Semmes.* Philadelphia: Jacobs and Company, 1913.

Merk, Frederick. *History of the Westward Movement.* New York: Alfred A. Knopf, 1978.

———. *Manifest Destiny and Mission in American History.* Cambridge, MA: Harvard University Press, 1995.

———. *The Monroe Doctrine and American Expansionism, 1843–1849.* New York: Alfred A. Knopf, 1966.

———. *Slavery and the Annexation of Texas.* Cambridge, MA: Harvard University Press, 1972.

Meyer, M. L., and W. L. Sherman. *The Course of Mexcian History.* 5th edition. New York: Oxford University Press, 1995.

Meyers, William H. *Naval Sketches of the War with California 1846–1847.* New York: Random House, 1939.

Miller, Robert G. "Yellow Jack at Vera Cruz." Prologue: *Journal of the National Archives* 10

(Spring 1978): 43–53.
Miller, Robert Ryal. *Mexico: A History.* Norman: University of Oklahoma Press, 1985.
———. *The Mexican War Journal and Letters of Ralph W. Kirkham.* College Station: Texas A&M Press, 1991.
———. *Shamrock and Sword: The Saint Patrick's Battalion in the U.S.-Mexican War.* Norman: University of Oklahoma Press, 1989.
Montejano, David. *Anglos and Mexicans in the Making of Texas, 1836–1986.* Austin: University of Texas Press, 1987.
Montgomery, H. *The Life of Major-General Zachary Taylor.* Philadelphia: Henry T. Coates, 1847.
Moore, H. Judge. *Scott's Campaign in Mexico.* Charleston: Nixon and Company, 1849.
Moorhead, Max L. *The Presidio: Bastion of the Spanish Borderlands.* Norman: University of Oklahoma Press, 1975.
Morgan, Robert J. *A Whig Embattled: The Presidency under John Tyler.* Lincoln: University of Nebraska Press, 1954.
Morison, Samuel Eliot. *"Old Bruin" Commodore Matthew Calbraith Perry.* Boston: Little, Brown, 1967.
Morris, E. Y. "James Pinckney Henderson." M.S. thesis. Austin: University of Texas, 1931.
Morrison, C. W. *Democratic Politics and Sectionalism: The Wilmot Proviso Controversy.* Chapel Hill: University of North Carolina Press, 1967.
Morrow, Josiah, ed. *The Life and Speeches of Thomas Corwin.* Cincinnati: Anderson and Company, 1896.
Murphy, Lawrence R. "The United States Army in Taos, 1847–1852." *New Mexico Historical Review* 47 (1) (1972): 33–48.
Myatt, Major Frederick. *The Illustrated Encyclopedia of 19th Century Firearms.* New York: Crescent Books, 1979.
Myers, William Starr. *General George Brinton McClellan.* New York: D. Appleton-Century, 1934.
Nackman, M. E. *A Nation within a Nation: The Rise of Texas Nationalism.* Port Washington: Kennikat Press, 1976.
Nance, John Milton. *After San Jacinto: The Mexican-Texas Frontier, 1836–1841.* Austin: University of Texas Press, 1963.
———. *Attack and Counterattack: The Texas-Mexican Frontier, 1842.* Austin: University of Texas Press, 1964.
Neeser, Robert Weldon. *A Statistical and Chronological History of the United States Navy.* New York: Macmillan, 1909.
Nelson, Anna Kasten. "Mission to Mexico—Moses Y. Beach, Secret Agent." *New York Historical Society Quarterly* 59 (July 1975): 227–245.
Nevin, David. *The Mexican War.* Alexandria, VA: Time-Life Books, 1978.
Nevins, Allan, ed. *The Diary of John Quincy Adams.* New York: Longmans, Green and Company, 1928.
———. *Frémont, Pathmaker of the West.* New York: Longmans, Green and Company, 1955.
———, ed. *Polk: The Diary of a President, 1845–1849.* New York: Longmans, Green and Company, 1952.
Nichols, Edward J. *Toward Gettysburg: A Biography of General John F. Reynolds.* Reprint. Gaithersburg, MD: Butternut & Blue, 1988.
———. *Zach Taylor's Little Army.* New York: Doubleday, 1963.
Nichols, Roy F. *Franklin Pierce: Young Hickory of the Granite Hills.* Philadelphia: University of Pennsylvania Press, 1931.
Nieto-Gomez, Anna. "Women in Mexican History." *Somos* (May 1979): 17–20.
Niven, John. *John C. Calhoun and the Price of Union.* Baton Rouge: Louisiana State University Press, 1988.
Noble, D. *Santa Fe: History of an Ancient City.* Santa Fe, NM: School of American Research Press, 1989.
Nolan, J. C. *Andrew Jackson.* New York: Julian Messner, 1949.
Northrup, Jack. "The Trist Mission." *Journal of Mexican American History* 3 (1973): 13–31.
Nugent, D., ed. *Rural Revolt in Mexcio and U.S. Intervention.* La Jolla: University of California, 1988.
Nye, Russell B. *George Bancroft: Brahmin Rebel.* New York: Alfred A. Knopf, 1944.
Oates, Stephen B. "Los Diablos Tejanos: The Texas Rangers in the Mexican War." *Journal of the West* 11(2) (April 1972): 487–504.
O'Brien, Frank M. *The Story of the Sun.* New York: D. Appleton and Company, 1928.
Ohrt, Wallace. *Defiant Peacemaker: Nicholas Trist in the Mexican War.* College Station: Texas A&M Press, 1997.
Oliva, Leo E. *Soldiers on the Santa Fe Trail.*

Norman: University of Oklahoma Press, 1967.

Olivera, Ruth R., and Liliane Crete. *Life in Mexico under Santa Anna, 1822–1855.* Norman: University of Oklahoma Press, 1991.

Oswandel, Jacob J. *Notes of the Mexican War.* Philadelphia: n.p., 1885.

Parker, William H. *Recollections of a Naval Officer.* New York: Scribner's, 1883.

Parks, Henry Bamford. *A History of Mexico.* Boston: Houghton Mifflin, 1970.

Parks, Joseph H. *General Edmund Kirby Smith, C.S.A.* Baton Rouge: Louisiana State University Press, 1954.

Parrish, Leonard D. "The Life of Nicolas Bravo, Mexican Patriot (1786–1854)." Ph.D. dissertation. Austin: University of Texas, 1951.

Parton, James. *Life of Andrew Jackson.* New York: Mason Brothers, 1860.

Patch, J. D. *The Concentration of General Zachary Taylor's Army at Corpus Christi, Texas.* No city: Mission Printing, 1962.

Patton, Alfred. "Recollections of Medical Service during the War with Mexico." *Indiana Journal of Medicine* 5 (1874): 145–150.

Peck, John James. *The Sign of the Eagle, A View of Mexico 1830–1855, Based on the Letters of Lieutenant John James Peck, with Lithographs of Mexico.* San Diego, CA: Union-Tribune Publishing, 1970.

Pemberton, John C. *Pemberton: Defender of Vicksburg.* Wilmington, NC: Broadfoot Publishers, 1987.

Perry, Oran. *Indiana in the Mexican War.* Indianapolis, IN: Burford, 1908.

Peters, DeWitt C. *The Life and Adventures of Kit Carson.* New York: D. Appleton and Company, 1858.

Peterson, Charles. *Utah: A Bicentennial History.* Chicago: W. W. Norton, 1977.

Peterson, N. L. *The Presidencies of William Henry Harrison and John Tyler.* Lawrence: University Press of Kansas, 1989.

Pico, Pio. *Don Pio Pico's Historical Narrative.* Translated by A. P. Botello, edited by M. Cole and H. Welcome. Glendale, CA: Arthur H. Clark, 1973.

Pierce, F. C. *A Brief History of the Lower Río Grande Valley.* Menasha, WI: George Banta, 1917.

Pitt, L. *The Decline of the Californios.* Berkeley: University of California Press, 1966.

Pletcher, D. M. *The Diplomacy of Annexation: Texas, Oregon, and the Mexican War.* Columbia: University of Missouri Press, 1973.

Pohl, James W. "The Influence of Antoine Henri Jomini on Winfield Scott's Campaign in the Mexican War." *Southwestern Historical Quarterly* 78 (July 1973): 85–110.

Polk, James K. *The Diary of James K. Polk.* Edited by M. M. Quaife. Chicago: McClurg and Company, 1910.

Poll, R. D., ed. *Utah's History.* Salt Lake City, UT: Brigham Young University Press, 1978.

Porte, Joel. *Representative Man: Ralph Waldo Emerson in His Time.* New York: Oxford University Press, 1979.

Porter, John B. "Medical and Surgical Notes of Campaigns in the War with Mexico, during the Years 1845, 1846, 1847, and 1848." *American Journal of Medical Sciences* 23 (January 1852): 13–37; 24 (July 1852): 13–30; 25 (January 1853): 25–42; 26 (October 1853): 297–333; 35 (April 1858): 347–352.

Pratt, Fletcher. *The Compact History of the United States Navy.* New York: Hawthorn Books, 1957.

Pratt, J. W. "The Origins of 'Manifest Destiny.'" *American Historical Review* 32 (July 1927): 795–798.

Presley, James. "Santa Anna in Texas: A Mexican Viewpoint." *Southwestern Historical Quarterly* 62 (April 1959): 489–512.

Price, Glenn W. *Origins of the War with Mexico: The Polk-Stockton Intrigue.* Austin: University of Texas Press, 1967.

Proctor, William G. "On the Diseases of the United States' Army on the Rio Grande." *Western Journal of Medicine and Surgery,* Third series, 1 (1848): 461–489.

Raat, W. Dirk, ed. *Mexico, from Independence to Revolution, 1810–1910.* Lincoln: University of Nebraska Press, 1982.

———. *Mexico and the United States: Ambivalent Vistas.* Athens: University of Georgia Press, 1992.

Ramirez, Jose Fernando. *Mexico during the War with the United States.* Columbia: University of Missouri Press, 1950.

Ramsey, Albert C., trans. *The Other Side: Or Notes for the History of the War between Mexico and the United States.* New York: John Wiley,

1850.

Ratliff, Eric A. "Life and Death in the Mexican Army: An Analysis of Skeletal Remains from the Battle of Resaca de la Palma, May 9, 1846." M.A. thesis. Austin: University of Texas, 1989.

Rea, Robert R. *Sterling Price. The Lee of the West.* Little Rock, AR: Pioneer Press, 1959.

Reavis, L. U. *The Life and Military Services of General William Selby Harney.* St. Louis, MO: Bryan, Brand and Company, 1878.

Reed, Nelson. *The Caste War of the Yucatán.* Stanford, CA: Stanford University Press, 1964.

Reeves, J. S. *American Diplomacy under Tyler and Polk.* Baltimore: Johns Hopkins Press, 1907.

———. "The Treaty of Guadalupe Hidalgo." *American Historical Review* 10 (January 1905): 309–324.

Regnery, Dorothy F. *The Battle of Santa Clara.* San Jose, CA: Smith & MacKay, 1978.

Reichstein, Andreas V. *Rise of the Lone Star: The Making of Texas.* Translated by Jeanne R. Wilson. College Station: Texas A&M Press, 1989.

Reid, Samuel C., Jr. *The Scouting Expeditions of McCulloch's Texas Rangers.* 1847. Reprint. Freeport, NY: Books for Libraries Press, 1970.

Reilly, James. "An Artilleryman's Story." *Journal of the Military Service Institute* 33 (1903): 438–447.

Reilly, Thomas W. "Jane McManus Storms: Letters from the Mexican War, 1846–1848." *Southwestern Historical Quarterly* 90 (July 1981): 21.

Remini, Robert V. *Andrew Jackson.* New York: Twayne Publishers, 1966.

———. *Andrew Jackson and the Course of American Democracy, 1833–1845.* New York: Harper & Row, 1984.

———. *Andrew Jackson and the Course of American Empire, 1767–1821.* New York: Harper & Row, 1977.

———. *Henry Clay: Statesman for the Union.* New York: W. W. Norton, 1991.

Revere, Joseph Warren. *Keel and Saddle; A Retrospect of Forty Years of Military and Naval Service.* Boston: Osgood, 1873.

———. *A Tour of Duty in California. An Account of Principal Events Attending the Conquest of California.* Boston: Francis, 1849.

Reynolds, Curtis R. "The Deterioration of Mexican-American Diplomatic Relations, 1833–1845." *Journal of the West* 11 (April 1972): 213–224.

Rhoades, J. L. *Scapegoat General: The Story of Major General Benjamin Huger, CSA.* Hamden, CT: Archon, 1985.

Richards, Leonard L. *The Life and Times of Congressman John Quincy Adams.* New York: Oxford University Press, 1986.

Richardson, R. N. *The Commanche Barrier to South Plains Settlement.* Glendale, CA: Arthur H. Clark, 1933.

———. *Texas: The Lone Star State.* Englewood Cliffs, NJ: Prentice-Hall, 1958.

Richardson, W. H. *Journal of Wm. H. Richardson, a Private Soldier in the Campaign of New and Old Mexico, under the Command of Colonel Doniphan of Missouri.* Third edition. New York: William H. Richardson, 1849.

Richman, Irving. B. *California under Spain and Mexico.* Boston: Houghton Mifflin, 1911.

Richmond, Douglas, ed. *Essays on the Mexican War.* College Station: Texas A&M University Press, 1986.

Ripley, Roswell S. *The War with Mexico.* New York: Harper and Brothers, 1849.

Rippy, J. F. *The United States and Mexico.* New York: Alfred A. Knopf, 1926.

Risch, Erna. *Quartermaster Support of the Army. A History of the Corps 1775–1939.* Washington, DC: Quartermaster's Historian Office, 1962.

Rives, G. L. *The United States and Mexico, 1821–1848.* New York: Scribner's Sons, 1913.

Robards, H. R. "The Diseases of the Army of Occupation in the Summer of 1846." *Western Journal of Medicine and Surgery,* Second series, 7 (1847): 185–196.

Robarts, W. H. *Mexican War Veterans.* Washington, DC: Brentano's, 1887.

Roberts, Brigham Henry. *The Mormon Battalion. Its History and Achievements.* Salt Lake City, UT: The Deseret News, 1919.

Robertson, Frank D. "The Military and Political Career of Mariano Paredes y Arrillaga." Ph.D. dissertation. Austin: University of Texas, 1955.

Robertson, James I. *Stonewall Jackson: The Man, the Soldier, the Legend.* New York: Macmillan, 1997.

Robertson, John B. *Reminiscences of a Campaign in Mexico by a Member of the "Bloody First."* Nashville, TN: York, 1849.

Robinson, Cecil, ed. *The View from Chapultepec: Mexican Writers on the Mexican-American War.* Tucson: University of Arizona Press, 1989.

Robinson, Fayette. *An Account of the Organization of the Army of the United States; With Biographies of Distinguished Officers of All Grades.* Philadelphia: E. H. Butler, 1848.

———. *Mexico and Her Military Chieftains, from the Revolution of Hidalgo to the Present Time.* Hartford, CT: Silas Andrus and Son, 1848.

Robinson, Jacob S. *A Journal of the Santa Fe Expedition under Colonel Doniphan.* Princeton, NJ: Princeton University Press, 1932.

Rodenbaugh, J. F. *From Everglade to Cañon with the Second Dragoons.* New York: D. Van Nostrand, 1875.

Rodenbaugh, T. F. *The Army of the United States.* New York: Maynard, Merrill, 1896.

Rodríguez O., Jaime E., ed. *The Mexican and Mexican American Experience in the 19th Century.* Tempe, AZ: Bilingual Review Press, 1989.

Rogers, F. B. *William Brown Ide: Bear Flagger.* San Francisco: John Howell Books, 1962.

Rogers, J. M. *Thomas Hart Benton.* Philadelphia: G. W. Jacobs and Company, 1905.

———. *The True Henry Clay.* Philadelphia: G. W. Jacobs and Company, 1902.

Roland, Charles P. *Albert Sidney Johnston.* Austin: University of Texas Press, 1964.

Romero, Matías. *Geographical and Statistical Notes on Mexico.* New York: G. P. Putnam's Sons, 1898.

Roosevelt, Theodore. *Thomas Hart Benton.* New York: Houghton and Mifflin, 1886.

Rose, Victor M. *The Life and Services of General Ben McCulloch.* Philadelphia: Pictorial Bureau of the Press, 1888.

Rosenus, Alan. *General M. G. Vallejo and the Advent of the Americans.* Albuquerque: University of New Mexico Press, 1995.

Rowan, Stephen C. "Recollections of the Mexican War, Taken from the Journals of Lieutenant Stephen C. Rowan, U.S. Navy, Executive Officer of the USS *Cyane*, Pacific Squadron, 1845-1848." Edited by George W. Tyler. *United States Naval Institute Proceedings* 14 (September 1888): 530–560.

Rowley, Ralph. "The Acquisition of the Spanish Borderlands: Problems and Legacy." Ph.D. dissertation. Albuquerque: University of New Mexico, 1975.

Ruiz, Ramon Eduardo, ed. *The Mexican War: Was It Manifest Destiny?* New York: Holt, Rinehart & Winston, 1963.

———. *Triumphs and Tragedy: A History of the Mexican People.* New York: W. W. Norton, 1992.

Russell, Carl. *Guns on the Early Frontier.* Berkeley and Los Angeles: University of California Press, 1957.

Salas, Elizabeth. *Soldaderas in the Mexican Military: Myth and History.* Austin: University of Texas Press, 1990.

Samora, J. *Gunpowder Justice: A Reassessment of the Texas Rangers.* Notre Dame, IN: University of Notre Dame Press, 1979.

Samporano, Frank N. "The Political Role of the Army in Mexico, 1821–1848." Ph.D. dissertation. Stoney Brook: State University of New York, 1971.

Sanborn, G. *The Life of Henry David Thoreau.* Boston: Houghton Mifflin, 1917.

Sanchéz, Joseph P. "General Mariano Arista at the Battle of Palo Alto, Texas, 1846: Military Realist or Failure?" *Journal of the West* 24(2) (April 1985): 8–22.

Sanchéz, Pedro. *Memories of Antonio José Martínez.* Santa Fe, NM: Rydell Press, 1978.

Sands, Benjamin Franklin. *From Reefer to Rear Admiral. Reminiscences of Nearly Half a Century of Naval Life.* New York: F. A. Stokes, 1899.

Sandwich, Brian. *The Great Western: Legendary Lady of the Southwest.* El Paso: Texas Western Press, 1990.

Santa Anna, Antonio López de. *The Eagle: The Autobiography of Santa Anna.* Edited by Ann Fears Crawford. Austin: Pemberton Press, 1967.

———. "Letters of General Antonio López de Santa Anna Relating to the War between the United States and Mexico, 1846–1848." Edited by Justin H. Smith. *Annual Report of the American Historical Association for the Year 1917.* Washington, DC: U.S. Government Printing Office, 1920.

Santoni, Pedro. *Mexicans at Arms: Puro Federalists and the Politics of War, 1845–1848.* Fort Worth: Texas Christian University Press, 1996.

Santos, Richard G. *Santa Anna's Campaign against Texas, 1835–1836.* Second edition. Salisbury, NC: Documentary Publications,

1968.
Scheina, R. L. "The Forgotten Fleet: The Mexican Navy on the Eve of War, 1845." *American Neptune* 30 (1970): 46–53.
Schlesinger, Arthur M., Jr. *The Age of Jackson*. Boston: Little, Brown, 1948.
Schoonover, T. J. *The Life and Times of General John A. Sutter*. n.p., 1895.
Schroeder, John H. *Mr. Polk's War: American Opposition and Dissent, 1846–1848*. Madison, University of Wisconsin Press, 1973.
Scott, Henry. *Military Dictionary: Comprising Technical Definitions; Information on Raising and Keeping Troops; Actual Service, Including Make-Shifts and Improved Materiel; and Law, Government, Regulation, and Administration Relating to Land Forces*. New York: Greenwood Press, 1968.
Scott, John A. *Encarnación Prisoners, Comprising an Account of the March of the Kentucky Cavalry from Louisville to the Rio Grande*. Louisville, KY: Prentice & Weissinger, 1848.
Scott, Winfield. *Memoirs of Lieutenant General Scott*. New York: Sheldon and Company, 1864.
Scudder, H. E. *James Russell Lowell*. Boston: Houghton Mifflin, 1901.
Sears, Louis Martin. *John Slidell*. Durham, NC: Duke University Press, 1925.
———. "Nicholas P. Trist, a Diplomat with Ideals." *Mississippi Valley Historical Review* 11(1) (June 1924): 85–98.
Sears, Stephen. *George B. McClellan: The Young Napoleon*. New York: Ticknor & Fields, 1988.
Sedgewick, John. *Correspondence of John Sedgewick*. New York: Battel, 1903.
Seitz, D. C. *Braxton Bragg*. Columbia, SC: State Company, 1924.
Sellers, Charles. *James K. Polk, Continentalist, 1843–1846*. Princeton, NJ: Princeton University Press, 1966.
Semmes, Raphael. *The Campaign of General Scott in the Valley of Mexico*. Cincinnati, OH: Moore and Anderson, 1852.
———. *Service Afloat and Ashore during the Mexican War*. Cincinnati, OH: Moore, 1851.
Settles, T. M. "The Military Career of John Bankhead Magruder." Ph.D. dissertation. Fort Worth: Texas Christian University, 1972.
Sewell, R. H. *Ballots for Freedom: Antislavery Politics in the United States, 1837–1860*. New York: Oxford University Press, 1976.

Shalhope, R. E. *Sterling Price: Portrait of a Southerner*. Columbia: University of Missouri Press, 1971.
Shearer, Ernest C. "The Carvajal Disturbances." *Southwestern Historical Quarterly* 55 (October 1951): 201–230.
Shenton, James P. *Robert John Walker, a Politician from Jackson to Lincoln*. New York: Columbia University Press, 1961.
Shepherd, Rebecca A. *A Biographical Directory of the Indiana General Assembly*. Vol. 1, 1816–1899. Indianapolis: Indiana Historical Bureau, 1980.
Sheridan, Thomas E. *Arizona: A History*. Tucson: University of Arizona Press, 1995.
Sherman, Edwin A. *The Life of the Late Rear Admiral John Drake Sloat*. Oakland, CA: Carruth and Carruth, 1902.
Side, Joseph C. *Fort Brown Historical: History of Fort Brown*. San Antonio, TX: Naylor, 1942.
Siemans, A. H. *Between the Summit and the Sea: Central Veracruz in the Nineteenth Century*. Vancouver: University of British Columbia Press, 1990.
Sierra, Justo. *The Political Evolution of the Mexican People*. Austin: University of Texas Press, 1963.
Simmons, M. *The Little Lion of the Southwest*. Chicago: Swallow Press, 1923.
Singletary, Otis. *The Mexican War*. Chicago: University of Chicago Press, 1960.
Skelton, William B. *An American Profession of Arms: The Army Officer Corps, 1784–1861*. Lawrence: University Press of Kansas, 1992.
Smiley, David L. *Lion of White Hall. The Life of Cassius M. Clay*. Madison: University of Wisconsin Press, 1962.
Smith, A. D. H. *Old Fuss and Feathers. The Life and Exploits of Lt.-General Winfield Scott*. New York: Greystone Press, 1937.
Smith, E. B. *The Magnificent Missourian: The Life of Thomas Hart Benton*. Philadelphia: Lippincott, 1958.
Smith, E. Kirby. *To Mexico with Scott: Letters of Ephraim Kirby Smith to His Wife*. Cambridge, MA: Harvard University Press, 1917.
Smith, Franklin. *The Mexican War Journal of Captain Franklin Smith*. Edited by J. E. Chance. Jackson: University Press of Mississippi, 1991.
Smith, George W., and Charles Judah. *Chronicles of the Gringos: The U.S. Army in the Mexican

War, 1846–1848. Albuquerque: University of New Mexico Press, 1968.

Smith, Isaac. *Reminiscences of a Campaign in Mexico*. Indianapolis, IN: Chapmans and Spahn, 1848.

Smith, Justin H. *The Annexation of Texas*. New York: Macmillan, 1911.

———. *The War with Mexico*. New York: Macmillan, 1919.

Smith, Ralph A. "Indians in American-Mexican Relations before the War of 1846." *Hispanic American Historical Review* 43 (1963): 34–64.

———. "The 'King of New Mexico' and the Doniphan Expedition." *New Mexico Historical Review* 38(1) (January 1963): 29–55.

Smith, S. Compton. *Chile Con Carne; or, the Camp and the Field*. New York: Miller and Curtis, 1857.

Spell, Lota M. "The Anglo-Saxon Press in Mexico, 1846–1848." *American Historical Review* 38 (October 1932): 20–31.

Spence, Mary Lee, and Donald Jackson, eds. *The Expeditions of John Charles Frémont*. Urbana: University of Illinois Press, 1973.

Spencer, I. D. *The Victor and the Spoils. A Life of William L. Marcy*. Providence, RI: Brown University Press, 1959.

Spurlin, Charles. "Ranger Walker in the Mexican War." *Military History of Texas and the Southwest* 9 (1971): 259–279.

Stanton, William. *The Great United States Exploring Expedition of 1838–1842*. Berkeley: University of California Press, 1975.

Steele, M. F. *American Campaigns*. Washington, DC: United States Infantry Association, 1943.

Stenberg, R. R. "The Failure of Polk's War Intrigue of 1845." *Pacific Historical Review* 4 (March 1935): 39–69.

———. "Polk and Frémont, 1845–1846." *Pacific Historical Review* 7 (June 1938): 211–227.

———. "President Polk and the Annexation of Texas." *Southwestern Social Science Quarterly* 14 (March 1934): 333–356.

Stephenson, Nathaniel W. *Texas and the Mexican War*. New Haven, CT: Yale University Press, 1921.

Sterling, W. W. *Trails and Trials of a Texas Ranger*. Norman: University of Oklahoma Press, 1968.

Stevens, Hazard. *The Life of Isaac Ingalls Stevens*. Boston: Houghton Mifflin, 1901.

Stevens, Isaac I. *Campaigns of the Rio Grande and of Mexico*. New York: D. Appleton and Company, 1851.

Stewart, Miller J. "Army Laundresses: Ladies of the 'Soap Suds Row.'" *Nebraska History* 61 (Winter 1980): 421–436.

———. *Moving the Wounded: Litters, Cacolets & Ambulance Wagons, U.S. Army, 1776–1876*. Fort Collins, CO: Old Army Press, 1979.

Stonesifer, Roy P. "Gideon Pillow: A Study in Egotism." *Tennessee Historical Quarterly* 25(4) (Winter 1966): 340–350.

Strode, Hudson. *Timeless Mexico*. New York: Harcourt, Brace and Company, 1944.

Sunseri, Alvin R. "New Mexico in the Aftermath of the Anglo-American Conquest, 1846–1861." Ph.D. dissertation. Baton Rouge: Louisiana State University, 1973.

Sutter, John A. *The Diary of Johann August Sutter*. San Francisco: Grabhorn Press, 1932.

Swift, L. *William Lloyd Garrison*. Philadelphia: G. W. Jacobs, 1911.

Talbot, Theodore. *Soldier in the West. Letters of Theodore Talbot during His Services in California, Mexico, and Oregon, 1845–53*. Edited by R. V. Vine and S. Lottinville. Norman: University of Oklahoma Press, 1970.

Taylor, M. L. "The Western Services of Stephen Watts Kearny, 1815–1848." *New Mexico Historical Review* 21(3) (July 1946): 169–184.

Taylor, Zachary. *Letters of Zachary Taylor from the Battlefields of the Mexican War*. Edited by W. K. Bixby. New York: Kraus, 1908.

Tays, George. "Fremont Had No Secret Instructions." *Pacific Historical Review* 9 (May 1940): 153–171.

Tennery, Thomas D. *The Mexican War Diary of Thomas D. Tennery*. Norman: University of Oklahoma Press, 1970.

Thomas, B. P. *Abraham Lincoln: A Biography*. New York: Knopf, 1952.

Thomas, Emory. *Robert E. Lee: A Biography*. New York: W. W. Norton, 1995.

Thomas, Jack Roy. *Biographical Dictionary of Latin American History*. Westport, CT: Greenwood Press, 1984.

Thompson, D. E. *Indiana Authors and Their Books*. Crawfordsville, IN: Wabash College, 1981.

Thompson, Waddy. *Recollections of Mexico*. New York: Wiley and Puttman, 1846.

Thoreau, Henry D. *Civil Disobedience and Other Essays*. Mineola, NY: Dover, 1993.

Thorp, T. B. *Our Army on the Rio Grande*. Philadelphia: Carey and Hart, 1846.

Thrapp, D., ed. *Encyclopedia of Frontier Biography*. Spokane, WA: Arthur H. Clarke, 1990.

Tijerina, Andrew A. "Tejanos and Texans: The Native Mexicans of Texas, 1820–1850." Ph.D. dissertation. Austin: University of Texas, 1977.

Timmons, Wilbert H. *Morales of Mexico: Priest, Soldier and Statesman*. El Paso: Texas Western Press, 1963.

Todd, Charles Burr. *The Battles of San Pasqual. A Study*. Pomona, CA: Progress Publishing Company, 1925.

Trass, A. G. *From the Golden Gate to Mexico City: The U.S. Topographic Engineers in the Mexican War, 1846–1848*. Washington, DC: Corps of Engineers, 1993.

Trennert, R. A. *Alternative to Extinction: Federal Indian Policy and the Beginning of the Reservation System, 1846–1851*. Philadelphia: Temple University Press, 1975.

Trimble, Marshall. *Arizona: A Panoramic History of a Frontier State*. Garden City, NY: Doubleday, 1977.

Turner, Henry S. *The Original Journals of Henry Smith Turner, with Stephen Watts Kearny to Mexico and California, 1846–1847*. Edited by D. L. Clarke. Norman: University of Oklahoma Press, 1966.

Tutorow, N. E. *The Mexican-American War: An Annotated Bibliography*. Westport, CT: Greenwood Press, 1981.

Twitchell, Ralph Emerson. *The Conquest of Santa Fe 1846*. Truchas, NM: Tate Gallery, 1967.

———. *The History of the Military Occupation of the Territory of New Mexico from 1846 to 1851 by the Government of the United States*. Denver, CO: Smith-Brooks, 1909.

———. *Leading Facts of New Mexico History*. Cedar Rapids, IA: Torch Press, 1912.

Tyler, Daniel. *A Concise History of the Mormon Battalion in the Mexican War 1846–1847*. Chicago: Rio Grande Press, 1964.

———. "Governor Armijo's Moment of Truth." *Journal of the West* 11 (April 1972): 307–316.

Tyler, L. G. *The Letters and Times of the Tylers*. Richmond, VA: Whittet and Shepperson, 1885.

Tyler, R. C. *The Mexican War: A Lithographic Record*. Austin: Texas State Historical Association, 1973.

Underhill, Reuben L. *From Cowhides to Golden Fleece*. Palo Alto, CA: Stanford University Press, 1940.

Upton, Emory. *The Military Policy of the United States*. Westport, CT: Greenwood Press, 1968.

Van Deusen, G. G. *The Jacksonian Era*. New York: Harper & Row, 1959.

Van Deusen, George William. "Our Artillery in the Mexican War." *Journal of the Military Service Institute* 18 (1895): 87–96.

Van Tyne, C. H., ed. *The Letters of Daniel Webster*. New York: McClure, Phillips & Co., 1902.

Vandiver, Frank E. "The Mexican War Experience of Josiah Gorgas." *Journal of Southern History* 13 (1947): 371–394.

Vásquez, Josefina Zoraida, and Lorenzo Meyer. *The United States and Mexico*. Chicago: University of Chicago Press, 1985.

Vestal, Stanley. *Kit Carson, The Happy Warrior of the Old West*. Boston: Houghton Mifflin, 1928.

Viola, Herman J. "Zachary Taylor and the Indiana Volunteers." *Southwest Historical Quarterly* 72 (January 1969): 335–346.

Walker, Samuel Hamilton. *Samuel H. Walker's Account of the Mier Expedition*. Austin: Texas State Historical Association, 1978.

Wallace, Edward S. "The Battalion of Saint Patrick in the Mexican War." *Military Affairs* 14 (Summer 1950): 84–91.

———. "Deserters in the Mexican War." *Hispanic American Historical Review* 15 (August 1935): 374–382.

———. *General William Jenkins Worth, Monterey's Forgotten Hero*. Dallas: Southern Methodist University Press, 1953.

Wallace, William. *Antoine Robidoux, 1794–1860: A Biography of a Western Venturer*. Los Angeles: Glen Dawson, 1953.

War Department. *Statistical Report on the Sickness and Mortality in the Army of the United States from January 1939 to January 1855*. Washington, DC: Nicholson, 1856.

Warner, Lee H. "Nathaniel Hawthorne and the Making of the President—1852." *Historical New Hampshire* 28 (Spring 1973): 21–36.

Weaver, M. P. *The Aztec Maya, and their Predecessors*. New York: Seminar Press, 1972.

Webb, James J. *Adventures in the Santa Fe Trade, 1844–1847*. Edited by R. P. Bieber. Glendale, CA: Arthur H. Clark, 1931.

Webb, Walter Prescott. *The Handbook of Texas*. Chicago: R. R. Donnelly, 1952.

———. *The Texas Rangers: A Century of Frontier Defense*. Austin: University of Texas Press, 1965.

———. *The Texas Rangers in the Mexican War*. Austin, TX: Jenkins Garrett Press, 1975.

Weber, David J. *The Mexican Frontier, 1821–1846. The American Southwest under Mexico*. Albuquerque: University of New Mexico Press, 1982.

———. *The Spanish Frontier in North America*. New Haven, CT: Yale University Press, 1992.

———. *The Taos Trappers*. Norman: University of Oklahoma Press, 1971.

Weems, John Edward. *To Conquer a Peace*. New York: Doubleday, 1974.

Weinberg, Albert K. *Manifest Destiny: A Study of Nationalist Expansion in American History*. Chicago: Quadrangle, 1963.

Welsh, Jack D. *Medical Histories of Confederate Generals*. Kent, OH: Kent State University Press, 1995.

———. *Medical Histories of Union Generals*. Kent, OH: Kent State University Press, 1997.

Wessels, William L. *Born to Be a Soldier. The Military Career of William Wing Loring of St. Augustine, Florida*. Fort Worth: Texas Christian University Press, 1971.

White, Leonard D. *The Jacksonians. A Study in Administrative History 1829–1861*. New York: Macmillan, 1954.

Whittier, John Greenleaf. *The Letters of John Greenleaf Whittier*. Edited by J. B. Pickard. New York: Cambridge University Press, 1937.

Wilcox, Cadmus M. *History of the Mexican War*. Washington, DC: Church News Publishing Company, 1892.

Williams, A., and E. C. Barker, eds. *The Writings of Sam Houston, 1813–1863*. Austin: University of Texas, 1938–1943.

Williams, T. H. *P. G. T. Beauregard: Napoleon in Gray*. Baton Rouge: Louisiana State University Press, 1954.

Willing, Wildurr. "The Engineers and the Mexican War." *Professional Memoirs* 7 (1915): 333–356.

Willson, Beckles. *John Slidell and the Confederates in Paris (1862–1865)*. New York: Minton, Balch, and Company, 1932.

Wiltse, Charles M. *John C. Calhoun: Sectionalist, 1840–1850*. New York: Bobbs-Merrill, 1951.

Wiltsee, Ernest A. *The Truth about Fremont: An Inquiry*. San Francisco: Nash, 1936.

Winchester, G. R. *James Pinckney Henderson*. San Antonio, TX: Naylor Press, 1971.

Winders, R. B. *Mr. Polk's Army: The American Military Experience in the Mexican War*. College Station: Texas A&M University Press, 1997.

Wise, Henry A. *Los Gringos; or an Inside View of Mexico and California*. New York: Baker and Scribner, 1849.

Wolcott, Roger, ed. *The Correspondence of William Hickling Prescott, 1833–1847*. Cambridge, England: Cambridge University Press, 1925.

Woodward, Arthur. *Lances at San Pascual*. San Francisco: California Historical Society, 1948.

Worth, William J. "Never before Published Letters of Famous General Worth, Written during Mexican War." *New York Times Magazine* (July 16, 1916): 10–11.

Wortham, Thomas. *James Russell Lowell's Bigelow Papers: A Critical Edition*. DeKalb: Northern Illinois University Press, 1977.

Wyllys, R. K. *Arizona: The History of a Frontier State*. Phoenix, AZ: Hobson & Herr, 1950.

Wynn, Dennis J. *The San Patricio Soldiers: Mexico's Foreign Legion*. Southwestern Studies Monograph 74. El Paso: Texas Western Press, 1984.

Wynne, James. "Memoir of the Rev. Antony Rey, S.J." *United States Catholic Magazine* 6(10) (1847): 543–552.

Yoakum, Henderson K. *The History of Texas, from Its First Settlements in 1685 to Its Annexation by the United States in 1846*. New York: Redfield, 1855.

Young, Kevin R. "Finding a Face: El Soldado Mexicano, 1835–1848." In *A Thunder of Cannon: Archeology of the Mexican-American War Battlefield of Palo Alto*. Edited by Charles M. Haecker. Santa Fe, NM: National Park Service, 1994.

Young, Otis E. *The West of Philip St. George Cooke, 1809–1895*. Glendale, CA: Arthur H. Clark, 1955.

Zeh, Frederick. *An Immigrant Soldier in the Mexican War*. Translated by William J. Orr, edited by William J. Orr and Robert R. Miller. College Station: Texas A&M University Press, 1995.

Zollinger, James P. *Sutter: The Man and His Empire*. Gloucester, MA: P. Smith, 1967.

Zweig, Paul. *Walt Whitman: The Making of a Poet.* New York: Basic Books, 1984.

Selected References in Spanish

Alamán, Lucas. *Historia de Méjico desde los primeros movimientos que prepararon su independencia en el año de 1808 hasta la época presente.* Mexico City: J. Mariano Lara, 1850.

Álbum mexicano: colección de paisajes, monumentos, costumbres y ciudades principales de la república. Mexico City: Celanese Mexicana, 1983.

Alcaráz, Ramón. *Apuntes para la historia de la guerra entre México y los Estados Unidos.* Mexico City: Tipografía de Manuel Payno, 1848.

Alessio Robles, Vito. 1934. *Saltillo en la historia y en la leyenda.* Mexico City: Editorial Porrúa, 1978.

Allesio Robles, Vito. *Coahuila y Texas desde la consumación de la independencia hasta el tratado de paz de Guadalupe Hidalgo.* Mexico City: Editorial Porrúa, 1979.

Almada, Francisco R. *Diccionario de historia, geografía y biografía sonorenses.* Hermosillo: Instituto Sonorense de Cultura, 1990.

Alvear Acevedo, Carlos. *La guerra del 47.* Mexico City: Editorial Jus, 1957.

Amaya, Juan Gualberto. *Santa Anna no fué un traidor.* Mexico City: n.p., 1952.

Arrangoiz y Berzábel, Francisco de Paula de. *Méjico desde 1808 hasta 1867.* Second edition. Mexico City: Editorial Porrúa, 1968.

Balbontín, Manuel. *Estado militar de la República Mexicana en 1846.* Mexico City: Ignacio Pombo, 1891.

———. *La invasión americana, 1846 a 1848.* Mexico City: Tip. de G.A. Esteva, 1888.

Bassols, Narciso. *Valentín Gómez Farías.* Mexico City: Secretaría de Relaciones Exteriores, 1933.

Bell Bravo, María Antonia. *La mujer en la historia de México.* Madrid, Spain: Encuentro, 1998.

Berruto Ramón, Federico. *En defensa de un soldado Mexicano.* Saltillo: Coleccion de escritores coahuilenses, 1957.

Bitar Letayf, Marcelo. *La vida económica de México de 1824 a 1867 y sus proyecciones.* Mexico City: Universidad Nacional Autónoma de Mexico, 1964.

Bocanegra, José María. *Memorias para la historia de México independiente, 1822–1846.* Mexico City: Imprenta del gobierno federal en el ex-Arzbispado, 1892.

Bonilla, Juan Dios. *Historia marítima de México.* Mexico City: Editorial Litorales, 1962.

Bosch García, Carlos. *Historia de las relaciones entre México y los Estados Unidos, 1819–1848.* Mexico City: Escuela Nacional de Ciencias Políticas y Sociales, 1961.

———. *Material para la historia diplomática de México y los Estados Unidos, 1820–1848.* Mexico City: Escuela Nacional de Ciéncias Politicas y Sociales, 1957.

Bravo, Ugarte José. "Don Nicolás Bravo y la defensa de Chapultepec." *Boletín del archivo general de la nación* 18(4) (October–December 1947): 421–460.

———. "Guerra a México de Estados Unidos, 1846-1848." *Historia mexicana* 1(2) (October–December 1951): 180–226.

———. *Historia de México.* Mexico City: Editorial Jus, 1959.

Bushnell, Clyde Gilbert. *La carrera política y militar de Juan Álvarez.* Mexico City: Miguel Angel Porrúa, 1988.

Bustamante, Carlos María de. *El nuevo Bernal Díaz del Castillo, o sea, Historia de la invasión de los anglo-americanos en México.* Mexico City: Secretaría de educacíon pública, 1949.

Cárdenas de la Peña, Enrique. *Tiempo y tarea de Luis Gonzaga Cuevas.* Mexico City: Contabilidad Mexicana, 1982.

Carreño, Alberto María. *El Colégio Militar de Chapultepec, 1847–1947.* Mexico City: Ediciones Victoria, 1972.

———. *La diplomacia extraordinaria entre México y Estados Unidos, 1789–1947.* Mexico City: Editorial Jus, 1951.

———. *Jefes del ejército mexicano en 1847. Biografías de generales de división y de brigada y de coroneles del ejército mexicano por fines del año de 1847.* Mexico City: Secretaría de Fomento, 1914.

Castillo Nájera, Francisco. *Invasión norteamericana, efectivos y estado de los ejércitos beligerantes, consideraciones sobre de campaña.* Mexico City: Editorial Jus, 1947.

Castillo Negrete, Emilio del. *Invasión de los norteamericanos en México.* Mexico City: Imprenta del editor, 1890.

Churubusco en la accion militar del 20 de Agosto de 1847. Mexico City: Museo Histórico de Churubusco, 1947.

Cosío Villegas, Daniel, ed. *Historia general de México.* Mexico City: Colegio de Mexico, 1994.

Cox, Patricia. *Batallón de San Patricio.* Mexico City: Editorial Stylo, 1954.

Cue Cánovas, Augustin. *Historia social y económica de Mexico (1821–1854).* Mexico City: Editorial F. Trillas, 1963.

Cuéllar Valdés, P. M. *Historia de la ciudad de Saltillo.* Saltillo: Universidad Autonoma de Coahuila, 1982.

Cuevas, Luis Gonzaga. *Porvenir de México: Juicio sobre su estado político en 1821 y 1851.* Mexico City: Imprenta de I. Cumplido, 1851.

Cuevas, Mariano. *Historia de la nación méxicana.* Mexico City: Editorial Porrúa, 1967.

de la Peña, Antonio, ed. *Algunos documentos sobre el tratado de Guadalupe y la situación de México durante la invasión americana.* Mexico City: Secretaría de Relaciones Exteriores, 1930.

Delgado, Jaime. *La monarquía en México (1845–1847).* Mexico City: Editorial Porrúa, 1990.

Diccionario geográfico, histórico y biográfico de los Estados Unidos Méxicanos. Mexico City: Antigua Imprenta de Murguia, 1888.

Diccionario Porrúa de historia, biografía y geografía de México. Sixth edition. Mexico City: Editorial Porrúa, 1995.

Discurso pronunciado por el presidente de la republica, General de division, Jose Joaquin de Herrera, el dia 1 de enero de 1851, en la apertura del congreso. Mexico City: Vicente Torres, 1851.

Echánove Trujillo, Carlos A. *Juan Crisóstomo Cano, héroe de Chapultepec, 1847.* Mexico City: Editorial Cultura, 1947.

Esquivel Obregón, Toribio. *Apuntes para la historia del derecho en México.* Mexico City: Antigua Librería Robredo, 1847.

Fernández Tomás, Jorge. *Ahí vienen los del norte; la invasión norteamericana de 1847.* (México: historia de un pueblo, no. 8) Mexico City: Secretaría de Educación Pública y Editorial Nueva Imagen, 1980.

Frías, Heriberto. *Episodios militares mexicanos: Príncipales campañas, jornados, batallas, combates y actos heróicos que ilustran la historia del ejército nacional desde la independencia hasta el triunfo definitivo de la república.* Mexico City: Editorial Porrúa, 1987.

Fuentes, Gloria. *El ejército mexicano.* Mexico City: Grijalbo, 1983.

Fuentes Díaz, Vicente. *La intervención norteamericana en México.* Mexico City: Imprente Nuevo Mundo, 1947.

———. *Valentín Gómez Farías, padre de la reforma.* Second edition. Mexico City: Edición del Comité de Actos Conmemorativos del Bicentenario del Natalicio del Dr. Valentín Gómez Farías, 1981.

Fuentes Mares, José. *Génesis del expansionismo norteamericano.* Mexico City: El Colegio de Mexico, 1980.

———. *Santa Anna, aurora y ocaso de un comediante.* Mexico City: Editorial Jus, 1956.

Gallagher, F. M. "Parte oficial de la acción de armas de Temascalitos." *New Mexico Historical Review* 3 (October 1928): 381–389.

Gaxiola, F. Javier. *La invasión norteamericana en Sinaloa.* Mexico City: Antonio Rosas, 1891.

Gayón Córdova, María. *La ocupación yanqui de la Ciudad de México, 1847–1848.* Mexico City: Consejo Nacional para la Cultura y las Artes.

Heroles, Jesus Reyes. *Mariano Otero: Obras.* 2 vols. Mexico City: Porrúa, 1967.

Instituto Nacional de Antropología e Historia. *Churubusco en la acción militar del 20 de agosto de 1847.* Mexico City: Instituto Nacional de Antropología e Historia, 1947.

Lerdo de Tejada, Miguel M. *Apuntes históricos de la heróica ciudad de Veracruz.* Mexico City: Vicente Garcia Tores, 1850–1858.

Ley organica de la guardia nacional. Mexico: Imprenta Ignacio Cumplido, 1848.

Livermore, Abiel Abbot. *Revisión de la guerra entre México y los Estados Unidos. Traducción, prólogo y notas de Francisco Castillo Nájera.* Mexico City: n.p., 1948.

López, Uraga José. *Sumária mandada formar a pedimento del Sr. Coronel del 4 Regimiento de Infantería.* Mexico City: Navarro, 1846.

Marchena Fernández, Juan. *Oficiales y soldados en el ejército de América.* Sevilla: Escuela de Estudios Hispano-Americanos, 1983.

Martínez Caraza, Leopoldo. *La intervención norteamericana en México, 1846–1848.* Mexico City: Panorama Editorial, 1981.

Mateos, Juan A., ed. *Historia parlamentaria de los congresos méxicanos de 1821 a 1857.* Mexico City: J. V. Villada, 1877.

Mestre Ghigliazza, Manuel. *Invasión norteamericana en Tabasco (1846–1847), documentos.* Mexico City: Imprenta Universitaria, 1948.

Millares Carlo, Agustín. *Repertorio bibliográfico de los archivos mexicanos y de los europeos y norteamericanos de interés para la historia de Mexico.* Mexico City: Biblioteca Nacional, 1959.

Molina, Ignacio. "El asalto al castillo de Chapultepec el día 13 de septiembre de 1847." *Revista Positiva* 2 (October 1, 1902): 444–464.

Moyano Pahissa, Angela. *México y Estados Unidos: orígenes de una relación 1819–1961.* Mexico City: Secretaría de Educación Pública, 1985.

Muro, Manuel. *Historia de la San Luis Potosí.* San Luis Potosí: Imprenta Moderna de F. H. González, 1910.

Negrete, Emilio del Castillo. *Invasión de los norteamericanos en México.* Mexico City: Imprenta del Editor, 1890.

Neve, Carlos D. *Historia gráfica del ejército mexicano.* Cuernavaca: Manuel Quesada Brandi, 1967.

Nieto, Angelina, Joseph Hefter, and Mrs. John Nicholas Brown. *El soldado mexicano 1837–1847. Organización, vestuario, equipo.* Mexico City: Ediciones Nieto-Brown-Hefter, 1958.

O'Gorman, Edmundo. *Historia de las divisiones territoriales de México.* Third edition. Mexico City: Editorial Porrúa, 1966.

Olavarría y Ferrari, Enrique. *México independiente, 1821–1855.* Vol. 4. *México a través de los siglos.* Edited by Vicente Riva Palacios. Mexico City: Editorial Cumbre, 1953.

Paredes y Arrillaga, Mariano. *Últimas comunicaciones entre el gobierno mexicano y el enviado extraordinario y ministro plenipotenciario nombrado por de los Estados Unidos sobre la cuestión de Tejas.* Mexico City: I. Cumplido, 1846.

Pasquel, Leonardo. *Biografía integral de la ciudad de Veracruz, 1519–1969.* México City: Editorial Citlaltépetl, 1969.

Peña Reyes, Antonio, ed. *Algunos documentos sobre el tratado de Guadalupe y la situación de México durante la invasión americana.* Mexico City: Secretaría de Relaciones Exteriores, 1930.

Prieto, Guillermo. *Memorias de mis tiempos, 1828 a 1853.* Mexico City: Editorial Pátria, 1948.

Rabasa, Emilio. *La evolución histórica de México.* Mexico City: Porrúa, 1956.

Ramírez, José Fernando. *México durante su guerra con los Estados Unidos.* Mexico City: Vda de C. Bouret, 1905.

Ramos, Roberto. *Bibliografía de la historia de México.* Mexico City: Instituto Mexicano de Investigaciones Económicas, 1965.

Rea, Vargas, ed. *Apuntes históricos sobre los acontecimientos notables de la guerra entre México y los Estados Unidos del norte.* Mexico City: Biblioteca Aportación Histórica, 1945.

Read, Benjamin M. *Guerra méxico-americana.* Santa Fe, NM: Cia Impresora del Nuevo Mexicano, 1910.

Rivera Cambas, Manuel. *Historia antigua y moderna de Jalapa y de las revoluciones del Estado de Veracruz.* Mexico City: Ignacio Cumplido, 1869–1871.

Roa Bárcena, José Maria. *Recuerdos de la invasión norte-americana.* Edited by Antonio Castro Leal. Mexico City: Editorial Porrúa, 1947.

Salvat Editores de México. *Historia de México.* México City: Salvat Editores de México, 1974.

Sánchez Lamego, Miguel A. *El Colegio Militar y la defensa de Chapultepec en septiembre de 1847.* Mexico City: n.p., 1947.

———. *Generales de ingenieros del ejército Mexicano, 1821–1914.* Mexico City: n.p., 1952.

Sánchez-Navarro, Carlos. *La guerra de Tejas: memorias de un soldado.* Second edition. Mexico City: Editorial Jus, 1960.

Santa Anna, Antonio López de. *Detalle de las operaciones ocurridas en la defense de la capital de la república, atacada por el ejército de los Estados Unidos del norte en el año de 1847.* Mexico City: Ignacio Cumplido, 1848.

———. *Mi historia militar y política 1810–1874.* Mexico: Ch. Bouret, 1905.

Secretaría de Defensa Nacional. *Guía del archivo histórico militar de México.* Vol. 1 (1821–1847). Mexico City: Taller Autográfica, 1948.

Secretaría de Guerra y Marina. *Apuntes para una bibliografia militar de México, 1536–1936.* Mexico City: Secretaría de Guerra y Marina, 1937.

Secretaría de Relaciones Exteriores. *Algunos documentos sobre el tradado de Guadalupe Hidalgo y la situación de México durante la invasión americana.* Mexico City: Secretaría de Relaciones Exteriores, 1930.

Sepulveda, Cesar. *La frontera norte de México: historia, conflictos 1762–1975.* Mexico City: Editorial Porrúa, 1983.

"La Situación política, militar y económica en la república mexicana al iniciarse su guerra con los Estados Unidos, según el archivo del general Paredes." Edited by Genaro García. In *Documentos inéditos o muy raros para la historia de México*. Second edition. Vol. 56. Mexico City: Editorial Porrúa, 1974.

Soto Estrada, Miguel. *La conspiración monárquica en México, 1845–1846*. Tepepan: EOSA, 1988.

Toro, Alfonso. *Compendio de la historia de México*. Mexico City: Editorial Patria, 1943.

Trens, Manuel B. *Historia de Veracruz*. Mexico City: Xalapa-Enríquez-Secretaría de Educación y Cultura, 1947–1950.

Trueba, Alfonso. *Santa Anna*. Third edition. Mexico City: Editorial Jus, 1958.

Valadés, José C. *Alamán, estadista e historiador*. Mexico City: J. Porrúa, 1938.

———. *Breve historia de la guerra con los Estados Unidos*. Mexico City: Editorial Patria, 1947.

———. *Santa Anna y la guerra de Texas*. Mexico City: Mexicanos Unidos, 1935.

Valázquez, P. M. *Historia de la San Luis Potosí*. San Luis Potosí: Academia de Historia Potosina, 1982.

Vargas Martínez, Ubaldo. *La ciudad de México (1325–1960)*. México City: Departamento de Distrito Federal, 1961.

Vasconcelos, José. *Breve historia de México*. Mexico City: Ediciónes Botas, 1936.

Velasco Márquez, Jesús. *La guerra del 47 y la opinión pública (1845–1848)*. Mexico City: Secretaría de Educación Pública, 1975.

Vígil y Robles, Guillermo. *La invasión de México por los Estados Unidos en los años de 1846, 1847, y 1848*. Mexico City: Tip E. Correcional, 1923.

Zorilla, Juan F., and Carlos Gonzáles Salas. *Diccionario biográfico de Tamaulipas*. Victoria, Tamaulipas: Universidad Autónoma de Tamaulipas, 1984.

Zorilla, Luís G. *Historia de las relaciones entre México y los Estados Unidos de América, 1800–1958*. Mexico City: Editorial Porrúa, 1977.

Index

Abolitionists, **1**, 123
Aburto, Juan, **1–2**, 131
Acapulco, 195
Adams, Henry, 304
Adams, John, 2
Adams, John Quincy, **2–3**, 2, 94, 145, 147, 171, 186, 276–277
Adams-Onís Treaty, 2
"Adventurers," 22
African Americans, **3**, 111
Agua Fria, 131
Agua Fria, Skirmish of, **3–4**, 132
Agua Nueva, **4–5**, 22, 27, 46, 54, 56, 69, 160, 273, 300, 301, 311
Aguascalientes, Plan of, **5**
Aguila, 195
Alamán y Escalada, Lucas, **5–6**, 209
Alamo, 122, 241, 248, 271, 307
Alcorta, Lino José, **6**
Alexander, Edmund Brooke, **6–7**
"All of Mexico" Movement, **7**, 90, 128, 134, 228, 289
Almonte, Juan Nepomuceno, **7–8**, 7, 14
Alvarado, **8–9**, 85, 115, 131, 143, 146, 195, 197, 226, 248, 263, 309, 310
Álvarez, Juan, **9–10**, 12, 13, 20, 99, 152
Alvarez, Manuel, **10**
"Amateur" soldiers, 22
American Flag, 13
American Pioneer, 13
American-Star, 13
Ampudia, Pedro de, **10–11**, *11*, 20, 42, 53, 55, 78, 81, 97, 115, 116, 138, 180, 184, 187, 188, 197, 207, 234, 291, 297, 309
Anahuac, 196
Anaya, Pedro María, **11–12**, 49, 213, 219, 311, 312
Anderson, Robert, **12**, 114
Andrade, Manuel, **12–13**
Anglo-American press, **13**
Anglo-Saxon, 13
Anti-war sentiment, 82, 88, 94–95, 110–111, 123, 125, 126, 145, 164, 167, 273–274, 295
Apache, 146, 200, 203, 245
Apache Canyon, **13–14**, 17, 155, 169
Arab, 14
Archuleta, Diego, 14, **14–15**, 17, 28, 40, 86, 105, 155, 169–170, 205, 267
Arispe Cotton Mills, 220
Arista, Mariano, xvii, xx, 10, 11, **15–16**, *15*, 44–45, 51–52, 53, 65, 98, 115, 116, 156, 180, 188, 207–208, 232–234, 274, 275, 291

Arizona, 16
Armijo, Manuel, 10, 13–14, **16–17**, 40, 155, 156, 169, 173, 201
Armistead, Lewis Addison, **17**
Army of Observation, **22–23**, 116, 269, 308
Army of Occupation, xvii, 13, 21, **23–25**, *23, 25,* 27, 28, 31, 33, 37, 38, 39, 43, 44, 47, 48–49, 51, 53, 57, 59, 62, 64, 67, 69, 71, 74, 78, 82, 85, 87, 90, 93, 99, 107, 113, 115, 116, 117, 119, 122, 124, 125, 126, 130, 131, 134, 135, 137–138, 142–143, 148–149, 150–151, 156, 163, 165, 165, 170, 171, 174, 175, 176–177, 180, 185, 187–191, 193, 196, 201, 203, 210, 211, 212, 213, 217–218, 222, 230, 231, 232–234, 235, 236, 241, 242, 247, 251–253, 255, 258, 269, 274, 276, 279, 284, 286, 290, 292, 300, 301, 302, 308, 309
  and Battle of Buena Vista, **53–56**, *54*
Army of the Center (Mexico), **20**
Army of the Center (United States), **27**, 135, 163, 186, 210, 255, 300, 301
Army of the East, 17, **20**, 49, 50, 51, 64, 72, 98, 148, 149–150, 152, 164, 212, 213, 222, 230, 247, 249, 275, 283, 285
Army of the North, xvii, xviii, xx, 10, 11, 15, 17, 28, 30, 42, 44, 45, 51, 53, 69, 85, 97, 98, 115, 152, 165, 174, 178, 180, 185, 188, 191, 197, 205, 210, 213, 219, 232–234, 246, 249, 269, 275, 283, 285, 309, 310
  Advance of, **18–19**
  and Battle of Buena Vista, **53–56**, *54*
  Retreat of, **19–20**
Army of the South, **20**
Army of the West, xviii, 13–14, **25–27**, 28, 40, 76–77, 81, 85, 86, 101, 102, 111, 133, 146, 153–154, 169–170, 192, 205, 221, 239–240, 250, 251, 267, 301, 309
  Kearny's March, **154–155**, 309
Arriaga, Ponciano, 128
Arroyo Colorado, **28**, 47
Arroyo Hondo, Skirmish at, **28–29**, 191
Atlixco, 131
Atlixco, Skirmish at, **29**, 312
Atocha, Alexander, J., **29–30**, 169, 219, 249, 309
Atristain, Miguel, 128
Aulick, John H., 140
Austin, Stephen, 271, 272
Aztec Club, **30**, 228

Baca, Tomás. *See* El Tomacito
Backus, Electus, **31**, 190

339

Bailey, T., 199
Baker, Edward Dickinson, **31–32**
Balbontín, Manuel, **32**
Balcárcel, Antonio de, 186
Balderas, Lucas, **32–33**, *32*, 109
Bancroft, George, **33**, 118, 196, 197, 219, 257
Bangs, Samuel, 13
Barbour, Philip Norbourn, 22, **33–34**
Barrera, Juan de la, 201
Bartlett, John Russell, **34**, 123, 126
Bartlett-Condé Agreement, 34, **34–35**, 122
Battle of Belén Gate. *See* Belén *garita*
Battle of Buena Vista, 4–5, 11, 12–13, 19, 24, 32, 43, 45, 46, 47–48, **53–56**, *54*, 70, 78, 82, 89, 94, 119, 125, 135, 152, 160, 162, 163, 165, 171, 173, 175–176, 178, 180, 185, 193, 203, 205, 210, 213, 216–217, 219, 220, 231, 234, 242, 247, 249, 268, 275–276, 293–294, 299, 300, 303, 311
Battle of Cerro Gordo, 11, 25, 31, 38, 39, 42, 51, 56, **71–74**, 89, 98, 99, 108, 117, 131, 136, 148, 150, 163, 164, 166, 170, 177, 183, 191, 211, 212, 217, 221, 230, 231, 232, 236, 240, 247, 253, 255, 277, 280, 284, 285, 294, 297, 299, 311
Battle of Chapultepec, 39, 56, 59, 67, **74–76**, *75*, 99, 107, 111, 136, 137–138, 139, 141, 142, 151, 156, 165, 166, 170, 175, 183, 191, 201, 212, 216, 217, 227, 232, 236, 253, 255, 259, 265, 266, 270, 276, 284, 311
Battle of Churubusco, 6, 12, 50, 56, 57, 59, 67, **79–80**, *79*, 89, 93, 99, 108, 111, 136, 139, 163, 175, 183, 211, 212, 216, 217, 226, 227, 231, 232, 236, 253, 255, 259, 265, 266, 274, 278, 294, 302, 311
Battle of Contreras, 20, 38, 45, 46, 50, 51, 56, 59, 67, **85–86**, 89, 99, 108, 111, 136, 148, 163, 170, 175, 180, 183, 210, 216, 217, 232, 236, 240, 241, 253, 258, 259, 265, 276, 283, 284, 302, 311
Battle of El Brazito, 101, 102, **107–108**, 238, 297, 310
Battle of El Molino del Rey, 9, 10, 12, 20, 32, 50–51, 59, 67, 74, 75, 96, 107, **108–110**, 117, 121, 126, 137, 142, 152, 164, 183, 212, 213, 230, 239, 253, 265, 266, 302, 311
Battle of Guaymas, **128–129**, 297
Battle of Huamantla, 22, 68, **141–142**, 273, 290, 297, 312
Battle of La Angostura. *See* Battle of Buena Vista
Battle of La Cañada, **159**
Battle of La Mesa, 67, 111, 113, 114, 154, **160**, 215, 244, 260
Battle of Los Angeles. *See* Battle of La Mesa, Battle of San Gabriel River
Battle of Mexico City, 68, 104, 126, 165, **183–184**, 212, 265, 270, 311. *See also* Veracruz-Mexico City campaign
Battle of Monterrey, xvii, 24, 31, 33, 42–43, 47, 48, 49, 51, 57–58, 65, 68, 69, 78, 81, 94, 110, 117, 119, 124, 125, 126, 134, 137, 138, 156, 165, 171, 175, 177, 180, 186, **187–191**, *188*, *189*, 193, 205, 212, 226, 231, 234, 235, 247, 255, 258, 268, 273, 275, 280, 284, 289, 290, 297, 302, 305, 310
Battle of Padierna. *See* Battle of Contreras
Battle of Palo Alto, xvii, xx, 10, 11, 15, 18, 21, 23–24, 31, 33, 39, 42, 44, 46, 47, 51, 53, 62, 64, 65, 78, 98, 99, 114, 116, 119, 125, 126, 165, 174, 177, 188, **207–208**, 212, 235, 236–237, 268, 269, 274, 275, 279–280, 289–290, 302, 309
Battle of Resaca de Guerrero. *See* Battle of Resaca de la Palma
Battle of Resaca de la Palma, xvii, xx, 10, 11, 15, 18, 21, 23–24, 31, 33, 39, 42, 46, 47, 51, 53, 62, 64, 65, 78, 98, 99, 116, 119, 125, 126, 165, 174, 177, 188, 212, **232–234**, 235, 268, 269, 275, 278, 279–280, 289, 297, 302, 309
Battle of Río Sacramento, 77, 81, 101, 103, 122, 138–139, **238–239**, 277, 311
Battle of San Cosmé *garita*, 59, 107, 143, 148, 183, 212, 230, 276, 311
Battle of San Gabriel River, 67, 111, 113, 114, 154, 160, 166, 215, **243–244**, 260, 311
Battle of San Jacinto, 248, 267, 307
Battle of San Pascual, 25, 36, 66, 111, 124, 154, 155, 192, 215, 240, **246**, 310
Battle of Santa Clara, **249–250**
Battle of Santa Cruz de Rosales, **250–251**, 277
Battle of Veracruz, 12, 24–25, 54, 56, 68, 71, 89, 140, 172, 211, 212, 240, 252–253, 254, 261, **285–287**, 310–311
Battles of Tabasco, **263–265**, *264*
Baz, Juan José, **35**
Beach, Moses Y., **35–36**, 44, 260–261, 299
Beale, Edward Fitzgerald, **36–37**, *36*, 66–67, 192
Bear Flag Revolt, **36–37**, 61–62, 67, 68, 118, 145, 204, 261–262, 284, 309
Bear Spring. *See* Ojo Oso
Beaubien, Carlos, **37**
Beauregard, Pierre Gustave Toutant, **38**, *38*, 72, 183, 214
Bee, Barnard Elliott, **38–39**
Belén *garita*, 104, 165, 183, 227–228, 270, 284, 311
Belknap, William Goldsmith, **39**
Bent, Charles, 14–15, 28, **39–40**, 105, 108, 110, 159, 173, 201, 205, 221, 222–223, 238, 251, 267
Bent, William, 39, 40
Benton, Thomas Hart, 3, 40, **41–42**, *41*, 117–118, 157, 169, 171
Bent's Old Fort, 39, **40–41**, 85, 86, 102, 154–155, 191–192, 308

Index   341

Bermúdez de Castro, Salvador, 5
Berra, Francisco, 43
Berryman, Ortway H., 278
Biddle, James, 42, 256
Bigelow Papers, 167
Billings, Eliza Allen, 42, 299
Bishop's Palace, Monterrey, 42–43
Bissell, William Henry, 43–44
Black, John, xx, 36, 44, 213, 256
Black Fort. *See* Citadel, Monterrey
Blake, Jacob E., 44–45, 274
Blanco, Santiago, 45, 55
Bliss, William Wallace Smith, 45–46, 56, 251, 269
Bocachicacampo, Skirmish at, 46
Bonham, Milledge Luke, 46
Bonita, 197   ital
Border. *See* Boundary
Borginnis, Sarah, 46–47, 52, 116, *298*, 299
Borland, Solon, 47, 159
Boundary, 34, 44, 111, 116, 122–123, 126, 176, 216, 238, 271, 276–277, 307, 308. *See also* Nueces River, Río Grande, Sabine River
Bowles, William Augustus, 47–48, 55
Boyd, Linn, 48
Bragg, Braxton, 48–49, 55, 190
Bravo Rueda, Nicolás, 20, 49–50, *49*, 74, 75, 79, 174, 180, 201, 209, 230
Breckenridge, John C., 162
Brevet rank, 50
Brinkerhoff, Jacob, 297
Brooks, Horace B., 50–51
Brooks, William Thomas Harbaugh, 51
Brown, Jacob, 51–52, 116, 207
"Brown Bess," 294
Buchanan, James, 30, 35, 40, 44, 52–53, *52*, 83, 93, 100, 118, 119, 136, 157, 257, 261, 278, 289, 296, 303
Buchanan, Robert Christie, 53, 233
Burnett, Ward B., 56
Burton, Henry S., 161, 275
Bustamante, Anastasio, 6, 56–57, 212, 248
Butler, Pierce M., 57
Butler, William Orlando, 57–58, *58*, 134, 141, 151, 159–160, 312

Cabrillo, Juan Rodríguez, 61
Cadwalader, George, 59, 80, 109
Calderón, José María, 247
Calhoun, John Caldwell, 60, 127
California, xviii, xix, 7, 25, 44, 49, 52, 57, 59–60, 60–61, 67–68, 85, 86–87, 101, 111, 113–114, 117–119, 123–124, 127, 128, 136, 146, 147, 153, 154, 160, 162–163, 169, 170, 171, 173, 215–216, 218, 219, 256–257, 261–262, 278, 280, 284, 307–308, 309, 310, 311
    Bear Flag Revolt, 36–37, 61–62, 67, 68, 118, 145, 204, 261–262, 284, 309

California Battalion, 59, 61–62, 66, 67, 118, 124, 145, 244, 250, 260, 262
Californian, 13
Californios, 59–60, 62, 67–68, 113–114, 118–119, 124, 136, 154, 155, 160, 162–163, 166–167, 186, 192, 215–216, 229–230, 243–244, 246, 249–250, 284, 310, 311
Camargo, 62–63, 130, 134, 188, 258, 309, 310
Camp followers, 18, 19, 54. *See also* Soldaderas
Campaigns of the Río Grande and of Mexico, 259
Campeche, 304
Campuzano, Antonio, 46, 63, 129, 199
Canales Rosillo, Antonio, 10, 15, 63–64, 65, 78, 113, 129–130, 184, 229
Canalizo, Valentín, 64, 72, 73, 148, 213
Cañoncito. *See* Apache Canyon
Carbajal, José María Jesús, 65
Carmelita, 195
Carmen, 65, 304
Carpender, Edward W., 278
Carrasco, José María, 65–66
Carricitos Ranch, Skirmish at, 66, 135, 145, 197, 207, 218, 238, 257, 274, 275, 290
Carrillo, José, 229–230
Carson, Christopher ("Kit"), 36, 37, 66–67, 118, 155, 157, 192, 246
Casey, Silas, 67, 75
Cass, Lewis, 58, 269
Castelar, Josefa, 297
Castro, José María, 37, 67–68, 113, 118, 136, 157, 166, 215, 308
Castro, Manuel, 204
Castro, Mauricio, 275
Casualties, 68–69, 90–91
Catana, Massacre at, 69, 303
Catholic Church, 69–71, *70*, 124, 142–143, 161, 173, 176, 181, 185, 212, 219–220, 220–221, 223, 234, 310, 311
Cazneau, William L., 261
Centralists (Mexico), 181
Cerro Gordo, 64, 149, 151, 195. *See also* Battle of Cerro Gordo
Chamberlain, Samuel, 4
Chapita, 66, 74, 274
Chase, Anna McClarmonde, 76, 266, 299
Chase, Franklin, 76
Chavallie, Michael, 229
Chaves, Manuel Antonio, 76–77
Chavez, Pablo, 159
Chavis, Pablo, 223
Chemuctah, 36, 66–67
Chihuahua (city), 77–78, 103, 107, 135, 221, 277, 294, 300, 301, 311
Chihuahua (state), 107, 122, 138–139, 145, 146, 169, 170, 219, 309, 310, 312
Chihuahua Expedition (John Wool), 301
Childs, Thomas, 43, 73, 78, 149, 190, 222

China, **78–79**
Citadel, Monterrey, **80–81**
Civil Disobedience, 273–274
Clark, Meriwether Lewis, **81**
Clark, William, 170
Clarke, Newman S., 80
Clay, Cassius Marcellus, 1, **81–82**, 121, 159
Clay, Henry, 2, **82**, 88, 218, 280
Clay, Henry, Jr., **82**
Clifford, Nathan, **82–83**, *83*, 254
Coahuila y Texas, **83–84**, 242, 271
Cochori, Skirmish at, **84**
Colegio Militar, 45, 74, 75, 201
Coleman, Ann, 52
Collado Beach, **84**, 286
Collins, John L., **84–85**
Colorado, **85**
Colt, Samuel, 290
Colt revolvers, 290, 294–295
Comanche, 146, 200, 266, 272–273
Comondu, 131
Congress, 104, 174, 244, 260
Conner, David E., 8–9, 14, 76, **85**, 131, 146, 148, 195, 196, 197, 198, 208, 248, 254, 259, 278, 308, 309–310
Cooke, Philip St. George, 16, **86–87**, 191–192
Cooper, James Fenimore, **87**
Coronado, Francisco Vasquez de, 16, 200
Corpus Christi, **87–88**, 95, 125, 126, 156, 193, 238, 241, 269, 291, 308
Corpus Christi *Gazette*, 13
Cortés, Hernán, 134, 181
Cortez, Rafael Ignacio, 70
Corwin, Thomas, 1, **88**
Couch, Darius, **89**
Court of Inquiry, Scott, **89–90**, 91
Couto, José Bernardo, **90**, 128
Crane, 96, 157
Craven, Tunis A. M., 84, 193, 199–200
Criolla, 259
Cross, Trueman, **90–91**, 113, 130
Cuevas, José María, 128
Cuevas, Luis Gonzago, **91**, 128
Cushing, Caleb, **91–92**
Cyane, 104, 123, 161, 174, 180, 186–187, 244, 245

Dale, 131, 166, 192–193, 258
Dallas, George Mifflin, **93**
Dalton, Patrick, **93–94**
Davis, Jefferson, 43–44, 82, **94**, 128, 171, 187, 190
Davis, John, **94–95**
Davis, Sarah Taylor, 94
Dayton, Wreck of, **95**
de la Rosa, Luis, **95–96**, *95*
De Russey, L. G., 237
Deas, Edward, 43
Delaware Indians, **96**, 146, 154

Dent, Frederick Tracy, **96**
Desertion, **96–98**. *See also* San Patricio Battalion
Diarrhea, **98**, 149
Díaz, Pedro A., 9
Díaz de La Vega, Rómulo, 72, **98–99**, 233
Díez de Bonilla, Manuel, 121
Dimick, Justin, **99**
Disturnell, J., 34
Dodson, Jacob, 3
Dominguez, Manuel, **99–100**
Dominguez's Spy Company, **100**, 140, 276
Donelson, Andrew Jackson, **100–101**, 151, 303
Doniphan, Alexander, 13, 25, 28, 77–78, 81, 84, **101–102**, 102–104, 107–108, 122, 133, 138, 139, 146, 152, 154, 155, 157, 203–204, 205, 216, 221, 238–239, 245, 267, 277, 310
Doniphan's March, **102–104**, *103*, 294, 311
Dos Amades, **104**, 297
Dosamantes, Maia de Jesús, 297
Dragoons, **104**
Drum, Simon H., 75, **104**
Du Pont, Samuel F., 63, **104–105**, *104*, 161, 199, 200, 245
Duncan, James, 80, 89, 90, 302
Duran, Augustín, 14, **105**, 205
"Dutch Mary," 299

Eagle, 13
Echeagaray, Miguel María, 74, **107**, 109
El Embudo Pass, Skirmish at, **108**
El Paso, 34, 102, 157, 250
El Rincón del Diablo, **110**, 190
El Tomacito, **110**, 146, 222–223
El Unico, 195
Emerson, Ralph Waldo, **110–111**, 274
Emory, William Hemsley, **111**, 126
Encinas de Aviles, Loreto, 297
Escopetas, 294
Ewell, Richard Stoddert, **111–112**
Expansionism. *See* Manifest Destiny

Falcón, Ramón, 91, **113**, 129–130, 234–235
Falmouth, 278
Fannin, James W., 281
Federalists (Mexico), 181, 185, 223
The Female Volunteer, 42
Ferrer, Vicente Suárez, 201
Fillmore, Millard, 36, 88, 119, 295
Flintlock muskets, 295
Flores, José María, 59, 68, **113–114**, 118–119, 160, 166, 199, 215, 243–244
Flying Artillery, **114**, 119–120, 208, 235, 236–237, 295
Ford, John Salmon, **114–115**
Forrest, French, **115**, 263
Fort Brown, 115–116, 255, 284
Fort Jesup, **116**, 150, 269, 308

Fort Marcy, **116**, 155
Fort Polk, **116–117**, 207, 217–218
Fort Pueblo, 192
Fort Tenería, **117**
Fort Texas, 46, 47, 49, 51, 171, 174, 207, 233, 274, 289–290, 308, 309. *See also* Fort Brown
Foster, John Gray, **117**
Frémont, Jessie Benton, 117–118
Frémont, John C., 3, 21, 36, 37, 40, 41, 53, 59, 61–62, 66, 67, 68, 96, 113, **117–119**, *118*, 123–124, 136, 146, 154, 157, 163, 166, 173, 186, 196, 199, 200, 204, 215, 244, 250, 260, 261, 262, 284, 308, 309, 311
French, Samuel Gibbs, **119–120**
Frontera, 263, 264–265

Gadsden, James, 121
Gadsden Purchase, 16, 201, 216
Gadsden Treaty, 16, 35, 111, **121**, 172, 232, 249
Gaines, John Pollard, 47, **121–122**, 138, 159
Galaxara, Skirmish at, **122**
Gaona, Antonio, 72, 100, **122**
Garces, Francisco, 200
García Condé, Pedro, 34, 77, **122–123**, 238
Garland, John, 184, 189
Garrison, William Lloyd, 1, **123**
Gillespie, Archibald, 36, 62, 118, **123–124**, 155, 157, 166, 229–230, 309
Gillespie, Robert Addison, **124**
Gilmer, Jeremy F., 116
Goliad, 248, 307
Gómez, Gregorio, 72, 73
Gómez Farías, Valentin, 12, 20, 35, 36, 71, **124–125**, 185, 212, 219, 219, 223, 231–232, 241, 248, 249, 310, 311
Gosiute, 281
Graham, Richard H., 125
Grant, Ulysses S., 28, 37, 88, 91, 96, **125–126**, *126*, 208, 303
Gray, Andrew Belcher, **126–127**, 192
Gray, Mabry B., **127**
"Great Western." *See* Borginnis, Sarah
Greeley, Horace, 126, 155
Green, Duff, 100, **127–128**, 151, 280
Gregory, F. H., 197
Griveaubal cannons, 294
Guadaloupe, 195, 196
Guaymas, 63, 195, 312
Guerra, Francisco de la, 59
Guerrero, Vicente, 56–57, 181
Guerrilla warfare, **129–132**, 149, 241, 254, 258. *See also* Texas Rangers
"Guerrillas of Vengeance," 241
Guerrrero, 196

Hale, William, 240
Hall, Willard Preble, **133**, 154

Hall flintlock rifles, 295
Halleck, Henry Wager, **133–134**, 174
Halls of the Montezumas, Mexico City, **134**
Hamer, Thomas Lyon, **134**, 141
Hamilton, C. S., 239
Hannegan, Edward Allen, **134**
Hardee, William Joseph, **135**
Hardin, John J., 55, **135**
Harney, William Selby, 72, **135–136**
Harrison, William Henry, 280
Harwood, William, 238
Hawkins, Edgar, 116
"Hawks of the chaparral," 129
Hawk's Peak, **136**
Hays, John Coffee, 43, 115, 122, 124, **137**, *137*, 175, 189, 254, 273, 289
Head, Mark, 238
Hébert, Paul Octave, **137–138**
Henderson, James Pinckney, **138**, 156, 187, 190
Hendley, Israel R., 191, 267
Henrie, Daniel Drake, **138**, 159–160
Heredia, José Antonio de, **138–139**, 238–239, 277
Herrera, José Joaquín de, xix, 5, 8, 12, 52, 90, 91, 125, **139**, 185, 209, 213, 230, 241, 257, 275, 275, 283, 308
Heywood, Charles, 200, 244, 245
Hill, Daniel Harvey, 22, **139–140**
Hitchcock, Ethan Allen, 100, **140**, *140*, 225–226
Holzinger, Sebastián, **140**
Home Squadron. *See* U.S. Home Squadron
Hooker, Joseph, **140–141**
Horacitas, Pedro, 239
Houston, Samuel, xix, **141**, 147, 151, 181, 184, 248, 271, 307
Howard, Tilghman A., 100
Howitzer and Rocket Company, 232, 240
Huger, Benjamin, **142**
Hughes, John Joseph, **142–143**, 176
Hunt, Henry Jackson, **143**, 183
Hunter, Charles G., 9, **143**
Hunter, G., 198

Ide, William Brown, 37, **145**
Immortal 14, **145**
Independence, 174, 244, 256
Indians, 21, 111, **145–146**, 170. *See also* Apache, Comanche, Delaware Indians, Gosiute, Klamath Indians, Paiute, Pueblo Indians, Shawnee, Shoshoni, Ute, Zuni
Ingraham, Duncan N., **146**
La invasión americana, 1846 a 1848, 32
Isabel, 196
Isthmus of Tehuantepec, 278
Iturbide, Agustín de, 6, 12, 15, 56, 64, 89, 122, 180, 181, 185, 205, 209, 226, 241, 248, 271, 275, 283

Jack Tier, 87
Jackson, Andrew, 2, 36, 48, 57, 60, 100, 127, 141, **147**, 171, 218, 254, 269, 275, 278, 284, 289, 296, 303, 307
Jackson, Samuel, **147–148**
Jackson, Thomas Jonathan ("Stonewall"), 75, **148**
Jalapa, 141, **148–149**, 160, 195, 285
Jararo, José María, 73
Jarauta, Celestino Domeco de, 1, 131, **149**, 160, 209, 254
Jarero, José María, **149–150**
Jefferson, Thomas, 170
Jesup, Thomas Sidney, **150**, 225
John Adams, 304
Johnson, Andrew, 91, 261
Johnston, Albert Sidney, **150–151**, 232
Johnston, Joseph Eggleston, 75, **151**, 214
Jones, Anson, 101, 127, **151–152**, 156, 271
Jornada del Muerto, **152**
Juárez, Benito, 10, 226
Juvera, Julián, 20, 55, **152**, 185

Kearny, Philip, 80, **153**
Kearny, Stephen Watts, xviii, 10, 13–14, 16, 17, 21, 25, 27, 28, 36, 37, 39, 40, 42, 59, 62, 66, 76–77, 81, 85, 86, 101, 102, 111, 114, 116, 119, 124, 133, 146, 150, **153–154**, *153*, 160, 161, 166–167, 169–170, 173, 192, 196, 199, 201, 203, 204, 205, 215, 221, 238, 239–240, 243–244, 246, 250, 251, 260, 267, 284, 301, 309, 310, 311
 Kearny's March, **154–155**, 309
Kendall, George Wilkins, **155–156**
Kinney, Henry Lawrence, 74, 87, 100, 127, **156–157**, *156*, 174
Kirker, James, 146, **157**
Klamath Indians, **157**

La Encarnación, 56, 81, 121, 138, **159–160**, 175, 185
La Hoya, Skirmish at, **160**
La Paz, 131, **161**, 193, 311
La Vallette, Elie A. F., 63, 129, 174
Laguna, 248, 310
Lally, Folliot T., 2, 131, 141
Lamy, Jean Baptiste, **161**, 173
Landero Bauza, José Juan, **162**, 213, 286
Lane, Joseph, 29, 114, 115, 122, 129, 131, 137, 141, 142, 149, **162**, 222, 230, 254, 290
Largo, Sarcilla, 204
Larkin, Thomas Oliver, 118, 123, 136, **162–163**, 186, 215, 257, 308, 309
Laundresses, 46–47, 299
Lawson, Thomas, 178
Lee, Robert E., 38, 51, 72, 80, 86, 117, 148, **163**, *163*, 165, 170, 183, 211, 214, 286
León, Antonio, 109, **164**, *164*

Levant, 186
Lewis, Meriwether, 170
Lexington, 161
The Liberator, 123
Libertad, 196
Lincoln, Abraham, 44, 81, 91, 119, 135, 143, **164–165**, 255
Llano, Manuel M., 187, 190
Lombardini, Manuel María, 19, 48, 55, **165**, 299
Longstreet, James, **165**
Loreto, **166**
Loring, William Wing, **166**
Los Angeles, **166–167**, 215, 260, 310
Louisiana Purchase, 170
Lowell, James Russell, 1, **167**

Mackenzie, Alexander Slidell, 30, **169**, 219, 249
Mackenzie, Samuel, 75
Magoffin, James, 14, 16, **169–170**
Magruder, James B., 72
Magruder, John Bankhead, 86, 87–88, **170**
Manifest Destiny, xvii, xix, 118, **170–171**, 218, 254, 276, 289, 295–296
Mansfield, Joseph King Fenno, **171–172**
Marcy, William Learned, 21, 22, 41, 90, 116, 131, 136, **172**, *172*, 219, 221, 251, 253, 269, 277
Marín, Tomás, 9
Márquez, Francisco, 201
Marshall, Thomas, **172–173**, 235
Marston, Ward, 249–250
Martinez, Antonio José, 14, **173**
Mason, Richard Barnes 62, **173–174**
Matamoros, 66, 74, 87, 98, 113, 122, 130, 137, **174**, 176, 184, 197–198, 207, 231, 234, 238, 281, 291, 292, 308, 309, 310
Maximilian, Emperor, 8, 170, 185, 221, 241
May, Charles, 208, 233
Mayans, 304
Mazatlán, 42, 133, **174–175**, 255–256, 257, 270
McClellan, George Brinton, **175**
McCulloch, Ben, 4, 54, **175–176**, 188, 229, 234–235, 273, 280
McElroy, John, 71, 142–143, **176**, 234
McGregor, John F., 304
McLane, Louis, 60
McNamara, Eugene, 70
Meade, George Gordon, **176–177**, 214
Medical practices
 Mexico, **177–178**
 United States, **178–180**, *179*
Mejía, Francisco, 51–52, **180**, 188, 244, 308
Melgar, Agustín, 201
Melville, Herman, 21
Mendez, Santiago, 304
Merchants War, 65
Merritt, Ezekiel, 37
Mervine, William, **180–181**, 186–187, 199,

229–230, 257
Mesilla Valley, 121, 122, 123, 249
Mexican-American relations, xvii
Mexican-American War
    causes, xviii–xx
    summary, xvii–xviii
Mexican Army, **17–21**
Mexican Claims Commission, 172
Mexican Spy Company. *See* Dominguez's Spy Company
Mexican War for Independence, 6, 12, 17, 49, 181, 248
Mexicano, 196
Mexico, 171, **181–182**
    Anglo-American press, 13
    casualties, **68**
    and Catholic Church, **69–71**, 70, 124, 142–143, 161, 173, 176, 181, 185, 212, 219–220, 220–221, 223, 234, 310, 311
    centralists, 181
    damages owed to United States, xix
    desertion, **97–98**
    federalists, 181, 185, 223
    and Indians, **145–146**
    instability, xvii, xviii–xix
    medical practices, **177–178**
    moderados, 125, 128, 139, **185–186**, 209, 212–213, 219, 223
    Navy, **195–196**
    puros, 124–125, 128, 181, 185, 219, **223**
    repatriation, **232**
    weapons, **294**
    women, **297–299**
Mexico City, 50, 59, 74, 78, 90, 122, 137, 153, **182**, *182*, 220–221, 222, 253, 297. *See also* Battle of Mexico City, Veracruz-Mexico City campaign
    Halls of the Montezumas, **134**
Micheltorena, Manuel, 113, 215
Mier, 131, 184, 258
Mier Expedition, 64, 138, 180, **184–185**, 213, 289
Military Society of the Mexican War. *See* Aztec Club
Mina Battalion, 32
Miñón, José Vicente, 20, 47, 121, 159, **185**, 220
Moctezuma I, 134, 181
Moctezuma II, 134
Model 1841 muskets, 295
Moderados, 125, 128, 139, **185–186**, 209, 212–213, 219, 223
Monclova, 83, 89, **186**, 300, 301, 310
Monroe, James, 186
Monroe Doctrine, 52–53, **186**
Monterey, California, **186–187**, 260, 293
Monterrey, 130, 137, 258. *See also* Battle of Monterrey
    Armistice of, **187**, 205, 219, 269, 301, 310

    Bishop's Palace, **42–43**
    Citadel, **80–81**
    Fort Tenería, **117**
Monterrey Gazette, 13
Montes de Oca, Fernando, 201
Montezuma, 195, 196
Montgomery, John B., 199, 243, 250
Montoyo, Pablo, 40, 159
Mora, Skirmish at, 191   bf 191
Mora y Villamil, Ignacio, 20, **191**, 246, 265
Morales, Juan, 213
Morelia Battalion, 183
Morelos, 196
Moreno, Francisco Rosendo, 247
Mormon Battalion, 16, 25, 86, 155, **191–192**, 311
Morris, Charles W., 263
Mule Hill, **192**
Mulejé, Skirmish at, 131, **192–193**
Munroe, John, **193**

Nájera, Juan, 189
National Bridge, 64, 141
National Palace, 134, 181, 182, 184, 253
National Road, 64, 71, 72, 78, 98, 99–100, 115, 131, 141, 149, 162, **195**, 216, 221, 222, 230, 232, 240, 254, 280, 285, 290, 302, 311
Native Americans. *See* Indians
Navajo Nation, 101, 146, 200, 203–204, 266, 310
Navy (Mexico), **195–196**
Navy (United States), **196–200**, *197*. *See also* U.S. Pacific Squadron, U.S. Home Squadron
Nevada, **200**
New Mexico, xviii, xix, 7, 13–15, 16–17, 25–26, 34, 37, 39–40, 44, 49, 52, 85, 86, 101, 102, 105, 108, 111, 116, 127, 128, 133, 145, 146, 147, 153–155, 161, 169–170, 171, 173, 193, **200–201**, 205, 218, 219, 221, 222–223, 232, 239–240, 256–257, 266–267, 278, 280, 301, 307–308, 309
    Jornada del Muerto, **152**
New Orleans *Picayune*, 155–156
New York *Sun*, 35–36
Niños Héroes, **201**
Nueces River, xix, 3, 11, 22, 116, 127, 137, **201–202**, 238, 271, 291, 293, 296, 307, 308

O'Brien, John Paul Jones, 55, **203**
O'Sullivan, John L., 171
Obispado. *See* Bishop's Palace, Monterrey
Ocampo, Melchor, 128
Ojo Oso, **203–204**. *See also* Treaty of Ojo Oso
Olompali, Skirmish at, 37, 68, **204**
Olvera, Agustín, 60
Oregon Territory, 52, 256, 308
Oronoz, José María, 20
Ortega, José María, 19, 55, 187, 190, **205**
Ortiz, Ramón, 232

Ortiz, Tomás, 14, 28, 40, 105, **205**, 267
Owen, Robert Dale, 7

Pacheco, Francisco, 19, 48, 55
Pacific Squadron. *See* U.S. Pacific Squadron
Padilla, Juan, 204
Page, H. W., 199
Paget carbines, 294
Paiute, 281
Palos Prietos, 174, 175, 270
Pánuco, **208–209**
Paredes y Arrillaga, Mariano, xix, 5–6, 8, 11, 12, 15, 49–50, 52, 57, 64, 91, 95, 125, 128, 139, 149, 190, 195, **209**, *209*, 241, 247, 249, 257, 275, 283, 308
    War Message, 292–293   bf 292–293
Parker, James, 259
Parras, **210**
Parrodi, Anastasio, 19, **210**, 266
Parrott, William S., **210–211**
Patterson, Robert, 72, **211**, 214
Pedregal, **211–212**
Pemberton, John Clifford, **212**
Peña y Barragán, Matías de la, 109, 183, **212**
Peña y Peña, Manuel de la, 44, **212–213**, 257, 311, 312
Pensacola, 196
Percussion rifles, 295
Pérez, Francisco, 55, 79, 109, 135, **213**
Perfecto de Cos, Martín, **88–89**, 199, 279
Perote, 195, 213
Perote Castle, 122, 138, 162, 184, **213–214**, 240, 249, 289, 290, 311
Perry, Matthew Calbraith, 9, 65, 85, 131, 143, 196, 198, **214**, *214*, 240, 263, 279, 285, 286–287, 304, 311
Personal Narrative of Explorations and Incidents Connected with the United States and Mexican Boundary Commission, 34
Petrel, 197, 208
Petrita, **214–215**, *245*
Pico, Andrés, 59, 62, 66, 119, 155, 192, **215**, 246, 310
Pico, Pío de Jesús, 61, 68, 166, **215–216**, *215*, 308
Pierce, Franklin, 46, 53, 58, 80, 91–92, 93, 94, 121, 131, 137, 172, **216**, 217, 253, 259, 261, 265, 311
Pike, Albert, 85, **216–217**
Pike, Zebulon, 170
Pillow, Gideon Johnson, 59, 73, 75, 86, 89–90, 141, 150, 170, 214, **217**, 311
    and Winfield Scott, 217, 253, 302, 312
Pineda, Manuel, 131–132, 161, 192–193, 199, 243, 244–245
Pino, Manuel, 14
Point Isabel, **217–218**, 309
Polk, James K., xvii, xviii, xix, xx, 2, 7, 8, 11, 13–14, 21, 22, 24, 25, 29–30, 33, 35, 36, 41, 44, 46, 48, 50, 54, 57, 62, 63, 66, 67, 71, 77, 82–83, 87, 89, 90, 93, 94, 95, 100, 107, 116, 118, 119, 123, 128, 134, 141, 142, 145, 147, 154, 162, 164, 169, 172, 186, 187, 191, 196, 210, 211, 216, 217, **218–219**, *218*, 228, 234, 235, 238, 240, 249, 251–252, 253, 254, 256, 257, 260, 265, 266, 269, 274, 275, 278, 280–286, 289, 296, 301, 302, 303, 307–308, 309–310, 312
    and Buchanan, 52–53
    War Address, **290–292**, 309
Polk, Sarah, 218
Polkos Revolt, 20, 35, 36, 69, 71, 124, 125, 185, 212, **219–220**, 223, 249, 261, 311
Ponce de León, Antonio, 107–108, 109
Porter, Caroline, **220**
Porter, Fitz John, 183
Portsmouth, 161, 243
Posada y Garduño, Manuel, **220–221**
Price, Sterling, 14, 25–27, 28, 105, 108, 110, 155, 159, 205, **221**, 222, 238, 250–251, 266, 267, 277, 310, 311, 312
Princeton, 278
Protocol of Querétaro, 95
Puebla, 122, 131, 137, 138, 141, 149, 162, 195, 216, **221–222**, 230, 245, 311, 312
Pueblano, 196
Puebla, Siege of, **222**
Pueblo de Taos, Skirmish at, 221, **222–223**
Pueblo Indians, 146
Puros, 124–125, 128, 181, 185, 219, **223**, 231, 278

Quartermaster departments
    Mexico, **225**
    U.S., 150, 156, 178, **225–226**, 261
Queretana, 196
Quijana, Benito, 191, **226**
Quitman, John Anthony, 7, 9, 75, 143, 177, 183–184, 198, 225, **226–228**, *227*, 265, 290

Ramos, 131, **229**
Rancheros, 129, 250. *See also* Californios
Rancho Dominguez, Skirmish at, **229–230**
Rancho Guadalupe, 127, 130, 229
Rangel, Joaquín, 109, 183, **230**
Rea, Joaquín, 29, 78, 122, 222, **230**
Reading, P. B., 60
Red River, 271
Reefer, 197
Reid, John, 245
Reily, John, **231**, 246–247
Rejón, Manuel Crecencio, 14, **231–232**
Reno, Jesse L., **232**, 240
Repatriation, **232**
Republic of the Rio Grande, 13
Requena, Tomás, 187, 188, 190

Revere, Joseph Warren, 199
Rey, Antony, 71, 142–143, 176, **234**
Reynolds, John Fulton, **234**
Reynosa, **234–235**
Richey, John A., **235**
Rico, Francisco, 59
Ridgely, Randolph, **235–236**
Riley, Bennett, 72, **236**
Rincón, Manuel E., 79, **236**
Ringgold, Samuel, 12, 114, 119, 208, 235, **236–237**, *237*
Río Calaboso, Skirmish at, **237**, 311
Río Colorado, **237–238**
Río Grande, xix, 3, 127, 137, **238**, 308, 309
Roberts, William, **239**
Robidoux, Antoine, **239–240**
Rockets, **240**. *See also* Howitzer and Rocket Company
Rogers, R. Clay, **240**
Romero, Tomás, 40
Rosas, Antonio, 278
Ruff, Charles F., 245–246
Russell, William H., 60

Sabine River, xix, 2, 22, 271, 276, 308
Saint Joseph's Island, **241**
Salas, José Mariano, 130, 190, 219, **241**
Saltillo, 77, 78, 83, 84, 113, 130, 131, 135, 159, 163, 184, 185, 188, 220, 235, **241–242**, *242*, 246, 293, 299, 300, *300*, 301, 310, 311
San Anita, 131
San Antonio, 184, 293, 300, 301, 307
San Antonio, Skirmish at, **243**
San Antonio Abad *garita*, 153, 183
San Francisco, **243**
San José del Cabo, 131–132, **244–245**
San José del Pozo, Skirmish at, **245**
San Juan Bautista, 136
San Juan de Ulúa, **245**, 285
San Juan, Skirmish at, **245–246**
San Luis Potosí, 56, 69, 152, 159, 165, 173, 178, 180, 205, **246**, 266, 269, 281, 283, 297, 301, 310, 310
San Patricio Battalion, 93, 136, 220, 231, **246–247**
Sánchez, Francisco, 249–250
Sánchez, José de la Cruz, 250
Sands, Joshua Ratoon, 65, 198, **247–248**
Santa Anna, Antonio López de, xvii, xviii, xix, 4–5, 6, 7, 8, 9, 10, 11, 12, 14, 15, 17, 18–19, 20, 27, 29–30, 36, 45, 47, 49, 51, 57, 63, 64, 69–70, 71, 72, 74, 75, 76, 77, 78, 79–80, 83, 85–86, 89, 90, 93–94, 95, 97, 98–99, 108, 109, 121, 124, 125, 139, 141, 148, 149, 152, 156, 159–160, 162, 164, 165, 169, 172–173, 174, 175–176, 180, 181, 183–184, 184–185, 187, 190, 191, 203, 205, 209, 210, 213, 219, 220, 222, 219, 223, 226, 230, 231–232, 235, 236, 241, 246, **248–249**, *248*, 261, 263, 265, 266, 267, 269, 270, 271, 273, 275, 277, 280, 281, 283, 290, 293, 297, 300, 301, 307, 308, 309–312
and Battle of Buena Vista, **53–56**, *54*
Santa Cruz de Rosales, 221, 312. *See also* Battle of Santa Cruz de Rosales
Santa Fe, 10, 13–14, 25, 28, 76–77, 86–87, 102, 116, 146, 153–155, 156, 200, 203, 205, 239–240, **251**, 267, 307, 309, 310
Santa Fe Trail, 77, 78, 84, 200, 236, 251
Saunders, J. L., 198
Savannah, 180, 186, 229
Schafino, Francisco, 247
Scott, Winfield, xviii, 1–2, 6, 9–10, 13, 17, 20, 21, 24, 29, 32, 32, 35, 38, 41, 45, 46, 49, 50, 51, 54, 57, 64, 70, 71, 73, 78, 79, 80, 84, 85–86, 89, 91, 93, 96, 98–99, 104, 111, 119, 121, 125, 130, 131, 135, 136, 137, 139, 140, 141, 143, 148–149, 153, 156, 163, 165, 170, 172, 173, 176, 183–184, 195, 211, 214, 216, 219, 221–222, 226, 230, 231, 232, 235, 236, 240, 245, 247, 248, 249, **251–253**, *252*, 254, 255, 261, 265–266, 269, 273, 274, 278, 280, 283, 285, 286–287, 294, 299–300, 301, 303, 310, 311, 312. *See also* Veracruz-Mexico City campaign
and Army of Occupation, **24–25**, 39, 51, 57, 59, 67, 74, 85–86, 99, 117, 122, 137–138, 142, 143, 148–149, 150, 151, 163, 165, 175, 196, 201, 212, 213, 222, 230, 232, 241, 251–253, 276, 284, 286, 290, 302
and Battle of El Molino del Rey, **108–110**
and Battle of Mexico City, 183–184
and Gideon J. Pillow, 217, 253, 302, 312
court of inquiry, **89–90**, 91
Scourge, 143
Scouts, 145–146, 156, 157, 175–176. *See also* Carson, Christopher ("Kit"); Crane; Delaware Indians; Texas Rangers
Scutia, Juan, 201
Secret agents, 260–261, 296, 299, 303
Selfridge, Thomas O., 166, 193, 199
Semmes, Raphael, 240, **253–254**, *253*, 259, 303–304
Sentinel, 13
Sequalteplan, Skirmish at, **254**
Sevier, Ambrose Hundley, 7, 83, **254**
Seymour, Horatio, 126
Shawnee, 146, 154
Sheldon, G. S., 200
Sherman, Thomas West, 55, **254–255**
Shields, James, 31, 32, 57, 72, 73, 80, **255**, *255*, 301
Shoshoni, 281
Shotguns, 295
Shubrick, W. Branford, 42, 62, 174, 199, 244,

255–256, 270
Silva, Mariano, 187
Sims, Alexander D., 7
Slavery, xx, 1, 3, 41, 42, 60, 82, 164, 167, 171, **256**, 270, 273–274, 289, 295, 307, 310. *See also* Wilmot Proviso
Slidell, John, xx, 44, 52, 211, **256–257**, *257*, 292, 308
Sloat, John Drake, 33, 37, 196, 199, 243, 256, **257**, 260, 308
Smallpox, **258**
Smith, Charles F., 189
Smith, E. Kirby, 22, 43, 87, 95, 302
Smith, Joseph, 281
Smith, Persifor Frazer, 80, 86, 141, 245, **258**, 265
Smith, W. T., 199
Snook, Joseph, 192
Soldaderas, 18, 19, 54, 225, 297–299
Soldado River, Skirmish at, **258–259**
Somers, 146, 240, 253, **259**
Sonora, 145
Sonora y Sinaloa, 16
Sonorense, 196
Soto la Marina, 197
Southampton, 244
Southern Pacific Railroad, 126
Spitfire, 197, 208, 267
St. Mary's, 147–148
Stanly, Fabius, 200, 258
Steele, Seymour G., 243
Stevens, Isaac Ingalls, **259**
Stockton, Robert Field, 36, 42, 59, 62, 67, 68, 104, 113, 114, 118–119, 124, 154, 155, 160, 166–167, 173, 196, 199, 229, 243–244, 257, **259–260**, *260*, 296, 310, 311
Storms, Jane Maria Eliza McManus, 35–36, **260–261**, 299
Surfboats, **261**
Sutter, John Augustus, 68, **261–262**, *261*
Sutter's Fort, 261–262, 284, 308

Tabasco, 85, 115, 146, 197, 248. *See also* Battles of Tabasco
Tacubaya, 265
 Armistice of, 74, 79, 80, 216, 219, 226, 227, 258, **265–266**, 311
Tafoya, Jesus, 159
Talcott, Henry, 240
Tamaulipas, 210, 226, 238
Tampico, 76, 85, 131, 146, 195, 197, 208, 210, 237, 248, 266, 278, 285, 310, 311
Taos Rebellion, 15, 27, 28, 37, 39, 40, 76–77, 105, 108, 110, 146, 159, 173, 191, 201, 205, 221, 222–223, 237–238, 250, 251, **266–267**
Tattnall, Josiah, 146, 208, 266, **267**, 279, 286–287
Taylor, Zachary, xvii, xviii, xx, 3–4, 11, 15, 17, 19, 21, 22, 25, 27, 28, 30, 31, 33, 34, 42, 43, 44, 45–46, 50, 57, 62, 63, 64, 66, 70, 78, 81, 90, 91, 94, 99, 103, 110, 114, 116, 121, 125, 127, 134, 135, 137, 138, 139, 140, 141, 159, 162, 165, 172–173, 174, 175–176, 186, 187, 197, 205, 207–208, 216, 217, 219, 220, 226, 229, 232, 234, 235, 246, 249, 251, 253, 254, 255, 257, 266, **268–270**, *268*, 273, 274, 281, 283, 285, 295, 299, 300, 301, 303, 308, 309, 311, 312
 and Army of Occupation, **23–24**, 39, 43, 44, 47, 48–49, 51, 53, 57, 64, 66, 69, 71, 74, 78, 82, 87, 90, 93, 99, 113, 115, 119, 124, 125, 126, 130, 131, 134, 135, 142–143, 150–151, 156, 165, 171, 174, 175, 176–177, 180, 185, 193, 203, 210, 211, 217–218, 231, 232–234, 235, 236, 241, 242, 247, 251, 255, 258, 269, 274, 279, 284, 290, 292, 301, 302, 308, 309
 and Battle of Buena Vista, **53–56**, *54*
 and Battle of Monterrey, **187–191**, 310
Téllez, Rafael, 174–175, **270**
Temple, William G., 9
Tenochtitlán, 180, 181
Terrés, Andrés, 183, **270–271**
Texas, xvii, xix, xx, 2, 22–23, 41, 44, 49, 52, 81, 82, 100–101, 116, 123, 125, 127, 128, 137, 138, 139, 141, 145–146, 147, 150–151, 156, 171, 186, 210, 218, 241, 248, 249, 254, 260, **271**, 280, 295, 296, 303, 307–308. *See also* Coahuila y Texas
Texas Mier Expedition. *See* Mier Expedition
Texas Rangers, 4, 22, 64, 113, 114–115, 122, 124, 127, 129, 130, 131, 137, 141–142, 156, 159, 175–176, 188, 207, 229, 234–235, **271–273**, *272*, 289–290, 295
Texas Revolution, 10, 83, 122, 141, 151, 165, 174, 175, 181, 238, 248, 271, 281, 289
Thoreau, Henry David, 170, **273–274**
Thornton, Seth B., 66, 74, 135, 207, **274**, 275, 309
"3 Million Dollar Bill," 254
Tibbatts, John W., 7
Tilghman, Lloyd, 44, **274**
Tlaxcala, 131
Todos Santos, Skirmish at, **275**, 312
Tornel y Mendivil, José María, **275**
Torrejón, Anastasio, 19, 66, 74, 100, 183, 207–208, 274, **275–276**, 309
Totten, George M., 261
Tower, Zealous Bates, 72, 183, **276**
Tower rifles, 294
Towers, Zebulon B., 72, 183
Traconis, Juan Bautista, 263
Transcontinental Treaty, **276–277**
Treaties of Velasco, xix, 141, 181, 248, 271, 307
Treaty of Cahuenga, **59–60**, 61, 119, 160, 215, 244, 311
Treaty of Guadalupe Hidalgo, xviii, 3, 7, 16, 27, 34, 53, 61, 82, 83, 85, 90, 91, 95, 126, **128**,

141, 149, 172, 185, 200, 201, 202, 209, 212, 213, 219, 221, 223, 226, 231, 232, 236, 243, 247, 250, 254, 271, 277–278, 281, 312
Treaty of La Mesilla. *See* Gadsden Treaty
Treaty of Ojo Oso, 146
Trías Álvarez, Ángel, 77, 107, 122, 238, 250, **277**
Tripler, Charles S., 179
Trist, Nicholas P., 7, 34–35, 90, 91, 128, 172, 219, 258, 265, **277–278**, *278*, 312
Trousdale, William, 75
Truxtun, **278**
Turley, Simeon, 28
Tuxpan, 197, 248, 254, **279**, 311
Twiggs, David E., 50, 51, 72, 73, 80, 131, 183, 214, 274, **279–280**, *279*, 301, 302
Tyler, John, 22, 60, 91, 100, 116, 127, 147, 260, 271, **280**, 295, 296, 308

Union, 196
United States
    casualties, **68–69**, 90–91
    desertion, **96–97**. *See also* San Patricio Battalion
    and European origins, xvii
    and Indians, **145–146**
    Manifest Destiny, xvii, xix, 118
    medical practices, **178–180**, *179*
    weapons, **294–295**
    women, *298*, **299**
Urrea, José, 6, 10, 64, 130, 174, 229, 266, **281**
U.S. Army, **21–28**
    recruitment, 21, *26*, *27*
U.S. Home Squadron, 115, 146, 147–148, 195, 196–199, 208–209, 214, 218, 248, 253–254, 259, 261, 267, 285, 308, 309–310, 311. *See also* Navy (United States), U.S. Pacific Squadron
U.S. Military Academy, 38, 234
U.S. Naval Academy, 33, 104
U.S. Pacific Squadron, 42, 174, 180–181, 186, 196, 199–200, 243, 244, 255–256, 257, 259–260, 309, 311, 312. *See also* Navy (United States), U.S. Home Squadron
Utah, **281–282**
Ute, 200, 266, 281

Valencia, Gabriel, 20, 45, 79, 85–86, 209, 249, **283–284**, *283*
Vallejo, Mariano Guadalupe, 37, **284**
Van Brunt, Gersham J., 264
Van Buren, Martin, 172, 280, 307
Van Dorn, Earl, 183, **284–285**
Vandalia, 166, 229–230
Vásquez, Ciriaco, 20, 72, 73, **285**
Vega, Rafael de la, 278
Veracruz, 38, 41, 44, 50, 78, 84, 85, 115, 125, 141, 162, 169, 175, 214–215, 240, 245, 248, 249, 252, 259, 261, **285**, 308. *See also* Battle of Veracruz
Veracruz-Mexico City campaign, 57, 64, 70, 89, 96, 99, 100, 104, 111, 114, 121, 126, 130, 135, 136, 137–138, 139, 140, 141–142, 143, 148, 149, 151, 153, 156, 162, 163, 165, 166, 170, 172, 177, 195, 196, 211, 212, 213, 221–222, 226, 230, 232, 236, 240, 241, 247, 253, 254, 255, 258, 259, 269, 273, 275–276, 278, 279–280, 285, 290, 294, 300, 301, 302, 311. *See also* Battle of Mexico City
Veracruzano Libre, 196
Verhaegen, Peter, 142
Victoria, 196, 310
Victoria, Guadalupe, 49, 181
Victoria, Manual, 61
Vidal, Luis, 107–108
Vixen, 197, 248
Vizcaino, Sebastian, 61

Walker, Joseph, 118, 200
Walker, Robert John, **289**
Walker, Samuel H., 22, 127, 131, 141–142, 160, 184–185, 207, 273, **289–290**
Walnut Springs, **290**
War Address of James K. Polk, **290–292**, 309
War Message of Mariano Paredes y Arrillaga, **292–293**
Washington, John Macrea, 55, 89, 203, **293–294**, 301
Watson, Henry B., 243
Weapons
    Mexico, **294**
    United States, **294–295**
Weber, Carlos María, 250
Webster, Daniel, **295**
West Point. *See* U.S. Military Academy
Whitman, Walt, **295–296**
Whittier, John Greenleaf, 1
Wickliffe, Charles Anderson, 100, **296**
Wilmot, David, 60, 256, **296–297**
Wilmot Proviso, 95, 164, 256, 295, 296–297, 310
Woll, Adrian, 184
Women
    Mexico, **297–299**
    United States, *298*, **299**
Wood, George T., 273
Wool, John Ellis, 3–4, 43, 47, 48, 53, 55, 56, 69, 77, 79, 84, 103, 131, 135, 136, 138, 170, 186, 203, 216, 255, 269, 293, **299–300**, *299*, *300*, 303, 309, 310, 312
    and Army of Occupation, **23–24**, 79, 150, 312
    and Army of the Center (United States), **27**, 163, 186, 210
    Chihuahua Expedition, **301**
Worth, William Jenkins, 4, 28, 43, 45, 50, 59, 72, 78, 89, 90, 98, 99, 100, 109–110, 156,

183–184, 187, *188*, 189, 190, 210, 212, 213, 214, 221, 254, 279, 280, 290, **301–302**, 311, 312
Wright, George, 109, **302**
Wright, Silas, 93
Wynkoop, Francis M., 160

Yell, Archibald, 4–5, 55, 69, 100, 216, 301, **303**

Yellow fever, xviii, 264, 286, **303–304**
Yucatán, 195, **304**

Zacatecas, 89
Zempoalteca, 196
Zozaya, María Josefa, 297, **305**
Zuni, 204